Divisions

Divisions

A New History of Racism and Resistance in America's World War II Military

Thomas A. Guglielmo

OXFORD
UNIVERSITY PRESS

OXFORD
UNIVERSITY PRESS

Oxford University Press is a department of the University of Oxford. It furthers
the University's objective of excellence in research, scholarship, and education
by publishing worldwide. Oxford is a registered trade mark of Oxford University
Press in the UK and certain other countries.

Published in the United States of America by Oxford University Press
198 Madison Avenue, New York, NY 10016, United States of America.

Library of Congress Cataloging-in-Publication Data
Names: Guglielmo, Thomas A., author.
Title: Divisions : a new history of racism and resistance in America's
World War II military / Thomas A. Guglielmo.
Other titles: New history of racism and resistance in America's World War II military
Description: New York, NY : Oxford University Press, [2021] | Includes index.
Identifiers: LCCN 2021016387 (print) | LCCN 2021016388 (ebook) |
ISBN 9780195342659 (hardback) | ISBN 9780190939908 (epub) |
ISBN 9780190940355
Subjects: LCSH: World War, 1939–1945—Participation, African American. |
Discrimination in the military—United States—History—20th century. |
World War, 1939–1945—Social aspects—United States. | United
States—Armed Forces—African Americans—History—20th century. | World
War, 1939–1945—Participation, Hispanic American. | World War,
1939–1945—Participation, Indian. | World War, 1939–1945—Participation,
Asian American. | United States—Armed Forces—Indian—History—20th
century. | United States—Armed Forces—Hispanic
Americans—History—20th century. | United States—Armed Forces—
Asian Americans—History—20th century.
Classification: LCC D810.N4 G84 2021 (print) |
LCC D810.N4 (ebook) | DDC 940.54/03—dc23
LC record available at https://lccn.loc.gov/2021016387
LC ebook record available at https://lccn.loc.gov/2021016388

DOI: 10.1093/oso/9780195342659.001.0001

1 3 5 7 9 8 6 4 2
Printed by LSC Communications, United States of America

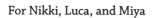

For Nikki, Luca, and Miya

CONTENTS

ACKNOWLEDGMENTS

Far too long in the making, this book might not have seen the light of day but for the support of so many generous and good people. I thank them here with great pleasure.

For help tracking down archival and other source material, many thanks to the late Walter Hill, Ken Schlesinger, Eric Van Slander, and Alexis Hill at the National Archives at College Park, Robert Glass at the National Archives at San Francisco, Guy Hall at the National Archives at Atlanta, Barbara Rust at the National Archives at Fort Worth, Gail Farr at the National Archives at Philadelphia, Richard McCulley at the National Archives at Washington, DC, Mary Brown at the Center for Migration Studies Archive, Joellen Elbashir at the Moorland-Spingarn Research Center at Howard University, Laura Mills at the Roosevelt University Archives, Savannah Wood at the Afro American Newspapers Archives, and the Inter-Library Loan staff at the Gelman Library at George Washington University. I also offer my thanks to Lizzie Cammarata, Jacqui Olson, and Gillet Rosenblith for research help and to Kimberly Probolus and Matthew Riemer for help with images.

For time to think and write, I thank Stanford University's Research Institute of Comparative Studies in Race and Ethnicity, Harvard University's Charles Warren Center, and George Washington's Columbian College Facilitating Fund and Dean's Research Chair.

Over the years, I've had the privilege and pleasure to present my work at a number of places where audience members challenged and encouraged me and, ultimately, made this a better book. For the opportunity to share pieces of this project, thanks to the École des hautes études en sciences sociales in Paris, the Institut d'histoire du temps présent at Université Paris 8, the Institute for Research on Race and Public Policy at the University of Illinois at Chicago, the DC-Area African American Studies Works-in-Progress Seminar, the Smithsonian Institution Contemporary History Colloquium, the Potomac Center for the Study of Modernity, Harvard

University, Stanford University, Bard College, the University of Delaware, New York University, the Berkshire Conference of Women Historians, the American Historical Association, the American Studies Association, the Association of Asian American Studies, the Council of European Studies, and the Society for Historians of American Foreign Relations.

Many colleagues and friends fielded questions, sent me sources, shared their own work, talked through ideas, invited me to speak, read chapter drafts, and encouraged and inspired me. Many thanks to Amin Ahmad, Eric Arnesen, Beth Bailey, Rick Baldoz, Nemata Blyden, Eduardo Bonilla-Silva, Mark Brilliant, Zoë Burkholder, Al Camarillo, Chris Capozzola, Patrick Chung, Daniel Coffeen, Liz Cohen, Matthew Countryman, Joe Crespino, Emilye Crosby, Silvia Álvarez Curbelo, Rachel Devlin, Jay Driskell, Jeff Edelman, Tyrone Forman, Brett Gadsden, Mike Galland, Ed Gitre, Dave Gutierrez, Melanie Haimes-Bartolf, Evelyn Brooks Higginbotham, Jennifer Ho, Bob Jefferson, Derrick Jones, Peniel Joseph, Andrew Kahrl, Katrina Quisumbing King, Peter Kolchin, Kip Kosek, Scott Kurashige, Dan Lee, Adriane Lentz-Smith, Amanda Lewis, Robert Lilly, Mara Loveman, Malinda Maynor Lowery, Ken Mack, Daryl Maeda, Laura McEnaney, James McNaughton, Chris Mihm, Natalia Molina, Kimberly Morgan, Kevin Mumford, Paul Murray, Jen Nash, Christopher Arris Oakley, Bibi Obler, Franklin Odo, Chris Parker, Pauline Peretz, Khary Polk, Russell Rickford, Dave Roediger, Tom Romero, Lucy Salyer, Josh Shannon, Jonathan Struthers, Rich Thomas, Steve Weissman, Scott Wong, Jeff Yamashita, James Zarsadiaz, and Susan Zeiger. For an expert reading of an early, partial draft of the manuscript and for her encouragement, many thanks to Susan Whitlock. For their support and fellowship, I am indebted to my students and colleagues in George Washington University's Department of American Studies, including those who were kind enough to read material: Colin Anderson, Sara Awartani, Francesco De Salvatore, Melani McAlister, Dara Orenstein, and Suleiman Osman.

Two friends deserve special recognition. Years ago, as I struggled mightily with this project, Cybelle Fox, in an act of signal generosity, read everything I'd written to that point and gave me invaluable feedback and encouragement, probably more encouragement than was warranted by the mess of half-baked writing she had to contend with. Similarly, an old friend from graduate school, Nathan Connolly, read a few draft chapters and, most important, expressed faith in me and this project. Given my great respect for him, it meant more than he knows, and it encouraged me to keep plugging away, believing again in this book's broader purpose. For throwing me a lifeline of sorts when I really needed it, heartfelt thanks to Cybelle and Nathan.

For putting into present-day practice some of the ideas in this book, I thank fellow members of the Race, Class, and Equity Group at the Capitol Hill Cluster School, including Marisol Bello, Chris Blanchard, Lisa Brooks, Ramona Burton, Asheley McBride, and Patricia Odom.

For personal insights on and images of the inspiring people I write about, my sincere thanks to Karyn J. Taylor, Colonel Carl C. Johnson, Robert McNatt, Toussaint Lynn, Alexander Lynn, Alex Carrillo Jr., Deborah Smullyan, and Charlotte Sherman.

Sincere thanks to Susan Ferber for believing in this project and in me, even after interminable delays, for her impeccable judgment in all matters editorial and beyond, for her superhuman responsiveness to emails at all hours, and for giving me the time and space to figure out what book I could and wanted to write. Thanks to two anonymous reviewers for their extraordinarily thorough and insightful reading of the manuscript and for their enthusiasm for it. Thanks to Jeremy Toynbee for shepherding the book through the production process, to Mary Becker for masterful copyediting, to Bob Land for proofreading, and to Ken Hassman for indexing. Finally, thanks to Oxford University Press and the *Journal of American History* for allowing me to republish parts of my article "A Martial Freedom Movement" here.

My deepest thanks go to my family members, whose love sustains me each and every day. For unwavering support over the years, I thank my grandparents, especially Grace and Angelo, my uncles, aunts, cousins, Mary, Andrew, Mackandal, Mike, Ron, and Andrea. Thanks to my mother, Maryloretta, for laying the foundation; to my father, Tom, for his inquisitiveness and sense of wonder; to my brother, Mark, for his fierce dedication to art and social justice, and for a goofiness that keeps all things in proper perspective; and to my sister, Jen, my closest intellectual confidante and comrade from day one, for her boundless heart and mind, in that order.

My wife, Nikki, and I met just as I began wrestling with this project's daunting demands. They never let up, even as we built a beautiful family together, juggling careers and dreams all the while. For her integrity, intelligence, steadiness, and love, thanks don't quite capture it. Finally, I thank my children, Luca and Miya, for being their inimitably awesome selves and for always reminding me that some things are more important than books, even one that takes nearly fifteen years to finish and concerns the deadserious subjects of racism and "World War Eleven," as they sometimes put it. Surprisingly, it was these reminders that freed me up, after many stops and starts and stumbles, to complete this book eventually. I dedicate it to them, and to Nikki, with all my heart.

LIST OF ABBREVIATIONS

ACLU	American Civil Liberties Union
CAIA	Council Against Intolerance in America
CIO	Congress of Industrial Organizations
COFEP	Committee on Fair Employment Practice
CPNNDP	Committee on Participation of Negroes in the National Defense Program
CRTC	Cavalry Replacement Training Center
FBI	Federal Bureau of Investigation
G-2	military intelligence staff of an army unit or of the War Department
G-3	organization and training staff of an army unit or of the War Department
JACL	Japanese American Citizens League
JAG	Judge Advocate General
KP	kitchen police or kitchen patrol
MIS	Military Intelligence Service
MOWM	March on Washington Movement
MP	military police
NAACP	National Association for the Advancement of Colored People
NCASAS	National Committee to Abolish Segregation in the Armed Services
NCCWL	National Citizens' Committee for Winfred Lynn
OCS	officer candidate school
OWI	Office of War Information
SPARS	United States Coast Guard Women's Reserve
STSA	Selective Training and Service Act
UDA	Union for Democratic Action
USO	United Service Organizations
WAAC	Women's Army Auxiliary Corps
WAC	Women's Army Corps

WAVES	Women Accepted for Volunteer Emergency Service
WDL	Workers Defense League
WMC	War Manpower Commission
WRA	War Relocation Authority
YCL	Young Communist League
YMCA	Young Men's Christian Association

Divisions

Chapter 18

Introduction

America's World War II military was a force of unalloyed good—and not simply because it helped save the world from Nazism and totalitarianism. It also managed to unify a famously fractious American people. At least that's the "good war" story many Americans have long told themselves, from the early days of war mobilization up until the present. Upon signing legislation for America's first peacetime draft in 1940, President Franklin D. Roosevelt predicted, "In the military service Americans from all walks of life . . . will learn to live side by side, to depend upon each other in military drills and maneuvers, and to appreciate each other's dignity as American citizens. Universal service will bring not only greater preparedness to meet the threat of war, but a wider distribution of tolerance and understanding to enjoy the blessings of peace."[1]

By war's end, if popular culture could be believed, Roosevelt's predictions had come true. Hollywood combat films and popular books showcased a seemingly limitless supply of plural platoons, many "quite consciously . . . composed of one Negro, one Jew, a Southern boy, and a sprinkling of second-generation Italians, Irish, Scandinavians and Poles." A long line of other commentaries celebrated America's troops as "a mixture of all the peoples in the world, a well-nourished, athletic, free-to-think, rather less frustrated and so somewhat better integrated mixture," and hailed the US Army "as an agent through which the variations, the superficial differences, the mannerisms and poses and artificialities of all kinds are faded out." In time, they praised returning veterans whose years in uniform had taught them, above all else, the need to "learn to live together regardless of race, color, creed, customs or domain."[2]

A balm against recurrent fears of a polarized nation, these stories about the adhesive powers of World War II military service live on. In his 1998 bestseller, *The Greatest Generation*, Tom Brokaw assured his readers that America's World War II GIs "were fused by a common mission and a common ethos," which was so uniformly profound that, more than half a century later, they still all "love each other." Completed six years later, the World War II Memorial on the National Mall, according to its website, "stands as an important symbol of American national unity, a timeless reminder of the moral strength and awesome power that can flow when a free people are at once united and bonded together in a common and just cause." Meanwhile, for decades, film and television have continued to produce World War II combat stories, which, for all their gore, celebrate "band[s] of brothers," in which time and again teamwork trumps tribe. Even scholars occasionally echo these themes, as did the author of *A Nation Forged in War: How World War II Taught Americans to Get Along*.[3]

Divisions tells a decidedly different story. It stresses not national unities but racist divisions as a fundamental feature of America's World War II military and of the postwar world it helped to fashion. Scholars and writers have skillfully explored some of these divisions.[4] But we still know too little about their full range, who built them, how, whom they divided precisely, and why. We know too little about the tireless and sweeping efforts, freedom movements of a sort, to redraw these divisions or to wipe them out altogether. And we know too little about the upshot and impact of these struggles between dividers and divided—these "wars-within-wars," in writer Ralph Ellison's evocative and apt phrase—on US troops, on the war effort, and on the nation as a whole.[5] This book tells these stories.

It follows a portion of the sixteen million young Americans who served in World War II as they metamorphosed from civilians to service members, as they received troop assignments and training, as they served in the United States and in theaters all around the world, and as the lucky among them returned home. This was a large, extraordinarily varied segment of the US population, whose ancestors or who themselves hailed from every corner of the globe. Indeed, one early wartime list of army inductees, organized by nativity, had eighty-three entries, including places as far-flung as Panama and Persia, Haiti and Hungary, Chile and China, Liberia and Latvia, and European and US colonial possessions everywhere in between.[6] The US military shoehorned this kaleidoscopic swath of humanity into a shifting set of "racial" categories, including colored or Negro, white, Japanese, Chinese, Puerto Rican, and American Indian.

The divisions or color lines that cleaved some of these people from others, in varying configurations, are the subject of this book. Who served?

Who fought? Who died? Who gave orders and who was forced to follow them? Who received the best ratings and jobs and pay and promotions? Who was court-martialed? Who received furloughs and leaves? Who received honorable or dishonorable discharges? Who ate at the officers' club? Who danced at the post's main recreation center? Who drank at the best pub in Cherbourg, France, or swam in the nicest pool in Calcutta? Shaping every imaginable aspect of military life, color lines often spoke definitively in all these matters and more.

What exactly did they have to say? The simplest and most fundamental answer is white supremacy. Taken as a whole, the US military constituted a sprawling structure of white domination in that it offered a grossly disproportionate share of power and prestige to those who could claim status as white. In comparison with all other people, whites had a much easier time joining the military—or a particular service or branch in it; breaking into the officer ranks and rising within them; receiving skilled, well-paid work and promotions; enjoying adequate recreational facilities on and off post, at home and abroad; fighting in combat and receiving the honor that came along with it; getting a fair shake in the military's criminal justice system; winning awards and decorations; and being discharged honorably, on time, and with access to invaluable GI Bill benefits.

But who were these white people exactly? And if their lives in the military had countless clear advantages, in relation to whom did they enjoy them? The answer is complicated, since the military's crisscrossing color lines defined whites and everyone else in less than clear-cut ways. By far the military's most foundational, ubiquitous, institutionalized, and consequential racist division split "colored" from white—or, in today's terms, black from white. Colored included anyone who was "Negro" or part "Negro," that is, anyone who had any discernible trace of "Negro" descent.[7] But the all-important white category was a moving target. At its most inclusive, it corralled everyone *not* colored, creating what some scholars today call a black-nonblack line. In these cases, the power of the black-white divide trumped, blurred, and even sometimes dissolved other lines, transforming a heterogeneous mix of people—Japanese Americans, Chinese Americans, Filipino Americans, Mexican Americans, Native Americans, Puerto Ricans, and others—into white insiders of a sort. One 1940 War Department memo regarding who would join white military outfits, for example, held that "[t]rainees of all races other than negro will be assigned the same as white trainees."[8]

A close parsing of the language, however, reveals that some of those "races other than negro" were not exactly white but would be assigned to outfits as if they were. Here, then, is a sign that the military established additional racist divisions—color lines within color lines, to paraphrase activist-intellectual W. E. B. Du Bois.[9] The most important of these were various versions of a white-nonwhite divide. They were less widespread, less institutionalized, and more capricious than the black-white ones, but at times they nonetheless narrowed the category of white to include, at its most exclusive, only those of supposed "pure" European descent. This meant that various groups within that "heterogeneous mix"—including Asian Americans, Latin Americans, and Native Americans—zigged and zagged between whiteness, nonwhiteness, and nominal whiteness, between insider, outsider, and a murky middle ground. None of these groups moved more frequently or more dramatically than Japanese Americans, thanks to their supposed ties to America's enemy in the Pacific. In fact, racist assumptions about these ties sometimes led to exclusions of Japanese Americans alone—a Japanese–non-Japanese line, which appears most obvious in the navy's outright ban on their enlistment throughout the war.

Overall, then, the military's complex of color lines—most notably, black-white, black-nonblack, white-nonwhite, and even occasionally Japanese–non-Japanese—did not simply constitute a structure of white domination. It was also a structure of black subordination—and often Japanese American and other nonwhite subordination, too.[10]

There was nothing static or inevitable about this structure. Some color lines originated during World War II, in direct response to its twists and turns. But even those lines that long preceded the war, especially black-white ones, had to be re-created affirmatively and continually throughout the conflict. As one landmark study of the wartime army put it, "[T]he formal rules, detailed and as elaborate as they were, and embodying past experience and long traditions of the Regular Army, were progressively inundated by a flood of new and rapidly modifying enactments required to meet the ever-changing situation presented by the rapid growth of the civilian Army and by the new demands of World War II."[11] In part as a consequence of this wartime flux, the military's various color lines shifted over time. The white-nonwhite divide generally blurred over the course of the war, often a fair amount. To a lesser but nonetheless important extent, the black-white divide did so as well, especially in the war's final year or so and especially overseas.

Erecting these divides was a group effort. Generally speaking, if some ordinary people, both in and out of uniform, proved enthusiastic builders, more powerful architects had the most say in the matter. These included on-the-ground commanders, who were sometimes granted the authority and discretion to craft racist divisions as they saw fit. In the main, however,

War and Navy Department leaders proved unquestionably the most decisive. Through their actions and inactions, they determined who joined the
military's ranks, who served in so-called white, colored, or other outfits,
which "races" mattered when it came to classifying inductees and how exactly this classification was conducted, and who received the most and least
advantages in uniform.

With a few important exceptions, the White House, Congress, and the
courts, including the Supreme Court, supported these leaders implicitly
or explicitly all along the way. President Roosevelt was instrumental in
forcing the navy to enlist more black people and in pushing the army to
desegregate a few facilities. But he was otherwise either uninterested in
the military's color lines or supportive of them. Southern Democrats in
Congress exploited their outsize institutional power to insist that the military maintain its black-white lines (they cared little about white-nonwhite
or Japanese–non-Japanese ones). At the same time, liberals in Congress
managed to pass a few laws that blurred them—or at least promised to.
None was more important than the 1940 Selective Training and Service
Act (STSA), which contained a seemingly straightforward and sweeping
civil rights clause: "[I]n the selection and training of men under this Act,
and in the interpretation and execution of the provisions of this Act, there
shall be no discrimination against any person on account of race or color."[12]
Had the military followed the letter of the law, or had the White House or
the courts forced it to do so, America's World War II armed forces would
have been far more egalitarian. After all, even the army itself conceded that
"[a]ny action . . . which brings an advantage or disadvantage to any person,
or which makes any discrimination between persons because of their race
or color would be in direct violation of the spirit and letter of this [Selective
Training and Service] Act."[13] But virtually no one in the federal government showed any interest in enforcing this law, though many of its main
branches had plenty of opportunities to do so.

The fate of the STSA, then, confirms a fundamental insight of numerous
legal scholars—that, in Noura Erakat's words, "the law is only as mean-
ingful as the political will underpinning its enforcement." It also shows
that, unlike what occurred in many other stories about state-sponsored
racism in this period, Congress, and southern Democrats in particular,
played no more than secondary roles.[14] Finally, the military's color lines
were not simply unjust, inefficient, and diametrically opposed to America's
stated war aims; they were also unlawful.

Military leaders and their supporters, however, saw things very
differently. In their view, they built these lines for one inescapable,

seemingly paradoxical reason: winning the war for Four Freedoms required unfreedoms.[15] In the case of the black-white divide, leaders claimed repeatedly that the morale, efficiency, and discipline of US troops, by which they invariably meant white US troops, demanded it. The implication was that whites would otherwise be too consumed by anti-black resentments and conflict to invest their all in the war effort. The black-white divide, from this perspective, was a wartime imperative, a precondition for victory. This argument was a damning admission about the depths of the nation's anti-black racism, and it painted a picture of the wartime military that contrasted sharply with popular notions of unity. But, truthfully, the black-white divide had more to do with leaders' own sentiments about black people's supposed inferiority as soldiers and as officers and their deep investments in white domination and black subordination. Both, they seemed to believe in their bones, were natural, essential, and virtuous features of American life. When the military itself—through the standardization, valorization, and geographical movement of its troops—proved at times to threaten these features, no matter how unwittingly, leaders redoubled their efforts to shore them up. Toward war's end, this white supremacist consensus showed cracks among some military brass, especially in the navy, but other leaders clung to it tenaciously through victory and beyond.

The white-nonwhite and Japanese–non-Japanese divides stemmed in part from their own particular logics. At times, military leaders also viewed them as essential to the war effort, none more so than when Japanese Americans and issues of national security were involved. If military brass viewed black people as threats to the nation for their supposed incompetence, Japanese Americans were seen as threats for another reason: their putatively indelible ties to the Japanese enemy and, relatedly, their always suspect, if not downright unattainable, Americanness. At other times, however, these leaders also viewed impermeable white-nonwhite and Japanese–non-Japanese divides—which variously targeted Asian Americans, Latin Americans, Native Americans, and more—as war-effort liabilities. They felt these lines damaged America's ties to its "darker" allies abroad, confirmed Axis propagandists' claims about the United States' race war for white supremacy, and encouraged various nonwhites to join hands in the struggle against the military's racist divisions. Of course, black activists and their allies made some of these same points about the black-white divide; that so few leaders seriously considered them offers another indication of their deeper commitments to it. If nearly all America's military brass viewed bright black-white lines as an undisputed war imperative, the value of white-nonwhite and Japanese–non-Japanese ones was more contingent, varying somewhat depending on the time, the context, and the people in question. Here, then, was one among many reasons that the latter divides were never as widespread, institutionalized, or consequential as the former.

* * *

The largely top-down efforts to draw divides constitutes only half the story. After all, no small part of the military's purpose in building racist boundaries in the first place was defensive; it sought to shore them up against black people's and others' constant efforts to rewrite or remove them. Furthermore, to the extent that these boundaries shifted or blurred over the course of the war, bottom-up struggles deserve a good deal of the credit. And yet the role of the military, and especially troops themselves, in civil rights histories is not well understood.[16] Wide-ranging battles against the military's racist divisions constitute an important chapter in the broader story of modern America's freedom movements.

These struggles were plural, because just as distinct color lines wended their way throughout the military, so too did distinct movements arise in response.[17] The largest of these involved black troops and an impressive array of allies, including black newspapers, civil rights organizations, unions, religious groups, liberals and leftists of various sectarian stripes, a select few military officials, and troops' families and loved ones, especially their mothers. Their primary target was the military's manifold black-white lines, or color lines altogether. The troops themselves tended to focus on those boundaries most common in their day-to-day lives in uniform—those involving, say, rank and promotions and jobs and recreational space. Their allies supported them in these battles, but also took the lead on broader policy fights about equal access to the military (though some strove to avoid fighting in the "white man's war") and its desegregation. Black activists and their supporters employed the broadest range of protest styles and tactics, working both inside formal institutional channels—letters and petitions to officials, editorials, congressional testimony, political lobbying, voting, and litigation—and outside them—boycotts, marches, strikes, sit-ins, and armed self-defense. They acted overtly and covertly, individually and collectively, and with and without the guidance and blessing of formal organizations like the NAACP. They tried their best as soldiers, hoping that heroic service in uniform might finally secure for them some semblance of fairness and decency and respect; and they tried their least, convinced that no amount of sacrifice in uniform would uproot Jim

Crow. Because troops often had less access to formal protest channels, they, more so than their civilian allies, practiced the most militant forms of resistance.

This activism, which took place throughout the United States and around the world, grew in visibility, significance, and coordination over the course of the war. By 1944 and 1945, for example, two national civilian organizations emerged in direct response to the increasingly spirited and combative protest of black troops themselves. They devoted all their energies to ending military racism: the Lynn Committee to Abolish Segregation in the Armed Forces and its successor of sorts, the National Committee to Abolish Segregation in the Armed Services (NCASAS). In their solitary martial focus, they appear to have been the first civil rights organizations of their kind.

Throughout most of the war, this movement faced formidable obstacles: little sympathy for, if not outright hostility to, their cause in the White House, in vast swaths of Congress, in the courts, and among military officers and the military's civilian leadership. And yet it scored some victories nonetheless, an indication of its reach and power. It managed to blur some of the military's black-white lines, including those related to enlistment, training camps, recreational spaces both on and off posts, in the United States and around the world, and even a few fighting units in western Europe. Perhaps more important, it succeeded in fundamentally and permanently shifting the conversation about military racism. For those advocating for integrated military units, for example, this was a fringe position at the start of the war but became a thoroughly mainstream one in black, liberal, and Left circles by its end—that is, within the span of four or five short years. By this point, even some pillars of white power in the military and Congress (and, eventually, the White House) came around to this view. Indeed, the postwar desegregation of the US military appears utterly inconceivable without an appreciation for African Americans' and their allies' tireless and extensive wartime activism around this and related issues. It laid the indispensable foundation for President Truman's landmark executive order 9981 in July 1948 and for the actual integration of troops that followed in fits and starts thereafter.

Facing their own set of military color lines, Japanese Americans and their allies also fought to resist and rewrite them. Their fight was more limited than that of African Americans, of course, because their population was much smaller and they lacked the same group-advocacy institutional infrastructure that black people had painstakingly built over many decades. Like many African Americans, most Japanese Americans were bereft of basic rights, though for some distinct reasons. Not only soldiers in an authoritarian army, they were also prisoners in detention camps and immigrants barred from naturalization. Despite these imposing handicaps, Japanese Americans still managed to resist military color lines with striking success.

The main actors in this struggle were ordinary Japanese Americans, both in and out of uniform, along with a variety of allies whose help they enlisted—from War Department brass like John J. McCloy to cabinet officials to the heads of federal agencies to congressional leaders. Some Japanese Americans wished to have nothing to do with a government and military that, without a whiff of due process, uprooted and incarcerated more than 110,000 of them. But those who embraced the opportunity to serve, or, more often, simply complied with conscription, fought to remove all color lines that concerned them, including the blanket bans or restrictions on their enlistment, the requirement that some serve solely in segregated combat units, and the singularly expansive levels of surveillance imposed upon them. Interestingly, a small subset of Japanese Americans also made their compliance with induction conditional on their receiving just compensation—reparations—for the wrongs of mass removal and mass incarceration.

Japanese Americans' tactics, like those of African Americans, were varied. They worked both within mainstream politics—writing letters, submitting petitions, meeting with government officials—and outside it—fighting with fellow soldiers who refused to distinguish between Japanese American soldiers and the enemy "Japs," conducting at least one large sit-down strike to protest their mistreatment in uniform, and sometimes, in the most extreme cases, resisting both voluntary enlistment and compulsory conscription, demanding repatriation and expatriation, and renouncing their US citizenship. While some organizations, especially the Japanese American Citizens League (JACL), attempted to corral these efforts, most activism occurred well beyond its grasp.

In the end, Japanese Americans' wartime struggle against military racism succeeded in greatly expanding their army enlistment, assigning large numbers of Japanese Americans to so-called white outfits, and helping to blur numerous color lines in uniform. These victories sometimes outpaced those of African Americans, even though Japanese Americans' activism was never as extensive as black people's. As will be shown time and again in the pages that follow, the state's institutional investments were much greater with black-white lines than with white-nonwhite ones, including those related to Japanese Americans. Indeed, sometimes military leaders thought that weakening the latter would strengthen the former—a trade-off they occasionally willingly made.

There were also miscellaneous struggles or moments of struggle involving people whom the military, at one time or another, excluded from the white category, included in the "colored" one, or both. Indeed, perhaps the most important of these struggles involved an assorted collection of inductees, whose official "racial" designation was the subject of great debate between the military and the men themselves. In many of these cases, the latter—who identified as Indian, Creole, Puerto Rican, Moorish American, and more—fought most fervently to be *not* black, since it was that category that occupied the deeply deleterious side of the military's most foundational and powerful racist divides. This point reminds us that these struggles against military racisms were as varied as the racisms themselves. Some people wished to keep color lines in place but simply to relocate themselves—and perhaps their fellows (however defined)—in relation to those lines; others wished to blur some color lines but not others; and still others fought to eliminate color lines altogether.

In part because of these varied racisms and varied responses, these struggles seldom intersected. There were, to be sure, fleeting, fascinating, pregnant moments when they did, especially among the military's two most subordinated groups—Japanese Americans and African Americans. Sometimes nonwhites expressed affinities for one another, joined forces in impromptu battles against white racisms, or even collaborated more formally, as when the NCASAS decried military "segregation and discrimination" aimed not simply at "Negro soldiers," but also at "soldiers of other minority groups," and sought to mobilize a broad swath of people—white, "Negro, Mexican, Chinese, Filipino, and Japanese"—for "concerted action."[18] But more frequently the military's multiple lines served to fracture its ranks, impeding efforts, both during the war and long after, to cross color lines and to build broad-based solidarities as, say, "darker races," workers, veterans, or Americans.

* * *

Divisions rests on a wealth of sources. It includes more than one hundred distinct collections at dozens of archives across the country, such as military, court, and other government documents; the records of numerous civil rights groups and of other nongovernmental organizations; and the personal papers of scores of wartime leaders, from Franklin Roosevelt, Harry Truman, and many of their top aides to an eclectic mix of others, including A. Philip Randolph, Rayford Logan, Carey McWilliams, George I. Sánchez, Dwight Macdonald, and many more. It draws on various oral history collections from the early postwar years and later. It includes published primary sources, such as a wide variety of big-city, small-town, black, Japanese American, and other newspapers, as well as memoirs, magazines, journal articles, and books. And it includes the vast secondary-source literature on the war.

Several concepts have helped me interpret these sources. The terms *division, line, boundary, divide,* and so forth, all of which are used interchangeably, refer to acts—individual, collective, or institutional, conscious or unconscious, implicit or explicit, formal or informal, symbolic, physical, affective, or behavioral—that distinguish some persons from other persons and, in the process, unite some persons with other persons. Acts of distinction, it must be remembered, are always simultaneously acts of assimilation—at once *both* inclusionary and exclusionary. These lines, boundaries, and so forth appear in numerous forms in the pages that follow—as jokes and as stories, as job structures and as patterns of promotion, as physical barriers in space, say a string between areas of auditorium seating, and as written and unwritten rules regarding social interactions. They also appear as formal policies about enlistment, unit assignment, and group classification and as day-to-day practices of association and disassociation.[19] Two elements make a line a "color line" or a boundary a "racist boundary." Racist distinctions are made on the basis of "race," that is, on the basis of ancestry, phenotype, supposedly inherent traits, or some combination, and they help produce or reproduce inequality and domination.[20]

These definitions suggest some of the advantages of *color line* or *racist boundary* as key concepts. Most important, they allow for a deep, textured analysis of social life. In the pages that follow, line-drawing or boundary-making happens on big and small scales, say, in everyday encounters between individuals, in the formal policies of state institutions, and in global developments, too. It involves both the "cultural" and "material" dimensions of life, and the intersections between the two. It concerns not simply whites and blacks or whites and nonwhites (or some analogue, such as people of color) arrayed along a single hierarchy or binary, which has been the main approach of the great majority of "race" scholarship for decades; instead, it involves a complex mix of categories, hierarchies, and binaries—hence my frequent use of "lines" and "boundaries" in the plural—all of which are constantly made (and sometimes unmade) in relation to one another.[21] As this observation would suggest, acts of line-drawing or boundary-making are also always in motion, always in process, always about "dynamic, unfolding relations rather than . . . static, unchanging things."[22] For example, in a classic "race relations" story, white discriminates against black, and both white and black are seemingly stable categories, ontologically uncomplicated. But in a boundary story, when white distinguishes itself from black, it discriminates, but it also reproduces and naturalizes the very idea of white and black. The color-line concept has one final, important advantage: in contrast to more technical, arcane language, it's familiar; a long list of social commentators have employed it for more than a century.

* * *

This book explores color lines in a particular setting at a particular time—the US military in and around World War II. This time and this place were critical because sixteen million people served, roughly one in nine Americans. Never before or since has such a large proportion of the US population been in uniform. Furthermore, these men and some women shared life-altering experiences at a young, impressionable age; the average GI, in 1944, was not quite twenty-six.[23] For these reasons and because, in the words of one postwar memo from President Truman's Committee on Civil Rights, "military service is the one place in the society where the mind of the adult is completely at the disposal of his government," "the minority group policies of the armed forces during World War II had a considerable impact upon the thinking of the American people." A careful, comprehensive reckoning with these policies and this thinking, in all their complexity, is long past overdue.[24]

At the same time, the wartime military, as an institution, had its quirks. It was deeply stratified beyond its racism, principally along lines of rank and gender. Indeed, commentators at the time and since have likened the divisions between officers and enlisted personnel to a "caste system" and a "highly stratified social system, in which hierarchies of deference were formally and minutely established by official regulation, subject to penalties for infraction, on and off duty."[25] Similarly, the World War II military was 98 percent male, assigned nearly all the relatively few women in its ranks to "the traditional female areas of office work, communications and health care," barred women from supervising men, and constituted a masculinist space par excellence, a "rite of passage that defined manhood."[26] The pages that follow will attempt at times to explain the military's racist divisions within the context of its other social boundaries, all of which intersected in complex ways.

The military was also a deeply authoritarian institution, especially for the vast majority of troops who found themselves among its enlisted ranks. If conscripted, one was forced to join. For those draftees and for everyone else, one was forced to follow orders and to remain in uniform, and had little formal recourse to push back or to dissent. This fact not only deeply shaped the various struggles to uproot or reroute the military's racist divisions, often pushing those struggles outside of established political and institutional channels. It also meant that it was a crime, even punishable by death in the most extreme instances, to escape these divisions through, for example, draft evasion, desertion, or temporary absence without leave. In the case of the World War II military, then, more than one million people had no choice but to subject themselves to the indignities, injustices, and violence of official state racism.

Furthermore, they were forced to do so all the while that they risked their lives to defend the United States and its allies against the Axis—for freedom no less. Some African Americans, Japanese Americans, and others well understood the excruciating ironies of the situation and responded by attempting to avoid service altogether. But far more people accepted the responsibility, even embraced it. That meant that only in the military did the US government deny a subset of its people the rights and privileges of citizenship at precisely the time that those same people performed the most solemn and dangerous obligation of citizenship: soldiering in time of war.

Finally, the military was a workplace—indeed, by far the nation's largest one during the war—but, again, with particularities. Like many capitalist workplaces, the military was a site of labor, wages, bosses, discipline, and divisions. One can, then, fruitfully reverse a Karl Marx analogy: an army of soldiers under the command of a military leader requires, like a real capitalist workplace, managers (officers) and foremen and overlookers (sergeants), who, while the work is being done, command in the name of the military leader. Understanding these connections, Americans during the war sometimes spoke of service personnel as "workers in uniforms."[27] But in other respects, the military was a less typical workplace. Not only was it more authoritarian than most, where workers had no formal rights to resist or to unionize or even to quit, but it also required around-the-clock labor. Save for the occasional leave or furlough, troops were always "on the job," in a sense, a true "24 hours' system" of "day and night work," whether drilling, training, fighting, garrisoning, sleeping, eating, bathing, or even relaxing off duty.[28]

* * *

Divisions proceeds by examining color lines, and the battles they generated, as servicemen and -women progressed through the military: in enlistment, in the organization of military outfits, in the official "racial" classification of all troops, in their training and service in the United States, in their travels and fighting overseas, and in their return home and their experiences of mustering out. Except for the chapters about classification and return, each of these subjects receives two chapters each—one that looks at black-white lines and the other principally at white-nonwhite ones.

In the end, the call and response of military racism and resistance discussed here cast a long and complex shadow over postwar American life, one that has not been fully examined or understood. On the one hand, it convinced or further convinced a growing number of American veterans to democratize the nation, invigorating a range of existing freedom struggles and laying the foundation for important civil rights gains to come, beginning with the desegregation of the military itself. On the other hand, the military's color lines also undermined these struggles and any hopes of building a more egalitarian nation. They traumatized, even killed, an unknowable number of nonwhite troops. They further naturalized the very concept of race. They deepened many whites' investments in white supremacy, especially anti-black racism. And they further fractured the American people and their politics. Seldom the stories we associate with the "good war," the Greatest Generation, or the US military, they deserve our undivided attention.

PART I

Enlistment

CHAPTER 1

c✍っ

The Jim Crow Boomerang

Perhaps the US military's most foundational color line involved enlistment—who could join the armed forces and who could not. Among able-bodied male adults, African Americans unquestionably faced the greatest restrictions during World War II. Roughly 10 percent of the US population in 1940, they made up less than 7 percent of all troops that served in World War II. Put another way, had African Americans accounted for a more proportional share of wartime GIs, the United States could have mustered roughly half a million additional troops—or, for example, three times the total number of Allied service members at D-Day. This is a startlingly large number, especially when one considers that crushing wartime personnel demands ultimately forced the military to greatly expand its definition of fitness to serve. In time, it drafted men with one eye or no teeth or no hearing in one ear or no external ears at all or no thumb on one hand or only three fingers on the other.[1]

To many military officials, evidently, classification as "Negro" or "colored" constituted a greater liability than any of these physical disabilities, since black people's underrepresentation in the armed forces was no accident. Instead, it stemmed from a sustained and deliberate effort among the military's most powerful leaders—sometimes supported and other times opposed by President Roosevelt, members of Congress, and the courts—to bar or to limit African American enlistment. They did so for two related reasons. They thought that black people, in the main, made pitiful soldiers and, therefore, that restricting their numbers would improve the overall quality of America's fighting forces. They also thought that the morale and efficiency of these forces required the strict segregation of African American troops, an arrangement that, in their view, the uncontrolled influx of black inductees would undermine. Military leaders' efforts to restrict or exclude black enlistment took many forms: service- and branchwide bans on black troops, a severe curb on their voluntary enlistment, chronically low "Negro quotas" in the draft, and chronically high rejection rates at induction stations.

And yet, as substantial as this underrepresentation was, it would have been worse but for black people's unstinting activism on the issue, with important if occasional help from others and from the broader demand for troops. A significant minority of African Americans, to be sure, wanted nothing to do with the "white man's war" and the forces fighting it. But many other black people battled vigorously for the "right to fight," by writing to political and military officials, composing editorials, signing and circulating petitions, bringing suits in court, testifying before Congress, and meeting with the president. In these efforts, a surprisingly diverse range of whites played a supporting role, from ordinary people to members of Congress, governors, cabinet officials, and even, on occasion, President Roosevelt and select military leaders. Some white people were motivated by a noble belief in every citizen's fundamental right to serve his or her country. Others, especially military leaders, realized that if one branch of service did not take its share of African Americans, another branch might have to make up the difference. Still others were diehard white supremacists, who recognized that black people's underrepresentation in the military meant whites' overrepresentation, not simply among troops but among casualties; they therefore feared the prospect of a "Negrofied" postwar America. Thanks in part to the work of this motley mix, African Americans chief among them, the military lifted all branch and service bans on black enlistment early in the war. As a result, black people's induction numbers, while never reaching proportional levels, rose dramatically across the military over the course of the war.

In the end, black troops' contribution to the war effort was unquestionably substantial—in all, more than one million men and women served. But it could have been considerably more substantial had military authorities not placed countless enlistment barriers in African Americans' way. What specific and concrete impact these additional troops might have had on the war will never be known, but the question is well worth pondering.

WAITING OUT THE WHITE MAN'S WAR

When World War II broke out and the US military began recruiting and drafting men for a life-or-death struggle against the Axis powers, surely it had a place for a young John Hope Franklin. Born and raised in Oklahoma, he graduated from high school as a sixteen-year-old valedictorian in 1931 and then moved to Nashville to attend Fisk University. Four years later, he moved on to Harvard, where he received a PhD in history in 1941. He was twenty-six years old. Soon, he would publish his first book on free black people in North Carolina; by 1947, his now-classic history of African Americans, *From Slavery to Freedom*, would appear.

Having seen the navy's full-page advertisements in the newspaper citing its desperate need for clerical help, Franklin hurried down to the local recruiting office to join up. He was more than qualified for the job: he had received numerous typing medals, was proficient in shorthand, could claim six years of secretarial experience, had completed coursework in accounting, and had achieved success as a young scholar. But the navy recruiter rejected Franklin out of hand. He told Franklin he was "lacking in [only] one qualification and that was color."[2] Franklin was black, and the navy refused to accept black recruits for any job save the most menial, as messmen.

But Franklin was undeterred. He moved on to the War Department, where he applied for a position as a historian, hoping to help research and write the army's official history of its war operations. Knowing that some white historians without his degrees and credentials had already been hired, Franklin was hopeful. Yet, as he later recalled, he "watched for the mail for weeks that stretched into months" but never received any War Department reply. "Perhaps . . . historians [there] were too busy to respond to a fellow historian's expression of interest in their enterprise. Perhaps once again I lacked that one essential prerequisite."[3]

In the end, Franklin never served in the US military. Although he entered the war years firmly committed to joining up and helping his country win the war, he soon concluded, after countless humiliations, that "the United States, however much it was devoted to protecting the freedoms and rights of Europeans, had no respect for me, little interest in my well-being, and not even a desire to utilize my professional services." Franklin "spent the remainder of the war years successfully and with malice aforethought outwitting my draft board and the entire Selective Service establishment."[4]

Franklin's eventual cynicism about the war effort and determination to avoid service in it were not entirely uncommon among African Americans during World War II. In the spring of 1941, a reporter for *PM*, an important New York City left-wing tabloid, journeyed uptown to 125th Street in Harlem to ask African Americans, "How does the Negro feel about the war?" Interviewing men on the street (no women appear to have been asked), the reporter found that the great majority expressed "sometimes profusely, sometimes hopelessly, always bitterly" that "they wanted no part of somebody else's war." Still incensed by World War I–era broken promises about "making the world safe for democracy" and infuriated by pervasive discrimination in the military, defense industries, and elsewhere, a segment of African Americans felt the same way, especially in the war's early years. At one January 1942 conference about black people's war participation, sponsored by the NAACP and the National Urban League, nearly all the attendees supported a resolution stating that "the colored people are not wholeheartedly and unreservedly all out in support of the present war." Stories about African Americans' low morale and their apathy toward a "white man's war" appeared frequently in mainstream magazines and in the black press. One *Harper's Magazine* article from April 1942, written by black journalist Earl Brown, reported that the "Negro to-day is angry, resentful, and utterly apathetic about the war. 'Fight for what?' he is asking. 'This war doesn't mean a thing to me. If we win I lose, so what?'" Five months later, in a *Nation* article, black scholar-activist Horace Cayton wondered whether the war, from African Americans' perspective, amounted to nothing more than "fighting for white folks."[5]

Government intelligence and public opinion studies painted a similar picture. One national survey of more than seven hundred African Americans, conducted in the first few months after the attack on Pearl Harbor, found that many black people "seem to feel disconnected and aloof from the war." Later polls from 1942 and 1943 based on interviews of several thousand African Americans in a range of cities—from New York and Chicago to Atlanta and Memphis—reported an "*almost even split* between those who say 'beat Germany and Japan' and those who argue for 'democracy at home.'" Yet another survey of black people in Baltimore and Cincinnati, in June 1942, found that a "frequently noted comment" in both cities was that "this is a white man's war." "We have no business in this [war] anyhow," said one domestic in Baltimore. "This is their war, not ours. They took our men in the other war, and what did we get out of it?" FBI reports from around the same time found similar sentiments in places as diverse as Huntington, West Virginia; Knoxville, Tennessee; and Chicago.[6]

This apathy, ambivalence, or hostility toward the war, born of deep racism-related resentments, occasionally expressed itself—as it did, eventually, in John Hope Franklin's case—as an effort to avoid military service.

Sometimes this involved the quiet refusal to register for the draft or to provide a correct address to Selective Service officials or to leave a forwarding address after a move. Sometimes it involved the determination to find work that offered a draft deferment. "I took this job because I hoped it would get me out of the draft," admitted one black welder in Boston, in early 1943. "I'd die before I'd fight in a Jim Crow army!" And sometimes it involved louder acts of defiance. In the wake of the 1942 Sojourner Truth riot, in which whites in Detroit violently barred black tenants from a new federal housing project, "the negroes are tearing up their draft cards," reported Attorney General Francis Biddle after a White House cabinet meeting.[7]

In some cases, black people's opposition to military service involved hoodwinking draft officials into classifying them as unfit to serve. One young black man, in a letter to his mother, reported: "[S]ome of the boys here in Harlem are talking about doing some crazy things to keep out of the war. One fellow knows some Russians, and he says they told him how the Russians in the last war used to cut off two or three fingers on each hand so they couldn't shoot a gun. Some more of them stuck something in their eyes so as they couldn't see. Some had their legs pulled out of joint, so that one leg would be shorter than the other. And a lot more took baths and went out in the cool air to catch pneumonia." Some African Americans cooked up their own choice methods of draft evasion: Redd Foxx, the future comedian, "ate pieces of soap bars to induce heart palpitations"; Malcolm X, then Malcolm Little, famously told the psychiatrist at his preinduction physical exam about his eagerness to join the army to "[o]rganize them nigger soldiers, you dig? Steal us some guns, and kill us crackers!"; and John Gillespie, future jazz legend "Dizzy," told psychiatrists that he had nothing against Germans, since it had been the American "white man's foot"—not any German's—that was "buried up to his knee in my asshole!" In all these cases, draft boards classified the men as 4-F, unfit to serve, and the men succeeded in avoiding induction.[8]

Occasionally black people openly defied Selective Service regulations, knowing full well that jail time could be a consequence. Soon after the passage of the Selective Training and Service Act (STSA), an organization sprouted up in Chicago calling itself the Conscientious Objectors Against Jim Crow. Led by a University of Chicago graduate student named St. Clair Drake, who would become an eminent scholar of black and urban life, it urged African American draftees to claim conscientious objector status, and therefore exemption from military service, on the basis of their opposition to segregation and discrimination in the armed forces. "We are ready, if it is necessary to do so, to go to jail or go to court to prove our point," Drake insisted. "We understand that quite a number of young men . . . will

Fig. 1.1 St. Clair Drake, c. 1947. Courtesy of the Roosevelt University Archives.

flatly refuse to join any national defense program . . . so long as discrimination exists."[9]

One such young man was Ernest Calloway, the educational director of the United Transport Service Workers of America (a labor union of railway station porters) and a member of Drake's organization. With his draft number soon to be called, he informed his local draft board in December 1940 that he would not accept "induction into military service under the present anti-democratic structure of the U.S. Army." Following Drake's lead, he claimed conscientious objector status and asked to be "exempted from military training until such time that my contribution and participation in the defense of my country can be made on the basis of complete equality." While sympathetic to his claims, his draft board rejected his request, though Calloway managed to avoid jail time. Draft and army officials dragged their feet for eighteen months, puzzling over how best to handle his potentially explosive case and wishing to minimize publicity. In the end, they found something defective about one of his elbows— perhaps that he swung it too aggressively in the army's direction—and declared him 4-F. He spent the rest of the war as a labor organizer on the home front.[10]

During World War II, Calloway's was the first well-publicized case of an African American protesting the Jim Crow military by resisting the draft, but it was not the last. Two years later, a local draft board ordered a Detroit physician named Edgar Keemer Jr. to report for induction in the army as an ordinary private. Keemer refused. Still smarting from his failed attempts to break into the all-white navy medical corps, despite his otherwise unassailable qualifications, he was also well aware that government policy typically allowed physicians to choose their branch of service. The FBI arrested Keemer for violating the STSA, but he was never convicted. As with Calloway, army and draft officials repeatedly postponed his hearing and eventually dropped his case, most likely because it highlighted the navy's rank discrimination against black doctors, it attracted the attention of the black and left-wing press, and Keemer secured the legal aid of the American Civil Liberties Union (ACLU), the NAACP, and the Socialist Workers Party.[11]

Calloway and Keemer were lucky at least in one respect: few African Americans who flouted draft requirements managed to escape both military service and jail time. Between 1941 and 1946, more than twenty-two hundred black people served time in prison for violating the STSA, a full 18 percent of the total. It is impossible to know what motivated these men in all cases. Surely the simple desire for self-preservation played a role at times—as did, in several high-profile cases involving dozens of black nationalists and small religious sects, a wholesale rejection of the United States and disavowal of US citizenship. In September 1942, for example, the FBI in Chicago arrested eighty-four members of three organizations— the Peace Movement of Ethiopia, the Brotherhood of Liberty for the Black People of America, and the Temple of Islam (the precursor to the Nation of Islam)—on sedition and draft evasion charges. Front-page stories in the Chicago newspapers and elsewhere offered sensationalistic details and patronizing stories about secret meetings with Japanese agents, dreams of a Japanese triumph over the Allies, and a new colored world in the making.[12] But in other cases African Americans defied the draft—and went to prison for it—to demand citizenship rights, not to disavow them. Lewis Jones, a Morehouse College graduate, spent three years in a federal prison rather than obey his induction order. "I am not a pacifist, nor a conscientious objector on any religious grounds," he explained in an October 1942 letter to the US Attorney's Office in New York City. "I am simply a colored American who insists on his constitutional right to serve his country as a citizen unsegregated, and unhumiliated in a jim crow army."[13]

ENDING EXCLUSIONS

Taken together, black people's opposition to military service during World War II was more common and varied than is often remembered. At the same time, it should not be exaggerated: many, many more African Americans, in the end, opted to enter the armed forces—or at least they tried to. They did so for a wide variety of reasons. For some, this willingness to serve came from a powerful and patriotic sense that, in the March on Washington Movement's (MOWM) phrase, "We Are Americans Too!" or from the sincere hope that wartime service might transform "part-time citizens" into full-fledged ones. In the letter to the editor that launched the well-known "Double V" campaign—"a two-pronged attack against our enslavers at home and those abroad who would enslave us"—James G. Thompson admitted that he was often treated like a "half American," but that he would nonetheless "die for the America that I know will someday become a reality." For other African Americans, the appeal of military service involved more mundane matters: the training, skills, and education that might come from it; or the clothing, food, and medical care; or perhaps most important, the pay, which was higher than that for many other jobs available to black people at the time. Still others joined up for the masculinist desire, in the words of one African American, to show that the "Negro is a Man among other men." No doubt many black people, like other Americans, simply complied with the draft, wanting to avoid arrest and imprisonment. Surely many African Americans joined the military for a combination of these and other reasons.[14]

But as Franklin's, Keemer's, and others' stories suggest, entering the armed services was never as straightforward as one might expect—especially when one was black. The most glaring obstacle for African Americans, at least in the early days of World War II, was that large swaths of the armed forces flatly refused to accept them. The navy, which for most of the nineteenth century included significant numbers of black people, barred their enlistment following World War I. When recruitment resumed in 1932, the navy restricted them to a single branch, the Messman Branch, where they shined shoes, washed dishes, prepared meals, and ironed clothes as stewards, cooks, and mess attendants. The marine corps—a "sister service" of the navy and, technically, a component of the Department of the Navy—maintained a rigid bar against all African Americans dating back to the late eighteenth century and remained firmly committed to that policy as World War II began.[15] The army, which included more than 400,000 African Americans during World War I, greatly and disproportionately reduced their ranks in the 1920s and 1930s, suspending black enlistment

and reenlistment for several years and restricting their service to a handful
of segregated units. These policies meant that vast stretches of the interwar
army, including its air corps, signal corps, field and coast artillery, and tank
corps, were effectively off limits to African Americans. By June 1940, then,
they were grossly underrepresented across the armed forces: while they
made up roughly one in ten Americans, they constituted less than one in
forty navy sailors, less than one in sixty-five army soldiers, and, excluding
the untold few that "passed," zero marines and zero airmen.[16]

These enlistment barriers were most infuriatingly visible to those
African Americans who volunteered to serve. One African American from
New Jersey, who wrote to Eleanor Roosevelt in 1939 for advice on how
to join the navy, was informed by navy officials that "men of the colored
race"—unless they are willing to cook and clean—"do not meet the best
interests of the United States Navy." A year later, another African American,
whose application to become an air corps pilot was initially accepted,
soon received a puzzling letter from a first lieutenant: "Dear Sir: Through
the most unfortunate circumstances, your application was allowed to be
completed because of our ignorance of your race. At the present time the
United States Army is not training any except members of the white race
for duty as pilots of military aircraft." And in November 1941, a twenty-
two-year-old named Albert James stopped by the army recruiting office
in downtown Manhattan, hoping to enlist as an army photographer. After
passing his mental and physical exams, he was placed on a waiting list,
because, as the desk sergeant suspected, "you're colored, aren't you?" In
a letter to President Roosevelt, James seethed at seeing "other enlistees,
white of course," accepted freely: "I do not see how I can raise my right hand
to God and swear to defend and uphold the principles of a government
which claims to be a democracy [but] which fosters racial discrimination
in its Army."[17]

Some African Americans had long railed against this discrimination.
Throughout the 1930s, for example, the NAACP wrote periodically to the
Navy and War Departments to protest their various restrictions on black
enlistment and service; and by the end of the decade, the *Pittsburgh Courier*
had become a leading voice on the issue, calling for "constant pressure . . . by
thousands of determined colored citizens and their white friends" to uproot the "forces of Negrophobism" in the military.[18] But the prospect of
a coming war—and America's related mobilization and preparedness
campaigns—offered black people newfound leverage in these struggles.
In June 1940, as Nazi Germany seized growing portions of Europe and as
Congress considered war preparedness bills, Roy Wilkins, assistant secretary of the NAACP, admitted to a supporter the difficulties involved in

"the over-turning of a long standing [military] tradition" to "secure the enlistment of Negro Americans in every branch of the armed service." But
"the events in Europe and the present vast national defense program," he
added hopefully, "may force the breaking down of some of the barriers."
After all, the *Philadelphia Tribune* surmised a few months later, "[r]acial discrimination in times of peace is stupid. When invasion threatens racial discrimination is suicidal." By 1940, growing numbers of black leaders, civil
rights groups, black newspapers, and others agreed, decrying "military
jim crowism" and demanding a "citizens'"—not a "white man's"—armed
forces.[19]

Black people differed, however, about the practical steps that might
lead there. Some thought that boycotting military service altogether was
the best protest strategy. Others debated whether to push for integrated
outfits or for segregated ones, which, some thought, might offer black
people a fuller range of officer and enlisted ranks and ratings. But in the
late 1930s and into 1940, when African Americans constituted such a disproportionately small share of military personnel, a range of black people
still tended to coalesce around two broad goals that addressed increasing
that share: they sought "full," "proportional," or "equal" representation
for African Americans in the military; and they wanted access to all its
branches, including those that had long excluded them, such as the air
corps and the marine corps. Supporting these positions, for example, were
not only big and small organizations from the National Urban League to
Washington, DC's black James Reese Europe Post of the American Legion.
They also included the NAACP, which was just beginning to advocate for integrated outfits, and the *Pittsburgh Courier* and the organization it helped
launch, the Committee on Participation of Negroes in the National Defense
Program (CPNNDP), both of which supported the formation of all-black
ones.[20]

This eclectic group fought for these shared goals by organizing and
mobilizing African Americans at the grass roots, by frequently publishing
editorials in the black press, by sending letters and resolutions to Congress,
the White House, military leaders, and the Democratic and Republican
National Committees, by testifying before and lobbying Congress, and
by meeting occasionally with President Roosevelt. Capturing the urgency
of these efforts was the renowned black civil rights attorney Charles
H. Houston, a World War I army veteran and leader in both the NAACP
and the CPNNDP. In June 1940, gravely concerned that the army was excluding too many African Americans from its ranks, he urged "every [black]
man and woman who has a son, brother or other relative within the draft
ages" to take action: "Get your friends and organizations to write and pass

resolutions by the thousands. Write to your local daily papers. Talk with your white friends against race discriminations when national unity should be the watchword. The [War Department] General Staff may be deaf as well as dumb, but if you protest loud enough and long enough, the voice of the people will be heard."[21]

Indeed it was, as victories, mostly modest, came first in Congress. With war raging overseas, Congress began to prepare the nation for its possible participation by increasing military appropriations and, eventually, by instituting the nation's first peacetime draft. All the while, black people shrewdly exploited their newfound importance as swing voters in the North and West to pressure their senators and House members to add civil rights protections to these laws, requiring the military to crack open its doors to them. In 1939, a Wyoming senator added to a bill to expand the national defense program a requirement that the War Department support civilian aviation training for black pilots. The understanding was that they would eventually gain entry to the heretofore lily-white air corps in the near future. In June 1940, the National Defense Act included a clause that promised "no Negro, because of race, shall be excluded from enlistment in the Army for service with colored military units." Three months later, in September 1940, thanks to lobbying on the part of the NAACP and the CPNNDP, the STSA boasted not one but two civil rights protections. The first, an amendment introduced by New York senator Robert Wagner, afforded any draft-age person "regardless of race or color . . . an opportunity to volunteer for induction into the land and naval forces of the United States," so long as those forces deemed him "acceptable." The second, introduced by New York congressman Hamilton Fish, who had commanded black soldiers during World War I, involved draftees and not voluntary enlistees. It provided that "in the selection and training of men under this Act, and in the interpretation and execution of the provisions of this Act, there shall be no discrimination against any person on account of race or color."[22]

The Fish amendment in particular would prove enormously important in forcing the army, and eventually all services, to accept a much larger share of black draftees and, as a result, to spread them more broadly across their various branches. But at the time, African Americans and their allies harbored justifiable doubts about the efficacy of these protections—or about how vigorously they would be enforced. The air corps managed to dodge the spirit of the 1939 amendment for several years, refusing to accept black pilots until 1941. The Fish amendment was, in the words of the Selective Service's sole race adviser, "probably the most definitely worded prohibition against discrimination found in any Federal law," yet the Wagner amendment's "acceptable" clause appeared to be its undoing. As NAACP leader Walter White fretted to a senator, "I fear that very few Negroes will prove 'acceptable' unless there is tremendous pressure or a very grave national crisis."[23]

Thanks to these uncertainties, black people turned their attention from Congress to military officials and especially to the commander in chief, President Roosevelt. In 1940, Roosevelt was locked in a presidential race that was closer than expected. His Republican opponent, Wendell Willkie, campaigned for black votes, in part by speaking out against the military's barriers to black enlistment. "I do not see any reason," he remarked in August, "why colored boys should not be trained as aviators the same as other boys." Roosevelt, by contrast, had said nothing publicly by the late summer, and some black voters took note. "Although Mr. Roosevelt is by law the Commander-in-Chief of the Army, Navy, and Marine Corps," wrote the *Pittsburgh Courier*, in late August 1940, "he has not said one word or lifted one little finger to end or even discourage the vicious system of discrimination against young colored America in these armed forces. . . . Today the Negro voter is completely disillusioned, and if the President does not know it now, he WILL know it on the morning of November 6, 1940."[24]

With the election nearing and the race tightening, Roosevelt in early September instructed the War Department to craft a statement that addressed some of African Americans' core concerns about the military: "colored men will have equal opportunity with white men in all departments of the Army." A week and a half later, on September 16, he made these points public in a statement he issued the day he signed the STSA. And at the end of the month, his wife, Eleanor, convinced him to meet with a group of prominent black leaders to discuss ways to remove anti-black barriers in the military—which were, in her view, "very bad politically besides being intrinsically wrong."[25]

The meeting took place at the White House on September 27. The three black leaders invited were Walter White of the NAACP, A. Philip Randolph of the Brotherhood of Sleeping Car Porters, and T. Arnold Hill, a former industrial secretary of the National Urban League. In addition to Roosevelt, they were joined by Frank Knox, the new secretary of the navy, and Robert P. Patterson, the assistant secretary of war. In the meeting's aftermath, during the final weeks of the campaign the White House press secretary created a political firestorm by implying falsely that Randolph, White, and Hill had approved the War Department's segregation policy. While this story has received considerable attention, many commentators have failed to note that the War Department's broader "negro" policy, as announced on October 9 (and as forecast by Roosevelt's statement on September 16), provided precisely the sort of access to the army for which many black people had been clamoring. Its first two points read: "The strength of the negro personnel of the Army of the United States will be maintained on the general basis of proportion of the negro population of the country"; and "Negro organizations will be established in each major [army] branch." This statement, then, marked an important, if sometimes overlooked victory for black activists. That, once achieved, some black leaders immediately and shrewdly pushed beyond it should not obscure this important fact. Indeed, when a more moderate group of black leaders, including Rayford Logan, the Howard University history professor and chairman of CPNNDP, met with the president a few weeks later, they readily admitted that the War Department policy was "just about what we are asking for."[26]

With access to the army seemingly taken care of, black people set their sights even more intensely on the air corps, the navy, and the marines. The first of these, formally a part of the army, appeared to be covered by the newly released War Department policy to establish "negro organizations" across all its major branches and by an earlier presidential statement that mentioned the future "formation of colored aviation units." Yet this point was not made explicit until January 1941, when the War Department announced it would open its doors finally to African Americans through the formation of the 99th Pursuit Squadron, a black flying outfit, of which the Tuskegee Airmen would later be a part. Its ground personnel would train at Chanute Field in Illinois and its pilots at a brand-new segregated field to be built at substantial taxpayer cost in Tuskegee, Alabama, only forty miles from an existing airfield for nonblacks.[27]

The decision to open the air corps to African Americans came from pressures internal and external to the army. Internally, once the War Department agreed publicly to take a proportionate share of black men and to spread them across all its major branches, the air corps' exclusion of black troops seemed to violate this new policy. The exclusion, if allowed to stand, would also have compelled the army's ground and service forces to take a larger share of African Americans to absorb some of the troops the air corps excluded. These branches objected to doing so, insisting, successfully in the end, that the air corps take its fair share.[28]

The external pressure came from black activists. Their campaign to gain equal access to the air corps, which dated back to World War I, involved some typical tactics—newspaper editorials, cover stories in the NAACP's monthly *Crisis* magazine, letters and resolutions to Congress, the president, and the military—and some less typical ones. In May 1939, two "dapper" black aviators from Chicago, Chauncey E. Spencer and Dale L. White, flew an old biplane on a daring journey from Auburn, Illinois, to Washington,

DC, hoping to convince Congress to open the air corps to black people.[29] This campaign came to a head in January 1941, when a Howard University student named Yancey Williams, represented by the NAACP, brought suit against the War Department for refusing to accept him into the air corps. Williams had a private pilot's license, had completed the requisite pilot training courses, and had passed his physical exam. But his application was turned down, Williams alleged, "on the ground that he is colored." Shortly after Williams filed his suit, however, the War Department announced the formation of its first black squadron (and the suit, it appears, was dropped).[30]

Opening up the navy and its marine corps to black enlistment took more time. The War Department's new "negro" policy did not extend to the Navy Department. Nor did the STSA's antidiscrimination clauses apply, at least for a time, since the navy did its own recruiting apart from the draft— and from its civil rights protections—until early 1943. Furthermore, the navy's leaders, during the early years of the war and in the first few months of America's involvement, categorically refused even to contemplate expanding African Americans' naval numbers and opportunities— and President Roosevelt, a former assistant secretary of the navy, initially seemed disinclined to force their hand. During the 1940 presidential election campaign, for example, while he helped pressure the War Department to drop some of its barriers to black army enlistment, he left the navy alone—his "pet arm," in Secretary of War Henry Stimson's begrudging phrase. In fact, the sum total of Roosevelt's effort to expand African Americans' role in the navy involved placing "a colored band on some of these ships, because they're darned good at it."[31]

But growing numbers of African Americans demanded change from the navy, especially after gaining greater access to the army and its air corps. For years, the *Pittsburgh Courier* had condemned "our lily-white navy," insisting presciently that "colored people can open up the navy to members of their race when they understand better the necessity and value of pressure politics." The broader black press came to agree, hammering the navy repeatedly for a "pots and pans policy" that restricted black enlistment to the Messman Branch. By late 1941, the navy began surveying these newspapers and found that dozens subscribed to this view, from well-known publications with national circulations like the *Pittsburgh Courier*, the *Baltimore Afro-American*, and the *Chicago Defender* to smaller, regional ones like the *Philadelphia Independent*, the *Minneapolis Spokesman*, the *Houston Informer*, and the *Seattle Northwest Enterprise*. A typical comment came from the *Kansas City Call* in October 1941: "Every time the Navy asks for Negro messmen our blood boils. If black boys can make up crack units in the Army, if some of them can rise to the rank of lieutenant, colonel and even general, if they are good soldiers on land, why wouldn't they be good soldiers on the sea?"[32] Civil rights organizations and leaders posed similar questions. In their two early White House conferences with President Roosevelt and with military leaders, in September 1940 and June 1941, Walter White and A. Philip Randolph asked not only about inclusion but also about integration within the navy. While White's NAACP held mass meetings, published pamphlets and editorials, and contemplated lawsuits to force the navy's hand, Randolph's famous threat to march on Washington in early 1941 included a demand for "abolishing discrimination in all government departments," including the navy.[33]

In time, this protest reached navy leaders, and eventually President Roosevelt himself. In the summer of 1941, with mounting calls for navy reforms and two weeks after the second White House conference in which Navy Secretary Knox apparently "had some rather brash remarks which got the colored people"—Randolph and White—"all churned up," Knox made his first concession. He established a four-person committee to examine whether the "enlisted personnel of the Navy and Marine Corps is

Fig. 1.2 Black officer's stewards serve a meal to the ship's white junior officers, c. April 1945. Courtesy National Archives, 80-G-K-3756.

representative of all United States citizens" and, if not, to suggest remedies. Later instructions made clear that the committee's focus should be on black people alone. Its majority report came back nearly six months later and called for no changes at all. In a rambling, disjointed memo, signed by two navy officers and a marine commander, it conceded that the navy placed rigid boundaries around all black men in order to prevent their mixing with or exercising authority over any enlisted whites. But these boundaries, far from constituting racial discrimination, were instead simply a "means of promoting efficiency, dependability and flexibility of the Navy as a whole." "For the good of the country, the efficiency of the Navy," it concluded, "no corrective measures are needed or desired."[34]

Addison Walker, the sole civilian on the committee and an aide to the navy's assistant secretary, saw things differently. In his minority report, dated December 31, 1941, he stressed that a "man's right to fight for his country is probably more fundamental than his right to vote" and that the "rights and privileges of . . . a group representing roughly 10% of the country's population, as is the case with the Negroes, comprise a social force that cannot be ignored." He warned, furthermore, that "the Negro today is not the cowed, humble, childlike person that his American ancestors were. With an emotional fervor, he is demanding equality of opportunity and this demand represents an expanding social force which can prove dangerous for iron clad restrictions unequipped with safety valves." He recommended, then, that the navy leadership consider a modest change: the creation of an experimental and segregated "assignment or rating for a negro combatant force," perhaps on a small vessel at a particular naval station or yard. "Such action would not relieve all criticism of the Navy by various members of the Negro race," Walker recognized. But "it would put the Navy in the strong position of doing something to broaden the opportunities for a minority group which is becoming increasingly articulate in its demands."[35]

Growing more sensitive to these demands, Roosevelt endorsed Walker's position a week later. This shift in view seems to have been at least a few weeks in the making. Just days after the attack on Pearl Harbor, Walter White fired off a telegram to Secretary Knox: "Please advise if radio and other appeals for enlistment in Navy include Negro Americans and if declaration of war and attack on America have caused or will cause any change in naval policy limiting service of Negroes to messmen division of Navy." White insisted on such a change. Unsatisfied with the navy's response—which seemed to support the status quo, in part because the "navy cannot take on the additional job of experimenting with social customs and traditions"—White then appealed to Roosevelt. He urged him to "issue an order to the Navy to abandon forthwith its policy of refusing to permit

Negroes to enlist save as messmen." The president asked for a reply from Mark Ethridge, the chairman of Roosevelt's newly created Committee on Fair Employment Practice, a product of White's and A. Philip Randolph's negotiating around the threatened march on Washington earlier in the year. Before composing his reply to White, however, Ethridge wrote the president, slamming the navy's "Negro" policies as "untenable and indefensible" and "not alert to one of the major moral issues of the present war." Echoing the views of Walker, he indicated that the navy could "at least explore the possibility" of finding other roles for black people. Convinced, Roosevelt wrote Secretary Knox on January 9, attaching Ethridge's letter and suggesting that "with all the Navy activities, the Bureau of Navigation might invent something that colored enlistees could do in addition to being messmen."[36]

A week later Knox asked the navy's General Board, its highest advisory group, for a plan to enlist five thousand African Americans outside of the Messman Branch, but the board claimed to be "unable to comply." Defending the status quo, it cited many of its traditional arguments: that accepting black people into its general service would lead to mixing with whites "on board ship life in particular close association," which would lower the "contentment, teamwork, and discipline in the service"; that black people, if they wanted to fight for their country, could join the army; and that the "white man is more adaptable and more efficient in the various conditions which are involved in the making of an effective man-of-war." When Knox passed these objections on to the president, Roosevelt, growing increasingly impatient with the navy's intransigence and with Knox's inability to overcome it, called the General Board's report "unsatisfactory" and "insufficient." He demanded further study. Channeling Addison Walker—who had, of course, simply repeated a point that African Americans had been making for years—Roosevelt stressed that African Americans made up almost one-tenth of the US population and were, as American citizens, "liable to military and naval service in the defense of their country." In the end, he rejected allowing black people to serve in all duties across the navy, since "to go the whole way at one fell swoop would seriously impair" its efficiency. But he did believe that "additional tasks" could be found for them in the navy.[37]

As the General Board returned to this question, demands for change grew more determined and widespread. Indeed, many African Americans' antipathy toward the navy seems to have crystallized in the first few months of 1942, but not simply because of its long-standing enlistment restrictions. News also broke that it had been partially responsible for the exclusion and then segregation of black blood donors from the Red Cross's national blood donor program and that it was not properly honoring—or, at first, even identifying—a black messman named Dorie Miller, who, while stationed at Pearl Harbor during the attack, fired an anti-aircraft machine gun at Japanese planes overhead and helped to carry an injured captain to safety, all amid falling torpedoes and a burning, sinking battleship.[38] In this new, increasingly charged moment, African Americans' protest letters, petitions, and resolutions flooded Knox's inbox; the black press insisted ever more adamantly that a "lily-white navy cannot fight for a free world"; beloved black heavyweight champion Joe Louis, upon joining the army, exclaimed, "I sure hope our boys will get their opportunity in the Navy equal with other boys"; and Arthur Mitchell, a black congressman from Chicago, declared from the floor of the House of Representatives, "I call on the American army, I call on the American navy, I call on the American government, yes, I call on white America to . . . let us go forth and save democracy for ourselves and for the world."[39]

By February and March 1942, black people's campaign to broaden the navy's enlistment opportunities also began receiving some high-profile white support. At a speech in New York City on March 19, former Republican Party presidential candidate Wendell Willkie, citing Dorie Miller, called for an end to the navy's bar against black enlistment outside the Messman Branch. Within a week's time, a mix of white newspapers from across the country—the *Des Moines Register*, the *Chicago Sun*, the *Hartford Courant*, the *Rutland (VT) Herald*—followed suit.[40] Meanwhile, inside the government, the War Department began pushing for navy reform as well. In the middle of February, Secretary of War Stimson began writing to Roosevelt to "force him to lay down the law to the Navy and make them take some colored marines." No civil rights advocate, Stimson feared that the navy's bar on black enlistment meant "the disproportionate number [of African Americans] which is thrown on us has given us a great burden."[41]

In late March, amid these expanding calls for change, the General Board relented. On March 20, it sent Knox a detailed plan for broader black enlistment, which, in its telling phrase, "would offer the least disadvantages." Eleven days later, Roosevelt approved the plan, though he objected to what he termed one "Ethiopian in the wood pile": that "several administrative authorities" would control such matters as the rate and size of black enlistment. Roosevelt insisted, instead, that he and Knox make those determinations. After they worked out these and other details in person, the navy finally announced its change in policy on April 7, 1942, a full seventeen months after the War Department promised to expand access to African Americans and some fourteen months after the air corps opened its doors to them for the first time: "Negro volunteers will be accepted for enlistment for general service in the reserve components of the U.S. Navy, the U.S. Marine Corps, and the U.S. Coast Guard"; and "all ratings in those three branches of the Naval Service will be opened to them."[42]

The limitations to the navy's policy changes became immediately apparent to many African Americans, in part because Secretary Knox emphasized them at his April 7 news conference: black men would be reservists, underlining the experimental and perhaps temporary nature of their wider inclusion in the navy; they would be strictly segregated from white personnel; they would be restricted to shore establishments and small boats and kept from serving, except as mess attendants, on the big ships in the fleet; and there was no promise about equal or proportional representation.[43] Because of these limitations, black people's views of the navy announcement were decidedly mixed. Some, like the National Negro Congress, hailed it as a "bold patriotic action in smashing age-old color restrictions"; others, like the Washington, DC, chapter of the NAACP, denounced it as "a demonstration of the Nazi attitude" and called for Knox's ouster; still others split the difference, as typified by a *Baltimore Afro-American* editorial: "Unlike some of our colleagues in the fight for equality, we are not going to kick Frank Knox in the face because he took

Fig. 1.3 William Baldwin, the first black recruit for the navy's General Service, June 2, 1942. Navy Secretary Frank Knox is to Baldwin's right. Courtesy National Archives, 208-NP-8B-2.

this action with reservations, and unlike other of our colleagues we are not going to heap upon him peans [*sic*] of praise, because we actually do not think he went as far as he should have gone or as far as public opinion would have permitted. But since he has gone further than any other secretary in the past fifty years we are going to give him a break and say: So far so good. But . . . we serve warning that we have just begun to fight."[44]

In truth, many black people applied this mixed message of praise, critique, and the promise of ongoing protest to all the armed services' early moves to end exclusions on black enlistment, not simply those in the navy. On the one hand, black protest, with some occasional white help along the way, scored some important early victories: for the first time ever black men could enlist in the marine corps; for the first time ever they could join the army in large, proportionate numbers that would be spread across all its branches, including the heretofore lily-white air corps; and for the first time in a generation they could enlist in the navy as something other than as messmen. On the other hand, black people began to turn their critical attention ever more pointedly from questions about access to military service to ones about the nature of military service—not least to the issue of their rigid segregation across all services.

But even regarding access, serious concerns remained. One involved black women. Starting in mid-1942, as the various services created new branches or auxiliaries for women—the Women's Army Auxiliary Corps (WAAC), the Women Accepted for Volunteer Emergency Service (WAVES), the US Coast Guard Women's Reserve (SPARS), and so forth—black people fought for black women's right to enlist. The WAAC (later WAC, or Women's Army Corps) accepted them from the outset, for example, but it took continuing black protest coupled with the pressures of another presidential election in 1944 before the WAVES and SPARS followed suit; the marines' auxiliary never did. In some cases, then, the complex interplay of anti-black racism and sexism conspired to erect and maintain boundaries to black enlistment that survived the war intact.[45]

THE OLIVE-DRAB CEILING

A much larger concern, simply because black men so greatly outnumbered black women in the military, was whether the former's broader enlistment opportunities were more symbolic than real; whether they would receive mere token representation or something more; whether they would receive proportional representation or something less. The answer, while varying across the military's assorted services and branches, lay somewhere

Fig. 1.4 Harriet Ida Perkins and Frances Wills, the first black WAVES to be commissioned, December 1944. Courtesy National Archives, 80-G-297441.

between token and proportional representation. But the case of the army, which of all services took the largest and fairest share of black people, shows that near-proportional representation was not the same as equal treatment. Even there, African Americans faced a series of complex and ever-changing barriers to entry, without which, for better or worse, they would have easily become overrepresented not underrepresented among soldiers.

The navy and the marine corps began to accept black enlistees on June 1, 1942, but their numbers were modest, especially when compared with those in the army. Many African Americans proved unwilling to join branches of the armed forces that had long excluded and demeaned them; and for that willing minority, rejection rates for physical and other reasons were high. By early 1943, African Americans' strength in the navy, negligible for so long, had increased significantly but was still modest: numbering nearly twenty-seven thousand in February 1943, black people constituted less than 2 percent of the navy's total strength (and a mere one-half of 1 percent of the army's roughly half million black soldiers at the time).[46]

But changes in the way the military procured its troops—and pressure from the White House and elsewhere—quickly led to a dramatic increase in African Americans' numbers in and, to a lesser extent, their share of the navy and marine corps. A December 1942 executive order forced these branches, beginning in February 1943, to do away with their separate recruiting efforts and their exclusive use of volunteers and to receive all future draft-age inductees—both those who were drafted and those who volunteered—through the Selective Service System; it also gave the newly established War Manpower Commission (WMC) control over the process. When the navy and marine corps began asking for relatively few black draftees in the early months of 1943, the WMC and President Roosevelt objected. In a February 1943 memorandum to Secretary Knox, Roosevelt warned him that "there is going to be a great deal of feeling if the Government in winning this war does not employ approximately 10 percent of negroes." It was perhaps the first time that Roosevelt insisted that the navy follow the army's plan of proportional black representation. In response, the navy and marine corps, starting in spring 1943 and continuing through the end of the war, inducted growing numbers and a fairer share of African Americans. But thanks in part to their long histories of exclusion and restriction, neither branch came close to Roosevelt's (belated) goal of proportional representation. By war's end, black people made up approximately 5 percent of the navy and 3 percent of the marine corps.[47]

In contrast, the army's ranks were 8 percent black by mid-1943 and between 8 and 9 percent for the rest of the war. But those percentages might have been a good deal higher. After all, the navy's and marine corps' early exclusions offered the army for a time a disproportionately large number of black men to choose from. Plus, throughout the war, African Americans were overrepresented among those men whom draft boards classified as I-A—fit to serve. This was not only because the navy and marine corps siphoned off white volunteers from this group. It was also because widespread employment discrimination left black people with fewer of the kinds of jobs that afforded them occupational deferments, because they were so woefully underrepresented on local draft boards and appeals boards, and because military authorities tended to keep many black soldiers far from the front lines, which meant rates of injury and death that were lower than those for whites. These factors, taken together, might have allowed over time for black people's total share of the army to rise above—perhaps well above—their share of the population.[48]

But it never did. The War Department policy, as stated clearly in October 1940, was that "the strength of the negro personnel of the Army of the United States will be maintained on the general basis of proportion of the negro population of the country." In other words, African Americans would be kept to a quota: the promise of proportional representation was also the promise to place firm limits—call it the olive-drab ceiling—on black army enlistment. "It is amazing that these announcements [of the quota] aroused scarcely any protest," noted a young lawyer named Milton Konvitz shortly after the War Department publicized its quota (and before he would begin working under Thurgood Marshall in the NAACP Legal Defense and Education Fund). "Here is an importation of . . . a practice made notorious toward the end of the Nineteenth Century when the Czarist government fixed a quota to govern the admission of Jews to the Russian universities and schools of higher learning. . . . Very quietly this obnoxious practice has been introduced in the United States, in the very institution designed to defend our democracy."[49]

In fact, some black people did protest the quota in time. An editorial in the NAACP's monthly, *The Crisis*, in October 1943, denounced "the enlistment and drafting of Negroes in accordance with a racial quota." But Konvitz's larger point, especially in the early days of the war, was correct. Some African Americans no doubt accepted the quota as protection against overrepresentation, a problem of real concern during World War I, when black people's share of total draftees exceeded their share of the population, especially in the South. Perhaps most important, at a time when they constituted less than 2 percent of the army's strength, the pledge to increase that paltry share seven or eight percentage points likely obscured for many black activists and their allies the quota's more retrograde and restrictive side. In fact, several years later, according to one *Pittsburgh Courier* survey, many black people still seemed satisfied with the quota. Asked, in the fall of 1943, whether the "10% induction of Negroes into the armed forces should continue to prevail," three-quarters of respondents said yes.[50]

War Department leaders insisted on firm limits to black enlistment for the same two, related reasons that the navy steadfastly banned it for a time. First, they had little faith in African Americans' abilities as soldiers. In the interwar period, the "semiofficial credo" of the army's officer corps was that black troops performed disastrously during World War I, due to

countless supposed liabilities, including carelessness, shiftlessness, se-
cretiveness, immorality, criminality, stupidity, and poor leadership skills.
These views permeated not only much of interwar American culture but
also numerous influential Army War College studies, in which so many
World War II army officers and leaders first encountered the "negro soldier"
as a putatively impenetrable problem. Reflecting these views was Secretary
Henry Stimson. At the very moment that his War Department formulated
its "negro policy," he wrote repeatedly in his personal diary about the "incompetency of the colored troops"; about how the "poor fellows had made
perfect fools of themselves" during World War I; about how "every time we
try to lift them a little bit beyond where they can go, disaster and confusion follows"; and about his efforts to dissuade President Roosevelt from
"placing too much responsibility on a race which was not showing initiative
in battle" and in whom "[l]eadership is not [yet] imbeded [*sic*]."[51]

War Department leaders also wished to limit black enlistment because of their unwavering commitment to segregation. They long feared
that black people's open access to the army would place such strains on
black units that some integration would have to result. In June 1940, as
Congress considered various military preparedness bills, Stimson's predecessor, Harry Woodring, strongly objected to one such bill that, in his
view, might have "result[ed] in the enlistment of Negroes . . . out of all
proportion to the colored population of the country." "Such a result," he
suggested, "would demoralize and weaken the effect of military units by
mixing colored and white soldiers in closely related units, or even in the
same units. . . . I have no objection whatever to negro troops but must
not be required to take them in such numbers as to prevent the proper"—
that is, segregated—"organization of the army." After Stimson succeeded
Woodring, he repeatedly made the identical argument. In early 1943, as
the WMC's chairman, Paul McNutt, pressured the army and navy to induct larger numbers of African Americans, Stimson adamantly resisted.
In several letters to McNutt, he argued that without carefully controlling
and limiting black enlistment, the army would be "forced to mix negro and
white enlisted personnel in the same units," which would "so gravely and
adversely affect the Army as to seriously impair the military effort."[52]

The army limited black enlistment in three principal ways—through
restrictions on voluntary enlistment; through race-specific draft calls,
which were chronically low for black people; and through rejections at induction stations. The other armed services used, to varying degrees, these
same methods. But the army was forced to be more creatively and secre-
tively restrictive than, say, the navy, because it both agreed publicly to
African Americans' proportional representation and had to abide by the

STSA's antidiscrimination protections throughout the war. Each of these restrictive methods generated immense controversy and protest—in some cases not only from black people wanting equal access to the military, but also from a diverse group of whites, some of whom, ironically, were die-hard segregationists who feared that whites' disproportionate share of the fighting and dying might lead to a "Negrofied" America. When one method proved too controversial, the army often employed another, trying throughout the war simultaneously to keep African Americans' numbers down and to cover its tracks while doing so. It had greater success with the former than with the latter.

The army's most long-standing method of restriction involved denying or greatly limiting African Americans' voluntary enlistment. This is how the army kept black people's numbers so low in the interwar years, and these barriers continued once the United States entered the war. In the frantic days following the attack on Pearl Harbor, when military recruiting stations stayed open around the clock and newspapers and radio beseeched men to join up, one black newspaper, echoing the black press in general, reported "Negro Recruits Not Wanted in Regular U.S. Army." Protest letters poured in to President Roosevelt. Receiving her share of these, Eleanor Roosevelt urged Secretary of War Stimson to take "steps to overcome the situation"—but to no avail.[53] From 1940 to 1945, the army accepted 1.4 million voluntary enlistees, only 2 percent of whom were black. Of course, some African Americans' reasonable reluctance to join the army surely depressed these numbers, but the army's own restrictions had a much greater effect. In early 1942, a draft official observed in private that voluntary enlistment, while completely closed to black people in the marine corps, was "practically closed" to them in the army and navy; ten months later, the Selective Service director conceded, again privately, that "the enlistment practices of the armed forces emphasize white recruiting." Indeed, the army's own postwar report on the "utilization of Negro manpower" readily admitted its wartime "reluctance to accept Negro volunteers." This, despite the fact that the STSA, according both to its wording and to the courts' interpretation of that wording, explicitly required that African Americans "be accorded privileges substantially equal to those afforded whites in the matter of volunteering."[54]

Black people, like other Americans, could also enter the army by another common route—the draft. It began soon after the STSA became law in September 1940, which seemed to promise equitable treatment not simply in volunteering but also in conscription. Yet for African Americans, new barriers to entering the army sprouted up just as soon as local draft boards did. The army's strict troop segregation policies required that separate race-specific calls be made for black people, on the one hand, and everyone else, on the other. Since the first draft call occurred in late October 1940, Roosevelt appears to have delayed instituting these race-specific calls for a month, so as not to raise "the problem of segregation one week before the [presidential] election." In the next six months or so of the draft's early operation, however, African Americans were conspicuously absent or significantly underrepresented among inductees. That is, they registered and were selected by local boards as fit to serve in large numbers, but the army inducted very few, if any, of them. The *Pittsburgh Courier* reported in late December 1940 that among the two hundred or so men the army would call in Washington, DC, for induction in January of the next year, not a single one was black. Similar stories appeared throughout the country. Indeed, by September 1941, the army had temporarily passed over nearly thirty thousand African American selectees, all of whom sat in limbo, having received one important draft document—a "Notice of Selection"—but not another—an "Order to Report for Induction." The problem, which waxed and waned over the course of the war, never went away. By early 1943, the number of those passed over had reached 300,000, and as late as October 1944, Selective Service director Lewis B. Hershey complained to Stimson about "the backlog of Negroes whom we have been unable to forward for induction because of insufficient calls for Negroes."[55]

For the first few years of the draft, War Department and Selective Service officials, and even President Roosevelt at least once, justified these delays in public as a consequence of temporarily inadequate training cadres and facilities for black troops. This was a problem that the army claimed to be working expeditiously to correct but that some black people saw, rightly, as a product of the army's insistence on segregated troops and camps. Privately these same officials recognized that a broader problem was the army's reluctance, born of its profound distrust of black soldiers, to create more black units for backlogged black draftees to join. In the final two years of the war, the War Department offered a new justification, albeit again in private: it needed fewer African American draftees because casualties and losses among black soldiers in battle were much lighter than those among whites, and thus blacks had to be replaced and inducted at lower rates.[56]

In the end, however, these shifting justifications missed the more enduring and fundamental cause of chronic black selectee backlogs: throughout the war the number of black men that local draft boards selected as fit to serve was always much higher than the number that the army was willing to induct. Indeed, while the War Department committed to taking no more than a proportional share of African Americans into the army—roughly 10 percent—black men's share of I-A registrants was always significantly higher than that—15 percent in January 1942, followed by 20 percent a year later, in January 1943, and a full 23 percent the year after that.[57] This mismatch partly explains the army's reluctance to take black volunteers in the first place, since they exacerbated its backlog problem: each black enlistee accepted into the army was one black selectee whose induction was delayed.

For those delayed African Americans, waiting around for their official order to report for induction was a major inconvenience. Many quit their jobs in anticipation of entering the army, only to be put off indefinitely. For many other black men, getting passed over in the draft was just the latest in a long line of national-defense-related outrages and snubs, uncomfortably akin to their exclusion from defense jobs and from the other armed services at the time. Inside the War Department, black adviser William Hastie chided his superiors for approaching the "utilization of the Negro soldier . . . as an unwelcome requirement . . . rather than as an opportunity to exploit a valuable military asset." He warned that "the accumulation of Negroes at the top of Selective Service lists, while whites far down the list are being called to service, will soon cause a nation-wide protest from white and colored citizens alike."[58]

In fact, that protest had already begun. Black activists in the press and civil rights organizations denounced the low or nonexistent draft calls for African Americans and the resulting backlog of black selectees.[59] What was new was that growing numbers of whites, and some very powerful ones at that, joined them. Some did so, at least in part, out of a principled belief in equality for all. In March 1942, a white missionary council from Danville, Illinois, sent Secretary Stimson a petition with more than one hundred signatures. It urged him to give "the Negro tenth of our population . . . its proportionate share of service, responsibility, and opportunity" in the army, "not only in the interest of unity and justice to the minority group but [also] in fairness to white men who must bear not only their proportionate share of service but also that of the minority group which is denied participation." Other whites demanded that more black men get drafted for decidedly less lofty ideals. "This 10% draft of the niggers is unfair," remarked one white person in Florida in the summer of 1942. "They ought to take them over there and let them get shot before the white men. Why should they take all of the white men in the army and put the niggers over here in good jobs in the defense plants to make good money?"[60]

Whatever their rationale and reasoning—and there seems to have been more of the latter than the former—by the spring of 1942 and continuing well into 1943, whites increasingly complained about African Americans' underrepresentation among draftees and their own consequent overrepresentation. Newspapers, civic clubs, labor and political leaders, and ordinary citizens, especially in the South, demanded that the military draft fewer white people and more black people. On the campaign trail in 1942, one senatorial candidate from Louisiana denounced draft boards for "depleting the white manhood in the South," leaving "our streets and roads populated by Negroes incited by northerners to seek social equality." During a race riot at the Alabama Dry Dock and Shipbuilding Company in Mobile in 1942, the *Chicago Defender* reported that "one of the chief 'soap box' orators who incited the mob shouted to those who gathered round him that 'We must see that the niggers are put in the army, so that white men can have these jobs."[61] Southern whites complained to their congressional representatives, military officials, and Roosevelt about "the white being sent overseas to be slaughtered; [and] the negroes being kept at home to multiply prodigiously, as is their wont."[62] Southern Congress members responded with protest letters of their own and with speeches on the floor of Congress about the "urgent necessity of drafting negroes into the armed services" and of leaving more white men, "the best blood of America," behind. If left unaddressed, warned one Louisiana representative, this "serious problem" would "produce an explosion."[63]

Fearing precisely that outcome, numerous government agencies and officials—not least the Selective Service itself—sought to address the problem. Concerned about the ever-present backlog of black selectees, Director Hershey began writing to Secretary Stimson and President Roosevelt as early as September 1941. "We must sooner or later," he insisted, "come to the procedure of requisitioning and delivering men in the sequence of their order numbers without regard to color." The Office of War Information, which in August 1942 reported confidentially about southern whites' concerns that "more of their men [were] being drafted than Negroes," issued a press release in early 1943 attempting to allay this concern. It stressed that black men's induction rates, the same or higher than their registration rates, were on par with white men's. At the same time, the WMC's chair, Paul McNutt, citing the backlog of 300,000 black selectees, wrote numerous letters to Stimson (and to Knox) promising an end to race-specific quotas and the induction of more African Americans. Roosevelt's adviser Jonathan Daniels, in a memo to the president, suggested that the increasingly popular notion that white men got drafted while black men got jobs had "some basis in truth." "Discrimination against Negroes in the armed services," he observed, "is resulting in a discrimination against white men in the sense that more white men are drafted into the services." Daniels suggested an investigation, though none seems to have followed.[64]

Among this diverse mix of protesters—from the black press to the WMC to white segregationists—the most potent argument against these draft practices was not that they were unjust to black people, to white people, or to both. It was that they were illegal. How could the Selective Service avoid "discrimination . . . on account of race or color"—something that the STSA expressly forbade —and use race-specific calls, which disregarded order numbers, delaying the induction of African Americans into the army and expediting the induction of everyone else? As the *Pittsburgh Courier* surmised, in December 1940, this had to be "a violation of the letter and spirit of the [Selective Training and Service] act."[65]

This point seems to have originated from within the Selective Service's own ranks. In late October 1940, no more than six weeks after the STSA's passage, the Selective Service's legal adviser in Illinois argued that the law's "clear intention" was that "there should be no differentiation between Negro and white male citizens" in the draft. "To defer Negroes on the basis that the Army has not called for them" would be to discriminate "against white persons called before their number was really due to be called, and would provide a reasonable ground [to sue] that would probably be sustained on appeal." And "numerous such appeals," feared the adviser, "might well shake the very foundations of the fine civic attitude supporting the Selective Service Act at the present time." Several months later a local board in Cuyahoga County, Ohio, sent a similar protest to draft headquarters in Washington: "We do hereby record our belief and opinion that the February Call for nine *white* men is unfair, unjust, and discriminatory against both the white and colored races. This arbitrary method of induction of men by color rather than by order number we believe is a flagrant and totalitarian violation of both letter and spirit of the law. . . . [W]e request that men of all colors be treated alike."[66]

Meanwhile, draft officials in Connecticut, backed by two state governors, Raymond Baldwin and his successor, Robert Hurley, publicly refused to abide the army's race-specific requisitions. They, too, considered them discriminatory and illegal. The governors threatened court action and, in the meantime, inducted men by order number alone, disregarding race entirely. "[Black men] are as eligible and fit for Army training, and as patriotic, as any other citizens, and must not be placed in any deferred status," Hurley declared in a public statement. "I find that this view is confirmed and written into the law of the land." As a result of his actions, Hurley received a flood of fan mail from appreciative African Americans across the country. One letter writer mused, "I sometimes wonder if in the next War to come, the black soldier will be given black rifles with black bullets, the white soldier given white rifles with white bullets, so as to differentiate the amount of slaughter accomplished by each. I wonder! I really wonder."[67]

Refuting Governor Hurley, a Selective Service spokesperson in Washington claimed that the army "can ask for men six feet tall with blue eyes and brown hair if it wishes, and it is the duty of local boards to supply those men." In time, however, national draft leaders had their doubts. When the Cuyahoga protest came in the mail, the director of Selective Service at the time, Robert Dykstra, forwarded it to Secretary Stimson, noting, "The general situation permits both Negroes who have volunteered for service and white men who have higher order numbers, but who are inducted with lower order numbers, to claim, whether justified or not, that there is discrimination contrary to the provisions of the [Selective Service] law." Shortly thereafter, Selective Service received word from the US Attorney General's Office that it would support and defend race-specific draft calls if they were challenged in court. Still, concerns lingered. The following year, in January 1942, Campbell Johnson, a black adviser to Director Hershey, claimed in a memorandum that separate race calls that delayed African Americans' induction were "probably a violation of the actual letter of the law." And in early 1943, while the WMC briefly controlled Selective Service, Paul McNutt's effort to end race calls once and for all stemmed in part from his doubts about their legality under the STSA.[68]

Even some officials within the War Department—the institution responsible for separate race calls and for delaying black men's induction—occasionally broached similar questions. In early 1941, as draft officials in Connecticut, Ohio, and Illinois rebelled against policies they viewed as illegal, an army assistant chief of staff wrote to Army Chief of Staff George C. Marshall, warning him that "unless the War Department made reasonably prompt provisions for the induction of Negroes legal action might compel it to do so." Secretary Stimson's race adviser, William Hastie, raised similar concerns a year later. In a memo to Undersecretary of War Robert Patterson, he insisted that the backlog of black draftees "invites court action by any white selectee chosen for induction ahead of eligible Negroes whose name precedes his."[69]

In time, southern segregationists, concerned about these white selectees, came around to these legal arguments. In the fall of 1943, Charles E. MacKenzie, a Democratic congressman from Louisiana, was appalled to find that his district's draft boards called men according not simply to draft number but to race, as a result inducting white fathers before single, childless black men. "Has it come to pass," he asked on the floor of the House, "that the color of a man's skin is the basis for his being deferred even if he is single and has no dependents?" Calling the draft arrangement discrimination against white fathers, McKenzie demanded that "the Selective Service follow the letter of the law" and induct men without regard to race or color. Some black and other commentators relished the delicious irony of a southern segregationist decrying race discrimination. The *Chicago Defender's* front-page headline read, "This Is News! Dixie Solon Flays Race Discrimination"; and the *New Republic* commented, "Representative McKenzie has not yet perfected any plan which makes it possible for his constituents to eat their cake and have it too. He is certain, however, that 'such discrimination is detrimental to the morale of the nation.' We may not be talking about the same thing, but you aren't kidding, Mr. McKenzie." The *Pittsburgh Courier's* response was more pointed: "Had the Army not insisted on segregated Negro troops in order to please the white South [thus delaying the induction of Negroes] there would not be such a disproportionate number of whites under arms."[70]

Arguably the most serious legal challenge to separate race calls and to the backlog of black draftees came not from a member of Congress or a governor, the Selective Service director or the chair of the WMC. It came, instead, from a thirty-six-year-old landscape gardener from Queens, New York, named Winfred William Lynn. In June 1942, when his local board in Jamaica reclassified him as I-A, he notified them that "[u]nless I am assured that . . . I will not be compelled to serve in a unit undemocratically selected as a Negro group, I will refuse to report for induction." When, in September, he was still ordered to report, Lynn made good on his promise. A month later, a federal grand jury indicted him on draft evasion charges. Lynn refused to back down. Represented by his younger brother, Conrad (a longtime activist in his own right), Lynn pleaded not guilty and petitioned for a writ of habeas corpus. He contended that he was being illegally detained, since his selection violated, among other things, the STSA. Echoing the views of Selective Service officials, among others, he argued that race-specific draft calls were necessarily discriminatory, since "the speed with which a man is called up depend[s] on his race as well as on his draft number." A federal judge in Brooklyn quickly dismissed the case, because Lynn had disobeyed his induction order. But then Lynn reluctantly joined the army, reported for service at Camp Upton on Long Island, and pursued his case from there.[71]

Apart from his brother Conrad, Lynn launched his fight entirely on his own, independent of any black or civil rights organizations. In his autobiography, Conrad recalled that the impetus for his brother's protest came from their family's "very strong feelings about the government's humiliating conscription practices." But as soon as his case reached the courts, Winfred Lynn attracted lots of support, which only grew over time. In

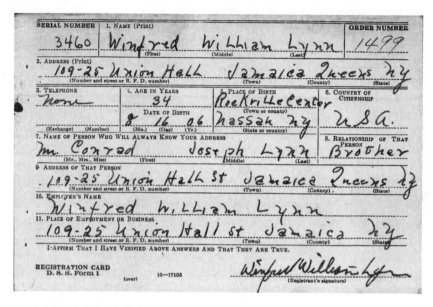

Fig. 1.5 Winfred Lynn's draft registration card. Courtesy Ancestry.com.

December 1942, when he appeared first before the Brooklyn judge, Arthur Garfield Hays joined his legal team, perhaps the most well-known civil liberties attorney of his day, who had represented the anarchists Nicola Sacco and Bartolomeo Vanzetti and the Scottsboro Boys. When Conrad too was drafted into the army in January 1943, Hays became the lead attorney on the case.[72]

Meanwhile, numerous organizations helped out in various ways. The ACLU, of which Hays was general counsel, led the legal fight. The NAACP, which at first had counseled Lynn against pursuing his case, fearing that it had little chance of success, eventually supported the case, raising money, releasing statements, attending mass meetings, and filing several amicus briefs on Lynn's behalf.[73] The black press, and a few left-wing periodicals such as *PM* and *The Nation*, also followed the case closely, while A. Philip Randolph's MOWM—and its group of white supporters, the Friends of the MOWM—made Lynn a cause célèbre through mass meetings, pamphlets, and speeches.[74] Eventually an umbrella organization emerged to spearhead these efforts—the Citizens' Committee for Winfred Lynn, soon renamed the National Citizens' Committee for Winfred Lynn and eventually the Lynn Committee to Abolish Segregation in the Armed Forces. Its list of sponsors was a who's who of the wartime non–Communist Party Left, including Socialist Party presidential candidate Norman Thomas, Christian pacifist A. J. Muste, the Trotskyist novelist James T. Farrell, union heads like Luigi Antonini and Willard Townsend, and black civil rights leaders of various political stripes such as Randolph, Roy Wilkins, William Hastie, and Anna Arnold Hedgeman. Through everything from cocktail parties to mass mailings, radio discussions to rallies, magazine advertisements to pamphlets, they helped make Winfred Lynn's case one of the war's leading civil rights causes.[75]

Supporters did so, in part, because they believed, as one pamphlet put it, that "the Winfred Lynn case may go down in history as the Dred Scott case did in the last century, as a major turning point in the history of the Negro . . . and the history of America." The hope was that the case might force the Supreme Court, a full decade before *Brown v. Board of Education*, to decide whether segregation was itself discrimination; whether the federal government, not simply the states, could impose segregation on US citizens across the land (and, in the case of the military, around the world); and whether a "jimcrow army [was] compatible with a war alleged to be fought for democratic aims." Yet, under Hays's direction, Lynn's fight, to the disappointment of some of his supporters, approached these broad questions through a much narrower one: Under the STSA, could "Negro American citizens . . . be selected and inducted, not strictly in their turn according to their numbers as determined by the impartial National draft lottery, but under separate 'Negro quotas' "?[76]

In January 1943, the US District Court in Brooklyn dodged this core question, but ruled against Lynn anyway. It found he had proved neither that "he was inducted under any order which calls for so many whites and so many colored" nor that he had suffered discrimination in violation of the STSA. A year later, in February 1944, the US Court of Appeals for the Second Circuit approached the issue more directly. In a two-to-one decision, it held that Lynn *was* in fact drafted in response to a "Negro quota" but that this procedure was perfectly legal, in part because it did not result "in calling him ahead of his turn in the draft." In a dissenting opinion, however, Judge Charles Edward Clark, a former dean of Yale Law School, sided with Lynn. Quoting from the testimony of New York City's director of Selective Service, who admitted that "Negro and white men are not called in turn or serially, but that the question of color has something to do with the time they are called," Clark concluded, "I do not see how such a result can be considered consistent with selection without regard to color." Further disputing the crux of the majority opinion, he added, "[STSA] requires that there be no discrimination, not that there be no legally disadvantageous discrimination."[77]

But the Supreme Court, taking an indirect route, let the circuit court ruling stand. On May 29, 1944, it refused to hear Lynn's case. It claimed that his original petition for a writ was now "moot," since he was no longer in the custody of the case's original "respondent," the commander of Camp Upton, Colonel Downer. In response, Lynn's attorneys, along with the NAACP through an amicus brief, petitioned the Supreme Court for a rehearing. But on January 2, 1945, with little fanfare and no explanation, the Court denied this final petition. Winfred Lynn's case was officially dead.[78]

Writing from the South Pacific, after the May 1944 ruling, Winfred Lynn retained a sense of humor about it all: "I'm not the least depressed about the events that are happening concerning the case. I am, as some people say, a brave man, nothing fazes me. Smile." But his brother, Conrad, was appalled. "Can you imagine that for a technicality?" he exclaimed in a letter from his army post in New York. "It . . . should be exposed in all its hypocritical evasiveness." Indeed, the high court's dodge raised a number of serious questions: Why was the moot point not broached earlier, since Winfred Lynn had left Camp Upton well over a year earlier, and the lower courts had never raised the issue? Why did the Supreme Court not simply substitute Lynn's current commander for Downer, in line with Federal Rules of Civil Procedure? Why, if habeas corpus was the one part of civil law that still applied to the military, could army authorities effectively nullify it by passing someone like Lynn from one commander to another?[79]

To Lynn's supporters, and surely others, the answer was obvious enough: the Court had deemed the case "too hot to handle." "When the U.S. Supreme Court resorts to a legalistic trick of this quality to dodge a case," noted one commentator at the time, "we may be sure it is a pretty hot one." In fact, signs of the case's fraught importance were evident all along. Before Lynn was indicted, the FBI and US attorneys in New York attempted at various times to convince Lynn to abandon his fight. Meanwhile, draft officials sought to persuade Conrad to do the same. A month before the Lynn case reached the district court level, Campbell Johnson, aide to Director Hershey, asked two friends of Conrad Lynn to convince him to abandon his fight. When that effort failed, Johnson traveled from Washington to New York to persuade Conrad himself, spending several hours with him and warning him, according to one report, that "Congress might repeal the antidiscrimination clause [in STSA] if the Lynn brothers insisted on pressing their case."[80]

Once Lynn's case reached the courts, it was not, in the words of one postwar Selective Service report, "lightly regarded by the Federal Government . . . especially the Legal Division at the National Headquarters of the Selective Service System and the Office of the Judge Advocate General of the Army. There was considerable feeling that had the case been tried on

Fig. 1.6 Winfred Lynn, c. early 1944. Courtesy Division of Rare and Manuscript Collections, Cornell University Library.

its merits, the separate calls' procedure might have been found illegal." As a result, the government sent a "bevy of officers" and "a platoon of lawyers" from Washington to attend and testify at Lynn's various court proceedings in New York. As Conrad Lynn recalled, the courtroom "glittered with brass." The government pulled few punches in defending its race quotas. In its brief to the Second Circuit, US attorney Harold M. Kennedy ended on this unmistakably ominous note: "It is our duty, we believe, to point out that if the existence of separate calls for White and Negro registrants to meet the requisitions of the armed forces is invalid and if all registrants, White or Negro, inducted under such calls are illegally in the armed forces, and subject to release by the courts under writ of habeas corpus, the security of the country is in peril."[81]

Precisely because these separate calls—and the resulting delayed induction of black men and expedited induction of others—proved so controversial, the army, and eventually the rest of the military, sought alternative ways to keep African Americans at or under their quota. Early in the war

mobilization it hit upon induction station rejections, which was the third
significant barrier the military erected to black enlistment. By classifying
and selecting men as fit to serve, civilians on local draft boards made preliminary judgments on these matters. But then "selectees" needed to clear
a final hurdle before becoming formal "inductees": they had to spend a day
at an induction center and pass a number of additional physical and psychological exams conducted this time by military personnel, not civilians.
Here the military had broad authority under the STSA to determine who
was and was not suitable for service. And it was here that it placed disproportionate numbers of black men in the unsuitable category. From
July 1942 through August 1945, military examiners at induction stations
rejected a staggering 56 percent of black selectees, a rate eighteen points
higher than that for whites.[82]

The ostensible causes of African Americans' high rejection rates were venereal disease and mental and educational deficiencies, all of which make
some sense when one considers the desperate conditions in which many
black people were forced to live. Venereal disease, one Selective Service
report pointed out, struck "areas of poorest housing, greatest ignorance,
lowest income and inadequate medical and public health service, regardless of race. Their more serious application to Negro registrants was due
not to any particular racial susceptibility to venereal diseases but rather
to the fact that larger numbers of this group lived under conditions which
produced venereal infection, and were without adequate educational and
medical services." Similarly, that so many black people, especially those
from the South, attended poorly funded, segregated schools with poorly
paid teachers had a predictably profound effect on their intelligence and
educational test results. Indeed, suggesting that poor schools made poor
test takers, one 1944 American Teachers Association study found that
African Americans from many northern states outperformed whites from
southern ones.[83]

Furthermore, some small portion of black men no doubt intentionally failed these tests to avoid service. Certainly many whites in the South
thought so. One white local board member from Georgia complained about
a "very intelligent negro [who] went for his examination, claimed to be illit-
erate, and they [the induction station examiners] put up the letter 'h' and
asked him what it was; he replied, 'I don't know, sir, but it looks like a plow
stock.'" Similarly, in a letter to the War Department, a congressman from
Louisiana wrote that he had heard "many reports when I was at home that
the negroes upon being asked if they could read or write had learned that if
they said 'no,' . . . they would get a ticket back home and I understand that
they are saying 'no' overwhelmingly."[84]

Black men's high rejection rates, however, reflected more than poor schools, inadequate health care, and a small minority of "malingerers" (whom government officials estimated at no more than 5 percent of overall rejectees). They also reflected the military's ongoing determination to limit the number of African Americans in its ranks. This strategy seems to have gotten its start in early 1941, amid increasing calls on the army to take more black selectees. In April, Army Chief of Staff Marshall received a memo from his deputy suggesting that "if the Army refused to induct illiterates the number of Negro selectees would be reduced." Sure enough, three weeks later the army instituted a new rule requiring that all inductees read, write, and compute at a fourth-grade level; and the number of black inductees dropped, since their rejection rates were significantly higher than those for whites. Demonstrating that none of this was purely coincidental was a matter-of-fact diary entry from Secretary Stimson in May 1942: "The Army has adopted rigid requirements for literacy mainly in order to keep down the number of colored troops."[85]

With this overall goal in mind, the army, and later the navy, rejected black selectees for reasons other than illiteracy. Indeed, endless flexibility was one of the strengths of this restriction method. In New York and elsewhere, psychiatrists at induction centers encouraged black men to speak "very feelingly" about segregation and discrimination and then rejected them for doing so. Author Richard Wright was classified as unfit to serve for his supposed "psychoneurosis" or, more particularly, for his "obsession" with the "problem of the Negro." In North Carolina, in one month, 41 percent of black selectees at Fort Bragg were rejected for flat feet, which had never before been a problem. In Georgia, the state director of Selective Service complained to national headquarters about induction centers' "exceedingly high" rejection rates of African Americans: "For a long while they rejected the Negroes for urethritis and when we kicked about that they switched to inadequate personality, we kicked about that and they switched to psychoneurosis. We have been kicking about psychoneurosis for a couple of months and now they are switching to other causes for rejections but the rejection rate, meanwhile, is steadily increasing." Summarizing these stories and others in a memorandum to the army in July 1943, an alarmed Campbell Johnson noted, "The opinion is prevalent that in some way the Army has passed down the word to induction stations to take only so many Negroes and the induction stations have moved from one reason for rejection to another in order to comply with these directions."[86]

In Georgia, a Selective Service official puzzled over how to explain the high rejection rates to increasingly exasperated local draft boards. "Frankly, I do not know what to tell them unless we give them the truth about the army not wanting negroes. It is my honest opinion that this [new visual] test was inaugurated for the purpose of disqualifying a larger number of negroes." The official's boss, the state director of Selective Service, agreed: "The men at the induction stations seem to have their orders and do not seem to have much discretion in the matter [of rejections]. The remedy, apparently, must come from top side." When Truman Gibson, Stimson's black aide, forwarded this message to Assistant Secretary of War John J. McCloy, he added that it represented the views of forty-four state Selective Service directors.[87]

For those whites already incensed about discriminatory draft calls, news about disparate rates of induction station rejection did not sit well. Across the South, according to one report from a Selective Service official, "local boards are on the verge of revolt because of the rejection of many Negroes whom they know from a life time of contact to be thoroughly capable of military service. . . . [They] have unofficially expressed the determination not to send forward any white selectees until the Army changes its policy regarding the acceptance of Negroes. They particularly

Fig. 1.7 Some African American "selectees" become "inductees" at Fort Benning in Georgia, April 1941. But throughout the war, the military rejected disproportionate numbers of black selectees at this stage. Courtesy National Archives, 161-SC-41-1067.

indicate that they will not move into the induction of white fathers until all Negro nonfathers have been processed properly." Meanwhile, ordinary whites, especially in the South, wrote Roosevelt, the War Department, draft officials, and their congressional representatives, complaining that "it is almost unsafe for a white woman to be on the streets on Saturdays or at night," since "so many negro's [sic] are turned down" for service and since white men are taken in their stead; or that too many blacks "are being sent home for such flimsy excuses as illiteracy. These negroes could be taught to read or write in a few weeks' or months' time." Congress members directed protest letters of their own to military and draft officials. "I was informed by reliable persons that negroes were being disqualified in great numbers because of physical disabilities or lack of educational standards," wrote one Louisiana House member to the War Department. "The negroes are walking the streets and rumors are rife of their bragging statements, and this does not go well with the Southern white people who have had to send their sons to the services. I greatly fear that this is going to lead to trouble."[88]

African Americans offered protests of a different kind. Selective Service official Campbell Johnson raised concerns about black men's rejection rates both because they were "complicating the problem of providing Negroes for military service" and because they were creating "a distorted statistical record of the health and intelligence of Negro men." Other black people focused their ire on the underlying causes of some rejections—and the rank hypocrisy of white southerners' supposed concern. Quoting a South Carolina draft official who held "the state's neglect in the past" responsible for the "great difference in the educational and physical standards of the Negroes as compared to the whites," the Pittsburgh Courier added, "In short, the white South is paying the penalty for ostracizing, segregating, disfranchising and discriminating against citizens of color, but it seems willing to keep paying it rather than lower the color bar and accept Negroes as brothers and equals."[89]

With different priorities, draft and military officials in Washington responded to these protests each in their own way. At the Selective Service national headquarters, draft leaders decided that if military officers at induction stations insisted on rejecting large numbers of the men that local draft boards deemed fit to serve, then they would have to select and call many more men than the military requested. They would, that is, have to add a buffer of sorts against presumed future rejections. After allowing steadily increasing overcalls, headquarters, in July 1943, eventually lifted all restrictions on their size, authorizing state directors to call as many men as it would take to fill military requisitions.[90]

The military, for its part, made changes here and there to reduce rejection rates. After all, it robbed the armed forces of all kinds of men, not simply those classified as "colored," most of whom the military was more interested in mustering. It began accepting and treating selectees with venereal disease; it introduced new testing to assess mental rather than educational qualifications; and it began to educate—rather than reject— illiterates through army- and navy-led twelve-week courses, which one commentator shortly after the war called "perhaps America's most successful broad-scale, adult literacy program."[91] Some of these changes, especially the literacy classes, helped all kinds of Americans and was downright transformative for some. Many black men, in particular, received a taste of decent schooling long denied them in the Jim Crow South and elsewhere.

In the end, however, African Americans' overall rejection rates remained stubbornly static for the last few years of the war. These measures never managed to reduce them appreciably, because, in truth, they were not supposed to. From the start, the military rejected large numbers of black men in an explicit effort to limit and cap their inductions. This fundamental fact never changed throughout the war.

* * *

Constant black activism and pressure, along with occasional help from white allies and white segregationist enemies alike, had a real impact. Most important, it broke down nearly every one of the military's exclusions against black enlistment, and it greatly expanded blacks' numbers and, to a lesser though still significant extent, the percentage of blacks in the military's various branches and services. Yet efforts to restrict black enlistment— through high rejection rates, severe restrictions on voluntary enlistment, and chronically low draft calls—continued throughout the war, sometimes in the face of broad and powerful resistance from national and local draft officials, members of Congress, state governors, and black protest and legal challenges.

Military leaders were more successful at protecting their anti-black restrictions than their anti-black exclusions for a variety of reasons. In a war in which "manpower" was desperately needed and which was supposedly about protecting freedom and democracy, the wholesale exclusion of African Americans from any of the military's branches and services fast became untenable. Early in the war mobilization, the War Department was forced to concede that black people deserved and would receive access to all branches of the army; the navy and marine corps managed to hold out a bit longer, but eventually caved to similar pressures. Furthermore, restrictions were less conspicuous and more complex than blanket exclusions, and thus more easily defended. For example, the army, toward the end of the war, sometimes justified its enlistment practices by pointing to black people's near-proportional share of *enlisted* personnel, when in fact its October 1940 policy statement promised proportional representation of *all* personnel, officers included. Or it would talk about draft numbers, which were often proportional to African Americans' overall population (if not to their I-A status), but it would ignore voluntary enlistment numbers, which certainly were not. Or later in the war, the navy would discuss its acceptance of a supposedly fair share of black draftees, but it would fail to mention that its induction rates for African Americans, because of years of exclusion, would had to have been much higher than that for black people to approximate an equitable share of overall navy strength. Finally, no doubt the military's most potent defense of restrictions was its claim that, without them, it might be forced to integrate black troops. Since virtually no prominent government authorities—no military leaders, hardly any Congress members, and certainly not President Roosevelt—seriously countenanced this sort of change, that argument must have held considerable weight. Indeed, this point likely explains why—even though not a few powerful southern Democrats in Congress spoke out against a military that, in their view, inducted too many white people and not enough black people—their protest was neither entirely unified nor sustained. Some of them, perhaps greater numbers over time, came to recognize that a core military policy that they cherished—segregation by military outfit—rested in part on another one that they loathed—black enlistment restrictions.

These policies of exclusion and restriction came almost entirely from military leadership—the highest-ranking generals and admirals and their civilian heads in the War and Navy Departments. One could be excused for assuming otherwise. The racist restrictions built into so many New Deal policies, including military ones, often came from their decentralized implementation and from the fact that the draft, for example, epitomized decentralization, since it was enacted at the grass roots through more than sixty-four hundred local draft boards, each of which had enormous discretion over who would be selected as fit to serve and who would be rejected or deferred. Indeed, one newspaper in New York City, in 1941, visited eighteen draft boards and found a "tangle of confusion and contradiction" regarding how they made their life-or-death decisions: "No two boards think or operate alike. What is reasonable and sufficient ground for deferment before one board is not before another a block away. Some are lenient, some are considerate, and some are about as tough as they come."[92]

But there is little evidence that African Americans' enlistment barriers came from these draft boards or from individual induction stations.

Indeed, these local officials often pushed in the opposite direction, as their forceful resistance to black quotas or to high rejection rates makes clear.[93] Instead, these barriers—either in the draft, at induction stations, or elsewhere—were always the handiwork of the most powerful leaders in the armed forces, who received protection from the courts, when necessary, and sometimes tacit, sometimes explicit support from the White House.

In the end, whether black people would have been better off with greater access to the military is not a simple question. Suffice it to say that if African Americans' service had its advantages and disadvantages, so too did their greater inclusion in the military. For example, if black troops received good pay, job training, education, health care, and some of the prestige attached to donning the uniform to fight in the war, they also faced vicious, sometimes deadly attacks for donning that same uniform and the daily humiliations and indignities of a Jim Crow military. If they traveled the country and the world, expanding their horizons and their sense of the politically possible, Jim Crow also followed them everywhere they went, reminding them that if, say, some Australians and Italians treated them with respect and dignity, many white Americans most certainly did not and would not. And if they received access to much-vaunted GI Bill benefits thanks to their service—reminding us, conversely, that the military's barriers to black entry were also long-forgotten barriers to the most generous welfare program in the country's history—this access proved decidedly limited in the postwar years.[94]

What can be said with certainty is that the manifold obstacles to entering the military which black people faced meant not simply that they were underrepresented in the armed services throughout the war and that far more would have served had these obstacles been removed or never been instituted in the first place. These obstacles also meant that more nonblacks served in their stead. Limits on black inductions necessarily meant an overrepresentation of nearly everyone else. The NAACP's *Crisis* had a name for this fact: "the Jim Crow Boomerang."[95]

CHAPTER 2

◦◡◦

Enlisting and Excluding
an "Enemy Race"

In the small border town of Del Rio, Texas, some Mexican Americans grew increasingly alarmed during the war. Roughly equal in number to the Anglo residents in town, they wondered why they comprised more than nine of ten draftees. Thinking these problems extended beyond Del Rio, civil rights leader George I. Sánchez surmised that "'anglos' are securing deferment for their young men by various subterfuges—such as designating them managers of stock raising and wool marketing activities in which these young men do not really participate." Another prominent statewide Mexican American leader, Alonso Perales, offered a much more troubling theory: "Some individuals who are prejudiced against the Mexican people are rushing our boys to the battle fronts in order that they may be the first to get killed and get rid of them that way." Not everyone accepted these theories, which proved hard to verify, because the Selective Service and the military collected no statistics on Mexican Americans, including them in the broader category of "white."[1] Nonetheless, while racism restricted black people's military enlistment, it may have had the opposite effect for other groups.

For some nonblacks, however, underrepresentation was more typical. The Selective Service System's official evaluation of its World War II–era practices concluded, "The greatest use was not made of some of the racial groups in the United States," focusing not only on African Americans, but also on black and white Puerto Ricans, among others. Regarding Puerto Ricans, in fact, the military proved so loath to muster those from the island, convinced they were "drastically inferior to continental troops," that it imposed higher standards on them and rejected them at exceedingly high rates. The report could also have mentioned Filipino Americans. For a brief period prior to the attack on Pearl Harbor, they were barred from joining all branches of the US Armed Forces. Hailing from a nation in the process of becoming independent from US colonization, Filipinos were "nationals," owing their allegiance to their colonizers without being full-fledged US citizens. As such, when the United States entered World War II, they were for a time, with few exceptions, forbidden from joining either the navy, which had earlier recruited large numbers of Filipinos for the Messman Branch exclusively, and the army, since the 1940 Selective Training and Service Act (STSA) applied only to citizens and aliens, not "nationals." "Natives of Guam and Samoa" faced similar exclusions.[2]

Of all nonblacks, however, Japanese Americans faced the most and most enduring racist barriers to joining up. These policies also changed dramatically and repeatedly over the course of the war, in response to numerous, sometimes competing forces, including fears of Japanese American disloyalty, Japanese American protest, the military personnel demands of total war, and the need to counter Japanese "race war" propaganda in Asia. The result was remarkable, and remarkably perplexing, variation. In the navy, to be sure, little changed: Japanese Americans were barred from enlisting and serving throughout the war. In the army, by contrast, Japanese Americans zigged and zagged between exclusion and inclusion, not once but twice, before and after the attack on Pearl Harbor. At times their access approximated that for white people; other times it was more restricted than that for black people. In the end, their share of the military was less than their share of the US population. Had there been no restrictions or exclusions, the armed forces would have had access to thousands more troops. At the same time, Japanese Americans' enlistment barriers had their own particularities, which bespoke the variety of racisms in wartime America and its military, as well as the variety of struggles that emerged to uproot them.

"A CLASS OF PERSONS NOT ACCEPTABLE"

The US military in the interwar years had virtually no people of Japanese ancestry serving in active duty. More than a thousand fought with the army during World War I, and several hundred Japanese immigrants served in the navy around the turn of the twentieth century, primarily as mess attendants. In the 1920s and 1930s, however, the army and navy permitted few Japanese Americans to join up. A 1940 tally of all enlisted men in the navy found miniscule numbers of Chinese, Puerto Ricans, American Indians, Samoans, Hawaiians, and Chamorros, but no Japanese Americans at all. The army, prior to the institution of the draft, accepted Japanese American voluntary enlistees in some locations but not in others. In late 1940, one magazine writer portrayed Japanese Americans as "bewildered as to the role America planned for them to play [in the military]. Had they not heard of racial discrimination? Were there not instances of rejection when one of their number patriotically attempted to enlist? In Santa Maria, California, he had heard that two American citizens, one a Chinese and the other a Japanese, had been abusively refused at the army recruiting office. And over the years he was aware of other such cases in the army, in the navy, and in the air corps."[3]

These barriers to entry reflected some military and political officials' deep-seated and often racist fears about Japanese American disloyalty, fears that would gain increasing power and prominence once the United States entered the war against Japan. Two years before the attack on Pearl Harbor, an Army War College study of the mobilization of Hawaiian military personnel argued, "The use of Japanese in any war is questionable and in a war with Japan they would constitute a serious liability. . . . [T]hey should not be considered for military service, except locally in case Japan is neutral or our ally." Around the same time, army officers and members of the War Department General Staff debated the so-called problem of Japanese American reserve officers in Hawaii: some thought they should be segregated in their own "special" unit; others preferred blocking their access to the reserve officer corps altogether, believing "their loyalty could never be trusted."[4]

In August 1940, as Congress debated the STSA and the wisdom of attaching an antidiscrimination clause to it, similar concerns resurfaced. Senator Lister Hill of Alabama quoted one War Department objection: "The population of Hawaii, totaling about 400,000, includes approximately 153,000 persons of Japanese racial origin. About three-fourths of them are American citizens by birth. A large number of these are, no doubt, loyal Americans, but it is well known that others are not loyal Americans. A law that would require acceptance of enlistment regardless of race or of American-born Japanese who are otherwise qualified would seriously cripple the military forces of the United States . . . in the event of any trouble in the Pacific." Senator Millard Tydings of Maryland agreed: "It would be unfortunate if the garrison in the Hawaiian Islands had a large percentage of Japanese troops, the loyalty of some of whom might be questioned, particularly in the event there should ever be a war between the United States and Japan. I think we had better leave this element [the antidiscrimination clause] out, let the Army run the Army, and not have so many generals in the United States Senate."[5]

Congress failed to heed Hill's and Tydings's warnings, however, passing the STSA with its civil rights protections intact. And the law led to growing numbers of Japanese Americans in the military. They were not in the navy or marine corps, both of which continued to exclude nearly all Japanese Americans from their ranks. These military services did not use the draft initially to procure troops and, therefore, did not have to abide by its antidiscrimination clauses. But the army was required to comply with them and, in part as a result, dramatically changed course on Japanese American induction. Army and Selective Service officials treated all draftees of Japanese descent like whites, indeed sometimes explicitly defining them as such. In October 1940, the army adjutant general declared in a memo to all commanding generals, "The status of citizens of oriental descent who are selected for induction will be the same as that of other citizens." In this context, "citizens" clearly meant everyone who was not black, among them "orientals" of Japanese descent. Two months later, Lewis B. Hershey, then Selective Service deputy director, noted that only two racial classifications mattered to draft officials—white and black—and while "all negroes or half-breeds may be classified as black," "all others, including . . . Japanese . . . will be listed as white." Thanks to these policies, thousands of Japanese Americans streamed into the army. In January 1941, one *Los Angeles Times* article noted, with a mixture of appreciation and condescension, that among the several hundred or so local men inducted into the army that month was a "diminutive Japanese 'nisei' (American-born) lad . . . who looked for all the world like a jiu-jitsu expert." On the eve of America's entry into the war, between three and four thousand Japanese Americans—all but a select few of whom were US citizens— served in the army.[6]

Then came the attack on Pearl Harbor. For a brief period, improvisation, confusion, and variation prevailed as a powerful, well-orchestrated campaign against Japanese Americans developed, particularly in the West. Of those Japanese Americans who were on active duty, some remained in their units and not much changed; but many others, especially those serving on the West Coast, were transferred inland, some were placed in inactive duty with the Enlisted Reserve Corps, and some were discharged from the service within the first few months of America's entry into the war. For those Japanese Americans joining the army—or wanting to—some local draft boards and recruiting stations barred Japanese American induction. The San Francisco Recruiting and Induction Station, for example, refused to induct a single Japanese American in December 1941; up to this point, its monthly average for the year had been nearly forty. In late January 1942, the War Department officially barred the further induction of "Japanese aliens." But Lewis B. Hershey, promoted to director of Selective Service, announced at the same time that local boards would continue accepting US citizens of Japanese descent, and many did so. In the first three months of 1942, the army inducted more than eighteen hundred Japanese Americans.[7]

Capturing the topsy-turvy nature of army policy at the moment was the experience of a young Nebraskan named Ben Kuroki. Shortly after the Pearl Harbor attack, his father, a Japanese immigrant, told him, "America is your country. . . . You fight for it." So he and his brother, Fred, drove 150 miles to the nearest army recruiting station in Grand Island. While the recruiting sergeant happily signed them up, he explained weeks later that the War Department now banned Japanese American enlistment. Undeterred, Ben and Fred tried another recruiting station, this time getting in. "[T]he next morning," Ben's biographer noted, "they stood up straight and tense, listening with ten others to the recruiting officer reading from his book, then saying, 'Now repeat after me.'"[8]

Ben and Fred were among the lucky ones, at least from their perspective. Exclusion was right around the corner, as one Selective Service report later suggested, voicing in the process many of the racist assumptions that guided so much wartime government policy toward Japanese Americans: "The Japanese will now require special consideration. Even though they are native-born citizens of the United States, there is a feeling that the racial ties of many of these men may prove stronger than the accident of their national birth and require the development of special policies for them within the Selective Service System."[9] While draft officials acknowledged Japanese Americans' citizenship rights, they stressed the limits to those rights. Given their supposed un-Americanness—the "accident of their national birth"—and their "racial ties" to Japan, "Japanese" would have to be treated differently from other Americans, even others with ancestral connections to enemy lands, such as those of Italian and German descent. Only "special policies" would protect the United States from the singularly dire threat Japanese Americans putatively posed.

In the early spring of 1942, just as the army began to exclude Japanese Americans from the West Coast and to plan their mass removal to inland camps, it began to settle on these "special policies." On March 30, at the informal request of the War Department, Selective Service confidentially instructed its state directors to stop accepting any further "registrants of Japanese extraction" and to "discontinue deliveries for such purpose." In a confidential message to Hawaii the next day, the army adjutant general ordered Hawaiian authorities to do the same. The army's induction of Japanese Americans, which averaged roughly six hundred a month in January, February, and March 1942, dropped to twenty-nine in April, four in May, two in June, and zero after that. In June, Secretary of War Stimson, in a letter to Hershey, made the army's exclusion policy official: "Except as may be specifically authorized in exceptional cases, the War Department will not accept for service with the armed forces, Japanese, or persons of Japanese extraction, regardless of citizenship status or other factors."[10]

All the while, the army was not content simply to keep Japanese Americans out. It also worked to expel many of those who had already found their way in, often prior to America's entry in the war. It is difficult to determine how many Japanese Americans the army discharged prematurely, but the number may have exceeded one thousand in 1942.[11]

Finally, in September 1942, draft officials, at the behest of the War Department, repurposed an existing classification, IV-C, to apply to "any registrant (whether a national of the United States or an alien) who, because of his nationality or his ancestry, is within a class of persons not acceptable to the land and naval forces for training and service." Significantly, while this category applied to other aliens besides those from Japan (those from enemy countries or from neutral ones, who sought an exemption from service), it applied to only one group of US citizens, or "nationals" in the Selective Service's telling language: Japanese Americans. In their case, "ancestry" trumped "nationality"—and citizenship.[12]

Indeed, it was precisely this trumping of the former over the latter that helps explain the War Department's decision to ban and expel people of Japanese descent from the army. The former policy seems to have begun in the G-1 division of the War Department, which was in charge of personnel issues. In a memo dated March 27, 1942, which recommended such a ban only days before it took effect, the director of military personnel wrote approvingly of the recent "trend of national policy" to place "citizens of Japanese extraction" in the "dangerous enemy alien category." He cited a long list of examples, including the confinement of Japanese Americans in "concentration camps." Within the army, he explained, the trend meant that "men of this class must be placed in the interior; cannot be assigned to Air Force, Chemical Warfare, Signal, or Armored Force installations; are to be kept away from localities from which they can gain important information; and are to be kept under surveillance in the Army."[13] Thanks, then, to their deep-seated, widespread, and baseless fears about Japanese Americans' dangerousness and foreignness, War Department leaders thought that these soldiers placed undue burdens on the army. For the sake of its all-important efficiency, Japanese American induction had to end.

That the War Department approved and implemented this blanket exclusion within a few short days reflects how these fears pervaded its top leadership. After all, six weeks earlier it had designed and provided the decisive endorsement for the mass removal and imprisonment of all West Coast Japanese Americans. In the words of its "final recommendation" for this momentous policy, "The Japanese race is an enemy race and while many second and third generation Japanese born on United States soil, possessed of United States citizenship, have become 'Americanized,' the racial strains remain undiluted." Subscribing to this view was, among others, Secretary of War Stimson. On February 10, 1942, he noted in his diary the "fact" that Japanese Americans' "racial characteristics are such that we cannot understand or trust even the [US] citizen Japanese."[14]

Starting at the end of March 1942, then, Japanese Americans—citizens and noncitizens alike—were, with precious few exceptions, henceforth barred from joining any part of the US Armed Forces. It is noteworthy that the fortunes of Japanese Americans and African Americans, at least concerning enlistment, moved in opposite directions at this moment, even if officials seem to have been unaware of the fact. Just one week after the army barred Japanese American enlistment, the final step in their exclusion from the entire military, the navy and marine corps lifted their ban on the enlistment of African Americans, opening all the military's major branches to them. If the end of black exclusion only brought a continuing, evolving story of restriction, however, Japanese Americans' treatment would prove even more ever-changing. Within the span of a few short months, they had already gone from being drafted and classified like white people to being expelled and excluded more than black people. More changes were on the way.

Meanwhile, the navy's long-standing and unwavering exclusion of Japanese Americans met with occasional protest from various quarters throughout the war, though especially in its last year or so. From within the Roosevelt administration, Harold Ickes, secretary of the Interior Department, and Elmer Davis, head of the Office of War Information (OWI), each at different times opposed the navy's ban. It provided the Japanese enemy, in their view, with a "basis for charging that the United States preaches democracy but practices race discrimination." The *Washington Post*, in an August 1944 editorial, chided the "Nordic Navy" for undermining "Americanism" at the "very top levels of command," and other newspapers, from the *Milwaukee Journal* to the *Berkshire (MA) Evening Eagle*, followed suit. Around the same time, the American Civil

Liberties Union (ACLU) began a year-long campaign to convince the navy to lift its ban, since it was "the only department of the Government which totally excludes Americans of Japanese ancestry for any position what-ever."[15] Japanese Americans themselves, especially by the last few years of the war, became increasingly vocal on the matter. In dozens of letters and petitions to political and military leaders, they insisted that every branch of the armed services, including the navy, be open to them. In March 1944, to cite one of many examples, the Amache Community Council from the Granada Relocation Center in Colorado wrote to Secretaries Knox and Stimson with eleven "requests," the first of which was "that equal opportunity for service and advancement in all branches of the Armed Forces and Services be opened and offered to Japanese American[s] . . . solely on the basis of individual merit and qualification."[16]

But the navy refused to budge on its ban—at least not publicly. In fact, the navy inducted several hundred or so Japanese Americans as seamen in its Coast Guard and an unknown number of top-secret linguists and others serving in special duty. According to one postwar article in the Japanese American Citizens League (JACL) newspaper, the *Pacific Citizen*, when the War Relocation Authority (WRA) proposed during the war that it announce Japanese Americans' service in the marine corps, it was told that the men would be discharged if it did. In the face of the growing critiques later in the war, the navy did not deny its ban of Japanese Americans, but tried simply to explain it away. Responding to the ACLU, for example, Acting Secretary of the Navy Ralph Bard offered this long-winded and convoluted defense of its policies: "It is impossible to accede to the proposal that the Japanese-Americans be made eligible for any of the various branches of the Naval Service. . . . This policy is dictated not by any fundamental distrust of the loyalty of this group as a class, but because of the peculiar conditions which are encountered in present naval warfare and which could make their presence particularly troublesome on active areas of combat, such as in the Pacific."[17]

In truth, this policy unquestionably arose from—and was maintained throughout the war in part because of—a "fundamental distrust" of Japanese Americans "as a class." No one epitomized this distrust better than Navy Secretary Frank Knox. Nearly a decade before the attack on Pearl Harbor, he suggested the need to "to intern every Japanese resident" in Hawaii as a "first military precaution . . . *before* the beginning of hostilities threatens." In his first month as navy secretary, he suggested to President Roosevelt that one among many ways to "impress the Japanese with the seriousness of our preparations" for war was to draw up "plans for concentration camps." After the Pearl Harbor attack—which Knox's navy proved completely unprepared for, despite his boast only three days earlier that wherever the Japanese might strike, it was "not going to be caught napping"—he attempted to deflect blame by publicly accusing local Japanese Americans of having performed "the most effective Fifth Column work of the entire war." He offered no evidence for the charge, but repeated it for two weeks following the attack, in a private discussion with the president, at a packed press conference, and at a cabinet meeting.[18]

The next few years failed to diminish Knox's near obsessive concerns about Japanese Americans' disloyalty, which he often used to justify the navy ban against them. In October 1942, when Roosevelt forwarded a critique of the ban to Knox, he wrote the president that the much bigger problem was the "very large number of Japanese sympathizers, if not actual Japanese agents, still at large in the population of Oahu, who, in the event of an attack upon the islands, would unquestionably cooperate with our enemies." Fourteen months later, when an Asian specialist wrote him to insist that "Americans of Japanese parentage . . . be drafted and placed in the Armed Forces exactly like" anyone else, Knox demurred, sounding a familiar alarm: "I am terribly worried over the constant menace which exists, for instance, in Oahu, where there are at large many Japanese-Americans, whose probable sympathies are still with Japan."[19]

The ban, for all intents and purposes, survived the war intact not simply because of these baseless fears about Japanese American disloyalty. After all, many War Department leaders shared them and yet eventually chose to induct Japanese Americans anyway, partly because some among these leaders grew to become unexpected champions of the cause. It appears that no one in a similarly powerful position in the navy ever assumed such a role.[20] African Americans' eventual inclusion in the navy offers another clue about the staying power of the Japanese American ban. Both President Roosevelt and the War Department came for different reasons to support black people's greater access to the navy, but they showed no similar inclination when it came to Japanese Americans. Whereas Roosevelt eventually insisted that the navy revise its policies regarding black induction, he seldom asked Knox about its Japanese American ban, and no doubt in part because of their scant political power, he seems to have made no effort to overturn it. Whereas Secretary Stimson implored the president to force the navy to "take some colored marines," he assumed an entirely different tack when it came to Japanese Americans. In a draft letter to the president from late 1942, in which he made the case for reopening the army to Japanese American enlistment, he added that the "Navy is faced with a slightly different situation, as the treachery of one man on board a ship has far direr possibilities than similar disaffection on the ground."[21]

"IT *IS* POSSIBLE TO SEPARATE THE SHEEP FROM THE GOATS"

If the navy held fast to its exclusion of Japanese Americans, how was it that Stimson and other War Department leaders did not, especially when their own fears of Japanese American "treachery" continued to haunt them? This story begins within days of their decision in late March 1942 to end all future inductions of Japanese Americans, when they started receiving calls to change course. On April 6, Delos C. Emmons, the commanding officer of the War Department's Hawaiian Department, requested authority to create a new unit made up not only of the Japanese Americans already in uniform there, but also of Hawaii's "young male citizens of Japanese parentage who desire to demonstrate their loyalty to the United States in a concrete manner." In other words, Emmons appears to have been requesting, in part, an exception to the War Department's week-old ban on Japanese American induction. Emmons thought that such a unit "would give a good account of itself." A month later, Milton Eisenhower, the director of the WRA, the new government agency charged with overseeing the "relocation centers," wrote Assistant Secretary of War John J. McCloy calling for Selective Service to accept Japanese Americans again. McCloy may have been especially receptive to these ideas, for two reasons. He had recently returned from a trip to Hawaii, where he had had a chance to witness "the serious dedication to task and country" of Japanese American volunteers assisting an army outfit in Oahu. While there, he also met with Emmons, who no doubt discussed his new combat outfit idea. Whatever the reason, McCloy forwarded Milton's letter to his older brother Dwight Eisenhower, then working for the War Department General Staff, adding a note that, revealingly, echoed Emmons's language: "I have felt for some time that it may be well to use our American citizen Japanese soldiers against the Germans. I believe we could count on these soldiers to give a good account of themselves."[22]

McCloy's, Emmons's, and Eisenhower's interest in the matter seems to have convinced the War Department to revisit the question of Japanese American enlistment. On July 1, 1942, it convened a board of officers to consider "the military utilization of United States citizens of Japanese ancestry." Two months later, the board recommended the continued exclusion of all Japanese Americans, save a few individuals for "intelligence or for specialized purposes." In other words, it endorsed the status quo. In doing so, it cited familiar concerns: that Japanese Americans were "such a distinctive class of individuals, so marked by racial appearance, characteristics and background, that they are particularly repulsive to the military establishment at large and the civilian population of the United States"; and that "the lone fact that these individuals are of Japanese ancestry tends to place them in a most questionable light as to their loyalty to the United States." The board did not discuss whether this distrust or repulsion was warranted, nor did it offer a shred of evidence to support either. Regardless, in mid-September, the War Department General Staff approved the report and its recommendation.[23]

If the purpose of the study was to settle the matter, however, it had the opposite effect. Indeed, even before the board finished its report, opponents of the ban spoke out. Dillon Myer, who succeeded Milton Eisenhower as WRA director, called the War Department in early September 1942, pleading with officials "from the depth of my heart . . . to use them [Japanese Americans]." At the same time, McCloy had the OWI send him a letter explaining the potential propaganda value of enlisting Japanese American soldiers, which he then promptly forwarded to the War Department's personnel division, which was in charge of the board study. "I feel that all avenues of possible utilization should be exhaustively considered," added McCloy, "before a decision is reached not to use them." Most surprisingly, the navy also lobbied the army to lift its ban, though it did so for a less surprising reason: it thought that drafting the "10,000 people of Japanese extraction" in Hawaii "would remove a lot of dangerous characters from the islands, and that so long as they are . . . used on fronts outside of the Pacific area, they will render good service."[24]

When the War Department balked at these suggestions, choosing to retain its Japanese American ban, opposition only grew. The opponents were a diverse group, coming from inside and outside the War Department and differing on many points, including whether Japanese Americans should be drafted or simply allowed to volunteer, whether they should serve in segregated or integrated units, whether enlistment should be open to all military-age men of Japanese descent or to US citizens alone, and whether they should be employed in combat or noncombat roles, in the United States or overseas. Uniting this camp was the conviction that the army's exclusion of Japanese Americans was wrongheaded and should end.

Among the first important challenges to the War Department's latest endorsement of the ban came from within. A collection of career army officers, who specialized in Japanese language and intelligence and who commanded the few Nisei at the time permitted to serve in the Pacific as translators and interpreters, swore by their men's loyalty and value to the war effort. Chief among this group was a colonel named Moses W. Pettigrew, who headed the Far Eastern Branch of the War Department's Military Intelligence Division. In an early October memo to his boss, he counseled fighting the Japanese American ban and the board report on which it was most recently based. The report, he argued, was irreparably flawed: it ignored the views of numerous generals who supported the enlistment of Japanese American soldiers; it failed to consult the War Manpower Commission about the "*necessity* . . . of . . . 15,000 military prospects"; it sought no opinion from those officers who actually commanded Japanese Americans and who "could have testified to the[ir] exemplary conduct"; and it did not yet know about the "Nisei soldiers on duty in Intelligence detachments in the only . . . places in which they have had a chance to engage in action against the Japanese . . . [who] have been officially commended by their Commanding Officers." In the end, Pettigrew strongly recommended that the original board, or a newly convened one, reconsider the ban on Japanese American enlistment in light of these facts. Elsewhere he called for rescinding all "existing restrictions against conscription and voluntary enlistment" of US citizens of Japanese descent. He even wished to allow Japanese aliens the right to volunteer for service.[25]

Meanwhile, similar requests to reopen army doors to Japanese Americans came from other quarters. In early October, Elmer Davis, the OWI director, wrote President Roosevelt to urge him to lift the ban. "It would hardly be fair to evacuate people and then impose normal draft procedures," Davis reasoned. But permitting "loyal American citizens of Japanese descent" to join the armed forces was sound military policy both at home—since "it *is* possible to separate the sheep from the goats"—and abroad—since Nisei soldiers would undermine Japanese propagandists' continued claims that America was fighting not an honorable war for the Four Freedoms but a "racial war" for white supremacy. Far East expert and Harvard professor Edwin O. Reischauer echoed this final point almost word for word in a memo, which was forwarded to McCloy within days of Davis's letter. He called for the "inclusion of large numbers of Japanese Americans in combat units." During the conflict, they "would be the best possible proof that this is not a racial war to preserve white supremacy in Asia, but a war to establish a better world for all." Afterward they "could be made into a tremendous strategical advantage in the great struggle to win the peace in Asia."[26]

Later that month, the governor of Hawaii suggested reinstituting Selective Service for Japanese Americans. The governor, citing the concerns of an Oahu local draft board, worried that its discontinuance violated the STSA; he also feared unrest in the territory "among those other racial groups whose sons, husbands and brothers have been drafted into service." A few weeks later, in mid-November, at its annual national convention, the JACL, believing that "Selective Service is the cornerstone of our future in this country," unanimously passed a resolution asking President Roosevelt and the US Army to afford "American-born-Japanese" "the same privilege of serving our country in the armed forces as that granted to every other American citizen." In effect, it asked that Japanese Americans' right to volunteer and be drafted into the service be restored. At that same conference, WRA director Dillon Myer, insisting that "all citizens have the right to fight for this country," continued lobbying for the increased use of Japanese Americans in the army. He met with Roosevelt's closest adviser, Harry Hopkins, earlier in the month, hoping to persuade the president on the matter.[27]

Of all these efforts, it was Elmer Davis's letter that seems to have had the most obvious impact. Shortly after receiving it, Roosevelt bumped into Davis at a luncheon and indicated he was "willing for citizens of Japanese descent to enlist in the Army for restricted duty." The implication seemed to be that "the men would be assigned to functions not normally handled by soldiers and if everything went well there they could later be assigned to more normal tasks." Perhaps army reform on the matter might have begun and ended there had Davis's letter not also resonated with the most powerful leaders in the War Department. Roosevelt forwarded Davis's letter to Stimson, who promptly passed it to McCloy for comment. McCloy, who would soon be collaborating closely with Pettigrew on pushing Japanese American enlistment, endorsed Davis's main points about their loyalty, their promise as soldiers, and their propaganda value. Stimson may have asked for more details, in part to provide Roosevelt with a substantive response to Davis's letter, because two weeks later he received a longer draft memo. Almost certainly coming from McCloy, it concluded, "In consideration of the rights of the American born Japanese and his reputed loyalty, and in further consideration of the propaganda effect of having Japanese in the United States service as outlined in Mr. Elmer Davis' letter, it is believed that the value of recruiting Japanese into the Army would outweigh the objections given in the report of the board of officers."[28]

Stimson, it appears, required little convincing. "I am inclined strongly to agree with the view of McCloy and Davis," he wrote to Army Chief of Staff Marshall in an undated handwritten note. "I don't think you can permanently proscribe a lot of American citizens because of their racial origin—We have gone to the full limit in evacuating them." Marshall evidently agreed. In an undated draft letter to Roosevelt, Stimson conveyed that he and Marshall had "reached the conclusion that the possible benefits accruing from . . . [Japanese American] enlistment in the Army outweigh opposing factors." The benefits included the "utilization of manpower"; the "increase of fighting power," since Japanese Americans "should prove to be, after suitable training, excellent fighters"; the "external psychological effect" of the "yellow man voluntarily fighting for the white," which would impress Asia and would provide "the whole world" with "further evidence of the success of democracy"; and "the internal psychological effect" of improving Japanese American morale and their prospects in postwar America. "There is no question in my mind," Stimson wrote, "that the Japanese problem in this country after the war would admit of far easier solution if voluntary enlistment were permitted."[29]

By mid-December, the War Department's organization and training division (G-3) had agreed on a plan to allow "citizens of Japanese ancestry whose loyalty is unquestioned" to volunteer for the army again—this time, for service solely in a combat team whose enlisted personnel were entirely Japanese American. On January 1, 1943, Marshall officially approved the plan, and on January 28, Stimson announced it publicly. "It is the inherent right of every faithful citizen, regardless of ancestry, to bear arms in the nation's battle," he declared. "When obstacles to the free expression of that right are imposed by emergency considerations those barriers should be removed as soon as humanly possible." Several days later, President Roosevelt agreed. "No loyal citizen of the United States should be denied the democratic right to exercise the responsibilities of his citizenship,

Fig. 2.1 Members of the 442nd Combat Team, whose formation was announced on January 28, 1943, training at Camp Shelby in July of that year. Courtesy of The Bancroft Library, University of California, Berkeley, WRA no. H-88.

regardless of his ancestry," he proclaimed in a much-quoted public letter to Stimson, which Dillon Myer, with the help of Elmer Davis, had written. "The principle on which this country was founded and by which it has always been governed is that Americanism is a matter of the mind and heart; Americanism is not, and never was, a matter of race or ancestry."[30]

Despite the lofty rhetoric, the "matter of race and ancestry" still deeply shaped and restricted Japanese Americans' access to the army. While the War Department rejected the board of officers' position that none but a few individual Japanese Americans were suitable for service, it implicitly accepted Davis's notion that "sheep" and "goats" could be distinguished. This was a remarkable admission given that the "evacuation" decision, not yet a year old at the time, and the War Department's contemporaneous defense of it in the courts rested on the point's presumed impossibility. At the same time, the military stopped well short of treating Japanese Americans, as the JACL wanted, like "every other American citizen" (by which it clearly meant nonblack citizens).[31] For those Japanese Americans wishing to, as Stimson put it, "bear arms in the nation's battle," they encountered a daunting and lengthy list of additional requirements beyond age and physical ability, which applied to everyone: They had to be US citizens (which in their case meant US-born, since Japanese immigrants were barred from naturalization); Japanese aliens were completely excluded from military service. They had to join the army, since the other services refused to accept them. They had to be men, since all branches of the military open to women were closed to Japanese Americans. They had to volunteer, since the draft remained off limits. They had to serve in combat, the deadliest of army assignments. They had to serve in a segregated outfit, whose only white personnel were commanding officers. They, much like African Americans at the time, had to contend with a firm quota of available army slots. And they had to undergo an extensive loyalty screening process that no other citizens—or aliens, for that matter—faced.[32]

Regarding this last point, all Japanese American volunteers had to complete minimally two forms—an application for voluntary induction, which all enlistees filled out, and a "Statement of United States Citizen of Japanese Ancestry," which was for Nisei alone. The latter's purpose, in the words of the Selective Service, "was to present to these registrants certain questions, the answers to which would reveal their connections with Japan, relatives in Japan, visits to Japan and a number of other factors peculiar to the racial background and education of the young Japanese American." The War Department's—and, in Hawaii, the Hawaiian Department's—Military Intelligence Division reviewed these statements, conferring with the FBI, the Office of Naval Intelligence, and, when appropriate, the WRA. It used an elaborate scoring system, which, for example, rewarded points to those who had Anglicized names, played baseball, were Christian, and joined the JACL and deducted them from those who had Japanese names, practiced Judo, were Buddhist or Shinto, and joined a Congress of Industrial Organizations union. It then divided men into those "acceptable" and those "not acceptable" for duty. The latter men kept their IV-C classification; the former appeared before local draft boards and were processed "for induction in the same manner as any other I-A man."[33] No longer an "enemy race" exactly, Japanese Americans, in the eyes of the War Department, remained a suspect one.[34]

But if the army's new opportunity for Japanese American enlistment came with considerable limits, it still constituted a shift in policy from near-total exclusion to somewhat greater inclusion. A complex mix of factors seems to have convinced the War Department to change course. First, greater inclusion of Nisei was, in Roosevelt's words, "the fullest and wisest use of our manpower [which] is all important to the war effort." This was a point that Pettigrew and Stimson also made. It came at a time of widespread concerns about personnel shortages in and out of the military, concerns that also led to the Mexican guest worker or Bracero program, the increased enlistment of women, the conscription of fathers, and growing pressure on the armed forces to take more black registrants.[35]

The War Department was also genuinely impressed with the salutary impact Nisei enlistment would have on its war in Asia. From its start, Axis propagandists abroad avidly contrasted America's democratic rhetoric with its racist realities, hoping to drive a wedge between the United States and its "colored" allies. In the Pacific, in particular, Japan hailed itself as the savior of the "darker races" and condemned America's "race war" for white supremacy. The US government, then, was eager to show the world—and especially its non-European friends—that its commitment to democracy was real. Making this point as well as anything, according to McCloy, Stimson, Davis, and other officials, was renewed Nisei enlistment. As Stimson wrote President Roosevelt, Nisei combat units would show the world not only "the yellow man voluntarily fighting for the white," but also the fallacy of Japan's anti-American claims.[36]

Japanese Americans' new enlistment opportunity also came in part from the War Department's confidence in their fighting abilities, a confidence that stood in stark contrast to its dim view of black soldiers. Stimson thought Japanese Americans would make "excellent fighters," McCloy predicted a "highly effective . . . corps d'elite," and Pettigrew claimed that a Nisei combat team "would have no superior in our entire army." Sometimes this supreme confidence stemmed from a grudging respect for the Japanese enemy—and its presumed ancestral or "racial" similarities with Americans of Japanese descent. As the final War Department memo that recommended lifting the ban noted, "Considering the fighting qualities which enemy Japanese have demonstrated there is no reason to believe that combat units of a high degree of effectiveness could not be developed from loyal personnel of this class."[37] The supposedly indelible blood ties that bound all people of Japanese descent, no matter where they were born or lived, led both to the exclusion of Japanese Americans from the army and to their later inclusion.

Belated acknowledgment of Japanese Americans' citizenship rights also played a role in this inclusion. Publicly, Stimson and Roosevelt stressed this argument—"It is the inherent right of every faithful citizen, regardless of ancestry, to bear arms in the Nation's battle," in Stimson's words. But these arguments appeared in private, too. Stimson's handwritten note to Marshall—"I don't think you can permanently proscribe a lot of American citizens because of their racial origin"—is the most obvious example, but there were others. In McCloy's memo to Stimson making the case for ending the ban on Japanese American enlistment, he spoke of "the fundamental rights of citizens to serve their country."[38]

Finally, allowing Japanese American army enlistment was part of a larger government effort at the time to separate "loyal" and "disloyal" Japanese Americans in the camps and to give the former greater opportunity to leave, lest they be permanently damaged by the whole traumatic experience, by disaffected foreign-born (Issei), or by both. "At present these people [loyal Japanese Americans] are in relocation centers where they are subject to the influence of dissident alien Japanese," McCloy told Stimson. "As a result of these undesirable contacts their future value as useful citizens may be seriously impaired." In Stimson's letter to Roosevelt, he echoed this point: "After completion of mass evacuation the indications were that . . . the great majority of the evacuees, whether citizen or alien, remained completely loyal to the United States. Since that time, as might be expected from such trying circumstances, some deterioration in this attitude has probably occurred." But Stimson thought military service could solve this problem—and improve Japanese Americans' postwar prospects, too. "When they returned, they would return with pride in their hearts that they had done their bit, instead of being released like lepers to find their places in a world all too eager to reject them."[39]

FROM ENLISTMENT TO CONSCRIPTION

Barely a week after Secretary Stimson announced the War Department's new willingness to accept Japanese American enlistees, McCloy sent him a short memo. He enclosed a brief summary of "editorial reaction" to the move and happily reported it was overwhelmingly positive. Indeed, if mainstream newspapers are any indication, many Americans applauded the new policy. It was "wisely undertaken" (*Minneapolis Morning Tribune*), a "tardy attempt to treat the Nisei with justice" (*Portland (ME) Press Herald*), an "encouraging beginning toward a more rational treatment" (*San Francisco Chronicle*), and "bad news for Hirohito" (*Portland Oregonian*). Rarely, but at times, newspapers even questioned the racist reasoning that collapsed all distinctions between people of Japanese descent in Japan and in the United States. "The characteristics responsible for Japan's national policies appear to be the result of education and environment rather than race," the *Galveston News* contended in February 1943. "It seems reasonable to suppose that a Japanese born and educated in this country is primarily American in his outlook on life."[40]

Some Japanese Americans also welcomed the army's new policies. From the camps came a story of four brothers at Minidoka in Idaho all proudly joining up, or of Harry Osaki of Gila River in Arizona, who, upon being accepted into the army, pronounced being "the happiest of my life," or of grand "send-off-celebrations" for enlistees.[41] But this welcome was much more pronounced in Hawaii, where Japanese Americans had been spared mass removal and mass detention. There, pressure to join up was enormous. Numerous "AJA" (American of Japanese Ancestry) organizations and "morale committees" began "virtually soliciting volunteers," in the words of one Japanese American. Some found the effort unseemly and "irritating," but many others were overjoyed at the chance, in the words of one enlistee, "to show our patriotism—to show that we are not afraid to die for this country."[42] Thanks to these and other motivations, thousands of young men rushed to enlist, surpassing the War Department quota of fifteen hundred Japanese Americans within a few hours. In two weeks, nearly ten thousand men had volunteered, an astonishing one-third of all military-eligible Japanese American men in Hawaii. When the portion of these men who were accepted and inducted for service set sail for training on the mainland in late March 1943, a massive, jubilant crowd—considered by one Associated Press report to be "probably the largest . . . in the city's history" at nearly twenty thousand and "composed almost entirely of Japanese-Americans"—bid them farewell. Most striking about the event, observed the *Honolulu Star-Bulletin*, was "not alone the size of

Fig. 2.2 Twenty-one-year-old Mitsuma Yokohari signs voluntary enlistment papers to join the 442nd Combat Team at the Granada Relocation Center in Colorado, February 10, 1943. Courtesy of The Bancroft Library, University of California, Berkeley, WRA no. E-741.

the crowd . . . [but] the pride of the families and friends of these young Americans—their pride that the youths are entrusted with the patriotic mission of fighting for their country and the Allied nations."[43]

Not everyone shared this excitement. Within the War Department, several prominent holdouts opposed the acceptance of Japanese American volunteers, such as General Dewitt of the Western Defense Command, who infamously told a House subcommittee, "They are a dangerous element. There is no way to determine their loyalty. . . . It makes no difference if he is an American citizen, he is still Japanese"—"a Jap's a Jap." Anti-Japanese American organizations on the West Coast—local chapters of the Veterans of Foreign Wars, the Native Sons of the Golden West, and even a breakfast club in East Los Angeles—agreed, calling the army's use of Nisei a "menace to . . . the nation." A handful of US Congress members, sometimes citing constituents' fears, expressed similar views: John Rankin from Mississippi, for example, was "shocked beyond expression" that the army chose to accept "these Japanese who aided in the fifth column work before the attack on Pearl Harbor." He considered the new combat team an "appeasement to the Japs," all the while that "our boys are being butchered by these brutal apes." A small minority of newspapers, such as the *Fort Worth Star-Telegram*, also opposed the army's use of Japanese Americans, since "the American Melting Pot is a marvel of alchemy in transmutation of racial characteristics . . . [but] the children of Nippon are not mixers and they have not mixed. They are Japs." Finally, ordinary people absorbed and shared these views. Nisei enlistment is "a very dangerous thing," wrote one woman from Savannah, Georgia, in a letter to the army in March 1943. "They are loyal to the Emperor of Japan and their fanatical outlook on life. . . . They would not hesitate at the opportune moment to knife our officers and turn their guns on our men fighting near them."[44]

The most widespread and consequential opposition to the War Department's new policy came from Japanese Americans themselves, often those residing in detention camps. Unlike Rankin, DeWitt, and others, they objected not to any "appeasement to the Japs," but to the federal government's continuing subjugation and humiliation of Japanese Americans, which many thought the new army plan exemplified.

As successful as the army's recruitment efforts were in Hawaii, they unfolded disastrously in the camps. Although War Department and WRA officials proved remarkably obtuse on the point initially, the whole experience of mass removal and mass detention hardly prepared many Japanese Americans to embrace voluntary enlistment. "In January 1943," a WRA report later acknowledged, "the residents of relocation centers felt like they had been discriminated against in the evacuation, that they had blundered in failing to protest it, that their future in the United States was being threatened from many quarters, that WRA and the government in general could not be trusted, and that the Army, in particular, was responsible for their present situation." Capturing this "atmosphere of insecurity and suspicion" was one Nisei at the Minidoka Camp in Idaho, who later asked, "How could the government and army, after branding us disloyal, after stripping us of our possessions and dignity, and imprisoning us in barbed wire concentration camps, how could they now ask us to volunteer our lives in defense of a country that had so wrongfully treated us?"[45]

Pondering this weighty question, many Japanese Americans found that the army plan raised countless others: Why had War Department policy suddenly shifted from exclusion to enlistment? Why were so many stipulations tied to it, including requirements that Japanese Americans volunteer and not be drafted, that they join a segregated unit, that they serve in combat, perhaps in "suicide missions," that they join the army alone and not the navy, marine corps, or air corps, and that they be male citizens and not Nisei women or Issei? If Nisei failed to volunteer, would they simply be drafted in time? If drafted, could they avoid service in the segregated combat team? Would the act of volunteering come with any guarantee that enlistees' citizenship rights would be restored, that their families would be protected, that they would be compensated in some way for their property losses and general hardship, or that they could return to the West Coast? Perhaps most fundamentally, given the uncertainties of the war and the profound injustices of mass removal and mass confinement, would Nisei futures lay ultimately in Japan or in the United States?

Many Japanese Americans worried, too, about the lengthy loyalty questionnaire that all draft-age Nisei completed as a prerequisite for enlistment. This coincided with the distribution of a separate though similar questionnaire from the WRA regarding possible resettlement outside the camps, which only compounded the bewilderment and anxiety of the moment. To begin with, authorities were unclear and inconsistent about whether completing the forms was even required. Instructions from the WRA's acting director in Washington, DC, explicitly said no, but some individual camp directors thought otherwise, even arresting and imprisoning men for their refusal to complete and submit the forms. At one camp, officials claimed erroneously that this refusal constituted a violation of the draft law and was punishable as such. In fact, no Nisei were being conscripted—they were being asked to enlist—and the "Statement of United States Citizen of Japanese Ancestry" was from the War Department, not the Selective Service, though stamped across the top was "Selective Service System." Japanese Americans also wondered why they alone had to fill out these questionnaires. Did the government, asked detainees at Tule Lake, "employ likewise an exclusive form for the purpose of inducting Negroes and other racial minorities, such as the United States citizens of German and Italian ancestry?"[46]

Then there were the form's actual questions, especially the final two, numbers 27 and 28. The former asked, "Are you willing to serve in the armed forces of the United States on combat duty, wherever ordered?" Nisei wondered whether answering yes was tantamount to enlisting—and whether a no answer permanently disqualified them from military service. The latter asked whether Nisei men would "swear unqualified allegiance to the United States of America" and "forswear any form of allegiance or obedience to the Japanese emperor." Many Nisei puzzled over how they could, in the words of Brooklyn-born Victor Moto, "renounce something I never had." They also feared that a negative answer might imperil their US citizenship. Many Issei, who had to answer a similar question and whom US law explicitly barred from naturalization, feared that an affirmative answer would leave them stateless, citizens of neither the United States nor Japan.[47]

Given these myriad, gravely important questions and concerns—and given the government officials' frequent inability to address them satisfactorily—confusion and conflict convulsed the camps in early 1943. Resistance to enlistment (and registration more generally) was most extensive and organized at Gila River, Manzanar, Jerome, Heart Mountain, and especially Tule Lake.[48] At Tule Lake, the government arrested more than one hundred protesters. Many hundreds flatly refused to complete the questionnaire, and similar numbers opted, instead, to apply for expatriation. More than a third of all Nisei men declined to swear unqualified allegiance to the United States, and as of April 1943, only fifty-nine men volunteered for the army—less than 3 percent of eligible Nisei.[49] Despite significant variation from one place to another, no camp was immune. "At nearly every center," one WRA report noted, "registration produced a crisis," since it "precipitated all the suppressed resentments growing out of evacuation and relocation center experiences." Even at Minidoka, which provided by far the largest number of volunteers, despite being one of the smaller camps, the army's enlistment program, according to one detainee's memory, caused "immediate turmoil and split the camp in two." In all, of nearly twenty thousand military-age Nisei men in the camps, fewer than twelve hundred volunteered for the army by early April 1943.[50]

Considering all that incarcerated Japanese Americans had been forced to endure, this was a remarkably high number. But it was well under the army's expected quota of roughly forty-three hundred from the continental United States. The War Department—especially those leaders like McCloy who had championed Japanese American enlistment and were "very anxious" that it succeed—was deeply disappointed. Since the plan's presumed value had much to do with its message, to be broadcast home and abroad, about America's happy and harmonious multiracial democracy, many Japanese Americans' widespread and well-publicized resistance was decidedly unhelpful. Indeed, anticipating this possibility as early as October 1942, McCloy cautioned Stimson, "It must be assured that a voluntary program will not fail, and prior to instituting such a program a survey should be made to determine the probable success of the program." The WRA conducted such a survey a month or so later, at least among camp officials. Despite its significant caveat that its estimates were "based primarily on . . . [its] 'feel' for the attitude prevailing on [its] Projects," it was bullish regarding enlistment. At Tule Lake, for example, which, again, had fewer than sixty volunteers, the WRA had projected more than one thousand.[51]

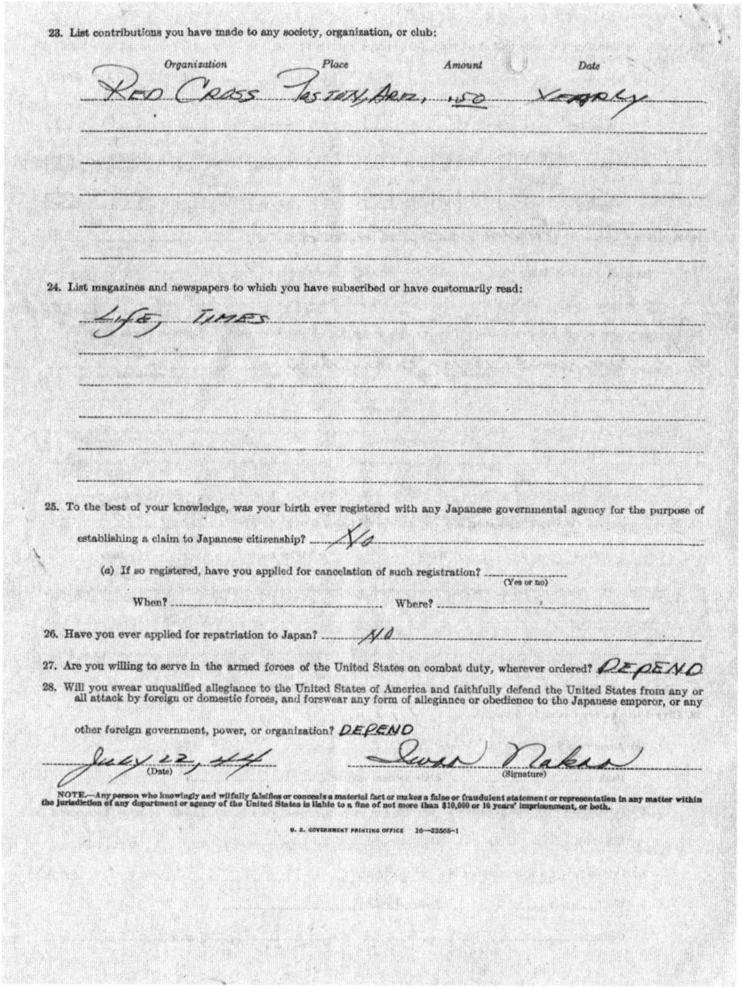

23. List contributions you have made to any society, organization, or club:

Organization	Place	Amount	Date
RED CROSS	POSTON, ARIZ.	1.50	YEARLY

24. List magazines and newspapers to which you have subscribed or have customarily read: Life, TIMES

25. To the best of your knowledge, was your birth ever registered with any Japanese governmental agency for the purpose of establishing a claim to Japanese citizenship? NO

(a) If so registered, have you applied for cancelation of such registration? ______ (Yes or no)

When? ______ Where? ______

26. Have you ever applied for repatriation to Japan? NO

27. Are you willing to serve in the armed forces of the United States on combat duty, wherever ordered? DEPEND

28. Will you swear unqualified allegiance to the United States of America and faithfully defend the United States from any or all attack by foreign or domestic forces, and forswear any form of allegiance or obedience to the Japanese emperor, or any other foreign government, power, or organization? DEPEND

July 22, 44 (Date) Iwao Nakao (Signature)

NOTE.—Any person who knowingly and wilfully falsifies or conceals a material fact or makes a false or fraudulent statement or representation in any matter within the jurisdiction of any department or agency of the United States is liable to a fine of not more than $10,000 or 10 years' imprisonment, or both.

U. S. GOVERNMENT PRINTING OFFICE 16—32565-1

Fig. 2.3 The "Statement of United States Citizen of Japanese Ancestry" of eighteen-year-old Iwao Nakao, an "internee" at the Poston Relocation Center, July 22, 1944. On both questions 27 and 28—about whether Nakao would willingly "serve in the armed forces of the United States on combat duty, wherever ordered" and "foreswear any form of allegiance or obedience to the Japanese emperor"—he answered "depend." Courtesy National Archives.

The War Department, working closely with the WRA and other government agencies, responded to Japanese Americans' opposition to enlistment with a mixture of carrots and sticks. It used the Espionage Act, the violation of which could result in fines of up to $10,000 and imprisonment for twenty years, to stifle dissent, intimidate protesters, and arrest and jail the most determined and fearless among them. At some camps, WRA officials threatened protesters with jail time, and even imprisoned some for supposedly violating the STSA and WRA camp regulations.[52] War Department leaders like McCloy also came to believe in the importance of making concessions to Japanese Americans. "While it may be a temptation, especially in these times, to administer 'rough justice' without regard for niceties," McCloy wrote a congressman in April 1943, "I have the very definite feeling that the degree of cooperation we will receive from our Japanese population will correspond very closely to the opportunities for service which we give them." Seeming to confirm this point was the stark contrast between how Japanese Americans in and out of the camps responded to enlistment. "It is my opinion," one of McCloy's top aides, Colonel William Scobey, wrote in March 1943, "that the difference in treatment of the Japanese on the mainland and in Hawaii is largely responsible for the difference in enthusiasm."[53]

As a result, McCloy's office successfully pushed for a series of War Department reforms in the spring and summer of 1943. On April 18, with McCloy's crucial support and lobbying, Nisei soldiers were permitted for the first time since mass removal to enter and travel within the Western Defense Command, a mere week after its commander, John DeWitt, told a House subcommittee that he would oppose any such move "with every proper means at my disposal."[54] On May 3, the War Department, notwithstanding a long list of conditions, lifted its sixteen-month-long ban on civilian Nisei working at army posts and establishments, something that McCloy's office had proposed seven weeks earlier and had been pushing for ever since.[55] On July 22, after months of preparation and lobbying by McCloy and his staff, the War Department announced that "American-born women of Japanese descent" would be accepted for enlistment into the Women's Army Corps (though they would be subject to a strict quota and to a loyalty screening process similar to the one that Nisei male enlistees faced).[56]

McCloy also began contemplating reinstating the draft for Japanese Americans. In a series of memos with the War Department General Staff's personnel chief throughout March, April, and May 1943, McCloy insisted that he carefully consider "the reinstitution of general Selective Service for all persons of Japanese ancestry, the disloyal as well as the loyal," citizens as well as aliens. The War Department had entertained the idea several months earlier, after Colonel Pettigrew, WRA director Myer, the JACL, and others advocated versions of it. And President Roosevelt's February 1943 public statement in support of Japanese American voluntary enlistment declared it a "natural and logical step toward the reinstitution of the selective service procedures." McCloy and others in his office came to see this reinstitution as both a reward for an enthusiastic embrace of enlistment and a punishment for the opposite. In the camps, army teams, which were always closely controlled by McCloy's office, told internees both that "reinstatement of the draft was not yet assured and would be contingent on the success of the voluntary induction" and that those who failed or refused to volunteer "will probably be taken"—that is, conscripted—"into the military service in due time."[57]

As with enlistment, McCloy received outside support for his position. The JACL continued its months-long push for reinstituting the draft for Nisei, and some other Japanese Americans joined in the effort, from well-known sculptor Isamu Noguchi to the New York–based Japanese American Committee for Democracy, whose motto read, "Unite! Crush Japanese Militarism—For Democratic Japan!" and whose advisory board included Albert Einstein and author Pearl Buck.[58] But McCloy's most important ally on the issue may have been Senator Albert B. "Happy" Chandler of Kentucky, who was leading a Senate subcommittee investigation of the WRA camps. In April 1943, pronouncing the enlistment program, which he had previously supported, a "complete failure," Chandler began considering reinstituting the draft, though for novel reasons: it would serve to reduce the camp population, thereby saving taxpayer money, and would answer growing, if specious, complaints about the WRA's "coddling" of imprisoned Japanese Americans. A month later, in early May 1943, after visiting six camps, holding hearings, and receiving McCloy's blessing, Chandler's subcommittee formally recommended drafting "Japanese of military age who are loyal citizens of the United States." The Senate Military Affairs Committee soon endorsed the proposal.[59]

In its inclusion of "loyal citizens" alone, the proposal was more limited than what McCloy had often considered. Yet it still met strong opposition from the War Department General Staff, especially from its personnel chief, Brigadier General M. G. White, who was in charge of these issues. White did not see Japanese Americans as among the "more desirable categories of personnel." He had concerns about their loyalty, which only grew after the enlistment debacle in the camps. As a result, he eyed any plan to conscript Japanese Americans warily, since it might upend the army's "fundamental need" to control and minimize the induction of Japanese Americans. Indeed, throughout the spring and summer of 1943, not only did White and other uniformed War Department leaders successfully scuttle any effort to reinstate the draft for Nisei, but they also blocked Japanese Americans' voluntary enlistment for a brief time, once the army's few segregated Nisei units had reached full strength. By early October 1943, a backlog of eighty or so Japanese Americans appeared, those who had volunteered and been cleared for army service but who had not yet been inducted. They therefore faced a situation similar to the one that African Americans faced, though on a much smaller scale.[60]

War Department leaders, McCloy included, were also concerned about the "serious administrative difficulties" that might come from drafting Nisei. They refused to send Japanese Americans to the Pacific theater, because of the "opportunities for [enemy] infiltration" and because of the "atrocities which Japanese-American soldiers would almost certainly be subjected to if captured." This meant that if Nisei were drafted and widely dispersed around the army, they would have to be pulled from any units destined for the Pacific, which, often coming in the "last stages of training . . . might seriously affect the unit's combat efficiency."[61]

A breakthrough came in the fall, when Japanese Americans of the 100th Infantry Battalion journeyed overseas to battlefronts in North Africa and Europe. As casualties mounted, the army quickly went from having a slight surplus of Japanese American troops to having a shortage, and the segregated nature of the 100th Battalion required that all enlisted replacements be Japanese American. The draft, which would compel reluctant or resistant Japanese Americans to serve, would solve this problem. As the War Department's adjutant general admitted in a private memo months later, "The primary reason for reinstituting Selective Service for Japanese Americans is to provide replacements for certain Japanese American combat units."[62] If that was the primary reason, however, an important additional one was that the performance of the 100th Battalion—and, to a lesser extent, that of other Japanese American soldiers and linguists in the army—convinced many War Department leaders of Nisei troops' trustworthiness. In pushing for enlistment, Stimson, McCloy, and others touted the presumed fighting prowess of Japanese Americans. But other leaders were not so convinced, awaiting the hard evidence of battle reports—what one major general called the "acid test" of Nisei loyalty. White, for example, repeatedly advised McCloy that reinstituting the draft should come only after "experience with [Nisei soldiers] . . . provides a sound basis" for evaluating them. When that experience proved exceedingly impressive, McCloy wrote and called White to underline the fact—the "extraordinary performance of [the] Japanese American battalion in Italy" "should prove that Americans of Japanese descent, properly screened, are no menace to our security." He also resumed his push to "consider whether we ought not reinstitute selective service for all Americans of Japanese descent."[63]

Within weeks, the War Department began to do just this, as generals across its various divisions weighed in on the subject. Finally, in late November 1943, the War Department General Staff recommended that "Selective Service be reinstituted for citizens of Japanese descent." As with enlistment, this recommendation came with several key caveats: that drafted citizens be inducted only after a careful loyalty screening by the War Department's Military Intelligence Division; that inducted men be assigned only to segregated Japanese American units as replacements for existing ones or as soldiers for new ones; and that, in contrast to McCloy's suggestion earlier in the year, the army maintain its ban on "alien Japanese" enlistment and conscription.

In mid-December, these recommendations became War Department policy, which was announced publicly a month later, on January 20, 1944.[64] One year after the army cracked open its doors to Nisei volunteers, then, it opened them wider to include draftees. Unlike the former policy shift, the latter owed something to Japanese Americans themselves—both as resisters and as soldiers. The War Department viewed the reinstitution of the draft as a way to appease troublesome resisters, to address the troop shortage their opposition had a hand in creating, and to reward and replace brave soldiers fighting and dying overseas.

THE ARMY DOOR SWINGS OPEN

Many whites did not seem all that concerned about the army's new draft policy. A few local draft boards were "somewhat averse" to conscripting Japanese Americans, refusing to believe they could be loyal, dependable soldiers. Others on the West Coast, according to one JACL complaint, drafted them in larger numbers "as a way of opposing and protesting the return of Japanese Americans" there.[65] More generally, drafting Nisei generated less public opposition from whites than enlisting them did. Perhaps it was the well-publicized battlefield successes of Japanese American soldiers; or the fact that Nisei had already begun re-entering the army through enlistment; or their relatively small and segregated numbers; or the way the Selective Service stressed, especially in the West, that drafting Nisei men might postpone the induction of many "pre–Pearl Harbor fathers."[66] Or perhaps it was that some whites thought all along that the more Japanese Americans fighting and dying overseas the better. As one letter-writer from Hawaii put it, "I'm glad they're putting them in. It always made me feel a little sick because our nice white boys were dying in the jungles while the Japanese-Americans were kept at home. . . . Putting them on the firing line and letting them taste what their homeland started is much to my liking. Let them do a little of the dying for a change."[67]

Among Japanese Americans, the draft, like enlistment, generated fierce debate and a broad range of responses. A segment of Japanese Americans welcomed the news. In Hawaii, some remained enthusiastic about military service and viewed their renewed inclusion in the draft as a major, democratic advance for which their "boys"—not War Department officials—deserved the credit. They expressed repeatedly that it was thanks to these Japanese Americans' loyalty that they became, as one person put it, "classed as real Americans both in birth and in deeds" and, in the words of another, no longer "looked upon as freaks that could not be trusted." Others simply approved of the draft as a way to spread sacrifice more evenly among Japanese American communities and, as one letter-writer expressed, "catch all the bums who didn't volunteer."[68] In the camps, some Japanese Americans also applauded the reinstitution of the draft—and their opportunity to be conscripted. "The acceptance of the nisei through the draft," gushed *The Irrigator*, the camp newspaper at Minidoka, ". . . prove[s] that America's faith in the nisei has been fully restored, and all our labors, protestations of loyalty to this country, our faith have not been in vain." Perhaps accepting this sentiment, one young man from Poston, desperate to be drafted despite being underweight, convinced the doctors to accept him on his fourth try.[69]

More Japanese Americans, perhaps most, accepted the reinstitution of Selective Service with some level of dissatisfaction, disgruntlement, or anger. In its safest version, they applauded or expressed gratitude for the new draft policy, but they also requested further reforms. In a statement sent to Secretary Stimson, the US Citizens Committee at Topaz called the reinstitution a "first great step," but recommended others, namely integrating Japanese American soldiers throughout the army and allowing them to serve in all branches of the military. Similarly, the "American Citizens of Japanese Ancestry at Heart Mountain Relocation Center" sent President Roosevelt, Stimson, Attorney General Biddle, and perhaps others a petition both hailing the reinstitution of the draft as a "big step toward the application of American principles in the treatment of minority groups" and asking for "careful consideration" of seven points, including the Topaz committee's two recommendations, but also others, such as the "full restoration of our civil and inalienable rights" and "protection of families in relocation centers." Other Japanese Americans questioned the wisdom of the draft or passed no judgment, but nonetheless used its reinstatement as an opportunity to press the government for equal treatment. As the Amache Community Council wrote Stimson, "We believe . . . that the rights and privileges of citizenship should, in all justice, be combined with the duties and obligations of citizenship."[70]

Whether their responses reflected a happy embrace of the draft, incensed resignation over it, or something in between, the great majority of

Fig. 2.4 Tom Oki, an "internee" and block manager at the Heart Mountain Relocation Center, explains new draft procedures for Japanese Americans to fellow block managers, March 1944. Courtesy of The Bancroft Library, University of California, Berkeley, WRA no. I-132.

Nisei men, in and out of camps, complied with the Selective Service. From February 1944 through the end of the war, the army inducted more than eleven thousand Nisei. While it is not clear how many of these men were draftees and how many were voluntary enlistees, all of them accepted military service.[71]

But not everyone did. A significant segment of Japanese Americans resisted the draft in overt and covert ways, often choosing many of the same strategies that African Americans (among others) employed. They had various motivations, including wanting to stay with and provide for family members; to avoid death in battle, something that was appearing more and more likely as Nisei casualty lists ominously lengthened; and in many cases, to take a principled stand against a military and a government that persecuted them. On the covert side, both in Hawaii and on the mainland, Japanese American young men scrambled to find essential war work—on docks, plantations, and farms—and, with it, a draft deferral; some took "heavy doses of *shoyu* (soy sauce)" or feigned mental illness to fail pre-induction physical and psychiatric exams; some tried to stay one step ahead of draft boards by "moving from one place to another when they received or were about to receive orders to report" for induction.[72]

More openly, some claimed prisoner-of-war status or attempted to renounce their citizenship and apply for expatriation to Japan in the hope that either would exempt them from conscription (in practice, neither did).[73] Across the camps, the War Department noticed, once the draft was reinstituted, a "marked increase in requests for expatriation." At Poston, an admittedly extreme case, more than five hundred Nisei filed for expatriation in the two months after the draft's reinstitution, dwarfing the total number from the previous twenty months combined. Certainly some of these men had genuinely given up on the United States and cast their future lot with Japan; others simply hoped to avoid conscription. "In many of these cases," McCloy wrote, "expatriation has been requested by individuals unable to speak Japanese and who have no relatives, property, or other apparent interests in [Japan]."[74]

Some Japanese Americans—more than three hundred in all—went further still, openly defying draft requirements, such as signing requisite forms or reporting either for their pre-induction physical exam or for induction itself.[75] Many of these men, much like black draft resisters Winfred Lynn, Ernest Calloway, and Lewis Jones, explained that they would willingly serve and fulfill the obligations of citizenship but only if they were first granted its attendant rights and privileges. While present at all camps, draft resistance along these principled lines developed most dramatically at Poston and Heart Mountain, which accounted for roughly two-thirds of all draft resisters who were criminally prosecuted. At Poston, a group of Nisei, led initially by a twenty-eight-year-old "camp mortician" and former University of Southern California student named George Fujii, decided in early February that they would openly oppose the draft and accept the consequences. "We, the Niseis, are willing to serve and bear arms at any time," they wrote in a letter to the secretary of state and in a mimeographed notice they posted around the camp. They concluded, however, that "until such time as all the wrong has been righted and adequate compensation made, we, the Niseis, should not be compelled to bear arms." In a later notice, they called on all "Niseis of draftable age" to "back our fight for constitutional rights" by refusing to report for pre-induction physicals until "we have reached our goal. (Fighting for our rights)."[76] At Heart Mountain around the same time, another group of Nisei calling itself the Fair Play Committee began holding regular and sometimes raucous protest meetings at the camp's mess halls. Soon the group settled on a clear position regarding the draft. In a March 4 mimeographed circular, it declared, "[U]ntil we are restored all our rights, all discriminatory features of the Selective Service abolished, and measures retaken to remedy the past injustices . . . we feel that the present program of drafting us from this concentration camp is unjust, unconstitutional, and against all principles of civilized usage." It therefore concluded, "We, members of the Fair Play Committee *hereby refuse to go to the physical examination or to the induction* if or when we are called in order to *contest the issue*."[77]

The federal government moved swiftly to stamp out resistance. It threatened draft protesters with criminal prosecution, tore down their circulars, forbade them to meet, worked closely and surreptitiously with the JACL to spy on camp communities, and made clear that those who requested expatriation would be drafted anyway. Later it considered whether such requests could amount to a voluntary renunciation of citizenship in the hope that it would discourage men from claiming loyalty to Japan in order simply to avoid the draft. And it attempted to guilt Japanese Americans into thinking that they had to accept the draft as an "obligation to their country" and that "the loyalty and sincerity of all American citizens of Japanese descent" would be judged on the basis of their "performance." When all efforts failed to snuff out resistance, agents of the US Marshals Service and the FBI swooped into the camps and arrested resisters and their leaders—real and alleged. Several hundred were eventually convicted of draft evasion—or of counseling, aiding, and abetting others to evade the draft—and sent to federal prison for up to five years.[78]

Eventually, the War Department, as with enlistment, responded to Japanese American protest by, among other things, significantly expanding Nisei access to army enlistment. In September 1944, for the first time since January 1942, it allowed loyal Japanese aliens to volunteer for the army. In January 1945, it lifted its mass exclusion of Japanese Americans from the Western Defense Command and elsewhere, following the Supreme Court decision in *Endo*, which raised serious questions about the government's right to detain loyal citizens. And in April 1945, it opened the army nurse corps to Nisei women. But most important, in the spring of 1944, it created many more openings for Nisei inductees by forming another Japanese American unit—the 1399th Engineer Construction Battalion—and by assigning more and more of them to nonblack, integrated outfits. The result was that, starting around May 1944, the number of Japanese Americans inducted into the army soared. Between July 1943 and April 1944, the army inducted an average of just over one hundred Japanese Americans a month. From May 1944 until the end of the war, that monthly average increased eightfold. More than half of all Japanese Americans who served during World War II joined up in this period.[79]

As the war began winding down first in Europe and then in the Pacific, and as the Supreme Court began questioning the government's treatment of US citizens of Japanese descent, some officials, echoing and responding to Japanese American protesters, pushed for further reforms. Most important, at Selective Service, its legal division insisted in a February 1945 internal memorandum that the loyalty screening for Japanese Americans was "inviting righteous criticism" and that it should be discontinued, along with all other "Regulations, Memoranda, and Selective Service forms now discriminating against Japanese Americans because of their ancestry." Convinced by these arguments, Director Hershey wrote Secretary of War Stimson on March 8, 1945. He proposed eliminating the loyalty statement entirely and "proceed[ing] with the induction of United States citizens of Japanese ancestry in exactly the same manner as other United States citizens."[80]

Significantly, the War Department refused, still believing that Japanese Americans represented a singular threat demanding "special" security measures. In an internal memo dated April 9, 1945, the Judge Advocate General wrote, "It cannot be denied that there are disloyal citizens of Japanese ancestry. If routine induction procedures were applied to them, they might find their way into our Army and thus have unlimited opportunities to commit sabotage, espionage and other acts of treachery. It is altogether proper that reasonable steps be taken to separate the loyal from the disloyal to the end that the men of our Army may be guarded against a traitor in their midst." The memorandum never explained why "routine induction procedures" seemed to root out all "traitors" except those of Japanese descent, but Stimson was convinced. He enclosed the opinion in his response to Hershey two weeks later, defending a draft policy that allowed the War Department to select "only those who are believed to be unaffected by attachments to Japan." "That this preinduction screening procedure has effected the selection of thoroughly loyal and excellent American soldiers of Japanese ancestry," he added, "is amply demonstrated by their record in the 442nd Infantry Regiment and the 100th Infantry Battalion, whose fame on the battlefields of Italy and France reflects credit not only to themselves but also to all loyal Japanese-American citizens in the United States."[81] To Stimson, then, Nisei soldiers' overseas exploits somehow confirmed rather than challenged the army's racist policies against them.

Not until well after the war with Japan ended did the US Armed Forces at long last begin dismantling some of its most exclusionary and discriminatory measures regarding Japanese American enlistment. In November 1945, the navy lifted its decades-old ban on Japanese American service, though it later clarified that its policy shift did not apply to the marine corps. A month later the War Department finally eliminated its loyalty screening of Nisei, declaring it "no longer necessary." A little more than a month later, Selective Service issued a directive to its local boards: all future Japanese American inductees would be "processed . . . in the same manner as any other United States citizen."[82] Again, this meant nonblack citizens.

* * *

In the end, as with African Americans, restrictive and exclusionary policies aimed at Japanese Americans led to their underrepresentation in America's World War II armed forces. Roughly 1 in 460 Americans, they constituted less than 1 in 600 of those who served in the war.[83] Put another way, had Japanese Americans served at a rate that was proportional to their share of the US population, the military could have counted on an additional 12,000 or so troops. While miniscule in comparison with the half million additional black people who might have otherwise served or to the sixteen million Americans who did, this number is not insignificant, especially when considering that in total war every soldier can make a difference.

Even more so than with African Americans, the navy bears greatest responsibility for the military's underutilization of Japanese Americans, though the army certainly built its share of barriers. With few exceptions, the navy, including its marine corps, refused to accept any Japanese Americans throughout the war. In contrast, the army inducted more than 23,000 from July 1940 through August 1945. Despite months of exclusion and years of restriction, Japanese Americans' share of total wartime army inductees—0.23 percent—more or less matched their share of the US population—0.22 percent.[84] If Japanese Americans were significantly underrepresented among inductees in 1942 and 1943, they were overrepresented in 1944 and 1945, which was, in part, a function of the navy's ban. Once Selective Service began accepting Nisei again, they, unlike other draftees (even African Americans, by this point), could not be distributed across the armed forces and were all channeled instead into the army.

Occasionally, a local draft board or, early in the war, an induction station attempted to keep Japanese Americans out of the army. But as with black people, by far the most consequential barriers of entry came from top military leaders and not from local officials exploiting their discretionary powers. The navy and marine corps bans perfectly reflected the views of Navy Secretary Frank Knox, who defended them until his dying day, in the spring of 1944. Neither his successor, James Forrestal, nor President Roosevelt ever appears to have wanted to shift course. As for the army, its ever-changing policies of exclusion and restriction stemmed from the

War Department's military and civilian leaders, who at times agreed and at other times fiercely disagreed about the desirability of Nisei enlistment.

Perhaps surprisingly, these military leaders often considered Japanese American and African American enlistment issues in isolation from each other and not as linked or similar in any way, despite the fact that some of these leaders, especially McCloy, were deeply involved in crafting policy for both groups. Numerous American officials, military ones among them, grew deeply concerned during the war about "Japanese-inspired agitation among the American Negroes" and the possibility, dire in their view, that the two groups might unite as fellow "darker races."[85] Indeed, once Nisei and black soldiers began crossing paths in southern training camps and on Italian battlefields, War Department leaders and army commanders endeavored at times to keep the two groups apart. There is evidence that at least one top War Department official considered these fears when recommending the continued exclusion of Japanese Americans from the army. But it is doubtful that these fears played any significant role in shaping enlistment policies. War Department leaders passionately debated Japanese American enlistment questions, and only very rarely did concerns about Japanese American–African American relations come up. Furthermore, had these concerns been especially salient, it is hard to explain why so many Japanese American soldiers were sent to train and serve among so many African Americans on southern army posts, even when one recognizes that the great majority of these posts were located below the Mason-Dixon line.[86]

Apart from how leaders approached these matters, the timing and mechanics of Japanese Americans' restrictions and exclusions both aligned with and diverged from those of African Americans. While both groups faced blanket bans, limited space in strictly segregated units, and draft backlogs, Japanese Americans served in some integrated outfits and were much more likely to face loyalty screenings and less likely to be disproportionately rejected at induction stations.[87] As for timing, both groups were barred from large swaths of the military prior to the institution of Selective Service in the fall of 1940; and both groups, after this point, streamed into the army for a time. But America's entry into the war affected the two groups very differently. For African Americans, the demand for troops and their ever-expanding activism eliminated nearly all remaining bans on their service and increased their induction numbers, first in the army and later beyond. For Japanese Americans, whose ancestral home was now at war with the United States, the opposite occurred: they soon found themselves expelled in large numbers from the army and barred from joining all parts of the US military. They regained access to the army, and only the army, in fits and starts over time. Toward war's end, however, while African

Americans continued to face manifold army restrictions, those targeting Japanese Americans began falling away. Despite loyalty screenings, which outlasted the war, the army began inducting large numbers of Japanese Americans beginning in the spring of 1944. At this time, black people's rejection rates at induction stations remained high, and their chronically low draft calls still created backlogs for many thousands of their draftees.

One critical reason for these convoluted variations in timing and mechanics is that while anti-Nisei and anti-black racist schemas helped explain, justify, and give rise to military barriers against both groups, these schemas fundamentally differed from each other. Military and other leaders viewed both African Americans and Japanese Americans as dire threats to the optimal functioning of the armed forces and, as such, to the life and future of the nation. But each group putatively posed a distinct threat. Put simply, African Americans were suspected of incompetence, Japanese Americans of disloyalty. The distinction should not be overdrawn: white leaders also questioned black people's allegiance to the nation, for example.[88] Still, when deciding who should be in and out of the military, these separate, group-specific schemas were unquestionably the most dominant and enduring throughout the war.

The disloyalty schema, which military leaders cited each and every time they restricted or barred Japanese American enlistment, had a soft and hard version. The latter held that, since not a single Japanese American could ever be trusted, Nisei had to be either barred completely from military service or screened and surveilled, and assigned the most harmless tasks on the most out-of-the-way posts. These "Jap's-a-Jap" views dominated the navy throughout the war and the army for some time following the attack on Pearl Harbor. But a softer version emerged and, at least in the War Department, came to dominate by the fall of 1942. It also argued that Japanese Americans represented a singularly disloyal group but that some members, perhaps even most, were loyal and dependable. It therefore supported allowing Japanese Americans to enlist and be drafted and to be placed in a range of different outfits, combat and noncombat, segregated and integrated—so long as they were subjected to a uniquely sweeping loyalty screening process.

Two men perfectly embodied these hard and soft schemas: John DeWitt and John J. McCloy, respectively. McCloy thought Japanese American "sheep" and "goats" could and should be separated; DeWitt, the commander of the Western Defense Command, saw nothing but "goats." But, again, drawing lines too distinctly would be a mistake. McCloy, for example, emerged as Japanese Americans' most indefatigable defender in the War Department only after he served as one of the key architects of Japanese

American mass removal and mass detention. Moreover, during the war, he occasionally referred in private to Japanese Americans as "Japs"—a slur that effectively erased any distinction between people of Japanese descent in the United States and those in Japan, a hallmark of the hard schema.[89]

Because these anti–Japanese American racist schemas revolved almost exclusively around questions of loyalty, the specifics of the war—whom the United States was fighting, how its prospects for victory looked, and so forth—deeply shaped Japanese Americans' enlistment opportunities in a way that was not the case for African Americans. It was the attack on Pearl Harbor and the ensuing US war with Japan that led the army to close its doors to Japanese Americans; it was not until the United States scored some major victories in the Pacific and until after the war there turned decisively in its favor that the army reopened those doors; and it was not until that war ended that the army dropped its remaining restrictions on Japanese Americans and the navy finally lifted its ban. Indeed, it seems highly likely that had the United States and Japan not been fierce adversaries in a "war without mercy," Japanese Americans would have gained far greater access to the World War II military. In contrast, African Americans' access was much less contingent on the war's specific developments. While the opening of the air corps and marine corps owed something to the war in a general sense—the greater need for troops, for example—the commitment to control and limit African Americans' entry into the military long predated the war and operated for the most part independent of its twists and turns.

Japanese Americans, like African Americans, staked out a similarly varied set of positions on enlistment restrictions and exclusions. Some Nisei, not unlike John Hope Franklin, viewed these policies as yet one more sign of shameful and entrenched state racism, and committed themselves to avoiding military service in myriad ways and at all costs; several thousand—much like the members of, say, the Peace Movement of Ethiopia—even went as far as rejecting the United States entirely and disavowing their US citizenship. Others, like James G. Thompson, author of the "Double V" slogan, believed that fulfilling citizenship's most solemn obligation would unlock its most prized rights and privileges. Still others, like the Heart Mountain draft resisters, made the former conditional on the latter: like Winfred Lynn, they promised to serve, but only after their full rights were granted.

Despite these similarities, Japanese Americans could not flex the same formal political muscle that African Americans could, and so they sometimes employed different protest tactics. Boasting a growing number of swing voters, deepening connections to urban North politicians, and an extensive network of black newspapers and civil rights organizations, those African Americans who sought greater enlistment opportunities tended to work through traditional institutional channels, testifying before Congress, meeting with the president, corresponding with political and military officials, writing editorials, circulating petitions, and bringing suits in court. Japanese Americans did many of these same things, including, perhaps most consequentially, the JACL's cultivation of a relationship with McCloy, which likely played some role in shifting his views on Nisei enlistment. But Japanese Americans, with none of the electoral power that northern African Americans enjoyed (thanks both to Japanese Americans' smaller numbers and to racist naturalization laws that prevented the immigrants among them from becoming voting citizens), also worked outside the formal political system, most notably in their mass resistance both to voluntary enlistment and to involuntary conscription.

Although fighting similar enlistment battles and at times employing similar tactics, Japanese Americans and African Americans seldom joined forces on the issue. To be sure, some of black people's biggest victories on the enlistment front—the STSA's antidiscrimination clause, for example— applied equally to all groups, including Japanese Americans, whose rapidly rising induction rates after its passage make clear. So groups' individual struggles need not have intersected in order for those struggles to have affected and benefited one another. Still, given the seeming similarity between struggles, given the amount of talk, not simply from anxious elites, but also from some "darker races" themselves about their dawning solidarity, and given the occasional instance of wartime cooperation between Japanese Americans and African Americans in and out of the military, it is worth asking why these groups' enlistment-related struggles did not overlap more.

One reason was that many members of each group seemed unaware of the others' related struggles. Some Japanese Americans, and especially the JACL, asked for the "same privilege of serving our country in the armed forces as that granted to every other American citizen," missing the fact that a large group of citizens also lacked these privileges. Or African Americans sometimes spoke as if only they encountered enlistment barriers, missing the fact that Japanese Americans for long stretches of the war also faced significant, sometimes greater, obstacles.[90]

Another reason was that some members of both groups opposed associating with the other, either because they harbored genuine feelings of, say, indifference, mistrust, disrespect, or hostility, or for the supposedly pragmatic reason that one pariah group could not afford to consort with another. In the case of Japanese Americans, the desire to disassociate from blackness came occasionally from the desire to associate with whiteness. In one letter to Secretary Stimson, for example, a young Nisei, recently resettled in Chicago, called for an end to all-Japanese American fighting units and to all bans on Japanese American enlistment in the air corps, navy, and marines so that Nisei could "mingle and train in the same camps with their caucasian buddies."[91] In an institution like the wartime US military, which lavished so many rights and resources on those who could lay claim to whiteness, this sort of politics held considerable seductive appeal.

But perhaps the most important reason was that just as African Americans' and Japanese Americans' enlistment problems diverged some, so too did their struggles to solve them. For starters, the timing differed for each group. African Americans' most formidable enlistment challenges, and their most determined activism against them, took place early in the war—indeed, well before America's entry—when their overall representation in the military was minuscule. Japanese Americans' efforts to open military doors took place later, especially in 1943 and 1944, after they had been completely excluded for some time and after the War Department began to enlist and conscript Nisei from the camps. So many of Japanese Americans' struggles involved the unique particularities of their experience, namely the prospect of having to fight for a country—in the name of democracy, no less—that had recently uprooted them from their homes and forced them into detention camps. The uniqueness of each group's situation militated some against their struggles intersecting. Finally, the uniqueness of each group's specific form of enlistment restriction or exclusion had a similar effect. While black people battled chronically low "Negro-only" draft calls, Nisei fought Japanese American–only loyalty statements and screenings.[92]

Even when struggles and proposed remedies seemed to offer the potential to overlap, they did not. It appears, for example, that Japanese American protesters made little use of the STSA's antidiscrimination clause, which provided that "in the selection and training of men under this Act, and in the interpretation and execution of the provisions of this Act, there shall be no discrimination against any person on account of race or color." This missed opportunity is surprising, given all the discrimination that Japanese Americans faced in their "selection" for service, discrimination that War Department officials, at least in private, readily conceded, and given that the clause was widely discussed during the war. If Japanese Americans had tried to exploit this provision in the law, the courts, as in Winfred Lynn's case, would have likely found creative ways around enforcing it. Indeed, a series of landmark Supreme Court cases on Japanese Americans' wartime treatment, especially *Korematsu v. United*

States and *Hirabayashi v. United States*, held that "discrimination, even against a group of American citizens, may be justified . . . when, under the war power, such measures are taken for the protection of the nation."[93] Nonetheless, for Japanese Americans protesting enlistment issues, the STSA's antidiscrimination clause was a statutory resource too potentially valuable to ignore. That Japanese Americans, it seems, did so underlines the separateness of their and African Americans' enlistment battles.

Despite this separateness, Japanese Americans, like African Americans, managed to play some role in shaping and reshaping military policy. Their widespread protest, coupled with their celebrated military service, broadened their army enlistment opportunities, most evident in their soaring army induction numbers beginning in the spring of 1944. In these efforts, they received help from a broader war context, in which military officials deemed it advantageous to counter Japanese race war propaganda by expanding Japanese Americans' ability to serve in the US Army. This point suggests a final difference between Nisei and African American enlistment struggles: throughout the war, black people tried—and sometimes succeeded at—exploiting this same wartime context, in part thanks to the fact that Japanese propagandists railed every bit as much against anti–African American as anti–Japanese American discrimination. Black activists often responded by arguing that only greater democracy at home would counter this propaganda and convince "colored allies" abroad of America's genuine commitment to the Four Freedoms. But these arguments seemed to have much less effect on black people's enlistment battles than on Japanese Americans', in part because exclusions against African American service collapsed either before the United States entered the war or shortly thereafter. Regardless of the reason, military officials decided that enlistment restrictions against Nisei troops hurt the war effort enough to do something about them—but that those against black troops did not.

PART II

Assignment

CHAPTER 3

☙

The Backbone of Segregation

African Americans encountered manifold enlistment barriers during World War II in part because of the military's deep and long-standing commitment to their segregation. The military believed that, without carefully controlling black people's induction numbers, it would be forced to do the unthinkable: integrate. But what precisely would integration have meant? What precisely did segregation mean? Who was segregated from whom exactly? When was this decided? And for what reasons? The answers to these questions turn out to be more complicated than they might seem.

Take black segregation, by far the best-documented and most widely discussed case. It was so extensive during the war that commentators at the time and since have spoken not of one military but of two: black and white. But this is misleading. The black military included thousands of white officers, and the white military integrated a diverse mix of groups that were typically seen—and that the military itself often officially classified— as not white, including American Indians, Chinese, some Filipinos, some Puerto Ricans, and even some Japanese Americans. The word "some" is significant here since nonblacks' access to so-called white outfits could vary a great deal from group to group and from time to time. This chapter and the next will investigate the complexities of this topic—"race" and individuals' assignments to military outfits—an important one because "this business of separation by unit," as two commentators put it in the immediate postwar years, was the "backbone of segregation."[1]

As America began to prepare for war in the late 1930s, the military required black troops to serve solely in "Negro" or "colored" units, in which all enlisted personnel were black and all their seniormost officers were white.

Military policy for some time, it was not particularly controversial among many African Americans, let alone anyone else. Instead, black people's main military concern, if they had any, centered on gaining equal opportunities to join and advance within its ranks. But over time growing numbers of African Americans, along with an increasingly vocal minority of whites and others, came to reject segregated military outfits out of hand and to support their abolition. This campaign became a core element of black people's wartime civil rights struggles, as they and their allies employed a broad range of tactics to dismantle military segregation, from drafting petitions to resisting the draft, from lobbying Congress and the president to building new national organizations devoted entirely to the issue.

Even so, if African Americans' enlistment struggles succeeded in opening military doors to hundreds of thousands of black troops, their efforts to abolish military segregation by war's end fell far short of this intended goal. The forces favoring the segregated status quo—Congress and the White House, military brass and military tradition, federal law and white public opinion—proved too formidable. Yet African Americans' and their allies' desegregation struggle had some enormously important longer-term effects. It convinced a growing number of both ordinary people and leaders to warm to a heretofore unthinkable idea: a mixed black-white military. Without this key change, the postwar desegregation of the armed forces would have been inconceivable.

AN EMERGING INTEGRATIONISM

In the summer of 1941, twenty-three-year-old Roger Samuel Starr made news. Living with his parents in their posh Park Avenue apartment, having graduated from Yale a few years earlier, he had become increasingly outraged by the discrimination that black people faced in America's developing defense program and had decided to do something about it. He submitted his Selective Service questionnaire to the local draft board and attached the following note.

> As a white, the Army wants to place me in a unit with white troops. Perhaps you can help me achieve something I should prefer. I should prefer to be placed with Negro troops, for then they would become mixed troops: American troops. Certainly there are others beside myself in this city who went to school with Negro boys, who learned beside them this history of our country and the theory of its government, and who want to be allowed to contribute their services to their country under conditions that do not hold that theory to ridicule.[2]

Having worked in publicity, Starr knew to also send his note to the editors of *PM*, the left-wing afternoon tabloid from which he had learned most about discrimination and segregation in America's armed forces. *PM*, in turn, published a glowing portrait of Starr, and the black press quickly followed suit.[3] Within days, fan mail poured in. Black writer Carlton Moss, who would soon write and narrate the well-known army documentary, *The Negro Soldier*, thanked Starr and assured him that "hundreds of other Negroes and progressive whites deeply appreciate and applaud your democratic stand." A married couple in Washington, DC, told Starr they admired his "spirit and imagination. Your letter to the draft board will have liberals all over the country saying to themselves, 'Why didn't I think of that?'" And one young white woman from Brooklyn reported that "all the boys"—with whom her brother served at Camp Upton on Long Island—"read or have heard of your statement" and "were pleased to hear such views expressed."[4]

NAACP leaders made the most of Starr's protest, since it captured one of their central arguments against Jim Crow: contrary to segregationists' claims, many whites opposed it. In fact, they had met with Starr six weeks or so before he drafted his letter, perhaps suggesting the idea in the first place. In late May, Starr had written Walter White, the NAACP's executive secretary, volunteering his services. "I haven't much money," he told White, "... but I do have a certain amount of time. I hope there will be some way in which your organization might find me useful. I can think of no work from which I would expect to find a greater personal satisfaction." After his letter appeared in the news, White shared Starr's story with the War Department and with Eleanor Roosevelt, insisting that "there are a good many others who share Mr. Starr's opinion."[5]

In the end, neither the commander in chief nor the War Department allowed Starr to join "Negro troops" or "mixed troops" or "American troops." The army drafted him in June 1943 as a private, and he served in a segregated "white" outfit in China with the Office of Strategic Services. He later recalled that his *PM* protest trailed him throughout his time in the army, barring him from admission into Officer Candidate School.[6]

The army refused Starr's request for one simple reason: it explicitly forbade the "intermingl[ing] [of] colored and white enlisted personnel" in the same outfits. Some version of this Jim Crow rule, while long unwritten, had been in effect for many decades. In two laws passed shortly after the Civil War, Congress required the army to create and maintain several black regiments. Black historian and civil rights activist L. D. Reddick wrote in the late 1940s that the decision "was not [at the time] looked upon so much as segregation; rather as a friendly and progressive move, as a recognition and reward for valor, so that henceforth and forever black soldiers would have a place in the American Army." Yet that place would be strictly segregated for many decades to come, as War Department and other government leaders interpreted these laws to mean that black soldiers could serve solely in these regiments—or in other similarly segregated ones. As a result, from the mid-1860s until Starr's protest and beyond, the only whites serving in otherwise all-black units were commissioned officers, the leaders of those units. Meanwhile all African Americans, with few exceptions, served in a limited number of segregated outfits in the Regular Army, the Organized Reserves, and the National Guard. During all their mobilization planning in the 1920s and 1930s, the War Department never considered departing from this tradition.[7]

The navy's policies were, for a time, more egalitarian than those of the army, but also more capricious. For most of the nineteenth century, substantial numbers of black men served alongside whites and others in an integrated navy. But by the turn of the twentieth century, as Jim Crow traversed the country, the navy began, wherever possible, to separate black people from everyone else in berthing, messing, and stationing. Beginning in the early 1930s, the navy restricted African Americans to a single branch—the Messman Branch—where they conducted only the most menial tasks as stewards, cooks, and mess attendants, wholly apart from white enlisted men (but not from the white officers whose shoes they shined, laundry they washed, and meals they cooked; or from some Asians, who were also restricted for a time to the Messman Branch). Taken together, as another world war loomed, the US Armed Forces strictly confined all black troops to a handful of outfits in the army and a single branch in the navy.[8]

In the late 1930s, few African Americans, or anyone else for that matter, forcefully opposed these policies. Instead, black people tended at the time to push for greater representation, not integration, in the US military. This approach was best represented by the *Pittsburgh Courier* and the organization it formed, the Committee on Participation of Negroes in the National Defense Program (CPNNDP). They argued that military leaders would never accept mixed units and so equal representation constituted the more realistic goal. This meant black troops' inclusion in all branches of the armed services, even those, like the army air corps and the marines, that had steadfastly barred them; but it also meant a grudging acceptance of—even a demand for more—segregated outfits within all branches. Beginning in 1938, for example, the *Pittsburgh Courier* repeatedly called for the formation of an all-black army infantry division and an all-black air corps squadron. In fact, it succeeded that year in convincing New York congressman Hamilton Fish, a white former commander of black troops during World War I, to introduce a bill in the House to create such a division.[9]

African Americans' support for these units seldom stemmed from any sympathy for segregation. It came instead from a pride in storied black outfits of the past, such as the "Harlem Rattlers" of World War I (the army's 369th Infantry Regiment). It also came from the desire to greatly expand the black officer corps—numbering in the single digits at the time—and to provide jobs and valuable technical training for thousands of young men struggling mightily during the Great Depression. As Rayford Logan, Howard University history professor, World War I veteran, and chair of the CPNNDP, put it in 1939, "I definitely advocate at least one colored division commanded from top to bottom by colored officers. . . . There is simply not going to be any mixing of colored and white troops in the American army. . . . We have merely the choice between colored troops commanded by colored officers or colored troops commanded by white officers. If the latter be integration, I'll take the segregation as much as I detest it."[10]

Even the NAACP's national leadership seemed at first to accept this approach, at least implicitly, despite its typically uncompromising opposition to segregation and avid support for Roger Starr. In 1935 and 1936, it called not for the dissolution of the army's all-black units but for their improved

Fig. 3.1 Rayford Logan, October 1948. Courtesy of Scurlock Studio Records, Archives Center, National Museum of American History, Smithsonian Institution.

status and treatment. In 1938, albeit through a poorly worded memo, it appeared to urge its branches, youth councils, and college chapters to support Fish's bill to create an all-black infantry division. In 1939, Walter White pressed President Roosevelt to increase African Americans' access to, not integration in, the armed forces. And in 1940, the NAACP worked every bit as hard as the *Courier* and the CPNNDP to add a nondiscrimination clause to the Selective Training and Service Act (STSA), a clause its leaders understood full well would not integrate a single military unit.[11]

Still, support for mixed outfits developed quietly all the while. Within the NAACP, some individual leaders and chapters chafed at the organization's support, tacit or otherwise, for military segregation. In 1936, the Chicago chapter chastised the national office for "condoning rather than condemning the policy of JIM CROW military units in the U.S. Army." It insisted, instead, on the "whole hog" approach of disbanding all such units. Two years later, "from all sides in the field, queries and criticism" greeted the NAACP's apparent endorsement of an all-black division. Thanks to this internal resistance, the national office in the spring of 1938, after some debate, eventually declared its opposition to this division. While wishing to avoid the appearance of "'cold-watering' the [*Pittsburgh*] *Courier*'s crusade," it decided that its "cornerstone philosophy" of integration permitted nothing less.[12]

Refusing to join the campaign for more black army units, NAACP leaders initially debated whether to insist on mixed ones instead. In one memo from October 1939 to the organization's national leadership, Walter White admitted "non-segregated units" were a "somewhat dangerous" subject. He asked, then, for advice on formulating a "realistic approach . . . in light of the Association's principles." White suggested proposing mixed outfits from states without a "fixed" Jim Crow policy. White's deputy Roy Wilkins, who had for some time appeared open to segregated units, considered White's proposal "useless," given the military's intransigence on the matter and its nationwide enlistment policies. Wilkins, echoing Rayford Logan and others, recommended fighting to ensure that black units received their fair share of black officers and combat assignments. Thurgood Marshall, the NAACP's assistant special counsel at the time, disagreed. He called for a categorical opposition to all "separate units existing in the armed forces at the present time, and to be set up [in the future]."[13]

In short order, Marshall's view, much closer to White's than to Wilkins's, won out. Beginning in the summer of 1940, the organization increasingly embraced and broadcast its opposition to Jim Crow outfits. At its annual conference in late June, William Hastie, a former federal judge, dean of Howard University Law School, and member of the NAACP's board of directors, first broached the subject. "There has been a lot of talk about whether we want black units in our existing military organization and in the new combat services," he declared. "I don't think we should be cowardly. . . . If we are good enough to fight and die for our country, it seems to me that we are good enough to fight and die side by side with anyone,—not in front, not behind, but side by side." The following day, perhaps inspired by Hastie's words, four hundred delegates and two thousand members passed a resolution insisting that "Negroes on the basis of their ability be integrated into every branch of the armed services without discrimination or segregation." Ten weeks later, the NAACP's board of directors voted to "contend for no segregation in the army and for the establishment of mixed units." In the interim, NAACP leaders made similar points in letters to members of Congress and military leaders. In correspondence with the newly appointed secretary of war, Henry Stimson, for example, Walter White rejected the secretary's assumption that black people endorsed the "well-established policy" of never mixing "the races" within army units. African Americans "opposed such segregation," White insisted, "not only as a matter of principle, but also because such segregation works definite hardships upon those segregated in addition to being a negation of every principle of Democracy which the Army of the United States and other branches of the armed forces, as well as the nation at large, are girding themselves to defend."[14]

In this early, modest effort to mix military units, the NAACP was not entirely alone. In 1939, a conference sponsored by a New Deal agency, the National Youth Administration, urged President Roosevelt to find a way to enlist African Americans "into all the armed forces without segregation." A year later, the Baltimore Afro-American proposed an idea similar to Walter White's, namely forming mixed military units for those mustered outside the South: "It is a little strange for men who have lived side by side on the same street all their lives, studied in the same school room, romped in the same playground, worked side by side at the same factory, suddenly to discover they must be separated as to color when the time comes to join our armed forces to protect their common heritage." Most important, around the same time, A. Philip Randolph, the prominent black labor leader, T. Arnold Hill, a former Urban League secretary, and Walter White recommended mixed military units at a brief White House meeting with President Roosevelt, Navy Secretary Frank Knox, and Assistant Secretary of War Robert Patterson. In a prepared memorandum, the black leaders outlined seven "important phases of the integration of the Negro into [the] military." The third read, "Existing units of the army and units to be established should be required to accept and select officers and enlisted personnel without regard to race." In the meeting itself, Randolph and White both stressed this point. A military "fighting allegedly for democracy," White insisted, "should be the last place in which to practice undemocratic segregation."[15]

The effort to mix military units, still quite limited at this point, grew considerably in the aftermath of this meeting. On October 9, after receiving President Roosevelt's approval, the White House announced the "War Department policy in regard to negroes." It covered a range of crucial issues, but the final point addressed troop segregation squarely: "The policy of the War Department is not to intermingle colored and white enlisted personnel in the same regimental organizations." While this had been army policy for decades, the statement "had the effect of pouring salt on old wounds," since, as one black newspaper later put it, the announcement "put on record officially for the first time in all our history . . . a statement setting segregation and discrimination as the policy for the United States Army." Making matters worse, the president's secretary, Stephen Early, in presenting the statement to the press, implied that White, Randolph, and Hill had signed off on the policy. When the leaders instantly struck back—denouncing Early's "phraseology," repudiating segregation, and condemning the president's policy as a "stab in the back of Democracy"— their statements made front-page headlines throughout the black press. That both this story and the War Department policy announcement broke amid the final month of an increasingly competitive presidential election campaign only further inflamed matters.[16]

These mid-October 1940 developments, taken together, quickly provided unprecedented urgency and attention to the issue of military-unit segregation and to the goal of abolishing it. The NAACP continued to lead the way. With Election Day approaching, it staged a dozen or so mass meetings at the end of the month, especially in areas where "the Negro vote is a potential factor." Everywhere, from Richmond to Kansas City, Chicago to Boston, the overriding goal was to "protest against the segregation in the Armed Forces." Meanwhile, the national office, for the first time, urged its six hundred branches, youth councils, and college chapters to "write President Roosevelt opposing segregation in the army, especially an army that is supposed to be fighting for democracy"; it appears that many local offices followed through. At the end of the month, when President Roosevelt, in response to this growing political pressure, offered NAACP leader William Hastie a civilian position to advise Secretary of War Henry Stimson on race matters, Hastie agreed. But he issued this public caveat: "I have always been consistently opposed to any policy of discrimination or segregation in the armed forces of this country. I am assuming

Fig. 3.2 William Hastie as civilian aide to the secretary of war, c. 1941. Courtesy National Archives, 208-NP-6BBB-1.

this position in the hope that I will be able to work effectively toward the integration of the colored man into the army."[17]

In the new year, with the election decided, the NAACP kept the pressure on. In mid-January, the War Department announced the formation of an "all-Negro pursuit squadron" in the army air corps, fulfilling a long-standing goal of the *Pittsburgh Courier*'s equal-representation campaign. Walter White vigorously protested this latest "surrender of the War Department to the segregation pattern." Later that month, in celebration of National Defense Day, it staged mass meetings in about twenty-five cities, calling for an "organized campaign of militant action" to uproot discrimination and segregation in the national defense program, which included the armed forces.[18]

But the clearest indication that a mixed military had gained greater prominence in black people's prewar civil rights agenda was the sudden involvement of new organizations and people. In Harlem in late October 1940, the Citizens' Committee for Equal Rights in National Defense held a rally and march. As many as six thousand people "from all levels of the economic scale and of all ages and political philosophies" attended. They unanimously demanded, in a statement to the president, "the equitable inclusion, without discrimination or segregation of Negroes in the complete program for national defense." Making similar demands around the same time were a growing and diverse list of black organizations, including the National Urban League, the National Council of Negro Women, the National Airmen Association, the Chicago Council of Negro Organizations, the Conscientious Objectors Against Jim-Crow, the Harlem Youth Congress, and some in the black press. "If the black man is good enough to shoulder a gun in defense of this country," the *Chicago Defender*, echoing Hastie, declared in January 1941, "he is good enough to march side by side with his white brethren and fight on the same front and in the same military unit."[19]

With passage of the STSA in September 1940, a smattering of individual African Americans also protested the military's Jim Crow units by refusing in one way or another to comply with the draft. In December 1940, labor organizer Ernest Calloway claimed to be a conscientious objector to army segregation; six months later, in July 1941, Herbert L. Wheeldin, an elementary school teacher in New Rochelle, New York, sought a deferment on similar grounds. The army "has not called for the organization of a Jewish army or Irish army," he told his draft board; "neither is there the justification or necessity for a Negro (Jim Crow) army." Langston Hughes eloquently captured the point in his poem "A Message to the President," appearing in March 1941:

> I don't like this Jim Crow army
> Or this Jim Crow navy,
> Or the lily-white marines
> Licking up the gravy. . . .
> Since, for our land's defense—
> If we have to fight—
> We ought to be together,
> Black and white.[20]

As Roger Starr's story suggested, some individual whites and white-led organizations, though few in number, joined Hughes's call for integration. In October 1940, writing in the Catholic weekly *America*, Father John La Farge condemned "our Jim Crow army," arguing that "what the country needs today is not segregation, but union." At the same time, the Socialist Workers Party resolved that "mixed regiments can protect the Negroes from special selection as a group for dirty or dangerous work, can unite the soldiers and build up a solidarity of Negro and white, and can help to undermine the system of Jim Crowism everywhere."[21]

Black leaders secured another meeting with Roosevelt, in June 1941—this time thanks to A. Philip Randolph's threat to organize a march on Washington involving tens of thousands of African Americans. The main issue was not solely, as is sometimes remembered, equal access to jobs in the burgeoning defense industries. "Equal integration in the fighting forces" was another important demand of the Negroes' Committee to March on Washington. This vague phrase allowed members of the equal-representation and mixed-military camps—Rayford Logan and Walter White, for example—to come together behind Randolph's march idea. And yet, at the June meeting, Randolph and White, according to the latter's recollection, reiterated to the president and military leaders their "adamant opposition to segregation" in the armed forces and "discussed practical means of abolishing" it. They also presented the president with a memorandum outlining a number of demands, one of which involved ending "all discrimination and segregation in the armed forces."[22]

AN ENTRENCHED SEGREGATIONISM

That the landmark victory coming out of this meeting—executive order 8802, which created the Committee on Fair Employment Practice (COFEP)—said nothing about mixed military units spoke to the formidable prewar obstacles that black activists continued to face on the issue. While the campaign for such units had grown considerably over the previous nine months, it remained limited. Few nonblacks were involved, and while growing numbers of African Americans and civil rights organizations like the NAACP were more committed than ever before to a mixed military, a diversity of views on the subject endured. Some conservative black leaders, like Frederick D. Patterson, the president of Tuskegee Institute, fretted about the "revolutionary tactics" employed to mix units, which might upset "the whole existing structure." Meanwhile black nationalist organizations, such as the Universal Negro Improvement Association, wished to extend, not end, segregation. In the early fall of 1941, it wrote Roosevelt, requesting "the organization of an African Expeditionary force to be made up of Negro units of the Army, National Guard, and draftees."[23]

These views created problems for black integrationists. "Divided opinion among Negroes on the question of segregation in the Army makes for great difficulty in solving this problem," admitted William Hastie in January

1941. "As long as people who are opposed to mixed units are able to point to Negroes as also agreeing with this position, our problem is extremely difficult." Indeed, later that year when a group of black newspaper editors met with the War Department, one official defended segregated units by noting that they had "been protested pro and con by letters which we have received from prominent societies and individuals of the Negro race. I think it is a problem which probably hasn't been entirely settled among your own people."[24]

A much more formidable obstacle to mixed military units was Congress. Article I of the Constitution gave this branch of the federal government the right "to make Rules for the Government and Regulation of the land and naval Forces." None of these "rules" required that the military place black people exclusively in segregated units. But some of them strongly indicated Congress's preferences on the matter. The National Defense Act, which passed in July 1940, included the following clause that simultaneously authorized African Americans' access to the army and segregation in it: "[N]o Negro, because of race, shall be excluded from enlistment in the Army for service with colored military units now organized or to be organized." A month later, when New York senator Robert Wagner proposed an antidiscrimination amendment to the STSA, several southern senators angrily denounced it as a devious ploy to mix units. In their view, the amendment "would put colored men and white men in the same company, make them sleep together in the same tent, make them eat together at the same table." All of this, in one Texas senator's words, violated laws "written in the Constitution of the [Anglo Saxon] race . . . written in the statutes of our blood." Ultimately, they pressured Wagner to repeatedly clarify that his amendment had nothing to do with mixed units and that he personally opposed the idea. Finally, Congress members communicated their segregationist commitments to military leaders directly. In a December 1941 letter, a Texas House member named W. R. Poage "earnestly plead[ed]" with Navy Secretary Frank Knox "to see that there is complete segregation of the [black and white] races" in the military. "You know that our [southern white] people have volunteered for military service more readily than the people of any other section of the Nation," he explained. "If they be forced to serve with Negroes, they will cease to volunteer; and when drafted, they will not serve with that enthusiasm and high morale that has always characterized the soldiers and sailors of the southern states."[25]

Southern Democrats like Poage, who were most fiercely invested in military-unit segregation, constituted significant portions of their party's caucus in the House and Senate throughout the New Deal period. They also held numerous committee posts across Congress, not least those related to the armed forces. By the late 1930s, they boosted this considerable power by forming an occasional "unnatural alliance" with conservative Republicans. As a consequence, they erected what scholar Ira Katznelson has called a "southern cage," which placed severe limits on federal policymaking in the New Deal period—especially that which touched on "Negro" matters. This meant that any effort on the part of the White House or the military to mix black and white outfits would have risked alienating many of the very powerful Congress members they relied on for legislation and key appropriations.[26]

But military leaders, who represented the third important obstacle to mixed units, likely caused legislators nary a concern on the issue. Both privately and publicly, these leaders never wavered from the staunchest fealty to segregated black and white units. In the navy, Secretary Knox and the uniformed admirals below him all insisted repeatedly that they "just could not mix white and colored personnel" or that "it would not be possible to integrate the Negro in the Navy." Similarly, Secretary Stimson spoke for any leader of consequence in the prewar army and War Department when he declared in a September 1940 diary entry, "I hope for Heaven's sake they won't mix the white and the colored troops together in the same units for then we shall certainly have trouble." Indeed, Stimson's new civilian aide, William Hastie, came quickly to chafe at this official intransigence. In September 1941, he presented his boss with detailed "recommendations concerning the integration of the Negro soldier into the Army." The last of these called for "the employment of soldiers without racial separation" at "some place in the Armed Services." "Many of the [army's] underlying problems . . . are inherent in the fundamental scheme of separate units for colored soldiers," Hastie argued. Well aware that upending this scheme would take time, he was nonetheless disturbed "that there is no apparent disposition to make a beginning or a trial of any different plan."[27]

As America prepared for war throughout 1940 and 1941, both the army and navy justified this lack of a "disposition" in more or less the same way. A range of leaders from both services argued that the vast majority of white troops adamantly opposed serving alongside—let alone, potentially, beneath—black people. The problem, according to navy brass, was the "confined quarters" and "close intimacy" of ship life combined with whites' widespread "race prejudice" and their consequent refusal to take orders from African Americans. For army leaders, it was the "racial conditions that exist in civil life" and the "social relationship between negroes and whites which has been established by the American people through custom and habit" over many years. To disregard these "realities" by mixing black and white troops, leaders reasoned, would destroy the efficiency, discipline, and morale of US fighting forces and gravely endanger the nation's security and perhaps its very existence. As one army colonel told a group of black newspaper editors on the day the United States declared war on Japan, "Experiments to meet the wishes of and demands of the champions of every race and creed for the solution of their problems . . . would result in ultimate defeat."[28] In this thinking, then, black and white segregated units were equal parts practical, patriotic, and, from the standpoint of the nation, existentially essential.

The word "enlisted" must be underscored, however, because while army and navy leaders claimed to oppose so-called race mixing, the practice, in fact, pervaded the military—in the form of white officers commanding black soldiers. This crucial point is a reminder that segregation—in the armed services, as elsewhere—was first and foremost a system of domination rather than separation. Mixing troops in the same units was unacceptable to many whites, leaders assumed, because it appeared to place them on equal footing with black people—or, indeed, on subordinate footing, in the event that African Americans were promoted over whites. Mixing white officers with black enlisted personnel, however, posed no such "problem." In this case, military hierarchy—officer over enlisted—perfectly reflected and added institutional force to racist hierarchy—white over black.

Military leaders, at times, disavowed any personal investment in the latter hierarchy. They even expressed occasional regret for its existence, speaking of the "harsh realities of this imperfect world." More often they presented themselves as impartial realists, whose sole purpose was to prepare the nation for possible war, not to solve a "social problem that has perplexed the American people throughout the history of this nation." There was something to this argument. In the run-up to America's entry in the war, both army and navy leaders faced an awesome task: to expand greatly and rapidly the nation's fighting forces as war raged overseas. It was "an inauspicious and dangerous time," in Secretary of the Navy Knox's words, to meddle with the military's most long-standing black-white line.[29]

These men were seldom impartial, however. With few exceptions, they believed deeply that supposed black inferiority required not only restricted access to the military, but also segregation and subordination therein. Such views about black inferiority, while appearing much more frequently in private than in public, were widespread. Stimson wrote repeatedly in his diary about the "incompetency of the Negro troops," for example. Secretary Knox, for his part, dismissed the idea of all-black crews since, as he wrote a friend, "you could not possibly find all the skills and crafts that are necessary if you had the entire negro population of the United States to choose from."[30] These ideas were as pervasive among senior officers as they were among their civilian superiors. One draft of a high-level War Department memo from September 1941 noted that the "[Negro] race . . . has not as yet attained the mental equipment to be employed in military functions other than those where brawn is [a] prerequisite."[31] Numerous other examples could be cited. The point is that military leaders' opposition to mixed units was not, in their view, based simply on a realist's calculation about what white enlisted personnel would tolerate at a profoundly perilous time. It was also an outgrowth of a set of tacit assumptions about black inferiority and subordination that virtually all military leaders at the time shared.

Perhaps the most significant obstacle to integrated outfits came not from the military or Congress, but from President Roosevelt. After all, he alone had the authority to mix any and all units he wished. As commander in chief, he could order military brass to do so, since Congress had not tied his hands, having never passed a law requiring that all black troops be segregated. In private prewar discussions with black leaders, Roosevelt seemed at times to support mixed black-white troops and even to promise their future formation. In his initial meeting with White and Randolph in September 1940, he discussed the need to "work into this [nonsegregation]": "Now, suppose you have a Negro regiment . . . here, and right over here on my right in line, would be a white regiment. . . . Now what happens after a while, in case of war? Those people get shifted from one to the other. The thing gets sort of backed into . . . gradually working in the field together, you may back into it." In a meeting a month later with another group of black leaders, he went further. Speaking with Rayford Logan and a few others, he insisted that he could not "put colored and white soldiers in the same company in southern camps." "But in the north," he pledged, according to Logan's diary entry, "I am going to mix the units. . . . I am going . . . to have a colored company in the same regiment with whites."[32]

Indeed, the White House seems to have considered this possibility. Two days earlier, amid the growing pre-election controversy over the War Department's "negro" policy, presidential aide James Rowe suggested to Roosevelt several moves to secure black votes. The last and most daring of these involved Roosevelt's promise to Logan a few days later: "a gradual beginning to end segregation. . . . For instance, there should be no problem if the races are mixed in a regiment quartered in the Northwest, where there is no racial feeling." Rowe noted that Roosevelt's closest adviser, Harry Hopkins, was considering the idea and that "consultation with persons like [William] Hastie . . . might give us a formula."[33]

Nothing came of Rowe's suggestion—and Roosevelt's promise— however. A week earlier Roosevelt had issued a public statement that seemed to capture his position on troop segregation better than his private pre-election pledges. "As to the policy of the War Department regarding the intermingling of White and Colored personnel," Roosevelt declared, "the thought in my mind, in approving the War Department's statement, was that in the present dangerous crisis, Negro Americans, as well as all other Americans, must make sacrifices to meet the emergency and that . . . we dare not confuse the issue of prompt preparedness with a new social experiment however important and desirable it may be." He concluded the statement by stressing that the issue of mixed black-white units "has had and shall continue to have my most serious consideration as President and Commander-in-Chief."[34] Once the pressures of the 1940 election passed and the pressures of the war mounted, however, Roosevelt moved on to other concerns—permanently, as it turned out.

Prior to America's involvement in the war, this active and passive support for the segregated status quo—from Congress and the military brass to Roosevelt himself—played out differently in the military's various services and branches. In the so-called lily-white ones, where leaders deemed the formation of new, separate black units impractical or impossible—the navy's general service, the marines, the WAVES (Women Accepted for Volunteer Emergency Service), the navy nurse corps, and so forth—all-out exclusion remained the rule. When black people tried to join any of these branches, the standard, matter-of-fact reply was "[T]here are no organizations made up of colored men [or, in some cases, women] . . . and none are contemplated."[35] In the army's ground and service forces, on the other hand, where a limited number of "colored" outfits had existed for years, simply expanding their numbers proved easier. So on the eve of America's entry into the war, while troop-assignment policies regarding African Americans varied some throughout the armed forces, the underlying, guiding principle remained the same: black enlisted personnel were to be kept exclusively in their own separate units.

INTEGRATIONISM EXPANDS

When the United States formally entered the war, in December 1941, attacks on this principle multiplied as the military swelled and, in time, hundreds of thousands of African Americans joined its segregated ranks. These attacks also became more pointed, as activists—African Americans and increasing numbers of others—began proposing specific ways to integrate the military, or at least parts of it. Some called for organizing a single mixed army unit—a division, a regiment, or a battalion; supporters sometimes differed on the point—made up solely of volunteers willing to join it, or for forming several mixed units in all branches of the military, or for mixing small black army units within larger "white" ones, or for keeping existing black army units intact but inducting new African Americans into fully mixed outfits, or for completely "intermingling" black—or often all—troops in all branches of the armed services.[36] Some activists pushed for several of these ideas at once or at different times during the war. At the outset, support for a voluntary mixed army unit was most widespread, but it was almost always understood and presented as simply a first step toward broader integration across the entire military. By early in America's war, this latter goal had fast become many blacks'—and a growing minority of nonblacks'—dominant demand.

On December 8, 1941, Claude Barnett, editor of the Associated Negro Press, proposed a voluntary black-white mixed army unit at a conference between the War Department and a large group of black journalists. It was the day after the Pearl Harbor attack, when Congress declared war on Japan. "I doubt whether many of us believe that separation of soldiers on the basis of race is necessary," he declared. "For one, I should like to see an experiment made with a mixed battalion in which white and colored soldiers might have an opportunity to volunteer to serve. . . . Perhaps war time is a good time to forget racial differences."[37] If military leaders' primary objection to mixed units rested, as they claimed, on whites' deep-seated segregationism, Barnett's proposal appeared to be the perfect response: those whites who opposed serving alongside black people would not be forced to do so. Several other editors and writers at the meeting expressed their hearty support.

Walter White and the NAACP quickly seized on Barnett's idea, hoping to secure a private meeting with Army Chief of Staff George C. Marshall to discuss it. They were not naive about their chances of success. "I share your pessimism and belief that only dire peril will make them [military leaders] yield to their prejudices," White confided to one black newspaper editor at the time. "But I also believe we must keep up unremitting pressure in order to get them to yield." In late December 1941 and early January 1942, White wrote two letters to Marshall (the first of which he also passed on to Eleanor Roosevelt, asking her to relay it to the president). He urged Marshall to organize a "volunteer division of the army open to all without regard to race or color," assuring him that a "gratifyingly high number of young white Americans" would join such a unit. He cited Roger Starr's story as proof. White also convinced numerous black newspaper editors to write letters of their own. One came from P. L. Prattis of the *Pittsburgh Courier*, for years the most committed of all newspapers to black people's equal representation—rather than integration—in the military. But its stance on the subject was evolving, thanks to changing circumstances and to the death of its longtime publisher and editor, Robert L. Vann. When the army announced that the formation of a new black division was well under way— one of the newspaper's central military-related demands—it adjusted its sights. Prattis's note to Walter White, dated December 29, 1941, suggests that the fight to abolish military segregation both underlay the modest request for a single voluntary unit and was gaining new supporters:

> We have fought for a Negro division because, as you know, the desire during the last twenty years has been to restrict Negroes to small work units. The division, even a Negro division, was a symbol of status.... However, now that such recognition has been forced, we should increase the pressure for a volunteer division without color lines and press on from there for planned integration by the War Department, not on a voluntary basis.[38]

The War Department promptly rejected the voluntary-division idea. Assistant Secretary of War John J. McCloy remarked privately that it represented the height of "unwisdom," and no military officials, with the possible exception of Undersecretary of War Robert Patterson, seriously considered it. When, in mid-January, William Hastie met with Secretary of War Stimson, neither a voluntary mixed division nor anything about integrated outfits seems to have come up.[39]

Supporters pressed on nonetheless. In January and early February 1942, numerous black newspapers and a few white publications endorsed a voluntary division, while Walter White, especially, continued to work tirelessly for it. He spent most of his time reaching out to whites, attempting to disabuse military leaders of the notion that only the smallest low-class minority among them supported mixed units. He sought and received endorsements from a collection of prominent southern whites, including Frank P. Graham, the president of the University of North Carolina, and Mississippi-born Mark Ethridge, the editor and publisher of the *Louisville Courier Journal* and chair of the newly formed COFEP. He passed these on to the War Department (as he did Roger Starr's fan mail). He spoke at colleges and universities, encouraging students to support the division. At the University of California at Berkeley, White recalled meeting a "blond, tousleheaded young giant," who remarked, "Ah want to be the first as a native of Jawja to volunteah for youah mixed division." And he wrote liberal, largely white organizations such as the Council Against Intolerance in America (CAIA) and the Union for Democratic Action (UDA), hoping to enlist their support in an all-out campaign of "letters, telegrams, petitions, and other communications to the President and the War Department."[40]

These efforts immediately paid off. By mid-February, officials in the War Department noticed that, "judging by the Chief of Staff's mail, the move for a volunteer mixed negro and white division seems to be growing to include representations from people of some importance." In addition to the fifty letters from "obviously negro organizations," they received notes from Dorothy Canfield Fisher, a well-known novelist at the time, Ruth Benedict, a prominent Columbia University anthropologist, and Katherine Devereux Blake, suffragist, peace activist, and educator; from leaders of the National Catholic Welfare Conference, the Federated Council of Churches of Christ in America, and the CAIA; and from numerous ordinary whites, some of whom were eager to join an interracial unit. In letters to Roosevelt, Stimson, and Knox, one Gerald White from New York wrote, "I am to be inducted into the U.S.M.C. [marine corps] which, I learned after I enlisted, restricts its membership to members of the white race. This does not satisfy me as being a bright, shining example of the democracy for which we are allegedly fighting." He asked to be transferred to a mixed unit, if one were organized.[41]

By March, the CAIA sponsored a "Victory through Unity" conference in New York City, at which five hundred people unanimously adopted a resolution urging the War Department to form a "mixed combat division of men of all creeds, faiths and colors." One white organizer suggested that the unit be called the "League of Nations Division," declaring, "A man who is good enough to fight for my country is good enough to fight alongside of me." Two months later, the UDA, whose chair was the renowned theologian Reinhold Niebuhr, launched a nationwide petition drive to "eliminate discrimination in the armed forces." One of its three demands included the formation of a "voluntary interracial unit" in the army. With the support of a wide range of big and small groups—from the NAACP and the Urban League to the Harlem Riverside Civilian Defense Volunteer Organization—the UDA had secured fifty thousand signatures by February 1943 and perhaps as many as twice that number a year later. This total, while well short of its goal of ten million, was substantial nonetheless. Most of these signatures came from ordinary people, but some also came from the governors of New Jersey, Utah, and Montana, New York City mayor Fiorello La Guardia, Massachusetts and Rhode Island bishops, distinguished academics like John Dewey, and movie stars like Joan Bennett.[42]

The larger campaign for a mixed army unit, though waxing and waning throughout the war's remaining years, generally expanded over time to include a wider array of people and organizations: Young Communist League (YCL) chapters across the country (one of its pamphlets claimed, in September 1942, that "the idea of forming a Voluntary Mixed Regiment

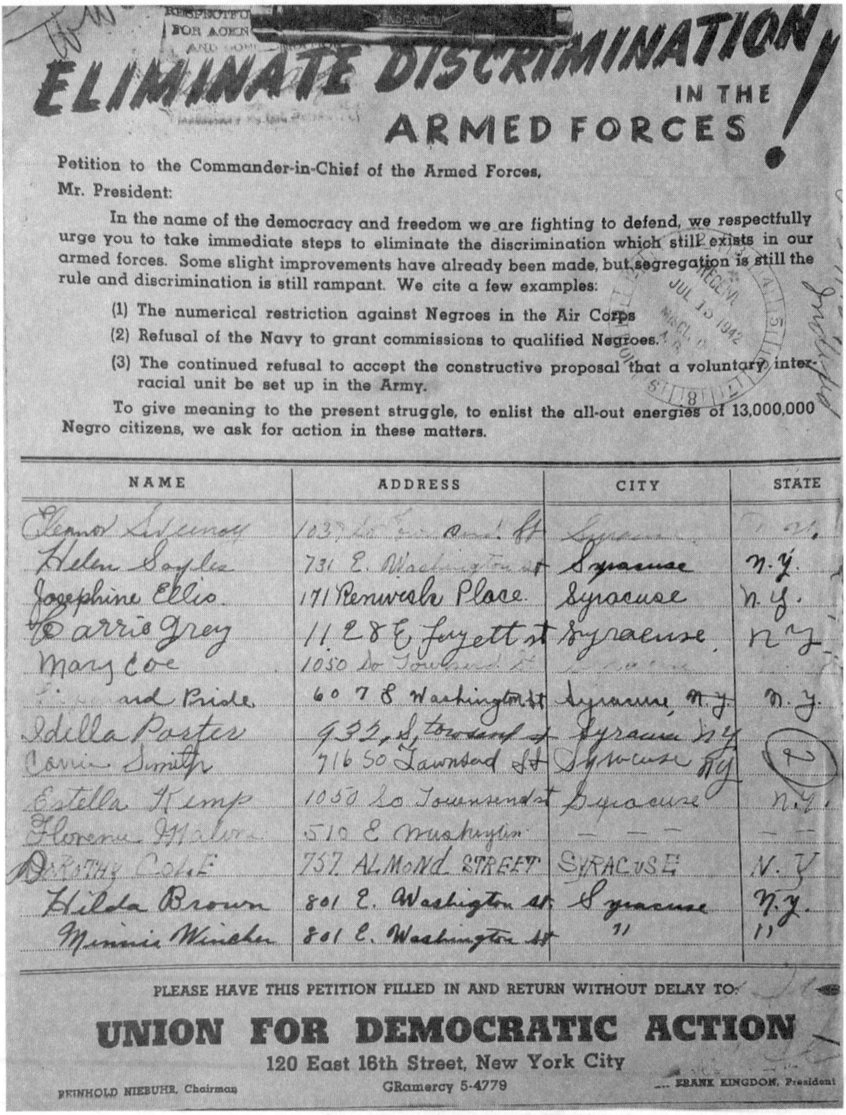

ELIMINATE DISCRIMINATION IN THE **ARMED FORCES!**

Petition to the Commander-in-Chief of the Armed Forces,
Mr. President:

In the name of the democracy and freedom we are fighting to defend, we respectfully urge you to take immediate steps to eliminate the discrimination which still exists in our armed forces. Some slight improvements have already been made, but segregation is still the rule and discrimination is still rampant. We cite a few examples:

(1) The numerical restriction against Negroes in the Air Corps

(2) Refusal of the Navy to grant commissions to qualified Negroes.

(3) The continued refusal to accept the constructive proposal that a voluntary interracial unit be set up in the Army.

To give meaning to the present struggle, to enlist the all-out energies of 13,000,000 Negro citizens, we ask for action in these matters.

NAME	ADDRESS	CITY	STATE
Eleanor Sweney	103 ...	Syracuse	N.Y.
Helen Sayles	731 E. Washington st	Syracuse	N.Y.
Josephine Ellis	171 Renwick Place	Syracuse	N.Y.
Carrie Grey	1128 E. Fayett st	Syracuse	N.Y.
Mary Coe	1050 So. Townsend E.		
... and Bride	6078 Washington st	Syracuse, N.Y.	N.Y.
Idella Porter	932 S. townsend st	Syracuse N.Y.	
Carrie Smith	716 So. Townsend St	Syracuse N.Y.	✓
Estella Kimp	1050 So. Townsend st	Syracuse	N.Y.
Florence Malone	510 E. Washington	— —	— —
Dorothy Cole	757 ALMOND STREET	SYRACUSE	N.Y.
Hilda Brown	801 E. Washington st	Syracuse	N.Y.
Minnie Winkler	801 E. Washington st	''	''

PLEASE HAVE THIS PETITION FILLED IN AND RETURN WITHOUT DELAY TO:

UNION FOR DEMOCRATIC ACTION
120 East 16th Street, New York City
GRamercy 5-4779

REINHOLD NIEBUHR, Chairman   FRANK KINGDON, President

Fig. 3.3 A petition to "eliminate discrimination in the armed forces," including support for "a voluntary interracial unit" in the army, July 1942. Courtesy of the National Archives, Record Group 407.

of Negro and white soldiers in the United States Army is catching on with the speed and power of a cannon shot!"); the fledgling Committee for a Mixed Army Unit, started by college students in the Philadelphia area and expanding to include prominent academics like anthropologist Ashley Montagu and noted black Communist Party leader Doxey Wilkerson; local groups such as the Bay Area Council Against Discrimination and the

Joint Anti-Fascist Refugee Committee in Jamaica, New York; a variety of publications like the *New Republic*, *PM*, and the *Harvard Crimson*; and ordinary people, who continued to send a steady stream of protest letters to the president and military leaders. In May 1942, even the Office and Facts of Figures, the federal government's domestic propaganda agency and the precursor to the Office of War Information, endorsed a "mixed volunteer unit" as a way to increase black people's support for the war effort.[43]

By the summer of 1943, at a time when bloody race riots convulsed scores of cities, towns, and military posts, a number of commentators

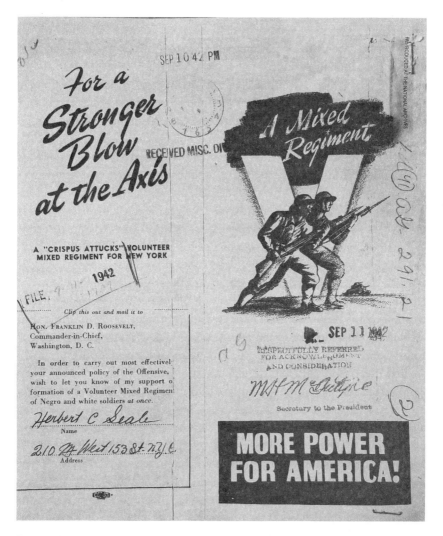

Fig. 3.4 A Young Communist League pamphlet in support of a "'Crispus Attucks' Volunteer Mixed Regiment for New York," September 1942. Courtesy of the Communist Party, USA.

suggested that the formation of such a unit might defuse tensions. In one July *PM* editorial, liberal columnist and educator Max Lerner urged the army, in light of its "sporadic riots and shootings," to "give Jim Crow an honorable discharge" by forming "an experimental mixed unit of Negroes and whites." Likewise, Walter White, who had for many months moved on to other civil rights projects, used the bloody summer of 1943 to renew his effort to create such a unit. Writing Stimson twice, he argued that recent riots were "born of repeated, unchecked, unpunished, and often unrebuked shooting, maiming, and insulting of Negro troops," all of which stemmed most fundamentally from segregation. White called not for any radical "overnight" changes, but for his modest proposal from two and a half years earlier: one voluntary mixed army division.[44]

In the early months of the campaign for this unit, a small minority of activists occasionally grumbled about this modesty. In a letter to Walter White in May 1942, A. C. MacNeal, the managing editor of the *Chicago Defender*, reprised a version of an argument he had made to the NAACP national office six years earlier, when he had led the organization's Chicago branch: since the "NAACP should be the one protest organization which should remain firm in the 'whole loaf' stand," he argued, it should not seek to integrate the military through "any backdoor . . . 'trial mixed regiment.'" But this sort of criticism was rare, because most supporters of the voluntary unit, not least White and the NAACP's national leadership, viewed it more as a means than an end: abolishing segregation across the entire army, or the military more generally—not a single unit—was their ultimate goal. The half loaf would beget the whole one. Indeed, MacNeal himself may have quickly come around to this position. A month after his letter to White, the Negro Newspaper Publishers Association, of which the *Chicago Defender* was a member, unanimously "endorsed the crusade for establishment of a voluntary interracial division as a forerunner to complete integration of colored and white citizens in all the armed forces of the nation."[45]

That the resolution mentioned "all the armed forces"—rather than simply the army—points to another potential source of conflict among activists. The campaign for a voluntary division often targeted the army alone and not the other military services and branches. Since some parts of the military excluded black people outright, while others segregated them into their own units, integrationists were not always entirely clear or consistent about what exactly they wished to integrate—the army, navy, marine corps, air corps, WAVES? For example, while the NAACP had, for several years, explicitly endorsed the wholesale abolition of all segregation across the military, its more modest demand that the army establish one mixed division seemed to have a parallel in its demand that the navy enlist

African Americans beyond the Messman Branch. Presumably this meant that it would acquiesce in the creation of separate black crews, so long as these crews served throughout the navy.[46]

Some clarity on this crucial question—How much of the military exactly did integrationists wish to integrate?—came in April 1942. Navy Secretary Frank Knox announced that African Americans would be permitted to serve outside of the navy's Messman Branch. At first, some black people celebrated the news. But within a few weeks, African Americans' criticism of the navy multiplied, for reasons that were, in the words of a *Time* magazine article, "plain as a battleship: new rule or no, Negroes still . . . must train and serve in segregated groups." In a telegram to the president, dated the same day as Knox's announcement, the local NAACP branch in Washington, DC, called "segregated Negro naval units" a "deliberate insult" and a "demonstration of the Nazi attitude." A few days later, the national office distributed a press release stressing the "disappointing" nature of the navy plan, which Walter White privately called an "inadequate, niggardly concession."[47] Randolph scored the navy policy since "it accepts and extends and consolidates the policy of Jim-Crowism in the Navy." Meanwhile, critical letters to Knox and Roosevelt poured in from across the country, and numerous black newspapers—and one or two white ones as well—blasted Knox for his "official proclamation of segregation." "Now that we have a separate Army, Navy, Marine Corps, Air Corps, and Coast Guard," a columnist for the *Cleveland Call and Post* joked, "I guess the next thing will be to give us a separate Congress and maybe a treasury." Some African Americans demanded Knox's resignation.[48]

Knox would remain at his post until his death, but some black people's dispute with the navy was revealing and significant. It showed that if the mixed-unit approach enjoyed widespread support throughout the war, the "whole-loaf stand"—the complete and immediate integration not simply of the army but of all the armed services, even those branches that long excluded African Americans—only grew in popularity over time among many black people, and eventually among some nonblacks, too. One early sign of this growing popularity among the former came from the *Pittsburgh Courier*. In the prewar years, it had long been the most vocal proponent of African Americans' equal representation in the military. Shortly after Pearl Harbor, it began supporting a single voluntary mixed unit, but by February 1943, it had cast away all moderation on the issue, demanding "a military New Deal": "We suggest that all segregated Negro units in all branches of the services be abolished. . . . The way to do this is not piecemeal but immediately, so that in a matter of a few weeks there will be no more racial units in any of the services, and Americans of all colors and creeds, and from all States will be serving side by side in all parts of the far-flung bat-tlefront." Another sign came from public opinion polls. One Office of War Information survey of a "representative cross-section" of four thousand black and white people in Birmingham, Raleigh, Oklahoma City, Chicago, and Detroit, conducted in March 1943, found that a full three-quarters of black respondents—66 percent in the South and 91 percent in the North—believed that "in the armed forces . . . white and colored men should be . . . in the same groups." Nine in ten white respondents disagreed.[49] What had once divided some black people now unified large numbers of them and divided them from the great majority of whites.

Also reflecting growing African American unity, black and some non-black activists began in the spring and summer of 1943 to organize increas-ingly around abolishing all Jim Crow units across the military. In August, the Save Our Soldiers Committee, a part of the NAACP's Brooklyn branch, sent dozens of petitions with hundreds of signatures to President Roosevelt calling for an "end [to] the discriminatory practices and segregation within the ARMED FORCES of the UNITED STATES." Making similar demands at the same time were two white-led Left and labor organizations—the Socialist Party and the Michigan Federation of Labor.[50]

A. Philip Randolph's all-black March on Washington Movement (MOWM) became an early leader in this struggle, asserting that the "abolition of segregation in the armed forces has become the central and dominating issue in the life of the Negro people of America today." Throughout the spring and summer of 1943, in letters to Roosevelt, his cabinet, and its supporters, and in press releases, posters, pamphlets, and mass meetings, the MOWM called on "every man, woman and child [to] unite in the cru-sade to . . . secure a National Proclamation from the President abolishing Segregation in the Armed Forces. Lincoln did it to save the union in 1864! Roosevelt can do it to save the Peace in 1943!"[51] The MOWM, especially its New York chapter, simultaneously worked on the Winfred Lynn case, which many of its supporters hoped would lead to mixed military outfits. It raised funds, staged rallies, published pamphlets, and eventually helped found the National Citizens' Committee for Winfred Lynn (NCCWL) in order to organize efforts to win the case.[52]

In 1944, this broader campaign to abolish segregated military units gained momentum and participants. In March, Roy Wilkins, assistant secretary of the NAACP, signaled that his organization was rethinking its primary two-year-long focus on forming a voluntary mixed division. In a letter to President Roosevelt, he called for "the abolition of segregation by race and color in America's fighting forces" (a point that its monthly publication, *The Crisis*, made with some regularity). Several months later, at its annual national convention, the NAACP reiterated its fundamental position—"the principal injustices which the Negro suffers in the Army and the Navy are outgrowths of the basic evil of segregation and will not be cured until separate Negro units are abolished."[53] Meanwhile, two Left youth organizations—the American Youth for Democracy (formerly the YCL) and the Southern Negro Youth Conference—presented petitions to President Roosevelt with as many as several thousand signatures between them, demanding an immediate end to "all discrimination and segregation against Negro youth, who are loyally serving, fighting and dying in the armed forces of the United States."[54] A new organization—the Lynn Committee to Abolish Segregation in the Armed Forces—which was established in the spring of 1944, replaced the NCCWL and took military integration as its primary goal. It boasted a long list of high-profile sponsors, including Randolph, executive director of the American Civil Liberties Union (ACLU) Roger Baldwin, and Socialist leader Norman Thomas. "Change segregation and discrimination in the armed forces," one of the group's pamphlets declared, "and you will change the face of America; you will make it possible for millions of Americans to know and respect each other—not as racial robots pulled by the strings of vicious anti-racial prejudice—but as human beings."[55]

As the 1944 presidential election approached, activists attempted to leverage it in their efforts to abolish military Jim Crow. In December 1943, representatives of twenty-five prominent African American groups— Randolph of the MOWM, White of the NAACP, Mary McLeod Bethune of the National Council of Negro Women, Max Yergan of the National Negro Congress, and others—declared that "any party that hopes to win the support of Negroes" must demand, among other things, their "full integration . . . into the armed forces without segregation." Later the following year, the Congress of Industrial Organizations Political Action Committee endorsed and amplified this demand. Meanwhile, organizations of black Democrats and black Republicans "condemn[ed] without reservation the treatment, discrimination, and segregation of Negro men and women in the armed forces of the United States" and recommended "end[ing] discrimination and segregation in the armed forces," respectively. In June, the Lynn Committee sent petitions to all presidential and congressional candidates, calling on them to inform voters whether they would "take steps to see that segregation is abolished in the armed forces," eventually hearing back from several dozen candidates who answered in the affirmative. And in October, some black newspapers, such as the *New York Amsterdam News*, opposed Roosevelt's reelection because of his ongoing refusal to reform the military's "pattern of segregation and discrimination that has led to the humiliation, mistreatment and murder imposed upon Negro servicemen."[56]

Just before the election and especially after it, some activists might have appeared to moderate their arguments in favor of abolishing all military segregation. As the war wound down and Congress began considering legislation for a permanent peacetime draft, they called for a mixed military after the war. If the purpose of voluntary mixed divisions was to accommodate those white GIs who opposed serving alongside black people, this idea of a peacetime mixed military addressed concerns that wartime was no time for social experiments. When "there is no longer such an emergency," wrote one *Chicago Defender* columnist, Congress should "eliminate any and all segregation, separation and humiliation of races in our Armed Forces of tomorrow." Endorsing this view—and often withholding support for any postwar conscription plan that did not explicitly outlaw segregated units—were NAACP leaders, from Walter White and Roy Wilkins to Grant Reynolds and William Hastie, as well as Mary McLeod Bethune, Channing Tobias, who was a race adviser for the YMCA, an Ohio-based civil rights group known as the Vanguard League, and others.[57] Encapsulating these efforts was black New York City congressman Adam Clayton Powell. In March 1945, he introduced a bill in the US House of Representatives "to prohibit race segregation in the armed forces of the United States after the termination of hostilities in the present war and the beginning of demobilization."[58]

This campaign for a seemingly more modest reform, like the mixed-division one before it, supplemented, rather than replaced, the broader struggle for an integrated armed forces. When, in March 1945, news leaked that the army had begun experimenting with black platoons fighting alongside white ones on battlefronts in western Europe, passionate appeals to expand the test case emerged from some powerful quarters. In May, fifty "civic, government, labor, religious, educational and fraternal leaders, Negro and white," joined Congressman Powell, California congresswoman Helen Gahagan Douglas, Bethune, and others in urging President Truman and the War Department to extend the "Army's organization of mixed Negro and white combat units . . . into every branch of the Armed Forces." The following month, the National Negro Congress circulated a statement to the same effect, which approximately five hundred "nationally prominent people" signed, including three senators and three dozen members of the House.[59]

This five-year push to mix military units seemed to find its first umbrella organization when, in late April 1945, the National Committee to Abolish Segregation in the Armed Services was founded. In mid-March, representatives of three New York City–based organizations—the MOWM, the Lynn Committee, and the Workers Defense League (WDL), a Socialist group that worked on labor and civil rights causes—had met in A. Philip Randolph's Harlem office. Noticing black GIs' expanding assault on "Jim Crow in uniform" and believing that it required the assistance of a nationally coordinated, interorganizational campaign, the leaders resolved to create one. Since all the military's race problems stemmed, in their view, from the "government's policy of segregating Negro and white troops," they took direct aim at that policy. In early April, Randolph, the WDL's national secretary Morris Milgram, and Willard Townsend, a black Congress of Industrial Organizations (CIO) leader, wrote more than fifty liberal, Left, and black organizations, inviting them to a two-day summit in northern New Jersey. They asked each organization to send two of its "most able representatives . . . to formulate a program of action to end race segregation and discrimination by the armed services." That the meeting was to take place only three weeks later spoke to its "utmost importance" in the eyes of its organizers.[60]

On April 28, at Goodwill Camp in Butler, New Jersey, representatives of twenty-five organizations convened. They included leaders of some of the most important liberal and Left groups of the day, such as the ACLU, American Council on Race Relations, American Jewish Committee, Anti-Defamation League, MOWM, NAACP, National Urban League, WDL, and a number of CIO unions. Smaller organizations, a number of which would become important in the postwar years, also attended, including the Congress of Racial Equality, Fellowship of Reconciliation, and Japanese American Citizens League. The delegates voted to establish a permanent organization and to call it the National Committee to Abolish Segregation in the Armed Services (NCASAS). They vowed "to cooperate with all existing organizations presently engaged in the fight [to end military segregation], and to enlist the support of organizations all over the country in the campaign." They discussed the need to reach out to the "white public and public officials," but also to a range of "minority groups, such as Negro, Mexican, Chinese, Filipino, and Japanese in order to secure concerted action." They brainstormed about possible plans of action, including distributing leaflets; organizing "street meetings" and letter campaigns; taking out newspaper ads; hosting radio broadcasts; appealing to the president to issue an executive order to abolish military segregation or to Congress to pass a law to that effect; staging mass meetings in San Francisco to coincide with the weeks-long conference, recently begun there, to negotiate and sign the United Nations charter, as well as elsewhere to build "mass pressure"; and holding Memorial Day services for soldiers who "died in the cause of freedom they did not enjoy." Finally, they unanimously adopted a resolution, which they sent to recently sworn-in President Truman, calling on him, as commander in chief of the armed forces, on the military leadership, and on Congress "to abolish every vestige of [military] segregation and discrimination now practiced."[61]

Despite its promising start, the NCASAS did not last. At its next meeting, in June, only one group had formally affiliated—the WDL—and by the fall, it had dissolved altogether. Some groups thought the goal of immediate and complete integration of the armed services was too ambitious; others thought that, as the war drew to a close, jobs had become the most pressing concern. Competition among organizations posed another problem. The NAACP, for example, chose not to affiliate, thinking that the NCASAS's goals overlapped too much with its own. And a lack of leadership plagued the organization from the start. Wilfred Kerr, the group's secretary (who also served as co-chair of the Lynn Committee), suffered from serious and debilitating "nervous strain" through much of the summer in 1945 and was likely unable to offer the fledgling organization much guidance. Randolph, the group's chair, like Kerr, was a driving force behind the formation of the NCASAS, but he failed to give it enough attention while juggling his responsibilities as leader of the Brotherhood of Sleeping Car Porters, the MOWM, and the National Council for a Permanent Fair Employment Practice Committee. By V-J Day, then, despite the growing energy and organizing around the issue, there was no unified national movement in opposition to segregated military units.[62]

Still, much had changed over the previous five or so short years. Many of the most prominent national African American leaders and civil rights groups were no longer divided over the question of equal representation or integration. They wanted both. Nor did they split over what integration would mean: not a single, mixed voluntary army unit, but the end of all segregated "Negro" (or, often, other) units across the entire armed forces. This demand—a fringe position at the start of the war—found by its end growing support not only among ordinary black people but also among liberal and leftist whites and others, many thousands of whom had organized, petitioned, written letters, and rallied on the issue. All in all, it was an object lesson in how political organizing, even when not immediately successful in attaining its stated goals, can still broaden people's sense of what is politically possible.

This expanding political imaginary and protest had other effects as well. In conjunction with the widespread and vigorous activism among black service members themselves, which more often targeted the pressing, everyday outcomes of Jim Crow units than the units themselves, it helped push military leaders to depart occasionally from their rigid policy of segregated outfits. In the final months of the war, fifty or so platoons made up of black enlisted men and white officers fought in western Europe within otherwise nonblack companies, the navy mixed crews on roughly two hundred of its noncombat auxiliary ships, and small numbers of black women served alongside other women in the navy's WAVES and the army and navy nurse corps. At the same time, the military also experimented—often in the final stages of the war—with integration in other venues, such as some army recreational facilities, army hospitals, army and navy officer candidate schools, and navy general-service basic training.[63]

Meanwhile, by war's end, army and navy leaders had begun at least considering more far-reaching changes to both services' foundational policy of segregated units. As for the army, these considerations dated at least as far back as the fall of 1942, when army colonel Edwin W. Chamberlain, disturbed by the massive waste and conflict that segregation generated, suggested a "radical" idea: place those black soldiers who had scored in the two lowest categories on army intelligence tests within white units on a one-in-ten basis; they would perform more menial jobs as cooks, orderlies, chauffeurs, truck drivers, and kitchen police. Higher-scoring African Americans would remain in separate black units. Chamberlain well understood the War Department's long-standing opposition to mixing white and black enlisted personnel. He thought his plan, however, was no different than the common practice of employing "Negroes as servants in a white household." After considering the plan, the army dismissed it when leaders of the army ground and service forces expressed opposition.[64] A year later, another army colonel, J. S. Leonard, as secretary of the Advisory Committee on Negro Troop Policies, suggested to Assistant Secretary of War John J. McCloy that "the elimination of segregation, in its various forms, . . . should be reviewed," in part because this was "the primary objective of the Negroes." But this suggestion, like Chamberlain's, went nowhere. Indeed, it was not until several weeks after the war's conclusion that army and War Department leadership agreed to a formal review of its race policies, including, in Chief of Staff George C. Marshall's words, a careful examination of "the practicability of integrating Negro elements into white units."[65]

The navy moved slightly farther and faster toward mixed units than the army did, a remarkable development given its total exclusion of black people outside of the Messman Branch just a few years earlier. A small committee of navy officers devoted to dealing with race-related problems had, soon after its formation in August 1943, concluded that segregated crews were wasteful, inefficient, and costly; it pushed to include and integrate some black sailors in the navy combat fleet. Financier James V. Forrestal, who replaced Frank Knox as navy secretary in May 1944, proved much more willing than his predecessor to consider and institute its proposals, beginning with the integration of noncombat auxiliary vessels. He was, in the words of one commentator, no "crusader for social justice, but, at the least, unlike his predecessor, he could read the writing on the wall which said that the old system was gone, perhaps forever." By the first few weeks of 1945, he resolved to go further than the mixed auxiliary ships. As conflict between white and black sailors and political organizing among the latter had grown increasingly disruptive, it appears that Forrestal and Admiral Ernest King, chief of naval operations, agreed on the complete, albeit gradual, integration of the navy's general service. By war's end, navy leaders "were laying plans" for this fundamental policy shift.[66]

Despite these real changes in attitude and policy across the military, unmistakable continuities remained at war's end. In July 1945, Forrestal conceded privately—and accurately—that the navy's reforms were merely "a start down a long road." Indeed, as the war concluded, only the smallest fraction of sailors had served any time at all in mixed crews: the navy's shift toward integration came late in the conflict as the navy was shrinking dramatically, discharging sailors by the thousands, a disproportionately large number of black people among them; and the shift did not apply to the navy's officer corps, its "sister service" the marine corps, or, most important, its Messman Branch, in which a shocking eight in ten black sailors still served. As for the army, its moves were even more limited. As Stimson's race adviser Truman K. Gibson astutely, and dispiritedly, observed in August 1945, the "basic [troop segregation] policies of the Army have remained essentially unchanged during the war."[67]

JIM CROW OUTFITS' ENDURING, INSTITUTIONALIZED SUPPORT

The military mixed so few black and white troops during the war because of several important and interrelated factors, some of which become especially clear when considered alongside the race reforms that the military did undertake, especially those involving broader black enlistment. As in the prewar years, Congress remained a major obstacle to mixed military units. In September 1944, a black church group asked Republican Hamilton Fish III, a New York congressman, for his help in integrating the military. An officer of black troops during World War I, Fish had since then pushed aggressively for their equal representation in the army. The mere thought of mixed outfits, however, enraged Fish: "What do you want to do—start another war before this one is over? Why, the entire South as well as the north would rise up in revolutionary fury." Besides, he added, "a bill to abolish segregation in the army wouldn't get three votes in Congress. It would be political suicide." In fact, nine months later, in June 1945, three senators and thirty-six House members declared their support for mixed units across the military, and their numbers were growing. Still, Fish had a point. When, in March 1945, Congressman Powell introduced a bill in the House to prohibit segregation in the armed forces six months after the end of hostilities, it received little public support, it never made it out of committee, and even Powell himself seldom spoke of it again.[68]

If Fish's and Powell's efforts show that congressional obstacles to mixing military units were national in scope, southern Democrats, as in the prewar years, remained pivotal. Indeed, the war years witnessed both the expansion of their power—non-southern Democrats, who lost seats in Congress following the 1942 midterm elections, became ever more dependent upon their southern colleagues to pass legislation—and a growing determination to wield it, especially on issues related to black people. Motivated by an "ever-more obsessive anxiety about race," they succeeded, for example, in weakening the president's COFEP, eventually defunding it completely in 1946, and in maintaining state control over soldiers' ballots. Both moves, intended to shore up white southern elites' economic and political power, offer a sense of how southern Democrats would have mobilized against any wartime attempts to mix military units. Whereas black enlistment divided southern Democrats, mixed outfits united them. After all, as Georgia senator Richard Russell put it, "There is no such thing as a little integration."[69]

For all its wartime tinkering with race policy, military leadership also remained a formidable obstacle to more far-reaching troop integration. When, in an end-of-the-war review, top-ranked army officers were asked to offer their opinion of segregated units, they expressed nearly universal support. Civilian leaders in the War Department held similar views, considering modest reforms only toward the end of the war. The navy proved more flexible on the issue but only up to a point. Forrestal and all the top admirals steadfastly refused to mix crews in any part of the wartime fighting fleet.[70]

As in the prewar years, these leaders leaned on a flexible mix of justifications, though the army and navy diverged some over time in this regard. As for the army, leaders claimed that black people preferred segregation and, for those who did not, "war is never agreeable, and whether we like it or not, we are engaged in a war for national survival in which the interests of the Nation must be paramount." They claimed that, because

African Americans had "comparatively low intelligence," integrating them throughout the military would dangerously dilute the fighting forces, "leav[ing] a commander with no outstanding units." They claimed that segregation did not mean discrimination, since "negroes are serving in every arm and branch of the service, eating exactly the same food as white soldiers, living in exactly the same type of quarters, and training with exactly the same weapons." They claimed that "the basic issues of this war are [not] involved in the question of whether Colored troops serve in segregated units or in mixed units and I doubt whether you can convince the people of the United States that the basic issues of freedom are involved in such a question." They claimed the "fundamental segregation instincts of the people generally . . . [made] it too much to ask the Army to change overnight."[71] Finally, and most important, they claimed, as they had for years, that troop discipline, morale, and efficiency—by which they often meant white troop discipline, morale, and efficiency—required black enlisted personnel's rigid segregation. At the war's outset, some leaders spoke breathlessly about how separate units "practically eliminated the colored problem." But even

Fig. 3.5 The Forty-First Engineers, a typical segregated black army outfit, on parade in a color guard ceremony at Fort Bragg in North Carolina, n.d. Courtesy National Archives, 208-NP-4HHH-2.

those leaders who came by war's end to question that assessment still saw integration, or "social revolution," as infinitely more problematic than its alternatives. "Segregation makes difficulties," Assistant Secretary of War McCloy conceded in 1944, "but mixing units would create even more upheaval, and we cannot take such risks."[72]

By war's end, while some navy leaders had diverged from these well-worn arguments, most had not. Most top brass continued to justify segregated crews in wartime, echoing many of the army and War Department leaders' concerns. Chief of Naval Personnel Admiral Randall Jacobs, for example, claimed that "you couldn't dump 200 colored boys on a crew in battle"; or the Marine Command was convinced throughout the war that mixing black and white marines "would bring dire results"; or Admiral King, in rejecting a proposal to mix the crews of mine ships and net tenders, argued that these vessels would face combat shortly and so demanded "the highest degree of experienced seamanship and precision work," something evidently beyond the supposed capabilities of black sailors.[73]

Beyond these segregationist impulses, attitudes, and assumptions, two additional factors help explain military leaders' persistent opposition to mixing black and white troops—in any small units in the army and in the wartime combat fleet in the navy. First, as in the prewar years, they were loath to antagonize southern Democrats in Congress, who controlled military spending and who strongly supported the segregationist status quo. "The army relies for necessary legislation, including appropriations, on two committees normally dominated in Democratic administrations by southerners and heavily pervaded by southern attitudes on race," noted two commentators on the war years, including one former lieutenant colonel in the army, in 1947. "Any sudden move away from the principle of segregation would probably bring reprisals." These concerns became especially acute among army leaders as they fought for Congress to pass a universal military training bill in the summer and fall of 1945.[74] Second, whereas in the case of enlistment the military's different branches and services battled one another, since exclusion in one part of the armed forces required greater inclusion in another, no such intramural struggles emerged over the question of segregated troops. The navy's experimentation with mixed crews, for example, might have given civilian activists an additional argument with which to hammer the army, but the navy was not doing any of the hammering, in public or in private. Whether one branch or service decided to integrate its troops had little to no bearing on any other branch or service. Thus, whereas the army and War Department had pushed hard against the navy's anti-black enlistment bars early in the war, no similar sort of intramilitary integrationist pressure developed during the war (or afterward).

President Roosevelt applied none of this pressure either, a third important reason that so little troop integration occurred during the war. Had the commander in chief demanded more mixing of army units and navy crews, it is likely military leaders would have consented. After all, while navy officers fiercely resisted opening the navy's general service to black people at the start of the war, Roosevelt succeeded in forcing them to do so. But the president appears never to have advocated for mixed military units. Throughout the war, military leaders sometimes claimed that their rigid unit-segregation practices simply followed the "Presidential directive" or the "President's policy."[75] To the extent that Roosevelt never demanded, requested, or even seriously considered anything else—despite his 1940 public promise that "intermingling of White and Colored personnel . . . shall continue to have my most serious consideration"—they had a point. In fact, Jonathan Daniels, the president's main aide on race matters, and Assistant Secretary of War John J. McCloy agreed, in a private phone conversation in September 1944, that the president and Secretary Stimson had, early in the war, "decided against mixed units, that they would adhere to the traditional policy of the Army in this respect."[76]

Roosevelt's wartime silence on—or outright opposition to—troop integration likely had several causes. Among them was his personal view that able-bodied, male citizens had a greater right to join the military than they did to serve in mixed units there. In correspondence with Navy Secretary Frank Knox in 1942, for example, he argued that black people were "liable to military and naval service in the defense of their country" but that this service need not be integrated: "I do not think it the least bit necessary to put mixed crews on the ships. I can find a thousand ways of employing them without doing so."[77] Furthermore, the staunch opposition to integrated troops of southern Democrats, whose support Roosevelt desperately needed for passage of his legislative agenda, must have only further cemented his personal convictions on the issue. Finally, there was the electoral calculus, something never far from Roosevelt's mind, especially in the run-up to the 1944 presidential election. Some whites in the South, disturbed by an administration that they perceived to be far too friendly to black people, warned Roosevelt to tread lightly on the "Negro problem." At the same time, growing numbers of black and liberal white voters in the North demanded that Roosevelt take a more courageous stand on civil rights, including mixing military units. Caught between these two competing voting blocs in the weeks before the election, Roosevelt offered military-related concessions to African Americans—for example, a pledge to integrate returning soldiers in army redistribution centers—but nothing related to mixed units. That the 1944 Republican Party platform and presidential candidate, Thomas Dewey, also refused to touch the issue provided little incentive for Roosevelt to risk alienating some white voters, southern Democrats in Congress, and military leaders.[78]

It was his successor, Harry S. Truman, coming to power after Roosevelt's sudden death in April 1945, who would eventually issue an executive order in July 1948 that led to the desegregation of the armed services. But not until another presidential election year and a full three years after the war's end did Truman show any sign that he supported—or countenanced—such a policy.[79] Throughout the war years, then, and across both the Roosevelt and Truman administrations, civil rights activists, at least on the issue of mixed military outfits, received little support from the White House.

Congress, the military leadership, and the president might have thought twice about this fact had more white Americans demanded change, as some did with increased black enlistment. Certainly, by war's end, the campaign for a voluntary mixed unit and then for broader integration had grown significantly and had come to include an impressive number of blacks and nonblacks alike. But it appears these people always represented a minority of the nation's population, albeit a vocal and active one. Three polls—one of nearly six thousand white enlisted airmen conducted in November 1942, another of forty-eight hundred white soldiers conducted four months later, and a third of two thousand white civilians in July 1943—all found that overwhelming majorities of whites favored separate units. Numerous other surveys of white civilians reported similarly broad support for other forms of segregation—in restaurants, neighborhoods, streetcars, and buses.[80] An inescapable point, then, is that the military segregated black and white units throughout the war in part because most whites preferred it that way.

But this is not to say, as military officials and others did, that these preferences required racial segregation, that, otherwise, whites' discipline, morale, and efficiency would have been fatally compromised or that "another war," in Hamilton Fish's words, would have erupted. The air force poll cited above had a fascinating, if puzzling, finding: while three-quarters of respondents thought that black and white people "should" serve in separate ground crews, a full 56 percent expressed no "personal objection" to serving in mixed ones. And in the army polling, as one later analysis noted, "there was a proportion of white soldiers, including many from the South, who professed no personal disapproval [of integration] but defended their support of separation as in deference to the opinion of others."[81] Moreover, once the army and navy began their modest experiments with mixed outfits,

they gathered copious evidence of the real-world feasibility, even desirability, of black-white integration. In Europe, for example, the army found
not only that black and white soldiers fought well in mixed companies, but
also that, according to one extensive poll conducted in June 1945, these
integrated experiences actually reduced "interracial" friction and improved
"interracial" understanding.[82] These poll results so thoroughly demolished
decades-long military justifications for segregated troops that the army
attempted to bury the results for months.[83]

Two final factors help explain the enduring power of black-white
segregated troop policies and the wartime failure to depart from them in
any substantial way. In contrast to the broadening of black people's enlistment opportunities, which constituted a return to earlier policies, the integration of black-white military units would have marked a signal break from
them. At a time of great change and existential uncertainty in the United
States, Congress, the president, and the military—and, it appears, many ordinary white people as well—found segregation's deep roots appealing and
were reluctant to modify one fundamental aspect of its fighting forces—
how they were organized. "We have taken as our basic policy that there
will be segregation of Negro regimental units," asserted John J. McCloy in
an April 1944 War Department statement. "This has been the policy of the
Army since the Civil War and even before. We are fighting a tough war and
our troops have to go against seasoned champions. Therefore . . . [w]e have
to go the tried way."[84]

Like tradition, federal law also appeared to side with segregationists.
While federal law, especially the STSA, seemed to require equal access—
or at least something approximating equal access—to enlistment, it
also required segregated military outfits, at least in some cases. Indeed,
in the Winfred Lynn case, his defense attorneys first attempted to attack segregated units, but they soon switched to the enlistment barriers
that draft quotas erected. This shift was unpopular among many original
supporters of Lynn, who hoped his case might undermine the legality and
constitutionality of segregation itself. But Lynn's main attorney, Arthur
Garfield Hays, thought otherwise. Because "the Supreme Court has time
and again held that segregation is lawful so long as accommodations are
equal," Hays argued that the much more realistic path to victory—or even
a hearing—was through a challenge of enlistment discrimination, not unit
segregation. Indeed, when the US Court of Appeals for the Second Circuit
ruled against Lynn, in February 1944, it declared unambiguously, "[T]he
appellant does not contend, and could not successfully do so, that after
selectees are lawfully inducted under the Selective Training and Service
Act of 1940 they may not be segregated into white and colored regiments.

Since July 28, 1866 federal statutes have made provision for separate Negro regiments."[85] Therefore, if the legality of the army's white and colored quotas was a matter of widespread dispute, the legality of its white and colored outfits was not. If Roosevelt, Congress, military leaders, and even large segments of the white public sought one more reason to oppose integrated black-white units, and it appears they did not, here it was, written indelibly in the laws of the land.

* * *

During the war, black people and their allies managed to mount an impressive and wide-ranging national struggle to desegregate the military. And while it failed to uproot the military's long-standing policy of segregated black units, it did enjoy several important successes. One was that, against all odds, it forced leaders, in and out of the military, to consider and, by the end of the war, to experiment more and more with mixed outfits. Given the power and entrenched nature of the opposition, it is hard to imagine any of these changes, modest as they might have been, occurring absent sustained and vigorous pressure from below. A related and perhaps even more important accomplishment was the way activists transformed black people's and growing numbers of nonblack people's approach to military segregation. By the late 1930s, it was a decades-old, taken-for-granted, noncontroversial foundation of America's armed forces. That changed dramatically over the course of a few short years, as protest steadily gained momentum and spread across broad swaths of wartime black, liberal, and Left America.

What changed? First, the interwar years were a time of political awakening for many black people, when a diverse range of antiracist activists sought to democratize—and often to integrate—workplaces and unions, voting booths and department stores, schools and housing, literature and music. As war mobilization began and thousands—soon many hundreds of thousands—of African Americans streamed into the military's swelling ranks, the armed forces became yet one more American institution to find itself the target of black people's strengthening civil rights struggles.[86] Second, the prospect of a mixed military spoke to a politically diverse collection of African Americans, liberals, and leftists. For liberals like many NAACP members and leaders, segregation denied black people's basic citizenship rights and polluted American democracy. For many leftists, various kinds of socialists and communists, it also bred divisions and distrust among an otherwise radicalizing working class. For them, integrating the military was one step toward integrating workers and transforming America's—and perhaps the world's—capitalist order.[87] Finally, the war, with the attendant intensified focus on unity and democracy and freedom and equality, made military segregation more conspicuous than ever. In his famous "Arsenal of Democracy" fireside chat, in December 1940, President Roosevelt warned ominously of "secret [Axis] emissaries [who] try to re-awaken long slumbering racial and religious enmities. . . . These trouble-breeders have but one purpose. It is to divide our people into hostile groups and to destroy our unity and shatter our will to defend ourselves."[88] Not a few Americans noticed, and were continually outraged, that the same could have been said, and increasingly was said, about America's own armed forces, an arsenal of division if there ever was one.

In the end, wartime activism paved the way for the postwar desegregation of the military. True, this much-celebrated policy change came about thanks to multiple factors—Cold War and Korean War imperatives, election-year politicking, the increasing power of black (and some liberal or antiracist nonblack) voters—but surely among them were the wartime struggles to abolish segregation in the military and to upend other forms of "Jim Crow in uniform." It is hard to understand or account for the postwar desegregation of the armed forces without appreciating the foundational work of these wartime activists. They changed hearts and minds, honed ideological arguments, established activist networks, experimented with different political tactics, and convinced growing numbers of people that a segregated military had no place in a true democracy.

CHAPTER 4

cⱴɔ

Separate Segregations

Throughout the war, African Americans and their allies often fought for the abolition of all military troop segregation on the basis of race.[1] But at times the goal seemed more limited: the abolition of anti-*black* segregation. In its early 1943 call for a "military New Deal," for example, the *Pittsburgh Courier* declared that "all segregated Negro units in all branches of the services [should] be abolished." Were these two camps, in fact, distinguishable? The *Courier* thought not. It contended that once black units were eliminated, "Americans of all colors and creeds, and from all States will be serving side by side in all parts of the far-flung battle-front."[2] It assumed, then, that the military assigned only black people to descent-specific outfits and, therefore, abolishing these outfits was tantamount to abolishing all troop segregation entirely. But was this, in fact, true?

According to some African Americans and their allies, the answer was clearly yes. They denounced military segregation for a wide range of reasons: it deflated black and "decent" white people's morale, dispirited "colored" allies overseas, widened petty racial divisions at home, confirmed Axis charges of American hypocrisy, trafficked in Hitler's toxic racial theories, fractured the working class, and trampled on the nation's purported democratic ideals and war aims. But some black people made an additional point: that military segregation was especially objectionable and unjust in that it targeted African Americans alone. A typical comment came from Channing Tobias, a black leader in the YMCA, in the spring of 1943: "It is absolutely impossible for the colored man not to be offended down to the very depths of their souls when they see Filipinos, Mexicans, Chinese and even native-born Japanese integrated into practically all arms of the services without discrimination and only the colored man completely segregated as if his presence were contaminating to other people."[3] In Tobias's view, then, only black people were "colored," and only "colored" faced "complete" military segregation.

Tobias had a point. From the start of the war to its end, African Americans faced the most rigid and widespread forms of descent-specific, military-unit segregation—that is, mandatory separation on the basis of one's descent or "race."[4] For black people, it was not simply that there were separate black units, but that there were, with rare exceptions, nothing but separate black units. All other groups always had much more variety regarding the outfits to which military authorities assigned them. Even in the case of Japanese Americans, the most thoroughly segregated of all nonblacks, one "relocation camp" newspaper accurately pointed out, "[t]he Negroes . . . are segregated in a more pronounced manner than the nisei will ever have to face."[5]

Even so, if Tobias meant to suggest, as the *Pittsburgh Courier* did, that no one but black people faced any troop segregation at all, then he was mistaken. The wartime army had at one time or another a surprisingly lengthy list of descent-specific outfits—made up not simply of African Americans, but also of American Indians and US citizens and aliens of Austrian, Chinese, Filipino, Greek, Japanese, Mexican, Norwegian, and Puerto Rican descent. True, many of these units represented only one of numerous places for, say, a Mexican, Chinese, or Greek recruit to serve, and thus did not involve mandatory separation. But in the case of others, the military, on the basis of descent, required inductees, or even voluntary enlistees, to join only particular descent-specific outfits. Throughout the war, then, while black people were the most "completely segregated" group, they were seldom the only segregated one.

Indeed, the story of nonblack troop segregation is largely unknown and remarkably complex. It varied over time and according to numerous factors, including, most important, descent or "race," of course, but also location of induction, timing of induction, gender, and even foreign-language ability. How and which ancestries mattered most hinged on everything from the particulars of the war to long-standing military policy, from the relative size of various descent groups to the curious unwillingness or inability of military leaders to consider how the policies targeting one nonwhite group might affect those of another.

NONBLACK, NON-JAPANESE OUTFITS

For decades prior to World War II, the organization of nonblack troops changed over time and differed between the army and navy. The latter had mixed crews throughout the nineteenth century, which included not just black sailors but also small numbers of Asian Americans, Native Americans, and Latin Americans.[6] By the first few decades of the twentieth century, as it began segregating (and excluding) black sailors, it also began extending these policies to other nonwhites. Immediately after World War I, for example, it experimented briefly (and, in the eyes of the navy, unsuccessfully) with an all-Samoan crew on a mine sweeper and all-Filipino crews on two destroyers. It also began restricting not just African Americans but also Filipinos and some other Asians and Pacific Islanders solely to the menial Messman Branch.[7]

As the navy moved from integration to segregation of a growing mix of nonwhites, the army eventually moved in another direction. During the Civil War it employed, beyond its "Negro" outfits, a broad range of descent-specific units, including New York's Irish Legion, Illinois's First and Second German Regiments, Wisconsin's Schwarze Jäger, and Kansas's Indian Home Guards.[8] In the postbellum years, the army had a series of Indian scout units, which fought in the "Indian wars" in the West. By the turn of the twentieth century, all but the "Negro" units had been disbanded. In World War I, a few National Guard outfits organized themselves around soldiers' ancestry—for example, New York City's largely Irish American "Fighting Sixty-Ninth" and the National Guard of Hawaii, which, in 1917, reorganized itself into separate Hawaiian, Filipino, Portuguese, Japanese, and "Anglo-Saxon" companies. But for the most part, the army—with the obvious and important exception of black people—barred "the formation of distinctive brigades, regiments, battalions or other organizations composed exclusively or primarily of members of any race, creed, political or social group."[9]

By 1940 and 1941, as the United States prepared for war, the army's and navy's policies regarding unit organization for nonblacks seem to have diverged somewhat. The navy's general service was open solely to whites, and so, according to one 1940 count, the 2 percent of its enlisted strength that the navy defined as neither "White" nor "Negro"—Chinese, Filipino, Samoan, Chamorro, Hawaiian, American Indian, and Puerto Rican—may have served, with some exceptions, in the Messmen Branch.[10] Indeed, as late as February 1942, one navy internal memorandum declared with more than a hint of pride, "The Navy of the United States is composed, except for messmen, of members of the white race."[11] It is worth emphasizing, however, that these members, if the 1940 breakdown accurately reflected navy policy and practice, nonetheless included broad swaths of the planet's people, including anyone it deemed nonblack from South or Central America, the Indian subcontinent, the Middle East, and all parts of Europe.

The army did things differently. As its ranks became ever more heterogeneous, thanks especially to the introduction of the draft in 1940, the army placed black people in "Negro" or "colored" units and everyone else in "white" ones. When army and draft officials faced occasional confusion about who precisely belonged to these broad categories, they explained that who was segregated from whom made all the difference: "All negroes or half-breeds may be classified as black. All others, including Filipinos, Mexicans, Chinese, Japanese, etc., will be listed as white, the reason for this being that the Army does not segregate these other men."[12] By the time the United States entered World War II, then, the navy organized itself around a white-nonwhite boundary (but seemed to define white fairly broadly), the army around a black-nonblack one.

Soon the war scrambled these seemingly straightforward lines. While the navy, as one official conceded in 1949, did not "keep accurate records on minorities," it seems that well before it began experimenting with white-black crews late in the war, it mixed other sorts of white-nonwhite ones as well.[13] For example, Chinese Americans, Puerto Ricans, and American Indians all served across the navy and marines throughout most of the war.[14] Perhaps the best-known collection of these service members—the Navajo Code Talkers—might seem to challenge this point. But while the Code Talkers trained as the all-Navajo 382nd Platoon in the marines, they then served in small teams in various regiments throughout the Pacific.[15] As it turns out, the iconic (albeit staged) image of Pima Indian Marine Ira Hayes—standing shoulder to shoulder with his white comrades in arms, raising the American flag at Iwo Jima—offers some sense of the level of integration that American Indians and some other nonwhites experienced in the World War II navy and marines.

The army's black-nonblack line also took some unexpected turns during the war. The War Department occasionally received requests to organize all–Mexican American, all–American Indian, all–Korean American, or all–Chinese American outfits, but it decided, in all four cases, that "integration with our armed forces is the best procedure in utilizing their services."[16] It largely stuck to this policy, dispersing hundreds of thousands of these troops across a wide variety of white army outfits. But the War Department also made occasional exceptions to the rule. In addition to several Native American units, the army and army air forces organized, in 1943, ten units—the 987th Signal Company and nine squadrons and companies that made up the Fourteenth Air Service Group—in which all enlisted personnel were Chinese Americans (officers were a mixture of whites and Chinese Americans). The purpose of these units, it appears, was to "further liaison relationships between American and Chinese troops" in China.[17]

The army made occasional exceptions with Mexican Americans, too. In early 1943, for instance, fearing that some Mexican American recruits were "without English, awkward, confused, unhappy," the army placed fifty-five of them in their own "special" "all Mexican platoon" with a "leader who could teach them in their own language, share their troubles, advise and encourage." But after basic training, the army scattered the men, three or four to a company, throughout an infantry regiment, reporting later that they had "fallen in on an equal plane with the English speaking men and more than hold their own." A longer-lasting exception was a single company in the Thirty-Sixth Infantry Division, which, at least initially, was composed solely of Mexican Americans, primarily from El Paso. It appears that the unit, like the "all Mexican platoon," emerged in part to address language barriers between some Spanish-speaking Mexican Americans and their English-speaking comrades.[18]

An even more significant blurring of the army's black-nonblack line came from its assignment of Puerto Ricans. To be sure, the army labored to impose this divide, placing "colored" Puerto Ricans in "colored" units and "white" Puerto Ricans in "white" ones, with the latter being by far the more numerous. Even so, the black-nonblack line remained murky, for at least two reasons. First, if the army dispersed "white" Puerto Ricans from the continental United States throughout regular "white" army units, it assigned "white" Puerto Ricans from Puerto Rico to outfits like the Sixty-Fifth Infantry Regiment, whose enlisted personnel were solely Puerto

Fig. 4.1 The Mexican American Company E, 141st Infantry Regiment at Camp Bowie in Texas, October 1941. Courtesy of Alex J. Carrillo Jr.

Rican and who were often kept separate from "continental" (read: whiter white) outfits. Second, units like the Sixty-Fifth Infantry, despite its official army designation as white, still had numerous members who, according to one War Department memo, "would have to ride the jim crow car in the [continental United States]." Indeed, when the army shipped the regiment to Panama, where the United States had previously promised "that no colored troops would be stationed," more than six hundred of its "unmistakably colored" men had to be reassigned to other "Puerto Rican units," perhaps "colored" ones.[19]

Also appearing to scramble the army's black-nonblack line were a series of "Free Battalions" it organized during the war. These units were composed of foreign nationals in the United States and their children who wished to help liberate their ancestral homelands from Axis control. By 1943, in response to President Roosevelt's politically inspired coaxing, the army had formed Austrian, Greek, Norwegian, and Filipino units—and had considered, but opted against, forming Italian, Polish, Czech, and Danish ones. By and large, the European units, often created as "special favors to foreign monarchs," fared poorly. Their connections

Fig. 4.2 Soldiers of the Puerto Rican Sixty-Fifth Infantry at Salinas, Puerto Rico, August 1941. Courtesy National Archives, SC 121824.

to unpopular past rulers or governments in exile stymied recruitment efforts, and soon the War Department, never thrilled with the idea of "foreign units" in the first place, began withdrawing its support. It quickly and unceremoniously disbanded the Greek and Austrian battalions, but the Norwegian Ninety-Ninth Infantry Battalion (Separate) survived the war intact, despite the fact that it repeatedly struggled to reach full strength as a consequence of too few "alien volunteers." Eventually the army resorted to assigning "all Norwegians reporting at reception centers to this unit," a clear sign that, at least for a time, they faced "mandatory separation."[20]

Some Filipino Americans appear to have faced the same. Following Japan's attack on Pearl Harbor and its invasion and occupation of the Philippines, many Filipinos in the United States demanded to "get a crack at the Japanese." The army responded, in part, by forming two Filipino infantry regiments—popularly known as the First and Second Fil—offering the roughly seven thousand men who joined the units "the eventual opportunity of fighting on the soil of their homeland."[21] Filipino Americans were not required to serve solely in these regiments—indeed, they had to

Fig. 4.3 The nucleus of the US Army's 122nd Infantry Greek Battalion at Camp Carson in Colorado, c. 1943. Courtesy Library of Congress, Prints and Photographs Division, LC-USW33-020998-C.

volunteer to join them—and perhaps as many as several thousand served in regular "white" army units instead. But it appears that some draft and army officials assigned Filipinos to the First and Second Fil, whether they volunteered for them or not. In at least one case, some Filipinos' integrated unit became segregated over time. In May 1944, growing antagonism between white replacement troops and Asian American soldiers from Hawaii convinced the army to reorganize the regiment into three battalions—one for whites, one for Filipinos, and one for a mixture.[22]

All told, the army began the war with a crystal-clear line when it came to the organization of its units—"Negroes" or "colored" on one side and everyone else mixed together on the other. Alternative lines soon appeared in the form of, say, an "all Mexican platoon" or a Chinese American company or a Puerto Rican regiment or a Norwegian battalion. At the same time, all these units were unlike "Negro" or "colored" outfits in that, with some variation across groups, Mexican Americans, Chinese Americans, Puerto Ricans, Norwegians, and all other nonblacks were never required to serve solely in descent-specific outfits. Indeed, in most cases, they did not. If hundreds of Mexican Americans, for example, served in Mexican American units, hundreds of thousands served in "white" ones.[23] With some notable exceptions, then, the army's black-nonblack organizational line seemed to hold throughout the war.

THE RISE OF JAPANESE AMERICAN SEGREGATION

But there was one further exception to this line that proved most significant of all. Among nonblacks, Japanese Americans faced the most extensive forms of descent-based segregation. But these policies, like those related to enlistment, also changed over the course of the war. At first Japanese Americans were completely integrated with nonblacks; then, starting in 1942, they moved increasingly toward greater segregation, only to move in the opposite direction in the final year of the war. Japanese Americans' troop assignments were complex, confounding, and capricious, for a variety of reasons: they developed alongside of and in response to specific and always-changing war developments; the core tenets of anti–Japanese American racism could push at once in both segregationist and integrationist directions; and Japanese Americans' relatively small numbers could make quick and repeated shifts in policy possible.

As with other nonblacks, the army did not segregate Japanese Americans on the eve of war. During World War I, the National Guard in Hawaii established a separate company for enlisted Japanese Americans, but no similar segregation on the mainland appears to have existed. In the interwar years, according to one army general, "the few Japanese who have served in the Army . . . were the subject of general"—that is, integrated—"assignment."[24] By 1940, the army was explicit that Japanese Americans would not be placed in descent-specific outfits and instead would be mixed with all nonblacks. In October 1940, shortly after passage of the Selective Training and Service Act, the War Department ordered that "the status of citizens of oriental descent who are selected for induction will be the same as other citizens," by which it meant nonblack ones. Two months later, the director of the Selective Service, Lewis Hershey, indicated that, on certain draft forms, "Japanese," like Mexicans, Chinese, and others, "will be listed as white," since, in contrast to its treatment of black people, "the Army does not segregate these other men."[25]

This integrationist policy toward Japanese Americans even weathered the attack on Pearl Harbor. Japanese Americans faced numerous hardships in the army at this time, from summary discharges to the eventual ban on their enlistment. But unit segregation was not one of them. Some whites would have preferred it. In February 1942, a newspaper reporter asked recent army selectees en route to their induction station whether they would willingly serve in a "mixed outfit." "Oh, sure," exclaimed a twenty-two-year-old from Brooklyn, Thomas Aniello. "I don't believe in that discrimination—except for the Japs." Indeed, a month earlier, the army did begin concentrating its recent Japanese American inductees in two training camps in the South. But those Japanese Americans who had already completed basic training were assigned to so-called white units, and the War Department issued very clear instructions, in January 1942, for all later inductees: once their training was complete, they would not be assigned to the armored force, the air force, the signal corps, and so forth, but "nor [would] they be grouped in specific units."[26] That Japanese Americans were allowed to serve neither in certain sensitive army branches nor as concentrated groups in particular outfits suggests the logic behind the army's integrationist policy: the racist fear of Japanese American disloyalty—which stood at the heart of so much army policy at the time, both regarding soldiers in uniform and civilians on the West Coast—also animated its integrationist decisions about the very organization of Japanese American troops. Whereas anti-black racism expressed itself in the form of segregated military outfits, anti–Japanese American racism expressed itself, at least early in the war, in the form of integrated ones.

Among the first challenges to this arrangement came from within the army, and perhaps surprisingly from an officer wishing to expand Japanese Americans' opportunities in uniform. In early April 1942, Lieutenant

General Delos Emmons, the army commander and military governor of Hawaii, wrote the War Department in Washington. He hoped to find a way for local soldiers of Japanese descent, who had been restricted since the attack on Pearl Harbor to labor units, to serve in combat outfits as well. These men, Emmons assured his superiors, "desire[d] to demonstrate their loyalty to the United States in a concrete manner." For reasons he did not explain, Emmons envisioned these new combat units as comprising only Japanese Americans. Inspiration for Emmons's segregationist suggestion may have come from his experience with the Varsity Victory Volunteers, a Japanese American manual labor support group, which he had established several months earlier and which had been working well at the time alongside an army outfit in Oahu. It may also have come from his belief that Japanese Americans could fight only in Europe or Africa, "where their physical characteristics will not serve to confuse our other troops."[27] Restricting Japanese Americans to segregated units made it easier to keep them all out of the Pacific theater and to avoid having to pull those from integrated units deployed there.

When the War Department quickly rejected Emmons's proposal, citing its policy of barring Japanese Americans both from combat outfits and from segregated ones, he tried again, adjusting his request somewhat. "It is recommended," he wrote in a May 11 telegram to the War Department, "that these [Japanese American] officers and soldiers . . . be distributed as far as practicable among [white] combat units or stationed as a [separate] unit at some interior post." Two weeks later Army Chief of Staff George C. Marshall shifted course and followed Emmons's segregationist suggestion. Breaking with army policy, decades old in the case of Japanese American troop integration, he authorized the formation of one combat unit from Hawaii "consisting of all officers and soldiers of Japanese ancestry." While, in the end, all of the unit's senior leadership would be white, all or nearly all of its enlisted personnel would consist of Hawaiians of Japanese descent.[28]

Sources are scarce as to why Marshall—and presumably the War Department—had such an abrupt change of heart. It is clear why Emmons—and, likely, his superiors in Washington—wished to ship a large contingent of Hawaii's Nisei soldiers to the mainland: fearing another Japanese attack on the islands was imminent, they questioned the "reliability of these [Japanese American] troops," who they also worried "would be shot immediately by the American [sic] troops." In Emmons's words, "A Jap in [an American] uniform is a Jap."[29] But the perceived urgent need to rid Hawaii of Nisei soldiers does not explain the decision to segregate them. Earlier that month the War Department had suggested the men's "transfer to the mainland for duty in Zone of Interior installations"; in other words, it proposed treating Japanese Americans from Hawaii the same as those on the mainland.[30] In the final days of May, however, for reasons that remain unclear, it quickly changed course, opting for segregation.

This change, regardless of its exact roots, would prove fateful. This provisional outfit would become the famed 100th Infantry—or "Purple Heart"—Battalion, which fought heroically in the European theater, helping in the process to expand army opportunities for all Japanese Americans. It also inaugurated an important army trend toward the ever more common segregation of Nisei troops.

In mid-1942, however, the 100th Infantry Battalion was, in its strictly segregated organization, the exception, not the rule. As Assistant Secretary of War John J. McCloy later pointed out, "At the time the 100th Battalion was reorganized . . . there were already on general assignment throughout the armed services a considerable number of Japanese Americans . . . scattered throughout the service commands in some tactical units. Their presence in units other than the 100th Battalion . . . was an indication that segregation as such was not the War Department policy."[31] Indeed, one official count from October 1942 revealed that the 3,857 soldiers of Japanese descent in the continental United States at the time were stationed at 160 different army posts all across the nation.[32]

If segregation would prove the way of the future, it was hardly preordained. As debates developed in and out of the War Department in the second half of 1942 about whether to reopen enlistment to Japanese American volunteers, debates also developed simultaneously about how these volunteers, and those Japanese Americans already in uniform, should be assigned. Should they be placed in segregated units like the 100th Battalion, in mixed units like the ones in which so many Japanese Americans served at the time, or in some combination? Suggesting the last of these options was someone named A. Lury in a July 1942 memorandum to a senior intelligence officer in the War Department. Lury recommended that "Nisei be brought into the armed service in two ways: creation of a single unit composed exclusively of Nisei; [and] individual enlistment and service in regular ranks." "The use of these two methods," he pointed out perceptively, "would answer possible charges of segregation." Among the integrationists was Harvard professor Edwin O. Reischauer, Asia specialist and future ambassador to Japan. In a September 1942 memorandum, which was forwarded to War Department leaders early the following month, he suggested forming a "special volunteer [combat] unit of Japanese Americans and other Americans who desired to serve with them," a version of the mixed unit that African Americans and their allies pushed for at precisely the same time. But Reischauer also seemed to believe that other Japanese Americans could serve in other, presumably mixed "combat units." Likewise, in its efforts to convince the army to treat Nisei like "every other American citizen," the Japanese American Citizens League also seems to have sided with integrationists, though they were more focused on regaining access to the military than on integration within it.[33]

But War Department leaders, especially those fighting to reopen army doors to Japanese Americans, seemed most inclined toward replicating the segregated model represented by the 100th Battalion. In Hawaii, soon after the 100th shipped out, all remaining Nisei soldiers there—those who had not been trained in combat: plumbers, carpenters, mechanics, equipment operators—were assigned to a segregated unit of their own—the First Battalion, 370th Engineer Special Service Regiment.[34] On the mainland, in June 1942, the head of the War Department's Military Intelligence Division recommended a "staff study . . . to determine the advisability of utilizing a small token force, composed of United States citizens of Japanese ancestry, both commissioned and enlisted, as combat troops in the European Theater." In September, this study flatly opposed the "military utilization" of Nisei—whether segregated or not. But Assistant Secretary of War John J. McCloy sought to keep the Japanese American "token force" idea alive. He wrote Secretary Stimson, in October, noting that while the army could "assimilate the [Nisei] total into many units of different types," he favored forming an "all-Japanese unit." It could "manifest its loyalty to the United States en masse, and this manifestation would provide the propaganda effect [in Asia and in the United States] desired."[35]

Stimson must have responded favorably, because McCloy soon asked an intelligence officer in the War Department's Far Eastern Branch, Colonel Moses W. Pettigrew, to study "the formation of a Nisei combat unit." When, a few weeks later, Pettigrew drew up plans for the unit, he too raised the possibility of assigning Nisei to units "in the same manner as other"—again, nonblack—"Americans." In the end, however, he also supported a "special combat unit," in his case a full, fifteen-thousand-strong infantry division, for which nearly "all existing commissioned and enlisted personnel of Japanese ancestry" would be made available. Such a unit, in Pettigrew's view, would boost Japanese American morale, have a "tremendous psychological value" at home and abroad, and be logistically simpler, since integrated units would have to screen Nisei members out before they moved to excluded areas of the West Coast or to the Pacific theater, where "(enemy) Japanese [could] infiltrate behind our lines in disguise."[36]

Soon the War Department General Staff and Stimson also endorsed a segregated unit—and advanced their own particular rationales for it. In addition to enumerating the same alleged logistical advantages, the former questioned Japanese Americans' loyalties and thought it would be easier to monitor a single segregated outfit than thousands of soldiers in assorted integrated ones. Interestingly, while McCloy supported segregation so that Japanese Americans could "manifest" their loyalty, the General Staff did so for fear they would manifest the opposite. Stimson, for his part, favored segregation because of the "fine esprit de corps" it would create among Japanese Americans and because, echoing his thoughts on the segregation of black soldiers, "friction and distrust . . . would inevitably decrease a mixed unit's fighting efficiency."[37]

By December the War Department General Staff had formally agreed to a plan to organize another segregated Japanese American unit along the lines of the 100th Battalion, but this time on a much larger scale. It would include one infantry regiment, one field artillery battalion, and one engineer company, all of which would be composed exclusively of Nisei enlisted men. Chief of Staff Marshall approved the plan on January 1, 1943, the War Department announced it publicly later that month, and President Roosevelt endorsed it in a public letter to Stimson in early February.[38]

Throughout its deliberations over the new Nisei outfit, soon to be named the 442nd Combat Team, War Department leaders seldom considered what Japanese Americans might think of its segregated nature. In raising the possibility that Nisei, leveling "charges of segregation," might oppose such a plan, the July 1942 memo from Lury was exceptional. Perhaps these leaders occasionally received assurances that, as at one early January 1943 meeting, "Nisei would have no objection to being put in a unit of their own." Indeed, in his message to President Roosevelt, Stimson assumed that an all-Nisei unit would foster, rather than undermine, a "fine esprit de corps." In a curious move, the War Department press release that announced the new "special" unit made it sound as if Japanese Americans themselves had asked for it. "This action has been taken," it claimed, "following study by the War Department of many earnest requests by loyal American citizens of Japanese extraction for the organization of a special unit of the Army."[39]

In fact, save one earlier Japanese American Citizens League (JACL) suggestion to form an all-Nisei "suicide battalion," which it had made in a desperate attempt to avoid mass removal, no evidence of any such requests seems to exist. Still, as War Department leaders had predicted, some Japanese Americans did accept segregation without seeming to think twice about it. In Hawaii in particular, while a few Japanese Americans groused about the "AJA [Americans of Japanese ancestry] unit"—"I'll be only too glad to serve if they will treat me as an American and not as an outcast as an AJA," one wrote in a private (censored) letter—these were lonely voices

Fig. 4.4 Members of the 442nd Combat Team train at Camp Shelby, June 1943. Courtesy Library of Congress Prints and Photographs Division, LC-USZ620-127110.

drowned out by the eager rush of thousands to enlist. Having faced neither mass removal nor mass detention, and being familiar with the segregated precedent set by the 100th Battalion, the Varsity Victory Volunteers, and perhaps even the World War I National Guard company, many Hawaiians of Japanese descent seemed to harbor few qualms about segregated service.[40]

As with enlistment, however, those on the mainland were another story entirely. JACL leaders Mike Masaoka and George Inagaki met with a top McCloy aide shortly before the War Department announced its segregated combat team and raised serious concerns. "We Japanese Americans were demanding equal rights, not special status," Masaoka recalled protesting, adding that "it was difficult to predict Nisei reaction to a call for volunteers for a segregated unit." In the end, however, despite misgivings among some leaders, and without time to survey its members, the JACL accepted the segregated plan. "In my lifetime there have been many decisions that I agonized over, that kept sleep away for long restless nights," Masaoka remembered years later. "[But] the decision to agree to a segregated combat team was not one of them."[41] Approaching the matter very differently was Jimmie Omura, longtime critic of the JACL and a writer at the *Rocky*

Nippon (later *Rocky Shimpo*), a Japanese- and English-language newspaper based in Denver. In no fewer than five blistering editorials and nearly as many letters to Secretary Stimson, all written in February 1943, Omura called the idea of a Nisei combat outfit a "disaster." "It would further segregate the Nisei in America and focus attention on the oft-repeated charge of unassimilability." "If there is a place for the Nisei soldier in Uncle Sam's army," he thought, "that position should be filled through the normal and common procedure akin to all races and nationalities here."[42] Omura's writings, not the JACL action, may have best approximated the true feelings of many mainland Japanese Americans on the segregation issue. In a National Opinion Research Center poll of approximately seventy-five Japanese Americans living outside the camps in Denver in March 1943, a full 89 percent of respondents thought "Caucasian and American-Japanese soldiers should . . . be put in the same units."[43]

Opposition to segregation was most pronounced and extensive in the camps. The army's recruitment efforts there were disastrous, leading to many hundreds of Japanese Americans refusing to complete government applications, to swear unqualified allegiance to the United States, and to

Fig. 4.5 Mike Masaoka (*second from left*), JACL leader and army corporal, poses with three of his brothers at Camp Shelby in Mississippi, April 1944. Courtesy Library of Congress Prints and Photographs Division, LC-USZ62-111188.

volunteer for the army. This disaster stemmed from multiple factors, but one of them has been too often overlooked: the War Department's decision to restrict Nisei volunteers to one segregated outfit. In early February, just as army teams began entering the camps to recruit volunteers, the War Relocation Authority (WRA) surveyed each camp and found that "almost without exception . . . the segregated nature of the Combat Team was particularly resented. It was interpreted as a further instance of discrimination against Japanese-American citizens, and on some projects references to 'Jim Crow' policies were made." At the Topaz camp, "evacuees" most wanted to know, "Why is separate combat unit necessary?" At Gila River, camp officials fretted about the "Jim Crow charges being circulated here." At Granada, what "seems to disturb the minds of the Nisei" was the decision "of segregating them apart from the regular combat units of the other Americans." At Heart Mountain, "most of them [Japanese Americans] question the feasibility of an All-Nisei Combat Unit, claiming they prefer fighting with other bloods." At Jerome, "after a week of discussions and unguided deliberations, evacuee reaction to the Army announcement still seems to center about the idea of segregation. Dissatisfaction over that feature was practically unanimous." At Minidoka, "expressions for gratification over Army recognition of Nisei are mingled with equally strong resentment of separate Army unit which is interpreted as segregation. Many young residents call it 'Jim Crowism.'" And at Rohwer, "many consider separate units racial segregation." One War Department memo later offered this summary: "there was an immediate and violent reaction by the evacuees in the relocation centers against the formation of a separate unit."[44]

This reaction did not soften over time. In late February, a member of McCloy's staff visited Manzanar and Poston and found army recruitment efforts stymied not only by a "general feeling of insecurity" and distrust of the War Department, but also by the issue of segregation: "many of the Nisei while perfectly willing to serve in the United States Army do not wish to serve in a segregated Japanese unit. They seem to feel that the segregation marked them as being apart from other citizens." By May 1943, McCloy, among the first and most vocal advocates for a Nisei unit, conceded that its "segregation feature was one of the formidable stumbling blocks that the Army recruiting teams ran up against when visiting the centers."[45]

The War Department scrambled to overcome Japanese American opposition in part by stressing two main points. The first was that, as Stimson insisted, "it is only because the War Department desires to aid the loyal Japanese Americans that a separate unit is being formed." "By giving loyal Japanese Americans an opportunity to form a unit of their own, of considerable tactical importance and for service in an active theater," another Stimson letter stressed, "Japanese Americans could, by an appropriate display of their loyalty and bravery, for all time set at rest the suspicions harbored by the uninformed elements of our population."[46] Since Japanese Americans already had a "unit of their own"—the 100th Infantry Battalion—the War Department never explained why a second one was necessary. The obvious answer is that all its top leaders, not least Stimson himself, shared these "uninformed" "suspicions." Much more than any "desires to aid loyal Japanese Americans," these suspicions explain the segregated unit's perceived necessity.

The second point was that the War Department was "not committed to a policy of segregation for Japanese Americans. . . . [T]here are well over two thousand Japanese Americans already in the Army serving in ordinary units in this country and abroad." What Stimson did not say is that, even at this point, roughly half of all Japanese American soldiers served in two segregated units—the 100th Battalion and the First Battalion in Hawaii— and that the War Department's commitments were continuing to move in this direction. Just as the formation of these two existing Japanese American units signaled a shift toward segregation, the formation of the 442nd Combat Team six months later only further confirmed it. Within a year of its formation, the army began using the team, in McCloy's words, as "an instrument of segregation," reassigning to the unit many of those two thousand or so Japanese Americans who had been scattered in hundreds of units and posts across the country.[47] Significantly, when the 442nd Combat Team, the 100th Battalion, and the First Battalion all reached full strength in the fall of 1943, the army began delaying Nisei inductions until room could be found for replacements to these units—and, with fewer and fewer exceptions, only these units. They were becoming, in McCloy's rueful words, "the one pool for all Japanese in the Army."[48]

As this comment suggests, all the while Japanese American resistance to segregation had begun to have its effects inside the War Department, especially among McCloy and his staff. They had supported—indeed, spearheaded—the combat team's formation, enthusiastically embracing its segregation as an unalloyed strength. When it proved to be among the unit's most glaring flaws in the eyes of many incarcerated Japanese Americans, they took note. As early as March 1943, six weeks after the combat team was first announced, McCloy's top aide, William Scobey, counseled his boss that "continuation of the segregation policy for [Nisei] soldiers in the Army would be of doubtful wisdom." By early May, McCloy agreed. In a memo to the War Department's head of personnel, he cited the recruitment problems that segregation caused in the "relocation centers," insisting for the first time that "it should be avoided if possible" going forward. While he and his staff remained committed to the 100th and the 442nd, they thought that segregating all or even most Japanese American troops was a serious mistake. In addition to alienating potential Nisei recruits, it denied the army precious personnel when the induction of perfectly qualified enlistees was delayed or denied, and it caused other inefficiencies when Nisei were transferred from integrated units to segregated ones. Of course, both points held even more true for black soldiers, but McCloy and his staff seemed blind to that fact. McCloy wrote of one air force technical sergeant who "was getting along well in an [integrated] air unit and now has been transferred to a [segregated] ground organization in which he has no connections and for which he has no particular bent."[49]

Soon this pressure from McCloy and his aides, who conveyed their new-found Nisei-integrationist leanings through internal War Department memos, conferences, and the like, prompted the War Department General Staff to consider, alongside the feasibility of reinstituting the draft for Nisei, the feasibility of their "general assignment"—or integration—across the so-called white army. Whereas the generals came to support the former, they unanimously opposed the latter. Following several weeks of memos and meetings on the subjects, the War Department General Staff recommended to Chief of Staff Marshall not only that "Selective Service be reinstituted for citizens of Japanese descent," but also that nearly all future Nisei recruits, thought to be ten thousand altogether, be assigned exclusively to current and future segregated units—first, to the 100th and 442nd as replacements and then, only after these needs were fully met, to "additional [segregated] combat and service units" to be designated as needed. This proposal was by far the most sweeping Japanese American–related segregationist plan that the army ever considered. On November 30, 1943, General McNarney, Marshall's deputy chief of staff, approved the plan. The War Department seemed bound for a dramatic expansion of Japanese American segregation.[50]

In formulating and ultimately adopting these recommendations, War Department brass cited a mix of old and new concerns: integration would "distribute thousands of foci of uncertainty with resulting anxiety in staging areas, lines of communication and actual combat"; it would disadvantage Nisei since their commanders would refuse to promote them to positions of authority over "American caucasian troops"; it might lead to "a violent display of [white] racial prejudice"; and it would continue to pose logistical problems, since Japanese American troops, they assumed, could not be deployed to the Pacific.[51] Provost Marshall General Allen W. Gullion raised a fascinating additional point that no one else seemed to pick up on: integrating Nisei would magnify African Americans' already growing outrage over their own segregation. As a result, Gullion thought "no one short of the Commander-in-Chief should order the general assignment of Japanese-Americans with its resulting emphasis on colored segregation."[52]

A RETURN TO "GENERAL ASSIGNMENT"

On the evening of January 20, 1944, the War Department announced the reinstitution of the draft for Japanese Americans, but its statement, and the first news reports about the move, made no mention of the equally significant plan to segregate nearly all these draftees.[53] Nonetheless, news soon began to circulate in and out of the camps to this effect. The following day, a WRA official telegrammed Minidoka camp administrators: "It is expected that the majority of nisei after basic training will be assigned to duty with the 100th Infantry Battalion or the 442nd Combat Team." Two days later, the *Salt Lake City Tribune* got closer to the truth. It stated that new Nisei draftees "will not . . . serve with other troops except as needed in military intelligence work."[54]

Japanese Americans responded to the reinstitution of the draft in various ways—from an enthusiastic embrace to a grudging acceptance to fierce defiance. While numerous issues informed these disparate responses, opposition to this widely expanding segregationist assignment policy was surely among them. In petitions, resolutions, letters, posters, meetings, newspaper editorials, and even draft resistance itself, a broad cross-section of Japanese Americans may not have agreed on the merits of Selective Service. They did share, however, a staunch opposition to segregated Nisei combat units. For some, this opposition stemmed more from the units' designation as combat than as segregated. At Topaz, for example, "young fellows felt that the Japanese Combat units are being used for landing spear heads," citing the ever-growing casualty rates of the 100th Infantry Battalion in Europe. For many Japanese Americans, the two issues were no doubt hard to disentangle. Regardless, opposition to Nisei segregation was widespread. Indeed, even among the minority of Japanese Americans who supported segregation from the start, some changed their minds fast. While the *Heart Mountain Sentinel*, in January 1944, defended army segregation as a salve against "lonesomeness for friends of kindred spirit and interest," two months later this same segregation was "a type of discrimination which sets a precedent endangering our struggle for equality and tolerance."[55]

Among those Japanese Americans who welcomed the draft news, some did so despite serious concerns about segregation. It was among the "weak points" of the army's new plan, conceded the *Minidoka Irrigator*, the official camp newspaper, but "the reinstitution of the draft" was nonetheless "beginning to open the door for further privileges for us and the rest of the minority groups." Similarly, some Japanese Americans applauded the War Department's move, while also making requests or demands of the government, among them the greater integration of Nisei troops. A late February petition from the "U.S. Citizens Committee" at the Topaz camp in Utah called the reinstitution of the draft a "great step . . . in recognizing the application of the Principles of American Democracy to all people regardless of race or color." The committee, however, was also "deeply disturbed about segregation of Nisei into their own units" and recommended that Japanese American draftees be mixed throughout all branches of the military. This way they "would assimilate with all free Americans . . . as one united brotherhood for democracy." Similarly, two days later, at Heart Mountain in Wyoming, nearly six hundred Nisei signed a petition to President Roosevelt in which, echoing the Topaz group, they also hailed the Selective Service move as "a big step toward the application of American principles." But they too had reservations. Since "many of us may be called any day, many of us may not return until victory is won, and some of us may never return," they asked the president to carefully consider seven points. The first of these made plain that "any further segregation from other Americans is unnecessary and undesirable, as it is much against our wishes to be segregated at all."[56]

Even the JACL, which had signed off on Nisei segregated troop assignments and which had long been among the government's most loyal defenders, paired its hearty support for reopening the draft with the insistence that future Nisei inductions be "unsegregated." "Just as this nation is a country composed of men of all racial ancestries," its newspaper the *Pacific Citizen* opined, "so must her army reflect multitudinous racial strains of the population." Several weeks later the JACL's Intermountain Council sent a resolution to McCloy. It thanked him for the new selective service opportunities, but asked that future draftees at least be given the option to join integrated outfits.[57]

Other Japanese Americans kept their views on the draft to themselves but pressed the War Department to integrate Nisei soldiers just the same. At the Granada camp in Colorado, in late February and early March 1944, the Community Council presented a wide-ranging list of eleven "requests" to numerous government officials, since "the rights and privileges of citizenship should, in all justice, be combined with the duties and obligations of citizenship." The second of these asked "that Japanese-American servicemen who are called to the colors hereafter be co-mingled with citizens of other racial extractions and not be assigned to segregated units." Similarly, in a poignant appeal sent to Secretary Stimson and General Emmons, forty-three Minidoka mothers "plead with heart-felt earnestness that our sons be granted the dignity of serving in the United States Army as free and equal American citizens, and they . . . not be segregated in any special combat unit."[58]

In the end, countless draft-age Nisei undoubtedly complied with the draft despite deep misgivings about the injustices they faced, including the segregated units. "It's known that many nisei resent their being segregated into special combat units," wrote one Japanese American columnist in the *Granada Pioneer*, the "evacuee" newspaper there. "Still, they are making and will continue to make the supreme sacrifices for rights that they are not quite sure they have." At Topaz, "a number of young fellows" willing to comply with the draft tried to leave the camps after its announcement. Loath to join the Japanese American outfits, they ran "the chance of getting lost in an all-American unit if drafted where Japanese Americans were scarce."[59]

But several hundred Japanese Americans openly defied the draft until the government fully restored their rights, which sometimes included not simply the right to live beyond barbed-wire prison camps, but also the right to serve in mixed units throughout the military. Journalist Jimmie Omura, who one year earlier had warned Stimson about Niseis' growing antipathy to their segregation in the army, wrote him again with another dire warning after the draft's reinstatement: A "general movement is on in relocation centers to petition for redress of grievances," which will involve a "refusal to bear arms." "Those who are protesting now, and I am inclined to believe that the great number hold this view," Omura added, "object to army segregation." He was right—both about some Niseis' planned resistance to the draft and about army segregation as one important motivation for it. At the Poston camp, for example, George Fujii, the most prominent draft resister there, launched his political organizing in response to the reinstitution of selective service with a circular that he posted around the camp with seven demands. The last of these was that the "Japanese soldier must be mixed with other Caucasian soldier [*sic*] to fight side by side." At Heart Mountain in Wyoming, in early 1944, a small group of Nisei formed the Fair Play Committee and organized regular protest meetings. Beyond mass removal and mass confinement, its largest grievance, in the words of one of its statements, was that "without rectification of the injustices committed against us nor without restoration of our rights as guaranteed by the Constitution, we are ordered to join the army thru *discriminatory procedures* into a *segregated combat unit!*" By early March, it declared that until these grievances were addressed, its members would not comply with the draft.[60]

Joining these Japanese American critics of Japanese American segregation were a growing number of white allies. Shortly after the War Department announced the reinstitution of the draft for Nisei, it received dozens of appeals, often in the mail but sometimes in person, "to allow draftees to serve in ordinary, un-segregated units." Such outfits were what "all thoughtful Nisei" wanted, one man from Elgin, Illinois, insisted. While the "segregation of American citizens according to ancestral lines is un-American, undemocratic," and at odds with the country's war aims, "racial intermingling will bring about better understanding between the racial groups that make up America," argued two men from the Chicago area. "We are missing a great chance by not breaking away now from the old pattern of Negro segregation in the army," argued one white activist from California. "But we are doing worse than nothing for the new policy of segregating those of Japanese parentage adds insult to injury."[61]

The federal government moved fast to stamp out protest in the camps while continuing its work to convince Japanese Americans and their friends of segregation's necessity. Having to make the case was often McCloy's office, which trotted out arguments that it simultaneously dismissed in private. At a War Department meeting in November 1943, McCloy's aide supported integrating Nisei draftees "in the same manner as any other [nonblack] inductee," but he argued publicly that "military considerations" required segregation. Well after McCloy himself stopped asserting that pulling Nisei troops from units deployed to the Pacific presented major logistical problems, his aides continued to contend to protesters that this process would be hopelessly disruptive and inefficient.[62]

All the while, McCloy and his staff persisted in their behind-the-scenes, months-long battle to assign more Nisei troops to white units. In early March 1944, as Japanese American protest against the draft and against segregation escalated in the camps, they strongly objected to the reassignment of more than eight hundred Japanese American troops from white units in the service commands to the 100th Battalion and the 442nd Combat Team, a process of deepening segregation that had been in the works for many months. McCloy worried that Stimson's February 1943 statement that "the War Department is not committed to a policy of segregation for Japanese Americans" no longer rang true. "The disturbing thought," wrote McCloy to the War Department's chief of military personnel, M. G. White, was that "the policies which we are, in fact, practicing are not consistent with the policy which has been expressed by the Secretary of War regarding segregation." The War Department, in his view, was "saying one thing and doing another." In the end, what McCloy requested, curiously, seemed something of a retreat from his earlier appeals: not "general assignment" for many future Nisei inductees but only for those "specially qualified personnel"—doctors, dentists, nurses, mechanics, and the like—"so that their special qualifications could be utilized."[63]

Ten days later, M. G. White responded with a newfound willingness to compromise, and not just on specialized personnel. "I am directing that a study be prepared to provide for the assignment of inducted Japanese Americans without discrimination," he promised. He wanted to assign future inductees first to the existing Nisei 100th and the 442nd combat units, but "any surplus remaining after these replacement requirements are met will be assigned without regard to racial considerations."[64]

Several weeks later, the War Department officially shifted course—in the novel direction of greater integration, not segregation. In an early April 1944 memo to Chief of Staff Marshall, White recommended the main thrust of the changes he had outlined to McCloy: the War Department's top assignment priorities for Nisei inductees should remain the same—finding, in addition to more linguists, soldiers for all-Nisei units like the 100th, the 442nd, and the 1399th Engineer Construction Battalion, a newly redesignated version of Hawaii's First Battalion. But when those priorities were met, White recommended that "surplus . . . be used as replacements to the European and North African theaters without being earmarked for specific units." Significantly, White estimated that a full 75 percent of all future Nisei inductees—more than eleven thousand men in total—would be among the "surplus" "available for general assignment." When the linguists, who also would be integrated, are added, White was recommending that more than eight in ten future Nisei soldiers—roughly half of their wartime total—serve in mixed outfits. When, by mid-April, the rest of the War Department General Staff and then Deputy Chief of Staff McNarney approved the plan, Nisei integration, not segregation, was reestablished as the army norm going forward.[65] These changes constituted a swift and significant reversal of War Department policy on Japanese American troop assignments. In the span of four short months, it moved from its most expansive segregationist policy back to a hybrid segregationist/integrationist one, with an increasing emphasis on the latter.

Why the change—especially at precisely the time that growing demands for an abolition of black or all segregation across the armed forces continued to fall on deaf ears? The reinstitution of Selective Service played an important, precipitating role. Because the navy, marines, and air corps refused to take any of the eventual thousands of new Nisei draftees, the army had to find a place to put them all. In time, the existing segregated units could take only a fraction of these men, forcing the War Department's hand: Would it create more such units, as it did with African Americans throughout the war and as its November 1943 policy envisioned? Or would it mix Nisei into any number of so-called white outfits across the so-called white army?

It chose the latter, it seems, in part because it was reminded at precisely this moment of the enormous logistical headaches and inefficiencies that segregation caused. At the very same time that M. G. White promised McCloy a reconsideration of Japanese American assignment policies, he was struggling to find ample and timely replacements for the existing Nisei combat units. Indeed, solving this problem was the primary reason for reinstating the draft for Japanese Americans in the first place; and the draft did solve this problem—eventually. But in early 1944, a temporary but nonetheless frustratingly long lag developed between drafting Japanese Americans and inducting them, causing the replacement shortages (and the transfer of those eight hundred or so Nisei troops from service commands to the combat units that irked McCloy and his staff). Explaining these complications, the War Department cited a convoluted set of Selective Service procedures, but the most fundamental problem was none other than segregation itself. Indeed, finding replacements for the Japanese American combat units would have been infinitely easier had they not been Japanese American. Had they simply been "unsegregated" army units open to any number of draftees, regardless of ancestry, the War Department's problems would have been solved, as it could have drawn from an infinitely broader pool of potential replacements. By opting for general assignment for more Japanese Americans, the War Department seemed to get wise to the fact that widespread Nisei segregation was more trouble than it was worth.

Several additional factors further facilitated the War Department's shift in this direction. First, of course, was the increasing pressure it received from McCloy and his office, which was itself partially a product of Japanese Americans' rising and increasingly outspoken opposition to their segregation. Although McCloy was a steadfast obstacle to change for African Americans, he helped advance it for Japanese Americans. Second, the shift was a return to an earlier policy of integration rather than a further departure from it. In contrast to the case of African Americans, for example, whose exclusive assignment to segregated army outfits dated back at least to the Civil War, separate Nisei units, which were never the sole place for Japanese American troops, were no more than two years old. Third, also in contrast to the case of African Americans, little pressure outside the War Department demanded segregated Nisei units. Whereas southern Democrats in Congress advertised their dogged determination to preserve "Negro" units, no groups in Congress made a similar stand regarding Nisei ones. Indeed, even Japanese Americans' most vitriolic detractors from the western states rarely demanded that Nisei soldiers be segregated, only that they be excluded from the West Coast and the broader Pacific theater.[66] Fourth, Japanese Americans' much smaller numbers in comparison with African Americans' assured the War Department that their general assignment would have minimal impact on the army as a whole. As it considered greater Nisei integration in the spring of 1944, the head of its Operations Division pointed out that "these personnel should not impose any racial problems because possibly not more than 10,000 Japs will be in the entire Army out of units composed exclusively of Japs."[67]

This line exemplifies a final key factor in the War Department's 1944 shift toward Nisei general assignment: War Department leaders could simultaneously support this cause and cling to the core tenet of anti–Japanese American racism—the notion that "Japs" and Japanese Americans were one and the same and thus forever suspect. In fact, at the start of the war, fears of Nisei disloyalty were cited as a reason for their integration, not against it.

In a war full of twists and turns regarding Nisei troop assignments, this 1944 swerve was the last of all. After this point, the War Department simply committed itself more fully to Japanese American integration. In June 1945, while it continued to exclude some Nisei troops from the "Pacific and Asiatic areas," it ordered that "otherwise Japanese-Americans may be assigned in the same manner as any other [nonblack] American replacements, either general service or limited service." By October 1945, "with the cessation of hostilities," the War Department personnel division considered "placing . . . enlisted personnel of Japanese descent in exactly the same status as other [nonblack] enlisted personnel," which would include completely integrated troop assignments. In December 1945, the War Department made it official, removing all remaining restrictions related to the "assignment of soldiers of Japanese descent," effectively mixing them across the entire "white" army.[68]

* * *

In comparison with black people, nonblacks as a whole faced limited segregated troop assignments during World War II. All these groups, from Chinese Americans and Puerto Ricans to Mexican Americans and Filipino Americans, had much greater access to integrated units than did African

Americans. By contrast, black people, throughout the war and with few exceptions, were forced to serve exclusively alongside other black people (and their white senior officers). Even Japanese Americans, the most segregated of all nonblack groups, never faced anywhere near this level of segregation in the army. They were completely integrated at the start of the war and increasingly so by its end, and even toward the middle, at the height of their segregation, significant numbers of Nisei soldiers remained in "white" units.

In a sense, then, the black-nonblack line held in the military's—especially the army's—wartime troop assignments: African Americans had exceedingly few if any opportunities to serve in integrated outfits; everyone else had either some opportunities or, more often, a great many. But this range was at times substantial and significant, and should not be obscured by too great a focus on the otherwise all-important black-nonblack divide. Huge differences separated Japanese Americans, who, for a time, faced considerable troop-assignment segregation, and, say, Mexican Americans, American Indians, and European ethnics, who faced none or virtually none at all.

But the story is more complicated still. Sometimes factors like gender, the time and place of induction, and even one's foreign-language abilities could help determine whether one served in a "white" or another outfit. Japanese Americans, for example, were much more likely to serve in the former if any of the following applied: they were women (once, that is, Nisei women were permitted to join the Women's Army Corps [WAC] in June 1943); they had the indispensable Japanese-language skills to serve as translators and interpreters; or they joined the army, roughly, before the summer of 1942 or after the spring of 1944. The chance of Puerto Ricans being integrated into a range of white units was greatly increased when the army inducted them in the continental United States rather than Puerto Rico.

Of course, one's ancestry, descent, or "race" mattered most when it came to these questions of integrated or segregated assignments. What, then, explains some of the great variations in these assignments based on descent? That is, what explains the variations both between blacks and nonblacks and among the latter? One answer is that leaders made no effort to avoid these variations by crafting comprehensive troop assignment policies that applied to all, or even some, nonwhite groups. Instead, as with enlistment, they often approached these different groups more or less in isolation. There were exceptions to this rule, of course—for example, General Gullion's fear that integrating Nisei troops would further antagonize black ones. Still, when it came to questions about segregated or integrated troop assignments, leaders nearly always tackled them on a group-by-group basis, with little sense of or concern about how policies regarding one nonwhite group might affect, support, or contradict those of another.

The most striking example of this point comes from Assistant Secretary of War John J. McCloy, mainly because he was deeply involved in crafting War Department policy regarding both African Americans and Japanese Americans. Indeed, according to his wartime diary, it was not wholly uncommon for him to address both issues on the same day. Yet he appears to have seldom considered these issues together or as related in any way, which expressed itself at times in the form of glaring inconsistencies. With equal amounts of passion, for example, he simultaneously denounced segregation (Nisei-white) and defended it (black-white). When engaged in the former, not only did he fail to consider black segregation, he actively erased it as a problem. In a common construction that he and other War Department leaders employed, integrating Nisei soldiers meant treating them "like everyone else" or "as any other inductee," which ignored what should have been an obvious fact to McCloy, of all people: not everyone was integrated. Many scholars have persuasively shown how "relational formations of race" undergird white supremacy and colonialism. But a kind of a-relational perspective can lead to similar ends. In discussing Japanese American issues while willfully ignoring African American ones, McCloy sought to erase not only the problem of black segregation, but also his responsibility to consider its solution.[69]

Troop assignment policies varied across groups also because they always had. By World War II, the military had long treated black people as exceptional in this regard, had long cordoned them off in their own particular units, and had long abandoned similar policies regarding other groups, if it had ever considered them in the first place. In a sort of anti-black path dependency, the military needed only to stick with the status quo to segregate African Americans more thoroughly—a lot more thoroughly—than any other group. And that is precisely what it did. This status quo had generated no shortage of powerful true believers—from southern Democrats and the military leadership to President Roosevelt and ordinary white Americans—who could not conceive of a military that did not segregate every last one of its black troops. This was not the case for any other groups, a fact that gave military leaders a lot more leeway to create ad hoc policies in their case—and to create some variation in the process.

Yet the war witnessed real change in troop assignment policy, which brings up a third factor in explaining policy variation: a group's real or imagined connections to America's wartime enemies and allies—and, crucially, how racist ideas shaped the meaning of those connections. That the United States fought against Japan and with China and the Philippines helps to account for why some Asian Americans gained greater access to "white" units than did others. But the United States fought Germany and Italy as well, and the military never segregated recruits of German or Italian descent—whether they were US citizens or not. The sometimes unstated assumption was that Italians and Germans in the United States were, for the most part, really Americans, and among those few who were not, their disloyalties could be readily detected. Not so for Japanese Americans, whose "racial ties" to Japan made them forever suspect, forever inscrutable, forever foreign—and sometimes segregated, too.[70]

A final key factor in policy variation involved the simple issue of numbers. In the army, for example, while African Americans, by the end of the war, comprised roughly one in ten inductees, Puerto Ricans constituted nearly one in two hundred; Japanese Americans, slightly more than one in four hundred; and Chinese Americans, Filipino Americans, and American Indians, approximately one in five hundred each. These numbers ensured that, while the integration of black troops would affect a significant portion of the army, the integration of all other nonwhite groups would not. Therefore, while McCloy, for example, dismissed the possibility of problems arising from Nisei (and other nonblack) integration, which "would mean a ratio of less than two [men] to a company," he feared the realization of "terrible prophecies" if hundreds of thousands of black troops mixed with whites. These fears also explain why the navy, when it began experimenting with integrated auxiliary ships at war's end, capped the percentage of black sailors on any one ship at 10 percent. It also explains why, when the army assigned Japanese American women to white WAC units, it limited their enlistment numbers.[71]

Regardless of these variations and their causes, who was responsible for nonblack descent-specific outfits? True, there were some popular and political demands for these units, the "foreign legions" especially. But for the most part, military leaders seem to have had a free hand to create—or not to create—these outfits. Recall that the War Department, for example, seemed more or less unilaterally to turn down several requests to form Chinese American, Korean American, Mexican American, and American Indian units. Conversely, when it decided to create a handful of Nisei outfits like the 100th and 442nd, it seemed again neither to solicit nor to receive much, if any, feedback from Congress or the White House. In contrast, both these branches of government, along with the military, played an important hand in protecting and greatly expanding the tradition of "Negro" or "colored" outfits.

Unlike what occurred in enlistment battles, African Americans and Japanese Americans did sometimes find common cause in fighting segregated units. A black newspaper spoke out against the formation of the 442nd Combat Team, insisting "that the proven method of Americanizing the army is to do away with racial units." For their part, some Japanese Americans leveraged the potent Jim Crow metaphor to decry not only their own segregation but, at least implicitly, black people's too. When "many of the young men [at Minidoka] objected to the creation of an all-nisei unit, classifying this as 'Jim Crowing,'" for example, they seemed to condemn "Jim Crowing" in all its forms and whomever its target. Sometimes Nisei made this point explicit, even without reference to Jim Crow. "The segregative plan of the Japanese-American," wrote one man to Secretary Stimson from the Jerome camp in Arkansas, "will inevitably lead to a duplication of the segregative treatment of the Negroes with all its social and moral evils." Sometimes Japanese Americans took an even broader view, which implicitly included African Americans among others, demanding that the military mix "multitudinous strains of the population" and suggesting that any advances they secured in the military would and should benefit "all minority groups."[72]

But the most significant connection between Japanese American and African American integrationist struggles came late in the war with the formation of the National Committee to Abolish Segregation in the Armed Services (NCASAS). The original impetus for this organization's formation was the "government's policy of segregating Negro and white troops," but that focus broadened over time. This happened no doubt in part because the JACL sent three members of its fledgling New York City office— Peter Aoki, Clara Clayman, and Ina Sugihara—to attend the inaugural New Jersey summit. Clayman, who had been a WRA official at Gila River and then was active in the Lynn Committee to Abolish Segregation in the Armed Forces for a time, joined the planning committee "to perfect plans for the organization." And Sugihara—who, upon moving to New York City in 1942, immediately began political organizing among Japanese Americans and African Americans, socialists and pacifists there—served on the "Committee on Statement."[73] Perhaps it was her input and perspective that gave the NCASAS's resolution its expansive scope: "it is totally inconsistent with the great sacrifices which all elements of our nation are making to establish, preserve and perpetuate freedom upon this earth that the Negro soldiers and soldiers of other minority groups should be subjected to segregation and discrimination." Perhaps it was the JACL contingent as a whole that also impressed upon the NCASAS the need to reach out to all "minority groups, such as Negro, Mexican, Chinese, Filipino, and

Japanese in order to secure concerted action." In the end, this organization did not last, but during its short life, the JACL appears to have been an early and active member—and it continued to speak out against all military segregation in the postwar years.[74]

In contrast, with the exception of Jews, no other "minority groups" seem to have been involved in these efforts.[75] That none faced much military troop segregation helps explain why. This point also explains why, for all their newfound connections, some African American and Japanese Americans continued to avoid or failed to consider cooperative efforts on the issue of segregated troop assignments. Like some black people, who mistakenly believed that they alone faced these troop assignments, some Japanese Americans showed a lack of awareness of, or blindness to, African Americans' plight on the issue. When, in late 1943, Mike Masaoka wrote to McCloy to oppose the further segregation of Nisei troops, he insisted that they, instead, "would prefer to be treated as all other Americans and not as a special class." In adopting the "all other Americans" construction, Masaoka, like McCloy and others in the War Department, unwittingly erased black people as "Americans" and black segregation as a problem worthy of attention.[76]

Sometimes African Americans and Japanese Americans sought to distance themselves from one another. In the rare instance when a black newspaper took note of and opposed Nisei segregation, it did so without ever mentioning black segregation or attempting to connect the issues at all, perhaps because it seemed to accept—or at least not to contest—the common, racist notion that Japanese Americans were especially suspicious and dangerous. "If there are doubts about Japanese loyalty," the *Baltimore Afro-American* offered, "it would appear safer to have them interspersed with other races than to confine them to a single unit. . . . If an army of eight million can't assimilate a few thousand Japanese-Americans, then the army is more afraid of the Japanese than most of us realize."[77]

As for Japanese Americans, a War Department official claimed that some of them "bitterly resented" their segregation in the army "on the theory that it places them on the same plane with colored people." Some evidence supports this observation. Reviewing the varied responses of incarcerated Japanese Americans to the news of the 442nd Combat Team's formation and the advent of voluntary enlistment for it, historian Takashi Fujitani points out that some Japanese Americans, "reflecting their understanding of African Americans as the most abjected group within the military, worried about themselves falling into the category of 'Negroes.'"[78] Indeed, when some Nisei lobbied the War Department for integration, they sometimes did so in a particularly limited way, by involving only themselves and whites. One man writing from Chicago "via the Colorado Relocation Center, Poston, Arizona," wished simply to train and fight with his "Caucasian buddies." When future draft resister George Fujii first circulated his demands around the Poston camp in early 1944, the last one called not for the abolition of all military segregation but simply for the "Japanese soldier [to] . . . be mixed with other Caucasian soldier [sic] to fight side by side." According to one internee's study of Topaz, this desire to be integrated with whites alone had a strategic side to it: "It is presumed in post-war times Japanese American comrades"—and presumably African American ones as well—"will be in a far less advantageous position to help in the program of restoring the Japanese minority to full acceptance in American communities than would their erst-while Caucasian comrades with whom they had faced death on the battle-fields."[79] Motivating Japanese Americans' fight for military integration of one kind or another was the desire by some to connect with black people and by others to push them away.

Whether in concert with African Americans or not, broad swaths of Japanese Americans, especially those in camps, actively and forcefully contested their segregation. They did so through letters and petitions, through editorials and resolutions, and, most dramatically, through a firm refusal to volunteer for, or even to be drafted into, the US Army. Toward war's end, they also began generating and garnering the support of some whites. But Japanese Americans, in pressing for general assignment, never produced anywhere near the same level of white attention and support that African Americans did; they never managed to sit down with President Roosevelt, members of Congress, or, beyond McCloy, with the highest levels of military leadership; they never tried to persuade Congress to consider legislation on the matter; they never launched a broad, nationwide campaign, including Left, labor, religious, civic, educational, and other organizations, to make their case. There are numerous obvious reasons for this: they were a much smaller, much less well organized, and much less politically connected group, and at least on the mainland, they were largely incarcerated.

Despite these formidable handicaps and despite Japanese Americans' inability to marshal the same sort of sweeping integrationist struggle that black people did, their activism arguably had a greater impact on military policy. In early 1944, the War Department shifted dramatically from a policy of increasing Nisei segregation to one of increasing Nisei integration. This shift would be hard to imagine absent McCloy's consistent pressure, which would be equally hard to imagine absent vigorous Japanese Americans' protest against their segregation, which eventually brought McCloy around on the issue. But, of course, that Japanese American activism on this issue succeeded where African American activism largely failed had little to do with the activists themselves. Instead, it had everything to do with the deep structural constraints on the latter. In their struggles to desegregate military troop assignments, black people battled the military, the courts, Congress, the White House, decades of tradition, and more. Japanese Americans contended mainly with the War Department or, in time, only parts of it.

PART III

Classification

CHAPTER 5

༄

The Boundaries of Blackness

In July 1943, Adjutant General J. A. Ulio, the chief administrative officer of the US Army, wrote Lewis B. Hershey, the director of the Selective Service System, with a seemingly straightforward request. Ulio wanted Hershey's agency "to investigate and determine the correct racial classification" of five men, all from New England and New York—James Barrows, Arthur F. Nicholas, Marcelino Gomes, James Pina, and William Rodriguez. Local draft boards had recorded each of them as either "Negro" or "white," but the army had its questions. Selective Service officials immediately got to work, examining draft registration cards, physical examination reports, and occupational questionnaires, and interviewing local school officials and town clerks. They might also have consulted medical officers, Red Cross officials, employers, birth, marriage, and death certificates, Military Intelligence, and the FBI, as they had in other cases.[1]

Both the high-ranking officials and the substantial effort involved in racial classification suggest its great importance. The US military's policies of assigning its inductees to descent-specific units explain why. What those policies required of the military was some system of classification on the basis of descent or "race." Since the army had "colored" outfits, for example, it had to decide who would join them by deciding who exactly counted as "colored."

In millions of cases, these decisions were routine and uncontroversial when the military, the Selective Service, and the inductee in question all agreed as to the latter's "race." But in hundreds of cases—involving people who identified as Indian, Creole, Puerto Rican, Cape Verdean, Mexican, Moorish American, Portuguese, white, and Negro—the story was infinitely more complicated. In these instances, men challenged their official race classification, or their placement in the segregated military, or both. Sometimes they also raised serious doubts about the authority of the military or Selective Service to classify inductees on the basis of race in the first place. This chapter explores these challenges. While relatively few in number, they nonetheless had some effect on national policy, and they shed light on the making and remaking of race—and on its ever-evolving meanings and boundaries.[2]

These stories highlight several important points. First, in responding to race-classification controversies, military and draft officials, whether fully cognizant of the fact or not, consistently acknowledged the critical local and social—rather than biological or essentialist—dimensions of race. They did so while at the same time upholding a racist set of government institutions. Second, a deeply marginalized and traditionally powerless set of racially ambiguous Americans nonetheless managed eventually to wrest some control over racial classification from the federal government. Third, this government, from local draft boards to the War Department, still retained immense power to determine which race categories counted, whom to slot into them, and on what basis. Finally, the most heated and most consequential race-classification controversies revolved around the meaning and membership of "colored"—not white. "Colored" people were by far the most thoroughly segregated and subjugated descent group in the US military. This meant that their race classification involved more than classification itself, but also assignment to "colored" outfits. Since membership in these outfits carried so many acute, sometimes deadly disadvantages—from menial jobs and harsher discipline to exclusion from senior officer ranks and separate and unequal post facilities—the stakes related to the "colored" category were unquestionably highest. As a result, the incentives to avoid it were substantial.[3]

A POLICY IS BORN

On September 16, 1940, President Roosevelt signed the Selective Training and Service Act (STSA). As nearly seventeen million young men registered for the draft a month later, confounding questions about racial classification and assignment immediately cropped up. On the back of registration cards, local boards examined registrants and made a check mark next to one of five "races"—"White," "Negro," "Oriental," "Indian," and "Filipino." One board member from Oregon wondered how best to classify "Hindus." Some boards in Colorado, insisting that "Spanish Americans" fit neatly into none

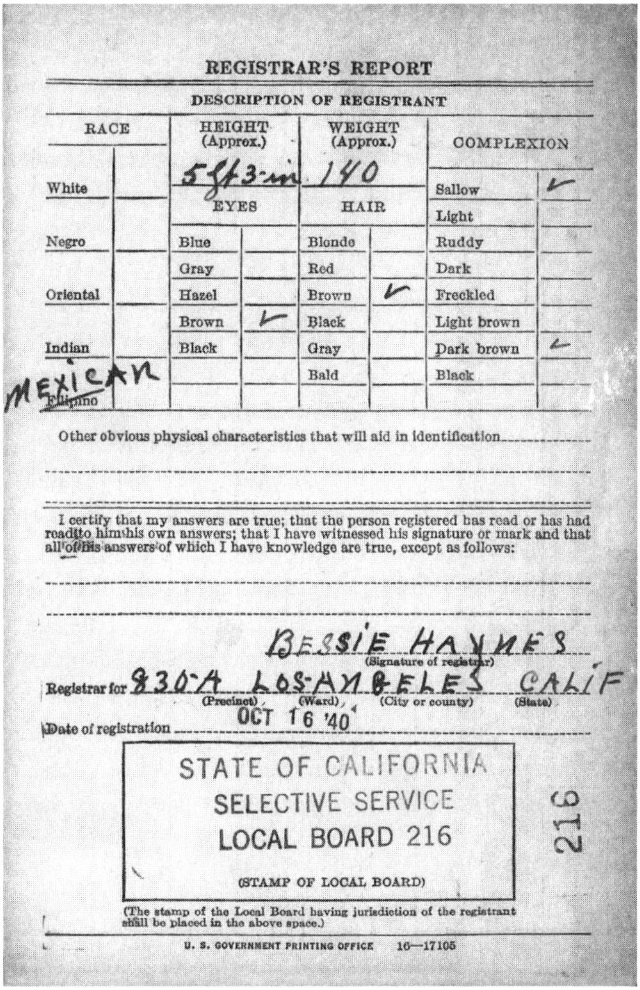

REGISTRAR'S REPORT

DESCRIPTION OF REGISTRANT

RACE		HEIGHT (Approx.)		WEIGHT (Approx.)		COMPLEXION	
White		5 ft 3 in		140		Sallow	✓
		EYES		HAIR		Light	
Negro		Blue		Blonde		Ruddy	
		Gray		Red		Dark	
Oriental		Hazel		Brown	✓	Freckled	
		Brown	✓	Black		Light brown	
Indian		Black		Gray		Dark brown	✓
MEXICAN				Bald		Black	
Filipino							

Other obvious physical characteristics that will aid in identification

I certify that my answers are true; that the person registered has read or has had read to him his own answers; that I have witnessed his signature or mark and that all of his answers of which I have knowledge are true, except as follows:

BESSIE HAYNES
(Signature of registrar)

Registrar for 930-A LOS ANGELES CALIF
(Precinct) (Ward) (City or county) (State)

Date of registration OCT 16 '40

STATE OF CALIFORNIA
SELECTIVE SERVICE
LOCAL BOARD 216
(STAMP OF LOCAL BOARD)

216

(The stamp of the Local Board having jurisdiction of the registrant shall be placed in the above space.)

U. S. GOVERNMENT PRINTING OFFICE 16—17105

Fig. 5.1 A Mexican American's draft registration card, on which the registrar wrote "Mexican" for race. Courtesy Ancestry.com.

of the five categories provided and unwilling to follow the instructions of the state Selective Service headquarters to count them as "White," created a sixth category: "Mexican."[4]

Once registration cards were filled out and boards tallied their registrants in something called minute books, another problem quickly arose. Curiously, these books shrunk the list of races from five to two—"White" and "Colored." Puzzled, a board member from Chicago wrote to the Selective Service national headquarters in Washington in November 1940, "Should Filipinos, Orientals and Indians be classified under the minute book heading 'White' and simply negroes under 'Colored,' or the reverse?

I deduce in my own mind that the whites are listed in one column and all other races in the second column, but would like to have confirmation."[5]

When the army began making calls for certain numbers of "white" and "colored" draftees, some boards wondered whom exactly to send. In late November 1940, the state director of Selective Service in Colorado sought advice from Washington: "Calls will specify whether they are for white or colored men. A negro is, of course, colored. Is this also applicable to Japanese, Indians, Filipinos, or others? Can such men be sent when white men are included in the call? Please advise." Finally, questions arose about who had the ultimate authority to make race classifications. In December 1940, a local board in King William County, Virginia, reported that while some of their registrants claimed to be Indians, it believed they were "of heavily mixed blood. . . . Please advise us whether this board has the authority to classify these registrants according to its own judgement or whether we shall take registrants' racial classification of themselves?"[6]

Selective Service and War Department officials in Washington—well aware that "the question of classification of men, whether white or black, seems to be presenting a difficulty"—scrambled to address these questions as best they could.[7] In November and December 1940, in several letters to state Selective Service officials around the country and at a meeting for state directors, draft officials in Washington made the same two clarifications: while registration cards listed five races, the army cared—and therefore draft boards should care—about only two: "white" and "colored"; and only "negroes" counted as "colored" and everyone else, "Filipinos, Mexicans, Chinese, Japanese, etc., will be listed as white." On December 23, 1940, the War Department confirmed these points— "Trainees of all races other than negro will be assigned the same as white trainees"—and added one more that would prove critical: "In questionable [race-determination] cases, the War Department will ordinarily be guided by the classification given these types by local boards concerned, since such local boards have the most intimate knowledge of ancestors and associates in communities."[8]

Within the first few months of the World War II draft, then, War Department and Selective Service officials appeared to formulate a clear set of policies regarding race and race classification: Which "races" really mattered? "Colored" and "white." Who was colored? Anyone "Negro" or "part Negro." Who was white or "as white"? Everyone else. Who should determine racial status in borderline situations? Local boards. And based on what criteria? A registrant's ancestors and associates. These policies would be tested soon enough, especially as the United States entered the war in December 1941 and as draft boards registered more than thirty million men and, of these, inducted roughly a third into the army and later the navy.[9]

WHO IS JAPANESE—AND MOORISH AMERICAN?

One surprisingly uncontested racial category was "Japanese." This category was originally folded into whiteness, at least in certain contexts, only to be separated after the attack on Pearl Harbor and after the United States entered the war against Japan. When it came to classifying incoming inductees, it is not exactly clear how military and draft officials defined "Japanese." But in time, they seemed to follow the precedent set by the Wartime Civil Control Administration and Western Defense Command, both of which decided in 1942 that anyone with the "slightest amount of Japanese blood" on the West Coast would face mass removal and mass detention.[10] The story of a young man named Charles Togo Ama suggests as much. Ama was the son of an "American Negro" mother and Japanese father, who left the family when Ama was young. As a result, Ama apparently knew little about Japan, "grew up as a part of the Negro race," "consider[ed] himself a Negro," and eventually graduated from historically black Morehouse College. In February 1941, he enlisted in the army as a "Negro" and was assigned to a "colored" Weather Detachment at Tuskegee Army Airfield in Alabama. In early 1943, however, he was transferred to Camp Shelby, because the army air forces now refused to accept people of Japanese descent. It is not clear whether he joined the recently organized Nisei 442nd Combat Team stationed at Camp Shelby, but the timing strongly suggests that he did.[11]

Perhaps draft and military officials sometimes made exceptions for those with "mixed blood," as the government eventually did when it came to "internment." Nonetheless, the Ama story suggests that in a battle of competing one-drop rules, "Japanese blood" sometimes won out. Indeed, this point squares with the recollection of one former member of the 442nd Combat Team, who remembered his company having "a lot of mixed races. . . . They had Japanese last names, so they were in our outfit. . . . A lot of guys from Texas were half Latino half Japanese. . . . One guy's father married a colored woman; he had kinky hair and everything, only lighter skin and Japanese last name. One guy his nickname was 'Haole,' because Japanese feature all over but his eyes were blue."[12]

Ama's allies at Morehouse College and elsewhere appear to have battled to have him reassigned to a "colored" outfit and, in effect, to have him redefined not as Japanese but as "Negro."[13] Few other people of Japanese

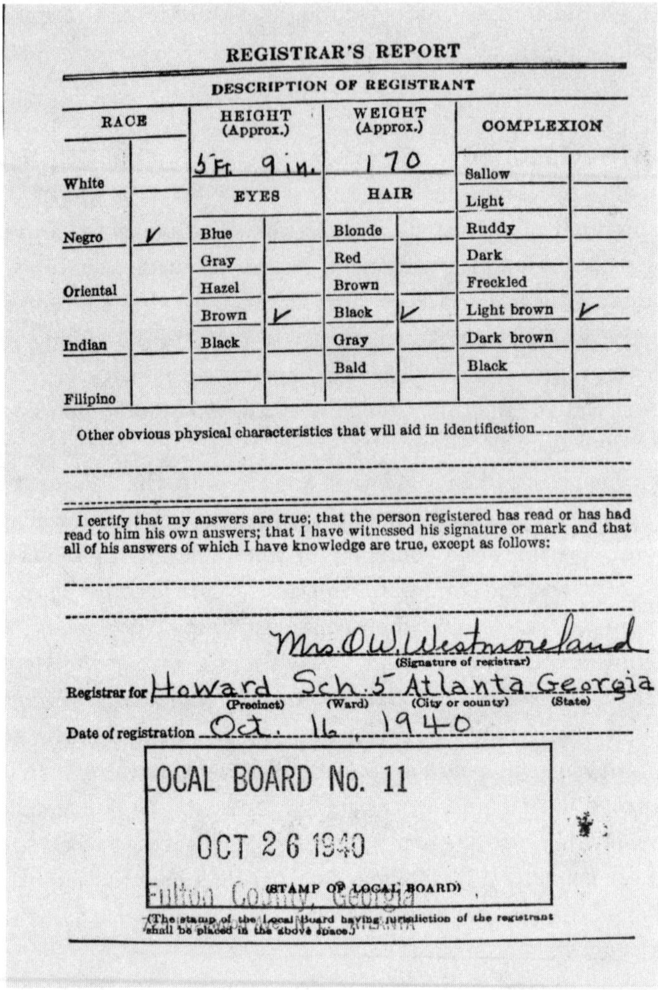

REGISTRAR'S REPORT

DESCRIPTION OF REGISTRANT

RACE		HEIGHT (Approx.)		WEIGHT (Approx.)		COMPLEXION	
White		5 Ft. 9 in.		170		Sallow	
		EYES		HAIR		Light	
Negro	✓	Blue		Blonde		Ruddy	
		Gray		Red		Dark	
Oriental		Hazel		Brown		Freckled	
		Brown	✓	Black	✓	Light brown	✓
Indian		Black		Gray		Dark brown	
				Bald		Black	
Filipino							

Other obvious physical characteristics that will aid in identification------------

----

I certify that my answers are true; that the person registered has read or has had read to him his own answers; that I have witnessed his signature or mark and that all of his answers of which I have knowledge are true, except as follows:

Mrs. O.W. Westmoreland
(Signature of registrar)

Registrar for Howard Sch. 5 Atlanta Georgia
(Precinct)   (Ward)   (City or county)   (State)

Date of registration Oct. 16, 1940 ------------------------

LOCAL BOARD No. 11

OCT 26 1940

Fulton County, Georgia
(STAMP OF LOCAL BOARD)

(The stamp of the Local Board having jurisdiction of the registrant shall be placed in the above space.)

Fig. 5.2 Charles Togo Ama's draft registration card. Courtesy Ancestry.com.

descent appear to have been involved in such controversies. While Nisei activism against military discrimination was widespread during the war, it did not seem to extend to racial determination issues. This point might seem surprising, given the high stakes involved. Many inductees classified as Japanese faced countless hardships—from summary discharges and extensive background checks to segregation in and exclusion from the military. Incentives existed to contest one's classification as Japanese, but few challenges seem to have emerged.

One reason is that determining Japaneseness did not involve potentially nebulous matters like "associates in communities." Instead, it likely involved the more clearly documented matter of nativity—where one or one's ancestors were born. Since Japanese immigration to the United States and its territories was largely a late-nineteenth- and especially early-twentieth-century phenomenon, Japanese-born immigrants were likely the parents (and less commonly the grandparents) of most "Japanese" inductees, making their ancestry easy to document for draft boards and military officials. That the army itself, in the form of the Western Defense Command, had to collect this information for "internment" purposes, and that the US Census at this time also made heretofore confidential information about Japanese Americans available to federal agencies, only added to the relatively straightforward nature of documenting Japanese ancestry.[14]

The obscure category "Moorish American" proved more difficult to verify and more controversial. Unlike "Japanese," this was not a race category that the government had created or employed, but one that a small number of draft registrants had claimed for themselves. Moorish Americans were an offshoot of the Moorish Science Temple of America, a quasi-Islamic organization founded in 1913 by a man who called himself Noble Drew Ali and who argued that "Negroes" were really "an olive-skinned Asiatic people who were the descendants of Moroccans." One dismissive War Department memo had other ideas. In its view, Moorish Americans were really a "group of American Negroes" who "purport[ed] to follow some tenets of the Mohammedan faith," who wore "fezzes and permit[ted] their beards to grow while the women w[ore] very long dresses," who "voluntarily set themselves apart from the rest of their communities by their beliefs and queer dress," and who were "particularly rabid on the question of race." "They strenuously resist the application to them of the racial designation Negro, calling it a 'slave name.'"[15]

When the Selective Service attempted to induct Moorish Americans, controversy ensued. In February 1944, for example, a Philadelphian named James Brown Bey (the War Department explained that "they suffix Bey to their names to avoid the use of a 'slave' cognomen") refused induction into the army "because Selective Service and the United States Army Officials designated him as a 'Negro.'" When, six months later, the government convicted him on draft evasion charges, sentencing him to five years in prison, Bey hired an attorney to press his case, filing one appeal after another. Like Winfred Lynn before him, he argued that the government violated the antidiscrimination clause in the 1940 STSA. But whereas Lynn saw this violation in the separate draft calls for and segregation of "white" and "Negro," Bey saw it in his classification and induction as the latter.[16]

Bey's attorney also corresponded with Selective Service and War Department officials, eventually convincing the former in Pennsylvania

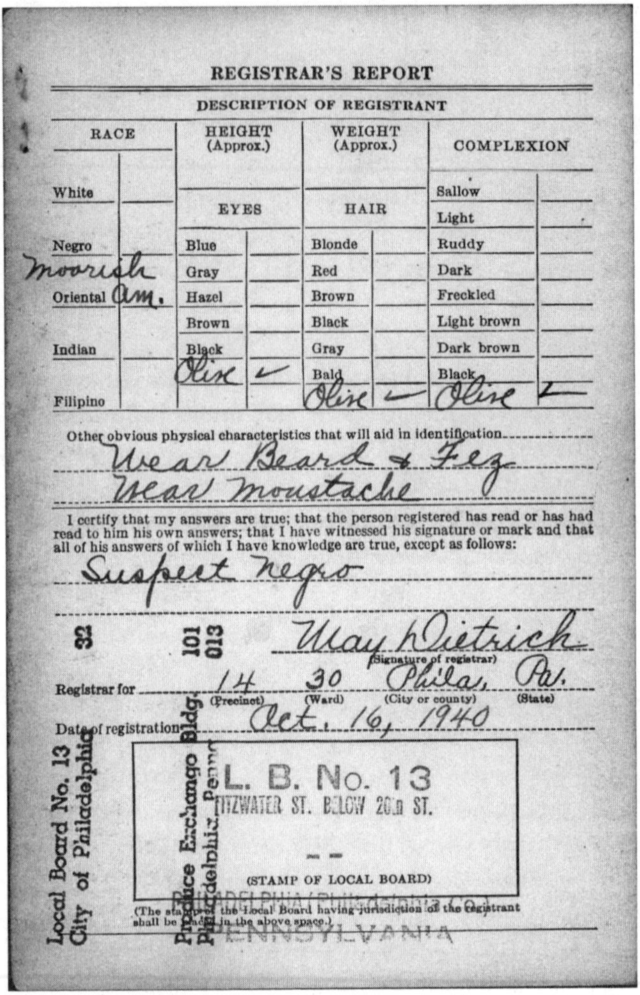

REGISTRAR'S REPORT

DESCRIPTION OF REGISTRANT

RACE		HEIGHT (Approx.)		WEIGHT (Approx.)		COMPLEXION	
White						Sallow	
		EYES		HAIR		Light	
Negro		Blue		Blonde		Ruddy	
Moorish		Gray		Red		Dark	
Oriental	Am.	Hazel		Brown		Freckled	
		Brown		Black		Light brown	
Indian		Black		Gray		Dark brown	
		Olive	✓	Bald		Black	
Filipino				Olive	✓	Olive	✓

Other obvious physical characteristics that will aid in identification

Wear Beard & Fez
Wear moustache

I certify that my answers are true; that the person registered has read or has had read to him his own answers; that I have witnessed his signature or mark and that all of his answers of which I have knowledge are true, except as follows:

Suspect negro

32 101 013 May Dietrich
(Signature of registrar)

Registrar for 14 (Precinct) 30 (Ward) Phila, (City or county) Pa. (State)

Date of registration Oct. 16, 1940

Local Board No. 13
City of Philadelphia
Produce Exchange Bldg.
Philadelphia, Penna.

L. B. No. 13
FITZWATER ST. BELOW 20th ST.

(STAMP OF LOCAL BOARD)

PHILADELPHIA (Philadelphia Co.)
PENNSYLVANIA

(The stamp of the Local Board having jurisdiction of the registrant shall be placed in the above space.)

Fig. 5.3 James Brown Bey's draft registration card. Note that the registrar, no doubt following Bey's wishes, wrote "Moorish Am." for his race, but acknowledged beneath that she "suspect[ed] negro."

to classify Bey as Moorish American. But the Selective Service's national leaders balked. After a conference in Washington, DC, in December 1944, they decided that "membership in the Moorish-American organization without some additional showing will not be considered relevant in determining race." Soon the War Department agreed. In a lengthy letter to Bey's attorney, Assistant Secretary of War John J. McCloy acknowledged that "one of the tenets of the Moorish-American organization is that there is no existence in fact of a Negro race." But McCloy asserted that "the Army cannot agree with this belief," since "determination by the Army of race is one of fact" and "since there is no 'Moorish-American' race." McCloy concluded, therefore, that the burden of proof lay with Bey: "In the absence of any showing that James Brown Bey is not a Negro within the customary and accepted meaning of that term, he will be classified as a Negro in the event he presents himself for induction." In the end, Bey was transferred from the Philadelphia County Prison to a federal penitentiary in Danbury, Connecticut, in July 1945, and presumably served the remainder of his sentence there.[17]

WHO IS WHITE?

In their quirky singularity, these cases involving Ama and Bey, while "headache[s]" for military and draft authorities, placed limited pressure on them. Controversies that arose around the all-important category of white were more widespread and perhaps a bit more troubling to government officials. From October 1940 through December 1945, local draft boards registered 28.5 million white men and inducted more than 7 million of them into the US Army. Who exactly was counted among these millions of so-called white people? These very data suggest some of the complications surrounding the question. In one table on registrants, Selective Service seems to have listed all non-"Negroes" as white; other tables indicated explicitly that "white" included "all races other than Negro"; and still other tables set "White" apart not only from "Negro" but also from "Chinese," "Japanese," "Hawaiian," "American Indian," "Filipino," "Puerto Rican," and "Other."[18]

Who was white, then, was no simple question, and it occasionally generated problems during the war. In a few rare cases, soldiers who had been classified as white and assigned to a white outfit nonetheless requested and received a transfer to a colored one. This happened with a Cuban-born inductee named Norberto González, because of mistreatment in the white unit, and with at least a half dozen or so Cape Verdeans from New England, "because of their racial characteristics." While these transfers were exceedingly unusual, they occurred frequently enough for the War Department to take a formal position on the matter: "It is the policy of the War Department to assign to colored units individuals whose records show them to belong to the white race, and who are black in color and have negroid features, provided they request such assignment and submit affidavits to that effect."[19]

A much more common problem occurred when a registrant or inductee claimed to be white and local draft boards disagreed and marked him down—say, on a registration card or on a physical examination form or in statistical reports—as something else. The problems were that much more serious when draft and War Department officials took the next step and attempted to assign a man claiming to be white to a black unit in the military. The first set of problems seems to have been more common than the second, but both surfaced during the war. In Hawaii, in October 1940, for example, a Portuguese man's "ire" rose "like the hackles of a game cock" when the local draft board insisted on recording his race as Portuguese, which the registrar wrote above the crossed-out Indian category "in precise handwriting." "The Portuguese are of the Caucasian race," the man insisted, "and therefore white."[20]

A similar sort of appeal came from a range of groups, most frequently Mexican Americans from the Southwest, Puerto Ricans from the island, and Creoles from Louisiana. Of all three groups, Mexican Americans seemed to have the surest claim to whiteness. Although their "proper" racial status was hotly contested and could shift dramatically from one realm or region to the next, matters seemed simpler with the military. Although they did so for, say, Chinese or Hawaiians or Puerto Ricans, army or draft forms, reports, and statistical tables seldom provided a separate "Mexican race" category. Selective Service officials in Washington and at state headquarters throughout the Southwest explicitly instructed local boards against using it.[21] Yet some local boards failed to listen. Problems first seem to have arisen in Colorado, but they spread to other parts of the Southwest. The Selective Service's official report of 1940–1941 found that "some 7,412 men were inducted . . . under an indefinite racial classification of 'Others.'" The report surmised that since "4,256 of these came from Texas, 2,266 from California, and 506 from Arizona . . . the question [is] whether or not they are actually people of Mexican racial stock." Southwestern states continued to have unusually high numbers of "other" inductees throughout the war.[22] One sociologist, writing about Texas, noted in 1942 that even "the Mexican of pure Spanish blood . . . registering for the Selective Service, has to wait twenty minutes while two school teachers consult over the problem as to whether or not he is white." In February 1941, one draft official in Montana complained to Lewis Hershey that a local board in Texas "refuse[d] to induct one of our registrants for the reason that they had no call for Mexicans"—only ones for whites and for Negroes.[23]

Some Mexican Americans deeply resented these practices, part of a long-standing and widespread Anglo effort to claim whiteness as theirs alone. As Francisco J. Flores of Laredo, Texas, complained in 1943, "[If] the name is Spanish, then they classify the selectee as 'Mexican'; if it is 'American' then the classification is, of course, 'white.'" "It is done in such a

Fig. 5.4 A retired army officer registers a man, possibly Mexican American, for Selective Service in Brownsville, Texas, February 1942. Courtesy Library of Congress Prints and Photographs Division, LC-USF34-022063-D.

way as to infer that we form no part of the 'White' race." At the same time, Mexican American civil rights leader George I. Sánchez informed a friend about ongoing complaints regarding the "classification of Spanish-speaking citizens as 'Mexicans' by the Army."[24] But in the end, whether draft and army officials classified their race as "Mexican," "white," or in some cases "Indian," virtually every last Mexican American served in so-called white units during World War II. Where one fit in the US Army hinged, as it turned out, on questions of Negroness, coloredness, or blackness, not on Indianness, Mexicanness, or even whiteness.[25]

Matters were a bit more complicated for Puerto Ricans. In the continental United States, the expectation was that they had to abide by racial-classification norms there and so fewer controversies seem to have arisen. But in Puerto Rico, where so-called race mixing had long been a part of the island's history, efforts to impose mainland US–style rigid racial taxonomies on the island's more fluid system not only was practically difficult, but also smacked of one more form of Yankee imperialism.[26] At first the War Department was undecided as to whether to segregate Puerto Rican draftees, but after initially experimenting with disregarding race entirely, it issued separate calls for "white" and "Negro" men as early as

January 1941. This policy, a reprise of the World War I approach, seems to have continued throughout the war. By one War Department count from May 1946, the army inducted some 86 percent of Puerto Ricans from the island into "white" units during World War II and 14 percent into "Negro" ones.[27]

This policy first became public in February 1941 when a Los Angeles black newspaper, the *California Eagle*, published a story entitled "Draft Brings Race Bias to Puerto Rico." Campbell Johnson, the Selective Service's one race adviser in Washington, and William Hastie, his counterpart in the War Department, were appalled. Having consulted with one another first, they penned memos to Hershey and to the War Department General Staff, respectively. Focusing on hemispheric ramifications, Johnson wrote, "[T]he Selective Service System and the War Department have perpetrated a serious injustice upon the people of Puerto Rico and have done the cause of our Pan American Good Will and Good Neighbor Policy great harm," since "one of the strongest barriers to the development of satisfactory international relations with South America has been the distrust which these countries have held toward the United States because of its racial policies." Hastie, who had served as a US District Court judge in the US Virgin Islands prior to the war, added, "Public relations in Puerto Rico are explosive at best. I believe the step now being taken by the Army will aggravate the situation." Some Puerto Ricans agreed with this assessment. Writing a special report for Rexford Tugwell, the governor of Puerto Rico, a "mulatto" government official warned that "to divide the Puerto Rican soldiers in white and colored, to start here a division of races that never existed, to bring to Puerto Rico the racial prejudices existing in the Continent, would constitute a dangerous menace to the stability of the Puerto Rican people."[28]

Further aggravating matters was that draft and War Department officials never settled on a consistent racial classification for Puerto Ricans. In the span of one year, army directives ordered that "[a] Puerto Rican is considered as of the White race" and that on various forms "Puerto Rican personnel have recorded in the race block a notation 'White or Colored' as applicable in addition to the race 'Puerto Rican.'" All the while, Secretary of War Stimson insisted that "Puerto Ricans, when called into military service in Puerto Rico, state whether they are white or colored, and their statements are, of course, taken as correct."[29] As for draft officials, their reports and official statistics often referred to Puerto Ricans as a "racial group" or "racial minority" that was somehow distinct from whites and other "races." These inconsistencies seem to have persisted. In July 1945, the War Department tallied its total number of Puerto Rican personnel. Whereas for those in the continental United States, it divided soldiers into "white" and "Negro" categories, those from the island were listed, significantly, as "colored" or "other than colored." Two years earlier, an African American correspondent for the *Chicago Defender* commented on the widespread results of this official confusion in a letter to Truman Gibson, a black adviser to the Secretary of War: "At least 20% of the Puerto Rican selectees classified as Negroes were of lighter complexion, had better hair and looked more Caucasian than some men whom I observed in the so-called white companies. . . . I saw men who were nearly my complexion in white companies and some lighter than you (looking about like Walter White [the NAACP executive secretary]) in colored companies."[30]

This confusion, and especially the official sense that all Puerto Ricans, regardless of their actual military assignment, constituted a nonwhite race of one kind or another, irked some Puerto Ricans, particularly the self-identified whites among them. In April 1943, one constituent wrote a telegram to Resident Commissioner Bolivar Pagán, Puerto Rico's single nonvoting member of the US House of Representatives: "Are you aware natives of Puerto Rico whether white or negro being classified at army camps under color or race as Puerto Ricans only. . . . No distinction being made. . . . Puerto Ricans proud of being American citizens, proud of their Spanish ancestry. . . . Could you not bring to the attention of the military that in Puerto Rico we also have the white race." Pagán immediately forwarded the telegram to Secretary Stimson, requesting "that steps be taken to clarify this situation." Meanwhile, Colonel Harry F. Besosa, the director of Selective Service in Puerto Rico, who had earlier approved of segregated race calls as "satisfactory to the majority of Puerto Ricans," wrote several letters to his boss in Washington, Lewis B. Hershey, on a similar point. Assuming all Puerto Ricans shared a single race was a "serious error due to a lack of knowledge and acquaintance with real data."

> Naturally an involuntary error or discrimination as to the classification of Americans from Puerto Rico as a non-white race will be resented, not only by the Puerto Rican-Americans, but also by all our neighbor Republics in the South, who, with the exception of Argentina and Chili [*sic*], are not as rosy cheeked and blonde as the North Americans, but tanned, brunette, and with pale complexions due to the Tropical Sun under which they are born and live, but still cannot be classified as non-white as they still are of the Caucasian race in their greater majority.

When draft officials in Washington ignored this advice and continued classifying all Puerto Ricans as nonwhite, Besosa wrote Hershey again: "For

God's sake, and as a matter of justice and truth, do not again place us in your Negro chapter."[31]

Some Louisiana Creoles, like Mexican Americans and Puerto Ricans, also claimed to be white and fiercely fought local draft boards' attempts to say otherwise. Controversies developed in various parts of the state, but were especially intense in Plaquemines Parish near the Mississippi Delta, where crafting color lines had long been a local art. Here, according to one FBI report, a group of people with a "light brown complexion" who lived in a settlement that local whites called "coon town" occupied an intermediate status between "whites" and "negroes." Apart from both groups, they had their own school, their own dances, and their own seating sections in the local Catholic church and theater, in both cases "alongside, but not amongst, the negroes." While they worked in the fields and on fishing boats with black people, they refused to eat with them at lunchtime or to drink from the same water jug on break.[32]

When, in the summer of 1942, the army ordered five men from the community to report for induction, they all refused. Local boards had classified them as Negroes and planned on delivering them to the military as such. But the men insisted on serving as whites, and when, in November, a federal grand jury indicted them for violating the STSA, they, like James Brown Bey, hired lawyers to press their case. In an especially perceptive letter to Hershey from December 1942, Edmond E. Talbot, a former US attorney for the Eastern District of Louisiana who was hired to represent the men, explained:

> In certain parishes in South Louisiana . . . the inter-marriage and co-mingling of various races has produced certain types which ever [sic] the Courts and the experts are at a loss to determine as to race. Italians, Indians, Spanish, French and, sometimes, negro blood often results in a type which classifies itself as white but which the Draft Board, for reasons of its own, classifies as colored mainly because some member of the Draft Board is of the impression that some colored blood existed in the family several generations back.[33]

But this was background. Talbot's real point was that, while boards clearly had the authority under the STSA to "determine whether a man is of the proper age to be included in the draft; whether he has dependents; whether or not he is an alien; whether or not he is a conscientious objector, and questions of that type," they did not have the "power or jurisdiction to classify any draftee as to color or race." Talbot reminded Hershey, "If any phase of induction is illegal, the Courts appear to be inclined to grant a writ of habeas corpus to the draftees involved and I sincerely believe that any attempt by a Local Board to classify as to color is an illegal exercise of the Board's authority."[34]

"Examined under protest at the induction center," the men were eventually found to be physically or mentally unfit for service, and the assistant US attorney in the area declined to prosecute.[35] It is unclear what effect Talbot's argument had on this decision. Regardless, some families retained Talbot's counsel in the event that local boards continued attempting to induct their sons into the "colored" army. It appears that by the fall of 1943—for reasons that, as we will see, had as much to do with Indians in Virginia as Creoles in Louisiana—local draft boards began forwarding controversial Creole cases to induction centers with men's race undetermined.[36]

In the end, registrants and inductees claimed whiteness for a variety of reasons—to assert their authentic sense of self, to avoid racial classification as Negro or Mexican or Puerto Rican, but also at times to avoid service in the so-called black military. On this last point, all Mexicans, the vast majority of Puerto Ricans, and at least some Creoles succeeded in either serving with white units or, in the case of the five men from Plaquemines Parish, not serving at all.

WHO IS INDIAN?

Draftees claiming to be white did not cause Selective Service and military authorities the biggest problems during World War II. That distinction went to men claiming to be Indian (or part Indian). Through November 1946, local draft boards inducted nearly twenty thousand American Indians into the army.[37] Most of these inductees came from western states such as Oklahoma, Arizona, New Mexico, and South Dakota. There, local boards seemed not to question their status as Indians, probably because the inductees had already been defined as such by some other arm of the US government, such as the Dawes Commission or the Office of Indian Affairs. But things were a lot more complicated primarily in the South, where, according to some proponents of the one-drop rule, American Indians had mixed with black people so extensively that they had vanished entirely. Where there had once been two "races"—"Indians" and "Negroes"—now there was only one—"Negroes." By the time the draft came to states like North Carolina and Virginia, then, local boards' racial classification of men claiming to be Indian was simply the latest chapter in a much longer, contentious story that often stretched back many decades, if not centuries.[38]

This was especially the case in Virginia, where among state elites protecting racial "purity" had long been an obsession. At the center of this story was the elderly, bespectacled Walter Ashby Plecker, a former "country doctor" and registrar of the state's Bureau of Vital Statistics since its inception in 1912. Consumed by the fear that "racial amalgamation" would contaminate white "purity" and imperil the nation, Plecker helped pass a series of strict state segregation laws in the 1920s. The most infamous of these was the Virginia Racial Integrity Act of 1924, which made it "unlawful for any white person . . . to marry any save a white person." He also made it his personal mission to enforce these laws by determining and recording all Virginians' "proper" racial status. He hoped to detect the thousands who "possess an intermixture of colored blood, in some cases to a slight extent, it is true, but still enough to prevent them from being white"—and from legally marrying and mixing with whites in schools, hospitals, theaters, and other public places.[39] Seeking any evidence of nonwhite status, he interviewed prominent white state residents and mined nineteenth-century county and federal records, including birth and death certificates, taxpayer lists, and US Census reports. He also closely monitored all the state's midwives, doctors, undertakers, and local registrars and explicitly, sometimes coercively, directed them how to classify people racially on birth, death, marriage, and divorce certificates, always demanding overwhelming "proof" of whiteness. He even sought, with mixed success, to convince US Census enumerators in 1930 and again in 1940 to follow his preferred racial classification schemes.[40]

One of Plecker's primary targets had long been the state's small Indian population. For years he doggedly maintained in state records, court testimony, speeches, and pamphlets that it was truly "colored," since, as he wrote categorically in 1930, "there are no native Virginia Indians unmixed with negro blood."[41] Predictably, then, as Virginia draft boards began registering and inducting men claiming to be Indian ten years later, Plecker insisted on having a say about these "mulattoes, styling themselves Indians." In a February 1941 letter to the state's director of Selective Service, he repeated his "unmixed with negro blood" claim and declared, "We classify all native people in Virginia claiming to be Indian as negro. . . . Even if any could show themselves to be Indians under the [US] Census, they would still be grouped with the colored group and would not be classified as white." Initially the state and some local boards seem to have followed Plecker's lead. In King William County in October 1940, for example, a local board registered twenty-one men as Indians. But after consulting with the state Selective Service office, which advised adherence to Plecker's views, the board called the men to the county courthouse in February 1941 to "prove their race."[42] In other counties, boards inducted or promised to induct Indians into black army units.

SURNAMES, BY COUNTIES AND CITIES, OF MIXED NEGROID VIRGINIA
FAMILIES STRIVING TO PASS AS "INDIAN" OR WHITE.

Albemarle: Moon, Powell, Kidd, Pumphrey.

Amherst: Adcock (Adcox), Beverly (this family is now trying to evade the
(Migrants to   situation by adopting the name of Burch or Birch, which was the
Alleghany and   name of the white mother of the present adult generation). Branham,
Campbell)   Duff, Floyd, Hamilton, Hartless, Hicks, Johns, Lawless, Nuckles
    (Knuckles), Painter, Ramsey, Redcross, Roberts, Southards
    (Suthards, Southerds, Southers), Sorrells, Terry, Tyree, Willis,
    Clark, Cash, Wood.

Bedford: McVey, Maxey, Branham, Burley. (See Amherst County)

Rockbridge: Cash, Clark, Coleman, Duff, Floyd, Hartless, Hicks, Mason, Mayse
(Migrants to   (Mays), Painters, Pults, Ramsey, Southerds (Southers, Southards,
Augusta)   Suthards), Sorrells, Terry, Tyree, Wood, Johns.

Charles City: Collins, Dennis, Bradby, Howell, Langston, Stewart, Wynn, Adkins.

King William: Collins, Dennis, Bradby, Howell, Langston, Stewart, Wynn,
    Custalow (Custaloe), Dungee, Holmes, Miles, Page, Allmond, Adams,
    Hawkes, Spurlock, Doggett.

New Kent: Collins, Bradby, Stewart, Wynn, Adkins, Langston.

Henrico and
Richmond City: See Charles City, New Kent, and King William.

Caroline: Byrd, Fortune, Nelson. (See Essex)

Essex and
King and Queen: Nelson, Fortune, Byrd, Cooper, Tate, Hammond, Brooks, Boughton,
    Prince, Mitchell, Robinson.

Elizabeth City
& Newport News: Stewart (descendants of Charles City families).

Halifax: Epps (Eppes), Stewart (Stuart), Coleman, Johnson, Martin, Talley,
    Sheppard (Shepard), Young.

Norfolk County
& Portsmouth: Sawyer, Bass, Weaver, Locklear (Locklair), King, Bright, Porter,
    Ingram.

Westmoreland: Sorrells, Worlds (or Worrell), Atwells, Gutridge, Oliff.

Greene: Shifflett, Shiflet.

Prince William: Tyson, Segar. (See Fauquier)

Fauquier: Hoffman (Huffman), Riley, Colvin, Phillips. (See Prince William)

Lancaster: Dorsey (Dawson).

Washington: Beverly, Barlow, Thomas, Hughes, Lethcoe, Worley.

Roanoke County: Beverly. (See Washington)

Lee and Smyth: Collins, Gibson (Gipson), Moore, Goins, Ramsey, Delph, Bunch,
    Freeman, Mise, Barlow, Bolden (Bolin), Mullins, Hawkins. - Chiefly
    Tennessee "Melungeons."

Scott: Dingus. (See Lee County)

Russell: Keith, Castell, Stillwell, Meade, Proffitt. (See Lee & Tazewell)

Tazewell: Hammed, Duncan. (See Russell)

Wise: See Lee, Smyth, Scott, and Russell Counties.

Fig. 5.5 A list of surnames that Walter Plecker distributed throughout Virginia in 1943 as part of his ongoing effort to identify all "mixed negroid Virginia families striving to pass as 'Indian' or white." Papers of John Powell, MSS 7284, Special Collections, University of Virginia Library.

But Plecker's views and actions had never gone uncontested. For years, various Indians had fought tirelessly to be recognized as such—and not as "negroes"—on state documents, in the US Census, and in some public institutions like hospitals and schools. In the process, they had sometimes enlisted the help of powerful white friends and state officials.[43] So when local boards in Virginia began raising questions about Indians' racial status at the start of World War II, Indians were ready to respond. In King William County, where problems first arose, two Indian communities—the Pamunkey and the Upper Mattaponi—struck back. The latter's chief wrote Virginia's governor, James H. Price, in February 1941, and pleaded, "The other time when the boys registered [during World War I] they registered as Indian, and went with the white, and now it seem [sic] that they want to send them with the colored. We don't mind our boy [sic] going if they can be sent right and not with the colored." A few weeks later, in a petition to Virginia's Selective Service director, the leaders of the state-recognized Pamunkey Indian Reservation made a similar request: "We . . . respectfully ask that . . . if and when any one or more of the [Pamunkey] Indians who have been registered . . . shall be called and inducted into the army of the United States they be assigned and placed in companies of white men."[44]

Responsibility for resolving this decades-long struggle over Virginia Indians' racial classification, at least as it related to the draft, fell to the state's director of Selective Service, Lieutenant Colonel Mills F. Neal. He was the founder and president of the M. F. Neal Tobacco Company in Richmond, the head of that city's Chamber of Commerce for a time, and an officer in the Virginia National Guard.[45] Sufficiently confused by the whole matter, he bought time by ordering local boards to postpone inducting all men registered as Indian in late February 1941. At the same time, he wrote the War Department's commanding general in the region and the Selective Service national headquarters, homing in on two critical questions: first, should "those persons who represent themselves as Indians" be delivered to induction stations as "white" or as "colored"?; second, do local boards have the lawful authority to racially classify registrants and inductees?[46]

On the first point, Neal was perfectly flexible, simply requesting explicit orders. "If it is the desire of the War Department that all such persons as described as Indians in the basic communication and other enclosures be inducted as Indians and delivered for induction under a call for White trainees," Neal wrote his commanding general, "this procedure will be followed. It is respectfully requested, however, that this headquarters be definitely advised in the matter." On the second point, Neal, like Talbot, the Creoles' lawyer, voiced real concerns: "It is the understanding of this headquarters that under Selective Service Regulations the Local Board appears to have performed its task when it determines that a man, without regard for his race, creed or color, is Class 1-A or some other class found applicable."[47] The local board had lawful authority, in Neal's view, to determine a man's eligibility for the draft, but not his race.

In their responses, both the War Department and Selective Service hewed closely to the policies outlined in December 1940, with a few minor adjustments. On the question of who should do the race categorizing, both agreed that, as the War Department's adjutant general explained, "It is the problem of the Selective Service System to deliver upon call specified numbers of whites and negroes. Consequently, it is encumbent [*sic*] upon the [local] board to make a finding of fact as to ethnic origin." Citing this policy, Hershey requested Neal to "instruct your local boards to make such ['ethnic'] determinations." As to how to classify Indians, the army emphasized the importance of "associates" rather than "ancestors." In a memo dated April 3, 1941, the adjutant general stated, "Members of the Indian race will be inducted as white trainees. It is for the local board to determine whether or not these registrants are Indians, and it will, of course, take into consideration whether their associates are Negroes and whether they are treated as whites in the social pattern of their community and state." Hershey added to this social understanding of race, a more biological, one-drop-rule dimension: "Under Army regulations a man is considered to be colored who has any ascertainable Negro blood."[48]

While the documentary record is largely silent for the rest of the year, it appears that Neal chose to ignore Hershey's request to determine Indians' race. Instead, he seems to have continued to postpone all Indian inductions, a decision made possible in part by the still relatively low army induction numbers prior to the United States' entrance into the war and the relatively few Indian registrants. He also surveyed the problem of race determination and Indians throughout the state, reviewed War Department and Selective Service policy, and met with some Indian leaders.[49]

Finally, on January 7, 1942, exactly a month after the attack on Pearl Harbor and just as army calls for inductees began to soar, Neal issued memorandum no. 336, intended to be the final word on the "procedure for classification of persons registered as Indians." Quoting from large sections of previous War Department and Selective Service policy memorandums, he finally accepted the requirement that "Local Boards . . . make a finding of fact as to the ethnic origin of each individual Registrant." He also concluded that of the 170 men registered as Indian in the state, "it appears impossible to classify them as a group" owing to "the wide variation in their ethnic origin." Therefore, local boards ought to secure from each Indian registrant "a sworn statement as to his ethnic origin" that would remain a part of his record. "In questionable, or border-line cases," local boards could delay induction for as much as sixty days to conduct a "thorough investigation . . . to insure a just determination of the proper classification of the Registrant." Neal concluded by reminding local boards that each registrant had the right to appeal "in the event they are dissatisfied with said classification." Something of a compromise, the new policy avoided blanket classifications of Indians as either all "colored," as Plecker and some local boards insisted, or all Indian, as some Indians and their allies requested. Instead, local boards would determine "ethnic origin" on a case-by-case basis, taking into account a registrant's own sworn statements and a "thorough investigation" of his "ancestors and associates."[50]

Such a solution meant that Virginia Indians—and a handful of other Indian communities in other mid-Atlantic states where policies came to mirror those in Virginia—faced a range of draft experiences thereafter. Some local boards accepted Indians as Indians, sometimes from the start, other times after a bit of struggle and political maneuvering. The Pamunkey were still sending petitions to the War Department, the Department of the Interior, and Colgate Darden, the Virginia governor, in the summer of 1942, "protesting their classification as negroes." By the end of the war, however, sixteen Pamunkey men had served in the armed forces, all as Indians. One lost his life.[51] Other Indians—such as the Nansemond, the Mattaponi, and the Upper Mattaponi in the tidewater region of Virginia, and several communities in North Carolina—seem to have received similar treatment.[52]

Some Indians were inducted by local boards as "Negro" and served in "colored" outfits without protest. Theodore Green reported many decades later to an interviewer, that, though he was "Native American," he served contentedly in a "black outfit": "In my outfit," he recalled, "I was the only one who was Native American but I thought it was really nice how I used to be able to do this and do that a little easier than the others."[53]

Other Indians, also inducted as "colored," were not as pleased with their unit assignment. Once in the military, some managed to get their status changed to Indian and transferred to "white" units. One Nanticoke Indian from Delaware wrote letters to family, friends, and prominent allies, seeking help in getting removed from "camp with A bunch of colored boys. . . . As this place is getting to be unbearble now." He eventually got his wish, reporting that "the first Sgt; called me in and show me a letter that he wrote in my behalf asking for records to be change as they enought proof that I was INDIAN and NOT COLORED The Major ask me if I wanted TO moved in the white barracks to night are waite and get moved to another camp I said I thought it would be best if I could be moved now."[54]

A similar story involved a group of Western Chickahominy living outside of Richmond, Virginia, in and around Charles City County. The community had been active from the start in battling local boards that were openly intent on inducting their young men as Negroes. Western Chickahominy leaders convinced Secretary of the Interior Harold Ickes to write Hershey on their behalf; they managed to meet face-to-face with national and state Selective Service officials; they hired an attorney, who, like Talbot and Neal, questioned local boards' authority to determine race; and they sent letters and petitions to President Roosevelt, the War Department, Governor Colgate Darden, and others. In their petition to the president in December 1942, which they submitted with the Rappahannocks, another small Indian community from the same Tidewater region of the state, they asked that he

> intercede on our behalf with local draft boards . . . to classify the members of such American Indian tribes as "Indian" and not as "colored" or "negro" as is being practiced by officials throughout Virginia; and further that such members of our tribes as may be drafted be assigned either to Indian Regiments or to White units; and not inducted into negro regiments. We hereby wish to proclaim our loyalty to the United States of America, and our willingness to fight on her behalf. We do, however, ask that as American Indians native to and residing in Virginia, we be not humiliated.[55]

The Western Chickahominy were fully prepared, then, when in March 1943 a local draft board inducted seven of their young men as Negroes and sent them "under protest" to Fort Meade in Maryland. There, the men refused to leave their barracks. After several months of coaxing from community leaders, their attorney, and influential white allies, the army eventually transferred the men to a "white" chemical depot company at Camp Sibert in Alabama.[56]

Some Indians inducted as "colored" but wishing not to serve as such were less successful at securing a transfer. One black soldier recalled that, while traveling by train to a Virginia port of embarkation, a member of his unit suddenly "went haywire . . . and was running up and down the aisle shouting, 'Me no "nigger," me Indian!' They got him off of that train like lightning. The men did not find it funny and his problem would have been solved tragically if he hadn't been removed fast."[57] It is unclear what in the end happened to this man or, more broadly, how many other men found themselves in similar shoes.

Outcomes varied widely in the few cases where Indians classified as "Negro" refused to serve until their racial designation was changed to Indian and until they were allowed to join white units. On one end of the spectrum was a group of Rappahannocks from Caroline County, Virginia, forty or so miles north of Richmond. Much like other Indians, they battled their draft authorities as best they could. They enlisted the help of anthropologists who wrote to prominent officials claiming that "to be classed a Negro is an obvious shock and blow to their traditions and tribal laws, and is placing them under the creed of an entirely different culture foreign to their tastes and aspirations." Their chief, Otho S. Nelson, worked tirelessly for weeks to gain legal counsel and the support of other local Indian groups, though, with the exception of the petition to President Roosevelt cited earlier, he largely struck out on both fronts.[58]

Despite these efforts, in January 1943 a federal court in Richmond sentenced three Rappahannocks—Oliver Wendell Fortune, Robert Purcell Byrd, and Edward Arnall Nelson—to two years in a federal reformatory for violating the STSA. Each had registered initially as Indian but their local draft board, citing birth and marriage certificates and attendance at black schools and churches, insisted on inducting them as Negro.[59] Robert Byrd, who reportedly worked as a teacher at a "school for colored children" for ten years, refused to "leave the county 'as a Negro,' because he was told that he would 'return as a Negro.'" Fortune told his tribal chief he would "go to the pen before he would take the negro status [and] . . . go down in history as negro."[60] All three men appealed their convictions, but the US Court of Appeals dismissed their cases. At least three other members of the same Rappahannock community, all relatives of Fortune, Byrd, and Nelson, also refused to submit to inductions and examinations as black people and served time for violating the STSA.[61]

But other Indians were more successful at challenging their race classification. Two cases are especially telling and would prove critical to Selective Service policy nationally. One involved a young Monacan from western Virginia and the other a group of six Waccamaw-Siouans in North Carolina. Monacans—at various times also called Issues, Cherokee Indians, Indian Mixed Race, even WIN (short for "white, Indian, Negro")—lived in and around Amherst County in the foothills of the Blue Ridge Mountains.[62] As with the Western Chickahominies, local draft boards made clear their intention to induct these men as Negroes, regardless of how they identified themselves. In January 1942, the local board in Amherst County informed a Monacan man that "the laws of this State very clearly fix the color of this race as 'Colored' and this Board therefore, will so classify said race to conform with the State laws." A year later the board, in the words of its chair, remained "determined to induct these people as negroes if they are inducted at all, because all members of this board know that they are a

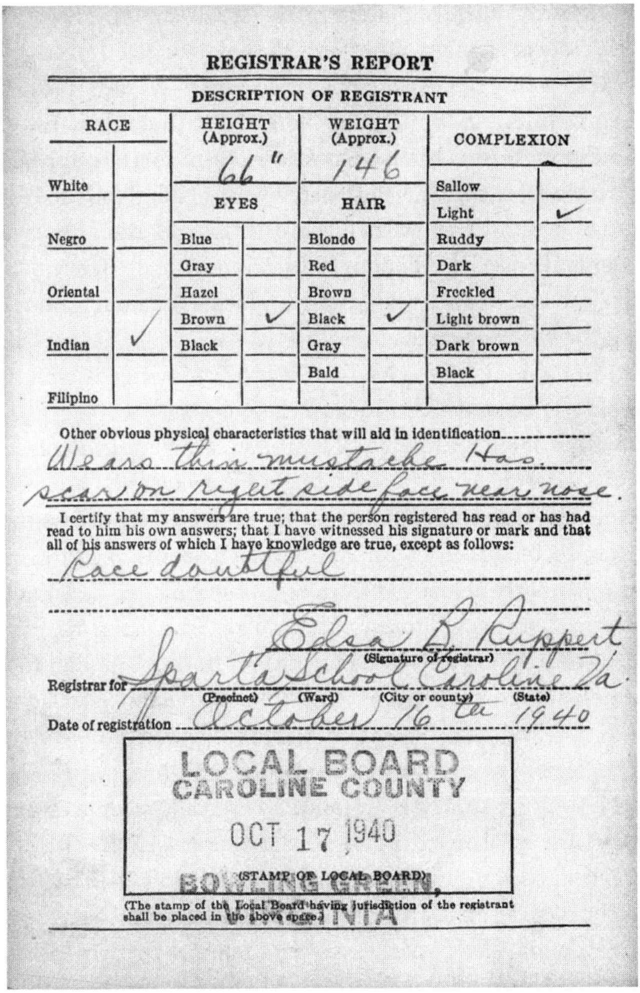

REGISTRAR'S REPORT

DESCRIPTION OF REGISTRANT

RACE		HEIGHT (Approx.)	WEIGHT (Approx.)	COMPLEXION	
White		66 "	146	Sallow	
		EYES	HAIR	Light	✓
Negro		Blue	Blonde	Ruddy	
		Gray	Red	Dark	
Oriental		Hazel	Brown	Freckled	
	✓	Brown ✓	Black ✓	Light brown	
Indian	✓	Black	Gray	Dark brown	
			Bald	Black	
Filipino					

Other obvious physical characteristics that will aid in identification..............

Wears thin mustache. Has scar on right side face near nose.

I certify that my answers are true; that the person registered has read or has had read to him his own answers; that I have witnessed his signature or mark and that all of his answers of which I have knowledge are true, except as follows:

Race doubtful

....

Edsa B Ruppert
(Signature of registrar)

Registrar for *Sparta School Caroline Va.*
        (Precinct)   (Ward)   (City or county)   (State)

Date of registration *October 16 1940*

LOCAL BOARD
CAROLINE COUNTY

OCT 17 1940

BOWLING GREEN,
(STAMP OF LOCAL BOARD)
VIRGINIA
(The stamp of the Local Board having jurisdiction of the registrant shall be placed in the above space.)

Fig. 5.6 Oliver W. Fortune's draft registration card, on which the registrar checked "Indian" for race but added "Race doubtful" below. Courtesy Ancestry.com.

mixed breed of people having perhaps more negro blood than any other strain."[63]

Yet by early 1943, the local board, despite its determination, had not yet inducted a single Monacan into the black military or any military. Many Monacan families, according to one local minister, "moved to Baltimore and other northern cities so that those entering the Army could be classed as white." Others chose to stay put and drew the draft process out through one protest after another. They enlisted the help of "outstanding White citizens," who signed and sent a petition to the local draft board and who wrote to Neal, the state governor, and others, insisting that Monacans should serve in the so-called white military, since they "never associated with Negroes, socially or any other way."[64] They also hired an energetic local attorney, William Kinckle Allen. Willing to represent only those men who "had no negro contamination," he gathered birth and marriage certificates to prove Indianness and nonblackness, wrote numerous appeals to Neal and Director Hershey, and traveled with several of his clients to Washington for a face-to-face meeting with Edward Shattuck, the Selective Service System's general counsel. All along, Allen argued that "while some of the Indians have mixed with the negro race, a far larger number have become mixed with the whites, or kept their own Indian strain pure. . . . Those who have kept their blood pure, or become intermixed with the white race, certainly should not be sent to camp with the negroes."[65]

These tactics bought time, but eventually, after months of delays and discussions between local boards, state headquarters, and officials in Washington, DC, the Amherst County local board and others in the area won out. It inducted several Monacans as black people in early 1943.[66] One of these was a nineteen-year-old from Lynchburg named William Branham Jr., whose racial status confused officials from the start. His draft registration card from June 1942 listed his race as "father one-half Indian" and "mother one-half white." Coming across this perplexing notation a month later, a clerk for Lynchburg Local Board No. 2 decided to place Branham's card "among those of negro registrants" after speaking with a former employer of the young man. When Branham was called to report for induction in April 1943, his local board ordered him to serve with Negroes. Branham refused and eventually, with the help of his father and Allen as his attorney, brought a civil suit against the board in the US District Court.[67]

In his complaint, filed in early June 1943, Branham denied having "one drop of Negro blood in his veins" or "any social relations with Negroes." As proof, he attached his birth certificate, which listed him as Indian, and the marriage licenses of his parents, grandparents, and a younger sister, all of whom were classified as Indian or white. He also claimed that "what little education he ha[d] was obtained in White Schools and he ha[d] never attended a Negro school," that the same local board that attempted to induct him as Negro classified his father as white, and that white ministers married his parents and grandparents. He also claimed that "irreparable, irremediable and irretrievable harm and injury will and would be done him if he were called as a Negro and delivered to the United States Army as a Negro with black buck Negroes from the City of Lynchburg" and that "being sent with negroes to army camps and to battlefields" would "change the whole tenour [sic], sentiment and soul of his life." In the end, then, he asked for two things from the court: that it "permanently and perpetually enjoin" his local board from calling him "as a negro to be delivered and inducted into the United States Army as a negro" and that it issue a "mandatory injunction" to the same board to call him "as he is registered, half white, half Indian, and to deliver him as a White trainee to be inducted into the United States Army as a White man."[68]

The case, *Branham v. Burton* (later *Branham v. Langley*, after Clarence G. Burton resigned as chair of the draft board and a local textile company manager took his place), appears on the surface to have been an utter failure for Branham. The US District Court in western Virginia dismissed the case in late June 1943, and the US Court of Appeals for the Fourth Circuit did the same five months later.[69] But Branham, it appears, actually prevailed. First, with one notable exception, no one disputed Branham's claims to be an Indian. Only the indefatigable Walter Plecker raised this issue with a memorandum that he had attached to Branham's birth certificate and that became an exhibit at the trial: "the Bureau [of Vital Statistics] declares that the certificate of birth of Willie Branham . . . is admitted into the birth files for statistical purposes only and is not accepted for establishing his race to be other than colored." But the defense seems not to have explored this point at the trial. Most important to Branham, he forced the Selective Service—fearful that local boards lacked the authority to determine race—to withdraw his initial induction order to report as Negro and to send him another one that left all race questions conspicuously blank. Indeed, it was precisely this last-minute adjustment that seemed to convince the federal judge to rule against Branham. As he put it in his ruling, "[T]here is no justiciable controversy, because the Local Board, before the institution of this action, cancelled its order requiring plaintiff to report for induction with negro inductees, and the current order to plaintiff to report for induction does not call upon him to report for induction as a negro trainee."[70]

A similar story, though with its own particularities, involved a group of people calling themselves variously Cherokees, Wide Awake Indians, and later Waccamaw-Siouans. Living in a swampy outpost about thirty-five miles west of Wilmington in the southeastern corner of North Carolina, they had long struggled, much like the communities in Virginia, to be recognized as Indians. Organized as the Wide Awake Indian Council, they used the courts and state legislature throughout the interwar years to build, maintain, and improve their own schools and churches, and they fiercely fought local whites' frequent attempts to classify them as black people. In the early 1920s, for example, Indian parents "threatened armed resistance" if white officials forced their children to attend "colored" schools, and in 1936, thirty-two Indian men "were arrested, fined, and some sentenced to work gangs because they refused to list or report their property for tax purposes. They explained to the court that 'they did not like the fact that their abstracts were listed in the same books as the colored people.'" All the while, local whites derided them as "self-styled Indians," insisting, much like Plecker in Virginia, that "there are no Indians" in the area.[71]

When local boards sprouted up in 1940, then, race classification was bound to be a problem. In late 1942 and early 1943, six men—Lonnie Wright Jacobs, J. D. Jacobs, Jolly Jacobs, Lofton Jacobs, Hezzie Patrick, and William Henry Young—refused to submit to a required pre-induction physical examination unless officials on hand changed the men's racial status from "Negro" to "Indian." Interestingly, while draft registration cards listed four of the men as "Indian," two—those for Patrick and Lofton Jacobs—listed them as "white."[72] The local draft board, located in the appropriately named town of Whiteville, argued that the "general public" considered the "Self-Styled Indians" really Negroes and refused to budge. When the state Selective Service director suggested sending the men to another county for induction, the board rejected the idea, ruing the day when "these individuals are permitted to serve in the Armed Forces as whites and later return to Columbus County." It reported furthermore that "other registrants in Columbus County . . . are claiming to be Indians but are considered Negroes."[73] Finally, the state Selective Service headquarters, following the course taken with Branham (and the Creoles), ordered the local board to send the men to the induction station with their race "undetermined," but this failed to placate the six Waccamaw-Siouans. On September 25, 1943, their very own special induction day, they refused to board the bus for Fort Bragg until their draft papers reflected an official and unambiguous recognition of their status as Indian.[74]

Like Oliver Fortune, the men were soon apprehended and stood trial for draft evasion, but their trial had a happier outcome than did Fortune's. For the case of *United States v. Lonnie Wright Jacobs, et al.*, the US District Court in Raleigh convened on November 2, 1943. Judge Isaac Melson Meekins, appointed by Calvin Coolidge in 1925, presided. The US attorney's office subpoenaed numerous witnesses to confirm the defendants' Negro status, including the clerk of the local draft board, a tax official, a clerk at the Columbus County Board of Commissioners, and the county schools' superintendent. But only the draft official testified for either side in court. Under questioning from the Indians' defense attorney, he admitted that his board knew full well that "the six young men . . . wouldn't go into the Army unless they went as they were, as Indians," that it still insisted on designating them as Negroes, and that it "had not given the defendants a hearing, to be present in person, to offer evidence, present affidavits, witnesses, etc., as to their side of the question."[75]

At this relatively early stage in the proceedings, Judge Meekins dismissed the case, stating, according to the recollection of the federal prosecutor, "that he was satisfied that the case was filled with prejudice, that he was not going to allow the defendants to be convicted of a crime upon such evidence, that they had not been given a full and fair hearing as to their race and contentions."[76] Selective Service officials in Washington interpreted Meekins's ruling more broadly. In a letter to Secretary of War Stimson in July 1944, Director Hershey argued that the federal court in North Carolina found "that the registrants were discriminated against because of their race and . . . that the local board had over-stepped its statutory and constitutional powers when, for purposes of selection, it arrogated from nowhere the power to determine race."[77]

THE NATIONAL PICTURE

Interestingly, there appears to be no record that Branham or at least five of the six Waccamaw-Siouans ever served in the World War II army, even though local boards classified each of the men as I-A and, after their trials, attempted to induct them again, this time without any reference to race from the start.[78] What explains this curious outcome—or various other outcomes described earlier, from Fortune's imprisonment and the Western Chickahominies' transfer to the Creoles' "undetermined" race status and the Pamunkeys' acceptance as Indians? Certainly the answers are, to some extent, particular to each case—the listing of Fortune's parents and grandparents as "colored" in official records or his enrollment in a black college, the state-recognized "tribal" status of the Pamunkeys, the vigilance of Western Chickahominies and the powerful allies they managed to mobilize on their behalf, the determination of young William Branham and his attorney, and so on. But growing out of these local stories is a larger national one that deeply shaped the outcomes of many race-determination controversies. Registrants' activism in Louisiana, Delaware, Virginia, and North Carolina caused serious tensions among, and eventually a split between, War Department and draft officials in Washington, DC. This split led in turn to a year of confusion and, in time, reforms on national race-determination policy. Coming too late for men like Fortune, these changes and confusion helped other racially ambiguous registrants avoid his fate.

This story begins, in some ways, back in early 1941 when Colonel Mills Neal, Virginia Selective Service director, first raised questions about local boards' authority to determine race. At the time, army and draft officials in Washington agreed that local boards, supposedly most knowledgeable about registrants' "ancestors" and "associates," could and should make these judgments. But by 1943, as race-related draft controversies mounted and began entering the courts, Selective Service officials reconsidered. In June, with the *Branham* case pending, General Counsel Shattuck wrote Hershey about "the relatively indefensible position in which the [Selective Service] System found itself when it was confronted with legal action regarding racial determination on the part of local boards or any other unit of the Selective Service." Sensing an imminent court defeat, he recommended the course of action followed in the *Branham* case (a course that he had helped craft): that draft boards induct men without reference to race and let the military deal with the confounding questions of racial determination. In an interoffice memo a month and a half later, the Selective Service's sole adviser on race issues, Colonel Campbell Johnson, sided with Shattuck: "[M]ajor responsibility for determining the race of registrants rests with the Armed Forces. I am fully aware of the complications which will arise, but I am of the opinion that these complications should rest most heavily upon the Branches of the Government which consider that they must make racial distinctions in carrying out their functions."[79]

Heeding this advice, Director Hershey revised draft policy in late August 1943. In a letter to the army's adjutant general and citing the *Branham* decision, earlier memoranda on race determination, and antidiscrimination clauses in Selective Service regulations and in the STSA, Hershey informed the War Department that he was rescinding earlier orders to local boards to determine racial status in all cases. He advised them instead to "forward registrants to induction stations with race undetermined in all questionable cases where the local board does not agree with the claims of the registrant." Hershey requested that the War Department notify all commanding generals in charge of induction that it was their responsibility going forward "to make the actual determination of race in questionable cases."[80] Selective Service sent amended instructions out to all local boards. On Form 221, for example, the "basic personnel document in the files of the armed forces," instructions under "Item 9—Race" read:

> If the local board does not agree with the claim of the registrant as to his race, it is the responsibility of the armed forces and not of the local board to determine the race of the registrant. Therefore, in the event of such disagreement, the local board should not fill in this item but should attach to Form 221 for transmission to the armed forces all information in the possession of the local board concerning the registrant's race.[81]

As the *Branham* solution became national Selective Service policy and local boards began sending Creoles, Waccamaw-Siouans, and others to induction stations with their race "undetermined," the War Department at first accepted its new race-classifying responsibility. Or, more accurately, it hoped to pass at least some of this responsibility on from local draft boards to local Red Cross chapters. The War Department apparently felt that the former had been "very unsatisfactory" in race-determination controversies. It also felt that Red Cross chapters were as well positioned as draft boards to investigate race classification from the perspective both of the documentary record—birth certificates, marriage certificates, and the like—and of "social acceptance" in local communities. But much like the Selective Service, the Red Cross soon resisted this responsibility as it too came to understand the stakes and the complexities involved. "Decisions on race determination involve serious social, economic, and legal considerations," the Red Cross stated in December 1943. "They must not be undertaken by [Red Cross] chapters."[82]

Soon after this announcement, the War Department backtracked on its promise to Selective Service to assume race-determination responsibilities in contested cases. In a confidential memorandum of January 1944, the adjutant general notified commanding generals across the country that "[r]egistrants reporting to the Armed Forces Induction Station or to a Reception Center for induction whose race has not been determined and so recorded . . . and whose race is not readily determinable with the information at hand will be returned to the local board . . . [as] 'Rejected—physically unfit,' if such is the case, or 'Status not determined because of incomplete records.'"[83] The War Department, in short, demanded a return to original race-determination policies.

For local boards stuck between conflicting orders from Selective Service and War Department officials, confusion and paralysis reigned. This fact must explain how perfectly fit I-A registrants like Branham and the Waccamaw-Siouans seem ultimately to have avoided induction. In North Carolina, for example, new army orders arrived just as the Columbus County local board, after extensive consultation between the assistant US attorney general, Tom Clark, and Selective Service in Washington and Raleigh, prepared to re-induct the six Waccamaw-Siouans without reference to race. Utterly confused, a draft official in Raleigh wrote Hershey in Washington, "It seems that this puts us right back where we were in the beginning and right up against the proposition of having the local board determine the ethnic origin of registrants." "The local board," according to draft officials in Washington, "would not hesitate to make this determination again in these race controversy cases were it not for the fact that the

Court said once that it was not in their power, and the further fact that to do so would be contrary to Selective Service instructions for filling in Form 221."[84]

As similar confusion hit other states and army induction stations rejected registrants whose race was undetermined, Director Hershey finally wrote Secretary of War Stimson, hoping to resolve matters.[85] In a letter dated July 19, 1944, he argued that the US District Court ruling in North Carolina in tandem with the War Department policy placed Selective Service in "an anomalous position": "local boards cannot legally make a determination contrary to the contention of the registrant, and the induction station will not accept the registrant for induction unless race is readily determinable from the information at hand." Doubting "that the armed forces may reject an otherwise acceptable registrant merely because the local board had not determined and recorded the race of the registrant," Hershey asked the War Department again to determine race in controversial cases.[86]

Two weeks later, Stimson refused to budge, claiming that local boards were best positioned to determine race by examining "conditions under which the individual lives in his home community." So Hershey tried again. But this time he spelled out in greater detail the dilemma local boards faced and, most important, offered a new solution. "Let us take the case of a registrant who claims that he is an American Indian," explained Hershey in an August 5 letter, "but who, by reason of the conditions under which he lives in his home community . . . is determined by the local board to be a Negro. In such a case the local board has three alternatives: (1) to determine that the registrant is of the Negro race; (2) to leave the question of race undetermined; or (3) to determine that the registrant is an Indian." Hershey noted that the federal district court in North Carolina had rejected the first option and the War Department the second, in both cases leaving "a registrant physically fit and liable to induction" out of the armed forces. Therefore, Hershey concluded that only the third option remained—one that Selective Service had never before proposed and yet many registrants had demanded from the start: "where racial status is in controversy" and where the local board can neither classify a registrant's race against his wishes nor avoid the race question entirely, then it must "in such cases resolve the question in favor of the claim of the registrant."[87]

Perhaps surprisingly, the War Department accepted this new proposal ten days later. In a letter to Hershey on August 15, Assistant Secretary of War John J. McCloy first reiterated his boss's—and, for several years, Hershey's—point that "the local board is better qualified to determine the race of a registrant because of their knowledge of his environment and home conditions than members of the armed forces who see the registrant for the first time when he reports to an armed forces induction station or reception center." But McCloy concluded that "unless conclusive evidence to the contrary is submitted," "[a] registrant, whose race determination has been based upon the claim of such registrant . . . will be found acceptable for military service if otherwise qualified."[88]

As a result of this exchange and agreement, Selective Service issued Policy Determination no. 241, titled "Controversy as to Race of Registrants," two weeks later. It stipulated that "where the registrant claims to be of one race and the local board is of the opinion or determined that he is of another race, the local board shall, nevertheless, complete Form 211 [sic: 221], showing the race of the registrant as claimed by the registrant and forward him for induction in the usual manner, transmitting to the induction station all information in the possession of the local board bearing upon the correct race of the registrant."[89] As the war ended a year later, this policy remained in place.

What effect this new policy had on remaining race-related draft controversies is not entirely clear, though the case of James Brown Bey in late 1944 showed that the federal courts and the War Department refused to allow inductees to claim any race they wished. Recall that McCloy told Bey's attorney, "The determination by the Army of race is one of fact" and "there is no 'Moorish-American' race."[90] What is clearer is that this simmering struggle between War Department and Selective Service officials over questions of race determination offered registrants slightly more say in the process over time; it also improved their odds of having the army pass them over entirely. As race determination became increasingly contentious, the army likely concluded that the induction of a smattering of Waccamaw-Siouans and Chickahominies and Creoles was not worth the hassle.

STATE, SOCIETY, AND RACE

In a broad sense, these varied classification stories involve two notoriously slippery abstractions—state and society—in their entangled making and remaking of a third—race. These stories, taken together, provide insights into all three.

It is remarkable that this smattering of people—so marginalized and numerically miniscule—played a role in shaping federal government policy, forcing high-level officials, from the secretary of war and the director of Selective Service to the assistant attorney general, to grapple seriously with their claims. One might, then, extend political scientist James Scott's helpful insistence that we "keep in mind not only the capacity of state simplifications to transform the world but also the capacity of the society"—even its most subordinated members—"to modify, subvert, block, and even overturn the categories imposed on it."[91] More generally, much like the battles over enlistment and troop assignments, the state's most powerful leaders never enjoyed free reign to dictate policy however they saw fit. Instead, they were forced to negotiate constantly with a diverse range of society's ordinary people who always insisted on—and sometimes succeeded in—having their say.[92]

These ordinary people seldom sought to create their own racial categories entirely. In this way, they were unlike, for example, writer Jean Toomer, who, in the 1920s and 1930s, insisted that he was neither white nor black but something new—a member of "the American stock or race."[93] They were also unlike those affiliated with today's "multiracial" or "mixed-race" movement, which tends to embrace fluid or "hybrid" racial categories. Instead, these racially ambiguous people, with the important exception of James Brown Bey and Moorish Americans, did not dispute the state's racial categories; they disputed the state's authority or accuracy in its slotting of people into them.

In these disputes, *white* and *Indian* were the locus of sometimes intense struggles, as various people organized themselves around the desire to be defined as one or the other (or, in the rare case of Branham, both). But the most contentious and consequential battles revolved as much around a negative identity—not colored or not Negro—as around a positive one—white or Indian or the rest. Therefore, while ordinary people's struggles to wrest from the federal government the power to self-classify are noteworthy and admirable, they should not be romanticized. Indians, for example, bravely battled against their subordination and forced disappearance, both core features of a centuries-old settler colonialist white supremacy.[94] But they sometimes did so by employing essentialist and demeaning notions of blackness. In other words, they fought one form of racism with another.

The consistent and spirited desire to be "not colored" came in part from the deep historical and structural roots of anti-black racism in the United States and around the world. In the Jim Crow South in particular, Indians had for decades been determined to avoid the colossal costs of black status there, and the World War II years simply witnessed a continuation of those struggles. But an equally important reason involved the specific institutional context in which these classification struggles emerged—the military. It segregated not on the basis of one's Indianness or Puerto Ricanness or even whiteness, but on the basis of one's coloredness. One could be defined as nonwhite and still be assigned to serve in white units. The same was not true for those defined as colored. That is, when it came to classification and the troop assignments based on that classification, the most important boundary divided colored from everyone else. Sometimes that "everyone else" was called "white"; sometimes it was not. But in all cases, people defined as colored occupied the deeply deleterious end of the military's most foundational and powerful color lines. It was those lines that further encouraged so many different kinds of people—from Creoles to Moorish Americans, Puerto Ricans to Indians—to desperately dodge coloredness.

How, then, in the case of official draft and military classification, did the state make and enforce these lines exactly—and define and determine race? As for defining race, ideas about biology and blood still held sway at times—recall, for example, Director Hershey's advice to local boards to define "Negro" as anyone with "any ascertainable Negro blood." But these ideas coexisted and sometimes were superseded by an implicit concession regarding race's critical social nature. When controversies arose, officials seldom considered closely examining bodies or measuring crania or drawing blood to clarify matters, as some local courts and other state agencies did at the time.[95] Instead, Selective Service and the military asked draft boards, or in some cases the FBI, military intelligence, and local Red Cross chapters, to gather information on ancestors, but also on associates and "home conditions"—where one, say, worshipped or worked or went to school. When these cases reached the federal courts, a school superintendent was more likely to be called to testify than an anthropologist. Ultimately, one's race, in the eyes of the state, often hinged on this social information. This is precisely why local draft boards (and, for a brief time, local Red Cross chapters) were tasked with classifying race in the first place.

This point might not appear wholly surprising. There is a long history, stretching back to the nineteenth century, of race-determination court cases turning on questions of "home conditions." Also, as Americans fought the Nazis overseas, scientific attacks on racial essentialism mounted, challenging efforts to rest race classifications on bodies and blood alone.[96] Still, one might not expect to find these quasi-social-constructionist ideas coming from the racist armed forces. The point serves as a crucial reminder that racial domination need not rely on biological or essentialist notions of race.

In the state's view, however, race was not simply social but also local— and the two points are inextricably linked. It viewed draft boards and, to a lesser extent, Red Cross chapters as social-information experts, because they were local institutions made up of local people—especially local white people—who presumably knew or could easily collect information about draftees' local associates and histories. Indeed, battles over race classification often pitted racially ambiguous local people not against a distant central state but against other local people, almost always white people serving as arms of the state. Would it be local board members or the inductees themselves who made the tough race classification calls? In this way, race classification was different from the enlistment and assignment stories of the early chapters. Only Washington's most powerful leaders decided who could join the military and in what sorts of segregated units they could serve. But when it came to the all-important task of racial classification, upon which these enlistment and segregated-assignment questions ultimately rested, local people prevailed. In a global age of global war, then, when capitalism, migration, colonialism, slavery, and genocide had long made race a national and transnational phenomenon, it retained a crucial local dimension.[97]

This dimension also explains why nearly all major race-classification controversies arose in the Jim Crow South—Louisiana, Virginia, and North Carolina. It was there that local state officials seemed most obsessed with policing racial boundaries, especially those surrounding "colored" or "Negro" people. In other parts of the country—Pennsylvania, in the case of James Brown Bey, is an exception here—it appears that racially ambiguous people had more freedom to define themselves and to avoid efforts to impose hard and fast racial categories on them. In Maine, for example, a Selective Service official discovered that a man whom it had already inducted as white possessed "colored blood to the extent of 25%." Unlike what occurred in the southern cases, this state official did not insist on the man's transfer to a "colored" outfit. The official "fear[ed] for the boy's future if he should be serving in Southern States with white troops and this situation [his 'colored blood'] revealed." But he also thought that "[i]t would be just as bad to have this boy transferred to a colored regiment as he can readily pass as a white man." In the end, the man appears to have stayed in the so-called white army.[98]

But race's local dimension had its limits. After all, if locals often decided how to slot others or themselves into race categories, it was the distant central state—say, the War Department, not the local draft board—that decided on what basis this slotting would take place and what race categories ultimately counted as legitimate or as "fact." This state determined, for example, that ancestors and associates mattered most in classifying by race and that "colored" was a real race but Moorish American was not. This state also determined who precisely belonged to its various racial categories. "White" was a moving target. Sometimes it included "Indians," "Filipinos," "Japanese," "Chinese," "Puerto Ricans," and "Mexicans," all of whom the military and the state more generally defined as nonwhite in other contexts. Other times it suggested that they would be counted "as white" but not necessarily defined as such. Other times it explicitly classified these groups as not white. As for "colored," the state defined it narrowly to include only "Negroes" but defined "Negro" broadly to include anyone with any Negro ancestry or "blood" at all.[99]

This narrowing of the "colored" category is significant in that it happened at precisely the time when some antiracist activists worked to expand the term to include—and to build solidarities across—a variety of nonwhites around the world.[100] The military undermined their efforts by stressing in a way that the most important color line was not between white and nonwhite, but between black and nonblack instead.

PART IV

Training

CHAPTER 6

ᴄᴧᴐ

Jim Crow in Uniform

The military's processes of enlistment, unit assignment, and racial classification offered numerous opportunities to draw color lines. These opportunities only expanded once inductees formally joined the military. As soon as civilians metamorphosed into uniformed servicemen and -women, they, like so many huddled masses, migrated to a new world—of rank and jobs, barracks and mess halls, post exchanges and service clubs, courts-martial and commendations, uniforms and the military salute. In all these matters and more, military personnel and others crafted an intricate and vast welter of color lines that not only divided so-called race from so-called race but also reinscribed the very notion and categories of race itself. What did these lines look and feel like? Who built them and why? What sorts of resistance did they generate? And did this resistance succeed in reshaping or removing any of these lines? This and subsequent chapters explore these crucial questions as they applied to military installations in the United States and on battlefields and in encampments around the world.

This chapter looks particularly at the military's black-white boundaries—so extensive and powerful in matters of enlistment, unit assignments, and classification—in the context of troops' training and stateside service. These boundaries, the handiwork of a wide range of actors, but none more important than military officers and especially leaders, wended their way through nearly every aspect of military life, creating a dense and powerful structure of white domination and black subordination—or, in the words of one wartime commentator, "Jim Crow in Uniform."[1] In the eyes of its creators, this version of Jim Crow was necessary both to win a war for freedom overseas and to shore up faltering white supremacy at home, faltering in part because of the military's own unwitting actions.

Like its civilian cousin, Jim Crow in uniform generated extensive protest. But unlike the considerable activism around enlistment and unit segregation, this protest had a broader grassroots reach; and it included, as its vital vanguard, large numbers of servicemen and -women, who employed the widest range of tactics, from armed resistance to boycotts, sit-ins to strikes, foot-dragging to courageous soldiering. In the end, this protest, with assistance from a select few military officials, managed to blur a small but important number of black-white lines. The number would have been higher had protesters not faced, as in the battle to mix military units, formidable opposition in the White House, in Congress, in the courts, and among military leaders.

DRAWING "DAMN FOOL LINES"

"It just don't make any sense," an African American soldier training at Camp Shelby in Hattiesburg, Mississippi, told a government official investigating the area in 1942. "We're all in the same army, wearing the same khaki, and they say we're fighting for the same thing. . . . [And] when those Japs and Wops start shooting they don't try to find out who is white and who is black before they aim. Yet they draw all kinds of damn fool lines and say 'black boys on this side, whites on the other.' "[2]

Spatial Segregation

Indeed, these ubiquitous black-white lines cropped up just as soon as civilians became service members. Young men and women who joined the military were officially sworn in at army reception centers, navy recruiting stations, naval training stations, and armed forces induction stations. While the place of induction varied, all recruits shared similar experiences there: they received a uniform, a battery of tests, a first job assignment, and some basic instructions in marching, saluting, the articles of war— and often the military's black-white lines. One corporal, recently back from service overseas, recalled matter-of-fact mixing between black and white recruits on their forty-five-minute train ride from New York City's Grand Central Station to the army reception center at Camp Upton on Long Island: they were "eating or drinking or playing music or shooting crap [*sic*]" and without any "natural—shall we say—segregation." That ended abruptly as soon as the men disembarked at the camp and officers ordered them to line up for physical examinations—with one queue for "white troops" and the other for "colored." Indeed, these reception-center divides were common practice across the United States throughout the war years. In 1941, War Department race adviser William Hastie observed that "a separate Reception Center or a distinct organization within a Reception Center is the present pattern for most Negro recruits in most places." Three years later not much had changed: in late 1944, army generals conceded privately that reception-center black-white divides were long-standing army policy, which they had no intention of changing.[3]

These divides followed African American troops to training camps, sometimes appearing on the very trip there. Train conductors and military and civilian police routinely forced black recruits to sit in the "colored" car upon entering the South. It was often no more than a cramped and crowded section of the baggage or smoking coach, which routinely denied black troops first-class seats or adequate—or sometimes any—eating and sleeping accommodations. In July 1941, a recently commissioned second lieutenant, Welton Taylor, left Chicago for Fort Sill in Oklahoma, where he would begin training with a mountain artillery unit. Expecting "an uneventful, if downright boring ride," he found that things changed when the train reached Oklahoma. There, an "elderly, white-haired conductor" told Taylor that state law required that he move to the "first car behind the coal tender." Taylor protested, but to no avail. "Livid," he later recalled, "I gritted my teeth, picked up my luggage and headed for the front of the train. 'It sure would be nice to enjoy a little democracy before I have to fight—or maybe even die—for it,' I spat out through clenched teeth as I passed my fellow officers and gentlemen."[4]

While these particular black-white lines were not technically the military's making, it shored them up in various passive and active ways. Taylor was frustrated because none of his fellow officers came to his defense. In other cases, it was the military itself that insisted on segregation. When Edward Soulds of Missoula, Montana, journeyed to Texas for infantry boot camp, it was a member of the military police, not a train conductor or civilian law enforcement, who moved him to the colored car in El Paso. This MP was simply following War Department policy. Federal courts at the time were divided over the applicability of Jim Crow state laws to interstate travel, which, after all, constituted the vast bulk of troop transports. And yet early in the war, the military leadership decided that its troops, when traveling on trains into or across the South, should respect Jim Crow laws and customs, "pending final determination of the question by the Supreme Court."[5]

Fig. 6.1 Welton I. Taylor, a field artillery officer at the time, at Fort Sill in Oklahoma, 1941. Courtesy of Karyn J. Taylor.

Once troops arrived at training camps and settled into their daily routines, black-white lines proliferated. Perhaps most immediately obvious was the strict spatial separation or ghettoization of black troops. In a few rare but important cases, this was achieved through so-called all-Negro posts, such as the Tuskegee Army Air Field in Alabama and Fort Huachuca in Arizona, both of which housed only black units (along with their white commanding officers, who lived in their own all-white sections of the post, ate at their all-white mess halls, and relaxed at their own all-white officers' clubs).[6] More often, black troops occupied a separate section of the post, carefully cordoned off from its main areas and from other troops by a river, fire break, stockade, parade ground, or a sort of no man's land. "It seems the army always arranged to have blacks back up against the woods someplace," recalled one African American soldier. "Isolated."[7] Commanders and others often explicitly marked these spaces on both their mental and physical maps as "Negro areas" or "Harlems" or, in one instance, "Monkey Point." Sometimes these areas also received their own formal names: Camp Robert Smalls at the Great Lakes Naval Training Center outside Chicago, for example, or Montford Point Camp at the Marine Barracks, New River (later renamed Camp Lejeune), in North Carolina.[8]

Alongside these large segregated military spaces, a dizzying array of smaller ones sprouted up. Throughout the armed services and across

Fig. 6.2 Six African American officers pose with their wives or sweethearts outside the officers' mess at Fort Huachuca during World War II. The fort was one of the few so-called all-Negro army posts at the time, so named because all the outfits on post had solely black enlisted personnel. Courtesy of the Smithsonian National Museum of African American History and Culture, Gift of Beverly J. Blackwood in memory of Charles J. Blackwood Sr.

the country, commanders forced black trainees to use separate—and in-variably unequal—barracks, latrines, water fountains, mess halls, drill halls, dispensaries, hospitals and hospital wards, post exchanges, rifle ranges, swimming pools, service clubs, churches, movie theaters, parade grounds, barber shops, shoe repair shops, tailors, haberdasheries, buses, gymnasiums, libraries, golf courses, guest houses, dental chairs, vending machines, and stockades. Sometimes black troops shared space with other troops but had particular time slots for their use of it, or they had sep-arate entrances, exits, seating areas, parking spots, and store windows. Sometimes "white" facilities were available and "Negro" or "colored" ones were not. One black soldier recalled that at Camp Shenango in Pennsylvania "there was a white PX [post exchange], but we could not use it. They set up a temporary situation in the barracks [for us] where a guy had some candy bars and a Coke. At the white PX, you could buy almost anything. We had nothin'."[9]

No army- or navywide directives required these black-white spatial patterns, nor did Jim Crow state laws or local ordinances, since military installations were, as federal property, not subject to them.[10] Instead, in-dividual post and station commanders often crafted these policies, so variations abounded. But very rarely could black service members es-cape spatial segregation entirely. The small number of black women ac-cepted into the military—often the Women's Army Auxiliary Corps (later renamed the Women's Army Corps, or WAC), since the navy, marines, and coast guard excluded them for most of the war—faced perhaps fewer black-white spatial lines than did men. Even so, they encountered their share of segregated dances, barracks, and officers' clubs and, on occasion, segregated classrooms, mess halls, and churches.[11] This variation by place was typical. Often an army post or naval station would insist on segrega-tion in some areas—say, barracks and mess halls—but not in others—say, post exchanges and recreation halls. Northern and western installations tended to be more integrated than southern ones. But the latter greatly outnumbered the former and, even so, for every Grenier Field in New Hampshire, which seemed to mix all its airmen irrespective of race, there was a Westover Field in Massachusetts, which drew distinct black-white lines in barracks, mess halls, chapels, and theaters.[12] There was a general move toward the greater integration of training space over time, especially by the final months of the war and especially in the navy. Prior to this point, the direction of change was more muddled. In the fall of 1942, for ex-ample, while one Indiana camp began for the first time mixing all trainees in shows, service clubs, post exchanges, and transportation, other posts in Alabama and Arizona began "increasing [their] segregation of Negroes."[13]

As in the civilian world, rank seldom shielded black military personnel from segregated space. In an important departure from past policy, the army integrated many of its officer candidate schools in 1941. But this mixing did not apply to black air corps pilots or naval officers, and even in the army, candidate-school integration had its limits.[14] One black officer candidate, for example, recalled attending school in North Carolina with integrated mess halls, training classes, and even latrines; but he also noted that he and the other black officer candidates slept at one end of the quarters away from everyone else and were, unlike whites, excluded from recreational halls.[15] More important, once one graduated from these schools and joined an outfit, Jim Crow spread in all directions. Some posts and stations had separate "white" and "colored" officers' clubs, messes, and quarters. Where this was deemed impossible, white officers simply ate and slept off post, or some commanders simply excluded black officers from white officers' spaces and required the former to eat or bunk with black enlisted men—a clear violation of the army's typically sacrosanct rules of rank.[16]

The line dividing Americans from their wartime enemies would seem even more sacrosanct, and yet black-white spatial boundaries sometimes scrambled that as well. Among African Americans' more maddening and memorable encounters with military Jim Crow came when German or Italian prisoners of war enjoyed access to white spaces long closed to them. The same soldier who bemoaned Jim Crow at Camp Shenango also bitterly remembered "German prisoners free to move around the camp, unlike black soldiers who were restricted. The Germans walked right into the doggone places like any white American. We were wearin' the same uniform, but we were excluded." In a 1944 letter to Truman Gibson, who succeeded William Hastie as the War Department's chief "Negro" adviser, one private stationed at Camp Barkeley in Texas protested the practice of segregating the latrines of black soldiers, on the one hand, and white American soldiers and German prisoners, on the other. "The tyrant," he wrote, dumfounded and disheartened, "is actually placed over the liberator."[17]

United States–enemy lines were scrambled in deference to black-white ones just as frequently off base as on, reflecting a key fact: the military's spatial segregation overlapped with and at times became indistinguishable from its widespread civilian variety.[18] This was especially the case when military commanders, as with train travel, forced black troops to follow Jim Crow customs and laws off base. Three WACs on leave from Fort Knox learned this lesson the hard way. In July 1945, finding the "colored" waiting room at the Elizabethtown, Kentucky, bus station overcrowded, the women settled in the white section instead. When a white civilian police officer accosted them and demanded that the "niggers" return to the colored section at once, an argument ensued. The officer soon took out his blackjack and beat the women across the head and face. The injuries to one of the women were so severe, according to the *Chicago Defender*, that she required two days of hospitalization. Even so, the post commander at Fort Knox, evidently more concerned with protecting Jim Crow than the three WACs in his charge, attempted to court-martial the women for violating state segregation laws. When the NAACP and others pointed out that no laws required segregated seating at bus stations, the commander charged the women with disorderly conduct instead. An army court-martial board eventually acquitted the women, but the entire story demonstrated the lengths to which some military commanders would go to buttress civilian Jim Crow.[19]

Sometimes this buttressing meant birthing it anew—transporting it to towns and cities with little if any history of black-white segregation. From Medford, Oregon, to Falmouth, Massachusetts, black troops found that Jim Crow spatial patterns often arrived in town just as soon as they did. In restaurants, USO clubs, bars, hotels, theaters, and train stations, at lunch counters, and on buses, sometimes signs—"No Service to Negroes" or "No Colored Trade Solicited"—told the story; sometimes it was a bartender or hostess insisting, "We don't serve colored" or "We don't serve niggers here!"[20] To be sure, some military commanders resisted these practices, placing, for example, a certain Jim Crow restaurant off limits to all troops until it agreed to serve everyone equally. But commanders' support for—and sometimes initiation of—Jim Crow spatial boundaries was more common. In Cheyenne, Wyoming, according to the recollections of one black veteran, "the few Negroes of the town were [initially] quite free to go about as they pleased. But when the Army moved in signs appeared all over town barring Negro troops from certain bars, hotels, and movies." In his memory, it was the army that "set up [these] discriminatory systems." In Fairbanks, Alaska, army commanders took a more comprehensive approach, placing the entire city off limits to black troops, in part to prevent their "fraternizing" with local white women.[21]

Forbidden Fraternizing

Indeed, male-female "fraternizing" afforded another opportunity for black-white boundary-making. The sex-segregated military tended to make these relations, at least on the home front, a lesser concern to whites than they were in the civilian world. But when men and women had the chance to interact socially across the black-white divide, white commanders often rushed to place obstacles between them. These obstacles appeared at Camp Forrest in Tennessee in the fall of 1944, when jazz musician Louis Prima came to town: black WACs were allowed to listen in their own Jim Crow section but were forbidden to dance. They appeared at Fort Huachuca in the spring of 1943, when the army temporarily quartered a group of white civilian women workers in the "colored troop housing area" and deemed it "necessary to place a high electrified wire fence around the area for their protection." And they appeared in a town outside of Philadelphia where, shortly after the attack on Pearl Harbor, an African American artillery regiment arrived to defend the area's booming war industries. When white locals warmly welcomed the men—hosting parties for the troops, visiting them in their barracks, and inviting them to their homes—the regimental commander grew increasingly alarmed. "Unless you have lived in the South," he later explained, "you can't understand the problem a thing like this raises. . . . I was afraid some of these Negroes might get ideas." He announced that "any cases of relations between white and colored males and females whether voluntary or not is [sic] considered rape and during time of war the penalty is death." After black troops and civil rights groups loudly protested the order, the War Department forced the local commander to rescind it. Still, he remained unapologetic, telling one newspaper reporter, "I may lose my command for this, but I would do the same thing again. . . . [J]ust a case of an officer being overzealous in his duty." Indeed, for numerous commanders, "duty" encompassed more than simply leading troops, carrying out orders, and defending the nation. It also included policing black-white fraternizing.[22]

"The Dirtiest Jobs"

That these commanders were nearly always white was hardly coincidental: the issue of rank constituted another crucial site of black-white lines. Black troops in all branches of the military found it exceedingly difficult, if not outright impossible, to receive commissions or to rise through the officer ranks. White officers up and down the chain of command crafted and endorsed these policies, since they widely and firmly believed that black people made pitiful officers, that black troops preferred or performed better under white officers, and that whites would never tolerate taking orders from a black superior.[23] By war's end, the marines failed to commission a single black officer, and the navy commissioned a paltry sixty or so (compared with several hundred thousand whites), and only late in the war.[24] The army, by contrast, had more than seven thousand black officers by

Fig. 6.3 The first black navy officers during World War II, February 1944. Courtesy National Archives, 80-G-300215.

war's end, a remarkable increase over its small handful in 1940.[25] Even so, the increase could have been much greater. According to Samuel Stouffer, in his classic study of the World War II army, *The American Soldier,* "Negroes, even those of equal educational and AGCT [Army General Classification Test] level, had much less chance to become [commissioned] officers." By March 1945, he found that while 11 percent of white army personnel held this rank, less than 1 percent of African Americans did—despite the fact that army surveys consistently found that the latter's desire to become an officer exceeded that of whites.[26]

Among this relatively small number of black army officers, promotions were also extraordinarily rare. Of course, many service members, regardless of race, griped about favoritism and unfairness in the military's promotion practices.[27] But African Americans' efforts to advance through the officer ranks faced uniquely insurmountable obstacles. In early 1943, the War Department announced that, since the beginning of the officer candidate program, one graduate had already achieved the rank of lieutenant colonel, a few had become majors, and hundreds were captains; but among them was not a single African American, because all black officers had stalled at the lieutenant rank, the lowest among officers. War Department policy required as much, which Truman Gibson privately admitted "limit[ed] seriously the promotion of Negro officers."[28] Indeed, throughout the war, African Americans—9 percent of the army at their height—never exceeded one-tenth of 1 percent of its generals.[29] Taken together, the military's myriad hierarchies of rank perfectly reflected and reinforced its black-white hierarchies of race.

For enlisted men and women, one's job or rating in the service, as much as one's rank, undergirded these hierarchies. Sometimes white commanders flatly denied black troops access to valuable job training and, therefore, to valuable jobs. In one instance, four black soldiers crossed the country to attend tire maintenance school in Akron, Ohio, only to be sent home by a white officer who refused to integrate classes there (an example of job boundaries reinforcing spatial ones).[30] Other times, the military provided African Americans training in countless invaluable skills—everything from physical therapy and auto mechanics to baking and plumbing—but not a suitable job in return. One black soldier, initially impressed by the "large number of Colored fellows attending technical schools with whites," quickly discovered that this training had little bearing on black troops' eventual assignment; they still received jobs as "part of the Officer's mess gang, pick and shovel detail, guard detail, or other tasks of menial nature only."[31] The upshot of these and other practices was that, as in the civilian world, black people held a disproportionate share of the most low-status and backbreaking labor. As the *Chicago Defender* put it in early 1945, "The dirtiest jobs are done by the darkest soldiers in the Army and Navy. Whether it has been glamorized with such terms as 'engineers' or 'port battalion' or 'construction battalion,' the job is still common labor."[32]

Job complaints pervaded the armed forces, of course, transcending racist boundaries. In a book about wartime life in the army, future playwright Arthur Miller noted that it teemed with "a mass of individuals each misfitted in his own mind to the job he is doing and filled with a yearning to work at something else which seems to him more romantic and satisfying." But finding "more romantic and satisfying" military work proved infinitely more difficult for black people than for whites, a point perhaps most easily appreciated in light of the experiences of the best-educated African Americans. Soldier Clinton O. Knox, a Harvard PhD, who would serve as the American ambassador to Haiti in the 1960s and 1970s, tended bar at the white officers' club at Camp McCain in Mississippi, an assignment that would have been utterly inconceivable for a white man with his education. Ewart Guanier, a New York University Law School graduate and a future Harvard professor, volunteered for the army in 1942. He then spent three long, infuriating years training, taking courses, and passing various specialized army exams to be a psychologist or an instructor in the War Department's Information and Education Division. But he was told time and again that someone with his qualifications was not needed at the moment. Eventually, in May 1945, a full three years after he joined up, the army sent Guanier to serve in Hawaii, but only after Congressman Adam Clayton Powell and NAACP leaders personally appealed his case to Secretary Stimson.[33]

Even when black and white troops shared the same job—if not the same unit—commanders ensured that other job-related color lines remained. Take the military police (or MP), for example. While early in the war years white MPs belonged to specially trained companies, the few black people allowed to join these ranks did so temporarily, as members of other units that were detached for special duty. More significant still, all white MPs were armed with manufactured billy clubs and .45 pistols, but their black counterparts were given "rudely fashioned and inoffensive-looking" clubs and were rarely permitted to carry firearms. One white general succinctly captured the rationale behind these policies: "the Negro is incapable of assuming the responsibilities of an M.P. without becoming overbearing."[34]

Fig. 6.4 A member of the "Military Police Colored" in Columbus, Georgia, April 1942. Courtesy National Archives, 111-SC-134951.

"You've Got to Teach a Nigger in Uniform,
That He's Still a Nigger"

Much like these entrenched employment hierarchies, a diverse set of symbols—from military dress and military salutes to post entertainment and everyday language—also helped mark and maintain black-white lines. At Camp Upton, one white officer warned his white troops, soon heading south for training, never to shake a "Negro's hand when he says goodbye," while one "Negro soldier" in Arizona complained that a white enlisted man refused to salute a black officer, not an uncommon occurrence. In Hawaii, in a bizarre trend that would expand overseas, white officers told locals that black troops had tails, a story that became "so widespread," in one African American soldier's memory, "that one of the local kids came peeking into the shower in order to see if one of the technical sergeants, Colored, had a tail." Also in Hawaii, USO entertainment for sailors stationed at Pearl Harbor included "two blackfaced comedians" who sold popcorn and "made humorous remarks." Meanwhile, the post exchange at Camp Claiborne in Louisiana sold a songbook with this poem, entitled "Watermelon Advice," tucked away in its back pages: "Oh, Ise a great big nigger / Ise black; that you can see / Oh, Ise a great big nigger /Just from the land of Africa / Ise a great big nigger / Some good advice to make / To tell all the white folks / How to eat a watermelon / Before I am too late."[35] Together, these diverse cases conveyed the sense that black people and white people were so profoundly unequal that the latter could not deign to shake hands with the former, could not possibly show deference to the former, could only imagine the former as ridiculous, undignified caricatures—or as animals.

As a pithy, seemingly unassailable statement of status, black troops' uniforms had the potential to transcend and muddle these distinctions. For this reason, many whites, in and out of the military, targeted them. Sometimes this involved insisting that black service members, while off post, remove "that soldier suit." Other times it involved modifying uniforms, even in subtle ways, to emphasize black-white difference. One black Seabee recalled that African Americans' and whites' identical navy uniforms so incensed the latter that they demanded the former replace their brass buttons with plastic ones.[36] Perhaps most often whites simply stressed that, uniform or no uniform, African Americans' subordinate status remained. "You've got to teach a nigger in uniform, that he's still a nigger," white southerners told one white journalist. Whites deemed this "education" especially vital when black officers were involved. "Every day since I've been in the Army," remarked one such officer, "some white person has reminded me through some word or act that, although I wear the uniform of an officer in the United States Army, I'm still nothing but a 'nigger.'"[37]

Perhaps the most common symbolic black-white boundaries involved the everyday use of language. One black officer objected to his regimental commander constantly referring to black troops as "you people" and to Benjamin O. Davis Sr.—the army's sole black general—as "your general," suggesting that Davis was "of an inferior class and not a general of the United States Army as any other general would be." A more common complaint was that white officers and white enlisted personnel routinely called black troops a litany of demeaning and difference-making names, including "nigra," "negra," "nigger," "darkie," "black bastard," "black son of a bitch," "Sambo," and "boy." In a June 1943 memo about "smouldering unrest" among black troops, Truman Gibson highlighted a number of causes, chief among them the fact that "many white officers now serving with Negro organizations . . . show a basic disrespect for Negroes generally and Negro soldiers particularly. Many use the expressions 'nigger,' 'Darkie' and 'boy' openly and freely." The purpose of such slurs, Gibson suggested, was to "impress daily on Negro soldiers . . . that they must 'remember their places.'"[38]

Along with the slur "nigger," "boy"—a term that could signal a messy mix of age, gender, and racial subordination—seems to have been a particular favorite among many white officers. One technical sergeant recalled that "all of my officers at these two southern camps"—Fort McLellan and Fort Benning—"were white and they had a great capacity for not remembering your name so substituted things like, 'Hey, you with the black face over there, boy.'" Another soldier, who trained at Fort Huachuca, remembered that his officers expressed "their belief in white supremacy with body language and tone of voice . . . [and with] their slave term, 'boy.'"[39]

Violence

These slurs and slights, especially when coming from enlisted personnel, could lead to another important form of black-white boundary-making: violence. What an African American GI referred to as the "almost daily name-calling and fisticuffs between black and white soldiers" constituted one everyday version of it.[40] Another version involved slightly less frequent, collective confrontations involving anywhere from dozens to thousands of troops. Erupting throughout the war years, though peaking in the spring and summer of 1943, these large-scale "riots" often pitted black troops, on the one hand, against white troops and white civilian and military police, on the other. Both these big and small acts of violence involved a host of complex issues, including overcrowded buses, abusive police, frayed nerves, inadequate recreational facilities, drinking, and rampant rumors. Related to all these matters, and sometimes explicitly at issue in these battles, were white troops' bottom-up efforts to police the military's black-white lines. For example, quotidian battles often involved whites calling their black comrades in arms demeaning terms. As for the major clashes, not a few began when white MPs thought African Americans had forgotten "their place" or when whites objected to black people's use of a post exchange or service club in posts like Camp Patrick Henry in Virginia, Camp Shenango in Pennsylvania, and Camp Beauregard in Louisiana.[41] In all these cases, white soldiers employed a tool most readily at hand—violence—to assist their commanders' more powerful efforts to divide "colored" and "white."

"Not Getting a Square Deal"

In the wake of violent incidents such as these, or even near-violent ones, how military authorities responded had a way of drawing and reinforcing black-white lines as well. At the navy's Camp Allen in Virginia in 1942 or 1943, for example, a "near riot broke out" when white commanders allowed white trainees "to march to the head of the movie line" and black troops objected. Whereas the whites involved received no punishment, all African Americans at the camp, whether they had attended the movie or not, were ordered out of their beds at midnight and "forced to drill until they nearly dropped of exhaustion." Similarly, after a large-scale disturbance involving hundreds of black troops and dozens of white police struck Alexandria, Louisiana, in January 1942, the *Pittsburgh Courier* complained that "instead of arresting those few, white and colored, responsible for the trouble, the military authorities arrested only the Negroes, permitting the whites to go scot free."[42]

These "disgraceful occurrences," in the *Courier's* words, were part and parcel of a much larger problem: a grossly unequal military justice system. For starters, the military more or less excluded black troops from its Judge Advocate General Department, which oversaw and reviewed all court-martial cases. More inclusive than the navy on this front, the army employed four or five black attorneys during the war, a time when the department included some twenty-eight hundred total.[43] One consequence of this utter lack of representation for black service members were glaring black-white disparities in punishment. "We know that many of our men are not getting a square deal," the NAACP grumbled in July 1944, "but unfortunately, the Army has so many regulations and technicalities under which charges can be brought and sentences imposed that it is difficult to prove prejudice or unfairness. . . . An outside civilian organization does not have much chance to do anything except to register a firm protest." One such example of this unfairness came in late 1943. While a white officer "convicted by a general court for stabbing a Negro soldier three times with a bayonet" received nothing but a reprimand, a group of black soldiers were sentenced from one to five years of hard labor for an unauthorized use of two army trucks.[44]

The white officer's tap on the wrist speaks to a broader phenomenon, indeed among the most fundamental black-white boundaries of them all: in the military's eyes, white life mattered more than black life. Yes, the military sought to keep black troops from the front lines, which complicates the point. But supporting it were the big and small indignities and injustices and brutalities that military Jim Crow, with little care or compunction, imposed on African Americans. Perhaps the most startling evidence of this point was the military's utter refusal to protect its black soldiers—or to punish those people who brazenly killed them: Private Felix Hall. Private Albert King. Sergeant Elvyn Hergrave. Private Ned Turner. Private Thomas Broadus. Sergeant Thomas Foster. Private James E. Martin. Corporal George Hall. Private Willie Jullis. Private Henry Williams. Private Larry Stroud. Private Raymond Carr. Private David Wood. Corporal Willie Lee Davis. Private Hollis Willis. Private Raymond McMuray. Private Edward Green.[45] These men were among the dozens of black troops killed while serving in uniform in the United States, nearly all of them unarmed and at the hands of white civilian and white military police officers. In nearly all the cases, the killers were either never identified or went free, thanks in part to a federal government that never seemed especially determined to get to the bottom of the homicides. "The record of the War and Justice departments in these cases," argued the *New Republic* in 1943, "has been one of constant evasion of their democratic responsibilities and surrender to Southern racial patterns. It must be remembered that in almost all these cases, regardless of how the blame has been fixed officially, it is inconceivable that a white soldier could have been shot for the same reasons or that wanton slayings of white personnel would be ignored by the Federal government as they have been ignored in the case of Negro troops."[46]

A Structure of White Domination and Black Subordination

In the real world and in real time, these various boundaries meshed and mingled with each other, one often supporting another. Major Charity

Adams, the first African American accepted into the WAC, likely knew as much. In 1944, she accepted an invitation to have a drink with a white male major at the officers' club at Fort Des Moines in Iowa. The evening went off without a hitch. But the next morning, one of Adams's commanding officers called her into his office. While she stood at attention for forty-five minutes, the colonel rebuked her for having the audacity to enter the club—and with a white man, no less. "So you are the Major Adams, the 'negra' officer who went into the officers club last night. . . . I don't believe in race mixing, and I don't intend to be party to it," he snapped. "Don't let being an officer go to your head; you are still colored and I want you to remember that. You people have to stay in your place. Why, your folks might have been slaves to my people . . . and here you are acting like you are the same as white folks." He concluded by forbidding her to ever use the officers' club again.[47] In this one instance, the colonel's attempt to patrol black-white boundaries—to keep "you people in your place" and to stress that "colored" differed qualitatively from "white folks"—involved rank (his insistence that Adams's "colored" status mattered more than her officer status), space (his exclusion of Adams from the club), language (his use of the term "negra"), and male-female relations (his opposition to "race mixing").

Taken together, for anyone training or serving stateside in the World War II–era US military—or for anyone who came regularly into contact with its many camps, stations, posts, and troops—black-white lines were impossible to miss. They were never universal, to be sure: some white military personnel and leaders crossed or dissolved lines during the war, a practice that increased in its final months. Still, these lines snaked their way through trains and buses, camps and camp towns, rank and job structures, fights and everyday language. They were formal, the commanding officer's written order to bar "all relations between white and colored males and females," for example; and informal, the unwritten yet seemingly inviolable rule that prevented black officers from outranking white ones in the same unit. They were also physical—say, a string separating black and white sections of a post movie theater or a partition in a post barber shop; social and behavioral—the fights pitting "colored" versus "white"; and symbolic—the notion that black men were really "boys."

These lines constituted a deep and sprawling structure of white domination and black subordination. Like its civilian cousin, Jim Crow in uniform helped to produce and reproduce the very categories of "colored," "Negro," and "white," making or remaking them tangible and concrete in a quotidian, commonsensical sort of way. It did so by depriving "colored" people of rights and resources, prestige and status; and, lest one forget, by offering white people a disproportionate share of these same things. When the military greatly restricted black troops' access to the officer corps or to promotions or to the best-paid jobs, for example, whites' access and opportunities expanded. Conversely, when black troops got the least desirable jobs or recreational halls or barracks, sometimes whites did not. While training at Fort Benning in Georgia, a white army lieutenant recalled that "we no longer were obliged to clean the barracks weekly with brooms and wet mops and window rags: Black troops did these things."[48]

Of course, at other posts, whites, facing their own rank-related hierarchies, worked these jobs too. Besides, anti-black racism's insidious tentacles also sometimes ensnared them. In 1943, for example, a white soldier was court-martialed for dancing with a young black woman in West Virginia. At some posts, furthermore, segregated facilities disadvantaged white people, as in the case of "a handful of Negro officers monopolizing a regimental officers' mess, while four times as many white officers packed into a building of the same size a mile away—uncomfortable but safe from contamination."[49] Even so, Jim Crow in uniform, at least in many respects, improved whites' military lives and prospects.

AUTHORING JIM CROW IN UNIFORM

The ongoing production of military Jim Crow was a group effort. At times, civilians played a role. When, for example, a new army hospital opened in Tuscaloosa, Alabama, in 1943, "no purposeful segregation of patients according to color" existed at first. But after a local congressman and a collection of influential white townspeople protested, the hospital commander instantly changed course. Soon, partitions ("from a point of two feet above the floor to a point about three feet below the ceiling") went up to divide white and "colored" patients in hospital wards; and the hospital toilets, washrooms, mess hall, restaurant, and chapel were all segregated in various ways. These changes, however, failed to satisfy the townspeople, who remained troubled that white nurses could still tend to black patients and that "no physical means was being provided to keep the colored [patients] from visiting the whites and the whites from visiting the colored." To allay these concerns, the commander created separate wards for black and white patients.[50]

Notably, the military did not initiate these black-white lines, even if the commander willingly implemented them in short order. Nor did the white patients, all military personnel, demand them. In fact, the commander testified that they "seemed more troubled about the segregation into wards than the colored patients." Instead, local civilians, fearful of "any appearance of 'social equality' between the Negro and white races," demanded them. These were not just any local civilians either, but Tuscaloosa's "best": doctors, lawyers, and even a close relative of the man in whose honor Northington General Hospital was named. They had the power and influence to enlist the help of their local congressman, who shared his and their concerns with War Department officials, and ultimately to get the hospital commander, a brigadier general in the army, to carry out their wishes, with haste no less.[51]

In other instances, white enlisted personnel, from privates and seamen to sergeants and petty officers, constructed and policed black-white lines. Among this broad group, military police or MPs often proved to be especially capable of and invested in the effort. To be sure, MPs—short for "Miserable Pricks," according to some soldiers—were a widely unpopular lot. But black troops reserved a special level of disgust and antipathy for many white ones. According to one Inspector General report, in 1943, "hundreds of questionnaires completed by Negro officers and enlisted men have been reviewed and there was no subject covered, except as to their attitude toward civil police, which invoked such odium and bitterness as was directed at white military police." It was MPs after all who often served as the on-the-ground enforcers of many black-white lines—on trains and buses, in camps and camp towns, in male-female interactions, and in violent, sometimes deadly, confrontations. According to many black troops, not only was the act of enforcement infuriating and unjust, but so too was the style, which often showed little regard for black people's dignity or rights as soldiers, citizens, or human beings. In a September 1941 memo to Secretary Stimson, William Hastie complained about the "bullying, abuse, and physical violence" that white MPs heaped on black soldiers. Two years later, Hastie's successor, Truman Gibson, made a similar point: "In large numbers of cases white military policemen have joined forces with local peace officers in the south who have been more interested in continuing a harsh and brutal treatment of Negroes than proceeding fairly and impartially."[52]

Still, if MPs had some say in making and enforcing black-white lines, they, along with other enlisted personnel and civilians, always amounted to lesser partners in the broader operation. Only officers and their leaders in the War and Navy Departments had the power to organize large and small military spaces, assign jobs and rank, commission and promote officers, mete out military justice, and the like.

As for officers—a broad category that included everyone from an army lieutenant or navy ensign in charge of a platoon or crew to an army general or a navy admiral in charge of a post, station, service command, depart-ment, division, and so on—the military granted them considerable dis-cretion and authority when it came to some black-white lines. This was especially the case regarding spatial segregation at posts and stations. As in the case of the Alabama army hospital, if some prominent Tuscaloosa citi-zens urged the commander to segregate, it was nonetheless the commander himself who ordered the changes. Indeed, War and Navy Department policy throughout most of the war held that "the burden of deciding whether or not there shall be some separation in the use of camp facilities is placed on the local command, with the assumption that local conditions will be taken into account."[53] Just as military leadership insisted that local draft boards had the vital local knowledge to make racial classification calls, it employed this same rationale when it came to local commanders and questions of spatial segregation.

But local commanders, and the officers below them, also shaped other black-white lines. They often decided whom to promote or to commission. They made the daily decisions about whom to punish for minor infractions. In more serious cases, they occupied all the key positions in the military justice system, deciding whom and whom not to prosecute, guilt or inno-cence, life or death, the length of sentences, clemency, and more. White officers were also every bit as likely as white enlisted men to employ racist language in talking to or about black troops.

Ultimately, however, leaders in the War and Navy Departments had the greatest authority and say regarding black-white lines at stateside mili-tary installations. After all, it was their formal and informal orders that established so-called all-Negro posts like the army's Fort Huachuca and the navy's Camp Morrow; it was their orders that restricted "the intermingling of [colored and white] races" at reception centers and officers' clubs;[54] it was their orders that either excluded African Americans from the officer corps or restricted their access; it was their orders that greatly limited black people's advancement through the ranks; and it was their lack of orders to redraw, smudge, or eliminate any of the other black-white lines that allowed them to live on.

EXPLAINING JIM CROW IN UNIFORM

Why did anyone, from a private or sergeant to an admiral or cabinet sec-retary, draw or fortify these black-white lines? What overlapping set of factors best explains their actions and inactions? Not among these factors was federal or state law. The latter had no jurisdiction over military affairs on military posts. Even so, while some commanders complied with Jim Crow laws in the South, others flouted civil rights laws in the North and West. For example, in Tennessee, Camp Tyson buses were segregated to conform with state laws; in California, Washington, and New Jersey, black-white segregation was required on some posts in violation of them.[55] Unlike these state laws, federal laws did govern military posts and policies. The antidiscrimination clause of the Selective Training and Service Act of 1940 (STSA)—that "[i]n the selection and *training* of men under this Act, and in the interpretation and execution of the provisions of this Act, there shall be no discrimination against any person on account of race or color"—seemed quite clearly to outlaw many of the military's black-white lines. Indeed, the army itself, in one of its training manuals for officers, appeared to suggest as much: "Any action . . . which brings an advantage or disadvantage to any person, or which makes any discrimination between persons because of their race or color would be in direct violation of the spirit and letter of this Act." More important, the federal courts seemed to agree. In its majority opinion against Winfred Lynn, in February 1944, the US Circuit Court of Appeals ruled "that Negroes must be accorded privileges substantially equal to those afforded whites in the matter of . . . training and service under the [Selective Training and Service] Act."[56] Given these statements, it appears that law, especially federal law, should have forbidden, rather than fostered, Jim Crow in uniform.

But existing military policy and custom, at least in some cases, required or "invited" black-white lines. For several decades prior to World War II, for example, the army and, to a lesser extent, the navy assigned "living quarters and messing facilities in accordance with organizational units."[57] Since these units were universally segregated, so too were their sleeping and eating arrangements. The segregation of other post facilities—exchanges, officers' clubs, recreation centers, and the like—also predated World War II, as did other boundaries involving, for example, rank and jobs. Why these black-white lines then? A preliminary answer is that, by the war years, they had long existed and simply lived on.

This explanation, however, only goes so far—mostly because these lines, not always as long-lasting as military leaders let on, constituted a "tradition" that authorities had to re-create actively throughout the war, a time when they jettisoned many military rules and customs in the face of explosive growth and total war's unyielding demands. Indeed, one such jettisoned rule, established by the War Department in February 1942, was that "commanders should avoid all practices tending to give the colored soldiers cause to feel that the Army makes any differentiation between him and any other soldier."[58] Why military authorities continually and affirmatively chose to draw black-white lines, even in the face of their own seemingly straightforward rules, requires an explanation.

The most complete and compelling explanation for these choices, and for Jim Crow in uniform writ large, comes from looking at whites' wartime sentiments about the present and future. One such sentiment, especially vital and widespread, also deeply shaped military policy regarding enlistment and assignment, among other matters: military leaders' conviction that the morale, discipline, and effectiveness of America's fighting forces—in truth, America's white fighting forces—required bright and bountiful black-white lines. Military leaders repeated these arguments whenever called on to defend Jim Crow in uniform. Citing their own public opinion polls that showed white troops, by wide margins, preferring "separate" "colored" and white outfits, service clubs, and post exchanges, these leaders insisted that segregation—or other lines related to rank and jobs, for example—lessened "interracial friction."[59] Buried in this reasoning was a paradox: winning a war for freedom required unfreedom—stark black-white divides at stateside installations as much as in military outfits and in enlistment.

But there was one more key sentiment, which extended beyond the military's leaders to its white enlisted rank and file and across civilian white America and which also informed demands for these divides and betrayed its own share of deep paradoxes. It was some whites' agonizing sense that military life, despite all the boundary-building, was subverting anti-black forms of white supremacy. Indeed, this boundary-building sometimes came in direct response to this sense of subversion.

Such subversion came in several forms. First, there was military standardization. In its efforts to operate as efficiently as possible, the military sought to standardize many things—from jeeps and buildings and screw threads to pants and shoes and people themselves. Even the common name for soldiers—"GI," short for "government issue"—or for their clothing—"uniform"—bespoke the "standardized nature of the military." One historian has discussed the ways the "army deliberately used the short haircuts, uniforms, and cramped communal traveling and living conditions to upset the men, to level their appearance, to make them look and feel the same." Such was "the leveling effect of the khaki uniform."[60] It was this leveling, this looking and feeling the same, that was so anathema to anti-black racism and white supremacy and that so concerned many white people, in and out of the military. Here, then, was a central contradiction in military life, not unlike one that animated capitalism: a simultaneous push toward both standardization and differentiation.[61] In the case of the military's black-white matters, the former, in the eyes of some, compelled the latter.

Exacerbating these concerns about standardization was the wide-spread wartime valorization of America's fighting men—those quintessential wartime heroes, super-citizens, and manly embodiments of the nation and state.[62] The military often strove to divorce or exempt black service members from this valorization by, for example, restricting their enlistment or their numbers on the front lines and impugning their fighting abilities. Nonetheless, more than a million black people managed to join up, and many thousands found themselves in combat roles of one sort or another, performing that most prized piece of wartime service: protecting the nation in war. The mere presence of so many black troops threatened to scramble some of the stark binaries, involving Americanness and citizenship and masculinity, that shaped and were shaped by anti-black racism.

Finally, there was the ever-present geographic mobility of military service, which imperiled the still-powerful local bases of this racism, especially in the rural South, where so many military training camps were located. There, it was sustained not so much by ordinance or statute as by personal relationships, not least those between black tenant farmers or sharecroppers and white landowners, on whom the former's livelihoods depended.[63] These informal mechanisms of white social control were ill prepared to deal with the influx of hundreds of thousands of heretofore unknown black people. Not only did they owe nothing to local white powerbrokers, but they were uniformed, sometimes armed, and at least ostensibly protected by the federal government. The military often tried to cleave to these local arrangements by, for example, providing local commanders considerable authority to craft black-white lines to comport with "local conditions."[64] And many commanders certainly exploited this authority to mitigate the destabilizing effects of military migrations. But concerns remained, so much so that powerful whites across the country, but especially in the South, urged the military throughout the war (and, ultimately, in vain) to refrain from moving black troops to their communities altogether.[65]

As these mitigation efforts suggest, the military built myriad black-white divides, sometimes in direct response to threats that itself—through standardization, valorization, and geographical movement—unwittingly posed to anti-black white supremacy. In other words, it was not simply that these lines, in the eyes of military authorities, best served the nation and the war effort by preserving the discipline, efficiency, and morale of its troops, or even just its white troops. They also existed because large swaths of white America, in and out of the military, harbored a profound conscious and unconscious investment in white domination and black subordination.

When the military itself seemed to endanger these entrenched aspects of American life, it redoubled its efforts to shore them up.

FIGHTING JIM CROW IN UNIFORM

But as it turned out, these military efforts, and the entire structure of black-white lines more broadly, produced one more deeply destabilizing effect: a powerful grassroots black struggle to dismantle these lines altogether. It was, in several respects, unlike the civil rights activism around enlistment and mixed military units. Its key actors were service members, not civilians. It drew support from a wide range of allies, but black servicemen and -women, often drawing on their distinctive experiences in uniform, were the central actors, planners, organizers, and mobilizers in the struggle. And it employed a broader array of protest approaches—from sit-ins and boycotts to strikes and armed self-defense—despite suffocating military repression, or sometimes because of it.

That black servicemen and -women mounted any challenge at all to these lines is remarkable. For one thing, black troops were hardly of one mind on the issue. An extensive army survey conducted in March 1943 found that four in ten black soldiers favored separate post exchanges and nearly five in ten supported separate service clubs. Black soldiers without access to any post exchange might have thought a separate one was better than none at all; and no doubt some, fearing persecution, chose to conceal their true feelings from the army. African American troops' views of segregation, furthermore, changed somewhat over the course of the war. By early 1944, both army and navy official publications acknowledged, "The idea of compulsory racial segregation is disliked by almost all Negroes, and literally hated by many."[66] Even so, some African Americans disagreed about Jim Crow in uniform, complicating efforts to dismantle it.

A much greater obstacle to black troops' activism, however, was state surveillance and repression—or fear of both. Outside the military, a rapidly expanding FBI, among other government agencies, investigated and hounded black activists and the black press, in a few rare but important cases indicting them on espionage and sedition charges. At the local level, civilian police, especially in the South, harassed, beat, and killed numerous black troops, whether they were protesting or not.[67] But it was inside the military, with its "sheer coercive power" over all troops, where repression against black service members in particular may have been most widespread and suffocating. African Americans served in units that often teemed with undercover military intelligence agents, their correspondence was carefully monitored, they could be shipped across the country and around the world as a way to squash activism, and they faced not only a military justice system in which few black people served, but also a maze of military rules, regulations, and laws that were equal parts complex and capacious. The catchall 96th Article of War, for example, which was used to punish many black troops, prohibited "all disorders and neglects to the prejudice of good order and military discipline, [and] all conduct of a nature to bring discredit upon the military service."[68] Even black troops' most moderate protest strategies, then, could lead them to be transferred to another camp or unit, restricted in their leave privileges, demoted, reprimanded, threatened, thrown in the stockade or brig, and formally court-martialed and dishonorably discharged.[69]

Understanding the massive powers arrayed against them, many black troops endured military Jim Crow, no matter how devastating or debilitating they may have found it. One lieutenant at Camp Van Dorn in Mississippi recalled that the men in his unit opposed the segregated post exchanges and theaters there, but chose not to do much more than talk about them. "They ran their mouths and let off a lot of steam," he explained, "but that was as far as it went." "Though justifiable," another black soldier said, "rebellion is more dangerous to us than resignation . . . [since] Army law is the white man's law."[70]

In the face of these very real dangers, a remarkable number of black troops still chose rebellion of one sort or another. For some, the decision was an easy one, made, in a sense, before they joined up and born of both the bitter and the inspiring memories of World War I—during which black soldiers became newly emboldened "torchbearers of democracy" and targets of American military racism at home and overseas. Rebellion was also a product of the more general, mounting black hope and activism of the interwar and war years. Sam Reed, a recent graduate of the University of Minnesota and former president of the St. Paul NAACP chapter, entered the army in 1942 determined to root out injustice wherever he found it. Soon after induction, while training at Camp Lee in Virginia, he wrote to the NAACP's national office, asking how he could be of service. "As long as we suffer discrimination, segregation and limitations solely because we are Negroes," he declared, "we must perforce protest and contest and fight."[71]

Their military experience politicized many other black people in new and profound ways. Perhaps it happened upon induction, since, as one black newspaper put it, "soldiers recruited to bring about human decency abroad are not going to tolerate jim crow at home." Perhaps it had something to do with the training experience itself, which helped forge comradely bonds between a diverse mix of black people from across the country and from various educational and class backgrounds, offering them the opportunity to share stories and compare notes about Jim Crow's many indignities and injustices and about how to respond.[72] According to William Hastie, training also "taught [a black person] to be a man, a fighting man; in brief, a soldier." Thanks to a long history of some African Americans and others conflating "manhood" rights with equal rights, this masculinist education carried with it an unmistakable political charge. "It is impossible to create a dual personality," Hastie continued, "which will be on the one hand a fighting man toward the enemy, and on the other hand, a craven who will accept treatment as less than a man at home." According to some commentators, the "manly" nature of military service promoted activism among female troops, as well. Some of the military's wartime race reforms, according to one *Pittsburgh Courier* editorial, arose thanks to "the manliness of men and women in the Services who insisted on a square deal."[73]

What politicized black troops perhaps more than anything else, however, was the idea of fighting—and, of course, the possibility of dying—for freedoms they had never known. Amid battles with military Jim Crow, black troops, often well before being deployed overseas, expressed with striking frequency a willingness to fight—and, if necessary, to die—for the cause. Every bit as important as the Double V campaign, which called for victories over both American racism and foreign fascism, black service members also launched a Single V campaign, which targeted primarily or even solely the former. "How can anyone expect me to cross the seas to North Africa, and to fight for the freedom of people everywhere, when I can't get a decent chance to live in my own town?" asked one black soldier. "I've decided that I'm ready to give my life to help straighten this out right here, because, as far as I can see, Jacksonville, Florida, is just as near heaven as any point in North Africa." One *Chicago Defender* columnist, who had talked to black troops of various ranks, summed up their feelings this way: "I just as soon die fightin' for democracy right here in Georgia, as go all the way to Africa or Australia."[74]

In some cases, this "fightin'" was literal. If some whites employed violence to build up color lines, some blacks used it to tear them down. In July 1944, for example, a small group of black soldiers, led by a young Sidney Poitier, destroyed a restaurant in Oyster Bay, New York, after its owner told them, "We don't serve Niggers here!" Similar protests-as-property-destruction took place throughout the war years at both civilian and military establishments: a tavern in Merced, California (March 1942); a restaurant in Bisbee, Arizona (c. June 1942); a movie theater at the Aiea Naval Barracks in Hawaii (December 1942); a recreation hall at a naval ammunition depot in Virginia (June 1943); and at post exchanges at Fort

Fig. 6.5 Black GIs spend downtime in May 1942 at a post exchange at Fort Huachuca in Arizona. Two years later, in June 1944, black soldiers twice stoned post exchanges at this fort in response to discrimination there. Courtesy National Archives, 111-SC-138788.

Huachuca in Arizona (June 1944), at Camp Beale in California (September 1944), and at Camp Claiborne in Louisiana (October 1944).[75]

Some black troops also resorted to violence as a vital form of self-defense. Nearly all their biggest and most dramatic examples of armed resistance— in which they stormed supply rooms and seized and fired guns at places like Camp Van Dorn in Mississippi (May 1943), Camp Stewart in Georgia (June 1943), Camp Shenango in Pennsylvania (July 1943), Brookley Field in Alabama (May 1944), and Camp Claiborne in Louisiana (August 1944)— were direct responses to physical, sometimes deadly, abuse at the hands of white officers, white civilian and military police, and white enlisted personnel.[76]

For local and national authorities, this armed resistance against military Jim Crow certainly reached frightening proportions, especially in the spring and summer of 1943 when civilian race riots also shook cities and towns across the country. Still, since armed self-defense and brawling were always such exceedingly risky protest tactics, many black troops opted against them. A safer—and, according to some, more effective—form of protest was excelling as a soldier. Given that military Jim Crow rested, in part, on deep-seated beliefs about black troops' inferiority, their success necessarily challenged some of its ideological foundations. As one NAACP pamphlet put it, reflecting what might be called a politics of soldierly respectability, "The man in uniform must grit his teeth, square his shoulders and do his best as a soldier, confident that there are millions of Americans outside of the armed services . . . who will never cease fighting to remove all racial barriers and every humiliating practice which now confronts him. But only by being a first-rate soldier can the man in uniform help in this battle which shall be fought and won."[77]

Many other black troops chose alternative, or additional, protest strategies. Still on the safer end of the spectrum was a broad range of covert, quotidian efforts to contest color lines. Some surreptitiously painted over, destroyed, or removed Jim Crow signs and screens on and off post, a practice that seems to have grown over the first few years of the war.[78] Some quietly gathered intelligence on camp conditions for civilian activists, who in turn used it to lodge complaints with military officials. And some black troops "goldbricked" and feigned illness, tactics that while fairly universal among all American troops during the war must at times have been born of and targeted specifically at military Jim Crow. One top-secret review of the Ninety-Second Division found that, during its training at Fort Huachuca in Arizona, a place of widespread discrimination, a "mass movement" of "straggling" emerged "suddenly and grew rapidly to large proportions." It involved more than two thousand soldiers, who "feigned physical ailments of a disqualifying nature."[79]

Perhaps the most common form of everyday protest, which at times was covert and anonymous for fear of military reprisal, was letter writing. Black troops addressed letters to political leaders, military officials, black and sympathetic white newspapers and magazines, civil rights groups, and loved ones. Letters poured in week after week and in such numbers that, according to the *New Republic*, they created an "ominous folkway" among African Americans, which expressed the unshakable "belief that sons and husbands and loved ones are subjected to humiliation and injustice in the army of American democracy."[80] These letters also did more. When, over and over again, black troops compared their treatment to that of slaves and dogs and animals, compared military life to hell, stressed that their "blood [was] boiling all the time," and denounced "denial, subjugation, persecution," they expressed emotions as well as beliefs—anger, outrage, disappointment, fear, dread. These emotions served to energize some civilians to act on soldiers' behalf. These emotions served to energize some civilians to act on soldiers' behalf, while also girding GIs, in the words of one soldier, "to contest wrong wherever it is found, abroad or as a cancer in our own nation."[81]

For some segment of black troops, contesting wrong meant escaping it. In January 1945, the US Border Patrol picked up Private James Albert Williams along the Rio Grande a full six months after he had fled Fort Meade in Maryland. Having had enough army Jim Crow for a lifetime, he had given up on the United States and was hoping to resettle in Africa. "I took the oath of allegiance with the understanding that I was fighting for freedom and democracy," he explained. "When I got into the Army, I found out there was no democracy. . . . I feel there is no future for me here in America."[82] It is hard to know how many black troops chose Williams's path of escape, but certainly some did. Military intelligence occasionally reported cases of "mass absence without leave" involving dozens, sometimes hundreds, of black troops, which was, of course, a broader problem for the US military, involving whites too. In comparison with white troops, however, black GIs had additional motivations to flee, to say nothing of a generations-long history of "escape, fugitivity, and maroonage." "The number of AWOL's has been found to bear a significant ratio to the amount of discrimination encountered," noted one black commentator; another discussed one black chaplain's "greatest problem": "keep[ing] men from 'going over the hill.' It is not the army routine that they mind. All Army men gripe about that. It's the internal stuff they have to take because they're colored, segregation in PX's, segregation in movies."[83]

Writing about a widely publicized AWOL case in the summer of 1941 involving a black engineer battalion, the *Baltimore Afro-American* declared, "[W]hen great batches of drafted men desert rather than serve in the army down in Dixie, the War Department will then do something. Passive resistance is an effective weapon." Indeed, as the war wore on, growing numbers of black troops tested this proposition. Sometimes this testing took the form of acts by individuals and small groups, almost too numerous to count. Targeting both military and civilian Jim Crow, the cases spiked in the wake of a July 1944 War Department order—itself a response to this activism—that seemed to prohibit racist exclusion or segregation in any post exchange or post theater or on any post bus. By this point, military intelligence reports noted with growing alarm not only that "a campaign is being conducted by colored personnel to test the effectiveness of the [July 1944] directive," but also that black troops were "extend[ing] their campaign for non-segregation to Southern, white [civilian] communities." Typical of both developments, according to the reports, were a long list of "disturbances," including sixteen black lieutenants demanding to eat in a whites-only, civilian café in South Carolina; black WAC members insisting on attending a whites-only dance at Camp Forrest in Tennessee; a black soldier stationed at Camp Gordon Johnston in Florida disobeying Jim Crow laws on nearby civilian buses; a black WAC first lieutenant refusing to leave the white section of the dining car on a Richmond–Rocky Mount train; and a black sergeant eating lunch in a white service club at Topeka Army Air Field.[84]

This "campaign for non-segregation" also involved collective actions, which may have inspired—and been inspired by—similar, contemporaneous civilian wartime protests spearheaded by organizations like the Congress of Racial Equality, the March on Washington Movement, and the NAACP. In March 1943, at Fort Belvoir in Virginia, five hundred black soldiers protested their segregated seating at a musical show by waiting for the act to begin and then marching out in unison and in "grim silence." Black troops sat in as well as walked out. In June 1943, at Camp Kearns in Utah, in what army officials called a "mass" and "premeditated" "disturbance," an African American quartermaster company occupied the white section of the post theater. The men refused to leave at first, then made "disrespectful and opprobrious remarks" on their way out. In a protest letter, they cited a common refrain: "If we have to die we just as soon die . . . on this side as over there." In perhaps the best-known case, 101 Tuskegee airmen at

Fig. 6.6 Some of the 101 black officers arrested for entering a "white" officers' club at Freeman Field in Indiana, April 1945. Courtesy of the Library of Congress Prints and Photographs Division, Visual Materials from the NAACP Records, LC-USZ62-138740.

Freeman Field in Indiana were arrested in April 1945 for insisting on using a white officers' club there.[85]

Boycotts of segregated space were especially common. In fact, the Tuskegee airmen had tried such a boycott at the Freeman Field officers' club shortly before their arrests. Black GIs staged other mass boycotts of segregated officers' clubs at Fort Huachuca (June 1942); segregated chapels at Fort Clark in Texas (May 1944); segregated seating at a USO show at Fort Jackson in South Carolina (April 1942); a segregated dance at Camp Gordon Johnston in Florida (September 1943); a segregated mess hall at Mather Field in California; and segregated post theaters at Walterboro Army Air Field in South Carolina (spring and summer of 1944), at Camp Forrest in Tennessee (winter 1943), at Camp Young in California (date unknown), and aboard a navy ship en route to Hawaii (circa 1944).[86]

Black troops' collective protest extended well beyond segregated recreational space. Sometimes it targeted white officers' racist rhetoric. In December 1944, at Vancouver Barracks in Washington, five hundred black soldiers marched out of a show in which a white lieutenant, singing "Old Man River," used the word "Nigger" instead of "Negro." Other times it involved civilian and military police abuse. In July 1943, in Jackson, Mississippi, a white civilian police officer beat a black soldier severely after forcibly removing him from MP custody. "It was the latest of a series of unbelievable brutalities permitted by city policeman against Negro servicemen and their families," according to one report from a black Urban League official. The next day most of the soldiers' comrades at the nearby Mississippi Ordnance Plant staged a "protest strike . . . milling around and refusing to obey their officers." When a detachment of heavily armed white MPs then arrived to maintain order, the protesting black soldiers broke down: "Beating their chests while tears of rage streamed down their faces, they advanced unarmed against the machine guns, shouting that if they were going to be killed for democracy they were willing to die for it in Mississippi."[87]

Rampant discrimination in job placement, workplace conditions, and promotions was also a prominent target of civil disobedience, sometimes collective. Regarding more individual-level, quotidian protest, one Navy Department study noted that it received so "many reports from all over the country of Negroes' refusal to do small deviations from the work for which they had been trained"—these "deviations" were a common form of discrimination against black service personnel—that "routine disciplinary handling was plainly not a practical, long-run solution." Work-related protest also involved groups of varying sizes. In July 1943, six WACs staged a five-day strike to protest their assignment scrubbing floors when they had been trained to do supply work instead and likely entered the military to escape domestic labor. In January 1944, members of a black truck regiment challenged their white officers' overworking of them, by, in the case of the unit's noncommissioned officers, requesting a demotion and transfer to another outfit and, in the case of the enlisted men, temporarily refusing to work.[88]

By the final year of the war, a series of high-profile "mutinies" or strikes highlighted the work-related black-white lines that many African American service members faced. Consider the Port Chicago Mutiny. At the navy ammunition depot in Port Chicago in northern California, black seamen loaded ammunition onto ships heading to war in the Pacific. It was dangerous work, made more so by the fact that white officers provided little instruction in the safe handling of highly explosive material. In fact, they encouraged the men to rush at times—"pour it on," as they would say—since the officers made five-dollar bets with each other about whose crew could work the fastest. On the night of July 17, 1944, disaster struck. A massive explosion—the worst of its kind on the wartime home front—shook fourteen counties, was heard eighty miles away, destroyed two munitions ships instantly, and killed 320 people, nearly two-thirds of whom were black. When the navy, not quite three weeks later, ordered traumatized African Americans back to work, several hundred refused.[89]

In their strike against workplace injustice, these sailors were not alone. A week earlier, dozens of members of an engineer company in Honolulu engaged in a work slowdown and then a brief strike in protest against the replacement of several black officers with white ones. Six weeks later, in September 1944, fifty-seven black soldiers struck at the Marana Army Air Field near Tucson to object to nineteen months of "dreary and menial" kitchen work, for which they failed to receive their rightful extra pay. In early March 1945, more than one thousand members of a navy construction battalion staged a two-day hunger strike at Port Hueneme in southern California, protesting, among other things, their commanding officer's refusal to promote them. Later that month, at Fort Devens in Massachusetts, sixty or so black WACs, trained as medical technicians, went on a sit-down strike for being forced "to mop walls, scrub floors, and do all the dirty work" at the post hospital.[90]

In all these struggles, black troops often relied on a large and indispensable network of allies. Occasionally these included nonblacks in the military. One white veteran, recently back from the war, recalled that when several hundred black soldiers marched out of a segregated post theater at Camp Young in California, one hundred whites joined them in solidarity.

Sometimes service members of color, some of whom faced their own forms of Jim Crow in uniform, also joined forces with black troops.[91]

But African American troops' most important allies were civilians—a diverse group, including a host of Left, labor, church, and civil rights organizations, the black press, a small handful of officials in the War and Navy Departments, and family and loved ones. Black GIs and their civilian allies—two groups that sometimes overlapped, as when soldiers joined the NAACP, for example—did not always see eye to eye. The former sometimes groused about civil rights groups being "bought and paid for" and about black newspapers writing inaccurate puff pieces about their experiences in uniform.[92] For their part, newspapers occasionally chided "lazy-thinking men in army and navy ranks" for using "discrimination as a pretext for lying down on the job" and they, along with civil rights organizations like the NAACP, sometimes advised black soldiers to "fight the enemy [abroad], [and] let civilians keep up the battle for citizenship on the home front."[93] Nonetheless, even when many servicemen and -women rejected this advice—spearheading their own "battle for citizenship" while in uniform— many sympathetic civilians still supported them in any way they could.[94]

In the early months of war mobilization, as harrowing stories proliferated about black trainees being "baited, bullied, humiliated, beaten, and . . . killed," especially in the South, this civilian support often began with a simple request or demand: protect our men (and some women) in uniform. Protection could mean many things, including arming black troops, moving them out of the South, preventing racist whites from commanding them, recruiting more black MPs, bringing perpetrators to justice, and simply pleading for unity and calm. Regardless, a variety of black civilians and others—in newspaper editorials, petitions, mass meetings, formal appeals and letters to military and government leaders, and the like—pushed these proposals forcefully. They did so throughout the war, as violent attacks on black troops remained a chilling constant. In a letter to Secretary of War Henry Stimson in June 1943, the president of the National Association of Negro Business and Professional Women's Clubs registered her "strongest protest" against the brutal mistreatment of "our sons, brothers and husbands" in army camps: "We believe that an organization that cannot control such misdeeds on its own soil and with its own people can do little to bring peace and understanding to other peoples of the world."[95]

Among the most important civilian defenders of black troops were their mothers. At a time when the nation showered praise on "war mothers" (who had sons in the military) or "gold star mothers" (who had lost sons in the military), some black women relied on the heightened ideological power of motherhood, and their direct link to soldiers, to make claims on the state, specifically to demand protection for their sons (and, sometimes, daughters) in uniform. In letter after letter to military and government officials to this effect, they began with something like "I am the mother of two sons in the service of their country" or "We the mothers . . . of the Negro soldiers that are now engaged in this present struggle for Democracy." They would often close not simply with a signature but also with another reference to motherhood: "A citizen of the USA and mother," "A worried mother," "A very worried Negro mother."[96]

Protection of black troops also meant their vigorous defense in the military justice system. Many black GI protesters—punished for anything from letter writing to armed self-defense—received considerable civilian support, including favorable press and formal representation in hearings, in court-martial trials, and in appeals. To cite one example, when four of the WACs who had taken part in the sit-down strike at Fort Devens were dishonorably discharged and sentenced to one year of hard labor, news of their sentences set off a firestorm of protest. Some African Americans had opposed the women's protest tactics; even the local NAACP, at first, deplored their "misguided" activism, believing they had "no right to strike in the armed services." But fierce opposition to their punishment was widespread. The *Pittsburgh Courier*'s editorial headline "Free the Four Wacs!" captured the mood of many black people and their allies, as dozens of angry letters poured into the War Department and to President Roosevelt from the NAACP, the National Council of Negro Women, the Workers Defense League, the Lynn Committee to Abolish Segregation in the Armed Forces, Congressmen Vito Marcantonio and Adam Clayton Powell, and scores of ordinary people. Within weeks, the army voided the WACs' courts-martial, restored them to duty, and removed their commanding officer.[97]

Sometimes soldiers' protests inspired civilians to join them. For example, one of the first national organizations devoted entirely to ending military Jim Crow in all its forms—the National Committee to Abolish Segregation in the Armed Services—emerged in part as a consequence of black troop activism. A small group of liberal and Left "leaders" scheduled the conference that established the umbrella organization only after noting "the wave of strikes among Negro servicemen" and feeling "it would be wise . . . to intensify the fight against army jim crow."[98]

No civilian organization was more deeply enmeshed in this fight than the NAACP. Toward the end of the war, the organization estimated conservatively that it had thirty thousand dues-paying members in the military—some of whom led local branches before joining up and others of whom opened new branches while in the service. Its monthly publication, *The Crisis*, regularly featured stories about troops from around the world donating a portion of their pay to the NAACP. They joined, donated, and opened branches no doubt because the organization, flooded with appeals from individual soldiers for help, answered the call. The NAACP battled tirelessly on other military-related fronts—to expand African Americans' enlistment opportunities and to integrate military outfits. It fought just as hard against the daily discrimination and humiliation that so many black troops faced. The national or local offices, or often both, corresponded regularly with troops, keeping each other apprised of their activities; investigated service member complaints; publicized their findings through their press releases, through articles in *The Crisis*, and by sharing their information with the black, liberal, and Left press; lobbied top military and political figures tirelessly for reforms; represented troops in court-martial proceedings and in attempts to overturn dishonorable discharges; joined hands with other organizations in these efforts; and may have, on occasion, helped service member activists formulate protest tactics and strategy.[99]

To appreciate the full extent of the NAACP's work alongside and on behalf of black troops, and the sometimes blurry lines between the two, consider the case of the hunger-striking Seabees at Port Heuneme. After serving twenty-one months in the Pacific and returning to the United States, where mail was not as thoroughly censored, the Seabees, some of whom were active members of the NAACP, organized a letter-writing campaign to the organization. They leveled numerous discrimination complaints and pleaded for help. The NAACP's Washington, DC, office responded by writing to Navy Secretary James Forrestal, ultimately succeeding in getting the navy to investigate the men's complaints. When the navy investigation claimed to have found no problems, members of the NAACP's Los Angeles branch conducted its own study, finding that the men were "on the brink of mutiny" thanks to long-standing and widespread discrimination. Roy Wilkins, acting secretary of the NAACP, then forwarded the report to Forrestal, amplifying demands for reform. The NAACP also sent the report and other relevant documents to the black and sympathetic white press and to select Congress members, many of whom placed added pressure on the navy. When this pressure trickled down to the Seabees themselves, they struck. That their hunger strike occurred just three days after the Los Angeles branch members visited them suggests that the latter may have played some role in proposing or planning the strike. What is clear is that, even though the strike—in conjunction with the NAACP-led civilian support—succeeded in getting the Seabees' commander and some of their other officers replaced, Wilkins continued for several months after the strike to write to Forrestal to advocate on behalf of the Seabees, and the Los Angeles branch continued to investigate their treatment.[100]

MODEST REFORMS

As this and other stories suggest, black GI activism made an impact. Sometimes it was tailored toward specific outfits' grievances, such as the reassignment of the commanders of the Seabees or of the sit-down-striking WACs, or the lifting of discriminatory orders, or the vacating of unfair punishments. More broadly, this activism compelled military leaders to rethink one of their most foundational and cherished racist assumptions: that the morale, discipline, and efficiency of the armed forces required stark black-white divides. In actions big and small—from mass mutinies and work stoppages to letter writing and sit-ins—black troops stood this logic on its head. Military leaders who long feared the possibility of white rebellion against too few color lines had to contend with the reality of black rebellion against too many of them. As a consequence, with little help from President Roosevelt or the courts and in the face of sometimes powerful opposition from southerners in and out of Congress, they began blurring some post boundaries between black and white troops. Their actions were limited in scope and came late in the war, but that they were undertaken at all is testament to the developing scale and force of black activism.

Throughout the first few years of the war, Roosevelt seemed completely indifferent to black service members' struggles against Jim Crow in uniform (in contrast to his work on enlistment but in line with his inactivity regarding mixed outfits). Indeed, even in the summer of 1943, with "an epidemic of racial tensions" convulsing military installations and cities across the country and abroad, he was conspicuously silent, despite the repeated urgings of some advisers to say or do something.[101]

As with the effort to mix military units, the president wrestled with competing political forces, a balancing act that only became more difficult over time. On the one hand, many white Democrats, not least elites in the South, grew increasingly fearful that white supremacy's days might be numbered and blamed Roosevelt and the national Democratic Party for the fact. Indeed, after the Supreme Court struck down the white primary in April 1944, "everywhere south of the Potomac," *Time* magazine observed, "the New Deal has lost a little more ground." Some prominent southerners at the time campaigned to draft Senator Harry Byrd of Virginia as the Democratic Party's presidential nominee. Roosevelt prevailed easily at the convention, but Byrd nonetheless received substantial support in primaries across the South.[102] As the 1944 presidential election approached, then, President Roosevelt could no longer take the solid support of the white South for granted. Moreover, he had to guard against antagonizing powerful southern Democrats in Congress.

On the other hand, white liberals' commitment to civil rights causes was growing, as was black people's electoral power, especially in several populous battleground states in the North, thanks to wartime migrations and ever-present political organizing. Both groups, but especially the latter, stressed that military Jim Crow would shape their voting behavior. One July 1944 "forecast" of "the Negro vote" noted that it had recently been "shifting back into the Republican column." The chief reason was "the outraged feeling of many colored citizens over the way that Negroes are treated in the Army." "Intimidation, discrimination, and segregation" there "have probably done more than anything else to dampen the ardor of the colored folk for President Roosevelt." A month later, another commentary stressed that the political importance of "discrimination in the service cannot be minimized, for it reaches into hundreds of thousands of Negro homes that have sent their sons to the wars to fight for freedom."[103]

Sensing an opportunity, the Republican Party, in contrast to the way it responded to mixed units, appeared to offer a real alternative to the Democrats, making further inroads with some black voters. Promising to address some aspects of Jim Crow in uniform, it ran full-page political ads in black newspapers. They condemned Roosevelt for standing by while "Negro soldiers [were] mobbed in [an] Alexandria, LA. jimcrow camp" and while a "Negro soldier [was] shot to death on [a] jimcrow N.C. bus." And the party's platform and presidential candidate, Thomas Dewey, promised "an immediate Congressional inquiry to ascertain the extent to which mistreatment, segregation and discrimination against Negroes who are in our armed forces are impairing morale and efficiency and the adoption of corrective legislation." Some black voters continued to eye the GOP as "the Same Old Party of Hoover & Co., steeped in the dangerous brew of isolation and reaction." But others endorsed Dewey, often citing military discrimination as a major factor. In late October 1944, the *Afro-American* newspaper chain, with editions in Baltimore, Washington, Richmond, Philadelphia, and Newark, published a long list of reasons it supported Dewey. The first was the "shocking and heart-sickening" "abuse and jim crow of the 800,000 colored soldiers in the Army of the United States."[104]

In the final weeks of the campaign, with the race appearing to tighten, several presidential advisers and cabinet members grew increasingly concerned about these and perhaps more military-related defections. They eventually convinced President Roosevelt to make some minor changes. "The situation among the Negro voters is still very serious," Attorney General Francis Biddle warned the president in late October. "The greatest resentment comes from Negroes in the armed forces, particularly those who have been in southern camps, and they are writing home about it."[105] And Roosevelt's all-purpose race adviser, Jonathan Daniels, wrote weekly memos to his boss in September and October suggesting last-minute ways to appease black voters by tinkering with Jim Crow in uniform.[106] In the end, Roosevelt approved a navy plan to accept for the first time a small number of black women into the WAVES (Women Accepted into Volunteer Emergency Services) and to integrate them into "training processes and living accommodations without making special or separate arrangements." He also ended a War Department plan to segregate returning black veterans.[107] But—consumed by other war matters, largely uninterested in the plight of African Americans, and fearful, in the words of one adviser, that southern whites' "impotent rumblings against the New Deal" might become "an actual revolt at the polls"—he left Jim Crow in uniform more or less alone.[108]

In some respects, the same could not be said of Congress. Some individual liberal Democrats and Republicans in the House and Senate, especially those from districts and states with large black voting populations, wrote a steady stream of protest letters to military leaders about training-camp color lines. They also proposed, by the last few years of the war, a half dozen or so bills and resolutions to dismantle aspects of them. One made the assault of any service member a federal offense; another sought to "prevent restaurants operated in connection with stations and terminal facilities of common carriers subject to the Interstate Commerce Act from discriminating against members of the armed forces on account of race or color"; and a third promised, six months after the end of the war, to prohibit "the separation of the races in the armed forces of the United States whether by means of separate quarters, separate mess halls, or otherwise." In the end, however, thanks to Congress's bloc of conservative Republicans and southern Democrats, none of these bills became law.[109]

But, in fact, Congress had already passed the STSA, which had the potential to effect far more sweeping changes than any of these failed bills. Passed in 1940, it plainly outlawed racial discrimination, presumably all forms of racial discrimination, in military training. And yet just as plainly, the courts—to say nothing of the military or the president—never enforced this provision, though activists certainly sought to require them to do so. Winfred Lynn's brother, Conrad, promised his brother and others that he would "test the 'training' phrase of the 'no discrimination amend-ment,'" seeking, in a sort of companion case to his brother's, a writ of habeas corpus once he entered boot camp. But according to Conrad's rec-ollection, the army, censoring his and his brother's mail, got wind of his plan. Already nervous about Winfred's suit against its enlistment practices, the army was determined to head off a court challenge to its Jim Crow training practices, too. It sought to limit the grounds upon which Conrad could bring his case by assigning him to "the first unsegregated training unit in the American armed forces!"[110]

Perry H. Hansberry's STSA-inspired challenge to racial discrimination in military training advanced a bit further than Conrad Lynn's. Hansberry was a twenty-three-year-old real estate broker and member of a promi-nent and politically active black family on Chicago's South Side, which in-cluded his father, who as a plaintiff won an important Supreme Court case against racial restrictive covenants in 1940, and his younger sister, future playwright Lorraine. Upon receiving his army draft notice in June 1944, he sought an injunction against his mandatory induction, claiming, like Winfred Lynn before him, that the government had violated the STSA's antidiscrimination clause in its treatment of black people. But Hansberry's case was broader than Lynn's. Drawing on all parts of this clause, it claimed not only unlawful discrimination in the selection but also in the training of African Americans for military service. Here, then, was Conrad Lynn's promised case from two years earlier. As Hansberry put it in his official complaint before the federal court in Chicago, he sought to restrain the government from, in part, placing him in a "segregated, Jim Crowed, dis-criminatory [army] camp in violation of the law." He wished to avoid "all manners of humiliation, disadvantages, segregation and other forms of limited privileges," which his brother Carl had recently faced as a soldier at Camp Bowie in Texas.[111]

Hansberry's case received some press attention and immediate assis-tance from Winfred Lynn's clutch of devoted civilian supporters. The Lynn Committee to Abolish Segregation in the Armed Forces also publicized the case as a clear companion to Lynn's, while also opening a Chicago branch to assist Hansberry's suit. Prominent Chicagoans such as writer Horace Cayton and union leader Willard S. Townsend soon joined it. But ultimately Hansberry's case, like Lynn's, ended in disappointment. It appears that the federal court in Chicago dismissed it in the fall of 1944 on the basis of a few technicalities. As with Lynn's case and other more well-known ones such as *Korematsu v. United States*, the US courts made it clear throughout the war that they would not interfere with racist military policy, regardless of what the law said.[112]

If the White House, Congress, and the courts, then, were of little to no help in battles against Jim Crow in uniform, that left military leaders to push and prod. Surprisingly, the navy, toward war's end, proved increasingly receptive. By this time, it was "trying sincerely and honestly to wipe out color lines," in the view of National Urban League's executive secretary, Lester Granger, who had become an informal race adviser to Navy Secretary James Forrestal in March 1945. This effort began with the integration of auxiliary ships, but it then moved to the training experience. After the navy began accepting black women into the WAVES, neither their living quarters nor their training program were segregated.[113] By the last few months of the war, the navy greatly expanded this integration. It shuttered its Jim Crow camps at the sprawling Great Lakes Naval Training Station and at all its specialist or "Class A" schools that heretofore had been open solely to black recruits. And it began, with a few exceptions, "assimilat[ing] Negro and white enlisted personnel" in all training activities and facilities.[114] These reforms, to be clear, had their limitations: they came only in the final weeks of the war after most sailors had already completed their training; they

Fig. 6.7 White patrons at the officers' club at the Naval Air Station in Beaufort, South Carolina, celebrate news of Japan's surrender, while black staff smile, August 14, 1945. By war's end, work hierarchies regarding who commanded whom and who served whom remained. Courtesy National Archives, 80-G-332964.

remained to some extent subject to the whims of local commanders and their "traditional autonomy" on "Negro" matters; and they left untouched numerous other stark black-white divides, such as those involving ratings and rank. Still, this was an important departure from Jim Crow training. The *Chicago Defender* called it, with some justification, a "major victory."[115]

Credit for this victory belongs in part to navy officials. The Special Programs Unit, the small and overworked group of officers who advised the Bureau of Naval Personnel on Negro policy, pushed hard for these reforms. And a growing number of their superiors, not least Forrestal, proved willing to listen to them and to experiment. But African Americans, especially those in uniform, were the most indispensable agents of change. It is no coincidence that the navy's boldest moves to blur black-white boundaries came in the wake of a spate of dramatic and large-scale black sailor protests—the mutiny at Port Chicago, the hunger strike at Port Hueneme, and others. These events challenged many navy leaders to reconsider their long-standing assumption that color lines cured more race problems than they caused. As Admiral Chester Nimitz, commander of the Pacific Fleet, noted toward the end of the war, "If you put all the Negroes together they'll have a chance to share grievances and to plot among themselves, and this will damage discipline and morale. If they are distributed among other members . . . there will be less chance of trouble." Here was a remarkable shift in beliefs—from the notion that discipline and morale demanded segregation, as navy officers firmly believed for most of the war, to its opposite. Neither this shift—nor the policy changes it enabled— could have occurred, it seems, without the widespread activism of African American sailors and marines and their many civilian allies. Writing two years after war's end, black scholar L. D. Reddick rightly observed that "the Negro people themselves" were "the greatest creative force of all" behind the important wartime shifts in the navy's "Negro policy."[116]

Similar shifts in thinking and policy, though more gradual and limited, occurred in the wartime army. They came from the same mix of internal and external pressures, activism within the War Department and, especially, black soldiers' protest outside it. As for the former, no one was more important than William Hastie. From the start of his work as an aide to Secretary Stimson, he stressed repeatedly the fundamental flaws of the army's entire approach to black soldiers' training and service—especially its fealty to "the traditional mores of the South," which demanded rigid black-white segregation "in tactical organization, in physical location, in human contacts." No radical, Hastie called not for the immediate, wholesale abandonment of this approach but, instead, for piecemeal reforms, such as the promotion of more black officers and the elimination of color bars in post theaters and exchanges. Without these reforms, he warned, black soldiers' "deeply-seated and keenly felt" bitterness "could . . . explode at any time. Only a spark is needed."[117]

But few War Department leaders heeded Hastie's advice or warning. In the early years of war mobilization, even as stories of black trainees' brutal mistreatment and plummeting morale piled up, some army brass looked away. In an April 1942 memo, a brigadier general credited segregation policies with having "practically eliminated the colored problem, as such, within the Army." When, within weeks, War Department leaders quickly upgraded their assessment of the "problem" to "explosive," they did not search for causes, as Hastie had, in their own Jim Crow policies.[118] Instead, they blamed African Americans themselves—their supposedly undisciplined troops and the "highly inflammatory" press and protest organizations—and a sinister and shadowy set of German, Japanese, and other "Axis-minded" agitators. Secretary Stimson claimed to have had "direct evidence" that a "good many of their [Negro] leaders have been receiving pay from the Japanese ambassador in Mexico," which supposedly explained black soldiers' objections to white officers. To the extent that whites were blamed at all, it was for a set of "inherent" and "hereditary" race prejudices, which seemed beyond their control.[119] Utterly frustrated for many months with these views and with the War Department's general intransigence on black-white matters, Hastie finally resigned in protest in early January 1943. The most immediate cause: the "reactionary policies and discriminatory practices of the Army Air Forces in matters affecting Negroes."[120]

Within the War Department, others carried Hastie's cause forward, especially his successor, Truman Gibson, and the army's sole black general, Benjamin O. Davis Sr. Neither man offered Hastie's broad-sweeping and fundamental critique of the War Department's policies, of which some black newspapers and soldiers claimed that Gibson and Davis were altogether too accepting. About Davis, the *Chicago Defender* bemoaned the "sorry comic opera spectacle [of his] running around the country making inspections in which he fails to see the plight of his black brother." In truth, both men, at least in time, worked behind the scenes to attack many of the same color lines that Hastie had, including those in post exchanges, post theaters, officers' clubs, and promotion policies. By the end of 1943, Davis in particular had grown increasingly exasperated with the army's glacial pace of race reform. In a memo to McCloy, he condemned the War Department for "regard[ing] colored soldiers as separate and distinct." The army's black-white race problems were "large enough and serious enough," in his view, that he proposed establishing a bureau at the highest, general-staff level

Fig. 6.8 Brigadier General Benjamin O. Davis Sr., August 1944. He was the sole black American army general during World War II and a member of the Advisory Committee on Negro (sometimes "Special") Troop Policies. Courtesy National Archives, 111-SC-192258-S.

that devoted its full attention to the "conditions surrounding the colored soldier." Black officers would have to be well represented, Davis added: "It is utterly impossible for any white man to appreciate what the colored officers and soldiers experience in trying to develop a high morale under present conditions."[121]

All along, Hastie, Gibson, and Davis were not simply advocating for particular race reforms. Like the black press, black soldiers, and others, they were also working at times to legitimize black protest itself, to convince white military leadership that it had little understanding of black

Fig. 6.9 Truman K. Gibson Jr., April 1945. He succeeded William Hastie as the civilian aide to the secretary of war, focusing, like Hastie, on matters related to black soldiers. Courtesy National Archives, 208-PU-77F-5.

experiences and so could not properly recognize the deep, tangled roots of their discontent or, implicitly, the justifiable motivations behind their activism. For white War Department leaders and white army generals who had long defined black protest as black misbehavior and long attributed the latter to flaws in black people themselves, this effort at reframing the meaning of black soldiers' activism was important.[122]

Still, in late 1943, the War Department passed on Davis's bureau proposal, which simply proved another of his charges: that it "refused to attempt any remedial action to eliminate Jim-Crow."[123] In fact, throughout 1942 and 1943, as black induction, disaffection, and protest all mounted, it left its army-post color lines firmly in place and simply tried to contain their rising costs. It established the Advisory Committee on Negro (sometimes "Special") Troop Policies, a small group of high-ranking officers charged with counseling the War Department General Staff about all things related to black soldiers. Davis served on this committee and aired most of his most pointed critiques of War Department policy at its meetings. The War Department tinkered with the training and selection of black soldiers and their officers. It insisted on handling all "breaches of discipline" "firmly, legally, and without compromising any standards of conduct." It redoubled efforts to protect ammunition and weapon stocks. It infiltrated black units with counterintelligence agents and carefully monitored "racial conditions." It sought to boost black morale by providing ample recreational facilities, entertainment, and spiritual support. And, in time, it moved black troops overseas.[124]

And yet black protest remained, often gathering steam over time. Varying some from post to post, it never went away. Eventually, it forced some War Department leaders, especially those on the advisory committee, to recognize that black-white lines had not "practically eliminated the colored problem," as many had initially thought, but fueled and magnified it, gravely compromising the war effort in the process. Some War Department leaders came to recognize the point that Hastie had made from the outset of mobilization, that Gibson and Davis continued to make after he had left, and that ordinary black soldiers and their civilian allies made in one form or another on a daily basis: the so-called colored problem was really a white racism problem, one that the War Department and army needed to address by eliminating or blurring some of their ubiquitous black-white lines. For example, in the wake of numerous "disturbances" in the spring and summer of 1943—boycotts and sit-ins and acts of armed resistance—the advisory committee secretary, Colonel J. S. Leonard, attributed some of this protest not to black troops' misbehavior or to outside agitators, but to their deep (and, implicitly, understandable) dislike of army policy—especially its segregation "in its various forms"—and to their growing determination to change it. Similarly, one War Department pamphlet released in early 1944 recognized that "most" black people despise "racial segregation" and for good reason: they know "from experience that separate facilities are rarely equal, and that too often racial segregation rests on a belief in racial inferiority." Toward the end of the war, even Assistant Secretary of War John J. McCloy, who headed the advisory committee and who had long feared "terrible prophecies" in the event of a desegregated army, recognized the "grave repercussions" of a segregated one.[125]

In time, much like their colleagues in the navy, though on a more limited scale, War Department officials began occasionally considering what had been utterly unthinkable for most of the war: that integration could help rather than hurt military efficiency and troop morale. An April 1945 study of Camp Plauche in Louisiana credited good "race relations" there, in part, to integrated recreation, sports, theaters, and post exchanges. Simultaneous experiments with integrated fighting units on the Western Front in Europe would lead to similar conclusions. It is no surprise, then, that shortly after the war's conclusion War Department leaders ordered a top-to-bottom review of its "Negro" policies, including the welter of army-post divides.[126]

These shifting views were in many ways a consequence of black people's protest and, even more important, their ongoing efforts in and out of the War Department to frame this protest as legitimate. They led by the final year or so of the war to some chipping away at Jim Crow in uniform. Often, the advisory committee proposed changes and the general staff approved them. The blurring of black-white boundaries came first in the realm of ideas and discourse. In February 1944, in direct response to black soldiers' activism, the War Department issued a booklet for officers entitled *Command of Negro Troops*. In straightforward language, it exploded many army officers' (among others') myths about innate black-white differences. "Most Negroes will differ somewhat from white people in their sensitivities, thoughts, and actions," it conceded, but these facts came from a "history materially different from a majority in the Army" and from "existing restrictions which limit their participation in the life of the community." They did not, that is, come from "mysterious inborn factors . . . whose presence or absence is a matter of racial inheritance."[127]

The booklet—to the extent it was followed, a point on which evidence appears mixed—also may have led to quotidian boundary blurring in other ways. For example, it informed officers that "most Negroes resent any word or action that can be interpreted as evidence of a belief that they are by birth inferior to members of other races." Therefore, it counseled against using "uncomplimentary references" such as " 'boy,' 'Negress,' 'darky,' 'uncle,' 'Mammy,' 'aunty,' and 'nigger,' " all of which "imply either racial hostility or a patronizing, condescending attitude." It also noted that African Americans resented attempts to assign them inherent superior abilities, as in the "compliments" they received about supposedly special musical, dance, and athletic talents. "Negroes see in such theories, no matter how well meant," the booklet asserted, "a tendency to place them in the position of a race apart." "A good rule," it advised, "is not to ask colored troops to show off by doing things at which white people think Negroes are especially talented as a race."[128]

Some War Department leaders' slight shift in views led to the blurring of training-camp spatial lines too, thanks to a series of directives, which began in early 1943 and grew somewhat clearer and more comprehensive over time. In one of its stronger iterations, a directive dated July 8, 1944, the War Department prohibited commanding officers from excluding any personnel on the basis of race from any post exchange, post theater, post bus, or section of a post bus. An additional directive from the summer of

1945 applied similar prohibitions to officers' clubs. By this time, at least some army and War Department leaders viewed these orders as banning all "segregation in [all] facilities on the post on account of race." Many others in and out of the army held similarly sweeping interpretations. One memorandum for McCloy that surveyed southern camps in the wake of the July 1944 order indicated that both black and white soldiers alike viewed it as a "radical change" from earlier segregation policies.[129]

So did many jittery and livid white southerners. A long list of US senators and House members, governors, city officials, newspaper editors, and ordinary people demanded that the War Department rescind its "anti-segregation ruling" immediately and stop "ruthlessly trampling on traditions and customs of long standing" in the South. "You have no right," a Louisiana congressman wrote Secretary Stimson, "to effect, or attempt to effect, changes in the life of the people of the Southland." Seventy or so white civilian employees at Fort Benning in Georgia also wrote Stimson in protest: "With our boys dying in blood and fire on the battlefields of the world FOR FREEDOM AND DEMOCRACTIC TRADITIONS, certainly it is no time to pass any orders, laws or regulations that will in any way interfere with peace and unity and the morale on the fighting front." The *Montgomery (AL) Advertiser* exclaimed, "Army orders, even armies, even bayonets, cannot force impossible and unnatural social race relations upon us."[130]

For their part, many black people and their allies welcomed the "no-segregation order" as a "courageous" departure from Jim Crow practices. William Hastie, from his new position as dean of Howard University Law School, wrote his former War Department colleague McCloy that "at no time during the last four years have I seen so much enthusiasm and good will generated by a particular bit of official action."[131] But it was black soldiers themselves who seized on the new policy, determined to make it real. They distributed copies of the written order from post to post to ensure that their comrades knew about it, even when local commanders refused to announce it. They also tested its enforcement by launching what military authorities called a full-fledged "campaign for non-segregation," demanding service in a wide range of "white" post facilities. When they determined that the order was not enforced, they often protested this fact to their commanders on the ground, in the process also enlisting the help of the NAACP, sympathetic Congress members, the black press, and others.[132]

As black soldiers' activism suggests, the War Department order proved more limited than its opponents feared and its supporters hoped. It was not until June 1945, for example, that War Department leaders clarified that local commanders' "administrative discretion should not carry the authority to exclude individuals [on the basis of race] from the right to enjoy recreational facilities" on army posts.[133] Still, that the order was issued and enforced at all was a direct consequence of black soldiers' ongoing efforts to demand nothing less.

* * *

In time, hundreds of thousands of black troops eventually left their training camps or their stateside service for staging areas and ports of embarkation on the East, West, and Gulf Coasts. They were finally heading to battlefronts and encampments overseas. Unsurprisingly, the military's tangle of black-white lines—and the battles to uproot them—accompanied them there. In the spring of 1943, for example, a black port battalion was stationed at the New Orleans Port of Embarkation, awaiting its deployment abroad. In letters home, members of the unit painted a dire picture of racism on and off post, but also of their determined efforts to fight back. They seethed over the violent, sometimes fatal, harassment of white MPs; over their treatment like dogs, animals, and "dumb brutes not men"; over officers calling them "Nigger," "black nigger," "God-Damn Nigger," and "Nigger Yankees"; over their inability to get promotions or furloughs; over their frequent trips to the stockade for minor infractions or, in their view, none at all; and over ubiquitous Jim Crow. In response, some kept their heads down, hoping to stay out of trouble; others refused "to put up with all that junk and demand[ed] the things that are right"; still others went AWOL or fought back in a steady stream of big and small altercations. Numerous men predicted more trouble to come. "If they don't move the 494th away from here," one soldier wrote, "there won't be any Louisiana."[134]

Even black troops' final moments on US soil could reflect and reinforce black-white lines. "[D]uring the four months we had at our Advanced Base Depot, we saw many units embark for overseas service," recalled one African American Seabee in the summer of 1944. "With band playing and colors flying they left, and we thrilled at the spectacle, looking forward eagerly to the day when we should sail away. The day came. We, too, must leave. But no band played, no flag waved as we marched away to war, down the tree lined streets of that little southern town." Boarding a troop transport for Europe around the same time, one black war correspondent "noticed that the Negro soldiers entered a different hole in the ship from the white troops."[135]

As a measure of just how humiliating, unjust, and terrifying many black troops' induction-to-debarkation experiences had been, their loved ones sometimes did not feel the same kind of fear and dread that many whites did as "their boys were shipped out . . . to do battle overseas."

In James Baldwin's arresting recollection, they felt, instead, "a peculiar kind of relief. . . . It was, perhaps, like feeling that the most dangerous part of a dangerous journey had been passed and that now, even if death should come, it would come with honor and without the complicity of their countrymen."[136]

CHAPTER 7

⌇⌇⌇

Bonds and Barriers

In November 1944, one Japanese American soldier wrote home about the hardships he faced while training at an army camp in Texas. In response, his correspondent asked, "You say they have racial discrimination there. I would like to know where you people stand. I mean Japanese. Are they classified as colored too?" It was a good question. Black-white lines deeply shaped "colored" or "Negro" troops' lives in their training and service in the United States. But what about the lives of everyone else on the so-called white side of those lines, especially those troops whom the military and the civilian world either consistently or occasionally categorized as non-white?[1] When a string divided "colored" from "white" at a post theater, who sat where? Or when the military prevented "colored" officers from commanding "white" troops, who led and who followed—or who was promoted and who was not? In these instances and more, were Japanese Americans white or colored or something else entirely? And what about other non-black minorities of Mexican or Filipino or Chinese or Native American or Puerto Rican descent? When it came to enlistment and unit assignments, the military never divided its panoply of personnel solely along the all-powerful black-white line but, instead, along a complex mix of them. To what extent did this complexity also apply to troops' lived experiences in uniform?

This chapter follows nonblack minorities through their training and service in the United States.[2] America's World War II military, from its top leaders to its enlisted personnel, simultaneously built and blurred a white-nonwhite divide alongside its black-white one. On the one hand, the blurring, which emerged on and off post and in a variety of units, stemmed from a host of factors, including the day-to-day intermingling of service members, the desire to counter Axis propaganda and to shore up "darker" ally support, the activism of nonblack minorities, and the counterintuitively unifying power of the black-white divide among nonblacks. On the other hand, this blurring had its limits. White-nonwhite lines cropped up in some of the same places black-white ones did—rank and job structures, fights and language, male-female relations and civilian space—and some different ones, too—especially anything related to national security and Japanese Americans. In the end, these lines remained in place throughout the war years, despite continuous blurring. They did so in part because of these racialized national security concerns, because of the power of civilian racist practices and investments, and because of the isolation and vulnerabilities that sometimes came from being one of a few nonblack minorities in a so-called white outfit.

"WHEN THE WAR STARTED, I BECAME A WHITE MAN"

The power and ubiquity of black-white lines sometimes forged unlikely connections among a heterogeneous mix of servicemen and -women, who were sometimes defined as white and other times simply as not black, not colored, or not Negro. In some cases, those lines essentially trumped and blurred other ones, most significantly the white-nonwhite divide, which snaked its way through so much of civilian life and parts of the military, too. Often this blurring came from within white units, where all members shared barracks, latrines, mess halls, service clubs, post exchanges, and the most intimate aspects of their round-the-clock military lives. But perhaps surprisingly, blurring also appeared when nonblack minority troops served in descent-specific units—say, the Japanese American 442nd Combat Team or even in "colored" ones.

As for white units, several scholars have made this argument about blurring with respect to Italians and Germans, Norwegians and Jews, English and Poles, Nordics and Mediterraneans, a remarkable story given the salience of intra-European racist divides in the prewar United States.[3] But at times, this blurring extended to others as well—Asian Americans and American Indians, Mexican Americans and Puerto Ricans. A host of factors—including the uniform experiences within white units, from barracks life, tests, and drills to marches, maneuvers, and carousing on leave—could unite service members not only across heretofore salient divides of region, religion, class, national origin, and European "races," but also across the color line that cleaved white from nonwhite.

Fig. 7.1 Enlisted men of the Twenty-Fifth Service Group relax in their barracks at the Greenville Army Air Base in South Carolina, July 1943. It was in these spaces, while training and serving, that some troops managed to bridge and smudge white-nonwhite lines. Courtesy of the Library of Congress Prints and Photographs Division, LC-USW3-035437-E.

Take American Indians, for example. Many years after the war, one Ojibwe man recalled "his first feeling of complete acceptance while serving in the Army during World War II." Anthropologist John Adair, having interviewed more than one hundred Pueblo and Navajo veterans decades earlier, in 1946, found that feeling to be widespread. Military life introduced "the Indian recruit . . . [to] something that he had never known before. He was accepted as an individual, and was judged as an individual, and not as one of a minority group." This acceptance derived from Indians' separation "from their cultural and natural environment and [their being] forced into the same way of life as millions of white men." In particular, they faced "the same training routine, the same garrison life with its monotony, and the escape from that monotony to the Post movie or to the PX to drink beer; or the more satisfactory escape to the towns when on passes, where liquor and women were at the center of attraction for Indians as well as Whites." Through it all, "some of the psychological barriers which had always been present in relations between the Indian and the White were torn down." By training and serving in white units, Native peoples and whites, according to scholars more recently, came to see themselves as "friends and brothers," "equals and friends."[4]

A similar process seems to have involved many Mexican Americans. Raul Morin, a young draftee from Texas, recalled his early days in basic training at Camp Roberts in California: "Finding ourselves [Mexican Americans] in a new setting away from the old surroundings, with new faces, new friends, and everyone in the same boat, put us on an equal status." This equality was a revelation to all those Americans who hailed from parts of the country "where minority groups were kept segregated, or where minority groups were small in number. Here for the first time in their lives they became acquainted and really got to know their fellow countryman of a different nationality and racial background."[5] Journalist Ignacio Lopez agreed, noting in 1946 that "every Southwest community has in it young men, formerly 'little' Americans but who were able to act as complete Americans for the three to four years [in uniform]. They know what it is to be released of the minority burden." As one Mexican American veteran summed it up, "In the service we were all equal. We were all Americans."[6] True, as one scholar has observed, "the emphasis in these accounts seems to be on being accepted as Americans rather than as white." Because these two categories were so often inextricably linked, however, inclusion in one often meant inclusion in the other. As soldier Ancieto Nuñez memorably put it, "When the war started, I became a white man."[7]

Military life in white units sometimes helped other nonblack minorities scale the related borders surrounding whiteness and Americanness. Fresh from completing six weeks of basic training at Camp Polk in Louisiana in 1942, Doroteo V. Vité, who described himself as a "Filipino rookie in Uncle Sam's Army," reported enjoying living among the "regular guys" in his white unit—"farmers and moonshiners from Alabama and Georgia, boatmen and fishermen from Mississippi, cowboys from Texas and Arizona, factory workers from Michigan and Illinois." This "close association" was providing "a wonderful opportunity" to establish "friendship, understanding and equality between the American and Filipino peoples."[8] Writing from an army airfield in Colorado in early 1944, Chinese American newspaperman-turned-airman Charles Leong remarked that the army was offering "GI Joe Wong . . . a 'Chinaman's chance' . . . a fair chance, one based not on race

Fig. 7.2 Tankmen of Chinese, English, French, Greek, Russian, and American descent at Fort Knox in Kentucky during World War II. Courtesy of the Library of Congress Prints and Photographs Division, LC-USW33-000871-C.

or creed, but on the stuff of the man who wears the uniform of the U.S. Army."[9]

This quotation highlights the masculinist meanings attached to soldiering that no doubt helped some male troops reach across the white-nonwhite line. But servicewomen experienced their own forms of white-unit bonding. Ruth Chan, the only Chinese American in her Women's Air Corps outfit, enjoyed full acceptance, something she had never experienced growing up in California's Central Valley. "While in the service," historian Judy Yung writes, "she was captain of the basketball team, given her first surprise birthday party, and promoted to corporal at the suggestion of the nurses under whom she worked as a secretary." Concepción Alvarado Escobedo, a Mexican American from Texas, had a similar experience in a white unit. Enlisting in the Women's Army Corps (WAC) in 1944, she, like Chan, joined an outfit with no co-ethnics and felt that everyone was treated "all the same." Reflecting years later on her time in the service, Escobedo said that she learned to "get along with other people. . . . [Before joining the WAC] I didn't have much experience with . . . Anglos or any other nationality or ethnic group. When I was at Randolph Field [in Texas], a lot of the women who were close to me were from the East—New York, New Jersey, northern states. . . . I didn't have any Mexican friends."[10]

Sometimes these friends in the service insisted on blurring the white-nonwhite divide when civilians sought to enforce it. On furlough from training at Camp Shelby in Mississippi, Puerto Rican New Yorker Manny Diaz and four white army friends, likely all members of the same white signal corps unit, went to a bar in nearby Biloxi. It was an act of socializing, which reflected the boundary-blurring that white units could foster. But not everyone took kindly to the blurring, especially in the Jim Crow South. When the men all ordered beers, only Diaz was served at the end of the bar. "Back there, boy," the bartender told him, evidently thinking Diaz was white enough to drink at the bar but not white enough to do so next to his friends. Diaz left in protest, and his buddies joined him. In fact, Diaz later recalled that one of them, Irish American Shorty Dolan, as incensed as anyone by the discrimination against his friend, hurled a bottle at "the window of the bar, the window shattered, and we started running."[11] One can only imagine how this harrowing, and perhaps thrilling, experience might have further bonded the friends.

In some cases, this bonding took time—and, occasionally, even conflict—to develop or emerged only within the smallest units, say, a platoon or squad, where face-to-face contact was an unavoidable reality. The same Manny Diaz, also while at Camp Shelby, slugged a white Texas soldier for refusing, despite several warnings, to stop stepping on Diaz's heel during a dress parade. While both men, as punishment, received two weeks of dreaded kitchen police (KP) duty, which amounted to "peel[ing] potatoes everyday [sic] for a couple of hundred soldiers," something un-expected happened. "Lo and behold, after two weeks," Diaz recalled, "this guy and I became good friends. . . . For the first couple of days, I wouldn't even talk to him. But I guess the hardship of being a KP brought us to-gether." Having trained alongside Mexican Americans at Camp Roberts in California, one white soldier from South Dakota reported a similar self-transformation: "The only Mexicans we ever saw back home were those that worked in the Railroad and lived in section houses. I always heard that they were not to be trusted, and if you turned your back to them, they would knife you in the back. But these fellows that I have known here at Roberts are just like other Americans." Private Katsutani, writing home from Camp Fannin in Texas to a friend in Maui, described incessant fighting within his company between the "boys from Hawaii" and a group of "haoles," or whites, sometimes involving bayonets and rifle butts. But Katsutani also noted that this conflict spared his own platoon, in which "the haoles . . . are really good guys." If comradeship overseas sometimes developed within

only the tightest of combat circles, something similar also occurred between whites and nonwhites at training camps in the United States.[12]

These varied forms of bonding within white units during training and
service in the United States could be transformative for some young nonblack minority servicemen and -women. Prior to their military life, many
of them had seldom interacted with or been accepted by members of their
locale's dominant descent group, however it was defined—white, Anglo,
American, or some combination. But bonding could take place in other
kinds of units as well, even so-called colored ones. Consider the case of the
Eightieth Naval Construction Battalion. It was "colored" in that all, or nearly
all, 750 or so enlisted men below a certain rank were classified as such.
But the unit's several hundred officers and petty officers were, without a
single exception, classified as white, including one Petty Officer First Class
Pablo Villareal of Laredo, Texas, presumably a Mexican American, and the
unit's senior medical officer, an Italian American lieutenant from Brooklyn
named Vincent J. Tesoriero. Interestingly, the unit also included "three
Chinese and ten Filipinos," nearly all of whom were messmen, but at least
one of whom appears to have been an electrician.[13]

Precious little is known about these men's experiences. But this unit,
while it trained in Virginia and Mississippi in the first five or so months of
1943, became the target of numerous complaints from its black members
about abusive white officers, discriminatory promotion policies, and
segregated barracks, chow halls, toilets, buses, beer parlors, and the Ship's
Service Store.[14] By March 1943, the men confided to a civilian ally that, in
her words, "serious trouble is likely to develope [sic] unless something is
done to rectify this situation."[15] Tesoriero, as one of the battalion's officers,
may have been the subject of the men's complaints, but surely not a victim
of the injustices underlying them. But what about Villareal and the small
number of Chinese and Filipinos? Did they also face promotion obstacles or
abusive officers? And where would any of them have eaten, slept, shopped,
or relaxed at the navy's Jim Crow installations in the United States? With
or without the "colored" men?

Definitive answers are difficult to come by, but some educated guesses
are possible. As for Villareal, the navy could be a tough place for Mexican
Americans, as we will see. But perhaps Villareal's authority over black
Seabees served to burnish his bona fides as white, or perhaps the ongoing
battles between the unit's black enlisted men and their white superiors,
Villareal among them, had a similar effect. Perhaps both dynamics were at
work. As for the Filipinos and Chinese, that nearly all these men served as
messmen placed them in an unambiguously subordinate position, indeed
one most likely to be occupied by and associated with black people in the

navy.[16] One might expect, then, that when navy officers, say, segregated "colored" men in barracks and beer parlors and bathrooms, they segregated Filipinos and Chinese alongside them. Perhaps they did on occasion. Yet, when the Seabee unit set sail for Trinidad in June 1943 and encamped there, segregation sprouted anew, sometimes dividing "Negroes," on the one hand, from whites, Chinese, and Filipinos, on the other.[17] Whether this particular divide also appeared stateside is unclear, but here was nonetheless a striking example of how a stark color line could simultaneously divide—black from not black—and unite—white with some nonwhite. Indeed, paradoxically, the former may have helped produce the latter.[18]

This uniting of whites and some nonwhites also happened in nonblack descent-specific outfits. Perhaps the most remarkable illustration of this point involves the well-known Japanese American 100th Infantry Battalion and the 442nd Combat Team, especially their training experiences, the bulk of which took place in 1943 at Camp Shelby in Mississippi, although the uniting in this case seems to have had less to do with the felt experience of soldiers themselves, as was the case for some American Indians, Mexican Americans, Chinese Americans, Filipinos, and others. It had more to do, instead, with the demands of Nisei soldiers' white officers, which themselves sometimes stemmed from the demands of War Department leaders above them and of Japanese American soldiers below them.

At Camp Shelby, where the number of Nisei soldiers soared from the single digits in late 1942 to more than five thousand in mid-1943, Japanese Americans had their own barracks and mess halls, since War Department policy required that unit members share these things.[19] Unlike black soldiers, however, they had free access to all other parts of and events in the camp's white section, including post exchanges, service clubs, and dances. While "the negro . . . is segregated in most instances," reported the director of post intelligence in July 1943, "all military organizations make absolutely no distinction between the yellow and white races at this station." Japanese Americans sported their own baseball squad, but unlike black soldiers, they played in white leagues. "We are treated like white soldiers out at Camp Shelby," remarked one Japanese American trainee.[20]

A similar pattern often prevailed in Hattiesburg, Mississippi, the town closest to Shelby. At first, ubiquitous black-white Jim Crow signs flummoxed Japanese American soldiers. Many of them came from Hawaii and the West Coast, where segregation, if it existed at all, was often subtler. "What are we?" 442nd member Richard Watada recalled wondering when encountering "white and colored toilets" for the first time. But the men's officers declared repeatedly that they were white; for some soldiers, it was the first thing they remembered hearing when they arrived at Shelby.[21]

Fig. 7.3 Members of the 442nd Combat Team salute the flag in a brief review at Camp Shelby in Mississippi, June 1943. Courtesy of the Library of Congress Prints and Photographs Division, LC-USZ62-127108.

Mike Masaoka, a public relations officer in the 442nd and a well-known leader in the Japanese American Citizens League, recalled, "Most of the officers—at least those who counted—insisted that we Nisei act, and be treated, as white." Hawaii senator Daniel Inouye, as an eighteen-year-old private three weeks into training with the 442nd at Shelby, remembered his captain telling his company, "Men, I have been instructed to tell you that during your time in this state, you will be treated by its people as white men."[22]

And so it was—for the most part. Between roughly January 1943 and April 1944, when large numbers of Nisei soldiers trained at nearby Camp Shelby, their relations with Hattiesburg's white civilians were never universally warm and friendly. But Nisei nonetheless occupied an honorary, if always precarious, white status in town. With some occasional exceptions, Japanese American soldiers (and their few family members who followed them to Mississippi) were permitted to ride in the white sections of rail cars, streetcars, and buses; to eat in white restaurants and cafés; to sit in the floor-level seats of movie theaters (rather than in the colored-only balcony called "nigger heaven"); to use white restrooms and water fountains;

to read in the white portion of the city library; to attend white churches and white Sunday school classes; to stay in white hotels; and to rent rooms in white homes. "We are considered as 'whites' in this south-lands," a private in the 442nd wrote his family back home in Maui in May 1943.[23]

That Hattiesburg's black-white lines resembled Shelby's in many respects was hardly coincidental. While the town's leaders ultimately decided these matters, local army brass influentially weighed in. As Nisei soldiers began streaming into town, the post commander at Shelby, Brigadier General Halloran, and the commanding officer of the 442nd, Colonel Pence, met frequently with town leaders, hoping to make Hattiesburg as hospitable a place for their troops as possible. In a town with such rigid lines between blacks and whites, this meant gaining acceptance for Japanese Americans among the latter. Indeed, when a group of especially "race-conscious" Hattiesburg leaders, increasingly uncomfortable with the growing number of Nisei in town, decided to ban them from white USO dances, Halloran objected vigorously and managed to have the ban revoked. In the end, town leaders responded by simply canceling all USO dances for the season, ostensibly on account of heat. But the army succeeded, at least in this case, in protecting Japanese Americans' honorary white status.[24]

This status appeared in other posts and post towns as well, though Shelby and Hattiesburg are the best-documented cases. Yoshiro Matsuhara, who later served in the Military Intelligence Service (MIS), recalled that, among the first things he heard upon arriving for infantry training in a Japanese American unit at Fort McClellan in Alabama, was that he was white and should board buses up front and avoid "Negro" post exchanges, canteens, and theaters. Lawrence Mori, a 442nd member, remembered an identical story about his training at Camp Wolters in Texas.[25] As at Hattiesburg, civilians elsewhere also accepted Japanese Americans as honorary whites at times, a fact that army authorities helped to make possible. Early in the war, a committee of white Little Rock citizens met with the commanding officer at nearby Camp Robinson to discuss its concerns about the Nisei training units stationed there. They objected to reports that the troops were "making social contacts" in "colored areas" and attending white USO dances, since the committee "had learned that Japanese were not accepted socially by the white people in the communities from which they came." But the post commander defended his Nisei troops. Believing firmly that "any discrimination on the part of the residents of Little Rock will impair their value as soldiers," he urged the committee to be patriotic and to drop its objections. It appears it did, since Little Rock's countless Jim Crow institutions seem to have accepted Japanese Americans by and large as white.[26]

Or perhaps the point, both in the army and in these southern communities, was not that Japanese Americans were white exactly, only that they were not colored. True, the effect could be the same either way— Japanese Americans frequented white spaces on and off post—but there was a difference: in one case whiteness included Japanese Americans, and in the other coloredness excluded them. Distinguishing between the two can be difficult, but at times the latter phenomenon was clearly at work. Note, for example, the intelligence report about Camp Shelby in which the "distinction between the yellow and white races" was simultaneously disavowed (at camp facilities) and underlined (in the phrase "yellow and white races" itself). Similarly, in official memoranda and correspondence, army and War Department authorities—even Japanese Americans' most ardent defenders, some of whom often insisted publicly on their whiteness—differentiated repeatedly between "white" or "Caucasian," on the one hand, and "Japanese American" or "Japanese," on the other.[27]

At Camp Shelby, this insistence on Japanese Americans' not-colored status more so than their whiteness had both bottom-up and top-down dimensions. As for the former, Japanese Americans and "colored" (or "Negro") people, interestingly, sometimes stressed the distinctions between each of their respective groups. In the process, they did their small part to reinforce those distinctions. One black soldier, serving as an undercover counterintelligence operative at Shelby, reported an instance in which "Japanese came to the negro table in the mess hall at the hospital, telling the negro troops that they preferred sitting with them rather than with the whites, but . . . the approach was not favorably received." Some Japanese Americans, who of course had much more to gain from these black-nonblack boundaries than did African Americans, scrupulously highlighted them. "As for [attending] negro dances," wrote one Nisei soldier in a June 1943 letter, "they are out of the question. We have orders not to fool with them. The [white] Southerners doesn't [*sic*] care to associate with anyone who fools with negroes. I'm going to be a real Southerner and hate the negroes like the devil."[28]

But this soldier's reference to "orders" is a reminder of who had the most power to define the not-colored status of Nisei troops: military authorities. This meant that Japanese American members of the 442nd Combat Team and the 100th Battalion training in the South were often barred from black spaces and from having much of anything to do with black soldiers or civilians. At Shelby, officers made these prohibitions exceedingly clear, as the letter writer suggested. "Our officers insist that we steer clear of

Negroes," reported another Japanese American private in the 442nd. "If we make friends with Negroes, we degrade ourselves in the eyes of the people, and in that degree, we ourselves are classified as low as the Negroes. So our officers say that we should not be seen with negroes or we'll be 'sorree.' "[29] In addition to these warnings, army authorities placed the "colored" section of Hattiesburg out of bounds for Japanese Americans (and for all nonblacks); fought to keep black Women's Army Auxiliary Corps members from being stationed at Shelby, presumably to prevent romantic ties from developing between black women and Nisei men; and closely monitored Nisei-black relations for any evidence of friendliness, collusion, or joint "agitation."[30] This monitoring consisted of poring over tens of thousands of pieces of censored mail, drawing on reports from civilians and undercover enlisted agents, and relying on the investigative work of the FBI, the War Department's Counter Intelligence Corps and Military Intelligence Service, and the Federal Security Agency.[31]

In the army, then, Japanese Americans serving in Japanese American units, whether defined as white or simply as not-colored (or not-Negro), were thrown together with whites from army post exchanges and service clubs to civilian restaurants and churches. These experiences, in some way, must have had an effect that was similar to that in white units: a blurring of the line between white and nonwhite.

A similar blurring occurred with other troops serving in descent-specific units. Members of these outfits, like those in the Japanese American units, did not tend to share barracks and latrines and dining halls with whites. So some of the day-to-day intimacy and familiarity that could dissolve social boundaries of various kinds did not occur. At the same time, like Japanese Americans but unlike African Americans, other nonblack minorities seem not to have faced additional segregated spaces on military posts. They must have mingled freely with whites or Anglos in service clubs, post exchanges, military buses, and so forth. A study of the army's sole Mexican American company found that, when it trained at Camp Edwards in Massachusetts, unit members "were looked upon as United States Army soldiers" and "were treated just like everyone else." This equal treatment took place both on the army post among fellow soldiers and in the surrounding area among civilians.[32]

In fact, even when some civilian communities were less welcoming, the military sometimes showed a willingness, as with Nisei troops, to fight for nonblack minorities' equal treatment. Before moving to Camp Edwards, the Mexican American company trained at Camp Bowie in Texas. A restaurant in nearby Brownwood refused to serve some of its members, who were attired in their army uniforms; its sign out front read, "No Mexicans or Dogs Allowed." Incensed, the company's white commander and a white army colonel placed the restaurant out of bounds for all service personnel, stripping it of countless customers. When the restaurant then relented, promising to serve all soldiers in the future, the officers lifted their ban, but they first fined the restaurant $500 for mistreating and humiliating its "American" soldiers.[33] Similarly, when members of the First Filipino Infantry, training in central California, faced universal exclusion from local restaurants, movie theaters, and hotels, the unit's white colonel met with the Chamber of Commerce and "laid down the law of cooperation with the army or else." As in Texas, the businesses soon "changed their tune." Both episodes underlined a key point: in the words of one Filipino soldier, "The army will go to bat for us."[34]

Indeed, the army may have been most likely to fight civilian discrimination when its nonblack members served in descent-specific units. In these cases, discrimination could and did undermine the morale not of a few people scattered throughout an outfit but of all or nearly all its members.

Fig. 7.4 Company I of the First Filipino Infantry at Camp Roberts in California, c. 1942. Shades of L.A. Photo Collection, Los Angeles Public Library.

This fact helps explain why white unit commanders sometimes acted quickly to defend their men and root out discrimination off post—from Japanese Americans in Mississippi and Arkansas to Mexican Americans in Texas to Filipinos in California—and to preserve the morale and effectiveness of their entire outfits.

All told, this blurring of the white-nonwhite line was varied and complex. It occurred on military installations and in nearby towns across the United States and in white units, in "colored" ones, and in a diverse assortment of descent-specific outfits in between. This uniting and blurring sometimes turned "Mexicans" into "Americans," or "Japs" into whites, or nonwhites into nonblacks. But in all cases at and around military installations throughout the wartime United States, the pervasive civilian divide that separated whites from everyone else dissolved somewhat.

This dissolving resulted from top-down policies, as in the case of military commanders "going to bat" for their men, from the bottom-up affective ties that emerged more organically in the day-to-day lives of white-unit barracks mates, and from ubiquitous black-white lines that, for all their divisiveness, also united a variegated mix of nonblacks. But there were several additional and related factors that further explain this blurring of the white-nonwhite line.

One such factor involved the activism of nonblack minority troops themselves. Fighting between whites and nonwhites could reinforce boundaries between the two groups, but it also constituted a bottom-up effort, sometimes successful, to resist their enforcement. Daniel Inouye recalls a time while he was training at Camp Shelby when "one of our boys got thrown out of a 69th Division PX [post exchange] and a couple hundred of us marched on the place with blood in our eyes. The MPs had to call up a couple of tanks to turn us back."[35] That commanders at the camp insisted on Nisei soldiers' equal access to all nonblack areas of the post no doubt came in part from Japanese Americans' demands for nothing less. Indeed, more broadly, most of the instances of officers defending their troops from discrimination on or off post also resulted from similar bottom-up pressure. This pressure manifested itself not only in the form of fisticuffs or complaints to one's officers, but also in the form of articles in major newspapers and magazines and letters and appeals to friends and loved ones, politicians and civilian civil rights groups, War Department officials and occasionally foreign governments.[36]

One of these officials was Assistant Secretary of War John J. McCloy, whose personal commitments to the success of some Nisei troops constitute another key factor in the blurring of white-nonwhite lines, at least for

Japanese Americans. He had advocated so forcefully for the army's use and integration of Japanese American soldiers and for the creation of Japanese American units that some members of the 442nd "claim[ed] Mr. McCloy as 'our father.'" Having battled with other leaders in the War Department over the use of these troops, he was "very anxious that this project succeed."[37] He and his staff sought to protect Nisei soldiers from any undue discrimination that might damage their prospects, often responding to the specific complaints that the soldiers themselves were making. Among other things, this meant ensuring that Jim Crow applied as little as possible to Japanese Americans, on or off post. Throughout the first nine months or so of the 442nd's training, therefore, McCloy and his assistant, Colonel William P. Scobey, closely monitored the unit's progress (including reading its censored mail, from which they learned what parts of Nisei soldiers' training lives needed amelioration), kept in constant contact with commanding officers on the ground at Shelby as well as with many of their superiors up the chain, and tried to eliminate discrimination where they could. They also traveled to Camp Shelby and settled matters in person. In October 1943, for example, McCloy and Scobey visited for two days, during which they not only inspected everything from the unit's command to its barracks and latrines, but also made a point of meeting the local USO chief to ensure that the opening of a new "Aloha USO" in Hattiesburg, which was meant to serve Nisei primarily, would not "prevent the acceptance of the Japanese Americans as all other white Americans" at other centers.[38]

McCloy was committed to this unit not simply because of the role he personally played in its formation. There was a broader reason, which helps further explain his and other War Department leaders' interest in blurring white-nonwhite lines for Japanese Americans—and for all nonblacks: the global "race" politics of the war. The US government, increasingly concerned about Axis propagandists, worried especially about how charges of racist hypocrisy, and the realities behind those charges, could weaken ties with America's "darker" allies around the world. Indeed, the reopening of Nisei enlistment in the army and the formation of the 442nd Combat Team in 1943 stemmed in part from this concern. So, too, did a weakening white-nonwhite divide at army installations in the United States. For one thing, Nisei units would show the world the supposed wonders of America's multiracial democracy through, in Secretary Stimson's words, "the yellow man voluntarily fighting for the white."[39] But this global message rose or fell depending on the outfits' performance. Disgruntled, demoralized, or half-hearted fighters would not suffice. It was, therefore, in the interest of all War Department officials, not simply McCloy and his staff, to push for

Nisei units' excellence, in part by minimizing the color lines they faced while training.

Furthermore, allied governments such as Mexico and China, in response to the complaints of service members themselves, attempted to leverage this fraught wartime moment to reduce discrimination against those troops. When Mexican American soldiers accused the US military of mistreatment, for example, the Mexican Embassy in Washington protested to the US State Department, which immediately appealed to military authorities. Or when the army denied commissions to qualified Chinese Americans, one US government official warned the War Department that it would "be conveyed back to Chungking"—China's wartime capital—"pretty promptly."[40] During the war, then, whittling away at some of the military's white-nonwhite boundaries served two related ends: it countered Axis propaganda against the United States and shored up America's ties to its "darker" allies. In this way, military leaders felt that America's war interests were best served by both a stark black-white divide and, at least to some extent, a blurred white-nonwhite one.

Indeed, in their view, the former at times required the latter, a final reason for the blurring. For example, the war years were rife with rumors about (and some limited evidence of) Japanese-black alliances, transnational and local and everything in between.[41] Officers at Camp Shelby in June 1943 conceded privately that "although the American-Japanese have not associated with Negroes to date, there was a real fear that they might be driven to this association through discrimination against them. . . . Such a situation would be most undesirable."[42] What exactly might be "undesirable" was left unspecified, but army officials clearly had their hands full with black soldiers' increasingly powerful and organized opposition, in and out of the military, to black-white boundaries. It seems likely that these officials dreaded the possibility that Japanese Americans might "be driven" to join these struggles on the black side. And, in fact, not a few Nisei, while training in the South, did associate and ally themselves with black people in one way or another. In this context, then, army officers' insistence on Nisei whiteness or nonblackness, indeed their explicit instructions for Nisei to avoid African Americans at all cost, was sometimes a straightforward effort to divide the army's two most subordinated groups from one another. To be sure, if the War Department had been greatly concerned about this "darker races" alliance, it would have kept its Nisei units out of Mississippi altogether, where black troops and black civilians were so numerous. Still, it appears the military's deep investment in the black-white divide convinced it, at least at times, to blur the white-nonwhite one.

"THEY THINK THEY'RE BETTER . . . JUST BECAUSE THEIR SKIN IS WHITE"

This sort of blurring, however, constituted only half the story. Some blurring was effected by well-educated cultural ambassadors of sorts, with both the tools and the desire to build bridges beyond their descent groups and across the white-nonwhite line. For example, Doroteo V. Vité had been, prior to enlistment, a PhD candidate at Columbia University in international relations and, in his telling, had dedicated his young life to improving relations between Filipinos and Americans. Similarly, Charles Leong, seemingly convinced of "GI Joe Wong's" "Chinaman's Chance," had a master's degree in journalism from Stanford and had cofounded the English-language *Chinese Press* to serve as "an interpretive medium for Chinese, Chinese-Americans, and Americans."[43] These men, and no doubt others, were primed to relish and broadcast not only white units' incorporation of nonwhites, but also the smudging of the white-nonwhite distinction.

This smudging only went so far, however. In fact, various versions of the white-nonwhite divide, while rarely official army- or navywide policy, still cropped up in different forms and in different outfits, some of which resembled the black-white lines that ensnared African American troops. These lines appeared most frequently in the case of Japanese Americans, about whom source material is richest, but they also surfaced in relation to a wide range of other nonblack minorities, including Chinese Americans, Filipinos, Puerto Ricans, Mexican Americans, Cape Verdeans, and others.

One set of lines involved the civilian world, the towns and cities within easy reach of military posts, where service members relaxed on leave or furlough. Some military commanders tried to shield their troops from these lines off post, but they were not always successful. For the Filipino service members who finally gained access to public accommodations in Marysville, the town near Camp Beale, those places slightly farther away were less dependent on soldiers' dollars and so freer to discriminate. In San Francisco, for example, one private reported that he and his fellow "Filipino soldiers on pass were unable to find a shop that would cut their hair at any price."[44]

Similarly, Japanese Americans in the South, despite their commanding officers' best efforts, still faced their own versions of civilian Jim Crow—what some called "Jap Crow." In Hattiesburg, Mississippi, color lines bent only so far to accommodate Nisei soldiers. Some locals worked to bar them from white USO dances and to keep their children out of Hattiesburg's white public schools. Though dances were canceled, the school effort succeeded. On September 13, 1943, Martha Sugi, the wife of a sergeant in the 442nd, arrived at Hattiesburg's Camp Grammar School to enroll her seven-year-old son, Rollin. But he was promptly turned away. "The constitutional law of Mississippi," the city's superintendent of schools later explained to Mrs. Sugi, "forbids attendance at the same schools of whites and colored children—colored, in this instance being any child not a member of the Caucasian race."[45] In the end, rather than send Rollin and other Japanese American children to a "colored" school, Japanese American military mothers established a separate one in a small Hattiesburg house (in which the wives of Nisei soldiers taught).[46] Here, then, was a particular version of the white-nonwhite line: it distinguished not only between Japanese American and white but also between Japanese American and colored. Similarly, Mike Masaoka recalled hearing of "instances when Nisei servicemen were ordered not to use either white or black restrooms," and an African American private remembered a public bus in rural Louisiana loading white soldiers first, then Japanese Americans, and finally African Americans.[47]

But the most common white-nonwhite line that Japanese Americans faced in the civilian South often excluded them from whiteness, while remaining mum about their relationship to coloredness or Negroness. In Little Rock, white citizens attempted to bar Nisei soldiers from the town's white USO dances. In Anniston, Alabama, near Fort McClellan, where 442nd replacement troops took their final training before heading overseas, few wives and sweethearts could visit, since white hotels would seldom accept them. Members of the 100th Battalion began their training in Wisconsin, where locals tended to welcome them: Nisei visited white homes, attended white churches, and dated and sometimes married white women. But when the unit moved to Camp Shelby in early 1943, its relations with civilians changed markedly, as the white-nonwhite line, once blurred in Wisconsin, brightened in Mississippi.[48] A War Department report from April, based on an analysis of several hundred censored letters from unit members, found a "torrent of vitriolic comment" about Mississippians' "lack of cordiality." When the 442nd arrived several months later, relations remained cool. In July 1943, an army intelligence officer reported that while "Jim Crows laws do not apply to the Japanese" (the report was written before Rollin Sugi's failed attempt to enroll in a white school), they "have not been generally accepted as social or racial equals by the white population of Mississippi."[49]

Sometimes these civilian white-nonwhite lines appeared not in spite of military authorities, but in part because of them. The authorities seldom if ever insisted on or enforced these lines against nonblack minority troops off military posts, as they often did with black soldiers. But their occasional indifference to them no doubt encouraged them to persist and spread. This indifference appears to have been most common in white units, in which only a handful of their soldiers—rather than all of them, in the case of descent-specific outfits—might have faced discrimination. For example, in two separate incidents in Texas, public accommodations refused to serve Mexican American soldiers in uniform. But in contrast to the Brownwood case, where the Mexican American unit's white commanders came to their defense, army authorities refused to act, even questioning whether the men's humiliating exclusion constituted discrimination at all, despite the protests of prominent Mexican American civil rights activists and of the Mexican Embassy in Washington, DC. "There was no discrimination shown in either case against a soldier, as such," the officers reasoned. "The discrimination, if any, was definitely against persons of Mexican extraction. The uniform had no bearing in either situation. Therefore, it is recommended that no further action be taken insofar as the Military is concerned."[50]

Here the military aided and abetted the construction and maintenance of civilian white-nonwhite lines. But the military built its own lines as well. These lines seldom took the form of spatial segregation, as they did in the case of black troops, but there were exceptions, especially, it appears, for Mexican American soldiers in Texas. At Camp Hood in Killeen, one black soldier recalled seeing outhouses marked for Mexicans, whites, and colored. One hundred miles away at Camp Bowie, near the town of Brownwood, the army housed all of one unit's Mexican Americans in the same tent, a move that the men disliked and interpreted as segregation.[51] And in Lubbock, a group of recent inductees were in town for medical examinations at the West Texas Recruiting and Induction Station, and an army sergeant separated the Mexican Americans, placing them all in the same hotel, since the other hotels in town apparently refused to accept them.[52]

Relations between men and women offered another occasion for dividing whites from nonwhites. USO dances in Arkansas and Mississippi at first attempted to exclude Japanese American soldiers. But eventually USOs devoted primarily to their use were established in both places and elsewhere, as were regular dances at Camp Shelby, to which the army shipped Nisei women from nearby detention camps for "state-sanctioned intra-ethnic dating."[53] Chinese Americans, it appears, were permitted at some USO dances, but some steered clear of them, disliking the discrimination that they faced—or that they feared facing—from white officers and white women. In at least one case, Chinese American women, like Nisei women, were brought in from afar for socializing with Chinese American troops.[54] Sometimes military authorities policed white male–nonwhite female relations by restricting the former under their command. Numerous army post commanders in Alaska, for example, explicitly forbade "the association of [white] soldiers with native women."[55]

At other posts, these top-down rules proved unnecessary, as white soldiers enforced them on their own. While training at Camp Mackall in North Carolina in the fall of 1943, a group of soldiers from Hawaii, "many of them dark-skinned" Asian Americans and Pacific Islanders, encountered violence when they flirted with white women in the area. Local whites, and perhaps some white soldiers too, refused to tolerate this "race mixing," and "a lot of fights" broke out. The largest of these, according to one report, involved "a thousand soldiers and five hundred civilians." "Don't let them push you Hawaiians around," friends and relatives urged the soldiers in letters from Hawaii. "We are just as good as they are maybe better." "I wonder if those white trash up there think you boys are coloreds."[56] Similarly, in the spring of 1944, white soldiers picked fights with Nisei soldiers at Camp Patrick Henry in Virginia to prevent them from dancing with white women. And a year later, at Camp Plauche in Louisiana, "ill feeling and friction" developed between Puerto Ricans and "Continental American soldiers" when the latter objected to the former dancing with "American girls."[57]

An even more common set of white-nonwhite lines involved rank and jobs. As for jobs, systematic evidence is limited, and gripes about work assignments were widespread among all troops. Still, it appears that the military sometimes reserved certain more menial positions for nonblack minorities. The navy, for example, restricted Filipino Americans and Chinese Americans to the Messman Branch for a time. One Filipino, who had served in this role during World War II, recalled "officers, some of them from the South," calling adult Filipinos "boy" and being "really very nasty, they thought you were . . . inducted to be their personal servant."[58] According to some reports, the navy also concentrated many Mexican Americans in the relatively low-status and low-pay rating of deckhand. Legendary labor and civil rights leader Cesar Chavez called his time as a deckhand in the navy from 1944 to 1946 "the worst of my life."[59] And in the wake of the attack on Pearl Harbor, the army ordered many Nisei soldiers to clean latrines, scrub horse stalls, and collect garbage.[60]

As for rank, the army's data on its wartime officer corps were often organized into two categories—either "Negro" and "White," or "Negro" and "Other than Negro."[61] It is hard to know, then, whether nonblack minorities had equal access to commissions. It appears doubtful. Complaints came from Chinese Americans, Mexican Americans, Puerto Ricans, and others about discriminatory obstacles to their admission to office candidate schools. The discrimination that one supremely qualified "native born American of Chinese stock" faced seems to have been typical, if not in its flagrancy then in its result. He received an interview only because "he writes his name in a fancy way so that the ordinary American on reading it would not be likely to assume that he is Chinese." But at the interview, an army officer told him point blank that "the Army has been selecting its [officer] candidates only from among Caucasian Americans." As an alternative, the officer said that the man could be considered for a noncommissioned rank, but only if his qualifications were twice as good as those for whites who would get commissions. In other cases, servicemen and -women were turned away because of a "lost" application, "too much of an accent," and minor infractions that had little effect on whites' advancement.[62] Some descent-specific units offered more opportunities for promotions and commissions, but only to a point. With the exception of Puerto Rican units, in which even the highest commanders were Puerto Rican, all other descent-specific units' officers were entirely or largely "Continental" white or Anglo, especially the highest ranking among them.[63]

This point, like the broader one about rank discrimination, is especially clear regarding Japanese Americans. The 100th Battalion's original officer complement was majority Nisei, but all the top commanders were white. Among the numerous Japanese American noncommissioned officers below them, furthermore, widespread grumbling occurred about their inability to advance into the commissioned ranks—their static status as "duration corporals."[64] Similarly, when the 442nd was formed, in early 1943, the War Department explicitly mandated that all its highest-ranking officers at the regimental, battalion, and company levels be "white American citizens."[65] In the Military Intelligence Service, white linguists became officers, and their Nisei colleagues, regardless of talent, remained corporals or sergeants. And in the WACs, where Japanese American women gained entry in the summer of 1943, they were explicitly excluded from the officer ranks. In all, at least twenty-three thousand Japanese Americans served in the armed forces by war's end, but less than 1 percent—fewer than two hundred in all—did so as officers.[66] As with African Americans, the boundaries of rank and "race" matched and fortified one other.

How this overwhelmingly white officer corps assigned everyday duties and privileges to their enlisted personnel—or how these personnel claimed privileges on their own—could also mark and maintain white-nonwhite lines. Again, evidence of this point appears clearest with Japanese Americans. As for enlisted men, white and Japanese American soldiers shared the same mess hall at Fort Snelling in Minnesota in 1945, but the former often tried to jump the line. Some whites even claimed openly that their white status entitled them to eat first. "The bastards!" one irate Nisei soldier fumed. "They think they're better than we are just because their skin is white." As for officers, Nisei also complained that, while whites were only 10 percent of the fort's troop strength, they received nearly all the passes to see "musical and stage attractions in the Twin Cities." Similarly, at Fort Meade in Maryland around the same time, while white officers allowed white platoons to watch movies and to play baseball in advance of the men's shipment overseas, they ordered Japanese American ones to do intense field training, including daily hikes of twenty miles and more.[67]

White troops' everyday teasing and harassment of some of their comrades constituted another set of white-nonwhite lines. Early on in training, a twenty-one-year-old Puerto Rican soldier was miserable, the subject of endless ridicule in his unit. The reason seems related in part to a supposedly insufficient manliness—his "slight physique" and his unwillingness to "join what he called the rough behavior of the others." But an equally serious problem involved racism: "though placed in a white battalion, he was considered Negroid by the southerners, who quickly let him know their antagonism." Similarly, a group of Cape Verdeans, "black in color," were evidently so unhappy in the white units to which they had been assigned, perhaps for the same racism-related reasons as the Puerto Rican, that they succeeded in getting transferred to "colored" outfits.[68]

Teasing and harassment often took the form of name-calling. Mexican Americans sometimes faced "slurring remarks in public," like "dirty Mexican" or "damn Mexican," from both their officers and barracks mates.[69] As for American Indians, whites in their units invariably called them "Chief." Some scholars have suggested that Indians tolerated, if not enjoyed, this practice, which was part of a broader pattern whereby GIs called their buddies "ethnic" names or slurs as a good-natured form of teasing that "united GIs more than it divided them."[70] This point surely held true for some Indians, but not all of them. One Native Alaskan sergeant in the army air corps recalled not only that there was general anti-Indian sentiment among the "mostly non-native people" with whom he served in the "lower forty-eight," but also that "a lot of natives just didn't cope[,] couldn't cope with being called names but that's what we had to put up with."[71] While Chinese Americans were called "damn Chinks," Japanese Americans faced a litany of racist names, including "Japs," "damned Japs," "goddamn Japs," "dirty Japs," "Oriental Creeps," "yellow bastards," "yellow-bellied so-and-sos," and "Tojo."[72]

Indeed, as with black troops, name-calling, teasing, and harassment could lead to large and small fights, which reflected and strengthened white-nonwhite lines. Some of these conflicts involved Chinese Americans and Hawaiians, and stemmed in part from battles over "white girls." Others, as in the case of several Zoot Suit Riots in 1943, also involved "girls" but pitted Anglo service members against Mexican American civilians off post, most famously in Los Angeles.[73] Similar altercations occasionally occurred on post as well. Just a month after the riots in Los Angeles, a brawl erupted near a latrine at the Lincoln Air Base in Nebraska between white southerners and Mexican Americans. "They didn't like one another," one sergeant reported at the time. Similarly, while training to be an engineer in the navy, Californian Ernie Gonzalez recalled white southerners once again causing problems. Hailing "from Texas and Oklahoma," they were pushing and tripping him. "I had six fights in two weeks and I won them all."[74]

Facing perhaps the most harassment of any nonblack troops, Japanese Americans may have fought more than any of them as well. At Shelby, several official reports attempted to downplay the number of altercations between Nisei and white soldiers, but Japanese Americans' censored mail suggests a steady stream of them. Indeed, Assistant Secretary of War John J. McCloy wrote several memos to army generals expressing his concern about the "increase in hostility between the white soldiers and the Japanese American soldiers" brought on primarily by the former "venting their feeling" against the latter "either in opprobrious terms or in more direct action."[75] Similar problems occurred elsewhere. Jesse M. Hirate, a member of the 100th Battalion, recalled "plenty of fights with other [white] outfits" during training at Camp McCoy in Wisconsin.[76] As some Nisei began training in integrated units toward the end of the war, problems persisted. At Camp Fannin in Texas, Japanese American soldiers wrote home about routine brawling with "haoles," or whites.[77]

This fighting need not necessarily have reflected or reinforced a line between so-called races. For one thing, fights also occurred within descent groups. Battling repeatedly at the start of their training, for instance, were "Kotonks" (mainland Japanese Americans, or Nisei) and "Buddaheads" (Hawaiian Japanese Americans, or "AJAs"). It also might seem plausible that other factors were more important than "race." Take the fights between Japanese Americans and whites, for example. "The reported incidents [between them]," argued McCloy to a concerned Eleanor Roosevelt in May 1943, "grow out of a Japanese enemy consideration rather than a Japanese racial consideration."[78]

But disentangling one from the other at this moment is nearly impossible. Perceived connections between Japanese Americans and the enemy were deeply rooted in ideas about race—not least the notion that Nisei, regardless of their US citizenship or their willingness to fight in the US Army, were still essentially committed to the enemy, indeed, were the enemy. This was quintessential "Jap's-a-Jap" reasoning, racist to the core. Moreover, white soldiers often embellished their fight-provoking insults and taunts by referencing the color "yellow"—as in "yellow bastards" and "yellow-bellied so-and-sos." While the term "yellow" could have simply meant cowardly, it also had a clear racialized meaning, which would not have been lost on many members of the wartime military—given the long history of "yellow peril" scares, the common equation of "Asian" or "Asiatic race" with "yellow race," or the equally common reference to the enemy Japanese as yellow. Indeed, the last of these had become so widespread during the war that Secretary of State Cordell Hull urged American newspapers and radio broadcasters to avoid using "terms of opprobrium and derogation such as 'yellow' and 'brown' in describing the Japanese because of the applicability of such terms also to the Chinese, Filipinos, and other of our Asiatic associates and friends who may be seriously offended thereby."[79]

If white-nonwhite lines appeared in the form of undue negative attention, as with harassment and fighting, they could also bring no attention at all, an everyday social ostracism that bespoke exclusion, a lack of belonging. The harassed and ridiculed Puerto Rican was, according to the same report, also sometimes simply ignored. When Japanese American brothers Ben and Fred Kuroki trained as part of a white army air corps unit at Sheppard Field in Texas, some of their comrades assumed they were Chinese American, since Nisei were excluded from that army branch. Even so, while they received a few curious glances and were the butt of ignorant remarks here and there, they were mostly treated as if they did not exist. "None of the hundred and twenty men in the barrack ever talked to them," wrote Ben Kuroki's biographer; "nobody ever smiled at them, nobody ever even said hello." This went on for three weeks, with Ben and Fred "enviously listening to the other guys talking loosely and friendly among themselves, always listening tensely for somebody to say something about them. Nights when they couldn't sleep at all, nights when they cried themselves to sleep." Similarly, George Aki, a chaplain with a group of 442nd replacement troops, recalled his first day at Camp Shelby, eating lunch with the other officers of his unit: "They were all white and talked to each other but not to me." Later Aki accepted his commanding officer's invitation to a party, but everyone there ignored him, and so he "chatted with the enlisted man who was serving the drinks."[80]

Like black-white lines, white-nonwhite ones also took symbolic form, beyond language and name-calling alone. For example, as was the case with black troops, uniforms could be a flashpoint of conflict and boundary-making. Some Japanese Americans were outraged to hear fellow American GIs remark that it was "a disgrace to the United States to permit a Jap to wear a uniform."[81] Or consider the 442nd's original arm patch design, a dramatic number replete with a bloody sword and a bursting bomb. Holding the sword was a "yellow gauntleted arm," which, as the official description noted for anyone missing the not so subtle symbolism, "represents the army of the Yellow Race taking up arms in defense of the National Colors of the United States."[82] That the bomb looked a lot like Japan's rising sun did not help matters. Outraged by the patch and its unmistakable racialized meanings, many members of the 442nd complained to anyone who would listen, including family members, unit and War Department leaders, and J. R. Farrington, Hawaii's congressional delegate. Soon McCloy got involved and managed to quash the production and use of the patch. Its central problem, as McCloy explained to Pence, was that the "keynote of the Japanese volunteers has been that they were Americans, not differentiated from their fellows, and this symbol of the 'yellow race' tends to emphasize such a distinction."[83]

As this episode and the ones involving "Jap" insults suggest, a final set of white-nonwhite lines concerned questions of national security and loyalty. One Chinese American army unit, while on maneuvers in rural Arkansas, was "surrounded by police and questioned about where they had obtained the army equipment, required to show identification, and detained until a white officer . . . came to verify their documentation."[84] Problems likely arose not because the unit was Chinese American, but because it was mistaken for Japanese American or Japanese. As in the case of enlistment and assignment policies, a particular set of training-camp white-nonwhite lines often distinguished Japanese Americans not only from whites but also from everyone else. In this sense, these lines might more precisely be called Japanese–non-Japanese.

They first appeared on and around US military posts shortly after the attack on Pearl Harbor. Panicked, some local commanders transferred all their Nisei trainees to the reserves; some trainees were discharged altogether; others were placed in "protective custody," supposedly because "the prejudice against Japanese on the part of the white enlisted men at this station might create a dangerous situation." In most places, Japanese Americans were kept away from "information of military importance" and from "vital military installations." In late January 1942, the War Department decided that all new Japanese American inductees would be sent to two inland training camps—Camp Robinson in Arkansas and Fort McLellan in Alabama—and would be excluded from certain security-sensitive branches of the army, namely "the Air Force, the Armored Force, the Signal Corps, and the Chemical Warfare Service."[85] By March, when Nisei induction was stopped altogether, all trainees of "Japanese extraction" were "dispersed in small numbers throughout the interior of the United States in such a manner as not to cause a severe burden upon any particular locality."[86]

While stationed there, new Japanese–non-Japanese lines appeared. At one post, for example, officers barred Japanese Americans alone from any job that involved the handling of classified documents. At another, all Nisei were ordered to give up their arms and ammunition and were confined to particular barracks. Throughout the war, Japanese American soldiers appear to have endured a singularly lavish level of scrutiny and surveillance (which is saying something, given the massive wartime military intelligence and counterintelligence apparatus). Writing of the 442nd at Camp Shelby, one intelligence officer noted, "Military authorities, through information from the censorship service, are more completely informed as to the state of mind of the individuals of this command than perhaps of any other unit in the Army."[87]

Among the more striking examples of the Japanese–non-Japanese divide on stateside military installations was an incident that took place at Fort Riley on Easter Sunday, April 25, 1943. On that day, President Roosevelt, on the road for more than a week on a secret inspection of training camps, stopped by for an open-air religious service with fifteen thousand troops, a lunch with officer candidates, and a tour of the post.[88] But not all troops were allowed to attend the events. Japanese American soldiers at the post's Cavalry Replacement Training Center (CRTC), roughly one hundred in all, were marched to the Motor Mechanics School Building and confined there for the length of the president's visit. Surrounding the building were "fifty armed guards with rifles and bayonets" and inside were six white officers with pistols and a submachine gun. The justification was that, in the estimation of several staff officers calling the shots, these soldiers were all "No. 1 subversives" and "potentially more dangerous than other personnel."[89] "Today, Easter Sunday, we experienced an action that I'll never forget as long as I live," wrote one of the confined soldiers to a friend. "Yup, we were in the same category as Prisoners of War. In fact, I felt like one. . . . I asked myself—what the hell is the use of wearing this uniform—they don't trust us and we aren't accorded the same privileges as the other men wearing the same uniform purely due to our racial ancestry."[90]

Numerous investigations of the event later revealed that other people were detained during the president's visit, including white and black civilian post employees and individual soldiers of various backgrounds, whom intelligence officers suspected of potential subversion. Conversely, the small number of Japanese American soldiers who were assigned to post headquarters and not to the CRTC faced fewer restrictions; in fact, a few seem to have attended the outdoor services with the president. Regardless, what makes the episode a vivid example of a Japanese–non-Japanese line is that Nisei (in the CRTC) were the only soldiers to be labeled "No. 1

subversives" and confined under armed guard solely on the basis of their "race" or ancestry.

In sum, this thicket of white-nonwhite lines was complex. The lines involved rank and jobs, fights and ostracism, day-to-day duties and privileges, name-calling and teasing, military uniforms and male-female relations. Most fundamentally they divided numerous nonblack minorities, including Chinese Americans, Puerto Ricans, American Indians, Mexican Americans, Filipinos, and especially Japanese Americans, from whites. Beyond this, they varied. Sometimes, as in the case of the Hattiesburg school or the Camp Hood outhouses, lines simultaneously divided a group not simply from whites but also from "colored." Other times, lines divided a group not simply from whites and "colored" but also from *all* other groups, as in the case of Japanese Americans and national security concerns. Still other times, lines referenced "American" or "Continental American," without explicitly mentioning whiteness or nonwhiteness. But, again, the category of American was too saturated with racist assumptions for these lines not to follow and to reinforce white-nonwhite ones.

There were still more descent divides on and around military installations in the United States, to be sure. Of these, the most important likely involved European "racial"—increasingly called "ethnic"—categories, as when, most commonly, Jewish troops faced harassment and prejudice in uniform. But these other boundaries seemed more likely than white-nonwhite ones to dissolve over the course of military training or service overseas, and they seldom revolved around questions of whiteness and nonwhiteness.[91] One study, based on interviews with 150 non-Jewish European-ethnic male veterans conducted in 1946, found that, despite the men's considerable anti-Semitic sentiment, they still made "many statements to the effect that the Jew was 'white after all,' or that there was 'no racial difference' between Jew and Gentile."[92] In the end, as America's World War II–era troops trained and served in the United States, the most salient and common descent divide—besides, of course, the ubiquitous black-white one—split white from nonwhite.

This divide generated varied acts of resistance, which sometimes resembled those of black troops. There were the frequent fights, protest letters, and determination to prove their bigoted naysayers wrong by shining as service members. One intelligence report on the 442nd in Mississippi observed that the discrimination the unit faced there, on and off post, did "not appear to have affected training, but on the contrary, possibly accentuate[d] the desire of the group to excel at soldiering."[93] There were also acts of protest as property destruction, as Manny Diaz and his buddies showed, as did various groups of Mexican American soldiers, who were enraged by civilian "Juan Crow" in Texas.[94] There were intentionally concealed forms of resistance or "infrapolitics": one Filipino former messman recalled that he struck back against bigoted white officers by making their coffee in old socks and by spitting in their food.[95] Unlike black troops, some Japanese American soldiers made requests or demands for expatriation or repatriation as protests against embittering army suspicion, hostility, and persecution.[96]

There was also occasional civil disobedience. It often took the form of small, everyday acts of insubordination, but at least in one case, it was much larger, resembling some of black soldiers' bigger protests like the collective work stoppages and hunger strikes that took place at roughly the same time.[97] In March 1944, a total of 103 Nisei soldiers, whom the army had recently transferred from noncombat to combat training, refused orders to march to the field house at Fort McClellan in Alabama. Eventually, army commanders put 28 of them on trial, ultimately convicting and sentencing 21 to anywhere from five to thirty years of hard labor. While the post commander offered a ready explanation for the men's action—they "have lived for several years in Japan and have become indoctrinated with the military philosophy of that country"—their motivations appear to have been far more complicated and principled than that. At precisely the time that some Japanese Americans in camps were taking a high-minded stand against conscription, these soldiers did the same against combat training and eventual service. Like some draft resisters, they stressed their willingness to serve in the US Army; indeed, they had for more than two years by the time of their sit-down strike. But before committing themselves to joining and training in a combat outfit, they wanted "to right the wrongs" of mass detention and of racist mistreatment in the army. Regarding the latter, some of the men were among those who had been detained at Fort Riley a year earlier. Many had been in the army prior to the attack on Pearl Harbor and so experienced the humiliation of being separated from their unit, sent inland, disarmed, and given menial jobs. And at least one of the men testified at his trial that "his action was in protest to continued displays of disrespect and attempts at humiliation by his superiors." He recalled, in particular, one sergeant barking at his outfit, "Get into line, you yellow——."[98]

A final, important form of activism involved making common cause with other nonwhites, including black people. To be sure, sometimes nonwhites fully embraced and defended their nonblack or honorary white status, which is—given the many benefits attached to it, especially in the Jim Crow South—hardly surprising. But others did the opposite, forging connections as and among nonwhites or the colored or darker races. How battle lines formed in some soldiers' fights offers a vivid illustration of this point. At Camp McCoy in Wisconsin in 1942, American Indians and Mexican Americans sometimes joined Japanese Americans in their battles against whites. Two years later, in the spring of 1944, when the 442nd prepared to deploy to the European theater, white soldiers scrapped with Japanese Americans, and black soldiers aided the latter.[99] And while training at Camp Fannin in late 1944, one Japanese American soldier from Hawaii reported, in a letter to his wife, frequent, bloody fights pitting "Mexican and American Japanese with other Kamainas [sic; native and non-native Hawaiians] against the whites."[100]

For those training in the South, some Japanese Americans—in particular, the "Kamainas" among them, who were accustomed to more fluid social boundaries—showed a striking willingness to embrace blackness and to challenge Jim Cow, at least off post.[101] In doing so, they fought white-nonwhite lines by, in a sense, connecting their struggle with the military's most subordinate of nonwhite groups. Given their officers' repeated and explicit instructions to avoid contact with black people, to say nothing of sweeping anti-black racism in the United States, these efforts, even if episodic, are noteworthy. Some Japanese Americans expressed sympathy for African Americans and disgust with Jim Crow and with a supposed democratic nation fighting a democratic war. One confidential army study—based on several hundred censored letters from members of the 100th Battalion at Camp Shelby to family and friends back home in Hawaii in March and April 1943—found "an increasing awareness of and indignation over the treatment of the negro in the South." One of these letter writers remarked that "negroes are treated just like rubbish down here. . . . Talk about democracy."[102] Months later intelligence reports continued to note as "unquestionably true" "that a great many of the Hawaiian Japanese-Americans sympathize with the negro in the South" or that they "have shown strong resentment toward the Jim Crow laws affecting negroes."[103] One newly enlisted volunteer in the 442nd from Honolulu explained this resentment in a letter home: we are told, he wrote, that "we cannot have any social intercourse with the colored. If we should have any sympathy for them, we must not voice or display [it]. . . . This may seem to be a simple social pattern to follow, however, the psychology of the men here will not permit this very easily. . . . We are full of principles and ideals. Among these, racial equality lies most prominently."[104]

One of these same reports also noted that "segregation of the white and black races in the South" put Japanese Americans "in the position of having to choose sides," and some actively battled the former by resolutely favoring the latter.[105] In cities and towns across the South, some Nisei soldiers, in open defiance of their officers, sat on the colored sections of buses, drank from colored water fountains, used colored toilets, bought movie tickets from the colored box office, sought housing in the colored section of town, befriended colored people, and fraternized with colored women.[106] When they witnessed an especially egregious form of white racism against black people, they occasionally took more drastic action. One Japanese American recalled that when he saw a white New Orleans bus driver push an older black woman to the ground and demand that she let whites board the bus first, he "grabbed the bus driver by the shirt and dragged him out of the bus." Then he and five buddies "kicked the hell out of him." Other times, they occasionally met privately with black people and commiserated about both groups' linked fate. In Hattiesburg, Mississippi, during a "drinking party" among a group of Nisei soldiers from New York, two black women, and a black soldier, a neighbor reported hearing one of the Japanese Americans shout, "[W]hen we come to town the white civilians give us hell; they treat us like negroes and animals, and kick us out of every place we go into. . . . [But] [d]on't you worry, when this war is over all that damn stuff will be straightened out; there will be no more race discrimination, you negroes and us japs will be just as good as the damn whites."[107]

In the end, despite this varied resistance and the blurring that it helped to promote, white-nonwhite military lines persisted throughout the war. Like a weaker version of the black-white divide, they too represented a structure of white domination and nonwhite—not simply black—subordination. As such, it helped to naturalize and concretize the otherwise abstract categories of white and nonwhite, in part by parceling out resources and status in a way that not only deprived the latter but favored the former. Like the black-white divide, the white-nonwhite one sometimes disadvantaged whites, too; recall, for example, white troops' more limited romantic options in Alaska, thanks to their commanders' restrictions on their dating "native" women there. But in the main, white-nonwhite lines helped the former and hurt the latter, as they were intended to do. For example, the military's clear and consistent practice of minimizing many nonblack minorities' access to the officer ranks only increased whites' opportunities there.

The concrete advantages that whites often gained from these white-nonwhite lines help explain their existence. Another important factor is that so-called white units, for all the genuine bonding they fostered, could also leave some of their nonblack minority members isolated and vulnerable to teasing, ostracism, harassment, name-calling, and official indifference to their plight. For example, the army seems to have been more likely to defend its Mexican American soldiers against discrimination when they were grouped together into a single outfit. Similarly, as dedicated as McCloy and his staff were to the 442nd's well-being and success, they seldom showed any similar concern for the individual Nisei or other individual nonblack minority soldiers scattered throughout countless so-called white units across the army. To have done so would have required a commitment of time, resources, and personnel that military officials likely never considered. They thought that problems would decrease with time—which in some cases they did—and that the success of these individual soldiers would not pack the same propaganda punch as, say, a heroic 442nd. Indeed, in initially fighting for these descent-specific units, War Department officials made precisely this point.

Another related factor involves the civilian world, which of course socialized so many service personnel before and after induction. When it came to black-white lines, military leaders felt they could not, in Army Chief of Staff George C. Marshall's words, "ignore the [civilian] social relationship between negroes and whites which has been established by the American people" over time.[108] Yet that is precisely what they did with nonblack minorities. After all, a segment of white "American people" had also "established" a "social relationship" with them, through, to cite simply two examples, Asian immigration exclusion and the violent dispossession of Native lands. And, in fact, racist civilian practices that targeted nonblack minorities in voting, housing, jobs, wages, public accommodations, policing, naturalization rights, land rights, colonialist projects, and more all continued into the World War II years and beyond. Products of this world, some white officers and troops sought, while in uniform, to protect the white power and advantage to which they had grown accustomed, in relationship not simply to black people but also to nonblack minorities.

Since the particulars of these white-nonwhite lines could vary from place to place, they had a regional dimension. Nonblack minority troops often faced the most discrimination, on and off military posts, in those areas of the country where civilian racism against them was most pronounced—for example, in Texas for Mexican Americans and in California for Filipinos. One exception to this rule involves white southerners, in and out of the South, who seem to have featured prominently in many efforts to build and police military white-nonwhite lines, efforts that entailed Japanese Americans in Mississippi, Alabama, and Arkansas, Chinese Americans in North Carolina, Mexican Americans' fights with white southerners in Nebraska and elsewhere, and a Filipino mess attendant's complaints about the white southern officers he served. At times, white southerners made a slippery-slope argument regarding nonblack minorities—that "any equality shown to [them] . . . by white people may result in the negroes in this vicinity increasing their demands." But sometimes white-nonwhite lines, those created by southern whites and others, stemmed from officers' and troops' deep-seated investments in white domination and nonwhite, not simply "Negro," subordination. At Camp Shelby, for example, one officer counseled his men that good soldiering required hating "Japanese and other non-white races."[109]

A final reason for the emergence and staying power of the military's white-nonwhite lines relates specifically to Japanese Americans—or rather to widespread feelings and beliefs about them. Pervasive, racist concerns about their loyalty shaped not only their enlistment and assignment, but also their training and service in the United States. From the top, War Department leaders, even Nisei soldiers' most loyal defenders among them, excluded Japanese American soldiers throughout the war from all but the most minimal command responsibilities and from certain security-sensitive branches of the army, all the while subjecting them to a uniquely draconian level of scrutiny and surveillance. From below, officers and fellow soldiers constantly questioned the loyalty of Nisei troops, calling them "Japs," claiming they did not belong in US Army uniforms, assigning them harmless and degrading tasks, and so forth. In all these cases, white-nonwhite lines—or, in some cases, Japanese–non-Japanese ones—stemmed from many whites' conscious and unconscious insistence that Nisei either were constitutionally incapable of true Americanness or would have to work harder than most anyone else to prove theirs.

* * *

At wartime military installations in the United States, a diverse group of nonblack minority service members—Japanese Americans and Chinese Americans, Puerto Ricans and Filipino Americans, Mexican Americans and American Indians—had this in common: they at once transcended a mix of white-nonwhite lines and remained circumscribed by them. None of these groups, however, had identical experiences, of course. Each could be differently placed on a continuum between one extreme—no boundaries with whites—and the other—numerous, formidable ones. Japanese Americans, for example, tended to cluster more toward the latter than the former pole, with their commander-imposed honorary-white (or nonblack) status balanced against the extensive top-down and bottom-up barriers they faced as so-called Japs. In contrast, American Indians tended toward the opposite, with more evidence of blurred white-nonwhite boundaries than bright ones.

Nonblack minorities' training-camp lives also resembled and differed from those of black troops. Both broad groups faced many of the same sorts of boundaries, involving rank and jobs, harassment and fights, male-female relations and civilian space, uniforms and everyday language; they also, in responding to these boundaries, employed some of the same protest tactics, from civil disobedience to violence to excellent soldiering. Indeed, thanks to this overlap, some nonblack minority troops occasionally sought and built connections with their black comrades. These affinities and associations were most evident among Japanese Americans. Unlike enlistment and unit assignments, where Japanese Americans and African Americans collaborated seldom or not at all, military training and service in the United States brought the two groups into closer contact, especially in the South, which at times produced alliances of a sort. Of course, it produced the opposite too, not least when white officers insisted that Nisei steer clear of "Negroes." But if proximity to coloredness pushed some Japanese Americans away, it drew others near. Recall, for example, the drinking party among black people and Nisei troops in Mississippi. For the latter, the fact that whites "treat us like negroes and animals" was not grounds to spurn African Americans but to talk and act in defense of "you negroes and us Japs" and, perhaps in the process, to narrow the distance between the two. If a nascent nonwhite identity or politics emerged with special force in certain times and places during the war years, America's military posts, despite their confusing, crisscrossing lines, were one such place.[110]

But these acts of solidarity at stateside military installations never extended too far, primarily because the differences between blacks' and nonblacks' lived experiences there remained profound. On the one hand, black troops rarely faced the national-security-related restrictions so common among Nisei troops. On the other hand, black troops experienced very little of the blurring that nonblack minority troops did. In relation to white-nonwhite lines, black-white ones were more expansive, in terms of the forms they assumed and the geographical areas in which they took root. They were more formal, in that they derived more often from the highest echelons of Navy and War Department power. And they were more spatial, encompassing nearly every corner of military installations, more violently and painstakingly policed, more likely to be imposed on civilian communities by military authorities, and far less likely to be opposed by foreign governments. Indeed, despite the fact that black people throughout the war years trumpeted the need to uproot anti-black racism to counter Axis propaganda and to appease "darker" or "colored" allies abroad, these allies, in truth, cared little about their concerns. In fact, some of them quietly worked to reinforce black-white lines in their own ways, as when Chungking sought to keep African American troops out of China or when the Mexican government seems to have helped exclude black soldiers from

Fort Bliss on its northern border, in part to protect black-white segregation in its border city of Ciudad Juárez.[111]

Still, the incomparably expansive black-white divide helped produce the incomparably expansive (and militant) efforts of black servicemen and -women to uproot it. Nonblack minorities resisted white-nonwhite lines. But their greater opportunities to transcend those lines, along with their much smaller overall numbers, meant that their activism as it related to US military installations never matched that of black troops in terms of its scope, reach, or impact.

PART V

Fighting

CHAPTER 8

☙

Deploying Jim Crow

In late 1943, First Lady Eleanor Roosevelt received two very different letters about African American soldiers' lives in England. The first came from Roland Hayes, an internationally renowned black tenor. He had just returned home from England, where he had performed at several "eminently successful" concerts with the help of a chorus of two hundred black soldiers stationed there.[1] But while overseas, he also toured several army camps and Red Cross clubs to gauge how black troops were faring. The general picture was dire. The men complained of incessant harassment and mistreatment by white American troops and officers, who spread lies about them among the English, barred them from pubs, routinely picked fights with them, locked them up for "talking with any English woman," and blocked their commissions and promotions. If changes were not made soon, one black corporal predicted ominously to Hayes, "awful trouble [is] coming."[2]

The second letter came from Lieutenant General Jacob L. Devers, who was the army's top commander in the European theater. It was a response to Hayes's, which Roosevelt had forwarded to the War Department (with the note that "the feeling among the colored people is very sad and I think they should be given a chance to prove their mettle"). "I have personally visited a great many of our colored units here in the Theater and . . . their morale is high," Devers assured Roosevelt. "Our system in regard to colored troops is a simple one. It is that we are all soldiers, colored and white alike. We have a common objective, i.e. to defeat the enemies of our country. There is no discrimination. There is no favoritism."[3]

These two portraits of the US military's colored-white lines in England are difficult to reconcile. Hayes, and the black troops he quoted, bemoaned the complex tangle of boundaries that crossed the Atlantic and took root in a foreign country. Devers, in contrast, categorically dismissed their existence. Whose perspective was closer to the truth, not only in England but wherever African American troops served around the world during the war? This chapter examines that question. It asks, most fundamentally, what happened to the US military's ubiquitous black-white lines as American troops moved overseas.

The answer is complex, befitting the contradictory claims of Hayes and Devers. On the one hand, the former was unquestionably right. The US military, with a slight, occasional assist from overseas locals and governments, transplanted its black-white lines all around the world. While not identical to those on the home front, these transnational lines also took multiple forms, involving everything from jobs and dances to courts-martial and minstrel performances. They also stemmed from the military's paradoxical goals of winning a war for democracy while at the same time protecting white supremacy. On the other hand, fully achieving this latter goal became more difficult overseas, not because the US military, as Devers suggested, finally foreswore favoritism for white people and discrimination against black people, but because of three overseas developments, all of which the military inadvertently helped bring about: non-Americans' warm relations with black Americans, the black-white comradeship of some American GIs, and the activism of black troops, which, like Jim Crow, traveled the wartime world. Taken together, these developments chipped away at the black-white divide. At war's end, Jim Crow in uniform was far from dead, but it lay moderately wounded just the same.

A FIXED PLACE

During World War I, as 200,000 black troops deployed to France, American segregationists, in historian Adriane Lentz-Smith's wise words, insisted "that black men's place remained fixed no matter where they traveled." This insistence grew even more urgent and adamant during World War II. More than a half million black troops served in overseas theaters all around the globe, from Trinidad to Tarawa, Ireland to India, Australia to Africa.[4] The military's black-white lines, so pervasive in the United States, stretched across oceans and continents. Long an avid traveler, Jim Crow—in this case, Jim Crow in uniform—had never before roamed so far and wide.

"The Unchallenged Modus Operandi"

Service members' first glimpse of this fact came aboard transports, which ferried American troops from ports of embarkation in the United States to battlefronts overseas. One young white soldier, David Brion Davis, later a preeminent scholar of slavery, recalled that his introduction to the subject took place en route to Le Havre, France, in the fall of 1945: "Still wobbly on the troopship from seasickness, I was given a billy club and sent down into the deep hold to make sure the 'Jiggaboos' there were 'not gambling.' Until then, I had not dreamed that the ship contained some two thousand black soldiers. After winding down endless circular staircases, I found myself, in effect, on board a slave ship—or what I imagine some slave ships to have been like, though the blacks were not chained together."[5] Indeed, on many—if not all—transports, the military assigned black troops to their deepest, dankest, least desirable areas, where they were confined to segregated quarters, bathrooms, and messes. If allowed on deck, black-white lines appeared there, too. In 1945, one member of a black naval construction battalion complained that on his thirty-five-day trip to the Pacific, commanders not only segregated church services, but also forced black troops to stand in the hot sun; whites had benches under shady tarps. As usual, rank seldom exempted African Americans from these indignities. One of the few black army colonels during the war, Howard Donovan Queen, told an interviewer in 1946 that, during his trip overseas two years earlier, he was lodged with the enlisted men of his unit, while several white officers, whom he outranked, slumbered in staterooms.[6]

As these stories suggest, the US military overseas carved up countless spaces according to the black-white divide. In Great Britain, where more than 130,000 black troops were stationed during the war, this practice was perhaps most extensive and unchanging.[7] In the summer of 1942, just as the first African American units began arriving there, US commanders, including Dwight D. Eisenhower, ordered "that discrimination against the Negro troops be sedulously avoided" and insisted, along the lines of Devers's assurances, that their "policy on Negroes" was "founded on fairness, justice, and common sense."[8] But that policy, with little variation across space or time, was often rigid black-white spatial separation. On posts and at more temporary encampments, it appeared in housing, messing, recreational facilities, at least one officer candidate school (OCS), and clubs for officers and enlisted men. In one instance, even trucks driven by black troops were parked separately from those driven by whites, according to an anonymous African American soldier's report. Off post, similar divides cropped up at Red Cross clubs, pubs, theaters, cafés, hotels, dance halls, restaurants, pools, and private parties. United States military commanders convinced or coerced British businesses to play along or issued passes or declared particular places "off limits" or "out of bounds" on a black-white segregated basis. In certain cases, white enlisted personnel lent their support by threatening or assaulting those Britons and African American soldiers who had the temerity to disregard these divides; at times, they destroyed the former's property for the same reason. These bottom-up and top-down efforts to draw spatial lines were not always successful, but they certainly made their mark on Britain and on the US troops (among others) there. In the words of one black GI, writing sometime in late 1943, "the net result" of these "bi-racial policies" was that "separatism is becoming so firmly entrenched as to be accepted as the unchallenged modus operandi" all over Britain.[9]

A similar separatism, though by no means universal, sprouted up all over the world. On and around posts, bases, and bivouac areas from Lille, France, to New Guinea in the South Pacific, US military commanders, as in the United Kingdom, segregated blacks from whites at mess halls, living quarters, post exchanges, canteens, clubs, bars, dances, USO shows, pools, beaches, and even, at least in one case, straddle trenches. Segregated Red Cross clubs and rest camps, for example, appeared in far-flung locations, including Casablanca, Algiers, Tunis, Cherbourg, Rome, Naples, Calcutta, Manila, Sydney, and Brisbane.[10] In the last of these places, an African American sergeant on furlough attempted to enter the city's American Red Cross club and was "accosted by an M.P. who refused his admission by stating, 'you can't go in here, boy, your Red Cross is on the other side of town.'"[11] Local commanders imposed Jim Crow practices, to cite simply a few examples, on cabarets in Marseilles, hotels in Genoa, brothels in Dagupan City, the Philippines, and restaurants in Nairobi.[12] As in Britain, they divided towns and neighborhoods into black or white "in-bounds" and "out-of-bounds" areas in New Zealand, Australia, Italy, Germany, and elsewhere. In Belgium, five members of an African American service unit, having mistakenly stumbled into the white section of town, were "treated as enemy soldiers and manhandled at the point of guns . . . walked six blocks with their hands over their heads . . . [while] MPs in charge of them were encouraged by other white soldiers to 'shoot them . . . we never did like those dark guys.'"[13]

All around the world this black-white spatial segregation was achieved sometimes through African Americans' exclusion from the only facilities available, or though temporary exclusion until black facilities could be built or arranged, or, most common, by the assignment of African American and white troops to their own respective spaces, places, and time slots. To provide a modicum of plausible deniability against charges of discrimination, the military often made these assignments not strictly on the basis of race but on the basis of units.[14] But because "colored" troops served only in so-called colored units, segregation by race and by unit were, for all practical purposes, one and the same. In any case, African Americans, as in the United States, invariably got the raw end of the deal—the older rest center, the sleepier leave town, the club in the "slum" neighborhood. When, in the summer of 1942, the US Army stationed separate black and white units on a country estate outside Sheffield, England, the latter were quartered in a mansion, while the former slept in tents outside.[15]

The military segregated space as much according to rank as to "race." As enlisted men knew all too well, officers enjoyed separate and better sleeping quarters, messes, service clubs, and more—or at least they were supposed to. But as was the case stateside (and on some transport ships), black officers, seldom enjoying the full range of advantages to which their rank entitled them, faced their own set of black-white spatial lines. In England, white MPs attempted to arrest a black officer for entering a town "laid aside for whites," despite the fact that these rules were supposed to apply to enlisted personnel alone.[16] In Italy, white Americans established an officers' club by invitation only with the sole purpose of excluding African Americans, since, in the words of one white commander, "a fight or unpleasant incident might result from the presence of colored officers in a club used by all."[17] Similarly, in the Pacific one African American captain noted rampant discrimination against "Negro officers in [officers'] clubs." On the South Pacific island of Efate, for example, he was allowed to use the officers' mess and club but "was obliged to eat by himself."[18]

When the imperatives of war compelled integration, sometimes the change was only temporary. Writing from Cherbourg, France, one month after its liberation, black war correspondent Roi Ottley observed that "no one here seems to have time for Jim Crow, nor do they seem to care." "But," he added ruefully, "the American Red Cross is now preparing to open a Jim Crow club. . . . The Army command forces them to do it." Similarly, while taking part in the invasion of Saipan in June 1944, a black marine recalled fleeting moments of cooperation between his black unit and a white division. But just as soon as the island was secured, the military built segregated camps for black and white troops, euphemistically labeled "Ammo" and "Depot" for the former and "Division" for the latter. "It was just like being in Mississippi," the marine recalled.[19]

The extent of these black-white spatial lines, often the work of local commanders, varied from place to place, and a host of factors led at times to their lasting blurring or wholesale erasure. But these lines often remained the norm for the US military—in all overseas theaters, for officers as much as for enlisted personnel, and from the war's beginning to end.

"We're Not Fighting for That Kind of Democracy"

As at home, many of these black-white lines—at beaches, bars, brothels, dances, clubs, and elsewhere—involved spaces where men and women interacted. In fact, while only a few of the military's stateside lines applied to these spaces, not so overseas. Jim Crow in uniform's worldly wanderings had lots to do with black men's relations with women, especially, but by no means exclusively, white women. (In part because so few black women went overseas, their relations with white men were not so pressing an issue among white Americans).[20] Many overseas deployments offered black male troops an opportunity, extraordinary for the time, to mix and mingle with a wide range of women. That so much of this socializing proved to be warm, respectful, caring, and loving caused immense anxiety among many white troops, their commanders, and some overseas locals and leaders, too.[21]

This anxiety was especially pronounced in Europe and Australia, where black troops' interactions with white women were most common. Take England, for example. From above, just as growing numbers of African American soldiers began arriving there in the summer of 1942, General Eisenhower confessed his concerns about their associations with English "girls" to a visiting Hollywood star, and British War Secretary Sir Percy James Grigg noted in a "most secret" memorandum to Prime Minister Churchill's War Cabinet that "from the point of view of the morale of our own troops . . . it is most undesirable that there should be any unnecessary association between American coloured troops and British women."[22] From below, while many ordinary Britons sympathized with African American soldiers, especially regarding their travails with a transplanted Jim Crow, "they drew the line at sexual relations."[23] For their part, many American white soldiers were dismayed and appalled by these relations, even casual friendships. A black journalist reported that in northern England, when a white soldier spotted an African American walking arm in arm with a local white girl, he "snatched off his hat and flung it to the ground. He broke into tears and kept repeating over and over, 'I'm from Georgia an' I jes can't take that!'"[24] According to censored letters from England, hundreds of white soldiers felt the same. One letter writer commented "with amazement and indignation on the fact that the English do not recognize the color bar, and that English girls associate with the negro troops." In a note to an English newspaper, a white corporal grumbled, "The white GIs just can't stand to see a nice looking white girl necking with a big black negro. We're not fighting for that kind of democracy."[25]

A related concern among white Americans was that this "necking" (and more) might promote the same behavior at home. Numerous military intelligence reports quoted white American soldiers remarking, for example, "Our men are afraid the colored soldiers are going to try the same practices on our women when they get back" to the United States or "There is going to be a lot of trouble back in the states with the colored lads. . . . You can see some of the nicest looking girls with them and when they get back home they will think they can do the same thing." Some reports also claimed that black soldiers, evidently well aware of whites' worries, taunted them. One soldier, for example, teased, "When we get back to the states, maybe we'll be taking your sister out."[26] Reflecting on his time in England, especially on "the excellent relations the U.S. Negro troops were enjoying with English white girls," a white lieutenant remarked ominously, "U.S. white troops, especially those from the Southern states . . . have repeatedly made statements to the effect that 'A few mass lynchings will be necessary when they get back to the states.'"[27]

Some of these troops, and their leaders, preferred not to wait until they returned home to nip black male–white female fraternizing in the bud. With occasional help from locals and leaders abroad, they sought to erect one barrier after another between black troops and white women. They lectured both groups or circulated flyers or wrote folk songs about the evils of miscegenation or the wisdom of following Jim Crow strictures in whatever far-flung location Americans found themselves.[28] They spread countless lies about "diseased, cruel" and subhuman black men, claiming that "cohabiting and reproducing" with them would spawn "freaks of nature."[29] White commanders occasionally issued formal antifraternization orders. In France, a black GI recalled that white officers' "almost psychotic terror" about these relations led to their campwide ban.[30] In the Pacific, the introduction of white women sometimes occasioned the introduction of stricter spatial segregation to keep black troops far away from them. "With the arrival of [white] Nurses and WACs [Women's Army Corps members] overseas," one black army sergeant serving in New Guinea complained to military intelligence, "there was an immediate discrimination against the negroes. Restrictions were placed upon them and they were not allowed to frequent areas where the women were, although the white troops were allowed to do so." Similarly, one army report of wartime racial practices in the mid-Pacific noted that while some post exchanges, athletic facilities, and theaters were initially mixed, segregation became instantly mandatory as soon as white American women arrived.[31]

When black servicemen's romantic relationships with white women moved toward marriage, many white officers stood in the way. Sometimes they put their objections in writing. In a January 1945 memo, a colonel for the main US air forces command in Europe stated that "[t]he policy of the headquarters regarding mixed [black-white] marriages" is that they are "against the best interests of the parties concerned and the service."[32] But often prohibitions were less formal or explicit. Commanding officers, nearly always white men, had to sign off on service members' requests to marry overseas, and when these marriages involved black men and white women, they seldom consented, coming up with one reason after another for failing to do so, for example, the need to respect the anti-miscegenation laws of the states from which the soldiers originated. One regimental commander in Britain simply refused to forward all requests for marriage between black GIs and white English women to his superior officers.[33]

When, despite these formidable obstacles, some black men and white women still managed to connect as acquaintances, friends, lovers, and, occasionally, newlyweds, the consequences could be severe. Women faced public shaming and ostracism, physical assault, arrest, and, if they worked for the US military, termination. In Italy, an "Italian-American Committee for the Preservation of the Italian Race" distributed leaflets in several major Italian cities that condemned those local women who, "dragging themselves in the gutter, dare to go out on the streets with Negroes, even dare invite them to their homes. Only the lowest type of people lower themselves thus; and the Italian people, already beaten and humiliated, should not allow that more mud be thrown on the land."[34] At one US Army rest center in Nancy, France, the American commanding officer fired any of his French female employees who disobeyed his order that they "not speak to colored boys."[35] In England, the British government used, among other laws, the Defense of the Realm Act, which supposedly targeted trespassing and loitering, to prosecute white English women for socializing with African American GIs. Also in England, a black correspondent relayed the story of a middle-aged white woman who volunteered at a Red Cross club for black troops in Manchester: "One night a group of white American soldiers stopped her as she made her way home alone. They warned her to stay away from the club, or they would give her the 'nigger cure.' . . . Then they cuffed her about and remarked, 'We string up women like you in Georgia!' "[36]

For black men, white Americans' opposition to their fraternizing produced a steady stream of taunts, harassment, attacks, arrests, and even death. A white private in Penzance, England, "observed a jeep, occupied by several Southern [white] soldiers, being driven down the street. Suddenly, the driver drove his jeep onto the sidewalk and one of the occupants stood up and swung a sledge hammer at three Negro soldiers who were walking along the sidewalk with English girls." At a Red Cross tent in France, a black veteran recalled that "a member of our regiment, Allen Leftridge, was talking to a French woman who was serving doughnuts and coffee. When a white MP ordered him not to stand there talking to this woman, Allen turned his back on him. He was shot in the back and killed."[37] Indeed, executions, though often occurring after formal proceedings, took place all over the world, where black soldiers were court-martialed and hanged for sexual relationships that they maintained were consensual or had never occurred. In one highly publicized case from the Pacific in 1944, the military executed six black members of an amphibious truck unit for allegedly raping two white army nurses, despite the men's repeated insistence that they were innocent, the flimsiest of evidence, and a summary trial.[38] Similarly, in Germany, according to the *Cleveland Call and Post*, rape charges leveled against three black GIs were "conceived by 'biased' Army officers, who completely disregarded the soldiers' plea that the woman involved consented to the acts in return for gifts." According to the *Chicago Defender*, the men's only crime "was [a] relationship not with a woman, but with a white woman. Death has become the penalty for crossing the color line."[39]

But if white Americans most vigilantly and violently protected the black-white color line when white women were involved, they did so with non-white women as well. After all, many of these lines regarding women were really about men—white men and what they perceived as their sexual prerogative. At the bustling crossroads between racism and sexism stood some white men's firm belief that women belonged to them alone. In Europe and Australia, this patriarchal proprietariness involved white women primarily. But where they were scarce, in North and West Africa, Asia, and the Pacific, for example, it encompassed nonwhite women as well. A black sailor told a war correspondent that while he served in Dakar, "there were few white women in the city, so the white G.I.s had colored girl friends—but violently objected to Negroes going out with colored girls!"[40] Black Urban League leader Lester Granger, having traveled throughout the Pacific to survey race relations in the navy toward the end of the war, noted that black and white marines clashed on the island of Guam in part because the former considered the "native women" their sole property.[41] Indeed, throughout the Pacific, the black enlisted men's officers in the Ninety-Third Infantry Division warned them, "Don't touch the women."[42] In the Philippines, where a white officer contended that "the sexual competition for women was even greater than in Europe," these prohibitions seem to have appeared especially frequently and starkly. The *Chicago Defender* quoted one black soldier there saying, "There was a dance to which we were all invited, white and Negro alike." But when some black soldiers approached Filipinas to dance, a white Captain shouted, "[Y]ou niggers are not going to dance with the Filipino girls."[43]

These objections to black male–nonwhite female fraternizing likely had several, sometimes overlapping causes. Among them may have been white officers' concerns that such fraternizing would offend local men, upon whom the US military often depended for vital labor. Or in other instances, if whites believed their own propaganda, some perhaps feared that, in dating the same women, they might expose themselves to black troops' putative pathologies. Or some whites fretted about possible off-spring. In the Pacific, for example, a marine major general thought that, whereas "the mix of Polynesians with white race produces a very desirable type, the mixture with the Negro" led to a "very undesirable citizen."[44] Or some men, motivated to fight the war to protect their mothers, sisters, wives, and sweethearts, sought to extend this "protection" abroad to other women. But perhaps the chief cause of white Americans' opposition to black male fraternizing with any women was their utter unwillingness to accept "colored" comrades, in the words of one white officer, "on a basis of social equality."[45] When men "shared" women, they shared social status, too, no matter the "color" of the women involved. And this sharing of status—the blurring of the black-white line—many white men refused to abide.

Disciplinary Measures

Black-white lines involving male-female relations bled into another im-portant set of divides concerning the military justice system. As noted, black troops' socializing with white and other women could lead to courts-martial and executions. Indeed, the black-white disparities for crimes like rape were staggering. In the European Theater of Operations, for example, black soldiers, roughly 10 percent of total army strength there, made up 43 percent of those charged with rape, 56 percent of those found guilty, 80 percent of those sentenced to death, and 87 percent of those executed.[40] In other words, at every stage of the criminal justice system, black troops charged with rape faced disproportionately severe treatment, which only grew more disproportionately severe with each fateful step toward the gallows. Data on other theaters are not as detailed, but gross disparities appeared there, too. According to the Fifth Army's statistics in Italy, from March through June 1945, black troops, 15 percent of all soldiers, suppos-edly committed 100 percent of rapes. Similarly, in the Pacific, where the US military executed eight men for rape, all were African American.[47]

This black-white military-justice divide involved more than rape alone. With few exceptions, whether the offense was dishonesty or misuse of military property or violence, military authorities sentenced black troops, proportionally speaking, far more frequently and more severely than whites. Again, the data on the European theater are most complete. For all general courts-martial (the most serious cases) from July 1942 through October 1945, black troops made up nearly one-quarter of all those convicted. But as with rape, the more serious the crime and punishment, the greater the disparities. Blacks constituted 32 percent of those men given life sentences, 74 percent given death sentences, and 79 percent of those executed. It appears that these inequities circled the globe. In the Pacific, black troops made up an even larger share of those executed—nearly nine in ten.[48]

One preliminary explanation for these shocking disparities is that the World War II–era military justice system was fundamentally—and, after the war, infamously—unfair to many different troops. Commanders had extraordinary influence over the process—for example, they decided whether to bring charges; they selected the prosecutors, the defense (who were not required to have any background in the law), and the jury; and they could control the proceedings to some extent in that they held the power to promote or demote all parties involved and to review their decisions in the end.[49] These systemic flaws—at least from the perspective of the accused—were only exacerbated overseas. The exigencies of war, for example, often rushed investigations, trials, and verdicts. A study of "executing soldiers in England" found that "the average capital case (supposedly the most carefully handled of all military prosecutions) took only one week to gather evidence and formally charge a defendant." Nearly all "trials lasted a single day, and most were over by early afternoon." Furthermore, commanders in the field, often removed from the watchful eyes of troops' families, friends, and allies, acted with much less oversight and accountability. In some of the same capital cases, loved ones of the accused did not learn about his legal troubles "until they received a 'non-battle casualty report' informing them of the execution." Here, then, were some of the reasons that, as the saying went, military justice is to justice as military music is to music.[50]

But this distinction between military justice and justice applied to all troops. It was much more pronounced when black soldiers were involved. The all-powerful officers in their cases—the judges, juries, and defense counsels, and the commander who selected them all—were often uniformly white. In Europe, in late 1943 and again in early 1944, the army's theater command "desired that wherever practicable, one or more Negro officers be detailed as members of all courts-martial before which are to be tried Negro personnel for the more serious crimes of violence or disorder and those involving inter-racial sensibilities."[51] But the practical effect of this directive is unclear. That the command asked that it not be reproduced and instead conveyed down the chain "orally" suggests not only its sensitive nature but also its vulnerability to being disregarded. In one particular instance when a black officer served on a court-martial in England, he was the lowest-ranking member, whom superiors could likely pressure to vote as they wished (death sentences required unanimous votes).[52] Furthermore, the Judge Advocate General (JAG) personnel, who oversaw and reviewed these trials, were likely even more lily white than the presiding court-martial officials. Indeed, it was not until the war's final months that the army assigned its first two black JAG officers to overseas work.[53] So the gross disparities in military justice abroad had a lot to do with the gross underrepresentation that African Americans faced in the system. Writing about rape cases in particular, the *Baltimore Afro-American* declared, "Put the shoe on the other foot and have colored personnel as prosecutors, witnesses, judge and jury, and rape figures for whites would be correspondingly higher."[54]

Another critical factor in these disparities was not simply white officers' monopoly on all positions of juridical authority. It was also their deep-seated prejudices concerning black people's supposed criminality, which shaped so many of their actions and judgments. The Ninety-Eighth Engineer Regiment—made up of black enlisted men and, with the exception of the chaplain, all white officers—provides a case in point. Its commander, Colonel C. W. Ball, a well-traveled career army officer with the Army Corps of Engineers, fancied himself a self-taught expert on black people. This so-called expertise, as he bragged, came from his "actual experience with raw jungle natives in the mines and bush of the Transvaal, Rhodesia, and German East Africa, native soldiers, Jamaica negroes, colored American soldiers of long service, river workers on the Mississippi and Ohio Rivers, and cotton hands in Texas." From this experience and from his time commanding his regiment in North Africa and England, he became convinced that "[a] veneer of white culture and what the Army has been able to instill does not alter basic facts." Therefore, "no disciplinary system devised can prevent these [black] soldiers from giving vent to their savage instincts except the extreme punishment as outlined in the Articles of War."[55]

No wonder, then, that there was—according to a black undercover agent with the Counter Intelligence Corps, whom the military placed in the unit—"frequent application of disciplinary measures, including courts-martial, where there was no need or justification for them." "[T]he men feel that their officers prosecute the possibilities of their guilt to the extreme," he concluded. "They believe the truth is twisted unnecessarily many times, that there are too many punishments; that in general the chief responsibilities of their officers are directed toward disciplinary actions." A white undercover agent sided not with his black colleague but with his superior, Colonel Ball, viewing the engineer outfit's problems as stemming from black men's addiction "to drinking wine which work them into a rage and bring out their animal instincts." Army intelligence officials ultimately recommended this "solution": "Quick trial and punishment of malefactors."[56]

These white officers' prejudices appear to have been widespread. As "Negro" aide to Secretary Stimson, Truman Gibson had numerous conversations with members of the JAG Department and overseas commanders about black troops and military justice matters, and he expressed precisely the same concerns as those of the black intelligence agent in England: "[M]any [white officers] believe that Negro soldiers possess certain inherent racial predispositions to commit crimes and particularly crimes of violence against women." These views, he thought, had led to "a tendency to impose excessively harsh and severe sentences on Negro soldiers."[57] Having covered the European theater during the war, African American *Stars and Stripes* reporter Allan Morrison agreed. "[C]olored soldiers were particularly vulnerable to prejudiced officers in the realm of the court-martial," he observed, since officers were "willing to believe in a Negro's guilt before it had been proven."[58] While serving in Paris in the wake of the cross-channel invasion, one white MP personally witnessed exactly this point. "The first time I went to testify [at a court-martial]," he recalled, "this [white] colonel was in charge. I said this guy wasn't guilty of selling anything. He was just picked up because he happened to be there. The colonel said, 'Was he a nigger?' He didn't say Negro, he said nigger. 'He was colored.' And he said, 'Well, if he's a nigger, he's guilty, too.'"[59]

Of course, officers' prejudices marred military justice for black troops in less explicit ways as well. In a meticulous study of rape cases involving US soldiers in northern France in the summer of 1944, historian Mary Louise Roberts demonstrates that it was precisely these prejudices—whether openly expressed or not, whether conscious or not—that so corrupted military justice at every possible turn. They help explain why "the US military inadequately investigated rape charges, concluded too quickly that the accused was black, arrived too easily at the identification of the alleged rapist, insufficiently probed the reputation of the accuser and witnesses, and erroneously assumed premeditated sexual violence on the part of black men."[60]

A final factor that helps account for the black-white lines in overseas military justice matters was locals' own anti-black racism. Many overseas locals embraced black troops with openness and kindness and love, but not everyone did, of course. This racism stemmed from colonialisms' self-serving lessons, transported back to the metropole through letters, memoirs, novels, poetry, word of mouth, and the like, about "natives"; from fascism's influences; and from some white American GIs' assiduous efforts to transplant Jim Crow overseas. But no matter its source, this overseas racism contributed to the grossly unequal military justice for black troops. It led to false accusations, false testimony, sexual blackmail (where, for example, a prostitute would overcharge a black client and "get him in trouble" if he refused to pay), and baseless fearmongering.[61] On New Caledonia in the Pacific, the Free French colonial governor there, without a shred of evidence, condemned African American troops as "the terror of white women."[62] For these reasons and others, what Roberts argued about some French also held true for other overseas people: they were white Americans' "deadly allies in racism."[63]

Overall, then, the *Baltimore Afro-American* was certainly right to caution its readers about military crime statistics. "As disturbing as they are, [they] cannot be taken as the complete picture. They must be read against a background darkened by prejudice, segregation, intolerance and even hate."[64] But these statistics were incomplete in another way as well. They involved only the military's most serious cases—general courts-martial. And while much less systematic information exists about the more day-to-day policing and punishment that black troops faced overseas, every indication is that, just as in the United States, stark black-white lines appeared here, too. Many black troops certainly thought so. Having traveled throughout the European theater in early 1944, NAACP leader Walter White reported back to the War Department: "Great unhappiness among Negro soldiers has resulted from their belief that they are punished more quickly and more severely than white soldiers," not simply in general courts-martial but in less serious "special" ones, too.[65] Similarly one black sergeant, recently back from three years of service in Australia and New Guinea, complained that "when one negro in his unit committed any offense, restrictions were placed upon all within the unit. [But] . . . when a white enlisted man committed an offense, he alone was punished." Occasionally white military officials confirmed the prevalence of these injustices, if not always intentionally. An Inspector General's report from Naples, Italy, contained this puzzling chain of events: "white soldiers had been irked by public manifestations of equality among negro soldiers and Italian civilians and had molested and insulted negro soldiers of this battalion. Among the remedial measures taken was a search for 'agitators' among the negro units."[66]

Race Wars

The molesting and insulting of black soldiers suggest another set of black-white lines—violent clashes between troops involving anywhere from a few soldiers to many hundreds. As in the United States, this violence often involved whites' frequent concerns, as in Naples, about "manifestations of equality" between black and white people—that is, smudging of the line between the two. As one black veteran years later perceptively pointed out, "When the fighting started, everyone on both sides was pulled in on the basis of color. It was a microcosm of America. Objectively, we [black and white soldiers] were striving toward a common goal. . . . Yet, at the critical point an appeal was made to color. Forgetting all reason, the herds grouped together to defend God knows what against 'them.'"[67]

In Britain and Ireland, black and white GIs squared off in hundreds of fights and a half dozen or so full-scale riots. Their causes, while varied and complex, often had at least this in common: whites' insistence on drawing and enforcing black-white lines, especially where white women were concerned. Violent clashes broke out as soon as African American troops began arriving in Britain and Ireland in large numbers in the spring and summer of 1942. In September of that year, numerous blacks stationed in Ireland wrote home, mystified: "I sometimes wonder who we are fighting. Did the War Department sent [sic] us here to fight against our white soldiers or against the Nazis?"[68] Serious conflict and some major rioting continued unabated through 1943. But as more and more GIs flowed into southern England in preparation for the D-Day invasion in June 1944, countless reports warned of a significant rise in "physical clashes" and "incidents of violence"—stabbings, brawls, riots, even the formation of white soldier "gangs" that terrorized black people and violently protected so-called white turf in English cities.[69] The biggest disturbance came just after the invasion, in Bristol, a port city in southwestern England. Over the course of a week white American paratroopers, resentful of African Americans dating local English women, started a series of fights that culminated in a massive brawl involving four hundred white and black American troops that lasted hours and left one soldier dead and several more seriously injured.[70]

These battles in Britain, which extended well beyond the end of formal hostilities in Europe, constituted one part of a larger, worldwide story.[71] In France, Italy, and Germany, combat against the Axis mitigated combat between black and white Americans. But even here, just as soon as the front lines moved on and base-section supply centers sprang up, so too did black-white conflict. One end-of-the-war army survey of race relations at its Delta Base Section in southern France noted "a constant procession of instances of friction between white and Negro troops as revealed by police records. They are of the nature of minor riots, fights, stabbings, shootings, murders and assaults. . . . They generally arise in bars and are frequently occasioned by indiscretion on the part of white soldiers who make slighting remarks regarding the Negroes or who express their resentment at seeing Negroes with French women." Similarly in Italy, it was well after the war in Europe had ended that "two near wholesale riots broke out" in and around Viareggio, a beach resort fifteen miles north of Pisa and home to the headquarters of the largely black Ninety-Second Infantry Division. In one of these, a black lieutenant and Bronze Star recipient from the division entered an officers' nightclub with a light-skinned black cast member of a USO show playing in the area. A white officer, thinking the woman was white, accosted her and the lieutenant and "demanded to know if [she] wanted to be 'with this N——.'" A fight ensued, and as word spread, "trucks of the 92d full of enlisted men culled from everywhere surrounded the place," but further fighting was averted.[72]

Australia also had its share of black-white clashes. When visiting in 1945, Walter White found that "the incessant conflict between white and colored American soldiers" completely confounded everyone "from Prime Minister Curtin . . . to barmaids and taxi drivers in Sydney." Brawls involving hundreds of black and white American troops, and sometimes Australians too, occurred in and around Brisbane, among other places. An army report written at the end of the war offered a familiar explanation: "Clashes between white and colored troops occurred in Australia due primarily to initial harassment of colored troops by white troops due to association of colored troops with white Australian girls and subsequent denial of entry into certain places of entertainment by [white] American military personnel."[73]

Finally, the Pacific also played host to the US military's mini–race wars. On Guam in late 1944, white marines, resentful of black sailors' associations with local Chamorro women and of their noncombat service work, harassed them by throwing empty beer bottles, bricks, smoke bombs, and hand grenades into their camp. They also called them "niggers," "night-fighters," and "black sons-of-bitches" and ran them out of Agana, the main town on the island. Tensions escalated on Christmas Day when whites shot two black sailors, killing one and seriously injuring the other, and when one black sentry "mortally wounded a white fellow marine who had been harassing him." As truckloads of armed blacks and whites mobilized for battle—or, in the case of the former, self-defense—large-scale bloodshed was avoided, but only after MPs, having failed to arrest a single white person to this point, apprehended more than forty black servicemen and charged them with unlawful assembly, rioting, theft of government property, and attempted murder. All men, initially court-martialed and imprisoned, were later released after an NAACP appeal.[74]

Similar sorts of competition over women sparked serious, bloody conflict in the Philippines as well. In the spring of 1945, one white lieutenant reported "numerous fights, shootings, and knifing [sic] among Negroes and whites at a house of prostitution in Dagupan." In Manila, a black correspondent noted that "not infrequently frictions and fistic brawls over women have occurred in the streets and quite often they have marred town social functions where white and colored soldiers have come together for a good time." And one black veteran recalled a particularly dramatic showdown "that just missed being a bloody war":

> [T]he 93rd [Division] vs. the [31st] Dixie Division. This white outfit was there when we arrived. I do not remember the name of the place but it was in the vicinity of the Dole Pineapple Company. Our men had been overseas for nineteen months without seeing any women to speak of so when the guys hit the Philippines they went hog wild. The Dixie Division couldn't stand the Filipino girls going for the Negro soldiers. After several days there were small battles. The ultimate finally arrived; the Dixie Division was lined up upon one side of the road for about two miles or more and the 93rd was lined up opposite them. Both sides had fixed bayonets, their guns were on load and unlock. It took the colonels of every battalion from both divisions to get their men and bring the situation under control. They were real busy riding or running up and down that road to keep down outright war.[75]

Rank Discrimination

While the veteran did not say, the colonels in his story had to have been white. As on the home front, black-white lines prevented nearly all African Americans from reaching these lofty ranks, even in so-called all-black divisions like the Ninety-Third. In an early 1945 memo to President Roosevelt from New Guinea, NAACP leader Walter White, having reviewed the division there, observed, "Some Negro officers have been kept as Second Lieutenants for nearly three years, while less educated and less able whites have been brought in and promoted over Negro officers."[76] When some black officers protested these barriers, their commanding officer told them, "There's something in your racial background that makes you inadequate to lead troops in an emergency." General Douglas MacArthur, the supreme Allied commander of the Southwest Pacific Area, avoided this sort of language, but also the larger problem of rank discrimination. He cited an Inspector General report on the subject of promotions in the division that supposedly cleared commanders of any wrongdoing, and he expressed "the greatest confidence in the integrity and judgment of the Division Commander in making these interior assignments."[77]

The other "Negro" infantry division, the Ninety-Second, drew similar sorts of black-white lines around its highest-ranking officers. Indeed, the division commander, Major General Edward Almond, who as late as the 1970s defended troop segregation on the basis of the "inherent difference in races," made no attempt to disguise these lines. Speaking to a *New York Times* correspondent in Italy in November 1944, a colonel beneath him admitted that "he does not foresee the time when his outfit will include Negro junior officers outranking white junior officers."[78] When Truman Gibson traveled to Italy in March 1945 to assess the division, he reported that, in a rare example of consensus, both black and white officers agreed that the unit's promotion policies discriminated against the former. He recommended revising them "so as to make it possible to promote Negro officers of demonstrated ability and confidence." "Negro officers should be used when qualified in staff and higher command positions," he added. "As rapidly as possible, a single standard for all officers should be approached in the 92nd Division." But Almond promptly ignored these recommendations. He was convinced that "the negro officer . . . lacks pride, aggressiveness, a sense of responsibility and has practically no command capacity above the grade of captain."[79]

Nonetheless, at least these two units had many scores of black officers each. Very few if any outfits across the armed forces could say the same, primarily because so many white commanders shared Almond's conviction both about black officers' supposed inadequacies and about all black soldiers' supposed need and desire to serve under whites. In the army, it was not until the summer of 1943 that its "Negro OCS" in Britain graduated its first class of fourteen black second lieutenants. It did so only after the army's highest-ranking black officer, Brigadier General Benjamin O. Davis Sr., noticed, on a visit to the theater, that "no colored solders were admitted . . . until I checked and found some with proper qualifications."[80] Problems persisted. In March 1945, Truman Gibson reported from Europe that some overseas commands still refused to forward African Americans' applications for OCS and, in directives about the school, referred to white prospective candidates alone. These practices help explain why, toward the end of the war, less than 1 percent of the army's overseas officers were black.[81]

Fig. 8.1 Major General Edward M. Almond inspects members of the Ninety-Second Infantry Division during a decoration ceremony in Italy, c. March 1945. Courtesy National Archives, 208-AA-47Y-1.

As for black women, the entangled barriers of racism and sexism meant that they constituted only the most miniscule share of this 1 percent. As of July 31, 1945, of the 4,510 black army officers abroad, a mere 85 were women—roughly one-third in the Women's Army Corps (WAC) and two-thirds in the army nurse corps. Months earlier, Mabel Staupers, the executive secretary of the National Association of Colored Graduate Nurses, protested this sorry state of affairs: "Colored nurses are still being accepted in very small numbers and are still restricted primarily to the care of colored troops and war prisoners. None have been accepted into the Navy." "At this time when we are continually hearing through the Daily Press and the Radio of the urgent need for nurses in both the Army and the Navy," she continued, with remarkable restraint, "it is difficult to understand these limitations."[82]

Overseas barriers to rank were even more insurmountable in the military's other services. The marines did not commission a single black officer during the war (in 1945, the marines had more than thirty-seven thousand active-duty officers); the navy commissioned only about sixty.[83] In fact, black sailors and marines often struggled in vain to rise beyond certain senior enlisted grades, let alone beyond that. Take the Thirty-Fourth Construction Battalion, for example, which built roads, warehouses, hospitals, and airstrips in the Pacific. When it embarked from Port Heuneme, California, in January 1943, the unit was rigidly segregated according to rank and "race." No black Seabees ranked higher than a petty officer second class, and all whites rated above this grade. When it returned from its first tour of duty more than twenty-one months later, these stark barriers remained. Despite the fact that the men, according to their commander, made a fine showing overseas, whites were promoted to chief petty officers and even commissioned, but not a single black Seabee was. Black Seabees remained permanently stuck, incapable of outranking any white men in their unit. In numerous protest letters to the NAACP, the outfit's exasperated men, many of whom had college degrees and extensive construction experience prior to entering the navy, condemned their "slave outfit" and their commander's open embrace of "white supremacy." Eventually they staged a two-day hunger strike to protest these injustices, especially those involving rank and promotions.[84]

Related to these matters were the black-white lines not simply in rank but also in the specific jobs black troops received. By the end of the war, nearly three in four black troops abroad served in only three army branches—the Corps of Engineers, the Quartermaster Corps, and the Transportation Corps.[85] Here, as on the home front, they did the less glamorous (if no less important) work of driving trucks, loading cargo, sorting mail, stocking and dispensing ammunition, and building roads, bridges, depots, and living quarters. Indeed, even those black troops in ostensible combat units often found themselves engaged in this work. Recounting his experiences in the Pacific as a lieutenant in the Ninety-Third Infantry Division, Welton Taylor wrote, "For us, there would be no glory, no hero's welcome, no medals on our chests. There would only be calluses, backaches, and the ubiquitous skin disease known as jungle rot. . . . Instead of using our skills as field artillerymen, we were functioning as stevedores, custodians, and warehousers assigned to housekeeping duty, nontactical."[86]

Some black troops denounced this "work-but-not-fight" policy, for reasons Taylor alluded to. At the peak of many Americans' idealization of the combat soldier as model manly, patriotic citizen, denying blacks access to the front lines also meant denying them this considerable prestige and status; it meant feminizing them as "housekeepers," who were "armed with shovels, pots and pans rather than guns"; it meant keeping them in a "servile, subservient place" akin to "slaves" or "coolies"; it meant depriving them of the chance to "defend the country" or "to be heroes"; and it meant symbolizing in the most unambiguous terms the conviction among so many military authorities that black soldiers were too weak, cowardly, and unreliable for the nation's defense.[87]

Unlike black people's menial positions on the home front, however, those positions overseas had a silver lining: they tended to keep blacks safely removed from the front lines. Taylor astutely recognized this fact: "I tried to cheer my men by reminding them that there was an upside to this humiliation: There would continue to be very few casualties among our ranks." He was right, not simply about members of his outfit but about all black troops. Roughly 7 percent of all wartime service personnel, African Americans accounted for less than 2 percent of all deaths.[88] Indeed, while black newspapers and civil right activists pushed tirelessly for African Americans' "right to fight," some black troops, especially those overseas, scoffed at this campaign. They wished to preserve the sole advantage of a monumentally disadvantageous military Jim Crow: physical survival. Encamped on the Solomon Islands in 1944, black soldiers accosted Enoch Waters, the *Chicago Defender* columnist, for his efforts to coax their unit into combat. "I don't know whom you folks think you're speaking for, but it certainly ain't us," the soldiers snapped. "You folks are sitting back at home and too old or too beat up to be drafted. It's easy to say let them fight and die." But, they asked bitterly, "[w]hy should we volunteer to sacrifice our lives for a Jim Crow Country?"[89]

Tales of Tails

One final set of crucial black-white lines involved symbols and discourse, conscious justifications and tacit beliefs. A share of these lines were identical to those at home: some whites' refusal to salute black officers or to respect blacks' uniforms, their everyday use of derogatory and difference-making language to describe black troops as "niggers" or "boys" or "jiggaboos" or "black sons-of-bitches," and their widespread beliefs that black soldiers were fundamentally distinct from themselves—more savage, animal, primitive, cowardly, lazy, unpatriotic, irresponsible, weak, timid, untrustworthy, and the rest.[90] That some theater commanders supposedly insisted that "any person subject to military law who makes statements derogatory of any troops of the United Nations will be severely punished for conduct prejudicial to good order and military discipline" clearly had little practical effect.[91]

As at home, sundry cultural productions spread these ideas far and wide: a minstrel show on Midway among white American Seabees at which a "fast steppin' dancer wow[ed] 'em"; handbills in Naples, which instructed locals "to justly scorn the Negro"; military memos and reports and guides, which with numbing regularity proclaimed all black troops to be "unsuited in all ways for actual combat"; official navy photographs of the "epic battle of the Philippines," which, according to one stinging critique in the black press, summarized African American sailors' contributions as thus: "1. Negroes wiped silverware. 2. Negroes snoozed away in their bunks. 3. Negroes prayed over their bibles";[92] and an unusual form of word-of-mouth war propaganda, in which white Americans spread scurrilous misinformation not about the Axis enemy but about their own purported comrades, maligning African Americans as "savages, cannibals, diseased, ragged," "rank morons, sexual fiends, veneral [*sic*] disease ridden, rapists, liars, thieves, [and] hygienic problems," and "the lowest racial group in the world; lower than even the coolie."[93]

In contrast to these examples, all of which appeared back home, perhaps the most outlandish lie proliferated primarily overseas. It concerned what some black soldiers bitterly referred to as the "animal angle": the notion that African Americans, more monkey than human, had tails. It surfaced here and there during World War I but really came into its own during World War II.[94] In Britain, black American soldiers wrote loved ones and allies back home about their white countrymen telling locals that "colored soldiers are still so close to the uncivilized stage that they have tails like a monkey." They complained to their chaplains, to American journalists abroad, and to each other about being approached on the street and "ask[ed] very innocently to be shown their tails," or about how "people are told that . . . we will grow tails, and we are direct descendents from monkeys," or about the humiliating and awkward moments that these lies produced. According to one black correspondent, writing from England, "A Negro major told me of being surprised when he visited a British home by the total concern for his comfort. The mistress of the house had placed a number of soft pillows in his chair. Every so often she would anxiously look in his direction. Before the evening was over he learned the reason. His hosts had been told by American soldiers that Negroes have tails!"

After the war, black troops preserved these infuriating memories for posterity. In late 1945, a black sergeant recalled that, upon arrival in England, kids would ask him and others in his outfit, "Have you got tails? Do they come out at night?" Decades later, a former member of the army medical corps recalled a memory of his time in England nearly identical to the black correspondent's earlier: "I met a very interesting family. This man and his wife befriended me and I was very appreciative because I didn't know anybody. The first time they invited me to dinner his daughter put a large pillow in my chair. I just figured what the heck, to make me nice and comfortable. So one day I asked her [the wife] and she said, 'Well they had told us you had tails and I didn't want you to sit on it. The whites had told us that you had this tail and you were monkeys.'"[95]

In every theater in which black Americans served, white Americans regaled wide-eyed locals with these "tales of tails." In France in 1944, a black corporal bristled at whites' "racial myths of colored soldiers with tails," and years later, a black veteran of the 369th Engineer Regiment recalled that his chaplain there "made it his business to visit in advance of every place we were going. He'd warn the people in those communities that in America white people did not associate with us and—I'm not kidding—that we had tails."[96] In Italy, a black GI noted on an army questionnaire, "Personally, I haven't seen a monkey tail on any human, and it really hurts when those damned Italians ask where it is." In the China-Burma-India theater, a newspaper reported, "The whites have told the Indians and Chinese that Negroes have tails. Indians have actually yanked up the coattails of Negro soldiers in Calcutta, Bombay and in Karachi to see for themselves if it is so." In the Philippines, a black soldier wrote his minister back home that American whites "are teaching the people [here] . . . that the Negro soldier has a tail like a dog that comes out at night and goes back in during the day." On the small atoll of Funafuti, in the South Pacific, one black veteran later recalled that his very first introduction to the place involved "natives" asking him, "Let me see your tail. The white marines had told them that all black people had tails." And in Australia, according to one private's letter, "one fellow was kind enough to drop his pants to let one of the Aussies see for himself that he did not have a tail."[97]

A Familiar and Unfamiliar Jim Crow

Taken together, the military's manifold black-white lines overseas closely resembled those at stateside training posts. Like the latter, the former wended their way through quarters and mess halls, post exchanges and officers' clubs, bars and brothels, rank and job structures, courts-martial and fights, and the ideas and assumptions animating everything from minstrel shows to military reports. Like the latter, the former could be formal—the prohibition on black-white marriages in certain European commands—and informal—the bright line dividing lower-ranked blacks from higher-ranked whites; physical—a string dividing a deck on board a navy ship bound for Trinidad; social and behavioral—whites' violent exclusion of black troops from so-called white spaces; and symbolic—the notion that "colored" soldiers had tails. And like the latter, the former constituted a vast structure of white domination and black subordination. It not only helped further naturalize the very idea of race and two of its master categories—black and white—but did so primarily by lavishing rights, resources, and status on the latter—from higher ranks and wages to better bunks and bars and more—and by depriving black people of the same.

But the black-white lines in the United States and abroad had their differences, too. One involved an exception to these gross disparities: keeping black troops from the front lines was a literal lifesaver; their casualty rates were significantly lower than were those for whites. Another difference was that, while some black-white lines blurred substantially overseas, others brightened in response. For example, in part because black men's access to nonblack women—especially white women—often expanded overseas, the military's black-white boundary building in this area did so as well.

Black-white lines' cast of busy builders differed in some ways from that on the home front. White enlisted personnel continued playing their part, primarily through the harassment and assault of black troops and the spreading of anti-black propaganda, and leaders in the War and Navy Departments remained critical, both in what they did and in what they did not do. Ultimately, they limited black troops' access to combat roles; they supported rigid barriers to black promotions; their unwavering commitment to segregated units led to segregation in other places and spaces, including overseas; and their unwillingness to enforce seemingly unambiguous policies—for example, one that required army commanders to "avoid all practices tending to give colored soldiers cause to feel that the Army makes any differentiation between him and any other soldier"—ceded enormous authority to commanders below them to craft black-white lines as they saw fit.[98] While this latitude existed stateside to some extent, it only grew overseas, thanks to the exigencies of combat. As one white officer of black troops in Europe and the Pacific recalled about his experiences there, "The attitudes of command in the lower echelons (regiments and below) became increasingly important in race relations. Units were more likely to be on their own. Poor communications, rapid movement, and long distances from headquarters often left matters of policy up to subordinate commanders."[99] Although these factors varied somewhat over time and from one theater to the next, the officer had a point. Much more so than on the home front, it was often overseas where the military's middle-manager level—commanders of bases, districts, sections, companies, battalions, regiments, and even up to divisions—enjoyed broadest authority to craft black-white lines as it wished. It was often these local US military authorities who segregated towns and recreation; forbade black-nonblack, or even occasionally black-black, fraternizing and marriage;

controlled court-martial proceedings; blocked black troops' commissions and promotions, as in the case of the Ninety-Second Infantry Division or the Thirty-Fourth Construction Battalion; and on occasion, even took the lead in slandering black troops to overseas locals.

Sometimes helping them along the way was one final group entirely absent on the home front: overseas locals and their governments. As for the former, especially in parts of Europe, they sometimes exacerbated an already unjust military court-martial system by too readily accusing black troops of crimes or assuming the worst about them, they had misgivings about their fraternizing with local women, and they cooperated in the segregation of space by barring African Americans from their bars and cafés, theaters and restaurants. To be sure, in the last of these cases, segregation could be a consequence of American coercion: some local proprietors in places like Britain and Australia excluded black patrons for fear that white Americans would otherwise boycott or ransack their businesses.[100] But in other cases, investments in black-white lines were, at least in part, homegrown, a function of colonialism's effects on the metropole or local iterations of global racist systems rooted in centuries of slavery and empire. No American arm-twisting, it appears, convinced a vicar's wife in Somerset, England, to suggest a set of best practices for British women now in the presence of African American servicemen; they included the directives that "white women, of course, must have no relationship with colored troops" and "on no account must colored troops be invited into the homes of white women." And in parts of France, some civilians' complicity in the scapegoating and railroading of African American troops stemmed in part from their "deeply-rooted racist sentiments, largely developed in relationship to the colonized peoples of western Africa."[101]

As for foreign governments, those allied with and dependent on the United States sometimes took an active role in assisting its efforts to smuggle and spread Jim Crow abroad. In Britain, Her Majesty's Government often yielded to the US military's colored-white segregationist wishes in a range of institutions under its control, including hospitals, recreational centers, living quarters, and troopships. The British War Office also instructed its soldiers to minimize their contacts with African American troops, and British army officers advised these same troops to "observe the amenities of Jim Crow" while in Britain. Finally, some local governments, "haunted by the spectre of interracial sexual relations," launched a "whispering campaign" to portray the American "darky [a]s a simple minded child" and reported, apprehended, and prosecuted British women and girls who engaged in these relations all the same.[102] Similarly, in Australia, authorities worked closely with the US military to station black servicemen in isolated rural regions and segregated urban neighborhoods and to keep them apart as much as possible from white Americans and white Australians in recreation and leisure.[103]

As with their citizens, however, these and other foreign governments sometimes drew black-white lines for their own distinct ends, having little if anything to do with American wishes. Indeed, sometimes they did so in opposition to those wishes. Numerous governments attempted to bar African American servicemen from entering their country or colonies, or, failing that, to carefully limit their numbers or their locations. A partial list of such governments and colonies spans the globe: Australia, Bermuda, Britain, Belgium, Chile, China, the Congo, Panama, Trinidad, and Venezuela.[104] The British government found itself in an especially tough spot. It wished to avoid unduly alienating "colored" colonial subjects by too slavishly supporting US black-white lines. At the same time, it buttressed and quietly insisted on some of them, and not just to avoid alienating its most important wartime ally in the United States. It also worried that blurred black-white lines might dampen wartime morale among white British troops or undermine its increasingly tenuous grip on its colonies. In India, for example, local British authorities, perhaps fearing "colored" connections between their imperial subjects and African American troops there, tried to keep rest camps for the latter, whether integrated or segregated, to a minimum.[105]

In the main, however, Jim Crow's wartime transnational travels came courtesy of white Americans' herculean efforts—those of enlisted personnel, War and Navy Department leadership, and especially local military commanders all around the world. Many white Americans proved deeply committed to building and fortifying the black-white divide in enlistment, in outfit assignments, and in training posts, a military commitment that, in one form or another, stretched back nearly a century. But the divide emerged on and around battlefronts and theaters of operation as well, where lives hung in the balance and where, one might have suspected, the US military had more important things to worry about. Yet nearly wherever it traveled overseas, it dutifully, methodically, even obsessively transported and transplanted the divide.

The reasons for this were similar to those on the home front, but with a few overseas twists. Some military leaders and field commanders continued to cling to their long-standing, genuine belief that bright black-white lines optimized troop efficiency, discipline, and morale. Only white officers, they thought, could get the most out of their "Negro" troops; only "physical segregation between Whites and Negroes," especially where women were concerned, would minimize friction between the two. Numerous

end-of-the-war army surveys of race relations around the world, for example, repeated these points.[106] But as on the home front, black-white
lines also emerged overseas from many white Americans' continuing, indeed intensifying, fear and suspicion that white supremacy might be on
the ropes, thanks in part to the military's own unwitting actions. In the
United States, these actions involved the standardization, valorization,
and physical movement of service personnel. All these factors also figured in overseas; in fact, the last of them, movement, was, in many white
Americans' minds, even more troubling in the international context. Here
black troops traveled not simply to other regions of the United States but
to other countries and continents, where many millions of people, so-
called whites among them, had little familiarity with and interest in US-
style Jim Crow. These fears and suspicions appeared perhaps most obvious
in relation to male-female interactions. But to appreciate their full scope
and scale and importance requires looking not simply at the building of
black-white lines abroad, but also at their blurring. Indeed, as on the home
front, these stories can only be told together, since each was so inextricably and dialectically linked to the other. The US military constructed the
black-white divide abroad because it also helped, often unintentionally and
indirectly, to chip away at it there.

"JIM CROW IS A WAR CASUALTY"

Such chipping away came primarily from three overseas developments,
all of which the US military inadvertently helped make possible. These
were non-Americans' friendliness toward black Americans, the occasional
black-white comradeship of American GIs, and the activism of black troops
themselves—like Jim Crow, another wartime American transplant—
which sometimes succeeded in compelling heretofore inflexible US military
commanders to modify or abandon their Jim Crow ways.

"They Received Us with Open Arms"

Wherever black American troops traveled, they bonded with locals. Seldom
schooled in the finer points of US racist ideas and practices, non-Americans
sometimes opened their homes, churches, dance halls, cafés, and hearts to
African Americans. This was certainly the case for the tens of thousands of
black American troops who spent some time in the United Kingdom during
the war. Many white Britons had had limited if any personal contact with

black people prior to the war and were perhaps taken in by the "polite, liquid-voiced, smartly uniformed Negro soldiers" and by the "happy opportunity . . . to thumb the nose of moral self-righteousness at the U.S."[107] Whatever the precise reason, many proved time and again to have little interest in the black-white "colour bar," inviting African Americans to dinner and church services, union meetings and choirs, picnics and community dances. Many hotels and restaurants, pubs and theaters happily welcomed African American business, even in the face of threats from white Americans not to do so. White British and African American soldiers

Fig. 8.2 An African American corporal with his new, likely foreign bride, 1945. Courtesy of the Library of Congress Prints and Photographs Division, Gladstone Collection of African American Photographs, LC-DIG-ppmsca-11494.

drank together and played "a lot of stud poker . . . and exchanged stories."[108] African American men and British white women dated, some married, and hundreds of "brown babies" were born. US military reports referred gravely to the "English girls" "proudly exhibiting their half-breed" children.[109]

Many African Americans embraced this boundary blurring. In one group of censored letters from Northern Ireland in September 1942, they gushed, "The Irish people treat us as if we were one of them"; "the girls invite us to parties, church, Sunday school and to other societies. . . . We appreciate it to the highest"; the people "have never heard of discrimination"; and "this is a great country here and the people are very friendly. . . . I am living the happiest days of my life." Having spoken to numerous black GIs in England, journalist Roi Ottley summarized their views "in the language of a Negro soldier: 'I'm treated so a man don't know he's colored until he looks in the mirror.' " One serviceman wrote to his former professor at Morgan State University that, whereas "in my own country I am merely a Negro, segregated, discriminated against, and denied the full rights of citizenship," "in England I am treated as an American citizen by the English."[110] In one army survey from November 1943 of American servicemen's attitudes in the European theater, 80 percent of black respondents reported a favorable view of the English people. Some black GIs expressed a desire to stay in Britain after war's end, and some did so.[111]

As conflicts erupted between white and black American servicemen in the United Kingdom, not least because of this boundary blurring, many Britons advertised their allegiances openly. According to an army intelligence report on a "small English village," eight- and nine-year-old children scolded white American soldiers on the street, saying, "You mistreat the black man." Pubs across Britain posted a sign: "For British people and coloured Americans only."[112] Some members of Parliament and civil rights groups like the League of Colored Peoples urged the British government to remind Americans that "the color bar is not a custom of this country."[113] When the US military prosecuted black soldiers whom Britons knew to be innocent, they organized grassroots campaigns in their defense, involving petitions with, in some cases, tens of thousands of signatures; they also wrote newspaper editorials and sent countless letters to the editor, their representatives, and US authorities.[114] One West Country farmer seemed to speak for a good many of his fellow countrymen and -women: "I love the Americans but I don't like the white ones they brought with them."[115]

Of course, relations between white Britons and black Americans varied some from one place to another, and some commentators thought that they cooled over time as a consequence, in part, of white Americans' influences.[116] Even so, no shortage of evidence—from censored soldiers' letters and army reports to journalists' and others' accounts—suggests that, at least for many white Britons, warm relations continued through the end of the war and beyond.[117] In late August 1945, black troops in Bristol were preparing to return home to America. When US army authorities fenced them in, hoping to prevent them from exchanging goodbye kisses with their local girlfriends, the latter—chanting "to hell with U.S. Army color bars!"—scaled the fences.[118] Here then was a perfect metaphor for black soldiers' experiences throughout the wartime United Kingdom: despite the US military's best efforts to shore up black-white barriers, some Britons defied them.

Other Europeans did as well. In France, some civilians, especially in the rural northwest in the wake of the Normandy invasion, contributed to the unjust prosecution of black GIs, but others here and elsewhere, in the words of two black soldiers, welcomed African Americans "with open arms" and made "no distinction between colors."[119] Black Americans dined in locals' homes, played with the children, took French classes in a chateau, and danced with, dated, and occasionally married French women. Sometimes grudgingly, numerous white American officers agreed that relations between French civilians and black American troops were "very amicable" or "too amicable"[120]

Similar boundary-blurring relations developed in Italy. One soldier, stationed in Piombino, a small city on the west coast, resolved to remain in Italy after the war, where "a colored man is treated as an equal and not like a dog [as] in Georgia." "The people in the [Italian] countryside and in the mountains were terrific to us," recalled one former black infantryman. "They cried tears of sorrow when we left for the front lines and cried tears of joy when we returned safely. . . . I have to this day some of these people as my best friends." Another former infantryman from a different regiment shared similar sentiments: "The Italians, given a chance at all, were most hospitable. On a moment's notice they would have a little party with dancing and wine. . . . I am sure the fondest memories the men of the 92nd Division have of the whole war are of Italy and its people."[121]

Even in Germany, black soldiers found that "Nazi-created anti Negro feeling is not a deep, living thing." A black gunner just back from the war appreciated that Germans questioned white Americans' horror stories about black people and "seemingly went out of their way to be congenial." "Strangely enough, here where Aryanism ruled supreme," observed *Ebony* magazine in 1946, "Negroes are finding more friendship, more respect and more equality than they would back home—either in Dixie or on Broadway."[122]

Fig. 8.3 African American soldier Ellis L. Ross enjoys a drink at the home of civilian friends in Italy, n.d. Ellis L. Ross Collection (AFC/2001/001/45353), Veterans History Project, American Folklife Center, Library of Congress. Courtesy of Carl Johnson.

Black troops sometimes found the same among whites and others outside of Europe, which similarly chipped away at Jim Crow's lines. A white American army officer reported that "the colored soldier" in North Africa was "accorded almost complete social equality for the first time . . . and letters to America were full of his emancipation among the native whites." In the Pacific, one black former pilot recalled fighting side by side with soldiers from Fiji, India, New Zealand, and Australia, and playing amiable poker games and volleyball matches with them behind the lines.[123] And in Australia—a settler-colonial "white man's country"—African American troops received a surprisingly warm welcome. A white American officer there observed that "the Australians accepted them [black GIs] enthusiastically, invited them into their homes, dated them publicly."[124] Black Americans agreed. In letters home, they raved about being "treated with as much respect, if not more respect" than "the white soldiers" and of Australians being "the most hospitable people in the world." "You hear all kinds of stories about Australians not liking blacks, but the citizens were cordial," recalled one member of a black quartermaster unit. "They received us with open arms. The people in Melbourne had Sunday teas in their homes and churches and would invite the black troops, and we went."[125]

In all these places, relations were never universally good. Sometimes they started well and deteriorated over time or were friendlier among some subset of the population—say, the working class or city folk—than others. Even when friendly, relations might have stemmed not from a high-minded commitment to antiracism or from sincere feelings of respect and love, but from black Americans' status as liberators or as conquerors or as well-paid Yankees or as temporary visitors or as service troops with easy access to coveted commodities like Spam, chocolate, nylon stockings, and cigarettes. Many whites in war-torn parts of the world were in desperate straits, and they knew that African Americans were in a position to help them; if treated kindly, the "Tan Yanks" perhaps would.

Even after granting these important caveats, this much is undeniable: from England to Australia, some African American troops—it is impossible to know how many exactly—still forged real attachments, friendships, and romances with whites. In the context of wartime Jim Crow America, these were, as many white Americans rightly appreciated, revolutionary acts of a sort. By transgressing the black-white divide, they fundamentally challenged its solidity, inevitability, naturalness, and wisdom. In the words of one black Red Cross worker in London, they "proved beyond the shadow of a doubt that it is possible for people of different shades of skin to live side by side in peace and harmony." Having served in a port battalion in Europe during the war, future civil rights leader Medgar Evers came to an identical conclusion. According to his brother, it was the act of "going with this French girl [that] made Medgar even more sure the racism we'd grown up with in Mississippi was unnatural and could be changed. It convinced him black and white could live in peace."[126]

"There Are No Color Lines in Fox Holes"

African Americans' experiences in and around battlefronts occasionally taught the same lesson. In the summer and fall of 1943, black reporters' dispatches from North Africa and Italy seem to have introduced an idea that reached near-cliché status by war's end: "there are no color lines in fox holes." Writing from Sicily in August, black war correspondent Ollie Stewart reflected on his first year overseas: "The common danger, the common foe and the hardship of battle are bringing American troops closer together." "Technically our army is separated by racial lines," he elaborated, "but actually every man in uniform has been brought together by our job. There are no color lines in fox holes or when a landing barge is being strafed or when a convoy is dive bombed. I have seen colored and white who glared at each other before a bombing get quite chummy after death whistled by in big hunks of shrapnel. . . . Men who had never eaten, slept or drunk with a different race now share the same bottle of wine, use fingers in the same rations and bunk in the same ditch or tent."[127]

Other accounts from the North African and Italian fronts shared Stewart's views. Two months later a front-page story in the *Baltimore Afro-American* reported that "colored troops are actually fighting side by side with troops of other races" in the Mediterranean theater and with great effect. "Authoritative sources" from the field (who, in truth, might have included Stewart himself) paid "tribute to the 'rank and file' soldier in this man's army. He is the chap really worth writing about. He doesn't give a damn what color his helpmate is. He has a feeling that there is a war to be fought and it takes all the races to get it over with. If he had any prejudice when he came over, it vanished with the exploding of the first bomb." NAACP leader Walter White told a similar story. Traveling as a war correspondent in North Africa and Italy for the *New York Post*, he wrote in March 1944 about American troops in and around Anzio: "Landings from and embarkations on the LSTs [landing ship, tank or, according to some sailors, 'large slow target'] at the beach under a virtually unbroken rain of German shellfire have to be made at such speed that no one has time to scrutinize his neighbor's face to tell whether he is white or Negro. No one cares." In January 1945, Roi Ottley published a story entitled "There's No Race Problem in the Foxholes." In Italy, where a "Negro outfit . . . holds down one wing of the front," white comrades "respected them" and "seemed to sense that equality of peril deserves equality of treatment and recreation. This feeling has been translated into a fraternizing between the races which will certainly carry over into civilian life." The following month, Sergeant Maurice Walker of the Ninety-Second Infantry Division in Italy put it most succinctly: "The front is a great leveling force."[128]

In his piece, Ottley contrasted the Italian front with the western one, where "the Negro soldier is doing little more than service work" and where, as a result, the black-white "barriers hold." But, in fact, exceptions appeared there, too, as more African Americans came to see combat toward war's end. On D-Day, the 320th Barrage Balloon Battalion was the only black combat outfit to land on the blood-stained beaches of Normandy. As medics, its members worked under incessant fire, while often nursing their own life-threatening injuries, to drag wounded men to safety, to extract bullets from bodies, to treat wounds, to amputate those limbs and feet too far gone to save, and to administer blood transfusions. "At that time," Waverly "Woody" Woodson, a member of the unit, later remembered, "they didn't care what color my skin was." Two months later, the white colonel of a white armored combat team made up of men from "Mississippi and the deep south" made a similar observation. "During a recent engagement a Quartermaster Truck Unit colored was attached" to his unit, and "the conduct of these colored men under fire was such that the best of comradeship developed." The same emerged when a black tank outfit joined General Patton's Third Army in France around the same time and performed bravely. Decades later, one member of the former unit stressed that, after the first few days of serving alongside whites, "there was no prejudice, because you don't have time for prejudice in a foxhole." At the time, black GI and *California Eagle* correspondent John Kinloch quoted a "tall weather-worn [white] Texan, dirt streaked across the red lines in his face": "Mighty proud of them colored boys in the tank outfit, mighty proud of 'em." "Good relations out here come the hard way," Kinloch concluded. "And they stick."[129]

The best-known example of these "good relations" came several months later, in early 1945. Facing a serious, months-long shortage of riflemen in the European theater and especially in the wake of the bloody Battle of the Bulge, the army, at long last, experimented with mixed outfits, which had become an increasingly popular demand among black people and some whites on the home front. The army retrained roughly twenty-five hundred black service troops who had volunteered for combat duty (forfeiting their stripes to do so); it reassigned them to fifty or so rifle platoons whose enlisted personnel were solely black and had them serve alongside whites in integrated companies in France and Germany.[130] The plan, first proposed by Lieutenant General John C. H. Lee, was an enormous success. "[S]ome of our commanders," Eisenhower later recalled, ". . . strongly objected [to the integration plan] on the grounds that some of our units were from the South and trouble would result. Our experience was just the opposite. There was not a single objection brought to my attention. On the contrary from all sides came heart-warming reports of the success of the experiment." A *Yank* article from February 1945 confirmed Ike's memory. "Hitler would have a hemorrhage," correspondent Ralph Martin wrote, "if he could see the white boys . . . bull-sessioning, going out on mixed patrols, sleeping in the same bombed building, sweating out the same chow line with Negro GIs." "When you're under battle conditions, and it's a toss up whose neck is next," he concluded, "there isn't any worrying about the differences in the color of your skin." Shortly after the war, a black member of one of these mixed companies summed up the matter well: "The white fellows treated us like brothers."[131]

In fact, the army, parts of which were finally considering integration as a postwar possibility, studied these units carefully (albeit from whites' perspective alone) and arrived at the same conclusions. In late May and early June 1945, it interviewed and surveyed nearly two thousand of the white officers and white enlisted men who served with black soldiers. Many of them, while at first harboring serious reservations about integrated companies, commended black troops as excellent soldiers and friendly comrades in arms. "Relations are very good," one company commander reported. "They have their pictures taken together, go to church services, movies, play ball together. For a time there in combat our platoons got so small that we had to put a white squad in the colored platoon. You might think that wouldn't work well, but it did. The white squad didn't want to leave the platoon. I've never seen anything like it." A platoon leader offered a similar response: "Got along fine in combat—teamwork couldn't have been better. A lot of the boys from the South didn't like the idea at first, but a few days fighting along with them changed their minds. Since we've been out of combat we haven't had any trouble and don't expect any."[132] Fearful that this evidence of black-white comradeship would only increase pressure

Fig. 8.4 Bound for the invasion of southern France, an interracial group of soldiers and sailors attend a religious service on the ship's deck, August 1944. Courtesy National Archives, SC-192720.

on it to mix more outfits or alienate southern Democrats or both, the army promptly buried the study for four months. Indeed, the delay would have been longer had Truman Gibson not left the study "probably accidentally" out where someone "grab[bed] a copy and release[d] it."[133]

In certain cases, this black-white comradeship outlasted combat, demonstrating that at times it could survive the potential "interracial" tensions of garrison life. Two months after one mixed outfit's fighting ended, its commander observed, "To date, there has never appeared the slightest sign of race prejudice, or discrimination in this organization. White men and colored men are welded together with a deep friendship and respect born of combat and matured by a realization that such an association is not the impossibility that many of us have been led to believe."[134]

This friendship and respect cropped up occasionally in fighting in the Pacific as well. In the summer of 1943, a Red Cross worker wrote home about an unusual sight on a hospital train in Australia: "Negro and white wounded together in the same trains, playing cards together, and on one bunk a white boy from Alabama—his accent so thick you could photograph it—and a colored soldier from Jersey. When men have been through war together their whole prejudices seem to vanish and it's as if they never existed." Fletcher Martin, a black war correspondent in the Southwest Pacific for two years, agreed. Back home, in March 1945, he told an Ohio audience that "at the front there is no discrimination; white and colored work together against the enemy." Martin may have been referring in part to a story he reported several months earlier about Private Ralph Hueca from Chicago, who "became the first colored unofficial member" of the Twenty-Fourth Infantry Division. During the battle to wrest control of the Philippines from the Japanese, members of the white unit passed Hueca, a truck driver, and one called out: "Hey fellow, you want to fight?" Indeed he did. According to Martin, he made his new comrades proud by fighting shoulder to shoulder with them, manning a machine gun "in the midst of three enemy banzai attacks, taking it over after four gunners had been bayonetted to death." Later, the outfit's commanding officer said he "wished he [Hueca] could remain with the unit."[135]

As Ottley predicted, all these instances of black-white comradeship involved combat—the stresses, dangers, and camaraderie distinctive to foxholes and front lines. Every so often it emerged behind these lines, too. In France, in the wake of the Normandy landings, the ceaseless work of building roads, laying communication wires, and shuttling supplies and equipment seemed to bring some white and black troops together—indeed, sometimes into the very same units. Among one such "mixed team," the men ate lunch "together full of geniality, good humor, conversation, and cheerfulness of nature."[136] A member of the famed Tuskegee Airmen told an interviewer in the early 1970s about "one incident I shall always remember [that] occurred in Italy while we were at Ramitelli."

> A white bomber squadron landed at our field because of weather conditions. They remained with us two or three days. Of necessity they had to eat with us, sleep with us, and a lot of guys gave up their beds and slept on pallets on the floor; they were our guests. We talked together, played cards together, had bull sessions together, did all of those things normally done by pilots and crews when they are socked in. . . . There were some good friendships developed in those few days. Some of the guys actually had tears in their eyes as they bid us goodbye. It was a good social experience. It stands out in my mind even today because it took an act of God, bad weather, to integrate the black and white air force for a few days.

From the Burma jungles in July 1944, four white soldiers wrote the army weekly *Yank* to commend "the many Negro outfits working with us." "They are doing more than their part to win this war," insisted the men. "We are proud of the colored men here. When we are away from camp working in the jungles, we can go to any colored camp and be treated like one of their own." And from an island in the South Pacific, one white private reported bonding among the black and white soldiers who worked at a post exchange: "We played tennis together, went to the movies together, ate meals together, and did everything except bunk together." "In the close association of the troops on the island," the man reported, "jim crow couldn't exist."[137]

These uplifting stories should be approached cautiously. Sometimes black-white comradeship had its spatial limits. As one black correspondent writing from Genoa put it, "Intolerances, which are seldom evident in the forward battle zones . . . have a way of creeping up in the rear zones where recreation, fraternization, and social mingling is the prime order of business." Sometimes its limits were, relatedly, temporal, lasting only as long as battles did. "Take D-days," wrote one black GI in his diary sometime in early 1945. "Everybody is buddies and everybody talk to you. If you don't have a fox hole in a raid maybe a white fellow call you to come get in his hole. That lasts like that during combat until the island start getting secure. Then it all change. A colored fellow can't get a lift in a jeep and six steps further on they pick up a couple of white fellows. Also colored man can't use the white man's latrine at the base. They gotta dig their own."[138] But most important, foxhole fraternalism's limits were structural. The War and Navy Departments committed few black GIs to combat and even fewer to the integrated kind. This meant that they effectively and systemically robbed hundreds of thousands of black troops of the opportunity, dangerous and miserable as it was, to sit in a foxhole, let alone to experience some of the boundary-blurring comradeship that sometimes accompanied it. Of course, millions of nonblacks, whites included, lost out as well.

Even so, for a small but important segment of black GIs, they either fought long enough on battlefronts to witness its leveling powers, or they experienced those seemingly rare moments when it cropped up behind the lines, too. On those occasions, the indelible black-white divide dissolved some, just as it did when black troops consorted and cavorted with friendly overseas locals. On those occasions, the *Chicago Defender*, while still guilty of wishful thinking, had a point: "In the brotherhood of battle . . . [i]n the common elementary struggle for life itself in the face of a ruthless foe, Jim Crow is a war casualty."[139]

Combating Jim Crow

To the extent Jim Crow was a casualty at all, however, black troops' and their allies' activism also had something to do with it. Despite facing even greater obstacles overseas, protest traveled there, too. It did not do so simply as a set of activist emotions, ideas, and practices brought from home, like so many olive-drab duffel bags. Protest was also a shrewd and courageous response to old and new conditions—the "changing same" of Jim Crow abroad.[140] In the end, despite the considerable power differentials between black GIs and their white commanders, the former—with the ongoing help of a diverse supporting cast, which sometimes expanded overseas to include ordinary locals—managed to wring concessions out of the latter. In the process, they blurred an admittedly small but nonetheless significant set of overseas black-white lines. If not killed in action, Jim Crow in uniform was at least moderately wounded.

Black GI activism faced many of the same hurdles that it did in the United States; those abroad simply tended to be higher and harder to clear. Deep dejection, for example, certainly evident on the home front, was often worse and more common overseas. In numerous military intelligence reports on black American troops, white and black officers alike reported dangerously low levels of morale and the "common belief among colored troops that they were fighting this war for nothing," that this was a "white man's war" or "Mr. Charlie's war."[141] In July 1945, one black warrant officer noted that the men in his quartermaster unit, which had been sent all over Europe often with little serious work to do, began calling itself the "Gypsy

Battalion" and developed a "defeatist attitude" and "subzero" morale. A few months earlier, a black chaplain confessed to an army intelligence officer, "It would make me happy to report that, in small part through my efforts, morale of the negro soldiers in those battalions with whom I served in the ETO [European Theater of Operations] had been superior. . . . It is my unhappy burden to report that matters have gone beyond anything that I could do."[142]

Sometimes the tandem traumas of war and racism exacted an even more serious mental and emotional price. Many psychological studies from the war years suffer from racist assumptions about the "negroid personality," from white psychiatrists' racist diagnoses, from the military's more general habit of maligning black troops, and even from some black servicemen's attempts to malinger. But their findings are worth considering, especially if viewed within the context of the military's myriad black-white lines.[143] A study of US Army hospitals on a Pacific island found black troops' rates of psychoneuroses and psychoses three to five times higher than those among white troops. Another, much larger study on the "ineffective soldier" and his "breakdown and recovery" featured several examples of black soldiers whose problems stemmed from their encounters with Jim Crow in uniform. In one case, JGS, a young, healthy, bright, junior college graduate from the Northeast, began developing "psychiatric symptoms" such as "nausea, headaches, tenseness, and stuttering" soon after joining the army, training in the South, and resisting its discriminatory policies. His condition only worsened when, shipped to North Africa and then Italy, he faced belligerent white GIs and white officers "who seemed to hate [black people] . . . more than the enemy." His stuttering grew so bad at times that he was unable to speak and was eventually hospitalized for a month in Italy and then again, at war's end, in the United States.[144]

Military repression, so expansive at home, also tended to be more severe overseas, mainly because black GIs there were subject to even greater forms of surveillance and were farther removed from their allies and, thus, more vulnerable to their commanders' repressive whims. These officers held near-total disciplinary authority over the black troops in their command, which many willingly wielded to stamp out even the most moderate forms of protest. In September 1942 in Trinidad, the commanding officer of the navy's Eightieth Construction Battalion invited a small group of black enlisted personnel to his office for "a little informal, off-the-record, get-together" to allow the men to "speak right up and get off what's on your chest." When the men were asked pointedly about "the racial situation on our base here," they shared their honest concerns about barriers to promotion and segregation. Afterward, the commander seemed appreciative, but the following day his superior "bawled" them out for "their petty complaints." "A few days later," one of the men recalled, "nineteen of us were dismissed from the service with discharges that read 'UNDESIRABLE by reason of UNFITNESS' and 'ORDINARY by reason of INAPTITUDE.' No charges. No trial. No court-martial. Just dismissal."[145] In other instances, so-called troublemakers were transferred to other units, sent to die on the front lines, demoted, court-martialed, and imprisoned. Wherever he traveled overseas—from Europe and North Africa to Asia and the Pacific—Walter White reported on white commanders abusing their authority in order to silence legitimate complaints about military Jim Crow.[146]

Despite these considerable obstacles, however, black troops' overseas lives could also facilitate protest. Some factors—like a more salient masculinism among servicemen, greater unity among black GIs, and the glaring disconnect between America's war rhetoric and its racist realities—also appeared at home. Others were more particular to serving abroad.[147] One involved how travel overseas exposed black troops to broad political solidarities—as, say, oppressed or colored peoples—and to broader political possibilities. In her survey of hundreds of black GIs' letters, *Pittsburgh Courier* columnist Marjorie McKenzie glimpsed men who were both "exhilarated by the freedom, respect and fair treatment that they have experienced abroad" and "militant and courageous in their demands and in the language they use to express themselves"; "[t]hey say they will not go back to the old ways." One black veteran recalled that when he first entered the service, he accepted racism as "just the way it was supposed to be." Wartime service in the Pacific changed all that: "It started coming to me after we got to Australia. I noticed the difference right then. The Australians called us the 'tan Yanks,' not niggers and monkeys. . . . There was nothing but white people [in Australia], but you was welcome. . . . It opened up a new world to me, opened up [my eyes] to the racial problems."[148]

The act of putting one's life on the line for the nation and seeing others do the same, some dying in the process, also inspired African American GIs to protest. On the home front, some black people had resolved to die in the United States, rather than overseas, in defense of democracy. Abroad, many black troops became ever more determined to gain some of those freedoms for which they and their buddies were supposedly risking and sacrificing their lives. Writing from Sicily, Ollie Stewart observed, "Our men talk of concrete thing[s] like homes with good plumbing, steady jobs, good schools, clean government with opportunity for all. In my travels . . . I find that colored soldiers expect to share these same rewards of victory in the same way they have shared the danger from the German ME-198's and eighty-eight millimeter guns." Having survived his first night in combat in the Pacific, one black infantryman put it more bluntly: "I ain't gonna take no shit off nobody from now on." "In a thousand subtle ways, in a thousand brutal ways, we were taught that we were not a part of American culture and history." But, he declared, "we were *making* history. . . . This was the ramrod that straightened the shoulders and lifted higher the heads of the young Negroes who made up the ranks of infantrymen in the Ninety-third Division." While hospitalized in New Orleans in 1945, a black army chaplain expressed a similar feeling to a white colonel: "The negroes with whom I served [in Europe] . . . have confessed to me matters that they would never breathe to you." "[M]y companions in arms," he continued, ". . . have pointed out to me that they are proudly and lawfully wearing the uniform of the United States Government and feel that they are entitled to the same treatment as other folks. . . . [T]he negro soldier . . . [has a] deep brooding in his heart and a dark smoldering resolve to start a new struggle, however hopeless, for the privileges that constitute his birthright."[149]

Drawing on these new and old motivations, black GIs' overseas activism was, as on the home front, extraordinarily varied. It took the form of strikes and sit-ins, boycotts and armed resistance, letter writing and desertion, splendid soldiering and infrapolitical goldbricking. It relied on a similar network of supporters, including the NAACP, the black and left-wing press, the few African Americans with any authority or influence in the military, loved ones at home, and so forth. But some overseas locals and local organizations, especially in Great Britain, also occasionally proved helpful. In the end, black GI activism had its modest but important impact on black-white lines.

Consider the nineteen members of the navy's Eightieth Construction Battalion who were summarily discharged for airing their objections to military Jim Crow in a meeting with their commanding officer. What preceded and followed this meeting speaks to some of the breadth and importance of GIs' and their allies' protest. Naval officers convened the fateful meeting in the first place because black Seabees had been chafing at their outfit's black-white lines for quite a while and sometimes succeeding in blurring them. On their trip to Trinidad, they complained to their commanding officer about a string that ran the width of the transport's deck, dividing white and colored space. Soon, after a protest and a "heated argument," it was taken down. Upon arrival in Trinidad to build an airfield, they opposed a lunchtime policy that allowed whites to eat first and required black people "to stand in line during the entire lunch hour, never having a chance to rest." The latter responded by boycotting the whole arrangement and refusing to eat. Soon they were granted a separate-but-equal accommodation, as segregated chow lines were introduced. Finally, when a ship's service store was built, it too had separate lines for black and white Seabees, which, "according to the battalion commander . . . was done as a 'favor' to the Negroes to speed up sales."[150] Again, blacks boycotted, opting to patronize the stores at a nearby air station and army post exchange instead, neither of which were segregated. Soon the navy store's lines were integrated. With this background in mind, it appears that the discharges had less to do with the meeting in question than with the black Seabees' long-running activism and their white officers' efforts to stamp it out.

The officers surely got more than they bargained for, because the discharged Seabees refused to go quietly, continuing and broadening their activism beyond their outfit. The men, especially Isaac G. McNatt, who would become a successful attorney and the first black city council member in Teaneck, New Jersey, worked hard to make their case before the American public. Over the course of more than a year, in late 1943 and 1944, they wrote newspaper and magazine articles, spoke on the radio, and enlisted the support of the black and liberal white press and of several civil rights and Left organizations, among them the NAACP, the Lynn Committee to Abolish Segregation in the Armed Forces, the American Civil Liberties Union, and the National Congress of Industrial Organizations War Relief Committee. Thanks to this support, they managed to get many of their former white officers and chiefs in the Eightieth Construction Battalion replaced. In December 1944, furthermore, they gained a hearing before the Navy's Board of Reviews, Discharges, and Dismissals. Represented by several prominent attorneys, including future Supreme Court Justice Thurgood Marshall, fourteen of the men had their discharges changed from "undesirable" to "honorable," which, among other things, offered them full access to the recently passed GI Bill. But in McNatt's words, their struggle was always "bigger than what happened to me and the other Seabees. . . . [Our] case has been decided in our favor, but I think that the fight has just begun. It will not end until Jimcrow conditions are abolished forever in our Army and Navy."[151]

These Seabees were not alone in their sometimes successful battles against those conditions. Overseas, from Corsica and England to the Philippines and Australia, black troops entered whites-only towns, attended whites-only parties, visited whites-only Red Cross clubs, lindy-hopped at whites-only dances, and bathed in whites-only officers' quarters.[152] Sometimes these actions—sit-ins, dance-ins, bathe-ins, and the like—forced whites to integrate these spaces; other times they were closed down altogether. In Oran on the Algerian coast, the American army officers' club there barred black men from dancing with white women. When a group of black officers disregarded the rule, the band stopped playing and all dances were canceled for a month, until the offending men shipped out. Sometimes African Americans, as in Trinidad, struck back against segregated spaces by boycotting them. In Cherbourg, France, in October 1944, when army officials designated one pub for white people and another for black people, the ten thousand African American GIs in the area—"to a man," according to one war correspondent—refused to patronize their Jim Crow pub. The segregation order was lifted a week later. Sometimes black troops opted instead to destroy these spaces. One African American veteran recalled fellow black GIs torching a "Jim Crow whorehouse" in Manila in 1945.[153]

Black GI activism paid dividends beyond segregated space alone. Black troops' armed and unarmed resistance to military police abuse often led to courts-martial, but it also convinced the army to assign more black MPs to black units.[154] When a port battalion in England refused to turn out at reveille to protest its officers' mistreatment of them, the theater command resolved not only to find and punish "the ring leaders of this mutiny," but also to replace the unit's leadership.[155] Or take the overseas experiences of Winfred Lynn, who continued his attacks on military Jim Crow long after his refusal to be drafted into a segregated outfit in 1942. Two years later, he served in a medical sanitary company in the Pacific. When a white officer ordered members of his unit to dig latrines for a white unit nearby, the men, Lynn included, said no. "Now we didn't have a latrine for ourselves," recalled Lynn, "and the boys couldn't see . . . digging a latrine for a white company, or any other company for that matter." Their commanding officer threatened to charge them with mutiny, but the men refused to back down, eventually prevailing: "We did not dig the latrine and we did not have any trouble."[156]

At times, this overseas activism also succeeded, as on the home front, in convincing at least some white officers to question their most basic assumptions about the military's black-white lines. In November 1944, a white navy officer, back from a six-months-long tour in the Pacific, noticed that when black sailors' commanders truly respected them and looked out for their welfare, they excelled. But "whenever any policy of segregation or discrimination existed, the men had a poor reputation. There were many cases where they refused to work, were insubordinate, and generally negligent in matters of cleanliness, discipline, and courtesy. To many white officers it appears that the most logical solution toward preventing racial difficulties is to keep white and colored separate. It has been proven to me that this only increases the chances for such difficulties."[157] That this was related by a navy officer perhaps makes sense, given that that service, more so than the army, increasingly experimented with integration by the war's final year. But army officers occasionally made similar arguments. In reviewing the Fifth Army's evolving wartime race policies in Europe, its commanding general found that integrated rest camps and recreational facilities reduced, rather than fomented, conflict between white and black troops.[158]

As the Seabees' story suggests, GI activism could also be a team effort. While black troops tirelessly protested the army's promotion policies, it seems to have been Brigadier General Benjamin O. Davis's actions that proved most decisive in opening the doors of Europe's OCS to them. Similarly, while numerous black officers in the Ninety-Second Infantry Division had long opposed segregated spaces, both on the home front and abroad, Truman Gibson may have been most influential at eliminating, albeit late in the war, the "color bar in any [of the division's] clubs, messes, rest centers, recreation facilities."[159] When it came to courts-martial, sometimes the spirited campaign of US-based civil rights activists or US politicians or overseas locals made the difference. In the rape case of Leroy Henry in England, for example, Britons' letters, editorials, and petitions on his behalf mobilized supporters on both sides of the Atlantic, eventually convincing General Eisenhower to vacate his death sentence and set him free.[160] Occasionally even white military personnel joined or led efforts to dismantle Jim Crow abroad. On an island in the Pacific, where white and black soldiers had worked together and had become unusually chummy, a southern white staff sergeant attempted to segregate tables at the mess hall, but to no avail. "The [white] guys from New York and Jersey, and, Hell, yes, even the guys from Texas and Alabama, shouted this moron down," reported one white private. "Jim Crow died a sudden death in that mess hall."[161]

Unlike reforms in the case of, say, enlistment, these scattered changes overseas did not result from activists' successful efforts to lobby the White House. Indeed, the few times President Roosevelt seemed even moderately engaged with military Jim Crow abroad, he was much more likely to prop it up than to tear it down. In response to a March 1945 wide-ranging memorandum from Walter White alleging numerous forms of discrimination in the Ninety-Third Infantry Division, Roosevelt sided with General Douglas MacArthur. "He is in no way prejudiced . . . by reason of race or color," he assured White. "[T]he discriminatory procedures which were reported to you . . . are without basis in fact."[162] In contrast, the War and Navy Departments occasionally helped blur black-white lines, especially, from time to time, in response to the urgent insistence of the few black advisers or high-ranking black officers, such as Truman Gibson and Benjamin Davis. But it was overseas commanders—of everything from theaters down to battalions—who often had the most authority over the US military's "race" policies and practices abroad. If they often used it to draw and fortify lines, some improvised in more egalitarian directions. In those instances where Jim Crow died at the Pacific mess hall, or the Cherbourg bar, or the Trinidad ship's store, it was local commanders, responding to the activists' pressures bubbling up from below, who served as the executioners.

* * *

At war's end, US troops journeying home were reminded once more of the war's muddled, ambiguous lessons—its bright and blurred black-white lines. On crowded transport ships crossing the Atlantic and the Pacific, some black GIs returned elbow to elbow with white comrades in arms, seeming to herald a new day for American race relations. In August 1945, the *Chicago Defender* featured a photo of black and white soldiers and the headline: "No Jim Crow on Homeward Voyage." Touting the long-term effects of foxhole fraternalism, the caption read, "There's no Jim Crow in the hold of this crowded Liberty ship homeward bound from Naples, Italy. These GIs have learned that there's no Jim Crow in foxholes and they are keeping up the inter-racial policy on their way back to the States—jammed together but happy to be on their way home."[163]

But other black servicemen and -women discovered that the Jim Crow that hounded them at home and followed them overseas also accompanied them on their return voyages to the United States. Four months later, the same newspaper ran another story about returning GIs, but this time the headline read, "White Face Passport to Come Home." It noted that navy commanders refused to allow 123 black GIs to board an escort carrier, the USS *Croatan*, in France, because the ship provided "no facilities to Jim Crow them" and because navy policy explicitly opposed "mix[ing] races." Despite protest both in Europe and in the United States—picketers met the *Croatan* as it docked in New York with signs that read, "Negroes on the Fighting Line. Why Not on the Croatan?" and "Jim Crow is Treason, Court-Martial Navy Officers"—the 123 men boarded another, slower, presumably segregated vessel for the trip home. Like the integrated one from Naples, it too was called a Liberty ship.[164]

In many ways, these mixed messages about black-white lines were simply the latest chapter in a longer story about the call and response of anti-black racism and resistance in the wartime US military. But there was greater blurring of black-white lines overseas. This in turn further convinced a good many white Americans to redouble their efforts to shore those lines up, which in turn further induced black people and their allies to push in the opposite direction, and so on.

In these cyclical battles, both sides returned home itching to fight on. Black troops were more determined than ever to finish Jim Crow off once and for all and, in the process, to make the Allies' stated war aims about freedom and democracy a postwar reality. "Everywhere I traveled in France, England, Italy and North Africa," Roi Ottley observed, "the [Negro] soldier was saying: 'I'm going to get some of that Freedom they are talking about when I get home.'" Writing from the Pacific, Winfred Lynn noted, "The boys that I have met aren't going to take as much as they did before when they get back to the states. At least this is something that this war has created."[165] Thanks to their overseas experiences, growing numbers of white troops seemed ready to join African Americans in these struggles. In the final months of the war, numerous black and white observers, from newspapers and magazines to officers and enlisted personnel, thought so. They argued that, in the words of one black sergeant in Italy, "the white American soldier has learned what artificial barriers of any sort mean and will be just as determined as the colored soldier to do away with them later." As one white lieutenant colonel put it, "From every continent and sea are returning the thousands of Southern white officers who have developed a solid respect for their Negro troops and are determined that henceforth these must receive in our country the rights, privileges and opportunities which they have helped to preserve for the rest of us." The *Chicago Defender* insisted, "The ten million white servicemen who are fighting alongside them are learning about Negroes for perhaps the first time in their lives and changing their minds about white supremacy. They can be the foundation of a new, really democratic America on their return home."[166]

"Can be" was the appropriate hedge, however, because other whites journeyed back to the United States with very different ideas, indeed. Some looked forward to a few "mass lynchings" to remind returning black service members of their "proper" place in America. One white sergeant, back home after serving for two years in Africa, Corsica, and Sardinia, told a military intelligence official that "almost all the [white] soldiers with whom he discussed the racial problem thought that there would be race riots in the United States after the war. He remarked that about nine out of every ten [white] soldiers with whom he talked on the boat returning to the United States said that they would welcome a racial clash due to their bitter feelings toward the negro."[167]

In the end, as the war drew to a close and millions of servicemen and -women came home, the future of the US military's black-white lines was anybody's guess. In the fall of 1944, a Red Cross official felt comfortable hazarding at least this much of a prediction: "[T]he members of the Armed Forces will enjoy tremendous prestige in their respective communities when they return,

therefore, the position they take on any public matter, including relations between the races, conceivably may determine whether peace and harmony or
conflict and strife shall prevail."[168] If the war showed anything, however, it
was not only that these GIs were an extraordinarily diverse lot but that, as
a result, it was hard to know what would prevail in the postwar years. It also
showed that "relations between the races" involved more than black and white
people and that any postwar prognosis would have to make room for nonblack
minorities like Japanese Americans and Chinese Americans, American Indians
and Puerto Ricans, Mexican Americans and Filipinos.

CHAPTER 9

✧

Brothers in Arms?

During the last year or so of the war, a curious subgenre of newspaper and magazine articles popped up in the United States. They celebrated the role that some of America's nonblack minority troops played on war fronts around the world, highlighting their manly heroism under fire and the "glowing comradeship" that bonded "white," on the one hand, with "red," "brown," and "yellow," on the other.[1] At the same time, they dwelled on distinctions between the two. Japanese American soldiers, for example, were not your run-of-the-mill doughboys, but "G.I. Japyanks," "Jap Americans," or "American Japs," whose friendships with white comrades constituted an act of "international understanding."[2] Similarly, an American Indian GI was not a "fighting Yank," but his best buddy, who "will risk his life for a white as dauntlessly as his ancestors lifted a paleface's scalp," who has a "special Indian quality [of] . . . imperturbability," and who "in thousands of Army psychiatric tests of men of all races [has] show[n] . . . the greatest resistance to mental strain."[3]

These portraits often came from civilian publications on the home front, but they accurately reflected the mixed messages that nonblack minority troops received overseas. As at training camps in the United States, they faced both bright and blurry white-nonwhite lines when deployed abroad. At times, the US military, from its civilian leaders to its enlisted ranks, remained determined to uphold distinctions between whites, on the one hand, and Asian Americans, Latin Americans, and Native Americans, on the other. This determination, evident in everything from military justice proceedings to military promotion patterns, stemmed primarily from long-standing civilian investments in these distinctions, which had deeply informed US immigration, colonial, and other policy for decades. It also emerged in response to the vicious race war in the Pacific and the virulent hatred the conflict engendered for America's archenemy there, Japan.

At the same time, overseas service also witnessed the continued blurring of white-nonwhite lines—the transformation of "Mexicans," "Puerto Ricans," "Indians," "Filipinos," "Chinese," and even "Japanese" into whites' buddies and brothers, comrades and fellow Americans. This process had begun on the home front but in many cases expanded and deepened abroad. While the overseas blurring often emanated, as it sometimes did with African Americans, from day-to-day battlefield bonding, it was America's military leaders and commanders who largely made it possible. In contrast to their treatment of black troops, they mixed nonblack minority service members much more closely and regularly with whites, committed far greater proportions of them to combat, and, in some cases, tirelessly celebrated their fighting performance. In doing so, they narrowed the white-nonwhite divide—but also deepened the black-white one in the process.

"NOT ONE WAR; TWO"

Like black-white lines, white-nonwhite ones also traversed the globe alongside the US military. For some troops, they appeared in the form of barriers to combat. In the case of Puerto Rican recruits from the island, for example, the War Department's local officials thought they were "not generally suited for front line duty" because of "lower educational and physical standards, racial and historical traditions and background, aptitude, etc." As a consequence, some all–Puerto Rican outfits, even supposedly combat ones like the Sixty-Fifth Infantry Regiment, were confined to "police duty in the Caribbean" for most of the war, much to the chagrin of many of the island's leaders, people, press, and even some of the troops themselves.[4]

In other cases, the white-nonwhite line appeared as too much "frontline duty," not too little. Consider, in the most obvious example, Japanese Americans. In Italy and France, receiving one harrowing combat assignment after another, some Nisei GIs—and their friends and family back home—came to wonder whether the army gave them "the suicide missions and blood baths as a matter of policy, to shield the white troops." In letters to their loved ones in uniform in Europe, Japanese Americans in Hawaii protested, writing, for example, "God will punish those who misuse human lives; lives are supposed to be saved; not put into unnecessary target of danger," and "The 100th Infantry boys have had more bullets whistling

around their ears, more artillery pounded on them than any [other] U.S. soldier."[5] Sitting in a foxhole one autumn day in the Vosges Mountains of
eastern France, amid the heroic, if deadly, rescue of a "lost" army battalion
from Texas, a 442nd private recalled thinking, "Are we being used? Are we
expendable goods? Are we cannon fodder?" The War Department's response
was that "the best troops are called upon to do the hardest fighting," but
the private's questions linger. According to one count, Japanese American
troops sustained 800 casualties to save 211 men from the white outfit; another count offered an even grimmer ratio: 189 rescued Texans in exchange
for more than 200 Nisei killed. Given these numbers, historian Takahashi
Fujitani has a point: "[This] particularly costly mission . . . undoubtedly
reveals as much about the low regard in which some high-ranking white
officers held the lives of Japanese Americans as it does about the latter's
heroism."[6]

That these officers, among others, remained virtually all white reveals
that white-nonwhite lines regarding rank and commissions, so prevalent in the United States, also ventured overseas. In the case of Japanese
Americans, the restrictions against their commissions or against their advancement softened some over time, especially in Europe, thanks in part
to battlefield successes. For example, Mitsuyoshi Fukuda steadily rose in

Fig. 9.1 Boy scouts at the Granada Relocation Center in Colorado hoist a flag to half-staff
at a memorial service for the first six Japanese American soldiers from the center killed in
action in Italy, August 5, 1944. Courtesy of The Bancroft Library, University of California,
Berkeley, WRA no. G-769.

the ranks from a second lieutenant to a captain and eventually to a major, becoming in the summer of 1945 "the first American of Japanese ancestry to command an infantry battalion in the history of the United States Army."[7] But he was an exception. One Japanese American linguist in the Pacific offered a more accurate description of his and his Nisei comrades' prospects for advancement: "When we go to the front, they [whites] become team leaders; we be the workers."[8] Indeed, by the end of the war, even though many Nisei soldiers had been overseas for more than a year, revealing regularly the "qualifications and trustworthiness which would be rewarded by commissioning were they of other than Japanese blood," their total number of officers remained paltry. By this point, while roughly 11 percent of white male army personnel were officers, less than 1 percent of Japanese Americans were the same.[9]

Other nonblack minorities faced similar rank-related barriers. Some Navajo Code Talkers resented the fact that, despite their vital overseas service, "hardly anyone got beyond" the rank of private or private first class. Similarly, some Mexican Americans wondered, as paratrooper Darío Villegas did, why "the majority of the Mexican people were privates up to maybe, staff sergeants (E-6) . . . and that's about it." Or consider the case of Filipino guerrilla units, which operated under the (sometimes nominal) control of the US Army Forces Far East and which emerged in the Philippines shortly after Japan's conquest there in early 1942. Some of these units, according to historian Christopher Capozzola, "operated on a colonial model, with strict control by white officers and subservient service by Filipino troops, along with an understanding that liberating US territory from Japanese control was an American colonial obligation, not a step toward Philippine national self-determination."[10]

Occasionally, nonblack minorities also faced white-nonwhite lines in the form of social exclusions of various sorts. Some Native Americans felt lonely and isolated in white outfits.[11] For Puerto Rican soldiers stationed in Panama, "Continental" army officers expressed "no objection" to segregating them in "dance[s] and other social activities."[12] Former 442nd infantryman Fred Kitada lamented that he and other Japanese American members of his outfit were barred from marrying the French and Italian women they fell in love with during the war. "Someone was going to say 'no,'" Kitada recalled, "either a chaplain or company commander or battalion commander."[13] Similarly, in May 1945, after the fighting in Italy ceased, a black war correspondent observed in Genoa that a white regiment, which had just finished fighting alongside Japanese American and African American units, "has established an exclusive club, bar, and theatre from which colored soldiers and troops of Japanese descent are excluded."

Perhaps similar exclusions help explain why Nisei troops farther south in Livorno appear to have started their own whorehouse (made up of "one madam and four girls") rather than simply frequenting those for other American troops—black or white—in the area.[14]

Like the black-white divide, the white-nonwhite one seemed at times to bisect the military justice system. The latter is tougher to track, because the army organized its court-martial statistics into two broad "racial" categories: colored and white, with all noncolored included among whites. But a review of those white men whom the military executed during the war reveals some troubling signs. In the European Theater of Operations, among the fifteen whites put to death were one Puerto Rican, two American Indians, and three Mexican Americans. Only a small fraction of all US troops there, nonblack minorities constituted a startling 40 percent of all white executions. A similar ratio existed in the Pacific, where a total of three whites were executed, one of whom was a Mexican American from Los Angeles.[15]

As with black troops, color lines appear to explain some of these striking disparities. It seems that nonblack minorities were every bit as underrepresented among the higher ranks of the military justice system as were African Americans. In the European theater, for example, a list of officers in the Judge Advocate General's office includes no obviously Spanish or Asian surnames.[16] Furthermore, scraps of evidence suggest that racist prejudices sometimes marred the criminal justice process when nonblack minorities were involved. For instance, when a French woman told a US Army lieutenant that a "short, heavy-set and dark complexioned" American soldier had raped her, the officer somehow deduced, evidently on the basis of this description alone, that her assailant was "either a Mexican or an Indian." Corporal Wilford Teton, a Shoshone Indian, was eventually charged with the crime, convicted, and given a life sentence. This, despite the fact that his accuser was unable to identify the attacker at first and only later became convinced of Teton's guilt because "she just knew" he was a rapist, and despite the fact that an Army Inspector General's report found that a white major had attempted to frame Teton.[17] Finally, it appears entirely possible that the overrepresentation of Mexican Americans in particular among those whites executed owed something to the fact that they were at the time "thrust . . . into the national consciousness as a criminal element in society." Their supposed criminality, according to historian Edward Escobar, "was a major reconstitution of the attributes that defined Mexican Americans as a separate race," both in and out of the military, one would suspect, as sailors' attacks on Mexican American youth in Los Angeles's Zoot Suit Riots showed.[18]

White-nonwhite lines also assumed various symbolic forms overseas. One subset involved the discursive connections that some Americans drew between other Americans and the Japanese enemy. The latter was no ordinary World War II adversary, according to numerous scholars, but unquestionably the most demonized, dehumanized, and nonwhite-racialized of them all. One need not disregard the Japanese military's own litany of well-documented biases and atrocities to insist on an equally well-documented fact: American officers and enlisted men (to say nothing of civilians) viewed Japanese in a different way than they did Germans and Italians. Japanese were lice and monkeys, rats and vermin, "Japs" and "Japes," "slant-eyed gophers" and "gooks," "yellow bastards" and "little brown men"; they were "subhuman, inhuman, lesser human, superhuman."[19] American troops collected their teeth, skulls, fingers, and ears, out of which they sometimes fashioned necklaces and rings, sometimes sending these macabre keepsakes to family members back home. Some attempted to blow apart Japanese genitalia and urinate in slain soldiers' mouths. While fighting in the Pacific, one marine veteran recalled in an unpublished memoir feeling "full of fear and hate, with the desire to kill, no not just kill, but to maim and give that 'Gook' a hurting lingering punishing death. . . . He's a savage animal, a beast, a devil, not a human at all and the only thought is to kill, kill, kill." Here then were, in historian John Dower's words, "patterns of a race war," an epic, merciless struggle pitting not simply one adversary against another but also white versus nonwhite ("yellow" or, less frequently, "brown"). [20]

Given this fact, whenever the US military connected a subset of Americans to Japanese, they also, in a sense, marked them as nonwhite. When American sailors posted a sign in the Pacific that read, "Kill Japanese, Kill Japanese, Kill the Yellow Race," a Chinese American sailor rightfully wondered not only what this killing had to do with "a war he understood as a struggle to safeguard democracy," but also why he and other Asian Americans were lumped together with Japanese—and, implicitly, separated from the evidently non-"Yellow" Americans.[21] Similarly, some US officers and enlisted personnel likened Japanese to American Indians, in particular. The common wartime phrase "the only good Jap is a dead Jap" was a clear—if, perhaps, not always conscious—reference to another saying from another race war: "the only good Indian is a dead Indian."[22] One marine colonel in the Pacific remarked to a journalist there, "What they [Japanese] have done is to take Indian warfare and apply it to the twentieth century. They use all the Indian tricks to demoralize their enemy." Finally, at a time when many American troops in the Pacific had come to believe that "the jungle was Jap"—that their Japanese foe was "a 'born' Jungle and night fighter"—the army weekly *Yank* kept highlighting some nonblack minorities' similar skills.[23] One article noted that, while most of "the Army's new jungle troops" "are ordinary guys, taken from city and farm, and possessing no special qualifications for the job," not so with "American Indians and Mexicans." For reasons left unstated, "these lads can melt through the jungle like water." Another article proclaimed that the Puerto Rican soldier "knows his jungle warfare."[24] In all these implicit and explicit, conscious and unconscious ways, then, the US military drew parallels between nonblack minorities and America's most detested non-white foe.

But the most common of these parallels involved Japanese Americans. Indeed, the discursive crux of anti–Japanese American racism concerned the categorical refusal to distinguish between Japanese and Japanese American. This popular notion shaped not only the mass removal and mass incarceration of all West Coast Japanese Americans, but also military policies, from enlistment restrictions to extensive security screenings. The notion also traveled overseas. In its most common form, the US military— its publications, its officers, its enlisted personnel—called a subset of its own soldiers "Japs," by far the most ubiquitous shorthand reference to the Japanese enemy. Sometimes the slur was employed as an act of den-igration and distrust, as when a general in the Pacific "remarked he didn't want any Japs" after the War Department assigned some Nisei linguists to his command. Sometimes it was used as an expression of demeaning humor, as when a white soldier came across a group of Japanese American soldiers in Italy and fell to his knees in mock horror: "My god. All is lost. The Japs have captured Naples." Sometimes it was blurted out more inno-cently, but reflected nonetheless the presumed interchangeability of "Japs" and Japanese Americans, as when a member of the rescued "lost" battalion in France remarked, "I never thought I'd be so damn happy to see a Jap." And sometimes, surprisingly, it appeared part and parcel of an admittedly backhanded effort to praise Nisei GIs. "Here's One Jap in New Guinea Who Happens to Be a Nice Guy" was the headline of a *Yank* article from late 1942. The article described a California-born interpreter of Japanese descent as "a stocky, cheerful college graduate who speaks flawless English," and added that "if his wishes come true there soon won't be any Japs in a posi-tion to drop bombs on loyal Americans" like himself. [25] Japanese American soldiers, and increasingly their commanders and comrades, resisted this equation of Japanese American and "Jap," and with some success, but they were never able to eliminate it entirely.

In fact, it appeared overseas occasionally in other ways. Nebraska-born Ben Kuroki, who managed to join the army air corps despite its exclusion

of Japanese Americans, flew fifty-eight missions as a gunner in North
Africa, Europe, and the Pacific, winning a Distinguished Flying Cross and
Air Medal and receiving glowing attention on radio programs, magazines,
and newspapers all across the country. But his heroism and celebrity did
not protect him from friendly fire. When he arrived on Tinian Island in the
Southwest Pacific in March 1945, an officer warned him, "Anything that
even looks like a Jap, the guards shoot first and ask questions later." A lieutenant then advised him not to "go anywhere unless one of the [white] boys
goes with you. . . . Better sew your sergeant stripes on all your clothes, too,
and don't forget to wear your sunglasses." Kuroki remembered thinking,
"It was going to be really lovely all right. Come back from a fifteen-hour
mission all pooped and beat-up trying to forget the fear—then sweat out

Fig. 9.2 Ben Kuroki, a decorated gunner, in June 1944, after his deployment in Europe and
before his deployment to Asia. Courtesy of The Bancroft Library, University of California,
Berkeley, WRA no. I-240.

getting shot by your own men. Not one war; two." When Kuroki entered his first mess hall in the Pacific, "everybody stopped eating to glare at him. A few mouths dropped open and one guy instinctively reached for his .45."[26]

Kuroki was exceptional, one of the few Nisei in the air corps at the time, but his experiences in the Pacific were not. Several thousand Japanese Americans also served there and in Asia as top-secret interpreters and translators for the Military Intelligence Service; and a few served with the Women's Army Corps (WAC). They, too, constantly ducked death, as fellow Americans, other Allied troops, and some civilians mistook them for the enemy. One Japanese American sergeant, serving with the First Marine Division on Peleliu, recalled, "I was much more worried about the marines shooting me than the Japs. You know how those marines are: if they see anyone who even looks like the enemy they fire. Whenever I was on patrol I had to be escorted by half a dozen marines or I'd be a dead duck. Despite my Army uniform I was fired on several times." On the eve of battle, some Nisei confronted their white comrades: "Take a good look, and *remember me*, because I'm going in with you!"[27] One white marine just back from the South Pacific admitted that the Nisei "had a tough time of it"; each was "captured eight or nine times—by our own men." In the end, the US military and other Allied forces felt compelled to assign most Nisei serving in the Pacific and Asia their own bodyguards to keep them safe, not from the Japanese but from their fellow Americans.[28]

Another symbolic, overseas white-nonwhite line involved the disparagement of nonblack minorities other than Japanese Americans. In the case of Chinese American GIs stationed in China, some of their white so-called comrades, according to one official unit history, "have a tendency to belittle the Chinese, their customs, their living conditions, food, etc., and automatically classify all people of the race as below par; as a result, they resent having to consider a large group of Chinese American soldiers as equals." Another unit history added that "the average GI looks down on them [Chinese American soldiers] and classes them as native or at least on a level with the native." When drunk, the latter called the former "slopies," which, as one Mexican American pilot later explained, was "short for 'Slopehead[s],' the GIs' epithet for the Chinese."[29] Similarly, in Panama in late 1943, a group of "continental officers" with "extensive association and dealings with Puerto Rican officers and troops" prepared and distributed a set of notes to "offer a full and complete understanding of the normal characteristics of Puerto Rican personnel" who were serving in the area. Among these characteristics were a "mixed racial background" of "Spanish, Indians, Negro, and sprinkling of Chinese," a preference to "delay action until tomorrow," a tendency to be "impetuous and volatile" and "to assault involving the use of deadly weapons," and an adherence to a "somewhat different standard of veracity." While the notes also "desired to impress that Puerto Rican officers and men are white," they assumed this status simply because "the Puerto Rican standard of differentiation between white and colored . . . is on an entirely different basic [sic] from that of the average Continental. To a Continental, a person with any colored blood is colored. To the average Puerto Rican, a person who has any white blood is white."[30]

These sentiments led to tension and conflict, which also drew boundaries between white and nonwhite or between their rough analogues—say, between "average GI" and Chinese or "Continental" and Puerto Rican. In the case of the last of these, a group of Puerto Rican officers took great exception to the notes, which, they warned, "are but one tangible bit of evidence to show the attitude of certain Continentals in key positions towards their people," all of which had "caused a tremendous amount of bad feeling on the part of all Puerto Ricans" and had created "a very tense situation" on and around Puerto Rico. Similarly, in Christopher Capozzola's telling, the Bataan Death March in 1942 "prompted a brutal race war, in which Americans and Filipinos, in language laced with racial epithets, stole one another's food, blamed each other for poor preparation and battlefield losses, and each accused the other of cozying up to the Japanese." And according to historian Scott Wong, one former Hawaiian National Guard infantry regiment, while serving in the Southwest Pacific, experienced so much "racial tension" between its white replacements from the mainland and Hawaiians of Asian descent that, in May 1944, the outfit "was reorganized to permit segregation of the white elements into separate units."[31]

Taken together, white-nonwhite lines overseas, much as on the home front, were varied and complex. They emanated primarily from commanders in the field, but white enlisted personnel also played a part. They took a range of forms, from too much combat to too little of it, from a disproportionately high number of capital-crime court-martial convictions to a disproportionately low number of commissions, and from sporadic comparisons with the "Jap" enemy to habitual equations with the same. They divided, at times, "Continental" from "Puerto Rican," or "Average American" from "Chinese," or "ordinary guys" from "Indians and Mexicans." But in all cases they distinguished, sometimes subtly and sometimes not, between those American troops' whose whiteness was secure and unquestioned and those whose whiteness was suspect or denied.

These white-nonwhite lines also varied somewhat from time to time and from place to place. Speaking broadly, overseas white-nonwhite lines tended to blur over the course of the war. The general who "didn't want any Japs" in his Pacific command, for example, "begrudgingly tolerated them at first," only to embrace them fully by the end of a campaign, by which point "he thought so much of them that he used to go personally to the transports and welcome each group as they came off the gangplank."[32] As this story suggests, the white-nonwhite divide also tended to be most pronounced behind the front lines, among rear-echelon troops or among combat soldiers enjoying a brief respite from battle. They also sometimes seemed more frequently to target those troops assigned to descent-specific outfits. Reflecting both these points, for example, was the mistreatment of members of the Chinese American air service outfits in China and of the Puerto Rican Sixty-Fifth Infantrymen Regiment while it served in Panama. Finally, some places more than others seemed to invite white-nonwhite line-drawing. Of all war theaters, the Pacific, with its "war without mercy," was the most likely to reinforce lines between white, on the one hand, and "Jap," "gook," "yellow," or "brown," on the other.

Indeed, the race war there was one reason for the military's overseas drawing of the white-nonwhite divide in the first place. Unlike the situation in other theaters, lines between ally and enemy in the Pacific mapped neatly onto this divide.[33] It did not simply ensnare Japanese or even those Americans who had ancestral ties to them. It also occasionally ensnared other "yellow" people, presumably anyone of Asian descent, and even Mexican Americans, Puerto Ricans, and American Indians, all of whom, some believed, shared essential "Jungle"-related characteristics with "Japs." The overseas white-nonwhite divide also stemmed from some white commanders' and white enlisted men's deep and long-standing investments in it, which had also shaped some troops' training camp experiences in the United States. When some white commanders prevented Japanese American soldiers from marrying white European women, for example, they might very well have been influenced by the fact that more than a dozen states back home explicitly forbade such unions.[34] Or anti–Chinese American sentiments and practices likely stemmed at least in part from decades of the same in the United States, as reflected in racist depictions in popular culture, exclusionary immigration and naturalization laws, violent efforts to expel Chinese and other Asian immigrants from the country, and more.[35] Of course, the military's color lines involving Puerto Ricans, Filipinos, American Indians, Mexican Americans, and others also owed something to decades of US colonial rule, which both rested on and reinforced these very lines.[36]

A final reason for the overseas white-nonwhite divide applies only to the rarest of cases: when one nonblack minority sought to secure his insider white status by stressing the outsider nonwhite status of another. Perhaps this dynamic helps explain why, for example, an American Indian, whom his fellows called "Chief," stabbed Ben Kuroki out of the blue one night in a drunken rage while both men served together in the Pacific, calling Kuroki a "Jap."[37]

BROTHERS IN ARMS

The white-nonwhite divide also broke down somewhat overseas, continuing a process that had begun tentatively and unevenly in and around training camps in the United States. As in the case of black-white lines, this process happened most often in combat or in its aftermath, but it also occurred elsewhere in both descent-specific units and in so-called white ones. This is in part a story of a beloved and popular topic: comradeship—the "fraternalism in war," the "brotherhood" of battle, the "human fellowship" or "community spirit" that troops develop, especially in combat, which sometimes allows them to dissolve the divides of "race" and class, religion and region, rank and sexuality, and more.[38] If at times there were "no [black-white] color lines in foxholes," the military's own policies and practices ensured that even fewer white-nonwhite ones cropped up there.[39]

Japanese American members of the 442nd Regimental Combat Team and 100th Infantry Battalion provide an excellent case in point. Whereas they encountered some stark white-nonwhite lines overseas, these lines faded substantially on and around battlefronts. Part of the credit for that ought to go to War Department leaders. They launched an impressively expansive public relations campaign—replete with press, still, newsreel, and radio coverage, micromanaged on occasion by Army Chief of Staff George C. Marshall himself.[40] It was all part of an effort to "continue the [publicity] buildup" of these outfits, a "buildup" that began with their formation in the United States.[41] The motivation had less to do with Japanese Americans' welfare. Instead, the army wished to "erase the impression that [it] . . . was discriminating against this racial group," while other government officials sought to portray the United States, to the "darker races" both at home and abroad, as a genuine multiracial democracy that "can produce and is producing young men of Japanese blood who willingly and effectively fight other men of their own race—the enemy."[42] Regardless, this celebration of Japanese American heroism not only won the day on the home front, but also won on the battlefront, where the military's own publications and leaders went "great guns for us," in the words of one Japanese American medic in the 442nd.[43] This unit, along with the 100th, was the subject of glowing features in *Yank* and *Stars and Stripes* and *CBI Roundup*;[44] received medals, honors, and tributes from their commanders and comrades;[45] and were even granted the distinct privilege of leading the US Army's V-J Day parade in Livorno, Italy.[46] By highlighting Japanese Americans' heroics, bravery, and "tough, loyal American" nature, this War Department public relations campaign helped blur the white-nonwhite line between "American" and "Japanese."[47] It had long been at the heart of anti-Japanese American racism, but symbolic shifts were afoot.

The War Department effected another, related shift. In stark contrast to the case of African Americans, it assigned large numbers of Japanese Americans to combat units. Even when those units were descent-specific, like the 442nd and 100th, it attached them closely to larger so-called white outfits. In doing so, it maximized the chances that comradeship would work its unifying magic on whites and Japanese Americans (and other non-black minorities) alike. In other words, while the commitment of the 100th and the 442nd to continual, immensely costly combat perhaps reflected a white-nonwhite line—a cheapening of Japanese American life—that same commitment allowed Nisei GIs to transcend that line.

It also helped that Japanese Americans' commanders in the 100th and 442nd insisted, as they had on the home front, that their men receive fair and respectful treatment from white personnel above and alongside them. When generals in the field expressed concerns about Nisei GIs' loyalty or fighting ability, the commanders vouched for their men unwaveringly. When interviewing prospective white officers for the units, they made sure that only those comfortable serving with Japanese Americans would be accepted. And when the 442nd or 100th were first attached to a new regiment or division, they made sure to introduce their men properly:

> Having been born in the United States, all of the men are citizens of the United States. Very few of them have been to Japan and most of them cannot speak Japanese. They are as thoroughly loyal as German Americans, Italian Americans, or any other American of foreign ancestry. . . . We count among our particular friends those units with which we have trained or with which we have fought. Of these are many American divisions that have the highest regard for the men of this unit. . . . They do not like to be called "Japs" or "Jap Americans." They are either soldiers or Japanese Americans (without the hyphen) or Americans of Japanese ancestry.[48]

More than anything else, it was the day-to-day fighting alongside one another in France and Italy, under these favorable conditions set by white officers and War Department officials, that bonded Japanese American GIs to their white comrades. As for the latter, many members of the 100th and 442nd reported that, in the words of one private first class, "[i]t was the uniform that counted, not name or face or whether French-American, Irish-American or Japanese-American. We all help and are friends; like brothers, only more." A sergeant agreed: "On that front all races in the army were pals. We shared everything that happened, danger and duty and sacrifice, mud and rain, food, sun. It was nothing when behind the lines out there, to see a six foot two white soldier go off for a long walk with a five foot two AJA [American of Japanese ancestry]. And when the AJA friends were sent home for hospital care or on furlough, the white soldiers gave them addresses of parents and relatives, begging them to visit." The battalion historian for the 100th reported its members forging a "sacred friendship" with the "white" Thirty-Fourth Division.[49]

Other sources confirmed this rosy picture. Newspapers and magazines across the country recounted stories about the warm, enduring bonds that Japanese American members of the 100th and 442nd forged with the

Fig. 9.3 Charles P. Carroll (*left*) and Noboru Hokame (*right*), who appear to have fought together in Europe, spend their convalescent furlough at Carroll's home in Chicago, March 1945. Hokame was a member of the 100th Infantry Battalion. "I'd rather fight with just one unit of Japanese-Americans than an entire Army of ordinary soldiers," Carroll said. "These boys mean business, and you have a better chance of coming out of a battle intact with them than anybody else I know in the Army." Courtesy of The Bancroft Library, University of California, Berkeley, WRA no. I-804.

white servicemen they met overseas: about "a friendship that began between three army buddies—two are Japanese Americans from Honolulu
and the third a Des Moines man—during the 'tough going' of Iowa's famed
34th 'Red Bull' division in Italy";[50] Norman Hiraoka spending Christmas
in New Hampshire with Raymond J. Winters, both of whom had become
"brothers-in-arms" and "fast friends when they met as wounded soldiers
aboard a home-bound hospital ship" from Europe;[51] two "wounded vets
and buddies"—Sidney Oshiro and Charles Fischer—at the latter's home in
Milwaukee;[52] Private Ray E. Dintini, who wrote from Italy about the heroism of the Nisei soldiers whom he fought beside and "to whom he felt
like a brother";[53] two Nisei soldiers and one of "Spanish descent" in San
Francisco, "who met in a foxhole, introduced themselves and later 'did the
town' together to celebrate their escape from death in battle";[54] and a troopship returning from Italy on which Japanese Americans mixed freely and
respectfully with other GIs. "It's a nice thing to see," wrote an army major
about the scene. "It makes you realize that the code that binds fighting men
doesn't draw the same kind of distinctions that they used to draw at home,
and maybe still do."[55]

The weakening of such distinctions was also evident in white GIs' continuous praise for their comrades and buddies in the 100th and 442nd.
This proved especially valuable toward the end of the war when Japanese
Americans began returning to the West Coast and, in some cases, faced
white hostility, harassment, and violence. When one white combat veteran,
home for no more than a few hours, picked up a newspaper and read about
"a Japanese-American veteran, a wearer of the Purple Heart, being ejected
from a barber shop in Arizona," he was outraged: "What kind of —— patriotism is that? I fought alongside those Nisei kids of the 100th Infantry
Battalion and I never saw an outfit with more guts. I'd like to spend about
10 minutes with that —— barber." One *Yank* correspondent, also recently
back from Europe, was even more forceful: "The best damned fighting men
in the world were the Japanese Americans in Italy. Let anybody say anything against them and the guys who fought with them will kill you. The
100th Infantry Battalion of 1300 men has 1247 with the Purple Heart.
They are fighting the war of 1776 in 1945. They are fighting for the right to
be American citizens."[56]

Indeed, many white GIs proved faithful allies in this twentieth-century
fight. Although some called Nisei soldiers "Japs," others insisted on something else entirely—their undeniable Americanness. Having endured
many baptisms by fire together on Europe's battlefields, white GIs called
their Nisei comrades "true American[s]," "damned good Americans," "real
Americans," and "better Americans."[57] At war's end, an entire company of

white infantrymen—117 in all—signed a petition hailing the "heroic and meritorious achievements of our fellow-Americans in the 100th Infantry Battalion and 442d Infantry Regiment."[58] At a time when Americanness had such close associations with whiteness, and Japaneseness with nonwhiteness, these GIs' "Americanization" of their Nisei comrades chipped away at the white-nonwhite divide.

This chipping away occurred for many of those Japanese Americans who served not in the 100th and 442nd but in so-called white outfits as well. Take Ben Kuroki, the much-decorated turret gunner in the army air corps. He faced some hostility from white (and, occasionally, other) comrades, but it seldom lasted, at least in Europe. "Under fire, a man's ancestry, what he did before the war, or even present rank, don't matter at all," he told an

Fig. 9.4 In combat together in Italy, Russell Buss (*left*) and Jack Kawamoto (*right*), a member of the 442nd Combat Team, are reunited at Dibble General Hospital in Palo Alto, California, July 1945. Buss remarked, "The Nisei is a brave, alert and excellent soldier. There are none better—none braver. I am proud of my Nisei buddies." Courtesy of The Bancroft Library, University of California, Berkeley, WRA no. -74.

audience in San Francisco between deployments in Europe and the Pacific. "You're fighting as a team—you're fighting for each other's life and for your country, and whether you realize it or not, you're living and proving democracy. . . . The tunnel gunner that helped me . . . was Jewish, I'm a Japanese-American, the bombardier of our crew was a German, the left Waist gunner was an Irishman. Later I flew with an American Indian pilot and a Polish tunnel gunner. What difference did it make? We had a job to do, and we did it with a kind of comradeship that was the finest thing in the world."[59]

Kuroki's problems with fellow servicemen proved more intractable in the Pacific's "race war," as his stabbing suggests.[60] Other Japanese Americans, however, experienced the boundary-blurring power of comradeship there, too. One Japanese American linguist, who served with the army's famed Merrill's Marauders, a special infantry outfit that worked deep behind enemy lines in the China-Burma-India theater, later recalled, "Once we proved our worth as soldiers . . . we were treated like brothers and no question about it at all. In fact we were greeted with open arms to be with them."[61] During the war, a white member of the same unit wrote home supporting this recollection—and offering a similar defense of Nisei GIs as those coming from Europe at the time: "We of the Merrill's Marauders wish to boast of the Japanese-Americans fighting in our outfit and the swell job that they put up. . . . Many of the boys and myself especially, never knew a Japanese-American or what one was like—now we know and the Marauders want you to know that they are backing the nisei one hundred percent. It makes the boys and myself raging mad to read about movements against Japanese-Americans by some 4-F'ers back home. We would dare them to say things like they have in front of us."[62] Finally, one Marine sergeant, having served with Japanese American linguists in the Southwest Pacific, wrote the newspaper *PM*: "There wasn't a single man in the outfit who didn't like and respect these boys"; they are "courageous, sincere, loyal and swell fellows."[63]

Nonblack minorities other than Japanese Americans also experienced overseas comradeship, transcending and smudging the white-nonwhite divide. As with Japanese Americans, sometimes troops expressed their bonding with fellows in the idiom of brotherhood. Speaking of his fellow American POWs in the Pacific, one Native American recalled that they felt "closer to each other than even our own brothers could be." Another Native American, who served in England, recalled his white comrades, whom he called his "pale-faced brothers," "treat[ing] us as brothers."[64] In memoirs and oral histories, several Mexican Americans reported similar recollections. A member of Merrill's Marauders remembered that "[w]hen you are in the outfit there is no discrimination there. If you're Catholic, Protestant or Jew it don't make no difference there because you are all going to be brothers in the foxhole." Another GI, who fought in the Philippines, recalled, "On the war front you don't see color. You are all the same. You are trying to take care of each other; you are brothers." And later reflecting on his squadron in China, a former fighter pilot wrote, "Several of them were to become as close as brothers to me, with that special camaraderie generated in combat by the unspoken, but understood, commitment to risk our lives for each other."[65]

Again, like Japanese Americans, other nonblack minority servicemen spoke of this camaraderie in terms besides brotherhood. Sometimes it was the military language of units, outfits, platoons, and squads. "The squad consisted of a German, a Frenchman, a Spaniard, a Mexican, an Italian, a Jew, and guys with names like Joe," a Mexican American wrote home from Luxemburg. Together they "had something to teach the world . . . how men of different breeds and creeds can live and work together when they must." Sometimes it was the language of masculinity or manliness. Another Mexican American, a former marine who served as a combat engineer on Okinawa and Saipan, later explained succinctly the bonds he forged with his mainly Anglo comrades: "We called each other 'men.'" Sometimes it was the language of friendship, as when one more Mexican American, a former waist gunner in the Mediterranean theater, "remember[ed] being the only Latino in his unit, but feeling comfortable and making friends with his fellow soldiers." Sometimes it was the language of equality. Many of the Chinese American combat veterans who spoke with historian Scott Wong "recalled that facing the enemy under fire equalized everyone in the unit regardless of rank, race, or ethnicity." Still other times it was equality alongside a newly undifferentiated Americanness. "At the front we were all on equal terms," a Mexican American noted. "We were accepted just like any other G.I. No one ever referred to us as being 'different Americans.'"[66]

But as it turned out, contrasting oneself or one's fellows with "different Americans" or different non-Americans constituted a final form of adhesive that stuck some servicemen together, even across the white-nonwhite divide. In other words, disunity bred unity, or particular kinds at least. Those different others could be officers, members of another service branch, "rear-echelon bastards," or pampered, clueless civilians back home. They could also be foreigners, from the enemy to any locals or "natives" whom US servicemen encountered abroad. Regarding the last, who seem to have been almost exclusively non-Europeans, sometimes US troops approached them with more condescension than contempt, ostensibly praising, for example, the "Fuzzy-Wuzzy" in Papua New Guinea for their help in fighting the enemy with the "best damned legs and backs we ever saw." Other times,

scorn for the "wild and wooly aborigines" led to the desire either to colo-
nize or to "say the hell with them." In the words of one private, the United
States "should keep these thousands of islands strewn throughout the wide
blue Pacific" to tap "a vast market composed of 150,000 natives" and "to
demonstrate to the world the colonizing abilities of our democracy." In
this instance, one sees how US troops sometimes both carried "the trace
of US settler colonialism" overseas and gradually grew into their role as
expert agents and "practitioners" of an expanding wartime, and in time
postwar, American empire. Regardless, in all these cases, involving everyone from officers and US civilians to overseas foreigners and so-called
Fuzzy-Wuzzies, some US troops bonded with each other through their
perceived distance from and superiority over various others.[67]

But among the most prominent of these others were American
servicemen themselves—African Americans. If, for generations, some
immigrants to the United States dissolved into the white masses "on the
backs of blacks," that is, by their designation and self-designation in opposition to African Americans, something similar happened in and around
World War II battlefronts. Historian Gary Gerstle has argued that the
military's white outfits, especially combat ones overseas, "became extraordinary vehicles for melding the many streams of Euro-Americans
into one."[68] They did so in part through the absence of African Americans
and through "white" unit members' contrast with them. But this melding
process may have been even more expansive still, including all nonblacks,
at least at times, not simply those of European descent. The military's
vast welter of stateside black-white lines did, on occasion, push many
Mexican Americans and Asian Americans, Native Americans and Puerto
Ricans toward that latter category. This dynamic occurred overseas as
well. In Trinidad, when one naval construction battalion set up a store,
a railing divided two separate shop windows. Black sailors were expected
to patronize one, whites, Chinese, and Filipinos the other. When, decades
later, a Mexican American sailor reflected on an encounter with African
American troops on Okinawa in which they refused to give him a ride,
he offered a ready explanation: they were rightfully hurt and angry, since
"they couldn't fight with *us*" and "they were not [treated] equal[ly] to the
rest of *us*."[69] In countless big and small ways, both at home and abroad,
the military encouraged its nonblack troops, whites and nonwhites alike,
to see themselves as one, undifferentiated "us" in opposition to the black
"them." Along with comradely bonds forged in the heat of battle, this too
sometimes whittled away at the white-nonwhite divide.

This point appears perhaps most evident regarding Japanese American
troops. Many whites' overseas acceptance of them as Americans, friends,

and brothers, and the overseas blurring of white-nonwhite lines, sometimes seemed to rest in part on Japanese Americans' explicit contrast with
African Americans. Consider the 100th and 442nd, whom some white
officers and enlisted men so warmly embraced during their joint fighting
in Europe, primarily in 1944 and 1945. At precisely this time, Japanese
Americans also fought alongside—indeed, for a few months, as part of—
the heretofore segregated black Ninety-Second Infantry Division in Italy.
One might think that the attachment of Japanese Americans to this unit in
the early spring of 1945 narrowed the distance between Nisei and "Negro,"
but the opposite was actually the case. The War Department decided to reorganize the unit by replacing two largely black regiments with white and
Japanese American ones, because it distrusted black combat troops and
trusted Nisei ones. When Army Chief of Staff George C. Marshall proposed
the idea, he thought "the 92d Division, the Negro troops . . . simply refused
to fight" but that "the Japanese regiment was spectacular."[70]

Indeed, intersecting with the War Department's celebration of the
100th and the 442nd was the simultaneous disparagement of the Ninety-
Second—in fact, each in a way magnified the other. At the exact time that
the army hailed these Japanese American troops as "the best damned
fighting men in the world," showering citations and awards and medals on
them, it publicly chided the black division for its "panicky retreats" and privately condemned it as an utter failure.[71] A semiofficial 1948 history of the
Fifth Army concluded that "[t]he Nisei of the 100th Battalion and the 442d
Regimental Combat Team . . . laid down their lives before the German machine guns in almost prodigal abandon. On the other hand the Negroes of
the 92d Division . . . did not perform as well as might be hoped." In his 1950
memoir, the Fifth Army's commander, General Mark Clark, agreed: while
the "100th Battalion fought magnificently throughout the Italian campaign," the Ninety-Second put in a "bad performance."[72]

During these campaigns in early 1945, the American press picked up
on and amplified the contrasts. The *New York Times* offered black troops
a fairer shake than some other publications, but a March 1945 article
entitled "Negroes' Courage Upheld in Inquiry" still featured this lede: "The
circumstances surrounding the American Ninety-second Division and
combat record present 'a rather dismal picture.'" Compare that with an editorial the same newspaper published a month later, devoted entirely to
Japanese American troops' unalloyed bravery and heroism. Focusing on
"action in Italy," it declared, "No soldiers we have sent abroad have a more
distinguished record than these Nisei." Several months later, with fighting
in Italy concluded, the *Times* chose again to contrast Japanese Americans
with African Americans. Writing of a troopship carrying more than

eighteen hundred soldiers returning home from Europe, it stressed the outstanding "fighting qualities of the Japanese Americans"; buried at the bottom of the story was a seemingly insignificant afterthought: "the 486th Quartermaster Company, a unit of 256 Negroes attached to a laundry outfit." These contrasts were evidently so common that—according to Mike Masaoka, a member of the 442nd—correspondents who "passed through" the Italian front asked him "why the Nisei had turned out to be exceptional soldiers while the black division was considered mediocre at best."[73]

Given the prevalence of these distinctions, it is perhaps no surprise that Jim Crow's defenders seized on them. In a rambling attack on the Committee on Fair Employment Practice before the Senate in June 1945, Mississippi senator James Eastland digressed to denounce black soldiers and to defend military segregation. The "utter and dismal failure" of the former, he argued, could not be blamed on the latter, since combat in Italy showed that a "Japanese-American division, trained in my state, distinguished itself in combat, and, further, saved a Negro regiment from annihilation." Three years later, Georgia senator Richard B. Russell reprised the same argument, this time to fend off African Americans' intensifying efforts to desegregate the military. "The nisei combat teams wrote a glorious page in the history of American valor," he declared on the floor of the Senate.

> With a racial pride that is unknown to some other minority groups they were not only satisfied but glad to serve with their own race and kind. . . . Instead of complaining they showed that there were no better troops in the American Army. They looked at their equipment and saw that it was the equal of that issued to any other American troops. They realized that their mess and quarters were the equal of those of any other American Army organization. They saw other nisei by their sides and felt no inferiority. When brought into contact with the enemy they did not refuse to fight because a white man was not in front of them or another white man by their side. Instead of "fading away in the face of enemy action," they took every objective they were ordered to take; and few if any other outfits of comparable size, whether of the Army, the Navy, or the Marine Corps, whether rangers or paratroopers, received more medals for heroism and achievement in action than did this segregated minority group.

He concluded by experimenting with a still-nascent "model minority" idea—that "exceptional" Asian Americans had something to teach "deficient" African Americans—which would only gain force over time: "It is a great pity that other minority groups do not emulate their [Japanese Americans'] example." Indeed, Eastland's and Russell's remarks reveal that the midcentury rise of this idea emerged in response not simply to world war and Cold War "international imperatives," but also to domestic ones—in this case, the perceived need to defend Jim Crow.[74]

Like later examples of the model minority idea, these speeches from Eastland and Russell contrasted African Americans with Japanese Americans not necessarily to narrow the gap between the latter and whites. Indeed, Russell, in particular, praised Nisei army outfits (and disregarded Japanese Americans' substantial protest against them) to justify the military segregation of both African Americans and Japanese Americans. But Russell was an exception. In so many other instances, the distinction between the two groups effectively leveraged Japanese Americans against African Americans, hoisting the former up, while pushing the latter down—strengthening black-white lines, while weakening white-nonwhite ones.[75]

True, the fighting records of the Ninety-Second, on the one hand, and the 100th and 442nd, on the other, appear to have been distinct. While commentators have long lauded these storied Nisei outfits, even the Ninety-Second's defenders have readily acknowledged problems.[76] But the source of such distinctions should be clear: in contrast to Japanese American troops, African American servicemen faced a far more extensive, debilitating, and humiliating set of boundaries, in and out of the military, in the United States and all around the world. They enjoyed none of the steadfast support of their own commanders, let alone senior War Department leaders. They were provided precious few opportunities to bond with nonblack comrades and to shine in combat. And when black troops did receive these opportunities and did shine, the military seldom broadcast or celebrated the fact. The successful experiment to integrate black platoons in white companies on the western front, for example, occurred at precisely the time that the military and the American press hailed the 100th and the 442nd and harangued the Ninety-Second. While the War Department tirelessly promoted Nisei troops' exploits in Italy, they buried similarly rosy reports of black riflemen in France.[77]

Had commentators in and out of the military recognized some of these foundational factors, they might have seen differential treatment as the root cause of the two groups' seemingly distinct fighting records in Italy. Indeed, some lonely voices attempted to make this point. When correspondents asked Mike Masaoka for his perspective on the matter, he answered, "The 92d's problem was in training and leadership. Little had been expected of it. Most of its officers were chosen with little thought other than the assumption that Southern whites knew how to handle blacks. The result was that the worst aspects of segregation were perpetuated. Under the circumstances, blacks had little incentive to assert themselves. The manpower they represented was largely wasted by official shortsightedness. By contrast, the Nisei felt they had something to prove. In pursuit of that objective they had the Pentagon's support. They had trained intensely, and their officers were caught up in the fervor."[78] But among military brass and America's white press, this perspective rarely appeared during the war.[79] As a result, when discussions turned to the Italian campaign of early 1945, the military and the press encouraged many Americans, in and out of uniform, to assume the worst about black combat troops and the best about Nisei ones—and to blur the white-nonwhite divide and to brighten the black-white one.

Sometimes this simultaneous blurring and brightening came from nonblack minorities themselves. Some Japanese Americans, for example, also stressed the distinctions between themselves and the black troops who fought alongside them (and, unlike Masaoka, failed to see the structural factors at play). One veteran recalled that black soldiers "always turned their backs to the enemy and ran. They never covered our flanks." "The ones that I saw at the emergency aid station when I took a buddy seriously wounded on the verge of life and death," another remembered, "were black soldiers with headaches and stomachaches."[80] One former member of the 100th told an interviewer in the late 1990s that "if the colored people did what the Japanese Americans did, I think they would have had a far more better response after World War II."[81]

At the same time, other Japanese Americans and other nonblack minorities approached matters more broadly: they chose to blur not simply the white-nonwhite line but the black-white one as well. Testifying before Congress in 1947, Mike Masaoka declared that the war years convinced Japanese Americans that "the problems of one minority are the problems of other minorities." And indeed, three years earlier, in a letter from Italy to Assistant Secretary of War John J. McCloy, he asked "what we may do to help further liberal War Department, War Relocation Authority, and general government policies regarding the treatment of Japanese Americans and other minorities."[82] Similarly, Private Richard Naito of the 442nd, while recovering from battle wounds he sustained in Italy, wrote to a Veterans of Foreign Wars chapter in Washington state that had rejected his application for membership: "Suppression of minorities . . . cannot be ignored. . . . The Japanese of today will become the Negro of tomorrow, the Jew of the next day, the Catholic of the next, and the Italian-American, Irish-American, Swedish-American, Polish-American, or Slavic-American of the next. . . . Our Chinese and other hundreds of millions of colored allies throughout the Pacific will know what we do here. They cannot be expected to help us win more quickly, if we make it plain that colored people are going to be regarded as inferior."[83] In these cases and through word and deed, Japanese Americans sought to blur lines not simply between white and nonwhite, but also between minority and majority, and between white and colored.

Taken together, weakening white-nonwhite lines appeared all around the world and in descent-specific outfits and in so-called white ones. They appeared especially on and around battlefronts, but also in prisoner-of-war camps, in field hospitals, on troopships, and even on furloughs back home. They turned "Japs" and "Mexicans" and "Chinese" and "Indians" into whites' fellow Americans, brothers, friends, and comrades, and they also, less frequently, turned black people into "colored" allies or minority "allies," too. In the process they narrowed the gap between white and nonwhite, continuing and intensifying a trend that began in training camps at home. This was a bottom-up phenomenon whereby, most commonly, fellow servicemen forged comradely bonds with each other under fire. But it was these men's commanders and the War Department officials above them who crucially set the conditions for this bonding. They either mixed nonblack minorities into white outfits or attached descent-specific units closely to these white ones; they assigned these troops, with some exceptions, to combat at the same rate as, or at a greater rate than, white troops; and in the case of Japanese Americans, they tirelessly sang their praises. These policies ensured that at least some nonblack minority troops would experience the full unifying and boundary-blurring powers of comradeship with whites.

But why, then, did the War Department and commanders in the field commit themselves to these policies and create these conditions when, for the most part, they steadfastly refused to do so for African Americans? One familiar reason involved the military's long-standing insistence on treating (or, more accurately, *mistreating*) African Americans unlike anyone else. This fact, coupled with the simple one that black troops so greatly outnumbered all nonblack minority groups, meant that, while the blurring of white-nonwhite lines took place around the edges of military life, the blurring of black-white ones would have changed military life more fundamentally. There was also the desire of US state officials, not least those in the military, to convince nonblack minorities at home and nonblack allies abroad of their sincere investment in democracy. Since, in this effort, they often deemed eliminating black-white lines too difficult or dangerous, they embraced even more wholeheartedly the blurring of white-nonwhite ones. If they balked at highlighting black soldiers' exploits to prove America's nonracist bona fides, then maybe those of Japanese American soldiers or Puerto Ricans or American Indians would do the trick. And chipping away at the white-nonwhite divide sometimes involved reinforcing the black-white one. In some cases, the valorization of Japanese American soldiers, for example, rested at least in part upon the denigration of black ones.

* * *

In many respects, the military's white-nonwhite lines overseas resembled those at home. Neither, for example, dissolved all differences among nonwhites, even among the nonblack minority ones. If some Japanese Americans complained about too much frontline fighting, some Puerto Ricans complained about too little of it. But perhaps the most important similarity between white-nonwhite lines at home and overseas was that, in both places, they proved strong and weak, bright and blurry—indeed, sometimes both at the same time. Blurring occurred at times only on the battlefront, where men faced "the pressure of imminent death," and even then, only among the tightest circle of comrades, who endured that pressure together for weeks and months and years at a time.[84] As one former member of the 442nd recalled, "There was so much discrimination against the Japanese Americans during the war, even while we were fighting, except for the combat troops and those were the front-line men who knew us." Or as one war correspondent put it, "The [100th] is looked on with admiration and respect by the white troops they associate with. Their officers say they don't know what the effect would be if the battalion was suddenly thrown into contact with white troops unfamiliar with their background."[85]

As this recollection suggests, however, these lines also morphed some overseas, where blurring, which had already begun at home, only intensified. Such was the case, it appears, with all nonblack minorities, though evidence is more plentiful for some groups—say, Mexican Americans and American Indians—than others—say, Chinese Americans. But the most dramatic case of further blurring abroad involves Japanese Americans. They moved from the most despised and distrusted of nonblack minorities to, in many cases, whites' faithful friends, brothers, and fellow Americans. Combat proved an ideal antidote to anti–Japanese American racism. As more and more Japanese Americans fought bravely abroad, "collect[ing]," in the words of GI-cartoonist Bill Mauldin, "enough metal in their bodies and on their chests to sink six battleships," suspicions and fears about their disloyalty became increasingly difficult to defend.[86] Not for everyone, of course, but for enough fellow Americans, especially venerated combat troops, to shift meaningfully the views and treatment of Japanese Americans in the military and beyond.

As on the home front, white-nonwhite lines differed from black-white ones overseas. In contrast to the latter, the former were far less pervasive, far less frequently rooted in space and far more often connected to America's Pacific enemy, far less fiercely and violently protected, and far less likely to be imposed on civilian communities. As on the home front, America's overseas military also sometimes brightened the black-white divide in order to blur the white-nonwhite one. This played out between black and Japanese American soldiers not only at and around Camp Shelby in Mississippi, but also on the battlefields of Italy. It is possible, however, that the opposite occasionally occurred overseas: that is, the white-nonwhite divide brightened as the black-white one blurred. An *Atlanta Daily World* headline from October 1944 blared, "Negro and White Marines Unite to Subdue Japs."[87] In either case, however, these two divides diverged.

But there were convergences, too. As on the home front, some overseas white-nonwhite and black-white lines resembled each other. They both, for example, involved some of the same matters, from rank and military justice to male-female relations and simian dehumanization. If some white Americans called Japanese and Japanese Americans "Japes," some also insisted, from Britain to Burma, that African Americans had tails.

It was these convergences that perhaps convinced Japanese Americans, on rare occasions, to join forces with black troops. In Italy, one African American member of the 812th Aviation Engineers recalled a fracas between white and black servicemen in which Nisei joined the latter: "We were fighting all over the road when a truck load of Japanese-Americans came along. The driver jammed on the brakes and they piled off of their truck. Numerically things were just about even, but hell those little Nisei didn't need us. They kinda gently pushed us aside and waded in; it was murder, they tore those patty boys up. . . . I will always remember that I saw whites outclassed in all ways by people of color."[88] That these acts of "people of color" solidarity were rare speaks, in the end, to the greater differences between the military's white-nonwhite and black-white lines abroad as much as at home.

Conclusion

As troops returned home from overseas battlefronts in 1944, 1945, and 1946, touching down on US soil in many cases for the first time in several years, some were instantly confronted by the racist lines that had long shaped their military lives. But they also encountered those lines' unexpected wartime twists and turns. In Boston, a decorated Tuskegee Airmen pilot recalled walking down the gangplank and a white soldier barking the following orders: "Blacks over here, whites over here." Similarly, another African American veteran reported hearing his friends tell him of "'White' and 'Colored' signs on the docks the minute they disembarked in U.S. ports." But a third black veteran, recently back from service in the China-Burma-India theater, shared a very different story. Talking to an interviewer in 1946, he marveled at the camaraderie among white and black troops not only aboard his transport crossing the Pacific, but also after its arrival on the West Coast: "I saw many white and colored soldiers shake hands with one another when the ship docked in Seattle, Washington, and as they parted for various separation centers, I left the service convinced that the United States can and should have a democratic army."[1]

Meanwhile, across the country in New York City, the *New York Times* reported that when Staff Sergeant Nubuo Tokunaga, a twenty-five-year-old member of the Nisei 100th Infantry Battalion, "walked down the gangway, he was loudly cheered by American troops" in apparent appreciation for his and his crack outfit's brave fighting in Europe. But should that story not have said "*fellow* American troops"? And did the cheering for Tokunaga confirm his Americanness or subtly question it by intimating that his heroism was somehow all the more remarkable for his presumed foreignness?[2]

Fig. C.1 US troops return home on the USS *Gen. Harry Taylor*, August 11, 1945. Courtesy Franklin D. Roosevelt Public Domain Photographs, Franklin D. Roosevelt Library, 195339.

These varied stories, along with some of the questions they raise, suggest only a few of the many ways that racist boundaries waxed and waned in the final stages of World War II military service. In the end, black-white lines, if blurred some, still defined many troops' last days in uniform. White-nonwhite lines also appeared here and there but still lacked the same institutionalization, reach, and force. And this broader complex of lines fundamentally shaped postwar America in numerous, complicated, and too often forgotten ways. They politicized a varied and substantial group of veterans, who returned home prepared and determined to democratize the military and the nation. But these lines also impeded their efforts, by further dividing Americans, further naturalizing race and racism, and more.

PARTING LINES

Those troops who returned to the United States to be redeployed elsewhere made a brief stop at what the military called redistribution stations. There they underwent several weeks of "painstaking occupational and

physical classification, mental and physical reconditioning, orientation, re-
doctrination," and, eventually, reassignment. The military wanted the process to unfold "without haste in an environment characterized by mental
and physical relaxation and comfort." Thus, in the War Department's plan
for these centers, for example, it selected "hotels of the highest type in the
most favorable locations," such as Miami Beach, Florida; Santa Barbara,
California; Hot Springs, Arkansas; and Lake Placid, New York. Or at least
those were the locations for white personnel. For black soldiers, it planned
wholly separate centers—and not in peaceful, bucolic resort settings, but
in hotels in the "mucky slums" of Harlem and on Chicago's South Side.
When the plan became public in September 1944, Secretary of War Henry
Stimson suggested that a returning black soldier's "effective rehabilitation"
would best take place, not among potentially hostile whites, but within
"the congenial surroundings" of "his own people."[3]

Many African Americans disagreed. In a flurry of editorials, resolutions,
and protest letters, they roundly denounced the plan. In one telegram
to President Roosevelt, a distinguished group of Harlem citizens, which
included Congressman Adam Clayton Powell Jr., NAACP leader Walter
White, and journalist George Schuyler, declared that "segregating Negro
soldiers who also have faced death on foreign battle fronts . . . is a reprehen-
sible act . . . [and] an insult to Negroes buried on foreign soil having died
in the belief that they were fighting for Democracy." Unfolding amid the
final months of the 1944 presidential election campaign, the controversy
over the redistribution plan became, in the words of President Roosevelt's
aide on race matters, one of the top two "hottest issue[s] among the Negro
voters today." Soon White and two other black leaders, Mary McLeod
Bethune and Channing Tobias, sat down with Roosevelt himself in the
White House, pressing their case to provide black troops with better and
integrated redistribution center options. Following this, Roosevelt, in an
exceedingly rare move, urged the War Department to offer the same.[4]

As a consequence of this mounting pressure, the War Department
quickly, if reluctantly, relented. In an October 8, 1944, press release, it
announced a revised plan. Unwilling to admit that soldiers would return on
an "integrated basis," it nonetheless explained that "Negro returnees will be
processed with white returnees through existing northern Redistribution
Centers." In most cases, those centers would be army camps instead of
luxury resorts, but some measure of integration had been achieved. In the
rare instances when returning black troops did get a taste of such resorts,
some seem to have been integrated. One *Baltimore Afro-American* front-
page headline from May 1945 blared, "Flash! Foxhole Dreams Come True
for GI's at Hotel Dennis." "As GI Joe enters the palatial world-famous hotel

[in Atlantic City], replete with its costly and magnificent furnishings," the article elaborated, "he first see[s] in actual practice the ideals of democracy for which he fought, for soldiers of all races and colors, with their wives, are enjoying the recreational facilities of the game room."[5]

Troops who returned from overseas not to be redeployed but to be discharged and "eased back into an almost strange civilian world" visited another set of military facilities: separation centers. Sometimes over a mere forty-eight hours there, "war-weary GI's" received "counselling on various problems," a physical examination, their discharge papers during a graduation-like ceremony, and their final pay. The name "separation center" was especially apt in some cases. At Fort Dix in New Jersey, among the largest of these facilities, numerous recently discharged black veterans complained of segregation. Winfred Lynn enjoyed mixing with white and black troops on board his troopship crossing the Pacific and aboard a train crossing the country. "We didn't encounter any segregation," he recalled, "until we reached Fort Dix—and then we really knew we were back in the United States."[6]

But policies and practices at separation centers seem to have varied some from service to service and over place and time. The navy's Great Lakes Separation Center outside Chicago seemed to process all men to-gether regardless of race. From Fort Warren in Wyoming to Camp Patrick Henry in Virginia, veterans reported the "question of color" being "for-gotten or at least shunted to the background." Even Fort Dix seemed to become more integrated over time. A *Baltimore Afro-American* investiga-tion in late 1945 revealed that, with the exception of unit designations, "all other procedure in discharging GI's is carried out on a non-racial basis." Indeed, to the extent that Dix changed, it may have involved the contin-uing activism of black soldiers—and even a few of their white comrades, too. Interviewed in 1946, one black veteran recalled a rope separating the white and "Negro" sections of the mess hall there. But when he and his black friends disregarded the divide and ate among whites, nothing came of it. Soon, some white soldiers joined in the impromptu protest, sitting and eating in the black area.[7]

Beyond the separation center experience of discharge, an even more dis-tinct and durable set of black-white lines wound their way through the type and timing of discharge. As for timing, the seemingly endless discharge delays—the "months of promises and retractions, official orders and re-vised orders," what historian Laura McEnaney has called "the travails of mustering out"—enraged a broad swath of America's troops. It prompted the formation of roughly two hundred "Bring Back Daddy" clubs at home and numerous soldier protests abroad, from Manila to Paris, London to

Yokohama.[8] But black troops faced a singularly onerous set of obstacles to discharge that stemmed directly from the singular set of racist boundaries that defined their time in uniform. The point system, which the military devised to determine which troops would be discharged when, favored those with combat experience. This seemed reasonable enough, except that the military had systematically relegated the vast majority of black troops to service units well behind the line. This meant that, on average, they accumulated points more slowly than their white comrades and so were discharged later. After Germany's defeat in May 1945, for example, "less than 1 percent of the three hundred thousand troops qualified to return home from the Pacific theater came from all-black outfits." While blacks' discharge rates may have improved over time, it is likely that they never achieved parity with those of whites. This was the case because, in addition to the point system, African Americans' strictly segregated units also delayed discharge. As one *New York Amsterdam News* editorial explained, "[T]he army admits that Negro personnel will not be replaced except by Negro personnel. There are fewer Negro replacements and so our boys will have to wait [to be discharged] because of race. If that is not discriminatory, nothing else is."[9]

Also discriminatory were the types of discharges that many African Americans received. Each serviceman and -woman, when separating from the military, received one of a variety of discharges, depending on his or her service branch and perceived performance while in uniform. Across the armed services, an honorable discharge was the best and a dishonorable one the worst. But there was an intermediate discharge of one kind or another as well: the army simply called it a discharge or a blue discharge, the navy referred to it as "a discharge under honorable conditions," and the marines had even more in-between categories. Which discharge a new veteran received mattered monumentally to his or her postwar life chances. Many GI Bill and other government benefits, for example, were off limits to those men and women who received a dishonorable discharge. Even those with an intermediate discharge often faced restrictions of one kind or another. Like the point system, this discharge typology, while nondiscriminatory on its face, proved anything but in practice, in large part because officers, in nearly all cases white officers, unfairly assigned a disproportionately large share of other-than-honorable discharges to African American troops. Both at home and overseas, these troops faced an unjust military justice system, which produced shockingly high court-martial rates that eventually turned into shockingly high dishonorable discharge rates. The same could be said about so-called blue discharges, many of which white officers used to silence and punish those black troops with the temerity to protest Jim Crow in uniform. One armywide count from December 1941 through June 1945 revealed that African Americans, never more than roughly 9 percent of the wartime army, received a full 22 percent of blue discharges. Veterans could and did appeal, the *Pittsburgh Courier* launched a vigorous protest campaign against them, and the NAACP established a Veterans Affairs Office to represent African Americans in these matters. But it appears that, during the war and beyond, anti-black discharge discrimination persisted.[10]

Another black-white boundary that shaped African American troops' final days in and early days out of uniform involved official military awards. Serving bravely in all theaters throughout the war, some black GIs and units received a measure of these honors—eight Distinguished Service Crosses (the army's second-highest award during World War II), nearly two hundred Silver Stars (the third-highest army award), and two Presidential Unit Citations (the highest valor award for military outfits). And yet, as with so much in the World War II armed forces, deep divides marred this otherwise uplifting story. During the war, the military awarded some 420 or so Medals of Honor, its highest award, but not a single one went to an African American. The eight Distinguished Service Crosses awarded to black soldiers constituted a tiny fraction of the total—in the case of the army, a mere 0.2 percent by 1947. "Brave white heroes in our armed services have been awarded the nation's highest decoration, the Congressional Medal of Honor, literally in batches by President Truman," remarked a *Crisis* editorial in December 1945. "The Crisis would not take one ounce of credit from these men. . . . Yet it does seem strange to Negro Americans that out of the nearly one million of their men in the armed services not one should have performed in such a manner as to be cited for the Congressional Medal of Honor."[11]

A thorough investigation of the matter, commissioned by the army in the 1990s, found "that the failure of an African-American soldier to win a Medal of Honor most definitely lay in the racial climate and practice within the Army during World War II." In particular, it pointed out that the army's racist policies of segregating black troops, keeping most of them far from the front lines, and insisting solely on white senior leadership gave black GIs "a much more limited chance . . . to win awards for valor." It also found that the prejudiced white commanders of the Ninety-Second Division, the one largely black outfit that saw the most combat, "had to [have] affect[ed] their judgment in awards." Indeed, on the basis of this report, President Clinton, at a White House ceremony in 1997, awarded seven African Americans Medals of Honor for their World War II heroism. Only one of them, Joseph Vernon Baker, was still alive to savor the moment. "History has been made whole today," Clinton nonetheless proclaimed, "and our nation is bestowing honor on those who have long deserved it."[12]

One final end-of-the-war black-white military line involved reenlistment. Given the depth and breadth of military anti-black racism, from induction through discharge, it might seem surprising to learn that, by war's end, "Negro veterans poured back into the service." Never more than one-tenth of wartime soldiers, they constituted a full one-fourth of all army reenlistments in the first year after the end of the war. Part of the reason stems from some reenlistees' hope that they would be sent back overseas, especially to Europe, to be reunited with a wartime love or simply to relive the greater freedoms there. According to a government report, black people's "trend to reenlistment slowed down when assignments to the desired areas were discontinued." Perhaps more important still were the many advantages that life in uniform afforded African Americans, rampant color lines notwithstanding. "For all the humiliations of segregated army service," wrote two commentators in 1947, "many [African Americans] remembered that it was only in uniform that they ever knew anything approaching a decent standard of living—shelter, warm clothing, and decent food; army medical service, insurance, and jobs." "The obvious interpretation of the high rate of Negro reenlistment," they concluded, "is not that the individual soldier loves Jim Crow military life more, but Jim Crow civilian America less." Regardless of their reasons, African Americans' reenlistment became so great that the War Department promptly shut it down "until such time as an acceptable white majority is restored."[13] At war's beginning, so too at its end, the US military restricted black participation.

All told, as America's World War II troops mustered out in 1944, 1945, and 1946, the African Americans among them continued to face a varied mix of black-white lines in redistribution centers and separation centers, in the timing and type of their discharges, in the awarding of valor medals, and in their opportunities to join back up. In all, the lines involved physical space (a mess hall or resort), material resources (a job and GI Bill benefits), prestige (decorations), and more. They were directly discriminatory—the War Department's initial refusal, for example, to allow black troops to attend what unquestionably were the nicest redistribution stations—and indirectly so—the discharge point system that disadvantaged black troops only because a separate military policy limited their combat experience. Like those overseas, some of these boundaries blurred over time, thanks to African Americans' activism, in and out of uniform. But there was only so much they could do. As the war wound down, Jim Crow in uniform, in all its insidious complexity, lived on.

As always, it was not clear where this left nonblack minorities. Throughout the war years, various white-nonwhite lines intersected with or ran alongside black-white ones. The same applies to troops' final days in the military, though the former remained less institutionalized and less widespread than the latter. In their many meetings and memos to resolve the redistribution plan controversy, for example, no one in the War Department or in the White House ever seemed the slightest bit concerned about Mexican Americans or Japanese Americans, Native Americans or Filipino Americans. When Stimson defended the plan as wholly consistent with "the War Department's long-standing policy not to force the intermingling of races," he thought only two truly mattered: "Negro" or "colored"—he used the terms interchangeably—and white. Where did this leave those troops who typically fit neatly into neither of these two categories? Officially, it appears they were treated as white, as had been the case on other occasions while they served in uniform. But what about unofficially? "When we were at the front," one Mexican American noted bitterly in 1945, "it didn't seem to matter, whether we were a Mexican, Italian, Greek, etc., but coming back to camp . . . the prejudice is still there, stronger than ever."[14] While this soldier likely spoke for other nonblack minority troops, the blurring of white-nonwhite lines that occurred in training camps—and, as he himself suggested, overseas—must have had longer-lasting effects in other cases. In the end, then, while the black-white line at redistribution centers blurred somewhat, the white-nonwhite one likely blurred even more, in large part because it was never formally imposed there.

The story at separation centers may have been similar. White-nonwhite lines also surfaced here on occasion, but it seems they were more short-lived or rarely uniform. Clerks, for example, sometimes recorded Mexican Americans' racial status as Mexican rather than white on their discharge papers. But sometimes clerks did not. Indeed, in a Tejano family of five discharged brothers, three were classified as white and two as Mexican.[15] Some members of the 442nd separated on the West Coast in late 1945 waited months for transports back home to Hawaii. In the meantime, according to some complaints, the Japanese Americans received inadequate medical treatment and restricted leave time and were forced to work the menial "garbage detail . . . in place of prisoners of war" and to endure the "Un-American attitude being inflicted upon them by the residents of communities adjacent to their military reservations." But Japanese American veterans protested these conditions, soon marshaling the support of the Japanese American Citizens League (JACL), Hawaiian leaders, and eventually the War Department itself, which "directed that the situation be corrected at once." Soon the JACL "reported that restrictive conditions . . . had eased."[16]

Regarding discharges, some Japanese Americans, like African Americans, received less than honorable discharges for resisting military racism.[17] And some groups, such as Puerto Ricans in Puerto Rico, likely faced similar disadvantages to African Americans in the military's point system, since they too tended to be kept from the front lines. These exceptions notwithstanding, however, nonblack minorities as a whole encountered few of the distinct and durable discharge-related racist lines that many African Americans did.

Not so with awards, at least in some cases. Mexican Americans and Native Americans seem to have been well represented among Medal of Honor winners, but Japanese Americans, like African Americans, were not. To be clear, the 100th Battalion, even before war's end, had already gained a reputation as "the most decorated unit in the history of the U.S. army," and the 442nd hauled in more than its share of medals as well. In all, an astonishing forty-seven Japanese Americans won the Distinguished Service Cross during the war, the army's second-highest award for valor.[18] But, curiously, not one was awarded the highest, the Medal of Honor, at the time.

Fig. C.2 A Japanese American corporal's service ribbons and qualification badge, 1943. Courtesy of the Library of Congress Prints and Photographs Division, LC-DIG-ppprs-00289.

Shortly thereafter, in March 1946, Private First Class Sadao S. Munemori, a squad leader in the 442nd, received the award posthumously. A thorough investigation of the matter of Asian Americans and the World War II Medal of Honor, conducted by a group of historians in the late 1990s, found that a whopping twenty additional Japanese Americans deserved the award. The group "did not find 'incontestable proof' of discrimination in military awards," but it did not specifically look for it. In the end, on June 21, 2000, President Clinton, in another White House ceremony three years after the one involving black World War II veterans and a full fifty-five years after the end of the war, presented twenty Japanese Americans (and two other Asian Americans) with the Medal of Honor. Only seven awardees were still alive. Clinton was again forced to acknowledge the injustice involved: "It is long past time to break the silence about their courage, to put faces and names with the courage, and to honor it by name."[19]

AFTERMATHS

Two years after the conclusion of World War II, the eminent black scholar L. D. Reddick decided to take stock. Reviewing several recent articles about African American soldiers during the war, he faulted them for not addressing what, to his mind, was the most obvious and pressing question of all: "whether the Army machine or Army experience . . . increased or decreased Jim Crow."[20] In a similar vein, one wonders how the numerous stories recounted in the preceding pages—of color lines drawn, redrawn, and blurred—shaped the US military, its veterans, and the postwar nation as a whole. The answer is complicated.

On the positive side of the ledger, countless returning veterans infused civilian freedom struggles, already swelling in power during the Depression and war years, with enormous energy and moral authority. The war years had profoundly changed many black GIs. They donned the official uniform of the US military, traveled America and the world, met new people, learned new skills, thrilled to new freedoms, and, yes, chafed and protested against old injustices and humiliations. In the process, they became ever more convinced that America could and must change and that they would be the primary agents of that change. Coming home at war's end, numerous black veterans resolved to "not take as much as they did before"; to "not return to the South to pick cotton for ten dollars a week"—or not pick it at all; to "never again fit into the serfdom of Southern feudalism or into the second-class status in Northern industrial cities"; to "no longer be satisfied with segregation and discrimination"; to "not bow and scrape"; to "not go back to the old ways" or to "business as usual."[21] Crossing the Pacific on a troop transport in late December 1945, an African American soldier predicted about his fellow black veterans that "when the moment came—and it would come—these men were going to be the cutting edge of a movement that would change America."[22]

That moment arrived sooner than he and others might have expected. All over the country, many black veterans quickly became indispensable leaders, organizers, and foot soldiers in surging postwar civil rights struggles. Whether their names are familiar—Medgar Evers and Robert F. Williams—or less so—Welton Taylor and George Leighton—they marched to courthouses across the South to register to vote; they organized chapters of the NAACP; they lobbied governments for fair employment and fair housing laws; they became litigants in civil rights cases of various sorts; they joined or launched local efforts to desegregate schools and pools, apartment complexes and movie theaters; they unionized their workplaces; and in the 1950s and 1960s, they cultivated a whole new generation of civil rights activists.[23]

A similar sort of political awakening occurred with nonblack minority troops as well, and for some of the same reasons—the wartime chance to represent the United States, to travel, to meet new people, to learn new skills. But in contrast to black veterans, many of them enjoyed greater freedoms inside the military than they ever had outside it, an experience that also politicized them in new and profound ways. Writing of Japanese American soldiers from Hawaii, historian Franklin Odo argued that "race relations could never be the same" after they "on the mainland and in Europe bought sex from white prostitutes, fed white beggars, fraternized and brawled with white GIs, married white women, and killed white enemies." Similarly, in the case of Native American veterans, according to several scholars, "the inclusion that [they] . . . found in the armed forces and the racial equality that seemed so sincere and all-pervasive" reinforced a desire for self-determination, equal treatment, or some combination of both. Writing shortly after war's end, a commentator on Mexican American veterans in Texas surmised, "They must have wondered sometimes, some of them, how it happened that their first experience with democracy was in fighting for it. . . . They must have wondered, too, about the man-made rules and customs that made them privileged to occupy the same trench or ship or plane with Anglo Americans when, perhaps, they were not allowed to attend the same schools, patronize the same theaters and restaurants, or hold the same jobs as Anglo Americans in their home towns. . . . It would be sheer, blind idiocy to think they have not resolved that this brighter better world for which they fought shall be a brighter, better world for their children."[24]

Much like African Americans, a mix of nonblack minority veterans also spearheaded postwar freedom struggles of various sorts. Native ex-GIs, for example, became active in tribal governments and, through spirted activism, quickly won the right to vote in New Mexico and Arizona, eliminated liquor prohibitions on Native Americans living on reservations, and demanded greater access to GI Bill benefits. Japanese American veterans, trading on their newfound status as war heroes, battled discriminatory veterans' organizations, employers, and alien land and naturalization laws and gained a modicum of redress for wartime mass confinement. And Mexican American veterans similarly returned fighting. Creating and helping to create new groups like the American G.I. Forum and the Community Service Organization or joining slightly older ones like the League for United Latin American Citizens, they fought against discrimination in the criminal justice system, cafés, schools, and housing.[25]

Military experiences convinced some white veterans to join these struggles as well. For some it was the act of traveling to and witnessing other less rigidly racist societies or fighting alongside "colored minorities" or rehabilitating with them in adjacent hospital beds or witnessing firsthand the ways that "blood and death . . . respected no man because of color." For others it was the evils of Nazi racism, the larger democratic and antiracist rhetoric of the war effort, or encounters with that other military caste regime that divided officer from enlisted personnel that convinced them to oppose "any system which grants unearned privileges to a particular class of individuals." Whatever the precise causes, some segment of white veterans returned home with a deepened or newfound determination to build a more egalitarian postwar America. One end-of-the-war informal survey of soldiers' postwar visions for the nation found, "above everything else, the need to wipe out racial and religious discrimination." New veterans' organizations, such as the American Veterans of World War II and the American Veterans Committee, were formed in part because "artificial barriers against our fellow men are crumbling under the impact of war. Bullets do not distinguish between color, race or creed. . . . These same democratic forces set in motion must be strengthened and reach their full function in peacetime." Other white veterans acted on these convictions, organizing "brotherhood days, weeks, and months," advocating for fair employment laws, speaking out against restrictive covenants in housing, and demanding a more democratic military and national guard.[26]

These varied postwar freedom struggles were never the sole product of the World War II military, of course; nor were they peopled exclusively or even primarily by veterans. In many cases, these struggles predated the war and also flourished on the home front among civilians. But a wide range of veterans still made up a vital new crop of activists that greatly strengthened and invigorated postwar America's assorted civil rights struggles. They were, unquestionably, the war's and the military's greatest gift to those fighting to birth the first true American democracy.

These struggles, intersecting with others abroad, may have helped birth or strengthen democracy there too. According to one scholar, for example, African Americans' wartime interactions with locals in Australia "were one factor behind the broader social and cultural shift that led eventually to the abolition of the White Australia Policy," a series of policies that restricted nonwhites from migrating to the country. Similarly, in Europe, North Africa, and elsewhere, black American soldiers' wartime encounters with colonized peoples, according to another scholar, "produced new sites of resistance to colonialism within and across nations."[27]

Back home, these civil rights struggles also produced a more egalitarian US military. Shortly after the war's end, in direct contrast to its beginning, no military service, for example, excluded any group on the basis of race. The practice of racist segregation by unit was well on its way out in the case of Japanese Americans and other nonblack minorities, and it was newly controversial in the case of African Americans. In fact, while the postwar black-white desegregation of the armed forces owed much to the Korean War, the Cold War, party politics, and the growing power of black voters and postwar protest, wartime activism, in and out of the military, laid the foundation. It did so by, among other things, forever changing people's views on the subject—those of African Americans, some military leaders and Congress members, and eventually President Truman—and by expanding their sense of the politically desirable and possible.

These were important advances, but the negative side of the ledger is longer and more significant. First, military color lines produced unspeakable trauma, suffering, and humiliation, which haunted some veterans long after the end of the war, if it did not kill them first. The distinguished historian John Hope Franklin recalled that his "older brother, a college graduate and high school principal . . . was abused by his white, uneducated staff sergeant, consigned to the kitchen brigade, and driven to an early grave, two years after the close of the war, by the insensitive, barbaric treatment of those who draped themselves in the flag and sang the national anthem even as they destroyed the nation's ideals and its people." Similarly, in *The Fire Next Time*, James Baldwin wrote, "Just before and then during the Second World War, many of my friends fled into the service, all to be changed there, and rarely for the better, many to be ruined, and many to die." And many of those who survived still faced serious challenges, even decades later. Interviewed in the 1970s, a black veteran recalled, "There are thousands of black ex-GIs who will not talk about World War II because for the black man it was humiliating, degrading, cruel—and not by accident. The treatment of the black was deliberate, contrived, and planned as well as the Normandy invasion, only the invasion is over but the wounds of the black are still raw."[28]

My grandfather-in-law's war story suggests that these lasting wounds were not black veterans' alone. Yasugo Kadomiya, born on Bainbridge

Fig. C.3 A portrait of a black soldier, having returned from war, 1945. The painter was fellow soldier Robert Smullyan Sloan. Courtesy of Deborah Smullyan and the Harvard Art Museums / Fogg Museum, accession no. 2004.194. © Robert Smullyan Sloan.

Island in Washington state, joined the army on his twenty-sixth birthday, January 13, 1942. What his experiences were like in uniform are largely unknown, except that on August 7, 1943, he and five other Japanese American soldiers stationed at Fort Francis E. Warren in Wyoming wrote to Secretary of War Stimson. They informed him that they wished to renounce their US citizenship and expatriate to Japan. Military racism seems to have played a decisive role. When the army investigated the men's requests, Kadomiya explained that "on several occasions in the United States Army I have been referred by officers as 'a goddam Jap.' An officer once told me that it is a disgrace to the United States to permit a Jap to wear a uniform." No doubt the other restrictions placed on Japanese American soldiers at the time—their mandatory movement inland, their constant surveillance, their loss of arms, and so forth—infuriated this willful, proud, and principled young man. In any case, the army rejected his (and the other) requests, but punished him just the same. It transferred him to a hard-labor battalion for the "potentially subversive," forced him to conduct menial tasks for the rest of the war, and eventually discharged him less than honorably, which restricted his access to invaluable GI Bill benefits, just as he was getting married and starting a family. When he died prematurely of alcoholism at fifty-eight, leaving a wife, a son who had recently graduated from MIT, and a small takeout restaurant on the north side of Miami, he had not been well for years. His embittering, if not downright traumatizing, experiences in uniform had to have played a role.[29]

Second, the military's racist lines unquestionably interfered with its efficient execution of the war, perhaps lengthening America's time in the conflict and costing American lives. To be clear, military leaders and civil rights activists hotly debated throughout the war whether color lines helped or hurt the Allies' chances against the Axis. Settling the matter definitively is impossible, since what the effects of a more egalitarian armed forces would have been in this period will never be known. What seems indisputable, however, is that military color lines—especially black-white ones—came with few benefits and considerable costs.[30] The military's restrictions against the enlistment of African Americans and Japanese Americans, or against their and other nonwhites' promotions and commissions, robbed it of hundreds of thousands of additional troops and untold numbers of people who, had they been given the chance, would have excelled as, say, combat troops or pilots or paratroopers or generals. Moreover, while military leadership often claimed that color lines minimized inefficiencies and strife, they often maximized both—in the form of the added administrative work required to run multiple militaries; in the form of the overuse and underuse of facilities, equipment, and people as a consequence of the same; in the form of countless disturbances and protests to dissolve or deepen racist divides; and in the form of lowered morale among many of those troops ensnared, enraged, and dispirited by them.[31]

Third, in drawing these color lines, the military made and remade the very idea of race, deepening belief in its taken-for-granted reality, what scholars Karen Fields and Barbara Fields have astutely called "racecraft." One might be tempted to discount the importance of this naturalization process, given that the concept of race had been around, by the war years, for at least a few centuries in the United States and beyond. But all racist regimes, less stable than they appear, require the constant making and remaking of race to live on. America's World War II military—sixteen million people strong, some 11 percent of the US population at the time—was among the nation's most important and bustling factories in this broader war production process. Along with the United States' colossal munitions industry, then, one might consider race to be the country's other great wartime "destructive creation." Speaking in the summer of 1944, NAACP leader Walter White both condemned this creation and unwittingly reflected its deep impact on so many Americans' thinking, including his own: "As long as our government insists on segregation in an army and navy allegedly fighting for democracy, the chasm between the races will be perpetuated and broadened with resultant bitterness on all sides. When ten or eleven million men return after the war is over, our government cannot escape responsibility for whatever happens since it is in large measure responsible for immature racial, political, economic and social thinking among these men whose every act they have directed for the period of their army and navy service."[32]

Fourth, this immature thinking most often looked on the ground like whites' deepening or newfound investment in white supremacy, especially its anti-black variant. Thanks in part to the US military's global movements, these investments appeared overseas. In France and England, for example, the United States' wartime presence seems to have contributed to the postwar "outburst of racial prejudices" and "growing racial discrimination" there. As for the United States, for every white veteran who returned home with a burning desire to redraw or remove America's color lines, there was another, or likely several, every bit as determined to protect those lines at all cost—especially, again, the black-white one. The most extensive army survey of soldiers' and veterans' views found that while some [whites] "felt that tolerance had been promoted by interracial contact in the Army . . . [a] larger group seemed to have reinforced their [prejudiced] pre-Army attitudes." Another study of a broader set of veteran and nonveteran opinion surveys in the postwar years found that, if the military did not worsen these prejudices, it also "seems to have had no moderating effect." Finally, in 1946, two eminent social scientists conducted extended, hours-long interviews with 150 white veterans from Chicago, finding widespread hostility toward black people in particular. One representative veteran, recalling his time in the service, remarked that relations with black GIs were fine "as long as they stayed in their place. We didn't associate with each other. They kept on the other side of the line." As this sentiment reflected, the authors found that claims "to have had no contact with Negroes in the army was *significantly* associated with outspoken and intense intolerance toward the Negro."[33] Just as Walter White and so many others had feared, military segregation—and racist divisions more broadly—seem in many cases to have "perpetuated and broadened" "the chasm between the races" rather than narrowed it.

Fifth, that this chasm was actually plural, not singular—that the military imposed not one color line but a bewildering mix of them—may have poisoned, or further poisoned, America's postwar politics for years to come. A War Department intelligence report from 1942 remarked, "In India the British have instituted as many as five or six grades of 'Jim Crow,' the reason for this being that the British found that the more classes there are, the easier it is to exploit the masses."[34] In other words, divide and conquer. Something similar happened in America's World War II armed forces, though save the crystal-clear intentionality. The military's many "grades of 'Jim Crow'" and many racialized "classes" greatly complicated the efforts of individual Americans and groups of them to imagine and to build broader solidarities. Compounding the problem was the military's unwavering insistence on the primacy of the black-white divide, especially its black-nonblack variant, in which black meant "Negro" or "colored" and white meant everyone else. By isolating black troops physically, materially, affectively, and symbolically, the military made it exceedingly difficult for anyone to imagine—let alone to construct—political bridges between black people, the nation's largest "racial minority," and other groups.

In this way, a fractured wartime military helped produce a fractured postwar America—and not simply between those, broadly speaking, fighting for or against white supremacy. There were also fractures among the latter. If a varied set of World War II veterans returned home with a newfound determination to democratize the nation, their freedom struggles tended to be just that—struggles in the plural, generally organized around particular identities such as Negro, Mexican or Latin American, Japanese American, and American Indian, and geared toward the particularities of each group's experience. The identity of "veteran" was a partial exception to this rule, but even here particularities appeared as separate veterans' groups emerged, sometimes in response to real exclusions, for everyone from African Americans and Chinese Americans to Jews and Catholics, to Italian Americans and Irish Americans. As historian Mark Brilliant put it in a slightly different context, these struggles often constituted "separate streams [that] . . . occasionally crossed" but seldom "converged into a civil rights movement"—or any mass movement—"river."[35] If veterans' experiences as wartime soldiers inspired them to join postwar protest struggles, these experiences may also have contributed to such struggles' largely parallel paths.

These parallel paths are especially noteworthy given the numerous promising Depression- and World War II–era efforts to cooperate across color lines—to build broad-ranging solidarities. Coalescing around an eclectic mix of expansive identities, from "workers" to "darker races" to simply "the people," a multihued collection of leftists, unionists, feminists, and civil rights activists organized and mobilized from Hawaii to Memphis, Los Angeles to New York, Winston-Salem to Detroit. They came together to fight fascism and imperialism, to advance civil rights and workers' rights, to mobilize for social democratic parties and candidates, and to imagine a new, more just world.[36] But such expansive solidarity appeared only intermittently in the military, and it often foundered in postwar civilian circles for numerous reasons, including the rise of the Cold War and the attendant attacks on the Left and on unions, and the particularities of distinct racisms throughout civilian state institutions and society. An additional, heretofore overlooked factor was the presence of deep and convoluted color lines in every aspect of millions of Americans' military lives—and the enduring fractures those lines produced.[37]

Finally, lost in this fracturing was a simple, but profound truth: military racism hurt everyone, or nearly everyone. *Divisions* has cataloged the manifold harms done to African Americans, Japanese Americans, and to a lesser extent other nonwhites. These harms endured in the form of skills not learned, promotions not won, wages not earned, wealth not accumulated, experience not gained, GI Bill benefits not received, mass movements not waged, and psychological traumas not resolved. But even white people, by far the biggest beneficiaries of the military's color lines, also paid a price, sometimes the ultimate price. They, too, suffered from a fractured polity and people that impeded broad mobilizations for potential lifesavers—from universal day care and health care to the wholesale restructuring of society—confirming another penetrating insight of W. E. B. Du Bois: "the problem of race discrimination always cuts across and hinders the settlement of other problems." Color lines, especially those between black and white, also ensured the overrepresentation of the latter among those who served, fought on the front lines, and died. According to one count, whites, who constituted roughly 90 percent of the US population in the war years, made up more than 96 percent of US World War II fatalities.[38] Viewed this way, military white supremacy crowned few true victors. So it has been with all forms of white supremacy.

NOTES

ABBREVIATIONS

ADW	*Atlanta Daily World*
AER	World War II Army Enlistment Records, Electronic Army Serial Number Merged File, ca. 1938–1946 (Enlistment Records), Record Group 64, https://aad.archives.gov/aad/fielded-search.jsp?dt=893&tf=F&cat=all
AGC	Alexander Gumby Collection, Rare Book and Manuscript Library, Columbia University, New York, NY
AGH	Adjutant General Headquarters Records, Formerly Classified General Correspondence, Record Group 492, National Archives at College Park, MD
AGS	Adjutant General's Section, Administrative Branch, General Correspondence, 1944–1945, Record Group 498, National Archives at College Park, MD
AJS	*American Journal of Sociology*
APRP	A. Philip Randolph Papers, Manuscript Division, Library of Congress, Washington, DC
ASR	*American Sociological Review*
BAA	*Baltimore Afro-American*
BLAC	Nettie Lee Benson Latin American Collection, University of Texas Libraries, University of Texas at Austin
BPR	Analysis Branch, News Division, [Army] Bureau of Public Relations, "Report of Trends in the Negro Press"
CABP	Claude A. Barnett Papers, Chicago History Museum, Research Center, Chicago, IL
CCP	*Cleveland Call and Post*
CD	*Chicago Defender*
CMS	Center for Migration Studies, New York, NY
CSL	Connecticut State Library, Hartford, CT
CT	*Chicago Tribune*
DMP	Dwight Macdonald Papers, MS 730, Manuscripts and Archives, Yale University Libraries, New Haven, CT
FDRL	Franklin D. Roosevelt Presidential Library and Museum, Hyde Park, NY
FDRP	Franklin D. Roosevelt Papers as President, Franklin D. Roosevelt Presidential Library and Museum, Hyde Park, NY

FGSP	Frank G. Speck Papers, American Philosophical Society, Philadelphia, PA
FORP	Fellowship of Reconciliation Papers, Swarthmore Peace Collection, Swarthmore, PA
GCMP	*The Papers of George Catlett Marshall*, ed. Larry I. Bland and Sharon Ritcnour Stevens (Lexington, VA: The George C. Marshall Foundation, 1981–). Electronic version based on *The Papers of George Catlett Marshall*, vol. 4, *"Aggressive and Determined Leadership," June 1, 1943–December 31, 1944* (Baltimore: Johns Hopkins University Press, 1996)
GCMRL	George C. Marshall Research Library, Lexington, VA
GPO	[US] Government Printing Office
HLSP	Henry L. Stimson Papers (micro), MS 465, Manuscripts and Archives, Yale University Libraries, New Haven, CT
HOHA	Hanashi Oral History Archive, Go For Broke National Education Center, Los Angeles, CA
HSTL	Harry S. Truman Library and Museum, Independence, MO
JAH	*Journal of American History*
JDP	Jonathan Daniels Papers, Southern Historical Collection, Louis Round Wilson Library, University of North Carolina at Chapel Hill
JJMP	John J. McCloy Papers, Archives and Special Collections, Amherst College Library, Amherst, MA
JNE	*Journal of Negro Education*
JNH	*Journal of Negro History*
LAT	*Los Angeles Times*
LDR	Lawrence D. Reddick World War II Project, Schomburg Center for Research in Black Culture, Archives and Rare Books Division, New York Public Library, New York, NY
MSRC	Moorland-Spingarn Research Center, Manuscript Division, Howard University, Washington, DC
NAACPR	National Association for the Advancement of Colored People Records, Manuscript Division, Library of Congress, Washington, DC
NARAII	National Archives at College Park, MD
NASE	National Archives at Atlanta, GA
NCSA	North Carolina State Archives, Raleigh, NC
NDL	Navy Department Library, Washington Navy Yard, Washington, DC
NJG	*Norfolk Journal and Guide*
NYAN	*New York Amsterdam News*
NYASN	*New York Amsterdam Star News*
NYHT	*New York Herald Tribune*
NYT	*New York Times*
NYTM	*New York Times Magazine*
PC	*Pittsburgh Courier*
PCC	Pacific Coast Committee on American Principles and Fair Play Records, Bancroft Library, University of California, Berkeley
PCCR	Records of the President's Committee on Civil Rights, Record Group 220, Harry S. Truman Library and Museum, Independence, MO
PCIT	*Pacific Citizen*
PNP	Philleo Nash Papers, Harry S. Truman Library and Museum, Independence, MO
RG 18	Records of the Army Air Forces, National Archives at College Park, MD

RG 44	Records of the Office of Government Reports, National Archives at College Park, MD
RG 46	Records of the United States Senate, National Archives at Washington, DC
RG 59	General Records of the Department of State, National Archives at College Park, MD
RG 60	General Records of the Department of Justice, National Archives at College Park, MD
RG 65	Federal Bureau of Investigation Records, National Archives at College Park, MD
RG 75	Records of the Bureau of Indian Affairs, National Archives at Atlanta, GA
RG 80	General Records of the Department of the Navy, 1798–1947, National Archives at College Park, MD
RG 83	Records of the Bureau of Agricultural Economics, National Archives at College Park, MD
RG 107	Records of the Office of the Secretary of War, National Archives at College Park, MD
RG 112	Records of the Office of the Surgeon General (Army), National Archives at College Park, MD
RG 126	Records of the Office of Territories, National Archives at College Park, MD
RG 147	Records of the Selective Service System
RG 159	Records of the Office of the Inspector General (Army), National Archives at College Park, MD
RG 160	Records of the Headquarters of the Army Service Forces, National Archives at College Park, MD
RG 165	Records of the War Department General and Special Staffs, National Archives at College Park, MD
RG 200	Records of the American Red Cross, National Archives Gift Collection, National Archives at College Park, MD
RG 208	Records of the Office of War Information, National Archives at College Park, MD
RG 210	Records of the War Relocation Authority, National Archives at Washington, DC
RG 228	Records of the Committee on Fair Employment Practice, National Archives at College Park, MD
RG 229	Records of the Office of Inter-American Affairs, National Archives at College Park, MD
RG 319	Records of the Army Staff, National Archives at College Park, MD
RG 337	Records of the Headquarters of Army Ground Forces, National Archives at College Park, MD
RG 389	Records of the Provost Marshal General, National Archives at College Park, MD
RG 407	Records of the Adjutant General's Office, National Archives at College Park, MD
RG 492	Records of the Mediterranean Theater of Operations, United States Army, National Archives at College Park, MD
RG 493	Records of the US Army Forces in the China-Burma-India, National Archives at College Park, MD

RG 494   Records of the US Army Forces in the Middle Pacific (World War II),
             National Archives at College Park, MD
RG 498   Records of Headquarters, European Theater of Operations,
             United States Army (World War II), National Archives at
             College Park, MD
ROC   General Correspondence (Formerly Classified), 1941–1945, Records of
             the Office of the Commandant, Pearl Harbor Navy Shipyard, Records
             of the Naval Districts and Shore Establishments, Record Group 181,
             National Archives at San Francisco, CA
RPPP   Robert Porter Patterson Papers, Manuscript Division, Library of
             Congress, Washington, DC
RWLP   Rayford W. Logan Papers, Manuscript Division, Library of Congress,
             Washington, DC
SCPC   Swarthmore College Peace Collection, Swarthmore, PA
SRE   Sociology of Race and Ethnicity
TIR   Army Service Forces, Office of the Commanding General, Technical
             Intelligence Report
TLV   The Library of Virginia, Richmond, VA
USDCEDL   Records of the United States District Court, Eastern District of
             Louisiana, New Orleans Division, Record Group 21, National Archives
             at Fort Worth, TX
USDCEDNC   Records of the United States District Court, Eastern District of North
             Carolina, Raleigh Division, Record Group 21, National Archives at
             Atlanta, GA
USDCEDP   Records of the United States District Court, Eastern District
             of Pennsylvania, Record Group 21, National Archives at
             Philadelphia, PA
USDCEDV   Records of the United States District Court, Eastern District of
             Virginia, Richmond Division, Record Group 21, National Archives at
             Philadelphia, PA
USDCNDI   Records of the United States District Court, Northern District of
             Illinois, Eastern Division at Chicago, Record Group 21, National
             Archives at Chicago, IL
USDCWDV   Records of the United States District Court, Western District
             of Virginia, Lynchburg, Record Group 21, National Archives at
             Philadelphia, PA
VHP   Veterans History Project, American Folklife Center, Library of
             Congress, Washington, DC
VOIIP   Voces Oral History Project, University of Texas at Austin
WDLR   Workers Defense League Records, Walter P. Reuther Library, Wayne
             State University, Detroit, MI
WP   Washington Post
WRADND   War Relocation Authority Daily News Digest, boxes 2-3, entry 5,
             Records of the War Relocation Authority, National Archives at
             Washington, DC
WRAWPR   War Relocation Authority Weekly Press Review, boxes 2-3, entry
             5, Records of the War Relocation Authority, National Archives at
             Washington, DC

INTRODUCTION

1. Charles Hurd, "400,000 by Jan. 1," *NYT*, Sept. 17, 1940, 1.

2. Quoted in John Morton Blum, *V Was for Victory: Politics and American Culture during World War II* (San Diego, CA: Harcourt Brace, 1976), 63; Ira Wolfert, *Battle for the Solomons* (Boston: Houghton Mifflin, 1943), 197; Donald Hough, *Captain Retread* (New York: Norton, 1944), 101; Joe McCarthy, "GI Vision of a Better America," *NYTM*, Aug. 5, 1945, 10. For secondary sources, see Benjamin L. Alpers, "This Is the Army: Imagining a Democratic Military in World War II," *JAH* 85 (June 1998): 143–147; Richard Slotkin, "Unit Pride: Ethnic Platoons and the Myths of American Nationality," *American Literary History* 13 (Sept. 2001): 469–498; Gary Gerstle, *American Crucible: Race and Nation in the Twentieth Century* (Princeton, NJ: Princeton University Press, 2001), 204–210. Gerstle makes the important point that, despite the claim above, many of Hollywood's plural platoons excluded black people.

3. Tom Brokaw, *The Greatest Generation* (New York: Delta, 1998), xxx; "Facts," National World War II Memorial, https://www.wwiimemorial.com/Facts/Facts.aspx (accessed Aug. 2, 2019); Thomas Bruscino, *A Nation Forged in War: How World War II Taught Americans to Get Along* (Knoxville: University of Tennessee Press, 2010). In fairness to Bruscino, whose book is excellent in many respects, he notes that African Americans were an exception to the argument, but it is a big exception and one that would not be expected given the book's subtitle. For a perceptive appreciation of popular World War II stories' emphasis on how "the cream of American manhood fought shoulder to shoulder," see Ann Banks, "Jim Crow's Last War," *NYT*, Feb. 16, 2003, sect. 7, 6.

4. See, for example, Robert L. Allen, *The Port Chicago Mutiny: The Story of the Largest Mass Mutiny Trial in Naval History* (New York: Amistad Press, 1993); Robert F. Jefferson, *Fighting for Hope: African American Troops of the 93rd Infantry Division in World War II and Postwar America* (Baltimore: Johns Hopkins University Press, 2008); Christopher S. Parker, *Fighting for Democracy: Black Veterans and the Struggle against White Supremacy in the Postwar South* (Princeton, NJ: Princeton University Press, 2009); Kimberley L. Phillips, *War! What Is It Good For? Black Freedom Struggles and the U.S. Military from World War II to Iraq* (Chapel Hill: University of North Carolina Press, 2012); Daniel Kryder, *Divided Arsenal: Race and the American State during World War II* (Cambridge: Cambridge University Press, 2000); Alan M. Osur, *Blacks in the Army Air Forces during World War II* (Washington, DC: GPO, 1977); Richard M. Dalfiume, *Desegregation of the U.S. Armed Forces: Fighting on Two Fronts, 1939–1953* (Columbia: University of Missouri Press, 1969); Ulysses Lee, *The Employment of Negro Troops* (Washington, DC: GPO, 1963); Morris J. MacGregor, *Integration of the Armed Forces, 1940–1965* (Washington, DC: Center of Military History, 1981); Sherie Mershon and Steven Schlossman, *Foxholes and Color Lines: Desegregating the U.S. Armed Forces* (Baltimore: Johns Hopkins University Press, 1998); Bernard C. Nalty, *Strength for the Fight: A History of Black Americans in the Military* (New York: Free Press, 1986); Susan L. Smith, *Toxic Exposures: Mustard Gas and the Health Consequences of World War II in the United States* (New Brunswick, NJ: Rutgers University Press, 2017); Mary Louise Roberts, *What Soldiers Do: Sex and the American GI in World War II France* (Chicago: University of Chicago Press, 2013); Luis Alvarez, "Transnational Latino Soldiering: Military Service and Ethnic Politics during World War II," in *Latina/os and World War II: Mobility, Agency, and Ideology*, ed. Maggie Rivas-Rodriguez and B. V. Olguín (Austin: University of Texas Press, 2014); Steven

Rosales, *Soldados Razos at War: Chicano Politics, Identity, and Masculinity in the U.S. Military from World War II to Vietnam* (Tucson: University of Arizona Press, 2017); Margarita Aragon, "'A General Separation of Colored and White': The WWII Riots, Military Segregation, and Racism(s) beyond the White/Nonwhite Binary," *SRE* 1 (Oct. 2015): 503–516; Takashi Fujitani, *Race for Empire: Koreans as Japanese and Japanese as Americans during World War II* (Berkeley: University of California Press, 2011); K. Scott Wong, *Americans First: Chinese Americans and the Second World War II* (Cambridge, MA: Harvard University Press, 2005); Christopher Capozzola, *Bound by War: How the United States and the Philippines Built America's First Pacific Century* (New York: Basic Books, 2020); Andrew Friedman, "US Empire, World War 2 and the Racialising of Labour," *Race & Class* 58, no. 4 (2017): 23–38.

5. Ralph Ellison, Introduction to *Invisible Man*, rev. ed. (New York: Vintage, 1989), xii. The US military employed several terms that, like *division*, had alternative meanings especially apposite to issues of race and racism. The Allies' code word for the invasion of Sicily, for example, was BIGOT. See Rick Atkinson, *The Day of Battle: The War in Sicily and Italy, 1943–1944* (New York: Picador, 2007), 34.

6. "Number of Enlistments and Inductions from July 1, 1940, thru December 31, 1941 Showing Nativity," Adjutant General's Office, Machine Records Section, Mar. 9, 1942, box 652, entry 389, RG 407.

7. I will call these boundaries "black-white," "Negro-white," and "colored-white" interchangeably. The "colored" category could signal a broader group of nonwhites but was often employed as a synonym for "Negro." "Black" is a more common term today, but was occasionally used during the war years as well.

8. Assistant Chief of Staff memo quoted in Edward S. Shattuck to Campbell C. Johnson, memo, Jan. 22, 1941, box 136, file 220, entry 1, RG 147, NARAII.

9. W. E. B. Du Bois, *Dark Princess* (1928; reprint with introduction by Claudia Tate, Jackson: University Press of Mississippi, 1995), 22.

10. Over the past several decades, scholars have debated which of these lines is predominating in the contemporary United States—or will predominate in the near future. But too little of this debate is informed by a deep knowledge of the past and its own tangle of color lines. For the debate, see, for example, Herbert J. Gans, "The Possibility of a New Racial Hierarchy in the Twenty-First-Century United States," in *The Cultural Territories of Race: Black and White Boundaries*, ed. Michéle Lamont (Chicago: University of Chicago Press, 1999), 371–390; Eduardo Bonilla-Silva, "From Bi-Racial to Tri-Racial: Towards a New System of Racial Stratification in the USA," *Ethnic and Racial Studies* 27 (Nov. 2004): 931–950; Frank D. Bean, Jennifer Lee, and James D. Bachmeier, "Immigration & the Color Line at the Beginning of the 21st Century," *Daedalus* 142 (Summer 2013): 123–140; Jennifer Lee and Frank D. Bean, *The Diversity Paradox: Immigration and the Color Line in the Twenty-First Century* (New York: Russell Sage, 2010), Jared Sexton, "People-of-Color-Blindness: Notes on the Afterlife of Slavery," *Social Text* 28 (Summer 2010): 31–56; David O. Sears and Victoria Savalei, "The Political Color Line in America: Many 'Peoples of Color' or Black Exceptionalism," *Political Psychology* 27 (Dec. 2006): 895–924; Nadia Y. Kim, "Critical Thoughts on Asian American Assimilation in the Whitening Literature," *Social Forces* 86 (Dec. 2007): 561–574; Moon-Kie Jung, "The Problem of the Color Lines: Studies of Racism and Resistance," *Critical Sociology* 41 (March 2015): 193–199. Only very rarely did wartime white-nonwhite lines exclude people of European descent from the former category, unless the military or local draft boards deemed them to have some non-European—especially "Negro" or Japanese—descent as well.

11. Samuel A. Stouffer, *The American Soldier* (Princeton, NJ: Princeton University Press, 1949), 1:412.
12. Selective Training and Service Act of 1940, Public Law 783, 76th Cong., 3d sess. (Sept. 16, 1940), 887.
13. Headquarters, Army Service Forces, *Leadership and the Negro Soldier* (Washington, DC: GPO, 1944), 2.
14. Noura Erakat, *Justice for Some: Law and the Question of Palestine* (Stanford, CA: Stanford University Press, 2019), 90. For a small sample of work on the importance of southern Democrats, see Jill Quadagno, *The Color of Welfare: How Racism Undermined the War on Poverty* (New York: Oxford University Press, 1994); Robert C. Lieberman, *Shifting the Color Line: Race and the American Welfare State* (Cambridge, MA: Harvard University Press, 1998); Ira Katznelson, *When Affirmative Action Was White: An Untold Story of Racial Inequality in Twentieth-Century America* (New York: Norton, 2005); Ira Katznelson, *Fear Itself: The New Deal and the Origins of Our Time* (New York: Liveright, 2013); David A. Bateman, Ira Katznelson, and John S. Lapinski, *Southern Nation: Congress and White Supremacy after Reconstruction* (New York: Russell Sage Foundation, 2018).
15. In a marvelous book, Ira Katznelson makes a similar argument about the entire New Deal period, during which the US government "had to navigate dangerous borderlands where freedom and the lack of freedom overlapped." But whereas Katznelson attributes much of this domestic unfreedom to the influence of southern Democrats in Congress, I see its source, at least in the case of the military, as more national in scope and as spreading across all branches of the federal government. See Katznelson, *Fear Itself*, 8. Rooted in slavery and settler colonialism, the United States, or what would become the United States, has long had these foundational and productive paradoxes, productive because freedom and unfreedom were co-constitutive. See, for example, W. E. B. Du Bois, *Black Reconstruction in America, 1860–1880* (1935; New York: Free Press, 1998); Edmund S. Morgan, *American Slavery, American Freedom: The Ordeal of Colonial Virginia* (New York: Norton, 1976); Tyler Stovall, *White Freedom: The Racial History of an Idea* (Princeton, NJ: Princeton University Press, 2021).
16. An enormous literature portrays World War II as a "seedbed" for the modern black civil rights movement. For a small sample, see Richard M. Dalfiume, "The 'Forgotten Years' of the Negro Revolution," *JAH* 55 (June 1968): 90–106; Merl E. Reed, *Seedtime for the Modern Civil Rights Movement: The President's Committee on Fair Employment Practice, 1941–1946* (Baton Rouge: Louisiana State University Press, 1991); Jacquelyn Dowd Hall, "The Long Civil Rights Movement and the Political Uses of the Past," *JAH* 91 (Mar. 2005): 1233–1263; Robert Rodgers Korstad, *Civil Rights Unionism: Tobacco Workers and the Struggle for Democracy in the Mid-Twentieth-Century South* (Chapel Hill: University of North Caroline Press, 2003); Glenda Gilmore, *Defying Dixie: The Radical Roots of Civil Rights, 1919–1950* (New York: Norton, 2008). On the war's positive impacts on Mexican American civil rights struggles, see Edward J. Escobar, *Race, Police, and the Making of a Political Identity: Mexican Americans and the Los Angeles Police Department, 1900–1945* (Berkeley: University of California Press, 1999); and Zaragosa Vargas, *Labor Rights Are Civil Rights: Mexican American Workers in Twentieth-Century America* (Princeton, NJ: Princeton University Press, 2005). For an alternative perspective— that the war harmed black civil rights struggles more than it helped them—see Harvard Sitkoff, "African American Militancy in the World War II South: Another Perspective," in *Remaking Dixie: The Impact of World War II on the American South*,

ed. Neil R. McMillen (Jackson: University of Mississippi Press, 1997), 70–92; and Kevin M. Kruse and Stephen Tuck, eds., *Fog of War: The Second World War and the Civil Rights Movement* (New York: Oxford University Press, 2012). On military-related activism, see Allen, *The Port Chicago Mutiny*; Jefferson, *Fighting for Hope*; Parker, *Fighting for Democracy*; Phillips, *War!*; Kryder, *Divided Arsenal*; Osur, *Blacks in the Army Air Forces*; Lawrence Scott and William M. Womack Jr., *Double V: The Civil Rights Struggle of the Tuskegee Airmen* (East Lansing: Michigan State University Press, 1992); Joyce Thomas, "The 'Double V' Was for Victory: Black Soldiers, the Black Protest, and World War II" (PhD diss., Ohio State University, 1993); Sarah Ayako Barksdale, "Prelude to a Revolution: African-American World War II Veterans, Double Consciousness, and Civil Rights, 1940–1955" (PhD diss., University of North Carolina, 2014); Dalfiume, *Desegregation of the U.S. Armed Forces*; Christine Knauer, *Let Us Fight as Free Men: Black Soldiers and Civil Rights* (Philadelphia: University of Pennsylvania Press, 2014); Mershon and Schlossman, *Foxholes and Color Lines*; Nalty, *Strength for the Fight*; Alvarez, "Transnational Latino Soldiering"; Fujitani, *Race for Empire*; and Thomas A. Guglielmo, "A Martial Freedom Movement: Black G.I.s' Political Struggles during World War II," *JAH* 104 (Mar. 2018): 879–903.

17. By "movement," I mean "conscious, concerted, and sustained efforts by ordinary people to change some aspect of their society" by working primarily outside formal political channels. See Jeff Goodwin and James Jasper, eds., *The Social Movements Reader: Cases and Concepts* (Malden, MA: Wiley-Blackwell, 2015), 3.

18. Planning Committee of National Committee to Abolish Segregation in the Armed Services, press release, Apr. 30, 1945, box 65, WDLR; Bertha Gruner, "Minutes of the Proceedings of Conference . . . in Order to Formulate a Program of Action to End Race Segregation and Discrimination by the Armed Service," n.d., 7, box 17, APRP.

19. Social science scholarship on boundaries is extensive. For an introduction, see Michele Lamont and Virag Molnar, "The Study of Social Boundaries in the Social Sciences," *Annual Review of Sociology* 28 (2002): 167–195; and Andreas Wimmer, *Ethnic Boundary Making: Institutions, Power, Networks* (New York: Oxford University Press, 2013). Especially influential to me has been Loïc Wacquant's insistence on the need to study "practices of division and the institutions that both buttress and result from them." See Loïc J. D. Wacquant, "For an Analytic of Racial Domination," *Political Power and Social Theory* 11 (1997): 221–234, esp. 229. On the point that boundaries are simultaneously inclusionary and exclusionary, see Devon Carbado, "Racial Naturalization," *American Quarterly* 57 (Sept. 2005): 639, 653; Moon-Kie Jung, *Beneath the Surface of White Supremacy: Denaturalizing U.S. Racisms Past and Present* (Stanford, CA: Stanford University Press, 2015), 70. Boundary-making also appears in acts of resistance against boundaries if resisters seek to overturn the hierarchical ordering attached to these distinctions, but not the distinctions themselves. On this point, see Wimmer, *Ethnic Boundary Making*, 57.

20. Taking these racist lines together, I refer to a "structure," which involves the mutually sustaining worlds of "resources"—in the military context, this would include, say, rank, jobs, pay, and recreational facilities—and "schemas"—ideas, attitudes, assumptions, stories, beliefs, sentiments, and so forth. See Jung, *Beneath the Surface of White Supremacy*, 21–51; William H. Sewell Jr., "A Theory of Structure: Duality, Agency, and Transformation," *AJS* 98 (July 1992): 1–29; Eduardo Bonilla-Silva, "Rethinking Racism: Toward a Structural Interpretation," *ASR* 62 (June 1997): 465–480.

21. The great majority of work on race and racism still revolves around a single binary—either white-black or white-nonwhite. This holds true for work on the World War II military as well. See, for example, Dalfiume, *Desegregation of the U.S. Armed Forces*; Kryder, *Divided Arsenal*; Katznelson, *When Affirmative Action Was White*, 80–112; Mershon and Schlossman, *Foxholes and Color Lines*; Steven White, *World War II and American Racial Politics: Public Opinion, the Presidency, and Civil Rights Advocacy* (Cambridge: Cambridge University Press, 2019). But building on older work, more scholars recently have been examining race and racism with regard to multiple, sometimes intersecting boundaries. On the World War II military, see Aragon, "'A General Separation of Colored and White.'" For an excellent, recent introduction to this broader work, see Natalia Molina, Daniel Martinez HoSang, and Ramón A. Gutiérrez, eds., *Relational Formations of Race: Theory, Method, and Practice* (Berkeley: University of California Press, 2019).

22. Mustafa Emirbayer and Matthew Desmond, *The Racial Order* (Chicago: University of Chicago Press, 2015), 79.

23. For the claim that service members during World War II constituted a larger share of the US population than in any other war, I have found service member numbers at "America's Wars," US Department of Veterans Affairs, Office of Public Affairs, May 2017, https://www.va.gov/opa/publications/factsheets/fs_americas_wars.pdf (accessed Aug. 1, 2019). For the GI's average age, see David M. Kennedy, *Freedom from Fear: The American People in Depression and War, 1929–1945* (New York: Oxford University Press, 1999), 710.

24. Robert K. Carr to Members of the President's Committee on Civil Rights, memo, June 10, 1947, box 37, PNP. We know a lot about racist divisions and the struggles they generated in twentieth-century state institutions of various kinds, involving housing, schools, welfare, immigration, deportation, miscegenation law, the census, the courts, empire, warfare, prisons, policing, and more. But the military is a singular case, which requires the singular focus it receives here. For a small sample of this extensive, outstanding literature, see N. D. B. Connolly, *A World More Concrete: Real Estate and the Remaking of the Jim Crow South* (Chicago: University of Chicago Press, 2014); Cybelle Fox, *Three Worlds of Relief: Race, Immigration, and the American Welfare State from the Progressive Era to the New Deal* (Princeton, NJ: Princeton University Press, 2012); Ruth Wilson Gilmore, *Golden Gulag: Prisons, Surplus, Crisis and Opposition in Globalizing California* (Berkeley: University of California Press, 2006); Adam Goodman, *The Deportation Machine: America's Long History of Expelling Immigrants* (Princeton, NJ: Princeton University Press, 2020); Kelly Lyttle Hernandez, *City of Inmates: Conquest, Rebellion, and the Rise of Human Caging* (Chapel Hill: University of North Carolina Press, 2017); Elizabeth Kai Hinton, *From the War on Poverty to the War on Crime: The Making of Mass Incarceration in America* (Cambridge, MA: Harvard University Press, 2016); Paul Kramer, *The Blood of Government: Race, Empire, the United States, and the Philippines* (Chapel Hill: University of North Carolina Press, 2006); Beth Lew-Williams, *The Chinese Must Go: Violence, Exclusion, and the Making of the Alien in America* (Cambridge, MA: Harvard University Press, 2018); Mae M. Ngai, *Impossible Subjects: Illegal Aliens and the Making of Modern America* (Princeton, NJ: Princeton University Press, 2004); Peggy Pascoe, *What Comes Naturally: Miscegenation Law and the Making of Race in America* (New York: Oxford University Press, 2009); Joel Perlmann, *America Classifies the Immigrants: From Ellis Island to the 2020 Census* (Cambridge, MA: Harvard University Press, 2018); Richard Rothstein, *The Color of Law: A Forgotten History of How Our Government Segregated America*

(New York: Liveright, 2017); Nikhil Pal Singh, *Race and America's Long War* (Berkeley: University of California Press, 2017); Keeanga-Yamahtta Taylor, *Race for Profit: How Banks and the Real Estate Industry Undermined Black Homeownership* (Chapel Hill: University of North Carolina Press, 2019).

25. Stouffer, *American Soldier*, 1:379; Lee Kennett, *G.I.: The American Soldier in World War II* (New York: Charles Scribner's, 1987), 84; Stouffer, *American Soldier*, 1:55. Military rank and social class bore some resemblance to one another. But "the class basis of war and the fact those who are most likely to fight are most likely to be poor or from the working class" held less true for World War II than for many other wars. For the quotation, see Simeon Man, *Soldiering through Empire: Race and the Making of the Decolonizing Pacific* (Berkeley: University of California Press, 2018), 11.

26. Susan M. Hartmann, *The Home Front and Beyond: American Women in the 1940s* (Boston: Twayne, 1982), 37; Allan Berube, *Coming Out under Fire: The History of Gay Men and Women in World War II* (New York: Free Press, 1990), 178.

27. "Protest Army Jim-Crow," *Fighting Worker*, Sept. 24, 1941, 1, 4. For the Marx analogy, see Karl Marx, *Capital: A Critique of Political Economy* (New York: Modern Library, 1936), 364. Thanks to Elizabeth Esch and Dave Roediger for introducing it to me. See David R. Roediger and Elizabeth D. Esch, *The Production of Difference: Race and the Management of Labor in U.S. History* (New York: Oxford University Press, 2012), 9; Elizabeth D. Esch, *The Color Line and the Assembly Line: Managing Race in the Ford Empire* (Berkeley: University of California Press, 2018), 16.

28. Marx, *Capital*, 282, 286. For recent ruminations on the "violent entanglements" between militaries and capitalism, see the "Militarism and Capitalism" special issue of *Radical History Review* 133 (Jan. 2019).

CHAPTER 1

1. I arrived at the half million estimate in the following way: 16,112,566 Americans served as military personnel during World War II. Ten percent of that number—the proportion of black people in the US population during the war years—is 1.61 million. But roughly 1.1 million black Americans—not 1.61 million—served as US military personnel during the war. The difference in those two numbers—1.61 million versus 1.1 million—is roughly 500,000. For the total number of US military personnel during World War II, see Anne Leland and Mari-Jana "M-J" Oboroceanu, "American War and Military Operations Casualties: Lists and Statistics," Congressional Research Service report to Congress, Feb. 26, 2010, 4. For the total number of African American military personnel during the war, see Ulysses Lee, *The Employment of Negro Troops* (Washington, DC: GPO, 1963), 211n30, 414; Morris J. MacGregor, *Integration of the Armed Forces, 1940–1965* (Washington, DC: Center of Military History, 1981), 7, 71; Alvan C. Gillem et al., "Policy for the Utilization of Negro Manpower in the Post-War Army," Nov. 1945, 18, box 442, entry 43, RG 165; Bernard C. Nalty, "The Right to Fight: African-American Marines in World War II," in *Marines in World War II Commemorative Series* (Washington, DC: GPO, 1995), 28. For African Americans' proportion of the total US population, see US Department of Commerce, Economics and Statistics Administration, Bureau of the Census, *We the Americans: Blacks* (Washington, DC: GPO, 1993), 4. For the total number of Allied troops at D-Day, see "D-Day, June 6, 1944," US Army, https://www.army.mil/d-day/ (accessed Jan. 15, 2020). For the US military's

expanding sense of who was fit to serve, see Rick Atkinson, *The Guns at Last Light: The War in Western Europe, 1944–1945*, vol. 3 of *The Liberation Trilogy* (New York: Picador, 2013), 19.

2. John Hope Franklin, *Mirror to America: The Autobiography of John Hope Franklin* (New York: Farrar, Straus and Giroux, 2005), 105.
3. Franklin, *Mirror to America*, 106.
4. John Hope Franklin, "Their War and Mine," *JAH* 77 (Sept. 1990): 578.
5. Gene De Poris, "What Have Negroes to Fight For?" *PM*, May 17, 1941, 16–17; Roi Ottley, "A White Folks' War?," *Common Ground*, Spring 1942, 278; Earl Brown, "American Negroes and the War," *Harper's*, Apr. 1942, 546; Horace R. Cayton, "Fighting for White Folks?," *Nation*, Sept. 26, 1942, 267–270.
6. Polling Division, Bureau of Intelligence, Office of Facts and Figures, "Negro Attitudes toward Certain War-Connected Problems," Mar. 9, 1942, box 1797, entry 164, RG 44; Surveys Division, Bureau of Special Services, Office of War Information, "The Negroes' Role in the War," July 8, 1943, box 1797, entry 164, RG 44 (emphasis in original); Bureau of Intelligence, Office of War Information, "Negroes and the War: A Study in Baltimore and Cincinnati," special report no. 16, July 21, 1942, 3, box 1784, entry 162, RG 44; Robert A. Hill, ed., *The FBI's RACON: Racial Conditions in the United States during World War II* (Boston: Northeastern University Press, 1995), 91, 292–294, 300–301.
7. E. Skolnick, "Weekly Assignment #4," Feb. 13, 1943, 11, box 1839, entry 171, RG 44; Francis Biddle notes on cabinet meeting, Mar. 6, 1942, box 1, Francis Biddle Papers, FDRL. For examples of "quiet refusal," see "Three Brothers Held as Dodgers of the Draft," *ADW*, Oct. 31, 1940, 1; "Two Draftees Not at Home," *NYAN*, Nov. 2, 1940, 1; Selective Service System, *Special Groups*, Special Monographs, no. 10, vol. 1 (Washington, DC: GPO, 1953), 82–83.
8. "'The Draft Finally Got Me,'" *BAA*, Sept. 21, 1940, 1; Gerald Robert Gill, "Afro-American Opposition to the United States' Wars of the Twentieth Century: Dissent, Discontent and Disinterest" (PhD diss., Howard University, 1985), 200; Manning Marable, *Malcolm X: A Life of Reinvention* (New York: Viking, 2011), 59; Dizzy Gillespie with Al Fraser, *To Be or Not . . . to Bop* (1979; Minneapolis: University of Minnesota Press, 2009), 120.
9. "Balks Call to Arms; Cites Jim Crow," *CD*, Jan. 11, 1941, 1.
10. "Balks Call to Arms," *CD*, Jan. 11, 1941, 1; "Red Cap, Drafted for Army, Asks to be Excused until Democracy Gets Going in Fighting Forces," newspaper clipping, n.d., box 318, CABP. On the outcome of Calloway's case, see Robert Bussel, *Fighting for Total Person Unionism: Harold Gibbons, Ernest Calloway, and Working-Class Citizenship* (Urbana: University of Illinois Press, 2015), 48–49. On Calloway's membership in Drake's conscientious objector organization, see "Swear They Will Not Fight for Uncle Sam," newspaper clipping, n.d., box 318, CABP.
11. On Keemer's case, see "Draft Case of Detroit Medic Again Delayed," *BAA*, Aug. 28, 1943, 5; "Tells Draft Board 'No,'" *BAA*, July 3, 1943, 1; "The Case of Dr. Edgar Keemer," *Militant*, June 19, 1943, in C. L. R. James et al., *Fighting Racism in World War II* (New York: Pathfinder, 1980), 257–258; and materials in folder 4, box II:A523, NAACPR. Keemer's principled willingness to defy authority continued well into the postwar years. Despite Michigan's anti-abortion laws, he made a name for himself as a safe and reliable abortion provider in Detroit and became, in time, an outspoken pro-choice advocate. See Eileen Shanahan, "Doctor Leads Group's Challenge to Michigan Anti-Abortion Law," *NYT*, Oct. 5, 1971, 28 (quotation); and Leslie J. Reagan, *When Abortion Was a Crime: Women, Medicine, and Law*

in the United States, 1867–1973 (Berkeley: University of California Press, 1998), 156–157.

12. "11 Held Here as Plotters for Japanese," *Chicago Sun*, Sept. 22, 1942, 1; "FBI Accuses 80 in Chicago of Part in Seditious Activities," *Chicago Herald American*, Sept. 23, 1942, 1; "12 Negro Chiefs Seized by FBI in Sedition Raids," *CT*, Sept. 22, 1942, 9; "Takahashi's Blacks," *Time*, Oct. 5, 1942, 25–26; Selective Service System, *Special Groups*, no. 10, 1:80–81. On the total number of blacks convicted of draft evasion during the war, Selective Service System, *Special Groups*, no. 10, 1:83. For government intelligence on these organizations, see, for example, "Japanese Inspired Agitation among the American Negroes," War Department intelligence report, July 12, 1943, box 15, entry 180, RG 107.

13. Lewis Jones, "Why I Won't Fight," *BAA*, Oct. 10, 1942, 1. For someone who seems to have straddled the line between a repudiation of and desire for US citizenship, see Thomas Parks, a twenty-five-year-old New Yorker. At his draft evasion trial, in 1942, he explained that his refusal to report for induction derived from his "part-time citizenship." Interestingly, one Thomas Parks, presumably the same one (also a New Yorker), co-wrote a letter to President Roosevelt desiring "a national home-land of their [blacks'] own on the continent of Africa." See Thomas Parks, interview by Lawrence D. Reddick, Sept. 4, 1946, box 5, LDR; "Draft Evader Swiftly Convicted," *NYT*, May 16, 1942, 4; Carlos Cooks and Thomas Parks to President Roosevelt, Feb. 23, 1942, box 3804, central decimal file 811.4016, 1940–1944, RG 59. After serving nineteen months at the Danbury Federal Penitentiary in Connecticut (where he helped to lead a number of strikes against segregation there), Parks was released, only to be drafted—and to defy his induction order—again. He was sent back to prison, this time for a four-year sentence. See Thomas Parks, interview by Lawrence D. Reddick, Sept. 4, 1946, box 5, LDR.

14. On "We Are Americans Too," see March on Washington Movement, "Why Should We March?," circular, n.d., box 5, APRP. For the "Double V" slogan, see *PC*, Feb. 14, 1942, 1. For Thompson letter, see James G. Thompson, "Should I Sacrifice to Live 'Half-American'?," *PC*, Jan. 31, 1942, 3. On the material benefits of military service, see Gunnar Myrdal, *The Negro Problem and Modern Democracy*, vol. 1 of *An American Dilemma* (1944; New Brunswick, NJ: Transaction, 2002), 419; Ira Katznelson, *When Affirmative Action Was White: An Untold Story of Racial Inequality in Twentieth-Century America* (New York: Norton, 2005), 105. For "Negro is a Man" quotation, see Horace Mann Bond, "The Negro in the Armed Forces of the United States Prior to World War I," *JNE* 12 (Summer 1943): 287.

15. See Bureau of Naval Personnel, "The Negro in the Navy," typescript, 1947, NDL; MacGregor, *Integration of the Armed Forces*, 4–6; William R. Mueller, "The Negro in the Navy," *Social Forces* 24 (Oct. 1945): 110–115; Nalty, "The Right to Fight."

16. See Lee, *Employment of Negro Troops*, 25–20, MacGregor, *Integration of the Armed Forces*, 5–7; L. D. Reddick, "The Negro Policy of the United States Army, 1775–1945," *JNH* 34 (Jan. 1949): 18; Bernard C. Nalty, *Strength for the Fight: A History of Black Americans in the Military* (New York: Free Press, 1986). On blacks "passing" as whites in the US military before and during World War II, a topic worthy of its own treatment, see W. L. White, *Lost Boundaries* (New York: Harcourt, Brace, 1947), 31–33; Arthur Miller, *Situation Normal* (New York: Reynal & Hitchcock, 1944), 92–93; Maurice E. (Jack) Wilson, Interview by Studs Terkel, n.d., in *"The Good War": An Oral History of World War II*, ed. Studs Terkel (New York: New Press, 1984), 70–71; Allyson Hobbs, *A Chosen Exile: A History of Racial Passing in American Life* (Cambridge, MA: Harvard University Press, 2014), 11, 219–220.

17. "U.S. Navy Does Not Want Us," *BAA*, Oct. 7, 1939, 9; Metz T. P. Lochard, "Negroes and Defense," *Nation*, Jan. 4, 1941, 15; Albert James to Mr. President, Nov. 27, 1941, box 1079, entry 363, RG 407.

18. "Our Lily-White Navy," *PC*, Feb. 27, 1937, 6. See also Lee, *Employment of Negro Troops*, 51–87.

19. Roy Wilkins to Samuel A. Reed, June 14, 1940, folder 2, box II:A654, NAACPR; "Racial Discrimination Suicidal When Invasion Threatens America," *Philadelphia Tribune*, Sept. 26, 1940, 4; "Negro Officers in the Army," *PC*, Oct. 19, 1940, 6; "Whose Army Is It?," *PC*, May 4, 1940, 6.

20. Florence Murray, *The Negro Handbook* (New York: W. Malliet, 1942), 60; "Only Four Officers," *Cleveland Gazette*, Apr. 23, 1938, 2; NAACP Secretary to Senator, Aug. 8, 1940, box II:A441, NAACPR; Thurgood Marshall to Secretary, memo, Aug. 9, 1940, box II:A647, NAACPR; "Let's Carry This Fight Through," *PC*, Mar. 5, 1938, 10; "Dr. Logan Sounds Warning," *PC*, Aug. 3, 1940, 12; "Courier's Plea for Fair Play in Draft Presented to the House," *PC*, Aug. 17, 1940, 1; "Text of Statement by Dr. Rayford Logan before Committee," *PC*, Aug. 24, 1940, 12. See also "The Right to Serve in the Army," *CCP*, Apr. 14, 1938, 6; "More Representation in Army and Navy," *NJG*, Mar. 5, 1938, 8; "Our Armed Forces," *NYAN*, June 1, 1940, 8; United Government Employees to President Roosevelt, resolution, Oct. 20, 1940, box 3, entry 99, RG 107.

21. "Mass Protests against Army Jim Crow Urged," *BAA*, June 22, 1940, 3.

22. Public Law 703, 76th Cong., 3d sess., July 2, 1940, 713; Selective Training and Service Act of 1940, Public Law 783, 76th Cong., 3d sess., Sept. 16, 1940, 885, 887. On civilian aviation training for blacks, see Lee, *Employment of Negro Troops*, 55–64. For the NAACP's and CPNNDP's lobbying, see Walter White to Roy Wilkins, memo, Sept. 7, 1940, box II:A112, NAACPR; Walter White to —— [House Members], Sept. 3, 1940, box II:A112, NAACPR; Walter White to Warren Barbour, Aug. 27, 1940, box II:A112, NAACPR; Walter White to Robert Wagner, Sept. 18, 1940, box II:A112, NAACPR; NAACP Secretary to Senator, Aug. 8, 1940, box II:A441, NAACPR; "Dr. Logan Sounds Warning," *PC*, Aug. 3, 1940, 12; "Courier's Plea for Fair Play in Draft Presented to the House," *PC*, Aug. 17, 1940, 1; "Want Safeguards in Service Bill," *PC*, Aug. 17, 1940, 13; "Text of Statement by Dr. Rayford Logan Before Committee," *PC*, Aug. 24, 1940, 12; Rayford W. Logan Diary, typescript, Aug. 31, 1940, Sept. 2, 1940, Sept. 4, 1940, Sept. 5, 1940, Sept. 6, 1940, box 3, RWLP.

23. Campbell C. Johnson, "The Mobilization of Negro Manpower for the Armed Forces," *JNE* 12 (Summer 1943): 302; Walter White to Warren Barbour, Aug. 27, 1940, box II:A112, NAACPR.

24. "Mr. Willkie and Mr. Roosevelt," *PC*, Aug. 10, 1940, 6; "The President and Precedent," *PC*, Aug. 31, 1940, 6.

25. For the tightening race, see David M. Kennedy, *Freedom from Fear: The American People in Depression and War, 1929–1945* (New York: Oxford University Press, 1999), 462. For the War Department statement, see Lee, *Employment of Negro Troops*, 75. For Roosevelt's statement, see Charles Hurd, "400,000 by Jan. 1," *NYT*, Sept. 17, 1940, 1. For Eleanor Roosevelt's influence and quotation, see Doris Kearns Goodwin, *No Ordinary Time: Franklin and Eleanor Roosevelt: The Home Front in World War II* (New York: Simon & Schuster, 1994), 168.

26. E. S. Adams to Commanding Generals, Oct. 16, 1940, box 810, entry 178, RG 160; Rayford W. Logan Diary, typescript, Oct. 25, 1940, box 3, RWLP.

27. Hurd, "400,000 by Jan. 1"; Alan M. Osur, *Blacks in the Army Air Forces during World War II: The Problem of Race Relations* (Washington, DC: GPO, 1977), 23–24;

MacGregor, *Integration of the Armed Forces*, 28. This black flying outfit was "to be trained under the supervision of 11 white officers and 15 white noncommissioned officers until such time that a sufficient number of black airmen could be trained to replace them. However, in accordance with Army Regulation 95-60, the Commanding Officer at Tuskegee had to be white." See MacGregor, *Integration of the Armed Forces*, 24.

28. Osur, *Blacks in the Army Air Forces*, 23–24; William H. Hastie, *On Clipped Wings: The Story of Jim Crow in the Army Air Corps*, NAACP pamphlet, July 1, 1943.

29. On the flight to Washington and the two pilots, see "Strictly Personal," *BAA*, May 20, 1939, 6; Nalty, *Strength for the Fight*, 135–136. On the broader protest against the air corps, see *Crisis*, July 1940, cover; Mr. Maletz to Mr. Clark, June 23, 1941, box 875, entry OP-45, RG 46; Mr. Lathrom to Mr. Fulton, July 15, 1941, box 875, entry OP-45, RG 46; Penn Kimball, "No Help Wanted . . . If You're a Negro," *PM*, May 7, 1941, 14.

30. "Rejected by Air Corps, Youth Sues," *BAA*, Jan. 25, 1941, 1; Julian P. Fromer, "Army Forms Negro Air Squadron as Youth Sues on Discrimination," *PM*, Jan. 17, 1941, 11; W. Robert Ming Jr., "The Negro in the Armed Forces," typed address to the annual NAACP conference, June 26, 1941, 11, box II:A23, NAACPR.

31. Henry Lewis Stimson Diaries, Jan. 17, 1942, microfilm, reel 7, HLSP; "Fragments on Back-Room Politics and Civil Rights," *American Heritage*, Feb./Mar. 1982, https://www.americanheritage.com/fragments-back-room-politics-and-civil-rights. On the navy and the marines, see Bureau of Naval Personnel, "The Negro in the Navy"; MacGregor, *Integration of the Armed Forces*, 58–122; Mueller, "The Negro in the Navy"; Nalty, "The Right to Fight."

32. "Our Lily-White Navy," *PC*, Feb. 27, 1937, 6; "Pots and Pans Policy Keeps Us Out of This," *BAA*, Apr. 16, 1938, 14; "In the Navy Messmen Only," *Kansas City Call*, in "Editorial Digest—Negro Papers, Aug.–Dec. 1941," Dec. 15, 1941, box 2, entry 131d, RG 80.

33. Negroes' Committee to March on Washington for Equal Participation in National Defense, "Call to Negro America," n.d., box 29, APRP. For the two meetings with Roosevelt, see "Fragments on Back-Room Politics and Civil Rights," *American Heritage*, Feb./Mar. 1982, https://www.americanheritage.com/fragments-back-room-politics-and-civil-rights; "Race Leaders Stand Pat on Job Demands," *CD*, June 28, 1941, 1; NAACP Press Release, Oct. 25, 1940, box II:A442, NAACPR. On the NAACP's early battles against the navy, see, for example, Anonymous, "The Negro in the United States Navy," *Crisis*, July 1940, 200–201, 210; "Army and Navy Chiefs Urged to Remove Color Bar in Armed Forces," *PC*, Aug. 3, 1940, 5; Thurgood Marshall to Frank Knox, July 26, 1940, box II:A654, NAACPR; "NAACP Mass Meeting PROTEST! Discrimination and Jim Crow in the Army, Navy, and Air Force," leaflet, c. Oct. 29, 1940, box II:A442, NAACPR.

34. Henry Lewis Stimson Diaries, microfilm, Jan. 18, 1941, reel 6, HLSP; Capt. Francis E. M. Whiting, Col. Thomas E. Watson, and Lt. Commander A. D. Chandler, Col. Watson Committee Majority Report, c. Dec. 24, 1941, box 2, entry 131d, RG 80.

35. Addison Walker to Secretary of the Navy, Dec. 31, 1941, box 2, entry 131d, RG 80.

36. Walter White to President Roosevelt, telegram, Dec. 9, 1941, box II:A654, NAACPR; Addison Walker to Walter White, Dec. 10, 1941, box 2, entry 131d, RG 80; Mark Ethridge to President Roosevelt, Dec. 31, 1941, box 339, Formerly Security Classified, General Correspondence of Chief of Naval Operations/Secretary of Navy, 1940–1947, RG 80; Franklin D. Roosevelt to Frank Knox, memo, Jan. 9,

1942, box 339, Formerly Security Classified, General Correspondence of Chief of Naval Operations/Secretary of Navy, 1940–1947, RG 80.

37. Frank Knox to Chairman, General Board, memo, Jan. 16, 1942, box 339, Formerly Security Classified, General Correspondence of Chief of Naval Operations/ Secretary of Navy, 1940–1947, RG 80; Chairman General Board to Secretary of Navy, Memo, Feb. 3, 1943, box 339, Formerly Security Classified, General Correspondence of Chief of Naval Operations/Secretary of Navy, 1940–1947, RG 80; Frank Knox to President, memo, Feb. 4, 1942, box 339, Formerly Security Classified, General Correspondence of Chief of Naval Operations/Secretary of Navy, 1940–1947, RG 80; Roosevelt to Secretary of the Navy, memo, box 339, Formerly Security Classified, General Correspondence of Chief of Naval Operations/Secretary of Navy, 1940–1947, RG 80. On Roosevelt's growing impatience, see Henry Lewis Stimson Diaries, microfilm, Feb. 21, 1942, reel 7, HLSP.

38. On the controversy around the blood donor program, see Thomas A. Guglielmo, "'Red Cross, Double Cross': Race and America's World War II–Era Blood Donor Program," *JAH* 97 (June 2010): 71–73. On Dorie Miller, see Francis Biddle to President, memo, May 1, 1942, box 1, entry 131d, RG 80; Ludlow W. Werner to Frank Knox, Feb. 13, 1942, box 1, entry 131d, RG 80; P. L. Prattis to Frank Knox, Mar. 13, 1942, box 1, entry 131d, RG 80; "U.S. Fails to Honor Hero Doris Miller," *California Eagle*, Mar. 19, 1942, clipping, box 1, entry 131d, RG 80; "Messman Hero at Pearl Harbor Should Be Honored," *Carolinian*, Mar. 21, 1942, clipping, box 1, entry 131d, RG 80; Arthur A. Allen to Walter White, Mar. 5, 1942, box II:A655, NAACPR; Assistant Secretary to Frank Knox, Mar. 13, 1942, box II:A655, NAACPR.

39. "Now Is the Time Not to Be Silent," *Crisis*, Jan. 1942, 7; Louis quoted in *PC*, Jan. 17, 1942, in navy newspaper transcriptions, box 1, entry 131d, RG 80; Mitchell quoted in *Kansas City Call*, Feb. 27, 1942, in navy newspaper transcriptions, box 1, entry 131d, RG 80. For a good summary of black popular opinion about the navy at this time, see "Negro Editorial Opinion Concerning the Navy: A Digest Embracing the Period 13 Dec. [1941]–28 Feb. [1942]," navy newspaper transcriptions, box 1, entry 131d, RG 80.

40. "Willkie, Citing Negro War Hero, Demands Navy End Racial Ban," *NYHT*, Mar. 20, 1942, 1A. For other newspapers, see navy newspaper transcriptions, box 1, entry 131d, RG 80.

41. Henry Lewis Stimson Diaries, microfilm, Feb. 16, 1942, reel 7, HLSP. Similar pressure may have come from Selective Service. See Selective Service System, *Special Groups*, no. 10, 1:94–95.

42. General Board Study of the Enlistment of Men of the Colored Race in Other than the Messman Branch, n.d., c. Mar. 20, 1942, box 339, Formerly Security Classified, General Correspondence of Chief of Naval Operations/Secretary of Navy, 1940– 1947, RG 80; Roosevelt to Knox, memo, Mar. 31, 1942, box 339, Formerly Security Classified, General Correspondence of Chief of Naval Operations/Secretary of Navy, 1940–1947, RG 80; Navy Department, "Navy to Accept Negroes for General Service," press release, Apr. 7, 1942, box 339, Formerly Security Classified, General Correspondence of Chief of Naval Operations/Secretary of Navy, 1940– 1947, RG 80.

43. "Navy Combat Units Opened to Negroes," *NYT*, Apr. 8, 1942, 11; "Navy and Marines to Enlist Negroes for General Service," *WP*, Apr. 8, 1942, 1.

44. National Negro Congress quoted in *Washington Afro-American*, Apr. 11, 1942, in navy newspaper transcriptions, box 1, entry 131d, RG 80; DC NAACP chapter

quoted in "Navy and Marines to Enlist Negroes for General Service," *WP*, Apr. 8, 1942, 1; "Anchors Aweigh!" *BAA*, Apr. 18, 1942, 12.

45. See, for example, Bureau of Naval Personnel, "The Negro in the Navy," 15–17, 98; "Negro Leaders Deny Approving Navy Program; Knox Refuted," *PM*, May 28, 1943, 11; Thomasina W. Johnson to Philleo Nash, memo, Sept. 29, 1944, box 27, PNP; Jonathan Daniels to President Roosevelt, memo, Oct. 12, 1944, box 14, JDP; Nalty, *Strength for the Fight*, 191–192.

46. Bureau of Naval Personnel, "The Negro in the Navy," 9; MacGregor, *Integration of the Armed Forces*, 68. For the army numbers, see Lee, *Employment of Negro Troops*, 415.

47. Roosevelt quoted in George Q. Flynn, "Selective Service and American Blacks during World War II," *JNH* 69 (Winter 1984): 20–21. For blacks' rising numbers in the navy, see Selective Service System, *Special Groups*, no. 10, 2:200. For blacks' overall proportion in the navy and marine corps, see Gillem et al., "Policy for the Utilization of Negro Manpower in the Post-War Army," 18; MacGregor, *Integration of the Armed Forces*, 71; Bureau of Naval Personnel, "The Negro in the Navy," 14; Nalty, "Right to Fight," 28.

48. On blacks' percentage of army strength, see Lee, *Employment of Negro Troops*, 415. On blacks' underrepresentation on Selective Service boards, see Selective Service System, *Special Groups*, no. 10, 1:34; Flynn, "Selective Service and American Blacks during World War II," 17–18. On blacks' lower death rates in comparison with others', see Department of the Army, *The World War II Rosters of the Dead (All Services)*, microfiche reference no. 601–607, May 1, 1983, Joint POW/MIA Accounting Command. Many thanks to Dan Lee for bringing this source to my attention.

49. E. S. Adams to Commanding Generals, Oct. 16, 1940, box 810, entry 178, RG 160; Milton R. Konvitz, "Legal Status of the Negro in the Army," *Guild Lawyer* 2 (Dec. 1940): 4–5.

50. "The Jim Crow Boomerang," *Crisis*, Oct. 1943, 294; Stanley Roberts, "Voters Satisfied with 10% Induction Rule," *PC*, Nov. 6, 1943, 4. For blacks' overrepresentation among World War I draftees, see Johnson, "Mobilization of Negro Manpower," 302; and Chad L. Williams, *Torchbearers of Democracy: African American Soldiers in the World War I Era* (Chapel Hill: University of North Carolina Press, 2010), 55. Johnson was quick (and right) to point out, however, that the War Department allowed far more whites than blacks to enlist voluntarily, and so the latter's overall proportion of the armed forces (10.7 percent) more or less matched its proportion in the population (9.9 percent in 1920).

51. Stimson Diaries, microfilm, Jan. 24, 1942, reel 7, HLSP; Stimson Diaries, Oct. 25, 1940, microfilm, reel 6, HLSP; Stimson Diaries, Sept. 27, 1940, microfilm, reel 6, HLSP. For "semiofficial credo" quotation, see Lee, *Employment of Negro Troops*, 44. On the widespread nature of anti-black racist beliefs among War Department officials shortly after World War I, see H. E. Ely, Memorandum for the Chief of Staff, Oct. 30, 1925, box 8, official file 4245g, FDRP.

52. Woodring quoted in Lee, *Employment of Negro Troops*, 69; Henry L. Stimson to Paul V. McNutt, Feb. 19, 1943, in *Black Soldiers in World War II*, vol. 5 of *Blacks in the United States Armed Forces: Basic Documents*, ed. Morris J. MacGregor and Bernard C. Nalty (Wilmington, DE: Scholarly Resources, 1977), 136–137; Stimson to McNutt, Feb. 20, 1943, box 1510, entry 360, RG 407.

53. *California Eagle*, Dec. 18, 1941, clipping, box 235, entry 188, RG 107; Eleanor Roosevelt to Henry L. Stimson, Dec. 20, 1941, box 1079, entry 363, RG 407. For

protest letters to President Roosevelt, see box 1079, entry 363, RG 407. On interwar enlistment restrictions, see Lee, *Employment of Negro Troops*, 23–49.

54. For "practically closed" quotation, see Selective Service System, *Special Groups*, no. 10, 1:95; Lewis B. Hershey to Oren S. Copeland, memo, c. Oct. 24, 1942, box 422, entry 1, RG 147, NARAII; Gillem et al., "Policy for the Utilization of Negro Manpower in the Post-War Army," 6. For the "2 percent" figure, see Lee, *Employment of Negro Troops*, 414. For the "substantially equal" quotation, see *Lynn v. Downer*, 140 F. 2d 401 (2d Cir. 1944).

55. James Rowe Jr., Memorandum for the President, Oct. 23, 1940, box 81, President's Secretary's File, FDRP; "Only D.C. White Draftees to Be Called in January," *PC*, Dec. 28, 1940, 3; Robert P. Patterson to Secretary of War, memo, Jan. 16, 1942, box 3, entry 99, RG 107; Selective Service System, *Special Groups*, no. 10, 1:94; Lee, *Employment of Negro Troops*, 91; Lewis B. Hershey to Mr. Secretary, Oct. 5, 1944, box 1508, entry 360, RG 407.

56. For the inadequate cadres and facilities defense, see Selective Service System, *Special Groups*, no. 10, 1:89; "24,000 to Be in Army by February," *ADW*, Dec. 12, 1940, 1; Lee, *Employment of Negro Troops*, 92; "Roosevelt Answers Courier," *PC*, Oct. 18, 1941, 3. For the reluctance to create more black units, see E. A. Adams to William H. Hastie, memo, Dec. 31, 1941, box 235, entry 188, RG 107. For justifications related to fewer black casualties, see G. B. Walker Jr., memo regarding "Induction of Negroes," Oct. 10, 1944, box 1508, entry 360, RG 407.

57. I have made these calculations based on data in Selective Service System, *Special Groups*, no. 10, 2:106–109.

58. William H. Hastie, "Survey and Recommendations Concerning the Integration of the Negro Soldier into the Army," c. Sept. 22, 1941, box 150, RPPP.

59. See, for example, "Secret Army Order Bared," *PC*, Nov. 23, 1940, 1; "Protest Scheme to Defer Colored Draftees," *PC*, Dec. 28, 1940, 22; "Protest War Department Plan to Segregate," *PC*, Jan. 4, 1941, 2; "Washington Denies Negro Draft Charge," *NYT*, Jan. 4, 1941, 6; "Discrimination in the Draft," *Crisis*, Jan. 1941, 7; "The Jim Crow Boomerang," *Crisis*, Oct. 1943, 294.

60. Eleanor S. Moore to Henry L. Stimson, Mar. 24, 1942, box 1077, entry 363, RG 407; Donovan Senter to Waldemar A. Nielsen, memo, Sept. 7, 1942, box 4, entry 207, RG 83.

61. Jerry Purvis Sanson, *Louisiana during World War II: Politics and Society, 1939–1945* (Baton Rouge: Louisiana State University Press, 1999), 265; "Draft Breaking Up Families in Dixie," *CD*, Dec. 18, 1943, 3.

62. F. C. Conroy to Sir, March 23, 1942, box 1077, entry 363, RG 407. See also Mr. and Mrs. L. M. Horne to FDR, Aug. 10, 1942, box 1074, entry 363, RG 407; W. M. Craft to FDR, box 1073, entry 363, RG 407; Anonymous to War Department, Feb. 9, 1943, box 1071, entry 363, RG 407.

63. A. Leonard Allen to Robert P. Patterson, Sept. 21, 1942, box 1073, entry 363, RG 407; "Congressman Urges Larger Draft of Negro Americans," *ADW*, Sept. 22, 1942, 1; Allen to Patterson, Oct. 10, 1942, box 1073, entry 363, RG 407. See A. L. Ford to Henry L. Stimson, July 31, 1942, box 1075, entry 363, RG 407; John H. Overton to Lewis B. Hershey, Aug. 10, 1942, box 422, file 170, entry 1, RG 147, NARAII; W. F. Norrell to Lewis B. Hershey, Oct. 2, 1942, box 422, file 170, entry 1, RG 147, NARAII.

64. Stimson quoted in Flynn, "Selective Service and American Blacks during World War II," 20. For the OWI report and press release, see "Negro Tensions: U.S.A., North and South," OWI Report no. 26, Aug. 27, 1942, box 1844, entry 171, RG 44;

and "Negroes Exceeding Quotas for Induction into Army," *NYASN*, Jan. 2, 1943, 1. On McNutt, see Lee, *Employment of Negro Troops*, 91; Henry L. Stimson to Paul McNutt, Feb. 20, 1943, box 1510, entry 360, RG 407; "McNutt Wants More Negroes in the Army," *NYASN*, Mar. 6, 1943, 3. On Daniels, see Jonathan Daniels to President, memo, June 26, 1943, box 13, JDP.

65. "Protest Scheme to Defer Colored Draftees," *PC*, Dec. 28, 1940, 22.
66. Baird V. Helfrich to Paul G. Armstrong, Dec. 2, 1940, box 32, file 070, entry 1, RG 147, NARAII; Local Board No. 13, Cuyahoga County, resolution, n.d. but c. Feb. 8, 1941, box 144, file 440, entry 1, RG 147, NARAII.
67. "Governor Hurley against Race Bar in Army," *Hartford Courant*, Feb. 19, 1941, 1; "State Short 67 Men of Draft Quota," *Hartford Courant*, Feb. 18, 1941, 1; Gordon C. Jackson to Governor Robert A. Hurley, Feb. 19, 1941, box 438, Robert A. Hurley Records, CSL.
68. Selective Service spokesperson quoted in "Action Illegal, Officials Claim, Hint Court Fight," *PC*, Feb. 22, 1941, 23. Dykstra quoted in Lee, *Employment of Negro Troops*, 91. On US Attorney General Office's opinion, see William H. Draper to Lewis B. Hershey, memo, Mar. 11, 1941, box 141, entry 1, RG 147, NARAII. Johnson quoted in Selective Service System, *Special Groups*, no. 10, 1:94. On WMC, see Lee, *Employment of Negro Troops*, 409.
69. Lee, *Employment of Negro Troops*, 92, 149.
70. "This Is News! Dixie Solon Flays Race Discrimination," *CD*, Nov. 27, 1943, 1; "Negroes in the Army," *New Republic*, Dec. 27, 1943, 904; "Wails from the South," *PC*, June 27, 1942, 6.
71. Winfred William Lynn to Local Board No. 261, June 28, 1942, box 30, series I, DMP; Dwight Macdonald, "The Novel Case of Winfred Lynn," *Nation*, Feb. 20, 1943, esp. 268, 269; Tom O'Connor, "Draft Law's Anti-Bias Clause Tested in Court Today," *PM*, Nov. 27, 1942, 18; "Draftee Hits Negro Quota," *PM*, Nov. 29, 1942, 19; "Hays Joins Negro's Fight against the Draft Act," *PM*, Dec. 4, 1942, 19; "Negro Gets Writ in Draft Law Test," *PM*, Dec. 24, 1942, 16; "Negro Is Denied Draft Writ Again," *PM*, Jan. 6, 1943, 17. On Conrad Lynn, see Simeon Booker Jr., "F.D. Snubs N.Y. to D.C. Pilgrimage," *BAA*, Sept. 19, 1942, 27; Conrad Lynn, *There Is a Fountain: The Autobiography of Conrad Lynn*, foreword by William M. Kunstler (Brooklyn, NY: Lawrence Hill Books, 1979).
72. Lynn, *There Is a Fountain*, esp. 92.
73. On the NAACP's initial reluctance to get involved in the Lynn case, see Lynn, *There Is a Fountain*, 93; Milton R. Konvitz to Dwight Macdonald, Apr. 21, 1944, box 904, series I, DMP. On the NAACP's eventual support, see Conrad Lynn to Dwight Macdonald, Mar. 18, 1943, box 30, series I, DMP; William H. Hastie and Thurgood Marshall, NAACP *amicus curiae* brief, *Lynn v. Downer*, Supreme Court of the United States, May 15, 1944, box 118, series II, DMP; Roy Wilkins to Bill Hastie, Oct. 13, 1943, box II:B148, NAACPR; Thurgood Marshall to Arthur Garfield Hays, Jan. 6, 1943, box II:B148, NAACPR; Colden Brown and Layle Lane to Roy Wilkins, Apr. 13, 1943, box II:B148, NAACPR; Roy Wilkins to Mrs. Johnson, Jan. 19, 1944, box II:B148, NAACPR.
74. For a small sample of the press's periodical treatment of the Lynn case, see Macdonald, "The Novel Case of Winfred Lynn"; Eunace B. Woodson, "Anti-Bias Draft Test Clause Reaches Boro Court," *NYASN*, Dec. 5, 1942, 18; "Negro Draft Issue Defeated in Court," *NYT*, Dec. 5, 1942, 11; "Draftee Challenges Army 'Quota' for Negro 1-A's," *CD*, Dec. 4, 1942, 1; "Charge of Racial Discrimination in Selective Service Call," *Social Service Review* 18 (Mar. 1944): 104; Dwight Macdonald, "Expect Federal Decision in Test of

Army Jim Crow," *Los Angeles Tribune*, Feb. 14, 1944, 3; Wilfred H. Kerr, "What I Would Like to See This Year," *Arkansas State Press*, Jan. 21, 1944, 4; "Rally Set for Thursday on Negro's Draft Fight," *PM*, Apr. 21, 1943, 12. On the MOWM's work, see "Negro Americans, Wake to Action!," flyer, n.d., box 422, entry 33, RG 228; Nancy Macdonald and Dwight Macdonald, *The War's Greatest Scandal! The Story of Jim Crow in Uniform*, pamphlet, n.d., 5–7, box 1067, entry 363, RG 407; Army Service Forces, First Service Command, Summary of Intelligence Information on Winfred William Lynn, Apr. 21, 1943, file no. 100, subject no. 205474, box 3017, entry HS1-89646273 (P186), RG 65; and materials in box II:B148, NAACPR; and boxes 26–28, APRP; and box 15, subseries A-3, series A, section II, FORP.

75. See "Support the Lynn Case!" (advertisement), *Nation*, July 1, 1944, 21; National Citizens' Committee for Winfred Lynn, *The Story of Winfred Lynn*, pamphlet, n.d., box 118, series II, DMP; Lynn Committee for the Abolition of Segregation in the Armed Forces, *The Story of Winfred Lynn*, pamphlet, n.d., box 118, series II, DMP; Wilfred H. Kerr to Friend, n.d., box 118, series II, DMP; A. Philip Randolph et al. to Friend, n.d., box 118, series II, DMP; Lynn Committee to Abolish Segregation in the Armed Forces, "Help Fight Jim Crow in Uniform! Come to the Cocktail Party," flyer, c. June 11, 1944, box 30, series I, DMP; Colden Brown and Layle Lane to Roy Wilkins, Apr. 13, 1943, box II:B148, NAACPR; Nancy Macdonald to Roy Wilkins, Nov. 11, 1943, box II:B148, NAACPR; National Citizens' Committee for Winfred Lynn, press release regarding "Segregation in Peace and War," c. Dec. 29, 1943, box II:B148, NAACPR.

76. National Citizens' Committee for Winfred Lynn, *The Story of Winfred Lynn*; Arthur Garfield Hays and Gerald Weatherly, Petition for Writ of Certiorari to the United States Circuit Court of Appeals for the Second Circuit, Apr. 22, 1944, box 118, series II, DMP. For the debate over strategy in the case, see Dwight Macdonald, "On the Conduct of the Lynn Case," *Politics*, Apr. 1944, 85–88; Arthur Garfield Hays, "Rejoinder by Mr. Hays," *Politics*, Apr. 1944, 88.

77. *Lynn v. Downer*, 140 F. 2d 398, 399, 402 (2d Cir. 1944).

78. Dwight Macdonald, "The Supreme Court's New Moot Suit," *Nation*, July 1, 1944, 13–14; "United States Supreme Court," *NYT*, Jan. 3, 1945, 33; Lynn v. Downer, 322 US 756 (1944). Cases similar to Lynn's did sprout up in the immediate postwar years. See, for example, "6 Injunctions Wrapped Up in Suit against Army Bars," *BAA*, Sept. 28, 1946, 1; "Afro's Suit Forces Army to Remove Jim Crow Ban," *BAA*, Oct. 12, 1946, 1.

79. Winfred Lynn to Nancy Macdonald, June 20, 1944, box 30, series I, DMP; Conrad Lynn to Nancy Macdonald, May 31, 1944, box 30, series I, DMP.

80. Lynn Committee to Abolish Segregation in the Armed Forces, "The Supreme Court's Great Moot Suit," press release, June 1, 1944, box 118, series II, DMP; "The Supreme Court's Moot Suit," *Politics*, June 1944, 133; Dwight Macdonald, "Expect Federal Decision in Test of Army Jim Crow," *Los Angeles Tribune*, Feb. 14, 1944, 3; Samuel Walker, *In Defense of American Liberties: A History of the ACLU* (New York: Oxford University Press, 1990), 165.

81. Selective Service System, *Special Groups*, no. 10, 1:50; Lynn, *There Is a Fountain*, 94; Harold M. Kennedy, Brief for Colonel John W. Downer, Respondent-Appellee, n.d., box 118, series II, DMP.

82. Selective Service System, *Special Groups*, no. 10, 2:118–119.

83. Selective Service System, *Special Groups*, no. 10, 1:102; and 1:161.

84. J. F. Chastain to Senator Russell, Mar. 15, 1943, box 1071, entry 363, RG 407; A. Leonard Allen to Robert P. Patterson, Oct. 10, 1942, box 1073, entry 363, RG

407. For some blacks intentionally failing tests, see Selective Service System, *Special Groups*, no. 10, 1:154.

85. For the 5 percent estimate, see *Special Groups*, no. 10, 1:154. On the memo to Marshall and the army's new rule, see Lee, *Employment of Negro Troops*, 92. On the drop in black inductees, see Selective Service System, *Special Groups*, no. 10, 1:145. For Stimson, see Henry Lewis Stimson Diaries, May 12, 1942, microfilm, reel 7, HLSP.

86. Campbell C. Johnson to Lt. Col. Johnson, memo, Oct. 2, 1940, box 422, file 170, entry 1, RG 147, NARAII; Gill, "Afro-American Opposition," 198–199; James N. Keelin to Colonel C. G. Parker, June 15, 1943, box 245, entry 188, RG 107; Campbell C. Johnson to Truman K. Gibson, July 8, 1943, box 245, entry 188, RG 107.

87. J. H. Shelton Jr. to Colonel Keelin, memo, June 11, 1943, box 245, entry 188, RG 107; James N. Keelin Jr. to Colonel Parker, June 15, 1943, box 245, entry 188, RG 107. For Gibson, see Lee, *Employment of Negro Troops*, 411.

88. Campbell C. Johnson to Truman K. Gibson, July 8, 1943, box 245, entry 188, RG 107; Mr. and Mrs. L. M. Horne to President Roosevelt, Aug. 10, 1942, box 1074, entry 363, RG 407; John H. Overton to Lewis B. Hershey, Aug. 10, 1942, box 422, file 170, entry 1, RG 147, NARAII; A. Leonard Allen to Secretary Patterson, Sept. 21, 1942, box 1073, entry 363, RG 407.

89. Campbell C. Johnson to Truman K. Gibson, July 8, 1943, box 245, entry 188, RG 107; "Wails from the South," *PC*, June 27, 1942, 6.

90. Lee, *Employment of Negro Troops*, 411.

91. Joseph Schiffman, "The Education of Negro Soldiers in World War II," *JNE* 18 (Winter 1949): 23. For more on these changes, see also Selective Service System, *Special Groups*, no 10, 1:101–102; Lee, *Employment of Negro Troops*, 263–270; Katznelson, *When Affirmative Action Was White*, 107–109; Paula S. Fass, *Outside In: Minorities and the Transformation of American Education* (New York: Oxford University Press, 1989), 139–151.

92. Gene DePoris and Sutherland Denlinger, "PM Finds a Snarl of Contradictions in Operation of the Draft," *PM*, Mar. 16, 1941, 13. For the total number of local draft boards, see Kennedy, *Freedom from Fear*, 632. For scholars who have mistakenly suggested that anti-black enlistment restrictions and exclusions derived from decentralization, see Katznelson, *When Affirmative Action Was White*, 100; James T. Sparrow, *Warfare State: World War II Americans and the Age of Big Government* (New York: Oxford University Press, 2011), 205.

93. A June 1945 Gallup poll found that slightly more blacks than whites agreed that "the draft has been handled fairly in your community." See Selective Service System, *Evaluation of the Selective Service Program*, Special Monograph no. 18, vol. 2 (Washington, DC: GPO, 1956), 365.

94. On black veterans' restricted access to GI Bill benefits, see David H. Onkst, " 'First a Negro . . . Incidentally a Veteran': Black World War II Veterans and the G.I. Bill of Rights in the Deep South, 1944–1948," *Journal of Social History* 31 (Spring 1998): 517–543; Kathleen J. Frydl, *The GI Bill* (Cambridge: Cambridge University Press, 2009), 222–261; and Katznelson, *When Affirmative Action Was White*, 113–141. There is a substantial, excellent literature on the welfare-related racist restrictions against black people, but none of it, as far as I can tell, explores the military's role. In addition to the work cited above, see, for example, Jill Quadagno, *The Color of Welfare* (New York: Oxford University Press, 1994); Michael K. Brown, *Race, Money, and the American Welfare State* (Ithaca, NY: Cornell University Press,

1999); Robert Lieberman, *Shifting the Color Line: Race and the American Welfare State* (Cambridge, MA: Harvard University Press, 1998); Cybelle Fox, *Three Worlds of Relief: Race, Immigration, and the American Welfare State* (Princeton, NJ: Princeton University Press, 2012).
95. "The Jim Crow Boomerang," *Crisis*, Oct. 1943, 294.

CHAPTER 2

1. George I. Sánchez to Elmore R. Torn, Jan. 2, 1942, box 28, George I. Sánchez Papers, BLAC; Alonso S. Perales to Paul J. Kilday, Nov. 24, 1944, in Alonso S. Perales, *Are We Good Neighbors?* (1948; New York: Arno Press, 1974), 283–284. See also Alonso S. Perales to Clare Boothe Luce, Apr. 15, 1944, in Perales, *Are We Good Neighbors?*, 277; George I. Sánchez to Roger Baldwin, Jan. 4, 1942, box 2, Sánchez Papers, BLAC; Special Services Division, Office of War Information, "Spanish-Americans in the Southwest and the War Effort," report no. 24, Aug. 18, 1942, 3, box 409, entry 33, RG 228. For an alternative theory—that "in the administration of the Selective Service Act, at least, it can never be alleged that discrimination against Latin Americans has ever been practiced"—see Pauline R. Kibbe, *Latin Americans in Texas* (Albuquerque: University of New Mexico Press, 1946), 223.
2. Selective Service System, *Evaluation of the Selective Service Program*, Special Monograph no. 18, vol. 1 (Washington, DC: GPO, 1950), 171; Harry Franqui-Rivera, *Soldiers of the Nation: Military Service and Modern Puerto Rico, 1868–1952* (Lincoln: University of Nebraska Press, 2018), 145–146; Clarence Senior, "Preliminary Analysis of Puerto Rican Selective Service Rejections," report, Social Science Research Center, University of Puerto Rico, Nov. 29, 1946, box 1144, entry 1, RG 126. On the Filipinos' status as nationals, see Rick Baldoz, *The Third Asiatic Invasion: Empire and Migration in Filipino America, 1898–1946* (New York: New York University Press, 2011), 194–204; Christopher Capozzola, *Bound by War: How the United States and the Philippines Built America's First Pacific Century* (New York: Basic Books, 2020). On "natives of Guam and Samoa" and the ability of some Filipinos who had served in the US Navy and Marines to enlist, see Edward Shattuck to John McI. Smith, memo, Mar. 14, 1941, box 141, entry 1, RG 147, NARAII.
3. "Nisei and the Draft," *Current Life*, Oct. 1940, 12. On Japanese Americans' service during World War I, see Lucy E. Salyer, "Baptism by Fire: Race, Military Service, and U.S. Citizenship, 1918–1935," *JAH* 91 (Dec. 2004): 854. On the navy's numbers, see "4000 Cooks and Waiters in U.S. Navy," *BAA*, Dec. 7, 1940, 5. On the army's acceptance of some Japanese American enlistees prior to the draft, see "Accessions Showing Japanese Race," Mar. 19, 1945, box 2166, entry 389, RG 407. See also James C. McNaughton, "Japanese Americans and the U.S. Army: A Historical Reconsideration," *Army History* (Summer/Fall 2003): 11; James C. McNaughton, *Nisei Linguists: Japanese Americans in the Military Intelligence Service during World War II* (Washington, DC: GPO, 2006), 4n2, 6n8, 8, 29.
4. Robert C. Blackstone, "Democracy's Army: The American People and Selective Service in World War II" (PhD diss., University of Kansas, 2005), 155–156; McNaughton, *Nisei Linguists*, 7n11.
5. *Congressional Record*, 76th Cong., 3d sess., 1940, 86, pt. 10:10889.
6. E. A. Adams to Commanding Generals, memo, Oct. 30, 1940, file 110, Legislative and Policy Precedent Files, RG 107; Lewis B. Hershey to Colonel Jarrell, Dec. 4, 1940, box 32, file 070, entry 1, RG 147, NARAII; "Second Group of Selectees

Enters Army," *LAT*, Jan. 21, 1941, 1. For estimates of the number of Japanese Americans in the army, see James E. Wharton to General Somervell, memo, Mar. 27, 1942, box 409, entry 360, RG 407; "Accessions Showing Japanese Race," Mar. 19, 1945, box 2166, entry 389, RG 407.

7. On San Francisco induction numbers, see Western Defense Command and Fourth Army, Assistant Chief of Staff for Civil Affairs, Wartime Civil Control Administration, Statistical Division, "Japanese and White Selectees Examined by the San Francisco Recruiting and Induction Station, by Month 1941," n.d., box 281, entry 208, RG 165. For the ban on Japanese aliens, see James E. Wharton to General Somervell, memo, Mar. 27, 1942, box 409, entry 360, RG 407. For Hershey's announcement, see McNaughton, *Nisei Linguists*, 48. For Japanese American induction numbers, see "Accessions Showing Japanese Race," Mar. 19, 1945, box 2166, entry 389, RG 407.

8. Ralph G. Martin, *Boy from Nebraska: The Story of Ben Kuroki* (New York: Harper and Brothers, 1946), 44, 48.

9. Selective Service System, *Selective Service in Peacetime: First Report of the Director of the Selective Service, 1940–1941* (Washington, DC: GPO, 1942), 262.

10. Selective Service System, *Special Groups*, Special Monographs, no. 10, vol. 1 (Washington, DC: GPO, 1953), 117; Lewis B. Hershey to Henry L. Stimson, June 1, 1942, box 445, entry 43, RG 165. For the message regarding Hawaii, see [J. A.] Ulio to Hawaiian Department, confidential message, Mar. 31, 1942, box 5, entry 406, RG 494. For Japanese Americans' dwindling induction numbers, see "Accessions Showing Japanese Race," Mar. 19, 1945, box 2166, entry 389, RG 407. For additional information about the War Department's decision to ban further Japanese American enlistments, see Alton C. Miller, Memorandum for the Assistant Chief of Staff, G-1, July 31, 1945, box 1735, entry 480, RG 389; and James E. Wharton to General Somervell, memo, Mar. 27, 1942, box 409, entry 360, RG 407.

11. I have been unable to find an official total number of Japanese American soldiers who were discharged by the US Army in this period. However, the army inducted 5,776 Japanese Americans between July 1940 (when data are first available) through September 1942. But as of October 1, 1942, the US Army included only 4,670 men. Even leaving aside the few Japanese Americans who might have joined the army prior to July 1940, it appears that the army somehow lost—likely discharged—many hundreds of soldiers in this period. For induction numbers, see "Accessions Showing Japanese Race," Mar. 19, 1945, box 2166, entry 389, RG 407; for the Oct. 1, 1942 count, see J. A. Ulio to John F. Embree, Nov. 5, 1942, box 652, entry 389, RG 407. For lower estimates of discharges—several hundred or so ooo Ambrose E. White to William P. Scobey, memo, July 10, 1943, box 652, entry 389, RG 407; "Army Will Review Cases of Nisei Barred from Draft," *PCIT*, Mar. 30, 1946, 3.

12. Selective Service System, *Problems of the Selective Service*, Special Monograph no. 16, vol. 1 (Washington, DC: GPO, 1952), 112.

13. James E. Wharton to General Somervell, memo, Mar. 27, 1942, box 409, entry 360, RG 407.

14. US War Department, *Final Report: Japanese Evacuation from the West Coast, 1942* (Washington, DC: GPO, 1943), 34; Peter Irons, *Justice at War: The Story of the Japanese American Internment Cases* (New York: Oxford University Press, 1983), 55.

15. Harold Ickes to Frank Knox, Apr. 7, 1944, box 51, entry 32, RG 80; "Nordic Navy," *WP*, Aug. 30, 1944, 6. For Elmer Davis, see Elmer Davis to President Roosevelt, Oct. 2, 1942, box 147, entry 360, RG 407. For newspapers like the *Milwaukee Journal* and the *Berkshire Evening Eagle*, see WRAWPR, no. 82, c. Sept. 6, 1944, box 3, entry 5, RG 210; "Nisei and the Navy," *Boston Herald*, reprinted in the *Berkshire Evening Eagle*, July 21, 1945, 6. For the ACLU, see "Navy Reiterates Ban on U.S. Japanese," *NYT*, Aug. 21, 1944, 17; "Protest Navy's Ban on Nisei," *York (PA) Gazette and Daily*, July 14, 1945, 7; ACLU, *In Defense of Our Liberties*, pamphlet, June 1944, 17, box 2, entry 8, RG 210; ACLU, *Liberty on the Home Front*, pamphlet, July 1945, 16, box 3, entry 8, RG 210.

16. Community Council, Granada Relocation Center to Henry L. Stimson, Mar. 8, 1944, box 1065, entry 363, RG 407; Community Council, Granada Relocation Center to Frank Knox, Mar. 8, 1944, box 49, entry 183, RG 107. For other examples of Japanese Americans' protests against the navy, see American Citizens of Japanese Ancestry at the Heart Mountain Relocation Center to President Roosevelt, Feb. 28, 1944, box 49, entry 183, RG 107; Frank Yamasaki and Seiko Yakaki, "Recommendations of Topaz Citizens for the Principles of American Democracy," c. Feb. 26, 1944, box 49, entry 183, RG 107.

17. "Nisei Served with Marines Despite Wartime Ban," *PCIT*, Nov. 17, 1945, 1; "Navy Reiterates Ban on U.S. Japanese," *NYT*, Aug. 21, 1944, 17. For additional evidence that some Japanese Americans did serve during World War II with the navy, marines, and coast guard, see G. B. Walker Jr., memo, Feb. 21, 1944, box 445, entry 43A, RG 165; Frank Knox to Director, War Relocation Authority, Mar. 18, 1944, box 2, entry 17, RG 210; Russell R. Waesche, "Report of the Interdepartmental Committee on the Employment of Americans of Japanese Descent as Seamen," n.d., box 2, entry 17, RG 210; "Contradictions in Policy," *PCIT*, Dec. 11, 1943, 4; "The Navy's Policy," *PCIT*, June 30, 1945, 4.

18. Fred Barbash, "After Pearl Harbor: How a Government Official's Baseless Claim Helped Lead to the Internment of Japanese Americans," *WP*, Dec. 12, 2016, https://www.washingtonpost.com/news/morning-mix/wp/2016/12/12/the-week-after-pearl-harbor-a-government-officials-ignominius-big-lie-and-the-internment-of-japanese-americans/ (emphasis mine); Greg Robinson, *By Order of the President: FDR and the Internment of Japanese Americans* (Cambridge, MA: Harvard University Press, 2001), 61, 77.

19. Frank Knox to President Roosevelt, Oct. 17, 1942, box 6, entry 47, RG 107; Frank Knox to Bruno Lasker, Dec. 23, 1943, box 51, entry 32, RG 80.

20. But navy officers sometimes spoke up in defense of Japanese Americans. See, for example, Robinson, *By Order of the President*, 64–65, 100; W. E. Crist to General Strong, memo, Jan. 4, 1943, box 1717, entry 480, RG 389.

21. Henry Lewis Stimson Diaries, Feb. 26, 1942, microfilm, reel 7, HLSP; Secretary of War to President Roosevelt, draft letter, n.d., box 147, entry 360, RG 407. Roosevelt also shared his own racist suspicions about Japanese American loyalty. See Robinson, *By Order of the President*, 120–124.

22. Delos C. Emmons to Adjutant General, Apr. 6, 1942, box 147, entry 360, RG 407; McCloy quoted and Milton Eisenhower's letter cited in McNaughton, *Nisei Linguists*, 86. For the JACL's lobbying of Eisenhower, see Mike Masaoka to Milton Eisenhower, Apr. 6, 1942, box 8, entry 183, RG 107. For the "serious dedication" quotation, see Franklin Odo, *No Sword to Bury: Japanese Americans in Hawaii during World War II* (Philadelphia: Temple University Press, 2004), 188. Emmons's

proposal would become the famed 100th Infantry Battalion, a story discussed in detail in Chapter 4.

23. T. J. Koenig and J. H. Lowell, "The Military Utilization of United States Citizens of Japanese Ancestry: Report of a Board of Officers," n.d., c. Sept. 1942, box 445, entry 43A, RG 165. For the date this report was approved, see I. H. Edwards, War Department disposition form, Dec. 17, 1942, box 147, entry 360, RG 407.

24. Conversation between Colonel Tate and Dillon Myer, Sept. 4, 1942, box 47, entry 183, RG 107; John J. McCloy to General Wilson, memo, Aug. 24, 1942, box 47, entry 183, RG 107; E. J. King to General Marshall, memo, July 15, 1942, box 445, entry 43, RG 165. For McCloy's solicitation, see Alan Cranston to Milton Eisenhower, memo, Aug. 19, 1942, box 1080, entry 222, RG 208.

25. M. W. Pettigrew to War Department General Staff, G-2, memo, Oct. 10, 1942, box 35, entry 208, RG 165; Pettigrew to John J. McCloy, memo, Nov. 17, 1942, box 147, entry 360, RG 407.

26. Elmer Davis to President Roosevelt, Oct. 2, 1942, box 147, entry 360, RG 407 (emphasis in original); Edwin O. Reischauer, "Memorandum on Policy towards Japan," Sept. 14, 1942, box 147, entry 360, RG 407.

27. Ingram M. Stainback to Harold L. Ickes, Oct. 31, 1942, box 47, entry 183, RG 107. For the JACL resolution, see Mike Masaoka with Bill Hosokawa, *They Call Me Moses Masaoka: An American Saga* (New York: William Morrow, 1987), 121. For slightly different wording of the resolution, see Eric L. Muller, *Free to Die for Their Country: The Story of the Japanese American Draft Resisters in World War II* (Chicago: University of Chicago Press, 2001), 43. Myer quoted in Muller, *Free to Die for Their Country*, 43. For the Hopkins meeting, see Robinson, *By Order of the President*, 167.

28. M. S. Eisenhower to John J. McCloy, Oct. 13, 1942, box 147, entry 360, RG 407; Memorandum for the Secretary of War, Oct. 28, 1942, box 147, entry 360, RG 407. See also John J. McCloy to Secretary of War, memo, Oct. 15, 1943, box 147, entry 360, RG 407. For McCloy's and Pettigrew's collaboration, see Pettigrew to McCloy, Nov. 7, 1942, box 35, entry 208, RG 165; Pettigrew to McCloy, Nov. 17, 1942, box 147, entry 360, RG 407.

29. "HLS" [Henry Lewis Stimson] to "CofS" [Chief of Staff Marshall], n.d., box 147, entry 360, RG 407; Stimson to Roosevelt, draft letter, n.d., box 147, entry 360, RG 407. For Marshall's support for this policy change, see "Reveal Gen. Marshall's Support of Nisei," *PCIT*, Jan. 25, 1947, 1.

30. I. H. Edwards, War Department General Staff, Disposition Form, Organization and Training Division, G-3, Dec. 17, 1942, box 147, entry 360, RG 407; War Department, Bureau of Public Relations, "Loyal Americans of Japanese Ancestry to Compose Special Unit in the Army," press release, Jan. 28, 1943, box 280, entry 208, RG 165; Franklin D. Roosevelt to Secretary Stimson, Feb. 1, 1943, box 47, entry 183, RG 107. War Relocation director Dillon Myer, with input from leaders of the Office of War Information, drafted the letter for Roosevelt. See D. S. Myer to John J. McCloy, Jan. 15, 1943, box 47, entry 183, RG 107; Thomas D. Murphy, *Ambassadors in Arms: The Story of Hawaii's 100th Battalion* (Honolulu: University of Hawaii Press, 1954), 109–110.

31. Masaoka, *They Call Me Moses Masaoka*, 121. On the courts, see Irons, *Justice at War*, 199–202; Muller, *Free to Die for Their Country*, 47.

32. Selective Service System, *Special Groups*, no. 10, 1:120; J. A. Ulio to Assistant Chief of Staff, G-2, memo, Jan. 20, 1943, box 22, entry 180, RG 107; Masayo Umezawa

Duus, *Unlikely Liberators: The Men of the 100th and the 442nd*, trans. Peter Duus (Honolulu: University of Hawaii Press, 1987), 58.

33. Both quotations in Selective Service System, *Special Groups*, no. 10, 1:120. For an excellent description of the screening process, see John T. Bissell to General Strong, memo, Jan. 23, 1943, box 1717, entry 480, RG 389; Takashi Fujitani, *Race for Empire: Koreans as Japanese and Japanese as Americans during World War II* (Berkeley: University of California Press, 2011), 125–162.

34. John M. Hall to Colonel Bicknell, memo, Aug. 13, 1943, box 22, entry 180, RG 107.

35. Roosevelt to Stimson, Feb. 1, 1943, box 47, entry 183, RG 107; Pettigrew to McCloy, memo, Nov. 17, 1942, box 147, entry 360, RG 407; Stimson to Roosevelt, draft letter, n.d., box 147, entry 360, RG 407. On the importance of additional military personnel, see also Office of the Provost Marshal General, Japanese-American Branch, "History of the Japanese Program," confidential report, n.d., 15, box 1717, entry 480, RG 389.

36. Stimson to Roosevelt, draft letter, n.d., box 147, entry 360, RG 407. See also Davis to Roosevelt, Oct. 2, 1942, box 147, entry 360, RG 407; McCloy to Stimson, Oct. 15, 1942, box 147, entry 360, RG 407; Memorandum for the Secretary of War, Oct. 28, 1942, box 147, entry 360, RG 407; Pettigrew to McCloy, Nov. 17, 1942, box 147, entry 360, RG 407; Crist to Strong, memo, Jan. 4, 1943, box 1717, entry 480, RG 389. For an especially incisive formulation of this point, see Fujitani, *Race for Empire*, 96–108. For other wartime instances of US government officials supporting civil rights to improve the country's image abroad, see Justin Hart, "Making Democracy Safe for the World: Race, Propaganda, and the Transformation of U.S. Foreign Policy during World War II," *Pacific Historical Review* 73 (Feb. 2004): 49–84; Thomas A. Guglielmo, "Fighting for Caucasian Rights: Mexicans, Mexican Americans, and the Transnational Struggle for Civil Rights in World War II Texas," *JAH* 92 (March 2006): 1212–1237; Ellen D. Wu, *The Color of Success: Asian Americans and the Origins of the Model Minority* (Princeton, NJ: Princeton University Press, 2013). For examples of the US government's concern about Axis propaganda's impact on America's domestic race relations, see Office of War Information, Bureau of Intelligence, Sources Division, "Axis Propaganda Intended to Undermine Relations between Whites and Negroes," July 21, 1942, box 1849, entry 171, RG 44.

37. Stimson to Roosevelt, draft letter, n.d., box 147, entry 360, RG 407; Memorandum for the Secretary of War, Oct. 28, 1942, box 147, entry 360, RG 407; Pettigrew to McCloy, Nov. 17, 1942, box 147, entry 360, RG 407; Murphy, *Ambassadors in Arms*, 109–110. *Collier's* magazine made a similar argument: "Judging from our boys' experience with the Jap soldiers on New Guinea and Guadalcanal, we can well afford to turn some Japanese-descended fighting talent against the original Japs." See transcription of "Nisei Soldiers" in Memorandum for Files, Mar. 26, 1943, box 47, entry 183, RG 107.

38. War Department, Bureau of Public Relations, "Loyal Americans of Japanese Ancestry to Compose Special Unit in the Army," press release, Jan. 28, 1943, box 280, entry 208, RG 165; "HLS" [Stimson] to "CofS" [Marshall], n.d., box 147, entry 360, RG 407; Memorandum for the Secretary of War, Oct. 28, 1942, box 147, entry 360, RG 407.

39. Memorandum for the Secretary of War, Oct. 28, 1942, box 147, entry 360, RG 407; Stimson to Roosevelt, draft letter, n.d., box 147, entry 360, RG 407.

40. John J. McCloy to Colonel Stimson, Feb. 6, 1943, box 48, entry 183, RG 107. Newspaper quotations come from WRAWPR, nos. 3–5, box 2, entry 5, RG 210; WRAWPR, no. 6, box 2, entry 5, RG 210.

41. War Department, Bureau of Public Relations, Press Branch, "1,000 in Relocation Centers Seek to Join Combat Unit," press release, Mar. 18, 1943, box 49, entry 183, RG 107; WRAWPR, no. 11, box 2, entry 5, RG 210.
42. Office of Censorship, General Information Summary, vol. II, no. 6, Apr. 15–30, 1943, box 12, ROC.
43. "Hawaii Hails Men Off to Fight Kin," *NYT*, Mar. 30, 1943, 5; *Honolulu Star-Bulletin* quoted in Duus, *Unlikely Liberators*, 58–59. On initial enlistment numbers, see Tamotsu Shibutani, *The Derelicts of Company K: A Sociological Study of Demoralization* (Berkeley: University of California Press, 1978), 39. On whites' resentment toward the attention Japanese American enlistees received in Honolulu, see Office of Censorship, General Information Summary, vol. II, no. 4, Feb. 15–28, 1943, ROC. McCloy thought that "there was too much fanfare when they [recent Japanese American inductees] left Hawaii." See Mar. 30, 1943, Diary of John J. McCloy, in box DY1, JJMP.
44. On DeWitt, see "General Opposes Return of Japs," *WP*, Apr. 14, 1943, 1. On anti–Japanese American organizations, see "Japs in Army Plan Protested," *LAT*, Feb. 10, 1943, A3; "Ban on Japs in Army Backed," *LAT*, Feb. 19, 1943, 8 ("menace" quotation). On the Oregon State Senate, see "Oregon Senate Would Deport U.S. Japanese," *PCIT*, Mar. 4, 1943, 1. On Rankin, see "'Coddling of Japs' Must End, Mississippi Legislator Warns," *LAT*, Feb. 4, 1943, 6; "Speech of Honorable John E. Rankin," Feb. 3, 1943, transcription, box 47, entry 183, RG 107; WRAWPR, no. 15, p. 3, box 2, entry 5, RG 210. For *Fort Worth Star-Telegram*, see WRAWPR, nos. 3–5, box 2, entry 5, RG 210. For Savannah woman, see Miss Clifford Geffekken to J. A. Ulio, Mar. 5, 1943, box 1068, entry 363, RG 407.
45. War Relocation Authority, "Army and Leave Clearance at War Relocation Centers," June 1943, 7, HSTL, https://trumanlibrary.org/whistlestop/study_collections/japanese_internment/documents/index.php?documentdate=1943-06-00&documentid=23&pagenumber=1; Minoru Masuda, *Letters from the 442nd: The World War II Correspondence of a Japanese American Medic*, ed. Hana Masuda and Dianne Bridgman (Seattle: University of Washington Press, 2008), 7.
46. War Relocation Authority, "Army and Leave Clearance at War Relocation Centers," 14, 61.
47. WRAWPR, no. 41, box 2, entry 5, RG 210. For a copy of the questionnaire, see "Statement of United States Citizen of Japanese Ancestry," DSS Form 304A, box 1722, entry 480, RG 389.
48. See Muller, *Free to Die for Their Country*, 41–63; Eric L. Muller, "A Penny for Their Thoughts: Draft Resistance at the Poston Relocation Center," *Law and Contemporary Problems* 68 (Spring 2005): 127–130; War Relocation Authority, "Army and Leave Clearance at War Relocation Centers"; Dorothy Swaine Thomas and Richard S. Nishimoto, *The Spoilage* (Berkeley: University of California Press, 1946), 63–81; Mae M. Ngai, *Impossible Subjects: Illegal Aliens and the Making of Modern America* (Princeton, NJ: Princeton University Press, 2004), 183–184; US Commission on Wartime Relocation and Internment of Civilians, *Personal Justice Denied: Report of the Commission on Wartime Relocation and Internment of Civilians* (Washington, DC: GPO, 1983), 191–195; Myron E. Gurnea, FBI Survey of Japanese Relocation Centers, c. Mar. 1943, box 1, entry 17, RG 210.
49. Muller, *Free to Die for Their Country*, 57; Thomas and Nishimoto, *The Spoilage*, 81; "Statistics on Forms Executed by Male American Citizens," Apr. 8, 1943, box 1, entry 183, RG 107; Selective Service System, *Special Groups*, no. 10, 2:202.

50. War Relocation Authority, "Army and Leave Clearance at War Relocation Centers," 20, 15; Masuda, *Letters from the 442nd*, 7–8. On the numbers at Minidoka, and for overall numbers, see "Statistics on Forms Executed by Male American Citizens," Apr. 8, 1943, box 1, entry 183, RG 107. Thomas and Nishimoto, *The Spoilage*, 61; War Relocation Authority, "Army and Leave Clearance at War Relocation Centers," 25; Selective Service System, *Special Groups*, no. 10, 2:202; William P. Scobey to John J. McCloy, memo, Mar. 16, 1943, box 47, entry 183, RG 107.

51. William P. Scobey to Colonel Booth, Feb. 20, 1943, box 22, entry 180, RG 107; Memorandum for the Secretary of War, Oct. 28, 1942, box 147, entry 360, RG 407; E. M. Rowalt to M. W. Pettigrew, c. Dec. 4, 1942, box 280, entry 208, RG 165. For the 4,300 figure, see John T. Bissell to General Strong, memo, Jan. 23, 1943, box 1717, entry 480, RG 389. Expecting a 30 percent rejection rate, the War Department wanted roughly 4,300 volunteers to yield 3,000 inductees.

52. John M. Hall to E. M. Rowalt, Feb. 1, 1943, box 47, entry 183, RG 107; Thomas and Nishimoto, *The Spoilage*, 68–72, 81; War Relocation Authority, "Army and Leave Clearance at War Relocation Centers," 15–18, 22, 35; Muller, *Free to Die for Their Country*, 56–58.

53. John J. McCloy to Senator Chandler, Apr. 24, 1943, box 32, entry 180, RG 107; William P. Scobey to John J. McCloy, memo, Mar. 16, 1943, box 47, entry 183, RG 107.

54. "Ban on Japs in West Eased," *LAT*, Apr. 19, 1943, 1; House Subcommittee of the Committee on Naval Affairs, *Investigation of Congested Areas: Hearings on H.R. 30*, 78th Cong., 1st sess., 1943, 739. For McCloy's lobbying, see William P. Scobey to John J. McCloy, memo, Mar. 16, 1943, box 47, entry 183, RG 107; John J. McCloy to General McNarney, memo, Apr. 13, 1943, box 12, entry 183, RG 107.

55. J. A. Ulio to Commanding Generals, memo, May 3, 1943, box 809, entry 178, RG 160; Scobey to McCloy, memo, Mar. 16, 1943, box 47, entry 183, RG 107. A similar ban was lifted for Issei five months later. See J. A. Ulio to Commanding Generals, memo, Oct. 7, 1943, box 809, entry 178, RG 160.

56. Vance L. Sailor to Commanding General, memo, July 28, 1943, box 1508, entry 360, RG 407; Scobey to McCloy, memo, Mar. 16, 1943, box 47, entry 183, RG 107; Oveta Culp Hobby to McCloy, memo, Apr. 7, 1943, box 17, entry 183, RG 107; M. G. White to McCloy, memo, June 15, 1943, box 17, entry 183, RG 107.

57. McCloy to White, memo, May 4, 1943, box 22, entry 180, RG 107; Roosevelt to Stimson, Feb. 1, 1943, box 47, entry 183, RG 107; War Relocation Authority, "Army and Leave Clearance at War Relocation Centers," 49; Scobey to McCloy, memo, Mar. 16, 1943, box 47, entry 183, RG 107; Scobey to Booth, Feb. 20, 1943, box 22, entry 180, RG 107.

58. Department of Justice, Special War Policies Unit, War Division, "Highlights in the Domestic Foreign Language Press: Japanese-American Press," report no. 11, 4, box 6, entry 8, RG 210; Isamu Noguchi, "Trouble among Japanese Americans," *New Republic* 108, Feb. 1, 1943, 142; Yoshitaka Takagi to Henry L. Stimson, Feb. 7, 1943, box 47, entry 183, RG 107.

59. For "complete failure," see WRAWPR, no. 14, box 2, entry 5, RG 210. For Chandler's initial support, see "Army Opens Ranks to Japanese Units," *NYT*, Jan. 29, 1943, 9. For his plans for and motivations behind reinstituting the draft, see Albert B. Chandler to John J. McCloy, Apr. 8, 1943, box 32, entry 183, RG 107; WRAWPR, no. 10, box 2, entry 5, RG 210. For Chandler's subcommittee's recommendation and work with McCloy, see "New Policy on Interned Japanese Urged by Senate Military Affairs Committee," *NYT*, May 8, 1943, 7; McCloy to

Chandler, Apr. 24, 1943, box 32, entry 183, RG 107. As commissioner of Major League Baseball after the war, Chandler would oversee and support its integration of black ballplayers. See Robert McG. Thomas, "A. B. (Happy) Chandler, 92, Dies; Led Baseball during Integration," *NYT*, June 16, 1991, 26.

60. M. G. White to McCloy, memo, May 22, 1943, box 22, entry 180, RG 107. See also White to McCloy, memo, Apr. 19, 1943, box 22, entry 180, RG 107; White to McCloy, Apr. 26, 1943, box 22, entry 180, RG 107; McCloy to General McNarney, Oct. 2, 1943, box 445, entry 43A, RG 165; McCloy to White, Oct. 12, 1943, box 445, entry 43A, RG 165.

61. McCloy to General McNarney, Oct. 2, 1943, box 445, entry 43A, RG 165; McCloy to Chandler, Apr. 24, 1943, box 32, entry 183, RG 107.

62. Adjutant General to Commanding General, First Service Command, memo, July 26, 1944, box 444, entry 43, RG 165. See also Harrison A. Gerhardt to M. G. White, Nov. 9, 1943, box 48, entry 183, RG 107; McNaughton, *Nisei Linguists*, 145; Selective Service System, *Special Groups*, no. 10, 1:124.

63. C. D. Herron to General Handy, memo, Nov. 17, 1943, box 471, entry 418, RG 165; White to McCloy, memo, May 22, 1943, box 22, entry 180, RG 107; Oct. 11, 1943, Diary of John J. McCloy, in box DY1, JJMP; McCloy to White, memo, Oct. 12, 1943, box 445, entry 43A, RG 165. For reasons that are not clear, McCloy's proposal now matched the Senate subcommittee's, excluding Japanese aliens and the "disloyal" from the draft.

64. M. G. White to Chief of Staff, memo, Nov. 27, 1943, box 445, entry 43A, RG 165. A copy of the December 13, 1943, memo is in box 1717, entry 480, RG 389. For the announcement, see "Japanese-Americans Will Be Drafted Soon," *NYT*, Jan. 21, 1944, 7.

65. Selective Service System, *Special Groups*, no. 10, 1:126, 132.

66. See, for example: WRAWPR, no. 53, box 2, entry 5, RG 210; WRAWPR, no. 54, box 2, entry 5, RG 210.

67. Office of Censorship, General Information Summary, vol. II, no. 4, Feb. 15–28, 1943, box 12, ROC. For public reception of the reinstitution of the Japanese American draft, see box 49, entry 183, RG 107.

68. Office of Censorship, General Information Summary, vol. III, no. 2, Jan. 15–31, 1944, box 12, ROC; Office of Censorship, General Information Summary, vol. III, no. 3, Feb. 1–15, 1944, box 12, ROC; Office of Censorship, General Information Summary, vol. III, no. 2, Jan. 15–31, 1944, box 12, ROC.

69. "On Equal Footing," *Minidoka Irrigator*, Jan. 22, 1944, 2; WRAWPR, no. 61, box 2, entry 5, RG 210.

70. Frank Yamasaki to Henry L. Stimson, Feb. 26, 1944, box 49, entry 183, RG 107; Frank Yamasaki and Seiko Yakaki, "Recommendations of Topaz Citizens for the Principles of American Democracy," Feb. 26, 1944, box 49, entry 183, RG 107; American Citizens of Japanese Ancestry at Heart Mountain Relocation Center to President Roosevelt, Feb. 28, 1944, box 49, entry 183, RG 107; Community Council, Granada Relocation Center to Henry L. Stimson, Mar. 8, 1944, box 1065, entry 363, RG 407.

71. "Japanese-Americans Inducted into the Army," box 1717, entry 480, RG 389; Army Personnel of Japanese Ancestry by Month of Enlistment or Induction, summary, XTM-23, n.d., box 2166, entry 389, RG 407.

72. On finding war work and draft deferrals, see Office of Censorship, General Information Summary, vol. III, nos. 2–6, Jan. 15–Mar. 31, 1944, box 12, ROC; Brian Masaru Hayashi, *Democratizing the Enemy: The Japanese American Internment*

(Princeton, NJ: Princeton University Press, 2004), 184. On *shoyu*, see Muller, *Free to Die for Their Country*, 85. On feigning mental illness, see Harrison A. Gerhardt to Deputy Chief of Staff for Service Commands, Mar. 24, 1944, box 49, entry 183, RG 107. On moving, see Selective Service System, *Special Groups*, no. 10, 1:135.

73. See especially McCloy to Secretary of State, May 11, 1944, box 445, entry 43A, RG 165; Muller, *Free to Die for Their Country*, 64–99; Hayashi, *Democratizing the Enemy*, 182–188; Muller, "A Penny for Their Thoughts," 134.

74. McCloy to Secretary of State, May 11, 1944, box 445, entry 43A, RG 165. On Poston, see Muller, "A Penny for Their Thoughts," 134–135.

75. Muller, *Free to Die for Their Country*, 4.

76. For "camp mortician," see "Japanese Respond to Induction Call," *NYT*, Mar. 27, 1944, 4. For letter and notice, see Muller, "A Penny for Their Thoughts," 137–138.

77. Muller, *Free to Die for Their Country*, 84.

78. Harrison A. Gerhardt to Dorothy Eley, Mar. 13, 1943, box 49, entry 183, RG 107. On the US government's efforts to stamp out resistance, see Muller, *Free to Die for Their Country*, 68, 89, 93–99; Muller, "A Penny for Their Thoughts," 141; Selective Service System, *Special Groups*, no. 10, 1:128–129; Haysahi, *Democratizing the Enemy*, 183–184; McCloy to Secretary of State, May 11, 1944, box 445, entry 43A, RG 165. President Truman eventually pardoned all Japanese American draft resisters in December 1947. See Muller, *Free to Die for Their Country*, 182. Members of other groups, like Puerto Ricans and American Indians, occasionally made principled antiracist and anticolonialist stands against conscription, too. See J. Edgar Hoover to Secretary of Interior, July 3, 1942, box 1144, entry 1, RG 126; "Puerto Ricans Hit Draft," *NYT*, Feb. 1, 1941, 8; Alison R. Bernstein, *American Indians and World War II: Toward a New Era in Indian Affairs* (Norman: University of Oklahoma Press, 1991), 24–34.

79. On aliens and the army nurse corps, see Alton C. Miller to Assistant Chief of Staff, G-1, memo, July 31, 1945, box 1735, entry 480, RG 389; Army Service Forces to Commanding General, Apr. 10, 1945, box 1717, entry 480, RG 389; G. B. Walker Jr., "Information on Japanese American Personnel," Apr. 9, 1945, box 444, entry 43, RG 165. On the lifting of mass exclusion, see Henry L. Stimson to The People Within the States of Arkansas, Colorado and Wyoming and the Public Generally, Public Proclamation no. WD2, Jan. 20, 1945, box 13, entry 183, RG 107; Irons, *Justice át War*, 341–345; Tom C. Clark to John A. Carver, Jan. 2, 1945, box 1727, entry 480, RG 389. On the creation of more Nisei units, see M. G. White to Chief of Staff, memo, Apr. 3, 1944, box 471, entry 418, RG 165. On Japanese Americans' induction numbers, see "Japanese-Americans Inducted into the Army," box 1717, entry 480, RG 389; "Army Personnel of Japanese Ancestry By Month of Enlistment or Induction," XTM-23, box 2166, entry 389, RG 407.

80. Selective Service System, *Special Groups*, no. 10, 1:134; Lewis B. Hershey to Henry L. Stimson, Mar. 8, 1945, box 1063, entry 363, RG 407.

81. Archibald King to Provost Marshal General, memo, Apr. 9, 1945, box 1063, entry 363, RG 407; Stimson to Hershey, Apr. 23, 1945, box 1063, entry 363, RG 407.

82. Robert P. Patterson to Lewis B. Hershey, Dec. 13, 1945, box 83, entry 102, RG 107; Selective Service System, Local Board Memorandum no. 179, Issued Jan. 27, 1943, As Amended Mar. 4, 1946, in Selective Service System, *Special Groups*, no. 10, 2:92. On the navy and marines, see "Navy Now Accepts U.S. Japanese," *LAT*, Nov. 11, 1945, 5; "Marines Retain Bar on Nisei," *NYT*, Nov. 17, 1945, 3.

83. For Japanese Americans' 1940 population numbers in the continental United States (126,947) and in Hawaii (157,905), see US Department of Commerce,

Sixteenth Census of the United States: 1940: Population: Characteristics of the Nonwhite Population by Race (Washington, DC: GPO, 1943), 5; Robert C. Schmitt, *Demographic Statistics of Hawaii, 1778–1965* (Honolulu: University of Hawaii Press, 1968), 120. For total 1940 population figures of the United States (131,669,275) and Hawaii (423,330), see US Department of Commerce, *Sixteenth Census of the United States: 1940: Population*, vol. 1, *Number of Inhabitants* (Washington, DC: GPO, 1942), 6. For the total number of US military personnel in World War II (16,112,566), see Anne Leland and Mari-Jana "M-J" Oboroceanu, "American War and Military Operations Casualties: Lists and Statistics," Congressional Research Service report to Congress, Feb. 26, 2010, 4. For the total number of Japanese American US military personnel in World War II (roughly 23,500), see Fujitani, *Race for Empire*, 391–392n32.

84. For aggregate Army induction numbers, see Lee, *Employment of Negro Troops*, 414.
85. "Japanese Inspired Agitation among the American Negroes," July 12, 1943, attached to Geo. V. Strong to Assistant Secretary of War, memo, July 13, 1943, box 15, entry 180, RG 107. For secondary sources that have looked at the real and imagined connections between Japan and African Americans in this period, see Fujitani, *Race for Empire*, 83–96; Ernest V. Allen, "When Japan Was 'Champion of the Darker Races': Satokata Takahishi and the Flowering of Black Messianic Nationalism," *Black Scholar* 24 (Winter 1994): 23–46; Marc Gallicchio, *The African American Encounter with Japan and China: Black Internationalism in Asia, 1895–1945* (Chapel Hill: University of North Carolina Press, 2000); George Lipsitz, *The Possessive Investment in Whiteness: How White People Profit from Identity Politics* (Philadelphia: Temple University Press, 1998), chap. 9; Reginald Kearney, *African American Views of the Japanese: Solidarity or Sedition?* (Albany: State University of New York Press, 1998).
86. See Fujitani, *Race for Empire*, 90–96.
87. When the 442nd was formed, Selective Service officials estimated that rejection rates of Japanese American enlistees for the unit would be in the 30–40 percent range. But that did not include those whom the War Department screened out for loyalty or security reasons. See John T. Bissell to General Strong, memo, Jan. 23, 1943, box 1717, entry 480, RG 389.
88. Other scholars have noted these differing schemas in other contexts. See, for example, Claire Jean Kim, "The Racial Triangulation of Asian Americans," *Politics & Society* 27 (Mar. 1999): 105–138; Moon-Kie Jung, *Beneath the Surface of White Supremacy: Denaturalizing U.S. Racisms Past and Present* (Stanford, CA: Stanford University Press, 2015), 35–37. For an example of state concerns about African American disloyalty, see Robert A. Hill, ed., *The FBI's RACON: Racial Conditions in the United States during World War II* (Boston: Northeastern University Press, 1995).
89. See, for example, the diary entries for Feb. 5, 1942, Mar. 24, 1942, Apr. 1, 1942, June 3, 1942, July 20, 1942, Sept. 7, 1942, Nov. 9, 1942, Dec. 2, 1942, Jan. 21, 1943, Feb. 2, 1943, Mar. 23, 1943, Apr. 22, 1943, May 19, 1944, June 8, 1944, Diary of John J. McCloy, box DY1, JJMP. It seems possible that McCloy's secretary composed his diary entries, which were often more of a schedule than deep, personal ruminations. But had he objected to the equation of Japanese American and "Jap," it might not have appeared—let alone appeared so frequently—in his diary.
90. Masaoka, *They Call Me Moses Masaoka*, 121; "The Negro in the United States Navy," *Crisis*, July 1940, 201.

91. George Okamato to Henry L. Stimson, Jan. 28, 1944, box 49, entry 183, RG 107. This effort to claim whiteness was an age-old strategy employed by a wide variety of marginalized people across a broad swath of time. Regarding Japanese Americans in the World War II years, see, for example, John Howard, *Concentration Camps on the Home Front: Japanese Americans in the House of Jim Crow* (Chicago: University of Chicago Press, 2008), 129; Charlotte Brooks, "In the Twilight Zone between Black and White: Japanese American Resettlement and Community in Chicago, 1942–1945," *JAH* 86 (Mar. 2000): 1655–1687.

92. On this point about the particularities of individual groups' experiences militating against broader cooperation and coalition-building, see Mark Brilliant, *The Color of America Has Changed: How Racial Diversity Shaped Civil Rights Reform in California, 1941–1978* (New York: Oxford University Press, 2010); Moon-Kie Jung, *Reworking Race: The Making of Hawaii's Interracial Labor Movement* (New York: Columbia University Press, 2006), 185.

93. Selective Training and Service Act of 1940, Public Law 783, 76th Cong., 3d sess., Sept. 16, 1940, 887; Archibald King to Provost Marshal General, memo, Apr. 9, 1945, box 1063, entry 363, RG 407.

CHAPTER 3

1. Charles Dollard and Donald Young, "In the Armed Forces," *Survey Graphic*, Jan. 1947, 67. For references to two militaries (or armies), one white and one black, see Nancy Macdonald and Dwight Macdonald, *The War's Greatest Scandal! The Story of Jim Crow in Uniform*," pamphlet, n.d. but c. May 1943, box 1067, entry 363, RG 407; John Hope Franklin, *From Slavery to Freedom: A History of Negro Americans*, 3d ed. (1947; New York: Knopf, 1967), 577; Ira Katznelson, *When Affirmative Action Was White: An Untold Story of Racial Inequality in Twentieth-Century America* (New York: Norton, 2005), 82.

2. Willard Wiener, "Park Ave. Youth Ready for Draft . . . If They'll Put Him in a Negro Unit," *PM*, July 24, 1941, 19; Roger Samuel Starr to Local Board No. 20, July 9, 1941, folder 6, box II:A650, NAACPR. Decades later Starr would become a controversial urban-affairs author and policymaker, a New-Dealer-turned-neoconservative who proposed in the 1970s that New York City solve its financial problems by denying essential city services to the South Bronx and other poor neighborhoods. See Bruce Lambert, "Roger Starr, New York Planning Official, Author and Editorial Writer Is Dead," *NYT*, Sept. 11, 2001, C17.

3. Wiener, "Park Ave. Youth Ready for Draft." For the black press coverage, see, for example, "White Writer Wants to Serve with Race Men," *ADW*, July 16, 1941, 1; Lania Davis-Gavin, "Philly Pepperpot," *Philadelphia Tribune*, July 31, 1941, 6; Bernice Calvin, "Mass Meeting Scores Release of Brutal Ft. Bragg M.P.'s," *CCP*, Sept. 6, 1941, 1B.

4. Carlton Moss to Starr, Aug. 2, 1941, box II:A650, NAACPR; Samuel and Lola Mermin to Starr, July 27, 1941, box II:A650, NAACPR; Clarice Selub to Starr, July 28, 1941, box II:A650, NAACPR.

5. Starr to Walter White, May 23, 1941, box II:A616, NAACPR; White to Eleanor Roosevelt, July 25, 1941, box II:A650, NAACPR; Eleanor Roosevelt to White, July 30, 1941, box II:A650, NAACPR.

6. Gail Buckley, *American Patriots: The Story of Blacks in the Military from the Revolution to Desert Storm* (New York: Random House, 2001), 257; Roger S. Starr enlistment record, AER, https://aad.archives.gov/aad/record-detail.jsp?dt=893&mtch=1&cat=WR26&tf=F&sc=24994,24995,24996,24998,24997,24993,24981,24983&bc=,

sl,fd&txt_24995=Roger+starr&op_24995=0&nfo_24995=V,24,1900&rpp=10&p
g=1&rid=3461959 (accessed Jan. 6, 2020).

7. Adjutant General E. S. Adams to Commanding Generals, memo, Oct. 16, 1940, box 810, entry 178, RG 160; L. D. Reddick, "The Negro Policy of the United States Army, 1775–1945," *JNH* 34 (Jan. 1949): 18. For more on army race policies prior to World War II, see Irvin Schindler to Executive to the Assistant Secretary of War, confidential memo, c. Aug. 3, 1944, box 37, entry 88, RG 107; Bernard C. Nalty, *Strength for the Fight: A History of Black Americans in the Military* (New York: Free Press, 1986); Horace Mann Bond, "The Negro in the Armed Forces of the United States prior to World War I," *JNE* 12 (Summer 1943): 268–287. For occasional exceptions to these rules, see Maj. Gen. George Van Horn Moseley to Walter White, Sept. 21, 1931, in *Blacks in the Military: Essential Documents*, ed. Bernard C. Nalty and Morris J. MacGregor (Wilmington, DE: Scholarly Resources, 1981), 94; "The Record: Why Negroes Are Segregated in Armed Forces," *NYAN*, Oct. 14, 1944, 1A.

8. See Historical Section, Bureau of Naval Personnel, "The Negro in the Navy," typescript, 1947, NDL; Morris J. MacGregor, *Integration of the Armed Forces, 1940–1965* (Washington, DC: Center of Military History, 1981), 4–6; William R. Mueller, "The Negro in the Navy," *Social Forces* 24 (Oct. 1945): 110–115.

9. "We'll Have to Fight," *PC*, Mar. 26, 1938, 10; "The Negro Division Is Logical," *PC*, June 11, 1938, 10. On Fish's bill, see "The Right to Serve in the Army," *CCP*, Apr. 14, 1938, 6.

10. Rayford W. Logan, "Segregation in Army Is a Basic Weakness," *NYAN*, Sept. 23, 1939, 5. Logan made this point frequently. See, for example, "Logan Points Out More Army Discrimination," *NJG*, Aug. 31, 1940, 10.

11. "U.S. Navy Refuses Enlistments in All but Menial Posts," *BAA*, Nov. 9, 1935, 11; Assistant Secretary [Roy Wilkins] to A. C. MacNeal, Mar. 31, 1936, box I:C377, NAACPR; Press Service of the NAACP, "Demand Hearing on Bills to Lessen Jim Crow in Armed Services," Apr. 22, 1938, box I:C377, NAACPR; Walter White to Roy Wilkins, Apr. 25, 1938, box I:C377, NAACPR; Roy Wilkins to Walter White, Apr. 26, 1938, box I:C377, NAACPR; Walter White to President Roosevelt, Sept. 15, 1939, box I:C376, box I:C377, NAACPR. On the NAACP's lobbying efforts in favor of the STSA, see folders 3–4, box II:A112, box I:C377, NAACPR.

12. "In Re 10th Cavalry, 24th Infantry," Mar. 2, 1936, box I:C377, NAACPR; Miss Jackson to Mr. White, May 26, 1938, box I:C377, NAACPR; Roy Wilkins to Walter White, Apr. 26, 1938, box I:C377, NAACPR; Roy Wilkins to Anderson S. Robinson, May 26, 1938, box I:C377, NAACPR.

13. Walter White to Roy Wilkins et al., memo, c. Oct. 18, 1939, in *Segregation Entrenched, 1917–1940*, vol. 4 of *Blacks in the United States Armed Forces: Basic Documents*, ed. Morris J. MacGregor and Bernard C. Nalty (Wilmington, DE: Scholarly Resources, 1977), 504; Roy Wilkins to Walter White, memo, Oct. 23, 1939, in MacGregor and Nalty, *Segregation Entrenched*, 505; Thurgood Marshall to Walter White, memo, Oct. 28, 1939, in MacGregor and Nalty, *Segregation Entrenched*, 506.

14. William H. Hastie, address at NAACP annual meeting, June 21, 1940, box II:A21, NAACPR; "Conference Resolutions," *Crisis*, Sept. 1940, 296; "White House Blesses Jim Crow," *Crisis*, Nov. 1940, 351; Walter White to Henry L. Stimson, Aug. 26, 1940, box II:A654, NAACPR.

15. Ulysses Lee, *The Employment of Negro Troops* (Washington, DC: GPO, 1963), 53; "Jim Crow Dooms England to Lose the War," *BAA*, Sept. 14, 1940, 4; "White House Blesses Jim Crow," *Crisis*, Nov. 1940, 351; "Report on Conference at the

White House, 27 September 1940," in *Black Soldiers in World War II*, vol. 5 of *Blacks in the United States Armed Forces: Basic Documents*, ed. Morris J. MacGregor and Bernard C. Nalty (Wilmington, DE: Scholarly Resources, 1977), 105–106.

16. E. S. Adams to Commanding Generals, memo, Oct. 16, 1940, box 810, entry 178, RG 160; Huntington Thomas to Assistant Secretary of War, Oct. 21, 1940, box 150, RPPP; "The Record: Why Negroes Are Segregated in Armed Forces," *NYAN*, Oct. 14, 1944, 1A; Stephen Early to Robert P. Patterson, memo, October 9, 1940, in Nalty and MacGregor, *Black Soldiers in World War II*, 31; "White House Blesses Jim Crow," *Crisis*, Nov. 1940, 351. For the black press's reaction, see, for example, "Army's Policy Called Jim Crow Attempt," *Los Angeles Sentinel*, Oct. 17, 1940, 1; "Leaders Charge 'Trick' to President's Army Edict," *ADW*, Oct. 15, 1940, 1; "White House Charged with Trickery in Announcing Jim Crow Policy of Army," *BAA*, Oct. 19, 1940, 12; "Jim Crow Army Hit," *NYAN*, Oct. 19, 1940, 1. For the White House's response, see typescript notes, Oct. 10, 1940, box 7, official file 93b, FDRP.

17. Walter White to Allen Jackson, Oct. 11, 1940, box II:A442, NAACPR; J. M. Tinsley to Walter White, Oct. 29, 1940, box II:A442, NAACPR; "White House Blesses Jim Crow," *Crisis*, Nov. 1940, 357; "Col. Davis Named General," *BAA*, Nov. 2, 1940, 2. For evidence of White House concern, see typescript notes regarding "White, Walter," "Randolph, A. Philip," and "Hill, T. Arnold," Oct. 10, 1940, box 7, official file 93b, FDRP; and typescript notes regarding "White, Walter," Oct. 16, 1940, box 7, official file 93b, FDRP.

18. Walter White to William Hastie, telegram, Jan. 17, 1941, box II:A112, NAACPR; Press Service of the NAACP, "We Are the Test of Democracy, Says Walter White in National Defense Day Message," Jan. 17, 1941, box II:A442, NAACPR; "Race to Stand as Test of Democracy," *BAA*, Jan. 25, 1941, 7.

19. Frank D. Reeves to Walter White, Oct. 29, 1940, box II:A442, NAACPR; Citizens' Committee for Equal Rights in National Defense to President Roosevelt, n.d., box II:A442, NAACPR; "Conscientious Objectors," *CD*, Jan. 18, 1941, 14. For additional black organizations' opposition to military segregation, see "Urban League Condemns Army Segregation," *PC*, Oct. 26, 1940, 23; typescript notes regarding "Foster, A. L.," Oct. 12, 1940, box 7, official file 93b, FDRP; "Women Want Equality in Armed Forces; Condemn Segregation," *NJG*, Nov. 9, 1940, 4; "Conscientious Objectors to Fight Jim-Crow Units," *CD*, Oct. 26, 1940, 5; "Youth Group to Protest Army's Jim Crow Policy," *New York Age*, Nov. 9, 1940, 12; "Council Votes to Oppose Jim Crow Air Unit," *CD*, Feb. 1, 1941, 3.

20. Letter to Editor, *NYAN*, July 19, 1941, 14; Langston Hughes, "Message to the President," *BAA*, Mar. 1, 1941, 3. On Calloway, see "NAACP Takes Up Calloway 'Draft Board' Case," *PC*, Jan. 18, 1941, 24.

21. "Catholic Organ Hits Segregation in the Army," *ADW*, Nov. 4, 1940, 6; Socialist Workers Party resolution reprinted in C. L. R. James et al., *Fighting Racism in World War II*, ed. Fred Stanton (New York: Pathfinder Press, 1980), 60–64.

22. Negroes' Committee to March on Washington for Equal Participation in National Defense, *Call to Negro America*, pamphlet, box 29, APRP; Walter White, *A Man Called White: The Autobiography of Walter White* (New York: Viking Press, 1948), 190; Harvard Sitkoff, *A New Deal for Blacks: The Emergence of Civil Rights as a National Issue* (New York: Oxford University Press, 1978), 321. See also Kenneth Robert Janken, *Rayford W. Logan and the Dilemma of the African American Intellectual* (Amherst: University of Massachusetts Press, 1993), 128–129.

23. "Editorial of the Month," *Crisis*, May 1941, 163; William L. Sherrill to Franklin D. Roosevelt, Oct. 3, 1941, box 4945, file 811.4016, central decimal file, 1940–1944, RG 59.

24. "Army Can Have Jim Crow in Selective Service Act," *Crisis*, Jan. 1941, 23; Conference of Negro Newspaper Representatives, Dec. 8–9, 1941, transcript, box 196, entry 188, RG 107.

25. US Constitution, art. 1, sec. 8; Public Law 703, 76th Cong., 3d sess., July 2, 1940, 713; *Congressional Record*, 76th Cong., 3d sess., Aug. 26, 1940, 10893, 10892; W. R. Poage to Frank Knox, Dec. 10, 1941, box 1, entry 131N, RG 80.

26. Julian E. Zelizer, "Confronting the Roadblock: Congress, Civil Rights, and World War II," in *Fog of War: The Second World War and the Civil Rights Movement*, ed. Kevin M. Kruse and Stephen Tuck (New York: Oxford University Press, 2012), 38; Ira Katznelson, *Fear Itself: The New Deal and the Origins of Our Time* (New York: Liveright, 2013), 16. On the proportion of southern Democrats in their party's House and Senate caucuses, see Katznelson, *Fear Itself*, 151.

27. Roscoe C. Giles to A. N. Vaughn, Jan. 21, 1941, box 312, CABP; Henry Lewis Stimson Diaries, Sept. 27, 1940, microfilm, reel 6, HLSP; William H. Hastie, "Survey and Recommendations Concerning the Integration of the Negro Soldier into the Army," c. Sept. 22, 1941, box 150, RPPP.

28. Addison Walker, memorandum, Dec. 6, 1941, box 1, entry E131d, RG 80; Lee, *Employment of Negro Troops*, 140; "Remarks of Colonel E. R. Householder," Dec. 8, 1941, box II:A647, NAACPR.

29. Addison Walker to Walter White, Dec. 10, 1941, box 1, entry E131d, RG 80; Lee, *Employment of Negro Troops*, 140; "Colored Folk Danger to What Navy?—Knox," *BAA*, May 17, 1941, 3.

30. Stimson Diaries, Sept. 27, 1940, and Oct. 25, 1940, microfilm, reel 6, HLSP; *Blacks in the World War II Naval Establishment*, vol. 6 of *Blacks in the United States Armed Forces: Basic Documents*, ed. Morris J. MacGregor and Bernard C. Nalty (Wilmington, DE: Scholarly Resources, 1977), 13.

31. Lee, *Employment of Negro Troops*, 147.

32. "Fragments on Back-Room Politics and Civil Rights," *American Heritage*, Feb./Mar. 1982, https://www.americanheritage.com/fragments-back-room-politics-and-civil-rights; Rayford W. Logan Diary, typescript, Oct. 25, 1940, box 3, RWLP.

33. James Rowe Jr., Memorandum for the President, Oct. 23, 1940, box 81, President's Secretary's File, FDRP.

34. David Welky, *Marching across the Color Line: A. Philip Randolph and Civil Rights in the World War II Era* (New York: Oxford University Press, 2014), 47–48.

35. Alan M. Osur, *Blacks in the Army Air Forces during World War II: The Problem of Race Relations* (Washington, DC: GPO, 1977), 21.

36. For some of these various proposals, see "Lincoln Conference Urges a Mixed Army," *BAA*, May 16, 1942, 1; "Form Mixed Army Now, Tobias Urges F.D.," *BAA*, Apr. 3, 1943, 1.

37. "Integration of Both Races in Army Units Held Very Unlikely," *BAA*, Dec. 13, 1941, 1. For a partial transcript of this meeting, see Conference of Negro Newspaper Representatives, Dec. 8–9, 1941, box 196, entry 188, RG 107.

38. Walter White to George C. Marshall, Dec. 22, 1941, box II:A651, NAACPR; White to Marshall, Jan. 2, 1942, box II:A651, NAACPR; White to Eleanor Roosevelt, Dec. 22, 1941, box II:A651, NAACPR; P. L. Prattis to White, Dec. 29, 1941, box II:A651, NAACPR. For other examples of black newspaper editors writing the War Department, see Carter Wesley to Marshall, Jan. 4, 1942, and William O. Walker to Marshall, Jan. 6, 1942, both in box II:A651, NAACPR.

39. John J. McCloy to General Adams, memo, Jan. 13, 1942, box 1079, entry 363, RG 407; Robert P. Patterson, Memorandum for the Secretary of War, Jan. 16, 1942, box 3, entry 99, RG 107.

40. White, *A Man Called White*, 221–222; Walter White to James Waterman Wise, Jan. 14, 1942, box II:A651, NAACPR; Mark Ethridge to White, Jan. 10, 1942, box II:A651, NAACPR; Frank P. Graham to White, Jan. 12, 1942, box II:A651, NAACPR.

41. W. T. Sexton to Assistant Chief of Staff, G-3, memo, Feb. 11, 1942, box 1078, entry 363, RG 407; Dorothy Canfield Fisher to General Marshall, Feb. 7, 1942, box 1078, entry 363, RG 407; Ruth Benedict to President Roosevelt, Feb. 7, 1942, box 1078, entry 363, RG 407; Katherine Devereux Blake to Marshall, Feb. 4, 1942, box 1078, entry 363, RG 407; Gerald White to Henry L. Stimson, Jan. 14, 1942, box 1078, entry 363, RG 407. For White's letters to the president and the navy secretary, see NAACP Press Release, Jan. 16, 1942, box II:A651, NAACPR.

42. "'Mixed' Division Urged on Army," *NYT*, Mar. 22, 1942, 9; "Asks U.S.A. Mixed Unit," *PM*, Mar. 22, 1942, 12. For the UDA petition campaign, see "Eliminate Discrimination in the Armed Forces," petition, box 1075, entry 363, RG 407; "La Guardia Raps Armed Service Jim Crow," *CD*, June 6, 1942, 7; "20,000 Whites Sign First Petition against Segregation," *BAA*, July 4, 1942, 3; "President Petitioned to End Race Bias; 50,000 Sign," *PC*, Feb. 13, 1943, 1; Walter White, "The Right to Fight for Democracy," *Survey Graphic*, Nov. 1942, 474; Ruth Danenhower Wilson, *Jim Crow Joins Up: A Study of the Negro in the Armed Forces of the United States* (New York: William J. Clark, 1944), 123–124.

43. Young Communist League, New York State, *For a Stronger Blow at the Axis*, pamphlet, box 1073, entry 363, RG 407. For more on this larger campaign for a mixed unit, see Young Communist League of Minnesota, "For a Mixed Regiment for the Defeat of Hitler," petition, box 1071, entry 363, RG 407; Edward K. Barsky to Henry L. Stimson, July 22, 1942, box 1075, entry 363, RG 407; John Henry Clark Jr. to Walter White, June 21, 1943, box II:A651, NAACPR; First Progress Report of the Bay Area Council against Discrimination, Aug. 1942, box 429, entry 33, RG 228; "Crimson Suggest Harvard Sponsor Mixed Regiment," *BAA*, Mar. 20, 1943, 24; "13 of These 15 Inductees Would Serve in 'Mixed' Outfits," *PM*, Feb. 18, 1942, 5; Max Lerner, "Drive Jim Crow from the Army," *PM*, July 15, 1943, 2; "The Negro: His Future in America," *New Republic*, Oct. 18, 1943, reprinted in *Primer for White Folks*, ed. Bucklin Moon (Garden City, NY: Doubleday, 1946), esp. 355; Bureau of Intelligence, Office of Facts and Figures, Survey of Intelligence Materials No. 25, May 27, 1942, 28, box 6, entry 3D, RG 208. On ordinary people, see the numerous letters in boxes 1070–1078, entry 363, RG 407.

44. "Drive Jim Crow from the Army," *PM*, July 15, 1943; Walter White to Henry L. Stimson, Aug. 6, 1943, box 1066, entry 363, RG 407; White to Stimson, July 14, 1943, box II:A643, NAACPR.

45. A. C. MacNeal to Walter White, May 12, 1942, box II:A654, NAACPR; "Publishers' Body Backs Mixed Army," *BAA*, June 13, 1942, 1.

46. Walter White to Franklin Delano Roosevelt, Dec. 17, 1941, box II:A654, NAACPR.

47. "Negroes to the Sea," *Time*, Apr. 20, 1942, 55; Washington NAACP quoted in *Washington Evening Star*, Apr. 8, 1942, transcription in box 1, entry 131d, RG 80; NAACP press release, Apr. 10, 1942, box II:A654, NAACPR; Walter White to *Chicago Defender*, Apr. 17, 1942, box II:A654, NAACPR. For navy announcement, see Navy Department, "Navy to Accept Negroes for General Service," press release,

Apr. 7, 1942, box 339, Formerly Security Classified, General Correspondence of Chief of Naval Operations/Secretary of Navy, 1940–1947, RG 80.

48. On Randolph, see "America Is Your Country Too," *Philadelphia Tribune*, Apr. 18, 1942, transcription in box 1, entry 131d, RG 80. On black newspapers' critiques, see, for example, transcriptions in box 1, entry 131d, RG 80; "What the Daily Press Thinks of the New Jim-Crow Navy Rules," *BAA*, Apr. 18, 1942, 3; "An Editorial," *CD*, Apr. 18, 1942, 1. On protest letters, see box 1, entry 131o, RG 80. On the CCP column, see W. O. Walker, "Down the Road," *CCP*, Apr. 18, 1942, transcription in box 1, entry 131d, RG 80. On demands for Knox's resignation, see, for example, "Navy and Marines to Enlist Negroes for General Service," *WP*, Apr. 8, 1942, 1.

49. "Wanted: A Military New Deal," *PC*, Feb. 6, 1943, 6; Surveys Division, Bureau of Special Services, Office of War Information, "The Negroes' Role in the War: A Study of White and Colored Opinions," July 8, 1943, 11–12, box 1799, entry 164, RG 44.

50. Save Our Soldiers Committee to President Roosevelt, petition, n.d., box 1066, entry 363, RG 407; Michigan Federation of Labor, resolution no. 45, c. Sept. 7, 1943, box 1066, entry 363, RG 407; A. Philip Randolph and Norman Thomas, "Victory's Victims? The Negro's Future" (New York: Socialist Party, 1943).

51. Welky, *Marching across the Color Line*, 141; "Negro Americans Awake to Action!," poster, n.d., box 422, entry 33, RG 228. See also A. Philip Randolph to Francis Biddle, Aug. 9, 1943, box 27, APRP; Randolph to Friend, Sept. 7, 1943, box 26, APRP ; National Headquarters of the March on Washington Movement, "Help Us Bury Jim-Crowism," petition to President Roosevelt, n.d., box 7, official file 93b, FDRP; "8 Point Program, March-on-Washington Movement," flyer, box 29, APRP; Resolution for Democracy in the Army, adopted Apr. 22, 1943, box 17, APRP; A. Philip Randolph, "March on Washington Movement Presents Program for the Negro," in *What the Negro Wants*, ed. Rayford W. Logan (1944; South Bend, IN: University of Notre Dame Press, 2001), 153; Macdonald and Macdonald, "The War's Greatest Scandal!"

52. A. Philip Randolph to Lawyers Citizens Committee, Oct. 19, 1943, box 27, APRP; Typed notes on National Steering Committee on Winfred Lynn Case meeting, Sept. 23, 1943, box 28, APRP; Doris [Grotwohl] to A. J. Muste, Sept. 24, 1943, box 15, subseries A-3, series A, section II, FORP; B. F. McLaurin to A. J. Muste, Oct. 26, 1943, box 15, subseries A-3, series A, section II, FORP; War Department, Army Service Forces, Headquarters First Service Command, Intelligence Report, Subject: Winfred William Lynn—Opposition to Segregated Army, Apr. 21, 1943, box 3017, entry HS1-89646273 (P186), RG 65; National Citizens' Committee for Winfred Lynn, *The Story of Winfred Lynn*, pamphlet, n.d., box 118, series II, DMP; A. Philip Randolph et al. to Friend, n.d., box 118, series II, DMP; "Will You Just Stand By," advertisement, *Crisis*, Apr. 1944, 123.

53. "Along the N.A.A.C.P. Battlefront," *Crisis*, Apr. 1944, 117; Resolutions Adopted at the War-Time Conference, NAACP, July 12–16, 1944, 1, box II:A28, NAACPR. For *Crisis* articles, see "The Jim Crow Boomerang," *Crisis*, Oct. 1943, 294; "First Bomber Pilots," *Crisis*, Jan. 1944, 7.

54. American Youth for Democracy, petition to Secretaries Stimson and Knox, n.d., box 1065, entry 363, RG 407; Clarence E. Lovejoy, confidential intelligence report on American Youth for Democracy's Trip to Washington, DC, Apr. 5, 1944, box 9, official file 4245g, FDRP; Elizabeth Lyman to Philleo Nash, memo, July 12, 1944, 25, box 1714, entry 149, RG 44.

55. Lynn Committee to Abolish Segregation in the Armed Forces, *Help Fight Jim Crow in Uniform!*, pamphlet, n.d., box 599, series II, DMP. On the shift to the Lynn

Committee, see "The Intelligence Office," *Politics*, June 1944, 157; Wilfred H. Kerr to A. J. Muste, Apr. 14, 1944, box 15, subseries A-3, series A, section II, FORP. For a small sample of additional evidence of other groups and individuals supporting mixed units, see "Congress of Race Equality Closes Detroit Meeting," *CD*, June 17, 1944, 2; L. D. Reddick, "What the Northern Negro Thinks about Democracy," *Journal of Educational Sociology* 17 (Jan. 1944): 300; Wilson, *Jim Crow Joins Up*, 123–124; "Drive J.C. from the Army," *BAA*, July 24, 1943, 1; "Oberlin Students Fight for Negro Rights," *CCP*, June 3, 1944, 10A.

56. "A Declaration by Negro Voters," *Crisis*, Jan. 1944, 17; Margaret Ryan to Philleo Nash, memo, Aug. 30, 1944, box 1714, entry 149, RG 44; "Along the N.A.A.C.P. Battlefront," *Crisis*, Apr. 1944, 116; Lynn Committee to Abolish Segregation in the Armed Forces, "4 Questions to the President," flyer, n.d., c. July 1944, box 30, series II, DMP; "The Record: Why Negroes Are Segregated in Armed Forces," *NYAN*, Oct. 14, 1944, 1A.

57. Harry McAlpin, "Uncovering Washington," *CD*, Sept. 9, 1944, 3. For the others, see Walter White, Tobias Channing, and Mary McLeod Bethune to President Roosevelt, Sept. 28, 1944, box 14, JDP; Grant Reynolds, "What the Negro Thinks of the War Department," *Crisis*, Oct. 1944, 316; "Along the N.A.A.C.P. Battlefront," *Crisis*, July 1945, 198.

58. *Congressional Record*, 79th Cong., 1st sess., 1945, 91, pt. 2: 2585.

59. BPR, May 5, 1945–May 19, 1945, box 223, entry 188, RG 107; "Army Frowns on Segregation," *CD*, June 23, 1945, 3; "2 U.S. Senators Fight Army Jim Crow Setup," *CD*, June 16, 1945, 2.

60. Willard S. Townsend, A. Philip Randolph, and Morris Milgram to Aron S. Gilmartin, Apr. 5, 1945, box 86, WDLR. On the initial meeting, see Wilfred H. Kerr to Morris Milgram, Mar. 12, 1945, box 65, WDLR.

61. National Committee to Abolish Segregation in the Armed Services, press release, Apr. 30, 1945, box 65, WDLR; Bertha Gruner, Minutes of Proceedings of Conference Called by A. Philip Randolph et al., n.d. but c. Apr. 29, 1945, box 17, APRP.

62. For "nervous strain" quotation, see Wilfred Kerr to Nancy and Dwight Macdonald, Sept. 5, 1945, box 25, series I, DMP. On Kerr's friendship with Lynn, see Doris [Grotwohl] to A. J. Muste, Sept. 24, 1943, box 15, subseries A-3, series A, section II, FORP. On the NCASAS's broader challenges, see National Committee to Abolish Segregation in the Armed Services, meeting minutes, Oct. 20, 1945, box II:A381, NAACPR; Walter White to Robert L. Carter, memo, June 6, 1945, box II:A381, NAACPR; Roger Baldwin to A. Philip Randolph, May 23, 1945, box II:A381, NAACPR; A. Philip Randolph to Roger Baldwin, June 12, 1945, box II:A381, NAACPR.

63. See MacGregor, *Integration of the Armed Forces*, 51–57, 94–98; Sherie Mershon and Steven L. Schlossman, *Foxholes and Color Lines: Desegregating the US Armed Forces* (Baltimore: Johns Hopkins University Press, 1998), 120–134; Historical Section, Bureau of Naval Personnel, "Negro in the Navy," 84, 92–93.

64. Lee, *Employment of Negro Troops*, 151–157. On the army intelligence tests, see Samuel A. Stouffer et al., *The American Soldier: Adjustment during Army Life*, vol. 1 of *Studies in Social Psychology in World War II* (Princeton, NJ: Princeton University Press, 1949), 492.

65. J. S. Leonard, Memorandum for the Assistant Secretary of War, Dec. 17, 1943, in MacGregor and Nalty, *Black Soldiers in World War II*, 286; George C. Marshall to John J. McCloy, memo, Aug. 25, 1945, in MacGregor and Nalty, *Black Soldiers in World War II*, 521.

66. L. D. Reddick, "The Negro in the United States Navy during World War II," *JNH* 32 (Apr. 1947): 214; MacGregor, *Integration of the Armed Forces*, 94, 98.

67. MacGregor, *Integration of the Armed Forces*, 96; Mershon and Schlossman, *Foxholes and Color Lines*, 140; Truman K. Gibson to John J. McCloy, Aug. 8, 1945, in *Planning for the Postwar Employment of Black Personnel*, vol. 7 of *Blacks in the United States Armed Forces: Basic Documents*, ed. Morris J. MacGregor and Bernard C. Nalty (Wilmington, DE: Scholarly Resources, 1977), 16.

68. "'GOP Not for End of Segregation in Army,' Says GOP Leader Fish," *CD*, Sept. 30, 1944, 1; "Army Frowns on Segregation," *CD*, June 23, 1945, 3. For the fate of Powell's bill, see H.R. 2708 (79th Congress; Introduced: Mar. 21, 1945), https://congressional-proquest-com.proxygw.wrlc.org/congressional/result/congressional/congdocumentview?accountid=11243&groupid=104012&parmId=16EE8A7F737&rsId=16EE8A1E5A9# (accessed Jan. 7, 2020). For Powell's reticence about his own bill, see Transcript of Lynn Committee and Schomburg Collection Forum on "Military Jimcrowism," Oct. 25, 1945, 32, box 5, LDR.

69. Katznelson, *Fear Itself*, 182; Robert A. Caro, *Master of the Senate* (New York: Vintage, 2003), 192.

70. MacGregor, *Integration of the Armed Forces*, 85, 91–92, 138–141, 158–161.

71. George C. Marshall to Dorothy Canfield Fisher (stamped "not used"), n.d., box 1078, entry 363, RG 407; Lee, *Employment of Negro Troops*, 155; George C. Marshall to Dorothy Canfield Fisher, Feb. 16, 1942, box 1078, entry 363, RG 407; John J. McCloy to William Hastie, July 2, 1942, in MacGregor and Nalty, *Black Soldiers in World War II*, 167; John J. McCloy to Herbert B. Elliston, Aug. 5, 1943, box 15, entry 88, RG 107.

72. R. W. Crawford to General Eisenhower, memo, Apr. 2, 1942, in MacGregor and Nalty, *Black Soldiers in World War II*, 161; Robert P. Patterson to General Bryden, memo, Jan. 10, 1942, in MacGregor and Nalty, *Black Soldiers in World War II*, 121; Agnes E. Meyer, "Conditions Improving, Yet Bitterness Mounts," *WP*, Mar. 26, 1944, B6.

73. Jacobs quoted in MacGregor, *Integration of the Armed Forces*, 84; "dire results" from Jean Byers, "A Study of the Negro in the Military Service," June 1947, typescript report, 258, box 571, entry 26, RG 319; King quoted in MacGregor, *Integration of the Armed Forces*, 91. For an exception, see Admiral Nimitz quoted in White, *A Man Called White*, 273–274.

74. Dollard and Young, "In the Armed Forces," 111. On the military's growing concerns about passing the universal military training bill, see MacGregor, *Integration of the Armed Forces*, 142.

75. Lee, *Employment of Negro Troops*, 76; Robert P. Patterson to General Watson, June 3, 1941, box 150, RPPP.

76. Osur, *Blacks in the Army Air Forces*, 7.

77. Franklin D. Roosevelt to Frank Knox, memo, Feb. 9, 1942, box 339, Formerly Security Classified, General Correspondence of Chief of Naval Operations/Secretary of Navy, 1940–1947, RG 80; MacGregor, *Integration of the Armed Forces*, 70.

78. On the growing concern among some white southerners about Roosevelt's stance on "Negro" issues, see William E. Leuchtenburg, *The White House Looks South: Franklin D. Roosevelt, Harry S. Truman, Lyndon B. Johnson* (Baton Rouge: Louisiana State University Press, 2005), 134–140. On some northern white and black voters taking civil rights issues more seriously in their voting

choices, see Eric Schickler, *Racial Realignment: The Transformation of American Liberalism, 1932–1965* (Princeton, NJ: Princeton University Press, 2016), 83, 102.

79. MacGregor, *Integration of the Armed Forces*, 292–294. On Roosevelt's concession, see "Hear Private Pledge from Roosevelt," *BAA*, Oct. 14, 1944, 3. On the Republican Party and Dewey, see Schickler, *Racial Realignment*, 243; and Warren Moscow, "Dewey Builds Up Party Platform on 2 Major Points," *NYT*, June 30, 1944, 11.

80. Research Branch, Special Service Division, Services of Supply, War Department, "Attitudes of Enlisted Men toward Negroes for Air Duty," Nov. 30, 1942, box 32, entry 501, RG 165; Stouffer et al., *The American Soldier*, 1:568; Surveys Division, Office of War Information, "The Negroes' Role in the War: A Study of White and Colored Opinions," memorandum no. 59, July 8, 1943, box 1799, entry 164, RG 44. A June 1942 Gallup poll found that a full 41 percent of respondents agreed that "negro and white soldiers [should] serve together in all branches of the armed forces." But that wording seems to have been too ambiguous to measure how many whites actually supported the black-white mixing of small units. Indeed, another Gallup poll from May 1948, which was more explicit in its wording, found support drop twelve points for military integration. Now, 29 percent of respondents agreed that "white and colored men [should] serve together throughout the U.S. armed services—that is, live and work together in the same units." See Schickler, *Racial Realignment*, 112 and his appendix 5.1 at http://assets.press.princeton.edu/releases/m1-10750.pdf (accessed Jan. 7, 2020). For polling data on restaurants, neighborhoods, streetcars, and so forth, see National Opinion Research Center, "Whites Look at Negroes and Negro Problems," n.d. but c. Dec. 1944, box 4, LDR; Hazel Gaudet Erskine, "The Polls: Race Relations," *Public Opinion Quarterly* 26 (Spring 1962): 139, 144–146.

81. Stouffer et al., *The American Soldier*, 1:580.

82. Stouffer et al., *The American Soldier*, 1:590–591; Research Branch, [Army] Information and Education Division, Headquarters, European Theater of Operations, "The Utilization of Negro Infantry Platoons in White Companies," report no. E-118, June 1945, 10, box 57, Adjutant General, General Correspondence, RG 493; [Army] Information and Education Division, "Opinions about Negro Infantry Platoons in White Companies of 7 Divisions," report no. B-157, July 3, 1945, box 212, entry 188, RG 107. On the navy, see Randall Jacobs to Commander in Chief, memo, March 6, 1945, in MacGregor and Nalty, *Blacks in the World War II Naval Establishment*, 265.

83. Mershon and Schlossman, *Foxholes and Color Lines*, 142–143; Charles Dollard, interview by Lawrence D. Reddick, June 27, 1946, box 1, LDR.

84. "The Army's Jim Crow Policy," *NYAN*, Apr. 22, 1944, 6A.

85. "Rejoinder by Mr. Hays," *Politics*, Apr. 1944, 88; *Lynn v. Downer*, 140 F. 2d 399–400 (2d Cir. 1944).

86. See, for example, Glenda Gilmore, *Defying Dixie: The Radical Roots of Civil Rights, 1919–1950* (New York: Norton, 2008); Jacquelyn Dowd Hall, "The Long Civil Rights Movement and the Political Uses of the Past," *JAH* 91 (March 2005): 1233–1263; Robin D. G. Kelley, *Hammer and Hoe: Alabama Communists during the Great Depression* (Chapel Hill: University of North Carolina Press, 1990); Robert Rodgers Korstad, *Civil Rights Unionism: Tobacco Workers and the Struggle for Democracy in the Mid-Twentieth-Century South* (Chapel Hill: University of North Carolina Press, 2003); Nikhil Pal Singh, *Black Is a Country: Race and the Unfinished*

Struggle for Democracy (Cambridge, MA: Harvard University Press, 2005); Thomas J. Sugrue, *Sweet Land of Liberty: The Forgotten Struggle for Civil Rights in the North* (New York: Random House, 2008).

87. For the liberal argument for integration, see, for example, Roy Wilkins, "The Old Army Game?," *Crisis*, May 1945, 145; Charles H. Houston, "The Negro Soldier," *Nation*, Oct. 21, 1944, 496; Walter White, "The Right to Fight for Democracy," *Survey Graphic*, Nov. 1942, 472–474. For the radical argument, see "Protest Army Jim-Crow," *Fighting Worker*, Sept. 24, 1941, 1; Arthur to Dwight Macdonald, Apr. 7, [1943], box 21, series I, DWP.

88. US Department of State, *Bulletin* 4, no. 80, publication 1544, Jan. 4, 1941, 5.

CHAPTER 4

1. "Fragments on Back-Room Politics and Civil Rights," *American Heritage*, Feb./Mar. 1982, https://www.americanheritage.com/fragments-back-room-politics-and-civil-rights; "Memo on Army Conference Held at White House, September 27, 1940," Sept. 28, 1940, box 150, RPPP; Robert P. Patterson to General Watson, June 3, 1941, box 150, RPPP; Henry L. Stimson Diary, June 18, 1941, microfilm, reel 6, HLSP; "Negro Americans Awake to Action!," March on Washington Movement poster, n.d., box 422, entry 33, RG 228; "Along the N.A.A.C.P. Battlefront," *Crisis*, Apr. 1944, 117; Lynn Committee to Abolish Segregation in the Armed Forces, *Help Fight Jim Crow in Uniform!*, pamphlet, n.d., box 599, series II, DMP; Planning Committee of National Committee to Abolish Segregation in the Armed Services, press release, Apr. 30, 1945, box 65, WDLR.

2. "Wanted: A Military New Deal," *PC*, Feb. 6, 1943, 6.

3. "Form Mixed Army Unit Now, Tobias Urges F.D.," *BAA*, Apr. 3, 1943, 1–2. For other examples of African Americans assuming only they faced military segregation, see "Score Army's, Navy's Segregation Policy," *PC*, Dec. 22, 1945, 20; "53,000 Recruits," *PC*, June 1, 1940, 6; "Conscientious Objectors," *CD*, Jan. 18, 1941, 14; "Recent Negro Reactions to the War," n.d., box 5, entry 207, RG 83; "Memorandum on Negro Morale," n.d., box 1553, entry 294, RG 208; John Sengstacke to Franklin D. Roosevelt, Feb. 7, 1945, box 239, entry 188, RG 107; Barbara Dianne Savage, *Broadcasting Freedom: Radio, War, and the Politics of Race, 1938–1948* (Chapel Hill: University of North Carolina Press, 1999), 252.

4. Segregation could be mandatory even if one had to volunteer to join a unit. The largely Japanese American 442nd, for example, was segregated because many Japanese Americans had no choice but to serve solely in this unit.

5. "A United Front," *Minidoka Irrigator*, Feb. 26, 1944, 2.

6. Regina T. Akers, "Asian Americans in the U.S. Military with an Emphasis on the U.S. Navy," Naval History and Heritage Command, https://www.history.navy.mil/browse-by-topic/diversity/asian-americans-pacific-islanders-in-the-navy/asian-americans-us-military.html (last modified Apr. 2017); "A Historic Perspective of Hispanic Sailors in the United States Navy: Admiral David Farragut and Bandmaster Jose Contreras," Naval History and Heritage Command, https://www.history.navy.mil/browse-by-topic/diversity/hispanic-americans-in-the-navy/historic-perspective.html (last modified Sept. 13, 2017); "Contributions of American Indians to the U.S. Navy: Serving the United States since Its Birth," Naval History and Heritage Command, https://www.history.navy.mil/browse-by-topic/diversity/american-indians.html (last modified Nov. 8, 2019).

7. Addison Walker, memorandum, Dec. 6, 1941, box 1, entry 131d, RG 80.

8. Army Service Forces, *Leadership and the Negro Soldier*, M5 manual (Washington, DC: GPO, 1944), 3.

9. Thomas A. Bruscino Jr., "Minorities in the Military," in *A Companion to American Military History*, vol. 2, ed. James C. Bradford (Malden, MA: Blackwell, 2010), 886. See also Bruce White, "Ethnicity and Race in the Military," in *The Oxford Companion to American Military History*, ed. John Whiteclay Chambers (New York: Oxford University Press, 2000), https://www-oxfordreference-com.proxygw.wrlc.org/view/10.1093/acref/9780195071986.001.0001/acref-9780195071986-e-0296; Ralph S. Kuykendall, *Hawaii in the World War* (Honolulu: Historical Commission, 1928), 41; Dave Gutierrez, *Patriots in the Barrio: The Story of Company E, 141st Infantry: The Only Mexican American Army Unit in World War II* (Yardley, PA: Westholme, 2018), 29.

10. "4000 Cooks and Waiters in U.S. Navy," *BAA*, Dec. 7, 1940, 5.

11. Chairman General Board to Secretary of Navy, memo, Feb. 3, 1942, box 339, Formerly Security Classified, General Correspondence of Chief of Naval Operations/Secretary of Navy, 1940–1947, RG 80.

12. Lewis B. Hershey to Harold H. Richardson, Dec. 5, 1940, box 33, file 070, entry 1, RG 147, NARAII.

13. Quoted in Desmond King, *Separate and Unequal: Black Americans and the US Federal Government* (New York: Oxford University Press, 1995), 123.

14. Lou Stoumen, "Puerto Rican Soldier," *Yank*, Mar. 31, 1944, 7; "A Separate VFW," *PCIT*, Dec. 15, 1945, 4; K. Scott Wong, *Americans First: Chinese Americans and the Second World War* (Cambridge, MA: Harvard University Press, 2002), 60. Some members of these groups served in very high-ranking positions. Gordon Chung-Hoon, a Hawaiian of Chinese descent, commanded a navy destroyer in the Pacific. See Akers, "Asian Americans."

15. Alison R. Bernstein, *American Indians and World War II: Toward a New Era in Indian Affairs* (Norman: University of Oklahoma Press, 1991), 49.

16. J. A. Ulio to Judge Johnson, Oct. 21, 1942, box 2581, entry 363A, RG 407; Adjutant General to Lloyd H. Stormo, May 11, 1943, box 444, entry 43, RG 165; Bernstein, *American Indians and World War II*, 22–24; Kenneth William Townsend, *World War II and the American Indian* (Albuquerque: University of New Mexico Press, 2000), 69–71; Henry L. Stimson to Elbert D. Thomas, Apr. 5, 1943, box 1068, entry 363, RG 407; Lili M. Kim, "The Pursuit of Imperfect Justice: The Predicament of Koreans and Korean Americans on the Homefront during World War II" (PhD diss., University of Rochester, 2001), 193–197, 236.

17. Wong, *Americans First*, 55–71, 148–192, esp. 164. In at least one case, a Chinese man served with an otherwise all-black New York (i.e., not yet federalized) Home Guard unit. See "Harlem's Home Guard . . . 599 Negroes and One Chinese," *PM*, Mar. 26, 1941, 15. On Native American units, see Elizabeth Shepley Sergeant, "The Indian Goes to War," *New Republic*, Nov. 30, 1942, 709; Flint Whitlock, *The Rock of Anzio: From Sicily to Dachau—A History of the U.S. 45th Infantry Division* (Boulder, CO: Westview Press, 1998), 21.

18. "Spanish Speaking Americans in the War," pamphlet, box 417, entry 33, RG 228; John W. McGilvray to Commanding General XXI Corps, Report of Investigation regarding alleged ill-treatment of Pvt Morales, April 12, 1944, box 93, entry 26e, RG 159. On the Mexican American company, see Gutierrez, *Patriots from the Barrio*. For evidence that this company did not remain all–Mexican American throughout the war, see *A Pictorial History of the 36th Division* (Austin, TX: 36th Division Association, n.d.), 31–33.

19. Howard E. Kessinger to Colonel Berry, memo, Aug. 28, 1943, box 37, entry 88, RG 107. For a taste of the complexities of Puerto Ricans' unit assignments, see Stoumen, "Puerto Rican Soldier"; Sonia S. Lee and Ande Diaz, "'I Was the One Percenter': Manny Diaz and the Beginnings of a Black–Puerto Rican Coalition," *Journal of American Ethnic History* 26 (Spring 2007): 56–57; Henry L. Stimson to Bolivar Pagán, Apr. 9, 1943, box 1070, entry 363, RG 407; Silvia Álvarez Curbelo, "The Color of War: Puerto Rican Soldiers and Discrimination during World War II," in *Beyond the Latino World War II Hero: The Social and Political Legacy of a Generation,* ed. Maggie Rivas-Rodríguez and Emilio Zamora (Austin: University of Texas Press, 2009), 116–117. On the racial breakdown of Puerto Rican service personnel, see Marcus Ray to Jack Miller, May 21, 1947, box 245, entry 188, RG 107; "Strength of Puerto Rican Personnel by Command and Race," July 1, 1945, box 1320, entry 389, RG 407; "Strength of Puerto Rican Personnel Outside Continental United States by Command and Race," c. July 1945, box 1320, entry 389, RG 407. On the race politics of Panama at the time, see Rebecca Herman, "The Global Politics of Anti-Racism: A View from the Canal Zone," *American Historical Review* 125 (Apr. 2020): 460–486.

20. See memo attached to Henry L. Stimson to President Roosevelt, Nov. 13, 1942, box 82, President's Secretary's File, FDRP. On Roosevelt's lobbying for these units, see Roosevelt to Stimson, memo, Nov. 17, 1942, box 82, President's Secretary's File, FDRP. For more on these units, see Carl Hartman, "End of the Australian Battalion," Overseas News Agency wire, June 1, 1943, box 1074, entry 222, RG 208; Alan Cranston to Archibald MacLeish, memo, Mar. 12, 1942, box 1078, entry 222, RG 208; Constantine Poulos to Alan Cranston and David Karr, memo, Dec. 30, 1942, box 1078, entry 222, RG 208; "Army Grows Cool to Battalion Idea," *NYT,* Jan. 9, 1943, 7; Robert Szymczak, "The Battalion That Never Was: Dr. Teofil Starzynski, the OSS, and the Polish Special Service Unit Project," *Polish American Studies* 66 (Autumn 2009): 47–72; Howard R. Bergen, *The History of the 99th Infantry Battalion, U.S. Army* (Oslo: E. Moestue, 1956); Gerd Nyquist, *The 99th Battalion* (Oslo: H. Aschehoug, 1981).

21. Bienvenido N. Santos, "Filipinos in War," *Far Eastern Survey* 11 (Nov. 1942): 249. See also J. M. Elizalde to Secretary of War, Dec. 8, 1941, box 2581, entry 363A, RG 407; and J. M. Elizalde to the President, Dec. 17, 1942, box 2581, entry 363A, RG 407. For the figure of seven thousand, see Christopher Capozzola, *Bound by War: How the United States and the Philippines Built America's First Pacific Century* (New York: Basic Books, 2020), 166.

22. On the need for Filipinos to volunteer to join the First or Second Fil and on their occasional assignment to these units regardless of their wishes, see Capozzola, *Bound by War,* 164. To arrive at the number of Filipinos serving in "regular" army units, I subtracted the 7,000 in the First or Second Fil from the total number of Filipinos whom the army inducted through November 1946 (11,651). Even when one subtracts those inducted after the end of World War II, that still leaves at least several thousand. For the 11,651 figure, see Selective Service System, *Special Groups,* Special Monograph no. 10, vol. 1 (Washington, DC: GPO, 1953), 113. For Filipinos, who served in "white" units, see Doroteo V. Vité, "A Filipino Rookie in Uncle Sam's Army," *Asia: The Journal of the American Asiatic Association* 42 (Oct. 1942): 565–566; O. N. Thompson to Adjutant General, memo, Mar. 14, 1944, box 445, entry 43A, RG 165. On the reorganized regiment, see Wong, *Americans First,* 150–151. It is also worth noting that nearly 200,000 Filipinos in the Philippines also fought as part of the formal US military during World War II, though they did

so in Filipino units attached to the US military and under its direct authority. See Capozzola, *Bound by War*, 208.

23. We will never have an exact number, since the US military did not collect statistics on troops of Mexican descent, save those of Mexican nativity.

24. Allen W. Gullion to Assistant Chief of Staff, G-2, memo, Nov. 2, 1943, box 445, entry 43A, RG 165. On the World War I years, see Kuykendall, *Hawaii in the World War*, 34; Ernest K. Wakukawa, *A History of the Japanese People in Hawaii* (Honolulu: Toyo Shoin, 1938), 205; Lucy E. Salyer, "Baptism by Fire: Race, Military Service, and U.S. Citizenship, 1918–1935," *JAH* 91 (Dec. 2004): 854.

25. E. S. Adams to Commanding Generals, Oct. 30, 1940, box 14, file no. 110, Legislative and Policy Precedent Files, RG 407; Lewis B. Hershey to Colonel Jarrell, Dec. 4, 1940, file 070, entry 1, RG 147, NARAII.

26. "13 of These 15 Inductees Would Serve in 'Mixed' Outfit," *PM*, Feb. 18, 1942, 5; H. B. Lewis to Commanding General, memo, Jan. 22, 1942, box 147, entry 360A, RG 407. See also E. S. Adams to Commanding Generals, memo, Jan. 23, 1942, box 5, entry 406, RG 494.

27. Delos C. Emmons to Adjutant General, memo, Apr. 6, 1942, box 147, entry 360A, RG 407. On the Varsity Victory Volunteers and the broader picture of Japanese Americans and the military in Hawaii at the time, see Franklin Odo, *No Sword to Bury: Japanese Americans in Hawaii during World War II* (Philadelphia: Temple University Press, 2004).

28. Delos Emmons to "WD CSA," secret telegram, May 11, 1942, box 5, entry 406, RG 494; George C. Marshall to Commanding General, Hawaiian Department, secret teletype, May 28, 1942, box 5, entry 406, RG 494. For the War Department's original rejection of Emmons's proposal, see J. A. Ulio to Commanding General, Hawaiian Department, memo, May 2, 1942, box 5, entry 406, RG 494. On white leadership, see Thomas D. Murphy, *Ambassadors in Arms: The Story of Hawaii's 100th Battalion* (Honolulu: University of Hawaii Press, 1954), 63.

29. Murphy, *Ambassadors in Arms*, 60; Odo, *No Sword to Bury*, 291n16.

30. Ulio to Commanding General, memo, May 2, 1942, box 5, entry 406, RG 494.

31. John J. McCloy to Assistant Chief of Staff, G-1, memo, Mar. 4, 1944, box 48, entry 183, RG 107.

32. Adjutant General's Office, Machine Records Branch, "Enlisted Men of Japanese Descent Now Stationed in the United States," Oct. 3, 1942, box 147, entry 360A, RG 407.

33. A. Lury to Lt. Col. Dusenbury, memo, July 20, 1942, box 35, entry 208, RG 165; Edwin O. Reischauer, Memorandum on Policy towards Japan, Sept. 14, 1942, box 147, entry 360A, RG 407. On the JACL, see Mike Masaoka with Bill Hosokawa, *They Call Me Moses Masaoka: An American Saga* (New York: William Morrow, 1987), 121.

34. Headquarters 1st Battalion, 370th Engineer Regiment, "Military History—All American Soldiers of Japanese Ancestry in Hawaii," Nov. 20, 1942, box 280, entry 208, RG 165; "Reinstitution of Selective Service in Hawaii, 1 April 1944," attached to M. G. White to Chief of Staff, memo, Apr. 3, 1944, box 471, entry 418, RG 165.

35. J. H. Hilldring to Chief of Staff, memo, June 26, 1942, box 445, entry 43, RG 165; T. J. Koenig and J. H. Lowell, "The Military Utilization of United States Citizens of Japanese Ancestry," n.d. but c. Sept. 14, 1942, box 445, entry 43, RG 165; Memorandum for the Secretary of War, Oct. 28, 1942, box 147, entry 360A, RG 407.

36. M. W. Pettigrew to John J. McCloy, memo, Nov. 17, 1942, box 147, entry 360A, RG 407.

37. John M. Hall to Colonel Bicknell, memo, Aug. 13, 1943, box 22, entry 180, RG 107; Secretary of War to President Roosevelt, draft letter, n.d., box 147, entry 360A, RG 407.

38. On details of the new unit, see I. H. Edwards to Commanding General, Army Ground Forces, memo, Jan. 12, 1943, box 1717, entry 480, RG 389. On Marshall, see Murphy, *Ambassadors in Arms*, 109–110. For the announcement, see War Department, Bureau of Public Relations, "Loyal Americans of Japanese Ancestry to Compose Special Unit in the Army," press release, Jan. 28, 1943, box 280, entry 208, RG 165. For Roosevelt's letter, see Franklin D. Roosevelt to Secretary Stimson, Feb. 1, 1943, box 47, entry 183, RG 107. War Relocation director Dillon Myer, with input from leaders of the Office of War Information, drafted the letter for Roosevelt. See D. S. Myer to John J. McCloy, Jan. 15, 1943, box 47, entry 183, RG 107.

39. Lury to Dusenbury, memo, July 20, 1942, box 35, entry 208, RG 165; W. E. Crist to General Strong, memo, Jan. 4, 1943, box 1717, entry 480, RG 389; Secretary of War to President Roosevelt, draft letter, n.d., box 147, entry 360A, RG 407; Bureau of Public Relations, "Loyal Americans of Japanese Ancestry to Compose Special Unit in the Army," Jan. 28, 1943, box 280, entry 208, RG 165.

40. Office of Censorship, District Postal Censor, Honolulu, T.H., General Information Summary, Mar. 15, 1943–Mar. 31, 1943, box 12, ROC. That few Japanese Americans in Hawaii seemed to object strongly to the 442nd's segregated nature, see censored mail reports in Office of Censorship, District Postal Censor, Honolulu, T.H., General Information Summary, Mar. 15, 1943–Mar. 31, 1943, box 12, ROC; Odo, *No Sword to Bury*, 221–228. On the JACL suggestion, see Masaoka, *They Call Me Moses Masaoka*, 123.

41. Masaoka, *They Call Me Moses Masaoka*, 123–125. Publicly, Masaoka echoed the War Department's justifications for segregation. See Mike Masaoka, "Why I Volunteered," *PCIT*, Feb. 4, 1943, 7.

42. James Omura, "Nisei Life: We Oppose a Nisei Legion," *Rocky Nippon* clipping, Feb. 2, 1943, box 47, entry 183, RG 107. For his letters and other editorials, see Omura to Henry L. Stimson, Feb. 5, 1943, Omura to Stimson, Feb. 15, 1943, Omura to Stimson, Feb. 21, 1943, Omura to Stimson, Feb. 23, 1943, all in box 47, entry 183, RG 107; Helen B. Chapin, Highlights in the Domestic Foreign-Language Press: Japanese American Press, report no. 11, c. Feb. 23, 1943, box 6, entry 8, RG 210; Helen B. Chapin, Highlights in the Domestic Foreign-Language Press: Japanese American Press, report no. 12, c. Mar. 13, 1943, box 6, entry 8, RG 210; Helen B. Chapin, Highlights in the Domestic Foreign-Language Press: Japanese American Press, report no. 13, c. Mar. 26, 1943, box 6, entry 8, RG 210. On Omura, see James Matsumoto Omura, *Nisei Naysayer: The Memoir of Militant Japanese American Journalist Jimmie Omura*, ed. Arthur A. Hansen (Stanford, CA: Stanford University Press, 2018).

43. National Opinion Research Center, survey no. 1, Mar. 19, 1943, box 7, entry 8, RG 210.

44. War Relocation Authority, "Army and Leave Clearance at War Relocation Centers," June 1943, 10, 54–57, HSTL, https://trumanlibrary.org/whistlestop/study_collections/japanese_internment/documents/index.php?documentdate=1943-06-00&documentid=23&pagenumber=1; John M. Hall to Colonel Bicknell, memo, Aug. 13, 1943, box 22, entry 180, RG 107.

45. William P. Scobey to Colonel Booth, Feb. 20, 1943, box 22, entry 180, RG 107; John J. McCloy to General White, memo, May 4, 1943, box 22, entry 180, RG 107.

46. Henry L. Stimson to Eleanor Roosevelt, Mar. 1, 1943, box 47, entry 183, RG 107; Stimson to Omura, Feb. 9, 1943, box 1717, entry 480, RG 389.
47. Stimson to Omura, Feb. 9, 1943, box 1717, entry 480, RG 389; Merritt B. Booth to Colonel Scobey, memo, Jan. 25, 1943, box 47, entry 183, RG 107; John J. McCloy to General McNarney, Oct. 2, 1943, box 445, entry 43A, RG 165.
48. McCloy to McNarney, Oct. 2, 1943, box 445, entry 43A, RG 165. The exceptions included Japanese-language translators and interpreters, Women's Army Corps members (this branch opened to some Japanese American women in July 1943), and those soldiers who remained in the service commands in the United States. A new, segregated unit of sorts was also activated at this time. In June 1943, the War Department placed the troops it deemed "potentially subversive" in the 525th Quartermaster Service Company. It had soldiers of German, Italian, Japanese, and other ancestries, but they were segregated along these lines. In March 1944, the unit was disbanded, and its hundred or so Japanese American members were reassigned to a new unit—Company B of the 1800th Engineer General Service Battalion. See Shirley Castelnuovo, *Soldiers of Conscience: Japanese American Military Resisters* (Lincoln: University of Nebraska Press, 2010).
49. William P. Scobey to John J. McCloy, memo, Mar. 16, 1943, box 47, entry 183, RG 107; McCloy to White, memo, May 4, 1943, box 22, entry 180, RG 107; John J. McCloy to General White, memo, Oct. 12, 1943, box 445, entry 43A, RG 165.
50. M. G. White to Chief of Staff, memo, Nov. 27, 1943, box 445, entry 43A, RG 165.
51. Allen W. Gullion to Assistant Chief of Staff, G-2, Nov. 2, 1943, box 445, entry 43A, RG 165; Harrison A. Gerhardt to Assistant Chief of Staff, G-3, memo, Dec. 22, 1943, box 445, entry 43A, RG 165; Harrison A. Gerhardt, Memorandum of Record, Nov. 1, 1943, box 48, entry 183, RG 107; George V. Strong to Assistant Chief of Staff, G-3, memo, Nov. 12, 1943, box 445, entry 43A, RG 165. For the views of the General Staff, see table attached to White to Chief of Staff, memo, Nov. 27, 1943, box 445, entry 43A, RG 165.
52. Gullion to Assistant Chief of Staff, G-2, Nov. 2, 1943, Nov. 2, 1943, box 445, entry 43A, RG 165.
53. For the War Department's press releases, see War Department, Bureau of Public Relations, Press Release for Radio, Jan. 20, 1944, box 48, entry 183, RG 107; War Department, Bureau of Public Relations, Press Release for Radio, Jan. 21, 1944, box 48, entry 183, RG 107. For press coverage in and out of the camps, see "Japanese-Americans Will Be Drafted Soon," *NYT*, Jan. 21, 1944, 7; "Jap-Americans in Draft Again," *WP*, Jan. 21, 1944, 2; WRAWPR, no. 53, week ending Feb. 2, 1944, box 2, entry 5, RG 210; Morris Burge, "War Department Announcement Welcoming News, Burge," *Extra Poston Chronicle*, Jan. 22, 1944, 1; "Draft: A Long Step," *Gila News-Courier*, Jan. 22, 1944, 2; "To Draft Nisei!!," *Granada Pioneer*, Jan. 22, 1944, 1; "Selective Service Opens for Nisei," *Heart Mountain Sentinel*, Jan. 22, 1944, 1; "Selective Service Open to Nisei," *Minidoka Irrigator*, Jan. 22, 1944, 1; "Call Nisei to Arms," *Manzanar Free Press*, Jan. 29, 1944, 2; "Questions and Answers about Selective Service," *Rohwer Outpost*, Jan. 26, 1944, 5; "Nisei Draft Approved by War Department," *Topaz Times*, Jan. 21, 1944, 1.
54. "Selective Service Open to Nisei," *Minidoka Irrigator*, Jan. 22, 1944, 1; "An Editorial . . . Selective Service," *Salt Lake City Tribune*, reprinted in *Topaz Times*, Jan. 29, 1944, 2.
55. Community Analysis to Dillon S. Myer, memo, Apr. 10, 1944, 6, box 48, entry 183, RG 107; "Into the Life of Every Man," *Heart Mountain Sentinel*, Jan. 29, 1944, 4; "Discriminatory Non-Discrimination," *Heart Mountain Sentinel*, Apr. 1, 1944, 4.

56. "A United Front," *Minidoka Irrigator*, Feb. 26, 1944, 2; Frank Yamasaki to President Roosevelt, Feb. 26, 1944, box 1065, entry 363, RG 407; American Citizens of Japanese Ancestry at Heart Mountain Center to Franklin D. Roosevelt, petition, Feb. 28, 1944, box 49, entry 183, RG 107.

57. "WACs Unsegregated," *PCIT*, editorial reprinted in *Manzanar Free Press*, Jan. 26, 1944, 2; Intermountain District Council Japanese American Citizens League, resolution, Feb. 24, 1944, box 49, entry 183, RG 107; Mike Masaoka to John J. McCloy, Nov. 10, 1943, box 49, entry 183, RG 107.

58. Community Council, Granada Relocation Center to Henry L. Stimson, Mar. 8, 1944, box 1065, entry 363, RG 407; "A Group of Mothers of the Minidoka WRA Center" to Delos Emmons, Feb. 21, 1944, box 49, entry 183, RG 107; Mothers' Society at Minidoka to Henry L. Stimson, Feb. 20, 1944, box 49, entry 183, RG 107.

59. Sueo Sako, "Just Incidentally," *Granada Pioneer*, Mar. 1, 1944, 2; Community Analysis to Dillon S. Myer, memo, Apr. 10, 1944, 6, box 48, entry 183, RG 107.

60. Omura to Stimson, Feb. 14, 1944, box 49, entry 183, RG 107; Eric L. Muller, "A Penny for Their Thoughts: Draft Resistance at the Poston Relocation Center," *Law and Contemporary Problems* 68 (Spring 2005): 136; Eric L. Muller, *Free to Die for Their Country: The Story of the Japanese American Draft Resisters in World War II* (Chicago: University of Chicago Press, 2001), 83 (emphasis in original).

61. Galen M. Fisher to Harrison A. Gerhardt, Jan. 24, 1944, box 47, entry 183, RG 107; Ralph E. Smeltzer to Stimson, Jan. 24, 1944, box 49, entry 183, RG 107; Harriet Yarrow to Stimson, Jan. 27, 1944, box 49, entry 183, RG 107; Rolland W. Schloerb to Stimson, Feb. 11, 1944, box 49, entry 183, RG 107; William Carr to Harrison A. Gerhardt, Apr. 7, 1944, box 47, entry 183, RG 107.

62. Harrison A. Gerhardt, Memorandum of Record, Nov. 1, 1943, box 48, entry 183, RG 107; Gerhardt to Dorothy Eley, Mar. 13, 1944, box 49, entry 183, RG 107; McCloy to McNarney, memo, Oct. 2, 1943, box 445, entry 43A, RG 165; Gerhardt to Eley, Mar. 13, 1944, box 49, entry 183, RG 107.

63. John J. McCloy to Assistant Chief of Staff, G-1, Mar. 4, 1944, box 48, entry 183, RG 107. Dillon Myer, director of the War Relocation Authority, also sided with McCloy and his staff. See Dillon Myer to McCloy, Dec. 22, 1943, box 22, entry 180, RG 107. On the secretary of war's expression of policy, see Stimson to Omura, Feb. 9, 1944, box 1717, entry 480, RG 389.

64. M. G. White to John J. McCloy, memo, Mar. 14, 1944, box 48, entry 183, RG 107.

65. M. G. White to Chief of Staff, memo, Apr. 3, 1944, box 441, entry 43A, RG 165.

66. "Policies of the Government as to the Resident Japanese," resolution adopted by the California delegation, Washington, DC, June 14, 1943, box 47, entry 183, RG 107.

67. Assignment of Citizens of Japanese Ancestry, memorandum for record, Apr. 12, 1944, box 471, entry 418, RG 165.

68. Harlan C. Parks to Assistant Secretary of War, memo, June 16, 1945, box 444, entry 43A, RG 165; Harlan C. Parks to Commanding General, Army Service Forces, confidential disposition form, Oct. 31, 1945, box 441, entry 43A, RG 165; Edward F. Witsell to Commanding Generals, memo, Dec. 10, 1945, box 441, entry 43A, RG 165.

69. McCloy to McNarney, Oct. 2, 1943, box 445, entry 43A, RG 165; Harrison A. Gerhardt, Memorandum of Record, Nov. 1, 1943, box 48, entry 183, RG 107. Only at the end of the war did McCloy begin to question the segregation of black troops. It seems entirely plausible that his experience with Japanese American

integration helped make this possible, though I have seen no evidence to this effect. On the relational point, see, for example, Natalia Molina, Daniel Martinez HoSang, and Ramón A. Gutiérrez, eds., *Relational Formations of Race: Theory, Method, and Practice* (Berkeley: University of California Press, 2019), 3; Moon-Kie Jung, *Beneath the Surface of White Supremacy: Denaturalizing U.S. Racisms Past and Present* (Stanford, CA: Stanford University Press, 2015), 69. For McCloy's diary, see Jan. 19, 1943, Jan. 26, 1943, Apr. 2, 1943, May 24, 1943, June 28, 1943, Mar. 11, 1944, box DY1, JJMP.

70. For the "forever foreign[er]" concept, see Mia Tuan, *Honorary Whites or Forever Foreigners: The Asian Ethnic Experience Today* (New Brunswick, NJ: Rutgers University Press, 1999).

71. McCloy to White, memo, May 4, 1943, box 22, entry 180, RG 107;Daniel Kryder, *Divided Arsenal: Race and the American State during World War II* (Cambridge: Cambridge University Press, 2000), 167n108. On induction numbers, see Selective Service System, *Special Groups*, no. 10, vol. 2, 113–134, table 55; on Japanese Americans' numbers, see Chapter 2, this volume. On the WACs' limitations on Japanese American enlistment, see Vance L. Sailor to Commanding General, Each Service Command, memo, July 28, 1943, box 1508, entry 360A, RG 407.

72. "Three Forward Army Steps," *BAA*, May 15, 1943, 4; District Intelligence Officer, Thirteenth Naval District to the Director of Naval Intelligence, memo, Mar. 30, 1943, box 2, entry 17, RG 210; Seichi H. Mikami to Henry L. Stimson, Feb. 5, 1943, box 47, entry 183, RG 107; "WACs Unsegregated," *Manzanar Free-Press*, Jan. 26, 1944, 2; "A United Front," *Minidoka Irrigator*, Feb. 26, 1944, 2.

73. Willard S. Townsend, A. Philip Randolph, and Morris Milgram to Aron S. Gilmartin, Apr. 5, 1945, box 86, WDLR; Planning Committee of National Committee to Abolish Segregation in the Armed Services, press release, Apr. 30, 1945, box 65, WDLR. On New York City's new JACL office, see Stephanie Bangarth, *Voices Raised in Protest: Defending Citizens of Japanese Ancestry in North America, 1942–1949* (Vancouver: University of British Columbia Press, 2008), 126. For Clara Clayman's work at Gila River, see Aron Hirt-Manheimer, ed., *The Dancer Within: Intimate Conversations with Great Dancers* (Middletown, CT: Wesleyan University Press, 2008), 3. For Clayman's work in the Lynn Committee, see Conrad Lynn to Dwight Macdonald, July 19, 1944, box 30, series I, DMP; Lynn to Macdonald, July 28, 1944, box 30, series I, DMP; Wilfred Kerr to Dwight Macdonald, July 22, 1944, box 25, series I, DMP. On Sugihara's activism in New York City and beyond, see Greg Robinson, *After Camp: Portraits in Midcentury Japanese American Life and Politics* (Berkeley: University of California Press, 2012), 90–91; Ina Sugihara, "Our Stake in a Permanent FEPC," *Crisis*, Jan. 1945, 14. On Sugihara's committee appointment, see Bertha Gruner, Minutes of Proceedings of Conference Called by A. Philip Randolph, et al., n.d. but c. Apr. 29, 1945, box 17, APRP.

74. Planning Committee of National Committee to Abolish Segregation in the Armed Services, press release, Apr. 30, 1945, box 65, WDLR; Gruner, Minutes of Proceedings of Conference Called by A. Philip Randolph, et al., n.d. but c. Apr. 29, 1945, box 17, APRP; "JACL Asks for Ending Segregation in the Army," *PCIT*, Apr. 30, 1945, 1–2; "JACL Opposes Segregation Proposals in Draft Measure," *PCIT*, Apr. 14, 1951, 2.

75. In addition to the Jews who represented non-Jewish organizations, the American Jewish Committee and the Anti-Defamation League attended the NCASAS

summit meeting. See Planning Committee of National Committee to Abolish Segregation in the Armed Services, press release, Apr. 30, 1945, box 65, WDLR .

76. Mike Masaoka to John J. McCloy, Nov. 10, 1943, box 49, entry 183, RG 107. See also Frank Yamasaki to Henry L. Stimson, Feb. 26, 1944, box 49, entry 183, RG 107; Ted G. Fujimoto to Henry L. Stimson, Jan. 26, 1944, box 49, entry 183, RG 107.

77. "Three Forward Army Steps," *BAA*, May 15, 1943, 4.

78. Telephone Conversation between Maj. Hughes and Col. Stacy Knopf, Mar. 21, 1944, box 22, entry 180, RG 107; Takashi Fujitani, *Race for Empire: Koreans as Japanese and Japanese as Americans during World War II* (Berkeley: University of California Press, 2011), 170.

79. George Okamoto to Henry L. Stimson, Jan. 28, 1944, box 49, entry 183, RG 107; Muller, "A Penny for Their Thoughts," 136; Community Analysis to Dillon S. Myer, memo, Apr. 10, 1944, 7, box 48, entry 183, RG 107.

CHAPTER 5

1. J. A. Ulio to Director of Selective Service System, July 30, 1943, box 1511, entry 360, RG 407; G. Tinsley Garnett to Adjutant General, Aug. 18, 1943, box 1511, entry 360, RG 407; Garnett to Adjutant General, Aug. 28, 1943, box 1511, entry 360, RG 407.

2. For a small sample of outstanding work that looks at battles over race classification as a window on the meaning and boundaries of race, see Christopher A. Ford, "Administering Identity: The Determination of 'Race' in Race-Conscious Law," *California Law Review* 82 (Oct. 1994): 1231–1285; Ariela J. Gross, *What Blood Won't Tell: A History of Race on Trial* (Cambridge, MA: Harvard University Press, 2008); Allyson Hobbs, *A Chosen Exile: A History of Racial Passing in American Life* (Cambridge, MA: Harvard University Press, 2014); Michelle Brattain, "Miscegenation and Competing Definitions of Race in Twentieth-Century Louisiana," *Journal of Southern History* 71 (Aug. 2005): 621–658; Peggy Pascoe, *What Comes Naturally: Miscegenation Law and the Making of Race in America* (New York: Oxford University Press, 2008).

3. This chapter focuses on the army and not the navy. The navy had its own race-classification controversies, but in part because the navy had free reign over its induction procedures until 1943, its controversies were not as well documented and publicized. For exceptions, see W. L. White, *Lost Boundaries* (New York: Harcourt, Brace, 1947), 31–32; and " 'Intolerance and Snobbery,' " *PC*, Feb. 3, 1940, 6.

4. Elmer Wooton to Director of Selective Service, telegram, Oct. 6, 1940, box 33, file 070, entry 1, RG 147, NARAII; Harold H. Richardson to C. A. Dykstra, Dec. 2, 1940, box 33, file 070, entry 1, RG 147, NARAII.

5. Stanley R. McNeil to Gareth N. Brainerd, Nov. 15, 1940, box 33, file 070, entry 1, RG 147, NARAII.

6. Harold H. Richardson to C. A. Dykstra, Nov. 25, 1940, box 33, file 070, entry 1, RG 147, NARAII; B. C. Garrett to State Headquarters, Dec. 6, 1940, box 33, file 070, entry 1, RG 147, NARAII.

7. Lewis B. Hershey to Colonel Jarrell, Dec. 4, 1940, box 32, file 070, entry 1, RG 147, NARAII.

8. Assistant Chief of Staff memo quoted in Edward S. Shattuck to Campbell C. Johnson, memo, Jan. 22, 1941, box 136, file 220, entry 1, RG 147, NARAII. For Selective Service officials' attempt to clarify race classification matters, see Lewis B. Hershey to State Directors of Selective Service, California, telegram, Oct.

16, 1940, box 36, file 300, entry 1, RG 147, NARAII; Hershey to Elmer Wooton, telegram, Oct. 7, 1940, file 300.2, entry 1, RG 147, NARAII; Gareth N. Brainerd to Major McNeil, Nov. 15, 1940, box 33, file 105, entry 1, RG 147, NARAII; Hershey to Harold H. Richardson, Dec. 5, 1940, file 105, entry 1, RG 147, NARAII.

9. Selective Service System, *Special Groups* (Washington, DC: GPO, 1953), Special Monograph no. 10, vol. 2, 102, 113.

10. John M. Hall to E. J. Ennis, Nov. 27, 1942, box 13, entry 183, RG 107; Karl R. Bendetsen to William P. Scobey, Nov. 1, 1942, box 13, entry 183, RG 107.

11. Forrester B. Washington to Truman K. Gibson, Feb. 10, 1943, box 179, entry 188, RG 107; Noel Parrish to Truman K. Gibson, Feb. 17, 1943, box 179, entry 188, RG 107. On Ama's enlistment, see AER, https://aad.archives.gov/aad/record-detail.jsp?dt=893&mtch=22&tf=F&q=   ama&bc=,sl,fd&rpp=10&pg=1&rid= 4463994&rlst=250725,3091809,   4463994,5375634,7048965,37092, 87399,2281341,2654729,3184814 (accessed Oct. 1, 2018).

12. Information Received from Colonel Washburne, typescript notes, Dec. 8, 1943, box 13, entry 183, RG 107; Fred Kitada, interview by Darrell Kunitomi, June 26, 2004, HOHA, part 3, http://www.goforbroke.org/ohmsviewer/viewer. php?cachefile=2004OH0461_03_Kitada.xml (accessed Oct. 15, 2018).

13. B. R. Brazeal to Truman K. Gibson, Feb. 12, 1943, box 179, entry 188, RG 107; Washington to Gibson, Feb. 10, 1943, box 179, entry 188, RG 107.

14. On Japanese immigration, see Erika Lee, *The Making of Asian America: A History* (New York: Simon & Schuster, 2015), 109. On the US Census, see Lori Aratani, "Secret Use of Census Info Helped Send Japanese Americans to Internment Camps in WWII," *WP*, Apr. 6, 2018, https://www.washingtonpost.com/news/ retropolis/wp/2018/04/03/secret-use-of-census-info-helped-send-japanese-americans-to-internment-camps-in-wwii/?utm_term=.c85a9d7adf8d.

15. Manning Marable, *Malcolm X: A Life of Reinvention* (New York: Viking, 2011), 82; Truman K. Gibson to Harrison A. Gerhardt, memo, Dec. 11, 1944, box 249, entry 188, RG 107.

16. For War Department quotation, see Gibson to Gerhardt, Dec. 11, 1944, box 249, entry 188, RG 107. For the Bey case and quotations, see Indictment, Aug. 22, 1944, *United States of America v. James Brown Bey*, criminal case no. 12360, USDCEDP; Statement of Questions Involved and Statement of the Case, n.d., *United States of America v. James Brown Bey*, USDCEDP; Petition to Withdraw Appeal, c. May 21, 1945, *United States of America v. James Brown Bey*, USDCEDP.

17. Gibson to Gerhardt, memo, Dec. 19, 1944, box 249, entry 188, record group 107; John J. McCloy to A. Bernard Hirsch, n.d., box 249, entry 188, record group 107; Return, c. July 17, 1945, *United States of America v. James Brown Bey*, USDCEDP.

18. For "headache" quotation, see Truman K. Gibson to Campbell C. Johnson, July 19, 1945, box 249, entry 188, RG 107. For total induction numbers, see Selective Service System, *Special Groups*, no. 10, 2:102; for tables and their inconsistent race classifications, compare 102–112 and 113–114; for tables that defined white as including "all races other than Negro," see 117–122.

19. On González, see Frank André Guridy, "Pvt. Evelio Grillo and Sgt. Norberto González: Afro-Latino Experiences of War and Segregation," in *Latina/os and World War II: Mobility, Agency, and Ideology*, ed. Maggie Rivas-Rodriguez and B. V. Olguín (Austin: University of Texas Press, 2014), 55. On Cape Verdean quotations, see Paul V. Toolin to Commanding Officer, Fort Devens, memo, May 31, 1942, box 1077, entry 363, RG 407; see also Commanding Officer, Fort Devens to Adjutant General, Mar. 21, 1942, box 1077, entry 363, RG 407. For War Department policy,

see Adjutant Generals Office to Commanding Officer, Fort Devens, memo, June 27, 1942, box 1077, entry 363, RG 407.

20. Moon-Kie Jung, *Reworking Race: The Making of Hawaii's Interracial Labor Movement* (New York: Columbia University Press, 2006), 77.

21. See, for example, Lewis B. Hershey to Directors of Selective Service, California, telegram, Oct. 16, 1940, box 36, file 300, entry 1, RG 147, NARAII; Joseph E. Weckler to George I. Sánchez, June 25, 1943, box 57, entry 1, RG 229; J. Watt Page to All Local Boards, memo, May 27, 1943, box 33, George I. Sánchez Papers, BLAC. For an example of the army, rather than the Selective Service, employing the "Mexican race" category, see John B. Cooley to Chief, Appointment and Induction Branch, Adjutant General's Office, memo, Feb. 28, 1944, box 1065, entry 363, RG 407. On the contested and capricious nature of Mexican American racial categorization, see, for example, Neil Foley, "Becoming Hispanic: Mexican Americans and the Faustian Pact with Whiteness," in *Reflexiones 1997: New Directions in Mexican American Studies*, ed. Neil Foley (Austin: University of Texas Press, 1998), 53–70; Neil Foley, "Partly Colored or Other White: Mexican Americans and Their Problem with the Color Line," in *Beyond Black & White: Race, Ethnicity, and Gender in the U.S. South and Southwest*, ed. Stephanie Cole and Alison M. Parker (College Station: Texas A&M Press, 2004); Linda Gordon, *The Great Arizona Orphan Abduction* (Cambridge, MA: Harvard University Press, 1999); Thomas A. Guglielmo, "Fighting for Caucasian Rights: Mexicans, Mexican Americans, and the Transnational Struggle for Civil Rights in World War II Texas," *JAH* 92 (Mar. 2006): 1212–1237; Cybelle Fox and Thomas A. Guglielmo, "Defining America's Racial Boundaries: Blacks, Mexicans, and European Immigrants, 1890–1945," *AJS* 118 (Sept. 2012): 327–379; Natalia Molina, *How Race Is Made in America: Immigration, Citizenship, and the Historical Power of Racial Scripts* (Berkeley: University of California Press, 2014); Julie M. Weise, *Corazon de Dixie: Mexicanos in the U.S. South since 1910* (Chapel Hill: University of North Carolina Press, 2015).

22. Selective Service System, *Selective Service in Peacetime: First Report of the Director of the Selective Service, 1940–1941* (Washington, DC: GPO, 1942), 261; Selective Service System, *Special Groups*, no. 10, 1:113–114.

23. W. Rex Crawford, "The Latin American in the Wartime United States," *Annals of the American Academy of Political and Social Science* 223 (Sept. 1942): 123; E. F. Bullock to Lewis B. Hershey, Feb. 7, 1941, box 144, file 420, entry 1, RG 147, NARAII.

24. Francisco J. Flores to George I. Sanchez, May 1, 1943, box 22, George I. Sánchez Papers, BLAC; George I. Sánchez to R. E. Smith, Feb. 8, 1943, box 33, George I. Sánchez Papers, BLAC; George I. Sánchez to R. E. Smith, May 14, 1943, box 33, George I. Sánchez Papers, BLAC.

25. If Mexicanness did not affect one's placement in the segregated military, it could prevent "many qualified Spanish speaking youths from obtaining officers' training," since "the entry 'Mexican'"—on Selective Service forms—"is assumed to mean that the individual is a citizen of Mexico and is therefore ineligible to become an officer." This matter will be taken up in Chapter 7. See J. Watt Page to All Local Boards, memo, May 27, 1943, box 33, George I. Sánchez Papers, BLAC.

26. Race-classification questions arose involving Puerto Ricans in the continental United States, but I have found no evidence of controversies there. For questions, see J. A. Ulio to Director of Selective Service, July 30, 1943, box 1511, entry 360, RG 407. On Puerto Rico and the complexities of race classification there, see Mara

Loveman and Jeronimo O. Muniz, "How Puerto Rico Became White: Boundary Dynamics and Intercensus Racial Reclassification," *ASR* 72 (Dec. 2007): 915–939; and Mara Loveman, "The U.S. Census and the Contested Rules of Racial Classification in Early Twentieth-Century Puerto Rico," *Caribbean Studies* 35 (July–Dec. 2007): 3–36.

27. John R. Deane to William H. Hastie, memo, July 20, 1942, box 245, entry 188, RG 107. On separate calls, see E. S. Adams to Lewis B. Hershey, Feb. 5, 1942, box 245, entry 188, RG 107; Campbell C. Johnson to William Hastie, June 21, 1942, box 245, entry 188, RG 107; William Hastie to Secretary of the General Staff, memo, June 23, 1942, box 245, entry 188, RG 107. For the May 1946 count, see Marcus Ray to Jack Miller, May 21, 1947, box 245, entry 188, RG 107.

28. *California Eagle* article, reproduced in Selective Service System, *Special Groups*, no. 10, 1:47; Campbell C. Johnson to General Hershey, memo, Mar. 10, 1941, box 136, file 220, entry 1, RG 147, NARAII; William Hastie to Secretary of the General Staff, memo, Mar. 10, 1941, box 245, entry 188, RG 107; Silvia Álvarez Curbelo, "The Color of War: Puerto Rican Soldiers and Discrimination during World War II," in *Beyond the Latino World War II Hero: The Social and the Political Legacy of a Generation*, ed. Maggie Rivas-Rodríguez and Emilio Zamora (Austin: University of Texas Press, 2009), 118.

29. Adjutant General to Commanding General, Second District, Air Forces General Training Command, memo, May 12, 1943, box 1512, entry 360A, RG 407; H. E. McCracken to Assistant Chief of Staff, et al., memo, May 27, 1944, box 471, entry 418, RG 165; Henry L. Stimson to Bolivar Pagán, April 9, 1943, box 1070, entry 363, RG 407.

30. "Strength of Puerto Rican Personnel by Command and Race," c. July 1945, box 1320, entry 389, RG 407; Deton J. Brooks Jr. to Truman K. Gibson, Aug. 12, 1943, box 37, entry 88, RG 107. On draft officials' reports and official statistics, see Selective Service System, *Special Groups*, no. 10, 1:4–7, 17; Selective Service System, *Special Groups*, no. 10, 2:113–114; Selective Service System, *Evaluation of the Selective Service Program*, Special Monograph, no. 18, vol. 1 (Washington, DC: GPO, 1950), 171; Selective Service System, *Selective Service in Peacetime*, 262; Selective Service System, *Selective Service as the Tide of the War Turns: Third Report of the Director of the Selective Service, 1943–1944* (Washington, DC: GPO, 1945), 206.

31. Bolivar Pagán to Henry L. Stimson, Apr. 5, 1943, box 1070, entry 363, RG 407; Robert C. Blackstone, "Democracy's Army: The American People and Selective Service in World War II" (PhD diss., University of Kansas, 2005), 170–171. See also Miguel Angel Maymon to Secretary of War, Feb. 6, 1944, box 1065, entry 363, RG 407.

32. Charles A. Kiester, "Dilworth Albert Denesse," Federal Bureau of Investigation report, Oct. 31, 1942, box 811, file 170, entry 1, RG 147, NARAII. On other Louisiana cases, see John Edgar Hoover to Oscar Cox, memo, Jan. 11, 1943, box 811, file 170, entry 1, RG 147, NARAII; Raymond H. Fleming to Lewis B. Hershey, Oct. 30, 1943, box 811, file 170, entry 1, RG 147, NARAII.

33. E. E. Talbot to Lewis B. Hershey, Dec. 18, 1942, box 57-1, Campbell C. Johnson Papers, MSRC.

34. E. E. Talbot to Lewis B. Hershey, Dec. 18, 1942, box 57-1, Campbell C. Johnson Papers, MSRC.

35. John Edgar Hoover to Oscar Cox, memo, Jan. 11, 1943, box 811, file 170, entry 1, RG 147, NARAII; and see Indictments and Notices of Nolle Prosequi for

Vincent Dennesse, Dilworth Albert Denesse, Delwood Rodie, Ernest Rodi, and Louis Demolle, cases 20827–20831, Criminal Cases, 1912–1978, entry ELA80, USDCEDL.

36. Raymond H. Fleming to Lewis B. Hershey, Oct. 30, 1943, box 811, file 170, entry 1, RG 147, NARAII.

37. Selective Service System, *Special Groups*, no. 10, 2:113–114.

38. On the state's racial classification of American Indians in the West, see Patrick Wolfe, *Traces of History: Elementary Structures of Race* (New York: Verso, 2016), 196–201; Gross, *What Blood Won't Tell*, 140–168. On the decades-long battles of Indians in the South to be recognized, see Mikaëla M. Adams, *Who Belongs? Race, Resources, and Tribal Citizenship in the Native South* (New York: Oxford University Press, 2016).

39. Pauli Murray, ed., *States' Laws on Race and Color* (1951; Athens: University of Georgia Press, 1997), 479; J. Douglas Smith, "The Campaign for Racial Purity and the Erosion of Paternalism in Virginia, 1922–1930: 'Nominally White, Biologically Mixed, and Legally Negro,'" *Journal of Southern History* 68 (Feb. 2002): 80.

40. On some of Plecker's tactics and views, see, for example, W. A. Plecker to Mary F. Adkins, Jan. 13, 1943, W. A. Plecker to John Collier, Apr. 6, 1943, and W. A. Plecker to John Collier, Oct. 26, 1943, all in General Correspondence Files, File 138, Series 6, Accession no. 61A9331, RG 75. On Plecker's "racial purity" campaigns, see Smith, "The Campaign for Racial Purity"; Pascoe, *What Comes Naturally*, 140–150; and Helen C. Rountree, *Pocahontas's People: The Powhatan Indians of Virginia through Four Centuries* (Norman: University of Oklahoma Press, 1990), 219–242.

41. Pascoe, *What Comes Naturally*, 148.

42. W. A. Plecker to Mills F. Neal, Feb. 25, 1941, box 427, file 220, entry 1, RG 147, NARAII; J. L. Adams to Governor Price, Feb. 18, 1941, box 427, file 220, entry 1, RG 147, NARAII. For previous work on Virginia Indians and the World War II draft, see Paul T. Murray, "Who Is an Indian? Who Is a Negro? Virginia Indians in the World War II Draft," *Virginia Magazine of History and Biography* 95 (Apr. 1987): 215–231; Kenneth William Townsend, *World War II and the American Indian* (Albuquerque: University of New Mexico Press, 2000), 87–102.

43. See, for example, Rountree, *Pocahontas's People*, 219–233.

44. J. L. Adams to Governor Price, Feb. 18, 1941, box 427, file 220, entry 1, RG 147, NARAII; Walter S. Bradley et al. to Colonel Mills F. Neal, Mar. 1, 1941, box 427, file 220, entry 1, RG 147, NARAII.

45. James Hoge Ricks to Robert Reeves Solenberger, Mar. 18, 1942, box 13, FGSP; "Col. Mills Neal, 79, Virginia Draft Chief," *WP*, Sep. 14, 1971, C6.

46. Mills F. Neal to Commanding General, Third Corps Area, Feb. 26, 1941, box 427, file 220, entry 1, RG 147, NARAII; Neal, Memorandum no. 94, Feb. 27, 1941, box 427, file 220, entry 1, RG 147, NARAII; Neal to Commanding General, Memo, Mar. 28, 1941, box 427, file 220, entry 1, RG 147, NARAII; Neal to General Hershey, Apr. 11, 1941, box 427, file 220, entry 1, RG 147, NARAII.

47. Neal to Commanding General, memo, Mar. 28, 1941, box 427, file 220, entry 1, RG 147, NARAII; Neal to General Hershey, Apr. 11, 1941, box 427, file 220, entry 1, RG 147, NARAII.

48. Adjutant General to Commanding General, memo, Apr. 3, 1941, box 427, file 220, entry 1, RG 147, NARAII; Lewis B. Hershey to Colonel Neal, Apr. 29, 1941, box 427, file 220, entry 1, RG 147, NARAII.

49. Mills F. Neal to Major Baker, Feb. 21, 1942, box 427, file 220, entry 1, RG 147, NARAII; Mills F. Neal to Chief Bradby, Aug. 5, 1942, box 427, file 220, entry 1, RG 147, NARAII.

50. Mills F. Neal to All Local Boards, memorandum no. 336, Jan. 7, 1942, box 427, file 220, entry 1, RG 147, NARAII.

51. Abe Fortas to General Hershey, Sep. 25, 1942, box 427, file 220, entry 1, RG 147, NARAII; Mills F. Neal to Chief Bradby, Aug. 5, 1942, box 427, file 220, entry 1, RG 147, NARAII; James R. Coates to Editor, *Norfolk Virginian Pilot*, May 17, 1946, box 13, FGSP.

52. Rountree, *Pocahontas's People*, 233; Christopher Arris Oakley, *Keeping the Circle: American Indian Identity in Eastern North Carolina, 1885–2004* (Lincoln: University of Nebraska Press, 2005), 57; Jeremiah James Nowell Jr., "Red, White and Black: Race Formation and the Politics of American Indian Recognition in North Carolina" (PhD diss., University of North Carolina, Chapel Hill, 2000), 82.

53. Theodore A. Green, interviewed by Joseph Sledge, June 6, 2002 (AFC/2001/001/6107), VHP.

54. Brewton Berry, *Almost White* (London: Collier Books, 1963), 99–100; C. A. Weslager, *Delaware's Forgotten Folk: The Story of the Moors and Nanticokes* (Philadelphia: University of Pennsylvania Press, 1943), 103–107.

55. Chief O. Oliver Adkins to President Roosevelt, Dec. 10, 1942, box 816, file 220, entry 1, RG 147, NARAII. For activism on the part of and on behalf of Western Chickahominy, see Harold L. Ickes to General Hershey, Feb. 9, 1942, box 427, file 220, entry 1, RG 147, NARAII; Harold L. Ickes to General Hershey, Mar. 4, 1942, box 427, file 220, entry 1, RG 147, NARAII; Chief O. Oliver Adkins et al. to War Department, Aug. 28, 1942, box 427, file 220, entry 1, RG 147, NARAII; O. Oliver Adkins et al. to Paul V. McNutt, Feb. 11, 1943, box 427, file 220, entry 1, RG 147, NARAII; Frank G. Speck to Paul V. McNutt, Feb. 13, 1943, box 816, file 220, entry 1, RG 147, NARAII; Cyrus W. Beale to Commanding General, July 14, 1943, box 816, file 220, entry 1, RG 147, NARAII.

56. Cyrus W. Beale to Commanding General, July 14, 1943, box 816, file 220, entry 1, RG 147, NARAII; Frank S. Sloan to Commanding General, memo, June 24, 1943, box 816, file 220, entry 1, RG 147, NARAII; Rountree, *Pocahontas's People*, 233.

57. Harry Duplessis, interviewed by Mary Penick Motley, in *The Invisible Soldier: The Experience of the Black Soldier, World War II*, ed. Mary Penick Motley (Detroit: Wayne State University Press, 1975), 331.

58. Lloyd G. Carr to Colgate W. Darden, Oct. 27, 1942, box 66, Colgate W. Darden Papers, TLV; Royal B. Hassrick to Indian Rights Association, Feb. 6, 1943, box 816, file 220, entry 1, RG 147, NARAII; Otho S. Nelson to Dr. Speck, Dec. 2, 1942, box 13, FGSP; Otho S. Nelson to Dr. Speck, Nov. 9, 1942, box 13, FGSP. Otho Nelson's first name is spelled "Otha" in a recent newspaper article, which quotes his daughter, but documents from the war years, including letters from him, spell his name "Otho." For the article, see Gregory S. Schneider, "The Indians Were Right, the English Were Wrong: A Virginia Tribe Reclaims Its Past," *WP*, Nov. 21, 2018, https://www.washingtonpost.com/local/virginia-politics/the-indians-were-right-the-english-were-wrong-a-virginia-tribe-reclaims-its-past/2018/11/21/2380f92c-e8f4-11e8-bbdb-72fdbf9d4fed_story.html.

59. See Indictment, Oct. 5, 1942, *United States of America v. Oliver Wendell Fortune*, criminal case 4036, USDCEDV; Judgment and Commitment, Jan. 12, 1943,

United States of America v. Oliver Wendell Fortune, criminal case 4036, USDCEDV; "3 'Indians' Are Sentenced in Draft Case," *Richmond Times-Dispatch*, Jan. 13, 1943, 5; "Three Indians Found Guilty of Draft Evasion," *ADW*, Jan. 19, 1943, 1; "'Indian' Draft Objector Sentenced," *BAA*, Jan. 23, 1943, 6. On evidence cited, see Mills F. Neal to Lloyd G. Carr, Nov. 2, 1942, box 13, FGSP.

60. "'Indian' Draft Objector Sentenced," *BAA*, Jan. 23, 1943; Otho S. Nelson to Frank G. Speck, Oct. 31, 1943, box 13, FGSP.

61. "'Indian' Is Held for Violation of Draft Law," *Richmond Times-Dispatch*, Feb. 14, 1943, 12; "'Indian' Held on Draft Count," *BAA*, June 10, 1944, 6; "Two 'Indians' Are Convicted," *BAA*, Aug. 5, 1944, 10.

62. For general information about the Monacans, see Bill McKelway, "Return of the Monacans: After Years of Scorn, Indians of Amherst Are Reclaiming Their Place, Their Pride," *Richmond Times-Dispatch*, Apr. 23, 1995, G1; Melanie Dorothea Haimes-Bartolf, "Policies and Attitudes: Public Education and the Monacan Indian Community in Amherst County, Virginia, from 1908 to 1965" (PhD diss., Virginia Commonwealth University, 2004); Samuel R. Cook, *Monacans and Miners: Native American and Coal Mining Communities in Appalachia* (Lincoln: University of Nebraska Press, 2000).

63. Amherst County Local Board to Homer Willis, Jan. 20, 1942, box 816, file 220, entry 1, RG 147, NARAII; F. C. Drummond to Bernard T. Franck, Feb. 16, 1943, box 816, file 220, entry 1, RG 147, NARAII.

64. Joe Jennings to Willard W. Beatty, Apr. 22, 1947, General Correspondence Files, File 138, Series 6, Accession no. 61A9331, RG 75; Bertha Wailes to Colonel Neal, Feb. 15, 1941, box 427, file 220, entry 1, RG 147, NARAII; Isabel Wagner to Whom It May Concern, Jan. 30, 1942, box 816, file 220, entry 1, RG 147, NARAII.

65. Wm. Kinckle Allen to Mills F. Neal, Jan. 22, 1942, box 816, file 220, entry 1, RG 147, NARAII. See also Allen to Homer Willis, Jan. 20, 1942, box 816, file 220, entry 1, RG 147, NARAII; Allen to Colonel Neal, Jan. 30, 1942, box 816, file 220, entry 1, RG 147, NARAII; Allen to Hershey, Feb. 16, 1942, box 816, file 220, entry 1, RG 147, NARAII; Allen to Director of Selective Service, July 13, 1942, box 427, file 220, entry 1, RG 147, NARAII.

66. Mills F. Neal to Director of Selective Service, Apr. 3, 1943, box 816, file 220, entry 1, RG 147, NARAII.

67. See Affidavit of Josephine P. Clement, June 16, 1943, *Branham v. Burton*, case no. 101, box 18, Civil Case Files (1938–1979), Accession no. 21-5W-6-4.3, USDCWDV; Judge A. D. Barksdale, Findings of Fact and Conclusions of Law, June 28, 1943, *Branham v. Burton*, case no. 101, box 18, Civil Case Files (1938–1979), Accession no. 21-5W-6-4.3, USDCWDV.

68. William Branham Jr. and Wm. Kinckle Allen, Amended Complaint, June 11, 1943, *Branham v. Burton*, case no. 101, box 18, Civil Case Files (1938–1979), Accession no. 21-5W-6-4.3, USDCWDV.

69. Judge A. D. Barksdale, Findings of Fact and Conclusions of Law, June 28, 1943, *Branham v. Burton*, case no. 101, box 18, Civil Case Files (1938–1979), Accession no. 21-5W-6-4.3, USDCWDV; *Branham v. Langley et al.* 139 F2d 115 (1943).

70. W. A. Plecker statement, June 1, 1943, attached to William Branham, Certificate of Birth, Exhibit D, *Branham v. Burton*, case no. 101, box 18, Civil Case Files (1938–1979), Accession no. 21-5W-6-4.3, USDCWDV; Judge A. D. Barksdale, Findings of Fact and Conclusions of Law, June 28, 1943, attached to William Branham, Certificate of Birth, Exhibit D, *Branham v. Burton*, case no. 101, box 18, Civil Case

Files (1938–1979), Accession no. 21-5W-6-4.3, USDCWDV; Edward S. Shattuck to Francis M. Shea, June 14, 1943, box 816, file 220, entry 1, RG 147, NARAII.

71. *Congressional Record*, 96th Cong., 2d sess., 1950, 96, pt. 13: A843; Patricia Barker Lerch, *Waccamaw Legacy: Contemporary Indians Fight for Survival* (Tuscaloosa: University of Alabama Press, 2004), esp. 72, 63.

72. See Frank P. Vixo, FBI Reports on Jolly Jacobs, Hezzie Patrick, J. D. Jacobs, Lonnie Wright Jacobs, and William Henry Young; all dated June 28, 1943, box 6288, Classified Subject File Correspondence, Central Files, RG 60; J. O. Carr to Charles R. Jonas, July 14, 1943, box 6288, Classified Subject File Correspondence, Central Files, RG 60; Charles R. Jonas to Director of Selective Service, Aug. 25, 1943, box 811, file 170, entry 1, RG 147, NARAII. See also Draft Registration Cards for Jolly Jacobs, William Henry Young, Hezzie Patrick, Lofton Jacobs, Lonnie Wright Jacobs, and J. D. Jacobs, Local Board No. 1, Columbus County, North Carolina, RG 147, NASE.

73. Charles R. Jonas to Director of Selective Service, August 25, 1943, box 811, file 170, entry 1, RG 147, NARAII. For the "self-styled Indians" quotation, see Information for Historical Record, Local Board No. 1 of Columbus County, n.d., box 36, Spencer B. King Jr. Files, 1940–1950, Selective Service System—State Office, Federal Records, NCSA.

74. Indictment, *United States of America v. Jolly Jacobs et al.*, Case file 8198, General Case Files, USDCEDNC.

75. "Indians Cleared of Draft Charge," *Raleigh (NC) News and Observer*, Nov. 3, 1943, 12; Chauncey H. Leggett to State Director of Selective Service, Nov. 13, 1943, box 811, file 170, entry 1, RG 147, NARAII.

76. Leggett to State Director of Selective Service, Nov. 13, 1943, box 811, file 170, entry 1, RG 147, NARAII.

77. Lewis B. Hershey to Secretary of War, July 19, 1944, box 1272, file 170, entry 1, RG 147, NARAII.

78. I have searched the AER, https://aad.archives.gov/aad/series-description. jsp?s=3360&bc=,sl,fd, and the military records at Ancestry.com. Curiously, a Lofton Jacobs—from a county bordering Columbus and whose birth year on enlistment records is two years later than that listed on the defendant Jacobs's registration card—entered the army as a "Negro" after the war on December 15, 1945. See AER, https://aad.archives.gov/aad/record-detail.jsp?dt=893&mtch=1 &cat=all&tf=F&sc=24994,24995,24996,24998,24997,24993,24981,24983&q=l ofton+jacobs&bc=,sl,fd&rpp=10&pg=1&rid=5072356 (accessed Apr. 6, 2020).

79. Selective Service System, *Special Groups*, no. 10, 1:75; Campbell C. Johnson to Major Hedrick, Aug. 3, 1943, box 816, file 220, entry 1, RG 147, NARAII.

80. Lewis B. Hershey to Adjutant General, memo, Aug. 28, 1943, box 816, file 220, entry 1, RG 147, NARAII. See also Hershey to General Fleming, Sept. 8, 1943, and Hershey to Colonel Neal, n.d., both in box 57-1, Campbell C. Johnson Papers, MSRC.

81. Selective Service System, *Special Groups*, no. 10, 1:76; William H. Krieg to Manpower Division, memo, Apr. 18, 1944, box 1272, file 170, entry 1, RG 147, NARAII.

82. H. Aubrey Elliott to William S. Hepner, memo, Aug. 30, 1943, box 1, Central File, 1935–1946, RG 200; "Request to Chapters to Make Investigations to Determine Race of Servicemen," Oct. 15, 1943, box 1, Central File, 1935–1946, RG 200; Robert E. Bondy to Area Administrators, Dec. 21, 1943, box 1, Central File, 1935–1946, RG 200.

83. C. W. Ardery to Commanding General, Fourth Service Command, memo, Jan. 18, 1944, box 57-1, Campbell C. Johnson Papers, MSRC.

84. Charles R. Jonas to Director of Selective Service, Feb. 29, 1944, box 1272, file 170, entry 1, RG 147, NARAII; William O. Sawyers to Colonel Dargusch, memo, July 6, 1944, box 1272, file 170, entry 1, RG 147, NARAII.

85. See Richard K. Mellon to Colonel Shattuck, Mar. 10, 1944, box 1272, file 170, entry 1, RG 147, NARAII.

86. Lewis B. Hershey to Secretary of War, July 19, 1944, box 1272, file 170, entry 1, RG 147, NARAII.

87. Henry L. Stimson to Lewis B. Hershey, July 31, 1944, box 1272, file 170, entry 1, RG 147, NARAII; Hershey to Secretary of War, Aug. 5, 1944, box 1272, file 170, entry 1, RG 147, NARAII.

88. John J. McCloy to General Hershey, Aug. 15, 1944, box 1272, file 170, entry 1, RG 147, NARAII.

89. Selective Service System, *Special Groups*, no. 10, 2:208–209.

90. John J. McCloy to A. Bernard Hirsch, n.d., box 245, entry 188, RG 107. See also *United States v. James Brown Bey*, Criminal Case File No. 12360, USDCEDP.

91. James C. Scott, *Seeing Like a State: How Certain Schemes to Improve the Human Condition Have Failed* (New Haven, CT: Yale University Press, 1998), 47.

92. Interestingly, many of the Virginia Indians discussed in this chapter finally received federal recognition as Indian tribes in 2018. The state giveth and the state taketh away, but not always in that order. See Jenna Portnoy, "Trump Signs Bill Recognizing Virginia Indian Tribes," *WP*, Jan. 30, 2018, https://www.washingtonpost.com/local/virginia-politics/trump-signs-bill-recognizing-virginia-indian-tribes/2018/01/30/8a46b038-05d4-11e8-94e8-e8b8600ade23_story.html.

93. Siobhan B. Somerville, *Queering the Color Line: Race and the Invention of Homosexuality in American Culture* (Durham, NC: Duke University Press, 2000), 131. See also Hobbs, *A Chosen Exile*, 18–19.

94. On settler colonialism in the United States, see, for example, Roxanne Dunbar-Ortiz, *An Indigenous People's History of the United States* (Boston: Beacon Press, 2014); Jodi Byrd, *The Transit of Empire: Indigenous Critiques of Colonialism* (Minneapolis: University of Minnesota Press, 2011); Wolfe, *Traces of History*.

95. The Immigration and Naturalization Service required a South Asian man who wished to naturalize during the war to take a blood test to determine his "racial" eligibility to do so. See Betty Moorsteen, "The Plight of Joaquim Rodrigues," *PM*, Mar. 4, 1945, 13.

96. See Gross, *What Blood Won't Tell*, 9–10. On race science, see Lee D. Baker, *From Savage to Negro: Anthropology and the Construction of Race, 1896–1954* (Berkeley: University of California Press, 1998); Elazar Barkan, *Retreat of Scientific Racism: Changing Concepts of Race in Britain and the United States between the World Wars* (Cambridge: Cambridge University Press, 1992); Tracy Teslow, *Constructing Race: The Science of Bodies and Cultures in American Anthropology* (Cambridge: Cambridge University Press, 2014).

97. For a similar point about the locale-specific nature of white supremacy in the Jim Crow South of this period, see J. Mills Thornton III, "Segregation and the City: White Supremacy in Alabama in the Mid-Twentieth Century," in *Fog of War: The Second World War and the Civil Rights Movement*, ed. Kevin M. Kruse and Stephen Tuck (New York: Oxford University Press, 2012), 51–69.

98. Richard F. Saville to Director of Selective Service, Aug. 25, 1941, box 136, entry 1, RG 147, NARAII; Carlton S. Dargusch to State Director of Selective Service, Sept. 10, 1941, box 136, entry 1, RG 147, NARAII.

99. Speaking of the state's awesome power to classify, sociologist Pierre Bourdieu has written, "By stating with authority what a being . . . is in truth . . . that is what he or she is authorized to be, what he has a right (and duty) to be, the social being that he may claim, the State wields a genuinely *creative*, quasi-divine, power." See Pierre Bourdieu, "Rethinking the State: Genesis and Structure of the Bureaucratic Field," *Sociological Theory* 12 (Mar. 1994): 12 (emphasis in original).

100. See Nico Slate, *Colored Cosmopolitanism: The Shared Struggle for Freedom in the United States and India* (Cambridge, MA: Harvard University Press, 2012).

CHAPTER 6

1. Nancy Macdonald and Dwight Macdonald, *The War's Greatest Scandal! The Story of Jim Crow in Uniform*," pamphlet, n.d. but c. May 1943, box 1067, entry 363, RG 407.

2. Special Services Division, Bureau of Intelligence, Office of War Information, "The Impact of Camp Shelby upon Hattiesburg, Mississippi," Nov. 23, 1942, box 7, official file 4245g, FDRP.

3. Transcript of Lynn Committee and Schomburg Collection Meeting on "Military Jimcrowism," Oct. 25, 1945, box 5, LDR; William H. Hastie, "Survey and Recommendations Concerning the Integration of the Negro Soldier into the Army," c. Sept. 22, 1941, box 150, RPPP. On generals' views, see transcript of telephone call between Jonathan Daniels and Colonel Davenport, Sept. 22, 1944, box 14, JDP. For general information about the early steps of joining the military, see US Office of Civilian Defense, *Introduction to the Armed Forces* (Washington, DC: GPO, 1944); Lee Kennett, *G.I.: The American Soldier in World War II* (New York: Charles Scribner's, 1987), 24–35.

4. Welton I. Taylor with Karyn J. Taylor, *Two Steps from Glory: A World War II Liaison Pilot Confronts Jim Crow and the Enemy in the South Pacific* (Chicago: Winning Strategy Press, 2012), 2. For other examples, see J. Todd Moye, *Freedom Flyers: The Tuskegee Airmen of World War II* (New York: Oxford University Press, 2010), 2–3, 41; Melton A. McLaurin, *The Marines of Montford Point: America's First Black Marines* (Chapel Hill: University of North Carolina Press, 2007), 38, 39, 42.

5. Joyce Thomas, "The 'Double V' Was for Victory: Black Soldiers, the Black Protest, and World War II" (PhD diss., Ohio State University, 1993), 259–260; Ulysses Lee, *The Employment of Negro Troops* (Washington, DC: GPO, 1963), 319–320.

6. Judge Hastie to Under Secretary of War, memo, Sept. 22, 1942, box 189, entry 13, RG 165.

7. Dempsey Travis, interview by Studs Terkel, in *"The Good War": An Oral History of World War II*, ed. Studs Terkel (New York: New Press, 1984), 152.

8. See, for example, Lee, *Employment of Negro Troops*, 98; McLaurin, *Marines of Montford Point*, 48, 98–99; Historical Section, Bureau of Naval Personnel, "The Negro in the Navy," typescript, 1947, 56, NDL.

9. Dempsey Travis, interview by Studs Terkel, in Terkel, *"The Good War,"* 152. See, for example, Lee, *Employment of Negro Troops*, 300–315; Morris J. MacGregor Jr., *Integration of the Armed Forces, 1940–1965* (Washington, DC: GPO, 1981), 35–45, 82–83; Sherie Mershon and Steven L. Schlossman, *Foxholes and Color Lines: Desegregating the U.S. Armed Forces* (Baltimore: Johns Hopkins University Press, 1998), 68–99; Ruth Danenhower Wilson, *Jim Crow Joins Up: A Study of the Negro in the Armed Forces of the United States* (New York: William J. Clark, 1944), 7; Charles Dollard and Donald Young, "In the Armed Forces," *Survey Graphic*, Jan. 1947, 67; William Y. Bell Jr., "The Threat to Negro Soldier Morale," typescript report, Oct. 1943, box 17, APRP; Isaac McNatt, "I Was a Seabee," *Politics*, June 1944, 137–138.

10. See Mershon and Schlossman, *Foxholes and Color Lines*, 123; Philip E. Brown to Adjutant General, memo, Oct. 16, 1943, box 1510, entry 360A, RG 407.

11. See, for example, Charity Adams Earley, *One Woman's Army: A Black Officer Remembers the* WAC (College Station: Texas A&M University Press, 1989), 164; Georgia Gaines to Franklin D. Roosevelt, Nov. 9, 1944, box 1268, entry 451, RG 389; Mary F. Kearney, interview by Lawrence D. Reddick, Apr. 11, 1946, box 1, LDR; Bessie Robinson, interview by Lawrence D. Reddick, n.d., box 1, LDR.

12. On Grenier, see Virgil L. Peterson to Deputy Chief of Staff, memo, May 19, 1943, box 1512, entry 360A, RG 407. On Westover Field, see Ben Yablonky, "Civilians Toss Charges of Army Jim Crow at Colonel," *PM*, Feb. 11, 1944, 6.

13. Judge Hastie to Under Secretary of War, memo, Sept. 22, 1942, box 189, entry 13, RG 165. On the Indiana camp, see George L. Banniester to Truman K. Gibson, Nov. 21, 1942, box 185, entry 188, RG 107.

14. MacGregor, *Integration of the Armed Forces*, 48–51; William H. Hastie, *On Clipped Wings: The Story of Jim Crow in the Army Air Corps*, NAACP pamphlet, Oct. 1943.

15. William Purnell Shelton, interview by Mary Penick Motley, n.d., in *The Invisible Soldier: The Experience of the Black Soldier, World War II*, ed. Mary Penick Motley (Detroit: Wayne State University Press, 1975), 56.

16. See, for example, Grant Reynolds, "What the Negro Soldier Thinks about This War," *Crisis*, Sept. 1944, 289; Special Services Division, Bureau of Intelligence, Office of War Information, "The Impact of Camp Shelby upon Hattiesburg, Mississippi," Nov. 23, 1942, box 7, official file 4245g, FDRP; E. T. Hall Jr., "Race Prejudice and Negro-White Relations in the Army," *AJS* 52 (Mar. 1947): 401; J. S. Leonard, "Digest of War Department Policy Pertaining to Negro Military Personnel," Jan. 1, 1944, 3, box 15, entry 88, RG 107.

17. Dempsey Travis, interview by Studs Terkel, in Terkel, *"The Good War,"* 151; Bert B. Babero to Truman K. Gibson, Feb. 13, 1944, in *Taps for a Jim Crow Army: Letters from Black Soldiers in World War II*, ed. Phillip McGuire (Lexington: University Press of Kentucky, 1983), 51.

18. For a few examples of white American civilians privileging white enemy prisoners of war over African Americans, see Rupert Trimmingham, "Democracy?," letter to editor, *Yank*, Apr. 28, 1944, 14; Lloyd L. Brown, "Brown v. Salina, Kansas," *NYT*, Feb. 26, 1973, 31.

19. "Three Wacs Slugged by White Police in Kentucky," *CD*, July 28, 1945, 1; "Demand Action against Dixie Cops Who Slugged Wacs," *CD*, Aug. 4, 1945, 1.

20. For examples of discriminatory signs, see Robert F. Jefferson, *Fighting for Hope: African American Troops of the 93rd Infantry Division in World War II and Postwar America* (Baltimore: Johns Hopkins University Press, 2008), 107; Charles E. Collier to NAACP New York City, May 26, 1943, box 221, entry 188, RG 107. For discriminatory staff, see "A Negro Soldier" to Adam Clayton Powell in McGuire, *Taps for a Jim Crow Army*, 55; Conrad Lynn to Dwight Macdonald, July 19, 1944, box 30, series 1, DMP.

21. Joseph Schiffman, "The Education of Negro Soldiers in World War II," *JNE* 18 (Winter 1949): 27; Ruth Gruber to Secretary of Interior, confidential memo, June 11, 1943, box 1512, entry 360A, RG 407. On white officers resisting segregation, see, for example, Bureau of Intelligence, Informal Report from Intensive Surveys Interviewer, Sept. 15, 1942, box 183, entry 188, RG 107.

22. War Department memo, confidential, Sept. 28, 1944, box 261, entry 189, RG 107; A. C. Knight to John Blandford, Mar. 22, 1943, box 212, entry 188, RG 107; "Army Takes Back 'Negro Warning,'" *PM*, Jan. 6, 1942, 4.

23. See, for example, Lee, *Employment of Negro Troops*, 213–219; Samuel A. Stouffer et al., *The American Soldier: Adjustment during Army Life* (Princeton, NJ: Princeton University Press, 1949), 1:580–586; Addison Walker, memorandum, Dec. 6. 1941, box 1, entry 131d, RG 80.

24. On the marines, see Bernard C. Nalty, *The Right to Fight: African-American Marines in World War II* (Washington, DC: GPO, 1995), 27. For varying estimates of the total number of black navy officers, see MacGregor, *Integration of the Armed Forces*, 98; Alvan C. Gillem et al., "Policy for the Utilization of Negro Manpower in the Post-War Army," Nov. 1945, 18–19, box 442, entry 43, RG 165; Historical Section, Bureau of Naval Personnel, "Negro in the Navy," 83. For the total number of white naval officers, see US Bureau of the Census, *Historical Statistics of the United States, Colonial Times to 1970*, part 2 (Washington, DC: GPO, 1975), 1141.

25. Gillem et al., "Policy for the Utilization of Negro Manpower in the Post-War Army," 17; Lee, *Employment of Negro Troops*, 415.

26. Stouffer et al., *The American Soldier*, 1:583.

27. Stouffer et al., *The American Soldier*, 1:259–269.

28. William H. Hastie, "Negro Officers in Two World Wars," *JNE* 12 (Summer 1943): 323; Truman K. Gibson to Roy Wilkins, Mar. 3, 1943, box II:A646, NAACPR. For more on the War Department's discrimination against black officers, see Jefferson, *Fighting for Hope*, 136–137; and J. S. Leonard, "Digest of War Department Policy Pertaining to Negro Military Personnel," Jan. 1, 1944, 3, box 15, entry 88, RG 107.

29. At the end of May 1945, for example, the army had fifteen hundred generals, only one of whom was African American—Benjamin O. Davis Sr. For the figure of fifteen hundred, see Stouffer et al., *The American Soldier*, 1:233.

30. "A Private" to *Pittsburgh Courier*, n.d., box 185, entry 188, RG 107.

31. James O. Austin to Elmer Davis, Aug. 1, 1943, box 8, entry 1, RG 208. On the invaluable skills the military taught its black troops, see Robert C. Weaver, "The Negro Veteran," *Annals of the American Academy of Political and Social Science* 238 (Mar. 1945): 128–129; Ira Katznelson, *When Affirmative Action Was White: An Untold History of Racial Inequality in Twentieth-Century America* (New York: Norton, 2005), 106–107.

32. "The 'Work-but-Not-Fight' Policy," *CD*, Feb. 10, 1945, 10. For more systematic evidence of anti-black discrimination in jobs and ratings, see Gillem et al., "Policy for the Utilization of Negro Manpower in the Post-War Army," 16; Stouffer et al., *The American Soldier*, 1:495; Lee, *Employment of Negro Troops*, 134; MacGregor, *Integration of the Armed Forces*, 98.

33. Arthur Miller, *Situation Normal* (New York: Reynal & Hitchcock, 1944), 22; Lawrence D. Reddick, "The Color of War," typescript manuscript, 25, box 4, LDR; "Ambassador Knox's Retirement Stirs Haitians," *BAA*, Apr. 7, 1973, 22; Ewart Guanier, interview by Lawrence D. Reddick, May 20, 1946, box 1, LDR.

34. Penn Kimball, "Why Army Had Race Rioting," *PM*, Jan. 23, 1942, 4; George V. Strong to Assistant Chief of Staff, G-3, memo, June 17, 1942, box 472, entry 418, RG 165.

35. Tom O'Connor, "Don't Shake a Nigger's Hand," *PM*, Aug. 6, 1941, 12; "A Negro Soldier" to Adam Clayton Powell, June 2, 1944, in McGuire, *Taps for a Jim Crow Army*, 53; Guanier, interview by Lawrence D. Reddick, May 20, 1946, box 1, LDR; Counter-Intelligence Section, B-7, District Intelligence Office, Fourteenth Naval District, "The Negro Problem in the Fourteenth Naval District," confidential

report, Aug. 15, 1943, 22, box 12, ROC; Truman K. Gibson to Chief, Army Exchange Service, Apr. 30, 1943, box 235, entry 188, RG 107.

36. "Soldier Beaten and Jailed in Miss.," *New York Age*, Dec. 11, 1943, 1; McNatt, "I Was a Seabee," 140.

37. Agnes E. Meyer, *Journey through Chaos* (New York: Harcourt, Brace, 1943), 26; Earl Brown, "American Negroes and the War," *Harper's*, Apr. 1942, 547.

38. TIR, no. 1818, Mar. 30, 1945, box 265, entry 189, RG 107; Truman K. Gibson Jr. to B. O. Davis, memo, June 30, 1943, box 243, entry 188, RG 107. See also William Eben Moss to Inspector General, May 21, 1943, box 529, entry 292A, RG 18; Shelton, interview by Mary Penick Motley, in Motley, *The Invisible Soldier*, 57; Army Service Forces, *Leadership and the Negro Soldier*, M5 manual (Washington, DC: GPO, 1944), 73; Thomas, "The 'Double V' Was for Victory," 228–257; O'Connor, "Don't Shake a Nigger's Hand"; Earley, *One Woman's Army*, 164; Jefferson, *Fighting for Hope*, 84; "A Soldier" to *Afro-American*, May 10, 1943, in McGuire, *Taps for a Jim Crow Army*, 170; Tom O'Connor, "Color Line Stands Out Everywhere at Army Shooting Scene," *PM*, Aug. 10, 1941, 12.

39. Willie Lawton, interview by Mary Penick Motley, in Motley, *Invisible Soldier*, 100; Nelson Peery, *Black Fire: The Making of an American Revolutionary* (New York: New Press, 1994), 140. See also "And the —— Engineers," *Time*, July 21, 1941, 44.

40. Lester Duane Simons, interview by Mary Penick Motley, in Motley, *Invisible Soldier*, 49.

41. See, for example, Army Service Forces, Camp Patrick Henry, Security and Intelligence Divisions, Racial Incident, Oct. 30, 1944, box 381B, entry 47, RG 319; Walter White to John J. McCloy, July 14, 1943, box II:A643, NAACPR; War Department, M.I.D., Army Service Forces, Headquarters Eighth Service Command, report about "Friction between White and Colored Soldiers at Camp Beauregard, Louisiana," Sept. 9, 1944, box 9, official file 4245g, FDRP. On the importance of violence to race-making and to boundary-making, see Mattias Smångs, "Doing Violence, Making Race: Southern Lynching and White Racial Group Formation," *AJS* 121 (Mar. 2016): 1329–1374.

42. McNatt, "I Was a Seabee," 137; "Asleep on Negro Morale," *PC*, Jan. 31, 1942, 6.

43. "Asleep on Negro Morale," *PC*, Jan. 31, 1942, 6. On the total number of black JAG officers in the army, see Gillem et al., "Policy for the Utilization of Negro Manpower in the Post-War Army," 17; Truman K. Gibson Jr. to John J. McCloy, memo, Nov. 24, 1944, box 213, entry 188, RG 107. On the figure of twenty-eight hundred, see "Army JAG Corps," "History," "Conflicts," https://www.goarmy.com/jag/about/history.html (accessed Dec. 11, 2019).

44. Assistant Secretary [Roy Wilkins] to Pfc. Dennard, July 31, 1944, box II:A646, NAACPR; Truman K. Gibson Jr. to Assistant Secretary of War, Dec. 20, 1943, box 15, entry 88, RG 107; Harold Preece, "Stiff Jail Terms for 65 Soldiers," *CD*, Dec. 11, 1943, 1. Even commentators generally partial to the military pointed out these injustices. See, for example, Meyer, *Journey through Chaos*, 345.

45. This partial list of names comes from a variety of sources: Walter White, "The Negro Waits to See," *Nation*, Oct. 21, 1944, 466–467; Florence Murray, "The Negro and Civil Liberties during World War II," *Social Forces* 24 (Oct. 1945): 212; "Police Kill Negro Held for Attack," *Anniston (AL) Star*, Mar. 3, 1944, 1; "Soldier Mob Victim," *BAA*, Mar. 18, 1944, 1; Alexa Mills, "A Lynching Kept Out of Sight," *WP*, Sept. 2, 2016, https://www.washingtonpost.com/sf/national/2016/09/02/the-story-of-the-only-known-lynching-on-a-u-s-military-base/?utm_term=.b44a142ae5aa; Lynn Committee to Abolish Segregation in the Armed Forces,

Help Fight Jim Crow in Uniform!, pamphlet, n.d. but c. late 1944, box 118, series II, DMP; "Racial Killings of Black Soldiers, 1941–1942: The War at Home," Civil Rights and Restorative Justice Project, Northwestern University School of Law, https://crrj.northeastern.edu/racial-killings-of-black-soldiers-1941-1942-the-war-at-home/ (accessed Dec. 11, 2019). Only today, three-quarters of a century after the fact, are organizations like the Civil Rights and Restorative Justice Project attempting to reexamine these cold cases.

46. "The Negro: His Future in America," *New Republic*, Oct. 18, 1943, in *Primer for White Folks*, ed. Bucklin Moon (Garden City, NY: Doubleday, 1946), 351.

47. Earley, *One Woman's Army*, 107–108.

48. Quoted in Kenneth D. Rose, *Myth and the Greatest Generation: A Social History of Americans during World War II* (New York: Routledge, 2008), 135.

49. Charles Dollard and Donald Young, "In the Armed Forces," *Survey Graphic*, Jan 1947, 68. For the West Virginia court-martial, see Conrad Lynn to Nancy Macdonald, Nov. 27, 1943, box 30, series 1, DMP.

50. Philip E. Brown to Adjutant General, memo, Oct. 16, 1943, box 1510, entry 360A, RG 407.

51. Brown to Adjutant General, memo, Oct. 16, 1943, box 1510, entry 360A, RG 407. On the hospital's namesake, see "Northington General Hospital Feature in U.S. Army Review," *Tuscaloosa Area Virtual Museum*, https://tavm.omeka.net/items/show/875 (accessed January 17, 2019).

52. Lathe B. Row to Inspector General, memo, Oct. 13, 1943, box 1510, entry 360A, RG 407; William H. Hastie, "Survey and Recommendations Concerning the Integration of the Negro Soldier into the Army," c. Sept. 22, 1941, box 150, RPPP; Gibson to Davis, June 30, 1943, box 243, entry 188, RG 107. For "miserable pricks" line, see Kennett, *G.I.*, 85.

53. War Department, *Command of Negro Troops*, pamphlet, no. 20–26, Feb. 29, 1944, 13, box 241, entry 26D, RG 159; Navy Department, Bureau of Naval Personnel, "Guide to the Command of Negro Personnel," n.d., 10, box 418, entry 33, RG 228.

54. Henry L. Stimson to President Roosevelt, memo, Sept. 20, 1944, box 1064, entry 363, RG 407.

55. Truman K. Gibson Jr. to Assistant Secretary of War, memo, Jan. 11, 1943 [*sic*; 1944], box 215, entry 188, RG 107. On California, Washington, and New Jersey, see Truman K. Gibson Jr. to Howard Peterson, memo, Aug. 28, 1943, box 235, entry 188, RG 107; Truman K. Gibson Jr. to Benjamin O. Davis, memo, June 30, 1943, box 243, entry 188, RG 107; "Army's 'Non-Segregation Order,'" *PC*, Sept. 9, 1944, 1. On military installations existing beyond the reach of state law, see Army Service Forces, *Leadership and the Negro Soldier*, 96.

56. Selective Training and Service Act of 1940, Public Law 783, 76th Cong., 2d sess. (Sept. 16, 1940), 887 (emphasis mine); Army Service Forces, *Leadership and the Negro Soldier*, 2; War Department, *Command of Negro Troops*, 1; *Lynn v. Downer*, 140 F. 2d 401 (2d Cir. 1944).

57. Henry L. Stimson to Andrew J. May, April 6, 1945, box 1063, entry 363, RG 407. On the navy and for "invited," see MacGregor, *Integration of the Armed Forces*, 83.

58. "Digest of War Department Policy Pertaining to Negro Military Personnel," Jan. 1, 1944, 2, box 15, entry 8, RG 107. On the relative recentness of some military racial policies, see General Benjamin O. Davis's comments in J. S. Leonard, "Minutes on Meeting of Advisory Committee on Negro Troop Policies," June 28, 1943, box 35, entry 88, RG 107. On the wartime need to re-create "tradition," see Stouffer et al., *The American Soldier*, 1:412.

59. War Department, *Command of Negro Troops*, 13.
60. James T. Sparrow, *Warfare State: World War II Americans and the Age of Big Government* (New York: Oxford University Press, 2011), 72; Thomas Bruscino, *A Nation Forged in War: How World War II Taught Americans to Get Along* (Knoxville: University of Tennessee Press, 2010), 77; Richard C. Brown, *Social Attitudes of American Generals, 1898–1940* (New York: Arno, 1979), 173. For a fantastic global account of US military–inspired standardization in this period, see Daniel Immerwahr, *How to Hide an Empire: A History of the Greater United States* (New York: Picador, 2019), 298–316.
61. See Lisa Lowe, *Immigrant Acts: On Asian American Cultural Politics* (Durham, NC: Duke University Press, 1997), 27–28; David R. Roediger and Elizabeth D. Esch, *The Production of Difference: Race and the Management of Labor in U.S. History* (Berkeley: University of California Press, 2012); Lisa Lowe, *The Intimacies of Four Continents* (Durham, NC: Duke University Press, 2015); Elizabeth D. Esch, *The Color Line and the Assembly Line: Managing Race in the Ford Empire* (Berkeley: University of California Press, 2018).
62. Sparrow, *Warfare State*, 12–14, 72–74.
63. For an especially trenchant treatment of this point, see J. Mills Thornton III, "Segregation and the City: White Supremacy in Alabama in the Mid-Twentieth Century," in *Fog of War: The Second World War and the Civil Rights Movement*, ed. Kevin M. Kruse and Stephen Tuck (New York: Oxford University Press, 2012), 51–69.
64. War Department, *Command of Negro Troops*, 13.
65. See, for example, Jason Morgan Ward, *Defending White Democracy: The Making of a Segregationist Movement and the Remaking of Racial Politics, 1936–1965* (Chapel Hill: University of North Carolina Press, 2011), 44–45. On the linkages between racism and geographical mobility, see Tim Cresswell, "Towards a Politics of Mobility," *Environment and Planning D* 28 (2010): 17–31; Elizabeth Stordeur Pryor, *Colored Travelers: Mobility and the Fight for Citizenship before the Civil War* (Chapel Hill: University of North Carolina Press, 2016); Genevieve Carpio, *Collisions at the Crossroads: How Place and Mobility Make Race* (Berkeley: University of California Press, 2019). Many thanks to Colin Anderson for bringing much of this literature to my attention.
66. Navy Department, "Guide to Command of Negro Naval Personnel," 10. For slightly different wording, see War Department, *Command of Negro Troops*, 11. For March 1943 survey, see Stouffer et al., *The American Soldier*, 1:568.
67. On surveillance and espionage and sedition charges, see Robert A. Hill, ed., *The FBI's RACON: Racial Conditions in the United States during World War II* (Boston: Northeastern University Press, 1995); Ira Katznelson, *Fear Itself: The New Deal and the Origins of Our Time* (New York: Liveright, 2013), 341–342; Kenneth O'Reilly, "The Roosevelt Administration and Black America: Federal Surveillance Policy and Civil Rights during the New Deal and World War II," *Phylon* 48 (1987): 12–25; Patrick S. Washburn, *A Question of Sedition: The Federal Government's Investigation of the Black Press during World War II* (New York: Oxford University Press, 1986). On civilian police harassment, see William H. Hastie, "A Report on Civilian Violence against Negro Soldiers," May 29, 1943, box 1066, entry 363, RG 407.
68. For "sheer coercive power," see Stouffer et al., *The American Soldier*, 2:112. On the 96th Article of War, see Harvey Clarence Carbaugh, "Pleading and Practice under the 96th Article of War," *Illinois Law Review* 13 (May 1918): 1. On military

intelligence agents, see Daniel Kryder, *Divided Arsenal: Race and the American State during World War II* (Cambridge: Cambridge University Press, 2000), 158–160. For an example of mail censorship, see Charles A. Briscoe to Director of Intelligence, memo, May 31, 1943, box 37, entry 88, RG 107.

69. Walter White to President, memo, Feb. 12, 1945, box 27, PNP.
70. Thomas, "The 'Double V' Was for Victory," 309; W. Y. Bell Jr., "The Negro Warrior's Home Front," *Phylon* 5 (1944): 276.
71. Sam Reed to Roy Wilkins, Dec. 10, 1942, box II:A643, NAACPR; "Bulletin: Sam Reed Coordinating Committee, Twin City Branches, NAACP," Jan. 3, 1942 [*sic*; 1943], box II:A643, NAACPR; Herman Taylor to Walter White, memo, Sept. 1, 1944, box II:A643, NAACPR. On the importance of World War I, see Adriane Lentz-Smith, *Freedom Struggles: African Americans and World War I* (Cambridge, MA: Harvard University Press, 2009); Chad L. Williams, *Torchbearers of Democracy: African American Soldiers in the World War I Era* (Chapel Hill: University of North Carolina Press, 2010).
72. "More and Better Riots Brewing," *BAA*, Aug. 16, 1941, 4; Marjorie McKenzie, "Pursuit of Democracy," *PC*, Feb. 10, 1945, 7.
73. William H. Hastie, "Survey and Recommendations Concerning the Integration of the Negro Soldier into the Army," c. Sept. 22, 1941, box 150, RPPP; "'Brass Hat' Awakening," *PC*, Apr. 14, 1945, 6. For some black people's long-standing equation of equal rights with "manhood" rights, see Steve Estes, *I Am a Man! Race, Manhood, and the Civil Rights Movement* (Chapel Hill: University of North Carolina Press, 2005). On the concept of "manliness" applying at times to women as well, see Tommie Shelby, *We Who Are Dark: The Philosophical Foundations of Black Solidarity* (Cambridge, MA: Harvard University Press, 2005), 34–35.
74. Alphonse Heningburg, "Two Worlds," *Common Ground* 4, no. 3 (1944): 51; Charley Cherokee, "National Grapevine," *CD*, June 19, 1943, 15. For examples of similar sentiments, see Peery, *Black Fire*, 173; "The War Department," *CD*, Sept. 20, 1941, 14; "Soldier Gets 25-Year Term," *CD*, Aug. 24, 1943, 1; Mack M. Greene to President Roosevelt, Mar. 21, 1943, box 1071, entry 363, RG 407; Truman K. Gibson Jr. to B. O. Davis, memo, June 30, 1943, box 243, entry 188, RG 107; Notes on Camp Sutton, North Carolina, Sept. 25, 1943, box 13, JDP; "The Army Must Act," *Crisis*, Sept. 1941, 279.
75. On the Oyster Bay story, see Conrad Lynn to Dwight Macdonald, July 19, 1944, box 30, series 1, DMP. On Merced, see "Calif. Soldiers in 2 Efforts to Wreck Jim Crow Tavern," *BAA*, Mar. 14, 1942, 9. On Aiea Naval Barracks, see Counter-Intelligence Section, B-7, District Intelligence Office, Fourteenth Naval District, "The Negro Problem in the Fourteenth Naval District," Aug. 15, 1943, 23, box 12, ROC. On Bisbee, see Peery, *Black Fire*, 156. On Virginia naval ammunition depot, see Historical Section, Bureau of Naval Personnel, "Negro in the Navy," 75. On post exchanges, see Notes on Fort Huachuca, box 13, JDP; J. M. Roamer, "Racial Situation in the United States," report, Sept. 30, 1944, 2, box 261, entry 189, RG 107; E. W. Gruhn, "Racial Situation in the United States," report, Oct. 20, 1944, 2, box 261, entry 189, RG 107.
76. For helpful overviews of black soldiers' mass wartime armed resistance, see James Albert Burran III, "Racial Violence in the South during World War II" (PhD diss., University of Tennessee, 1977); Kryder, *Divided Arsenal*, 133–207; Lee, *Employment of Negro Troops*, 348–379.
77. Hastie, *On Clipped Wings*, n.p.
78. Charles A. Briscoe to Director of Intelligence, memo, June 17, 1943, box 37, entry 88, RG 107; J. M. Roamer and E. W. Gruhn, "Racial Situation in the United States,"

report, Jan. 17, 1945, 4–6, box 261, entry 189, RG 107; Army Service Forces, Office of Chief of Transportation, Intelligence and Security Division, memo, Aug. 22, 1945, box 261, entry 189, RG 107; "Riot Threatens," *BAA*, Aug. 5, 1944, 2; "Protested to Mistreatment in Dixie Camp," *CCP*, Oct. 28, 1944, 12B; Thomas, "The 'Double V' Was for Victory," 263–265; Hill, *The FBI's RACON*, 332.

79. Proceedings of a Board of Review Appointed by Commanding General, 92d Infantry Division, June 24–25, 1945, 5, box 28, entry 109, RG 319; TIR, no. 2961, Aug. 4, 1945, box 265, entry 189, RG 107; TIR, no. 593, March 27, 1945, box 265, entry 189, RG 107; TIR, no. 1462, Jan. 10, 1945, box 265, entry 189, RG 107. On white GIs' own goldbricking, see Gerald F. Linderman, *The World within War: America's Combat Experience in World War II* (Cambridge, MA: Harvard University Press, 1999), 187; Bill Mauldin, *Up Front* (1945; New York: Norton, 2000), 15.

80. The Editors of *New Republic*, "The Negro: His Future in America," in *Primer for White Folks*, ed. Bucklin Moon (Garden City, NY: Doubleday, 1946), 352–353.

81. For "blood . . . boiling all the time" quotation, see "A Negro in the Army," *New Republic*, June 26, 1944, 851. For the "contest wrong" quotation, see "Negroes in the Army," *New Republic*, Dec. 25, 1944, 872. For many more letters that express similar sentiments, see McGuire, ed., *Taps for a Jim Crow Army*.

82. Thomas, "The 'Double V' Was for Victory," 177.

83. Bell Jr., "The Negro Warrior's Home Front," 276; J. Saunders Redding, "A Second Look," *BAA*, Aug. 7, 1944, 4. For military intelligence reports, see E. W. Gruhn to Commanding General, Army Service Forces, memo, May 19, 1944, box 381d, entry 47, RG 319; and E. W. Gruhn to Commanding General, Army Service Forces, memo, May 31, 1944, box 381d, entry 47, RG 319. For desertion rates, see John Whiteclay Chambers II, "Desertion," in *The Oxford Companion to American Military History*, ed. John Whiteclay Chambers II (New York: Oxford University Press, 1999), 212. For "escape, fugitivity, and maroonage" quotation, see Robin D. G. Kelley, "Beyond Black Lives Matter," *Kalfou* 2 (Fall 2015): 331.

84. J. M. Roamer, "Racial Situation in the United States," report, Aug. 12, 1945, 1, box 380, entry 47, RG 319; J. M. Roamer, "Racial Situation in the United States," report, Sept. 30, 1944, 3, box 261, entry 189, RG 107; J. M. Roamer, "Racial Situation in the United States," report, Sept. 9, 1944, 2, box 380, entry 47, RG 319; J. M. Roamer, "Racial Situation in the United States," report, Sept. 30, 1944, 3–4, box 261, entry 189, RG 107; J. M. Roamer, "Racial Situation in the United States," report, Jan. 2, 1945, 5, box 261, entry 189, RG 107. For the July 8, 1944, directive, see J. A. Ulio to Commanding Generals, memo, July 8, 1944, box 241, entry 188, RG 107.

85. On Fort Belvoir, see "Abuse Soldiers in Own Theatre," *BAA*, March 20, 1943, 5. On Camp Kearns, see Lathe B. Row to Inspector General, memo, Aug. 12, 1943, box 92, entry 26e, RG 159; Virgil L. Peterson to Adjutant General, Aug. 31, 1943, box 185, entry 188, RG 107; The Colored Men of Kearn,[sic] Utah, to Sir, June 9, 1943, box 185, entry 188, RG 107. Many scholars have discussed the incident at Freeman Field. For a useful primary source, see "Chronological Summary, Events at Freeman Field," box 443, entry 43, RG 165. On wartime boycotts and sit-ins occurring outside the military, see August Meier and Elliot Rudwick, *Along the Color Line: Explorations in the Black Experience* (1976; Champaign: University of Illinois Press, 2002), 344–353.

86. "Airmen Boycott J. C. Club," *BAA*, March 24, 1945, 1; Jefferson, *Fighting for Hope*, 85; E. W. Gruhn to Commanding General, Army Service Forces, memo, May 31, 1944, box 381d, entry 47, RG 319; "Jim Crowed Soldiers Boycott USO Show," *CD*,

April 11, 1942, 5; Negro Soldier to *BAA*, Sept. 27, 1943, in McGuire, *Taps for a Jim Crow Army*, 19–20; Bombardier, "The Story of the 477th Bombardment Group," *Politics*, June 1944, 141; Ernest E. Johnson, "Troops Boycott Jim Crow Theatre, Officers Slip In," *BAA*, Aug. 5, 1944, 9; Taylor with Taylor, *Two Steps from Glory*, 62; "Gittleson," interview by Lawrence D. Reddick, Dec. 7, 1945, box 1, LDR; Aaron Henry with Constance Curry, *Aaron Henry: The Fire Ever Burning* (Jackson: University Press of Mississippi, 2000), 61.

87. J. M. Roamer, "Racial Situation in the United States," report, Jan. 2, 1945, 3, box 261, entry 189, RG 107; William Y. Bell Jr., "The Threat to Negro Soldier Morale," typescript report, Oct. 1943, box 17, APRP.

88. Historical Section, Bureau of Naval Personnel, "Negro in the Navy," 67; "6 WACs Resign," *BAA*, July 10, 1943, 1; "Prevent Soldier Strike at Ga. Infantry School," *ADW*, Jan. 19, 1944, 1. For suggesting the point about black women's desire to escape domestic work, I thank Nathan Connolly.

89. For the "pour it on" quotation, see *Mutiny? The Real Story of How the Navy Branded 50 Fear-Shocked Sailors as Mutineers* (NAACP Legal Defense Fund, March 1945), 6. On the explosion's impact, see "Ship Blast Loss Near $7,000,000," *LAT*, July 20, 1944, 4. The best account of this story remains Robert L. Allen, *The Port Chicago Mutiny: The Story of the Largest Mass Mutiny Trial in U.S. Naval History* (New York: Amistad, 1993).

90. For "dreary and menial" quotation, see "The Tucson Strike," *Politics*, Oct. 1944, 285; for "mop walls, scrub floors, and do all the dirty work," see "Jim Crow in Uniform: Current Notes," *Politics*, May 1945, 150. Each of these cases got extensive coverage in the black, the left-wing, and often even the mainstream press and they are, for the most part, well documented in military and NAACP records. The smallest sample of these vast materials follows: On Honolulu slowdown and strike, see "Statement of Facts in the Case of William R. Allen et al.," March 30, 1945, box II:B18, NAACPR; "Facts on Mutiny Revealed," *PC*, Feb. 17, 1945, p. 1. On Marana, see E. W. Gruhn, "Racial Situation in the United States, 23 Sept. to 14 Oct. 1944," confidential memo, Oct. 20, 1944, box 261, entry 189, RG 107. On Port Hueneme, see "Port Hueneme Seabees End Hunger Strike," *LAT*, March 5, 1945, 1; and Norman O. Houston and Moody Staten to Roy Wilkins, memo, March 5, 1945, box II:B196, NAACPR. On Fort Devens, see Charles H. Houston to Mary McLeod Bethune, Apr. 26, 1945, box II:B159, NAACPR; Sandra M. Bolzenius, *Glory in Their Spirit: How Four Black Women Took on the Army during World War II* (Urbana: University of Illinois Press, 2018).

91. "Gittleson," interview by Lawrence D. Reddick, Dec. 7, 1945, box 1, LDR.

92. [Unknown] to Walter White, n.d. but c. Oct. 8, 1943, box II:A646, NAACPR. For black soldiers' critiques of black newspapers, see Jefferson, *Fighting for Hope*, 134–135; Peery, *Black Fire*, 133–134.

93. "We Want Our Soldiers Back Alive," *CD*, Nov. 27, 1943, 14; "The Camp Stewart Rebellion," *BAA*, June 26, 1943, 4.

94. This civilian support suggests that if, as several scholars have argued, the words of established black institutions seemed at times to tamp down mass militancy, their actions sometimes encouraged it. See Lee Finkle, "The Conservative Aims of Militant Rhetoric: Black Protest during World War II," *JAH* 60 (Dec. 1973): 693–713; and Harvard Sitkoff, "African American Militancy in the World War II South: Another Perspective," in *Remaking Dixie: The Impact of World War II on the American South*, ed. Neil R. McMillen (Jackson: University Press of Mississippi, 1997), 70–92.

95. "Hitlerism at Home," *PC*, Aug. 23, 1941, 6; Ruth A. Handy to Henry L. Stimson, May 27, 1943, box 1068, entry 363, RG 407.

96. Thelma Hobbs to War Department, June 16, 1943, box 1067, entry 363, RG 407; Mothers to Eleanor Roosevelt, June 21, 1943, box 1067, entry 363, RG 407; Rachel Golden to War Department, June 10, 1943, box 1067, entry 363, RG 407; Mattie B. James to FDR, June 26, 1943, box 1067, entry 363, RG 407; Nannie Mae Wilson to FDR, Nov. 18, 1944, box 1064, entry 363, RG 407.

97. "Devens WAC Strike Ends," *BAA*, Mar. 24, 1945, 1; "Free the Four Wacs!," *PC*, Apr. 6, 1945, 6. For black press coverage, see BPR, Apr. 2, 1945, Apr. 9, 1945, and Apr. 16, 1945, all in box 223, entry 188, RG 107. For the protest letters, see box 1063, entry 363, RG 407. For resolution of the controversy, see Robert H. Dunlop to Arthur Crookham, Apr. 30, 1945, box 1063, entry 363, RG 407.

98. Morris Milgram to Willard S. Townsend, March 19, 1945, box 65, WDLR.

99. For the figure of thirty thousand, see Roy Wilkins to Rear Admiral Denfeld, Mar. 26, 1945, box II:B196, NAACPR. For black GIs opening new NAACP branches, see Dorothy A. Autrey, "The National Association for the Advancement of Colored People in Alabama, 1913–1952" (PhD diss., University of Notre Dame, 1985), 186. For examples of the *Crisis* articles, see "Along the N.A.A.C.P. Battlefront," *Crisis*, Feb. 1944, 51; "Along the N.A.A.C.P. Battlefront," *Crisis*, Sept. 1944, 294; and "Along the N.A.A.C.P. Battlefront," *Crisis*, Oct. 1944, 323. On the NAACP activities, see especially the vast materials in boxes II:B12 to II:B23 and boxes II:B153 to II:B198, NAACPR. For the possibility that the NAACP occasionally helped GIs formulate protest strategies and tactics, see Bernard C. Nalty, *Strength for the Fight: A History of Black Americans in the Military* (New York: Free Press, 1986), 161, and the example of the Seabee hunger strike below.

100. Norman O. Houston and Moody Staten to Roy Wilkins, memo, Mar. 5, 1945, box II:B196, NAACPR; Roy Wilkins to James Forrestal, Mar. 13, 1945, box II:B196, NAACPR.

101. Memo for President from Jonathan Daniels, June 22, 1943, box 13, JDP. See Kryder, *Divided Arsenal*, 228–233; Charles W. Eagles, *Jonathan Daniels and Race Relations: The Evolution of a Southern Liberal* (Knoxville: University of Tennessee Press, 1982), 104–105.

102. Quoted in Ward, *Defending White Democracy*, 64. On Byrd and the Democratic National Convention, see William E. Leuchtenburg, *The White House Looks South: Franklin D. Roosevelt, Harry S. Truman, Lyndon B. Johnson* (Baton Rouge: Louisiana State University Press, 2005), 134–135.

103. Earl Brown, "The Negro Vote, 1944: A Forecast," *Harper's*, July 1944, 152–153; Edward A. Harris, "The Negro Faces November," *New Republic*, Aug. 28, 1944, 242. On liberal whites' growing electoral power, see Eric Schickler, *Racial Realignment: The Transformation of American Liberalism, 1932–1965* (Princeton, NJ: Princeton University Press, 2016), 95–97.

104. BPR, Oct. 23, 1944, box 223, entry 188, RG 107; "Congressional Inquiry Wanted!," *New York Amsterdam News*, Mar. 31, 1945, 14; "Future versus Past," *CD*, Sept. 23, 1944, 1; "The AFRO Is for Dewey and Here Is Why," *BAA*, Oct. 28, 1944, 1.

105. Quoted in Richard M. Dalfiume, *Desegregation of the U.S. Armed Forces: Fighting on Two Fronts, 1939–1953* (Columbia: University of Missouri Press, 1969), 89. On the tightening presidential race, see Katznelson, *Fear Itself*, 217.

106. Jonathan Daniels to President Roosevelt, memo, Sept. 21, 1944, box 14, JDP; Jonathan Daniels to President Roosevelt, memo, Sept. 28, 1944, box 14, JDP; Jonathan Daniels to President Roosevelt, memo, Oct. 5, 1944, box 14, JDP.

107. Chief of the Bureau of Naval Personnel to Commanding Officer, Dec. 8, 1944, in *Blacks in the Military: Essential Documents*, ed. Bernard C. Nalty and Morris J. MacGregor (Wilmington, DE: Scholarly Resources, 1981), 151; President Roosevelt to Henry L. Stimson, Sept. 28, 1944, box 14, JDP.

108. Jonathan Daniels to President Roosevelt, memo, Sept. 28, 1944, box 14, JDP.

109. "The GI Assault Bill," *CD*, Dec. 9, 1944, 12; H. R. 2651, 79th Cong., 1st sess., March 16, 1945; Henry L. Stimson to Andrew J. May, Apr. 6, 1945, box 1063, entry 363, RG 407. On Congress's bloc of conservative Republicans and southern Democrats, see Julian E. Zelizer, "Confronting the Roadblock: Congress, Civil Rights, and World War II," in Kruse and Tuck, *Fog of War*, 32–50; Katznelson, *Fear Itself*, 192–194.

110. Conrad Lynn, *There Is a Fountain: The Autobiography of Conrad Lynn*, foreword by William M. Kunstler (Brooklyn, NY: Lawrence Hill Books, 1979), 96, 98; Conrad Lynn to Dwight Macdonald, Mar. 18, 1943, box 30, series I, DMP.

111. *Perry H. Hansbery v. Franklin Delano Roosevelt, et al.*, complaint, Civil Action Case 44C720, USDCNDI. For background on Hansberry and his well-known family, see "Perry H. Hansberry Sues," *Arkansas State Press*, July 14, 1944, 1; "Inductee Starts Federal Suit for Army Jim Crow," *CD*, July 1, 1944, 3.

112. On press attention, see preceding note and "Negro Files Suit to Bar His Induction," *CT*, June 22, 1944, 14; "Woll Appointed Friend of Court in Negro's Suit," *CT*, July 14, 1944, 12. On the Lynn Committee's support, see their *Help Fight Jim Crow in Uniform!*, pamphlet, n.d., but c. late 1944, box 118, series II, DMP. On the outcome of Hansberry's case, see handwritten note on J. Albert Woll and Kenneth S. Nathan, Motion to Dismiss, *Perry H. Hansberry v. Franklin Delano Roosevelt, et al.*, Civil Action Case 44C720, USDCNDI. On the *Korematsu* case, see Peter Irons, *Justice at War: The Story of the Japanese American Internment Cases* (New York: Oxford University Press, 1983).

113. James T. Moutoux, "Finds Navy Trying Sincerely to Make Jim Crow Walk Plank," *PM*, July 15, 1945, 9; "No Jim Crow for WAVES," *PM*, Dec. 29, 1944, 14.

114. Randall Jacobs, Chief of Naval Personnel to Commandants All Naval Districts and All Recruit Training Commands, memo, June 11, 1945, in *Blacks in the World War II Naval Establishment*, vol. 6 of *Blacks in the United States Armed Forces: Basic Documents*, ed. Morris J. MacGregor and Bernard C. Nalty (Wilmington, DE: Scholarly Resources, 1977), 296; William M. Fechteler to Commandants All Naval Districts and All Recruit Training Commands, memo, June 25, 1945, in MacGregor and Nalty, *Blacks in the World War II Naval Establishment*, 299.

115. Historical Section, Bureau of Naval Personnel, "Negro in the Navy," 20–21; "The Navy's New Order," *CD*, July 21, 1945, 12.

116. Quoted in Walter White, *A Man Called White: The Autobiography of Walter White* (New York: Viking Press, 1948), 272–273; Lawrence D. Reddick, "The Negro in the United States Navy during World War II," *JNH* 32 (Apr. 1947): 218.

117. William H. Hastie, "Survey and Recommendations Concerning the Integration of the Negro Soldier into the Army," c. Sept. 22, 1941, box 150, RPPP.

118. R. W. Crawford to General Eisenhower, memo, Apr. 2, 1942, in *Black Soldiers in World War II*, vol. 5 of *Blacks in the United States Armed Forces: Basic Documents*,

ed. Morris J. MacGregor and Bernard C. Nalty (Wilmington, DE: Scholarly Resources, 1977), 161.

119. George V. Strong to Assistant Chief of Staff, G-3, June 17, 1942, memo, box 472, entry 418, RG 165; Stimson Diary, May 12, 1942, microfilm, reel 7, HLSP; Virgil L. Peterson to Assistant Chief of Staff, G-3, memo, Sept. 11, 1942, box 148, entry 360A, RG 407; Crawford to Eisenhower, memo, Apr. 2, 1942, in MacGregor and Nalty, *Black Soldiers in World War II*, 161; John J. McCloy to Herbert B. Elliston, Aug. 5, 1943, box 15, entry 88, RG 107.

120. Hastie, *On Clipped Wings*, n.p.

121. "The New Navy Policy," *CD*, Mar. 25, 1944, 12; B. O. Davis to John J. McCloy, memo, Nov. 10, 1943, in MacGregor and Nalty, *Black Soldiers in World War II*, 291–293. See also Truman K. Gibson Jr. to Assistant Secretary of War, Aug. 23, 1943, in MacGregor and Nalty, *Black Soldiers in World War II*, 273–279; Gibson to Assistant Secretary of War, Dec. 20, 1943, box 15, entry 88, RG 107; Gibson to John J. McCloy, memo, Nov. 2, 1944, box 15, entry 88, RG 107; Minutes of the Advisory Committee on Negro Troop Policies, Feb. 22, 1943, box 15, entry 88, RG 107.

122. For a good example, see Gibson to McCloy, memo, Nov. 2, 1944, box 15, entry 88, RG 107. Citing the work of anthropologist Richard Bauman, Charles L. Briggs has written that "narratives do not simply describe ready-made events; rather, they provide central means by which we *create* notions as to what [has taken] place." See Charles L. Briggs, ed., *Disorderly Discourse: Narrative, Conflict, & Inequality* (New York: Oxford University Press, 1996), 22–23.

123. Davis to McCloy, memo, Nov. 10, 1943, in MacGregor and Nalty, *Black Soldiers in World War II*, 291–293.

124. George C. Marshall to Commanding Generals, Army Air Forces, Army Ground Forces, Army Service Forces, memo, n.d., c. July 13, 1943, box 1511, entry 360A, RG 407. For a helpful discussion of these reforms, see Kryder, *Divided Arsenal*, 153–163.

125. J. S. Leonard to Assistant Secretary of War, Dec. 17, 1943, in MacGregor and Nalty, *Black Soldiers in World War II*, 285–286; War Department, *Command of Negro Troops*, 11. For "terrible prophecies," see Kryder, *Divided Arsenal*, 167n108; for "grave repercussions," see John J. McCloy to Secretary of War, memo, June 4, 1945, box 37, entry 88, RG 107.

126. For April 1945 study, see J. M. Roamer, "Racial Situation in the United States, 14 to 28 April 1945," May 7, 1945, box 261, entry 189, RG 107. On army review, see George C. Marshall to John J. McCloy, memo, Aug. 25, 1945, in MacGregor and Nalty, *Blacks in the United States Armed Forces*, 521.

127. War Department, *Command of Negro Troops*, 9, 1, 6.

128. War Department, *Command of Negro Troops*, 9–11.

129. Meeting of the Advisory Committee on Special Troop Policies, May 15, 1945, box 35, entry 88, RG 107; J. S. Leonard to Assistant Secretary of War, memo, Oct. 3, 1944, box 443, entry 43, RG 165. For July 8, 1944, order, see J. A. Ulio to Commanding Generals, memo, July 8, 1944, box 241, entry 188, RG 107.

130. Thomas L. Bailey to Henry L. Stimson, telegram, Aug. 30, 1944, box 1064, entry 363, RG 407; John Sparkman to Stimson, Aug. 30, 1944, box 1064, entry 363, RG 407; Leonard Allen to Stimson, Sept. 1, 1944, box 1064, entry 363, RG 407; Audie S. Ellis to Stimson, Aug. 31, 1944, box 1064, entry 363, RG 407; *Montgomery Advertiser* quoted in John Hope Franklin, *From Slavery*

to Freedom: A History of Negro Americans, 3d ed. (1947; New York: Knopf, 1967), 590.

131. "Army's 'No-Segregation Order,'" *PC*, Sept. 9, 1944, 1; "The Army Seizes the Pershing Hotel," *CD*, Sept. 16, 1944, 12; William H. Hastie to John J. McCloy, Sept. 5, 1944, box 39, entry 88, RG 107.

132. J. M. Roamer, "Racial Situation in the United States," report, Sept. 30, 1944, 3, box 261, entry 189, RG 107. Black soldiers' efforts to enforce this order is discussed above. For evidence of allies' help in the matter, see, for example, box II:B57 and box II:B194, NAACPR; Vito Marcantonio to John J. McCloy, Dec. 21, 1944, box 1064, entry 363, RG 407; Benjamin J. Davis Jr. to Henry L. Stimson, Feb. 2, 1945, box 1063, entry 363, RG 407.

133. John J. McCloy to Secretary of War, memo, June 4, 1945, box 37, entry 88, RG 107. Stimson officially confirmed McCloy's interpretation shortly thereafter. See Lawrence P. Scott and William M. Womack Sr., *Double V: The Civil Rights Struggle of the Tuskegee Airmen* (East Lansing: Michigan State University Press, 1992), 242.

134. Charles A. Briscoe to Director of Intelligence, NOPE, memo, May 31, 1943, box 37, entry 88, RG 107.

135. McNatt, "I Was a Seabee," 138; Mark A. Huddle, *Roi Ottley's World War II: The Lost Diary of an African American Journalist* (Lawrence: University Press of Kansas, 2011), 37.

136. James Baldwin, *Notes of a Native Son* (1955; Boston: Beacon Press, 1983), 101.

CHAPTER 7

1. Office of Censorship, District Postal Censor, Honolulu, T.H., General Information Summary, Nov. 15, 1944–Nov. 30, 1944, 15, box 12, ROC.

2. The term "nonblack minority" is not ideal. Some scholars prefer "minoritized" to signal the socially constructed process through which some people become "minorities." The term is also vaguely expansive in that it could reference all humanity, since anyone can be a minority given one dimension of their identity or another. I nonetheless use it here for the purposes of economy. *Nonblack minority* is my shorthand term for two groups: nonblack nonwhites, those people whom a broad collection of wartime institutions and individuals, both in and out of the military, defined as neither black nor white; and borderline whites, whom a broad collection of wartime institutions and individuals, both in and out of the military, defined as sometimes white and sometimes not white. Native Americans and Asian Americans tended to be in the former camp, Mexican Americans and Puerto Ricans in the latter. But as this and other chapters attempt to show, all these groups at times straddled the military's white-nonwhite lines and were "whitened" in a sense by its black-white ones. As I have argued elsewhere and as this book further confirms, that broad collection of institutions and individuals overwhelmingly agreed that people of European descent—Italians, Jews, Poles, Slavs, Greeks, and others—should be defined as white, unless they were deemed also to have "Negro" or Japanese ancestry.

3. Thomas Bruscino, *A Nation Forged in War: How World War II Taught Americans to Get Along* (Knoxville: University of Tennessee Press, 2010); Deborah Dash Moore, *GI Jews: How World War II Changed a Generation* (Cambridge, MA: Harvard University Press, 2004); Gary Gerstle, *American Crucible: Race and Nation in the Twentieth Century* (Princeton, NJ: Princeton University Press, 2001), 220–237.

4. Maya Mikdashi, "What Is Settler Colonialism?," July 17, 2012, http://www. jadaliyya.com/Details/26604/What-is-Settler-Colonialism   (accessed   Nov. 20, 2019); John Adair, "The Navajo and Pueblo Veteran," *American Indian* 4 (1947): 6–7; Kenneth William Townsend, *World War II and the American Indian* (Albuquerque: University of New Mexico Press, 2000), 140; Alison R. Bernstein, *American Indians and World War II: Toward a New Era in Indian Affairs* (Norman: University of Oklahoma Press, 1991), 58.

5. Raul Morin, *Among the Valiant: Mexican-Americans in World War II and Korea* (Los Angeles: Borden, 1963), 87.

6. Lopez and the Mexican American veteran quoted in Margarita Aragon, "'A General Separation of Colored and White': The WWII Riots, Military Segregation, and Racism(s) beyond the White/Nonwhite Binary," *SRE* 1 (Oct. 2015): 510.

7. Aragon, "'A General Separation,'" 510; Nuñez quoted in Maggie Rivas-Rodriguez, ed., *Mexican Americans and World War II* (Austin: University of Texas Press, 2005), 182.

8. Doroteo V. Vité, "A Filipino Rookie in Uncle Sam's Army," *Asia: The Journal of the American Asiatic Association* 42 (Oct. 1942): 565–566.

9. Judy Yung, *Unbound Feet: A Social History of Chinese Women in San Francisco* (Berkeley: University of California Press, 1995), 253. On Leong, see Ellen D. Wu, *The Color of Success: Asian Americans and the Origins of the Model Minority* (Princeton, NJ: Princeton University Press, 2014), 66–67.

10. Yung, *Unbound Feet*, 260; Joanne Rao Sánchez, "The Latinas of World War II: From Familial Shelter to Expanding Horizons," in *Beyond the World War II Hero: The Social and Political Legacy of a Generation*, ed. Maggie Rivas-Rodriguez and Emilio Zamora (Austin: University of Texas Press, 2009), 84–85. On the point that masculinity sometimes helped unite men across social boundaries, see Luís Alvarez, "Transnational Latino Soldiering: Military Service and Ethnic Politics during World War II," in *Latina/os and World War II: Mobility, Agency, and Ideology*, ed. Maggie Rivas-Rodriguez and B. V. Olguín (Austin: University of Texas Press, 2014), 78.

11. Sonia S. Lee and Ande Diaz, "'I Was the One Percenter': Manny Diaz and the Beginnings of a Black–Puerto Rican Coalition," *Journal of American Ethnic History* 26 (Spring 2007): 56–57.

12. Lee and Diaz, "'I Was the One Percenter,'" 56–57; Morin, *Among the Valiant*, 100; S. Katsutani to Irene Shimabuku, Dec. 11, 1944, letter transcribed by Office of Censorship, USA, box 9, entry 47, RG 107. On comradeship abroad, see Gerald F. Linderman, *The World within War: America's Combat Experience in World War II* (New York: Free Press, 1997), 263–299.

13. For Villareal, see *Log of the Cruise: 80th USN Construction Battalion, 1943–1944* (Providence, RI: Bickford Engraving & Electrotype, n.d.), 63, https://www.history.navy.mil/content/dam/museums/Seabee/Cruisebooks/wwiicruisebooks/ncb-cruisebooks/80%20%20NCB%20%201943-44.pdf; for Tesofiero, see *Log of the Cruise*, 5; for who appears to be a Chinese American electrician, Y. G. Yung, see *Log of the Cruise*, 13. For the "three Chinese" quotation, see Historical Section, Bureau of Naval Personnel, "The Negro in the Navy," typescript, 1947, 77, NDL.

14. See Isaac McNatt, "I Was a Seabee," *Politics*, June 1944, 137–138; Historical Section, Bureau of Naval Personnel, "Negro in the Navy," 77–79; and materials in folder 4, box II:B196, NAACPR.

15. Eartha M. M. White to Walter White, Mar. 20, 1943, Box II:B196, NAACPR.

16. See Jesse Quinsaat, "An Exercise on How to Join the Navy . . . and Still Not See the World," in *Counterpoint: Perspectives on Asian America*, ed. Emma Gee (Los

Angeles: UCLA Asian American Studies Center, 1976), 103–104; Jason Luna Gavilan, "Of 'Mates' and Men: The Comparative Racial Politics of Filipino Naval Enlistment, circa 1941–1943," in *Critical Ethnic Studies: A Reader*, ed. Nada Elia et al. (Durham, NC: Duke University Press, 2016), 326–343.

17. "Affidavit from Paul Belcher and Wilson Belcher," Oct. 28, 1943, box II:B196, NAACPR; "Statement from 9 Seabees at NAACP Office on Oct. 25, 1943," Oct. 27, 1943, box II:B196, NAACPR.

18. On the state drawing lines that simultaneously unite and divide, see Moon-Kie Jung, *Beneath the Surface of White Supremacy: Denaturalizing U.S. Racisms Past and Present* (Stanford, CA: Stanford University Press, 2015), 69–70.

19. On War Department policy, see Henry L. Stimson to Andrew J. May, Apr. 6, 1945, box 1063, entry 363, RG 407. On Japanese American soldiers' numbers at Shelby, see O. F. Roettger to Adjutant General, memo, Nov. 24, 1942, box 281, entry 208, RG 165; and James P. Dale, Memorandum for the Officer in Charge, July 8, 1943, box 23, entry 180, RG 107.

20. James P. Dale, Memorandum for the Officer in Charge, July 8, 1943, box 23, entry 180, RG 107; John Howard, *Concentration Camps on the Home Front: Japanese Americans in the House of Jim Crow* (Chicago: University of Chicago Press, 2008), 127; Confidential "Intermingling of Races" memo, June 26, 1943, box 380, entry 47, RG 319.

21. Richard Watada, interview by [Robert Horstein?], HOHA, May 2, 2004, video, tape 3, 28:24, http://www.goforbroke.org/learn/archives/oral_histories_videos. php?clip=44703; Edward Tamanaha, Interview by [Ross Segawa?], HOHA, Apr. 16, 2004, video, tape 2, 10:35, http://www.goforbroke.org/ohmsviewer/viewer. php?cachefile=2004OH0429_02_Tamanaha.xml.

22. Mike Masaoka with Bill Hosokawa, *They Call Me Moses Masaoka: An American Saga* (New York: William Morrow, 1987), 143; Daniel Inouye, *Journey to Washington* (New York: Prentice Hall, 1967), 96.

23. C. W. Pence to Colonel William P. Scobey, May 20, 1943, box 48, entry 183, RG 107; John Lansdale Jr. to Assistant Secretary of War, memo, Oct. 15, 1943, box 6, entry 47, RG 107; Robert Hirano to Mr. and Mrs. Takeo Hirano, May 16, 1943, quoted in Military Intelligence Division memo, May 25, 1943, box 87, entry 26e, RG 159.

24. Courtney H. Hodges to John J. McCloy, March 22, 1943, box 47, entry 183, RG 107; S. L. A. Marshall to Scobey, May 21, 1943, box 17, entry 183, RG 107; Joseph S. Dougherty to Inspector General, memo, June 19, 1943, box 87, entry 26e, RG 159. On the "honorary white" concept, see Mia Tuan, *Forever Foreigners or Honorary Whites? The Asian Ethnic Experience Today* (New Brunswick, NJ: Rutgers University Press, 1998).

25. Yoshiro Matsuhara, interview by [Steven Wasserman?], HOHA, Apr. 30, 2005, video, tape 3, 24:30, http://www.goforbroke.org/learn/archives/oral_histories_ videos.php?clip=56003; Lawrence Mori, interview by [Richard Hawkins?], HOHA, Aug. 5, 2001, video, tape 3, 18:21, http://www.goforbroke.org/learn/archives/ oral_histories_videos.php?clip=19001.

26. F. B. Mallon to Commanding General, Seventh Corps Area, March 20, 1942, box 147, entry 360, RG 407. See also Jason Morgan Ward, "'No Jap Crow': Japanese Americans Encounter the World War II South," *Journal of Southern History* 73 (February 2007): 75–105.

27. See, for example, John J. McCloy to General McNair, September 23, 1943, box 22, entry 180, RG 107; L. J. McNair to Assistant Secretary of War, memo, September

25, 1943, box 22, entry 180, RG 107; John J. McCloy to General McNarney, memo, October 2, 1943, box 445, entry 43A, RG 165.

28. James P. Dale, Memorandum for the Officer in Charge, July 8, 1943, box 22, entry 180, RG 107; "Morale of Japanese Hawaiian Soldiers," August 12, 1943, 6, box 23, entry 180, RG 107.

29. H. Isonaga to Phyllis Tam, May 2, 1943, box 87, entry 26e, RG 159.

30. James P. Dale, Memorandum for the Officer in Charge, July 8, 1943, box 22, entry 180, RG 107.

31. See, for example, John B. Terry to William P. Scobey, memo, c. Aug. 26, 1943, box 48, entry 183, RG 107; Mail Service Section, "Correspondence of the 100th Infantry Battalion," c. May 1943, box 87, entry 26e, RG 159; War Department, M.I.D., Headquarters Eighth Service Command, Army Service Forces, Office of Director of Intelligence Division, "Subject: Japanese Hawaiian Volunteer at Camp Shelby," May 14, 1943, box 87, entry 26e, RG 159.

32. Dave Gutierrez, *Patriots from the Barrio: The Story of Company E, 141st Infantry: The Only All Mexican American Army Unit in World War II* (Yardley, PA: Westholme, 2018), 60.

33. Gutierrez, *Patriots from the Barrio*, 31.

34. Manuel Buaken, "Life in the Armed Forces," *New Republic*, Aug. 30, 1943, 279–280.

35. Daniel Inouye, "written interview" by Brooke Barnhill, Feb. 1997, at http://ba-ez.org/educatn/LC/OralHist/inouye.htm (accessed Mar. 15, 2019).

36. See, for example, Buaken, "Life in the Armed Forces"; Pvt. Chew C. Yuen to Commander in Chief, US Army, Nov. 24, 1942, transcribed letter in Adjutant General's Office, Record of Communication Received, box 1069, entry 363, RG 407; Mauro Garcia to Henry Wallace, July 6, 1943, box 1067, entry 363, RG 407; "Notes on Puerto Ricans and Puerto Rican Troops," n.d. but c. Oct. 1943, box 93, entry 26a, RG 159.

37. Larry Mizuno to John M. Hall, Nov. 23, 1943, box 47, entry 183, RG 107; William P. Scobey to Colonel Booth, Feb. 20, 1943, box 22, entry 180, RG 107.

38. John J. McCloy to General McNair, Sept. 23, 1943, box 22, entry 180, RG 107.

39. Henry L. Stimson to President Roosevelt, draft letter, n.d., box 147, entry 360, RG 407.

40. Owen Lattimore to R. T. McDonnell, June 1, 1943, box 381, entry 47, RG 319. On the Mexican state's involvement, see, for example, materials related to incident in Lubbock, Texas, in March 1944, in folder "Adjutant General 291.21 (Sept 1, 1944–Sept. 30, 1944)," box 1508, entry 360a, RG 407. For a small sample of scholarship about foreign governments pressing for civil rights gains in the wartime United States, see Karen J. Leong, "Foreign Policy, National Identity, and Citizenship: The Roosevelt White House and the Expediency of Repeal," *Journal of American Ethnic History* 22 (Summer 2003): 3–30; Thomas A. Guglielmo, "Fighting for Caucasian Rights: Mexicans, Mexican Americans, and the Transnational Struggle for Civil Rights in World War II Texas," *JAH* 92 (Mar. 2006): 1212–1237.

41. See "Japanese-Inspired Agitation among the American Negroes," attached to George V. Strong to Assistant Secretary of War [McCloy], memo, July 13, 1943, box 15, entry 180, RG 107; "Japanese Racial Agitation among American Negroes," n.d., box 472, entry 418, RG 165. For a sample of secondary sources that have looked at the real and imagined connections between Japan and African Americans, see Takashi Fujitani, *Race for Empire: Koreans as Japanese and Japanese as Americans during World War II* (Berkeley: University of California Press, 2011), 83–96; Ernest V. Allen, "When Japan Was 'Champion of the Darker Races': Satokata Takahishi

and the Flowering of Black Messianic Nationalism," *Black Scholar* 24 (Winter 1994): 23–46; Marc Gallicchio, *The African American Encounter with Japan and China: Black Internationalism in Asia, 1895–1945* (Chapel Hill: University of North Carolina Press, 2000); George Lipsitz, *The Possessive Investment in Whiteness: How White People Profit from Identity Politics* (Philadelphia: Temple University Press, 1998), chap. 9; Reginald Kearney, *African American Views of the Japanese: Solidarity or Sedition?* (Albany: State University of New York Press, 1998).

42. Joseph S. Dougherty to Inspector General, memo, June 19, 1943, box 87, entry 26e, RG 159. Not all military authorities were concerned about the possibility of "Negro"-Nisei alliances. Some simply noted African Americans' "friendly interest in Japanese Americans" without expressing any fear about the former's ulterior motives. See S. L. A. Marshall to Colonel Scobey, memo, April 8, 1943, box 48, entry 183, RG 107. Others feared increased agitation among African Americans if Japanese Americans were not similarly segregated. See Allen W. Gullion to Assistant Chief of Staff, G-2, Nov. 2, 1943, box 445, entry 43A, RG 165.

43. Doroteo V. Vité, "Filipinos Stand Loyal," letter to editor, *NYT*, Dec. 14, 1941, E9; Wu, *Color of Success*, 66.

44. Buaken, "Life in the Armed Forces," 279.

45. C. W. Pence to Colonel William P. Scobey, May 20, 1943, box 48, entry 183, RG 107; John Lansdale Jr. to Assistant Secretary of War, memo, Oct. 15, 1943, box 6, entry 47, RG 107.

46. Masaoka, *They Call Me Moses Masaoka*, 143; William Theodore Schmidt, "The Impact of Camp Shelby Mobilization on Hattiesburg, Mississippi" (PhD diss., University of Southern Mississippi, 1972), 100–101.

47. Masaoka, *They Call Me Moses Masaoka*, 143; Robert F. Jefferson, *Fighting for Hope: African American Troops of the 93rd Infantry Division in World War II and Postwar America* (Baltimore: Johns Hopkins University Press, 2008), 129.

48. Thomas D. Murphy, *Ambassadors in Arms: The Story of Hawaii's 100th Battalion* (Honolulu: University of Hawaii Press, 1954), 81–82. On Anniston, see George Aki, "My 30 Months (1944–1946)," typescript memoir, VHP, https://memory.loc. gov/diglib/vhp/story/loc.natlib.afc2001001.11135/pageturner?ID=pm0001001.

49. Mail Service Section, "Correspondence of the 100th Infantry Battalion," c. May 1943, box 87, entry 26e, RG 159; James P. Dale, Memorandum for the Officer in Charge, July 8, 1943, box 23, entry 180, RG 107.

50. L. A. Hummell to District Commander, District No. 1, Eighth Service Command, memo, July 15, 1943, box 1068, entry 363, RG 107.

51. Harry Duplessis, interview by Mary Penick Motley, in *The Invisible Soldier: The Experience of the Black Soldier, World War II*, ed. Mary Penick Motley (Detroit: Wayne State University Press, 1975), 328; Ruben Ali Flores, "Edward Lopez Prado," n.d., VOHP, https://voces.lib.utexas.edu/collections/stories/edward-lopez-prado.

52. "Report of the Investigation Relative to Alleged Segregation of Latin Americans at the West Texas Recruiting and Induction Station, Lubbock, Texas," Aug. 8, 1944, box 1508, entry 360a, RG 407.

53. Howard, *Concentration Camps*, 138. See also Kathryn Close, "'An Ordinary American,'" *Survey Graphic*, Feb. 1945, 52; and James C. McNaughton, *Nisei Linguists: Japanese Americans in the Military Intelligence Service during World War II* (Washington, DC: GPO, 2006), 113.

54. Meghan K. Winchell, *Good Girls, Good Food, Good Fun: The Story of USO Hostesses during World War II* (Chapel Hill: University of North Carolina Press, 2008), 65; K. Scott Wong, *Americans First: Chinese Americans and the Second World War*

(Cambridge, MA: Harvard University Press, 2002), 174; Howard, *Concentration Camps*, 141.

55. E. J. Will to E. H. Craven, memo, May 11, 1943, box 1067, entry 363, RG 407; and S. B. Buckner Jr. to Adjutant General, memo, June 23, 1943, box 1067, entry 363, RG 407.

56. Wong, *Americans First*, 151; Office of Censorship, District Postal Censor, Honolulu, T.H., General Information Summary, July 15, 1943–July 31, 1943, 17, box 12, ROC.

57. James M. McCaffrey, *Going for Broke: Japanese American Soldiers in the War against Nazi Germany* (Norman: University of Oklahoma Press, 2013), 177; Army Service Forces, Office of the Chief of Transportation, Intelligence and Security, Nov. 14, 1945, box 264, entry 189, RG 107.

58. Quinsaat, "An Exercise on How to Join the Navy"; Gavilan, "Of 'Mates' and Men."

59. Jacques E. Levy, *Cesar Chavez: Autobiography of La Causa* (New York: Norton, 1975), 84. On Mexican Americans being restricted to jobs as deckhands and painters, see Kent Miller, "Military Honors Planned for Cesar Chavez," *Navy Times*, Apr. 19, 2015, https://www.navytimes.com/news/your-navy/2015/04/19/military-honors-planned-for-cesar-chavez/.

60. McCaffrey, *Going for Broke*, 36–37; McNaughton, *Nisei Linguists*, 55.

61. Samuel A. Stouffer et al., *The American Soldier: Adjustment during Army Life* (Princeton, NJ: Princeton University Press, 1949), 1:501–502; Alvan C. Gillem et al., "Policy for the Utilization of Negro Manpower in the Post-War Army," Nov. 1945, 7, box 442, entry 43, RG 165.

62. Owen Lattimore to R. T. McDonnell, June 1, 1943, box 381, entry 47, RG 319. On the supposedly lost application, see folder "Ho, George Ping," box 92, entry 26e, RG 159; for "too much of an accent," see Gutierrez, *Patriots from the Barrio*, 34; on minor infractions, see Lee and Diaz, "'I Was the One Percenter,'" 57.

63. On the Puerto Rican exception to this rule, see the officer corps of the Sixty-Fifth Infantry Regiment: Louis Büttner to David B. Falk, memo, Feb. 16, 1944, box 93, entry 26e, RG 159.

64. Mail Service Section, "Correspondence of the 100th Infantry Battalion," c. May 1943, box 87, entry 26e, RG 159. On the 100th's original officer complement, see Fujitani, *Race for Empire*, 207.

65. I. H. Edwards to Commanding General, Army Ground Forces, memo, Jan. 12, 1943, box 1717, entry 480, RG 389; and D. T. Sapp to Commanding Generals, American Ground Forces, Third Army, Seventh and Eighth Service Commands, restricted memo, Jan. 2, 1943, box 1717, entry 480, RG 389.

66. Army Personnel of Japanese Ancestry by Month of Enlistment and Induction, Summary, XTM-23, box 2166, entry 389, RG 407. See also McNaughton, *Nisei Linguists*, 130, 147; Tamotsu Shibutani, *The Derelicts of Company K: A Sociological Study of Demoralization* (Berkeley: University of California Press, 1978), 62; M. W. Pettigrew to McCloy, memo, Nov. 17, 1942, box 147, entry 360, RG 407.

67. Shibutani, *The Derelicts of Company K*, 250, 247, 127.

68. S. Kirson Weinberg, "Problems of Adjustment in Army Units," *AJS* 50 (Jan. 1945): 277; Adjutant General's Office to Commanding Officer, Fort Devens, Mass., June 27, 1942, box 1077, entry 363, RG 407.

69. Cameron County Local Board No. 1, Brownsville, Texas, to State Director of Selective Service, memo, July 26, 1943, box 529, entry 292a, RG 18; Jose Alvarado Garcia, interview by Carol Apt, Nov. 16, 2012, video, 54:35, VHP, http://stream.media.loc.gov/vhp/video/afc2001001_087312_mv0001001_640x480_

800.mp4; Daniel L. Schorr, "'Reconverting' Mexican Americans," *New Republic*, Sept. 30, 1946, 412.

70. Quoted in Moore, *GI Jews*, 80. On the "Chief" nickname, see Townsend, *World War II and the American Indian*, 140; Bernstein, *American Indians and World War II*, 40.

71. Richard Frank, interview by Roselyn Darby, part 1, audio, 6:17, VHP, http://stream.media.loc.gov/vhp/audio/afc2001001_011749_sr0001001.mp3.

72. For "damn Chinks," see Ralph G. Martin, *Boy from Nebraska: The Story of Ben Kuroki* (New York: Harper, 1946), 51. On the various epithets directed at Japanese Americans, see Robert Hirano to Mr. and Mrs. Takeo Hirano, May 16, 1943, quoted in Military Intelligence Division memo, May 25, 1943, box 87, entry 26e, RG 159; John J. McCloy to Eleanor Roosevelt, May 31, 1943, box WD1, JJMP; Jeffrey T. Yamashita, "Becoming 'Hawaiian': A Relational Racialization of Japanese American Soldiers from Hawaii during World War II in the U.S. South," in *Relational Formations of Race: Theory, Method, Practice*, ed. Natalia Molina, Daniel Martinez HoSang, and Ramón A. Gutiérrez (Berkeley: University of California Press, 2019), 195.

73. On the Zoot Suit Riots, see Edward J. Escobar, *Race, Police, and the Making of a Political Identity: Mexican Americans and the Los Angeles Police Department, 1900–1945* (Berkeley: University of California Press, 1999); Luis Alvarez, *The Power of the Zoot: Youth Culture and Resistance during World War II* (Berkeley: University of California Press, 2009); Eduardo Obregón Pagán, *Murder at the Sleepy Lagoon: Zoot Suits, Race, and Riot in Wartime L.A.* (Chapel Hill: University of North Carolina Press, 2003); Catherine S. Ramirez, *The Woman in the Zoot: Gender, Nationalism, and the Cultural Politics of Memory* (Durham, NC: Duke University Press, 2009); Elizabeth R. Escobedo, *From Coveralls to Zoot Suits: The Lives of Mexican American Women on the World War II Home Front* (Chapel Hill: University of North Carolina Press, 2013).

74. Testimony of Sergeant John Gloria, Taken at Army Air Base, Lincoln, Neb., Sept. 2, 1943, box 93, entry 26e, RG 159; Corina Kellam, "Ernest George Gonzalez," c. Dec. 18, 2000, VOHP, https://voces.lib.utexas.edu/collections/stories/ernest-george-gonzalez.

75. John J. McCloy to General McNair, Sept. 23, 1943, box 22, entry 180, RG 107. For evidence of fights in reports based on censored mail, see Office of Censorship, District Postal Censor, Honolulu, T.H., General Information Summary, Nov. 15, 1944–Nov. 30, 1944, 15, box 12, ROC.

76. *Japanese Eyes . . . American Heart: Personal Reflections of Hawaii's World War II Nisei Soldiers* (Honolulu: Tendai Educational Foundation, 1998), 61.

77. District Postal Censor, Honolulu, T.H., General Information Summary, Nov. 1, 1944–Nov. 15, 1944, 11, box 12, ROC.

78. John J. McCloy to Eleanor Roosevelt, May 31, 1943, box WD1, JJMP.

79. Cordell Hull to Bryon Price, Jan. 8, 1942, box 3804, file 811.4016/318A, central decimal file, 1940–1944, RG 59.

80. Murphy, *Ambassadors in Arms*, 91; Aki, "My 30 Months (1944–1946)," 2.

81. Quoted in Shirley Castelnuovo, *Soldiers of Conscience: Japanese American Military Resisters in World War II* (Lincoln: University of Nebraska Press, 2010), 64.

82. Harry B. Farr to Commanding General, memo, July 23, 1943, box 47, entry 183, RG 107; "Japanese American Combat Team Gets Special Insignia," *PCIT*, Aug. 28, 1943, 1.

83. John J. McCloy to Colonel [Pence], Sept. 5, 1943, box 47, entry 183, RG 107. McCloy's use of the term "Japanese" above also drew a similar distinction.

84. Wong, *Americans First*, 164–165.

85. H. B. Lewis to Commanding General, Northwest Sector, et al., memo, Jan. 22, 1942, box 147, entry 360a, RG 407; E. S. Adams to Commanding Generals, memo, Jan. 23, 1942, box 147, entry 360a, RG 407.

86. James E. Wharton to Assistant Chief of Staff, G-1, memo, Mar. 28, 1942, box 147, entry 360a, RG 407.

87. H. P. Stewart to Commanding General, IX Corps, memo, Oct. 2, 1943, box 280, entry 55, RG 337. See also Joseph S. Dougherty to Inspector General, memo, June 19, 1943, box 87, entry 26e, RG 159; McNaughton, *Nisei Linguists*, 114; Castelnuovo, *Soldiers of Conscience*, 23–32; Bill Hosokawa, *Nisei: The Quiet Americans* (1969; Niwot: University Press of Colorado, 1992), 401.

88. W. H. Lawrence, "President Gets Big Lift Visiting Training Camps," *NYT*, Apr. 25, 1943, E8; "Quiet Easter at Fort Riley," *NYT*, Apr. 30, 1943, 7.

89. Unknown to unknown, Apr. 25, 1943, box 87, entry 26e, RG 159. See also Joseph S. Dougherty to Inspector General, memo, June 19, 1943, box 87, entry 26e, RG 159; Smith W. Brookhart to Inspector General, memo, July 28, 1943, ibid.; McCloy to McNair, Sept. 23, 1943, box 22, entry 180, RG 107.

90. Unknown to unknown, Apr. 25, 1943, box 87, entry 26e, RG 159.

91. Bruscino, *A Nation Forged in War*, 83; Moore, *GI Jews*, 81. On the discrimination American Jewish GIs faced, see Vito Marcantonio to Henry L. Stimson, Jan. 20, 1944, box 1065, entry 363, RG 407; Jacob Fish to War Department, July 11, 1943, box 1067, entry 363, RG 407; Betty Sandler to War Department, Apr. 25, 1943, box 1068, entry 363, RG 407.

92. Bruno Bettelheim and Morris Janowitz, *Social Change and Prejudice Including Dynamics of Prejudice* (London: Free Press, 1964), 246.

93. James P. Dale, Memorandum for the Officer in Charge, July 8, 1943, box 23, entry 180, RG 107.

94. Aragon, "'A General Separation,'" 513.

95. Quinsaat, "An Exercise on How to Join the Navy," 104. On "infrapolitics," de-fined as "low-profile forms of resistance that dare not speak in their own name," see James C. Scott, *Domination and the Arts of Resistance: Hidden Transcripts* (New Haven, CT: Yale University Press, 1990), esp. 19.

96. Castelnuovo, *Soldiers of Conscience*, 65.

97. See Shibutani, *The Derelicts of Company K*, 140; Levy, *Cesar Chavez*, 85.

98. "U.S. Japs Refuse Army Discipline," *Baltimore Sun*, Mar. 23, 1943, 2; Duus, *Unlikely Liberators*, 152–153; Castelnuovo, *Soldiers of Conscience*, 47; "Army Disrespect Jap-American Soldier Raps," *Salt Lake Telegram*, Apr. 14, 1944, 2.

99. Murphy, *Ambassadors in Arms*, 78; McCaffrey, *Going for Broke*, 177.

100. T. Ohashi to N. Ohashi, Nov. 21, 1944, transcribed by Intelligence Division, box 16, entry 47, RG 107.

101. On social boundaries in prewar Hawaii, see Moon-Kie Jung, *Reworking Race: The Making of Hawaii's Interracial Labor Movement* (New York: Columbia University Press, 2006), 55–105.

102. Mail Service Section, "Correspondence of the 100th Infantry Battalion," c. May 1943, 2–3, box 87, entry 26e, RG 159.

103. James P. Dale, Memorandum for the Officer in Charge, July 8, 1943, box 23, entry 180, RG 107; Lathe B. Row to Inspector General, Sept. 17, 1943, box 1510, entry 360a, RG 407.

104. H. Isonaga to Phyllis Tam, May 2, 1943, box 87, entry 26e, RG 159.

105. James P. Dale, Memorandum for the Officer in Charge, July 8, 1943, box 23, entry 180, RG 107.
106. See, for example, James P. Dale to PIO consolidated report, June 11, 1943, box 22, entry 180, RG 107; Confidential "Intermingling of Race" report, June 26, 1943, box 380, entry 47, RG 319; Minoru Masuda, *Letters from the 442nd: The World War II Correspondence of a Japanese American Medic*, ed. Hana Masuda and Dianne Bridgman (Seattle: University of Washington Press, 2008), 16; Duus, *Unlikely Liberators*, 74; Murphy, *Ambassadors in Arms*, 94; Ward, " 'No Jap Crow,' " 96–97; Arvarh E. Strickland, "Remembering Hattiesburg: Growing Up Black in Mississippi," in *Remaking Dixie: The Impact of World War II on the American South*, ed. Neil R. McMillen (Jackson: University Press of Mississippi, 1997), 156.
107. Mike N. Tokunaga, interview by Hawaii Nikkei History Editorial Board, n.d., in *Japanese Eyes . . . American Heart*, 373; Confidential "Intermingling of Race" report, June 26, 1943, box 380, entry 47, RG 319.
108. George C. Marshall to Henry L. Stimson, memo, Dec. 1, 1941, box 10, entry 99, RG 107.
109. F. B. Mallon to Commanding General, Seventh Corps Area, Mar. 20, 1942, box 147, entry 360, RG 407; E. L. Kanwit, L. L. Foster, and W. C. Leland to Truman K. Gibson, memo, June 14, 1943, box 186, entry 188, RG 107.
110. Confidential "Intermingling of Race" report, June 26, 1943, box 380, entry 47, RG 319. On this point, see also Allison Varzally, *Making a Non-White America: Californians Coloring outside Ethnic Lines, 1925–1955* (Berkeley: University of California Press, 2008), 158–182.
111. George S. Messersmith to Secretary of State, memo, May 26, 1943, box 3805, file 811.4016/542, central decimal file, 1940–1944, RG 59; and Stephen E. Aguirre to Secretary of State, memo, May 18, 1943, box 3805, file 811.4016/536, central decimal file, 1940–1944, RG 59; on Chunking, see, for example, W. E. Bennett to Commanding General, Advance Section #3, Nov. 30, 1944, box 57, Adjutant General, General Correspondence, RG 493.

CHAPTER 8
1. "London Dailies Rave over Soldier-Choir," *BAA*, Oct. 16, 1943, 8.
2. Roland Hayes to Eleanor Roosevelt, Nov. 8, 1943, box 32, AGS.
3. Eleanor Roosevelt to George C. Marshall, Nov. 23, 1944, box 32, AGS; Jacob L. Devers to Eleanor Roosevelt, Dec. 22, 1943, box 32, AGS. The Devers quotation is a textbook example of what sociologist Moon-Kie Jung calls "symbolic perversity": "a knowing-unknowing" about "the suffering of . . . racial others," which results in a "depraved indifference to racial inequalities—depraved for its knowingness but indifferent in usually unknowing, unreflexive ways." See Moon-Kie Jung, *Beneath the Surface of White Supremacy: Denaturalizing U.S. Racisms Past and Present* (Stanford, CA: Stanford University Press, 2015), 143.
4. Adriane Lentz-Smith, *Freedom Struggles: African Americans and World War I* (Cambridge, MA: Harvard University Press, 2009), 131. On African American troops' overseas numbers, see Alvan C. Gillem et al., "Policy for the Utilization of Negro Manpower in the Post-War Army," Nov. 1945, 17, box 442, entry 43, RG 165.
5. David Brion Davis, "Re-Examining the Problem of Slavery in Western Culture," *Proceedings of the American Antiquarian Society* 118 (2009): 247–248. Troop transports, it should be emphasized, were seldom comfortable for any enlisted personnel.

6. Charles H. Robinson to Commander Quigley, Mar. 8, 1945, box II:B196, NAACPR; Colonel Howard Queen, interview by Lawrence D. Reddick, May 7, 1946, box 1, LDR. See also "Affidavit from Paul Belcher and Wilson Belcher," Oct. 28, 1943, box II:B196, NAACPR; Timuel Black, interview by Studs Terkel, in *"The Good War": An Oral History of World War II*, ed. Studs Terkel (New York: New Press, 1984), 279; Corporal Charles Pitman, interview by Mary Penick Motley, in *The Invisible Soldier: The Experience of the Black Soldier, World War II*, ed. Mary Penick Motley (Detroit: Wayne State University Press, 1975), 120; Brendan I. Koerner, *Now the Hell Will Start: One Soldier's Flight from the Greatest Manhunt of World War II* (New York: Penguin, 2008), 78.

7. Graham Smith, *When Jim Crow Met John Bull: Black American Soldiers in World War II Britain* (New York: St. Martin's Press, 1987), 4; Neil A. Wynn, " 'Race War': Black American GIs and West Indians in Britain during the Second World War," *Immigrants & Minorities* 24 (Nov. 2006): 328.

8. Fred A. Meyer to Commanding General, Services of Supply, European Theatre of Operations, memo, July 16, 1942, box 148, entry 360, RG 407; C. R. Landon to Base Section Commanders and All Commanding Officers, memo, Aug. 7, 1942, box 53, AGS.

9. Anonymous letter attached to Truman K. Gibson Jr. to Assistant Secretary of War, memo, Dec. 17, 1943, box 204, entry 188, RG 107. Evidence abounds on the US military's export of black-white spatial segregation to wartime Britain. For a small sample, see Outgoing Message from Headquarters, Services of Supply, European Theatre of Operations, Nov. 29, 1943, box 32, AGS; Jacob L. Devers memo, Oct. 12, 1943, box 53, AGS; G. M. Alexander to Commanding General, memo, Oct. 6, 1943, box 53, AGS; C. R. Landon to Base Section Commanders and All Commanding Officers, memo, Aug. 7, 1942, box 53, AGS; Fred A. Meyer to Commanding General, memo, July 16, 1942, box 53, AGS; A. C. Kincaid to Commanding General, memo, n.d., box 34, entry 501, RG 165; W. E. Hart to Commanding General, memo, July 31, 1945, box 34, entry 501, RG 165; Claude W. White to Commanding General, memo, Aug. 22, 1945, box 34, entry 501, RG 165; "First Negro OCS in ETO Turns Out 14 Looeys," *Yank*, July 2, 1943, 5.

10. See interviews in Motley, *The Invisible Soldier*, 50–52, 78, 91, 163, 188, 338; TIRs in box 265, entry 189, RG 107; memos from commanding officers in box 34, entry 501, RG 165; army's reports on the black press in box 223, entry 188, RG 107; Clark N. Bailey to Commanding General, Chanor Base Section, memo, Feb. 6, 1946, box 3, European Theater of Operation Public Relations Section Decimal File, 1943–1945, RG 498; Walter White, *Rising Wind* (Garden City, NY: Doubleday, Doran, 1945), 71–75, 97.

11. TIR, no. 2790, July 17, 1945, box 265, entry 189, RG 107.

12. BPR, Dec. 18, 1944, box 223, entry 188, RG 107; BPR, July 3, 1945, box 223, entry 188, RG 107; TIR, no. 247, Apr. 28, 1945, box 265, entry 189, RG 107; Warren Bryant, interview by Mary Penick Motley, in Motley, *The Invisible Soldier*, 253. For "in-bounds" and "out-of-bounds" areas, see Alex Martin Jr. to Ted [Poston], Sept. 14, 1944, box 204, entry 188, RG 107; W. T. O'Reilly to Adjutant General, memo, Sept. 3, 1945, box 33, entry 501, RG 165; Anonymous letter to Dave E. Satterfield, May 26, 1945, box 1062, entry 363, RG 407.

13. War Department, "Racial Situation in the United States," Jan. 28, 1945, 16, box 261, entry 189, RG 107.

14. See, for example, C. R. Landon to Base Section Commanders and All Commanding Officers, memo, Aug. 7, 1942, box 53, AGS.

15. Captain Frank P. Dunnington, Confidential Report of Investigation, c. Oct. 13, 1942, box 53, AGS.

16. Clause R. Preston to Commanding Officer, memo, Sept. 25, 1943, box 204, entry 188, RG 107.

17. Truman K. Gibson to O. L. Nelson, memo, March 12, 1945, box 15, entry 180, RG 107.

18. TIR, no. T/PFI-750, Dec. 18, 1944, box 265, entry 189, RG 107.

19. Mark A. Huddle, *Roi Ottley's World War II: The Lost Diary of an African American Journalist* (Lawrence: University Press of Kansas, 2011), 60; Cowie Taylor, interview by Roland Schaedig, VHP, n.d., video, 34:35, http://stream.media.loc.gov/vhp/video/afc2001001_050909_mv0001001_640x480_800.mp4.

20. Gillem et al., "Policy for the Utilization of Negro Manpower in the Post-War Army," 17. As of July 31, 1945, there were 888 African American women stationed overseas out of a total of roughly 505,000 African American troops there.

21. As Allan Bérubé explained years ago, overseas service afforded combat troops new opportunities for "romantic and even sexual intimacies between men." See Allan Bérubé, *Coming Out under Fire: The History of Gay Men and Women in World War II* (New York: Free Press, 1990), 188. While finding some evidence of these intimacies among African American troops, none of it involved "interracial" relationships. See two anonymous brothers, interview by Lawrence D. Reddick, n.d., box 1, LDR; Herbert S. Ripley and Stewart Wolf, "Mental Illness among Negro Troops Overseas," *American Journal of Psychiatry* 103 (Jan. 1947): 510.

22. Smith, *When Jim Crow Met John Bull*, 106; Thomas E. Hachey, "Jim Crow with a British Accent: Attitudes of London Government Officials toward American Negro Soldiers in England during World War II," *JNH* 59 (Jan. 1974): 68.

23. Lucy Bland, "Interracial Relationships and the 'Brown Baby Question': Black GIs, White British Women, and Their Mixed-Race Offspring in World War II," *Journal of the History of Sexuality* 26 (Sept. 2017): 426. See also Mary Louise Roberts, "The Leroy Henry Case: Sexual Violence and Allied Relations in Great Britain, 1944," *Journal of the History of Sexuality* 26 (Sept. 2017), 416–417 Sonya O. Rose, *Which People's War: National Identity and Citizenship in Britain, 1939–1945* (Oxford: Oxford University Press, 2003), 75–79, 252–253; Wendy Webster, "'Fit to Fight, Fit to Mix': Sexual Patriotism in Second World War Britain," *Women's History Review* 22 (2013): 607–624.

24. Huddle, *Roi Ottley's World War II*, 97.

25. "Extracts on Negro Morale," March 1–15, 1944, box 43, Historical Division, Administrative File 1942–Jan. 1946, RG 498.

26. Military Attache Report, no. 579, Aug. 17, 1944, box 30, PNP; "Extracts on Negro Morale," March 1–March 15, 1944, Historical Division, Administrative File 1942–Jan. 1946, RG 498; TIR, no. 696, July 12, 1945, box 265, entry 189, RG 107. On black troops similarly taunting a notorious southern segregationist senator back home, see Jason Morgan Ward, *Defending White Democracy: The Making of a Segregationist Movement and the Remaking of Racial Politics, 1936–1965* (Chapel Hill: University of North Carolina Press, 2011), 49.

27. Military Attache Report, no. 579, Aug. 17, 1944, box 30, PNP.

28. Huddle, *Roi Ottley's World War II*, 44; Walter White to War Department, memo, Apr. 22, 1944, box 58, PNP.

29. Horace Evans, interview by Lawrence D. Reddick, n.d., box 1, LDR.

30. Alfred Duckett, interview by Studs Terkel, in Terkel, *"The Good War,"* 370–371.

31. TIR, no. 2790, July 16, 1945, box 265, entry 189, RG 107; O. N. Thompson to Adjutant General, memo, Aug. 7, 1945, box 33, entry 501, RG 165. For a similar point about the concomitant appearance of both white women and hardened color lines in a different context—the US West—see Susan Lee Johnson, *Roaring Camp: The Social World of the California Gold Rush* (New York: Norton, 2000), 276–313; Linda Gordon, *The Great Arizona Orphan Abduction* (Cambridge, MA: Harvard University Press, 1999), 183–184, 307.

32. James D. Givens to Headquarters, Strategic Air Forces in Europe, memo, Jan. 8, 1945, box 1063, entry 363, RG 407.

33. C. W. Ball to Commanding General, Eastern Base Section, memo, May 28, 1943, box 1379, AGH. See also Peggy Pascoe, *What Comes Naturally: Miscegenation Law and the Making of Race in America* (New York: Oxford University Press, 2009), 198; Renee C. Romano, *Race Mixing: Black-White Marriage in Postwar America* (Cambridge, MA: Harvard University Press, 2003), 22–24; Susan Zeiger, *Entangling Alliances: Foreign War Brides and American Soldiers in the Twentieth Century* (New York: New York University Press, 2010), 80–126; Jane Dailey, *White Fright: The Sexual Panic at the Heart of America's Racist History* (New York: Basic Books, 2020), 123–125.

34. Huddle, *Roi Ottley's World War II*, 178. For a slightly different translation, see Walter White to War Department, memo, Apr. 22, 1944, box 58, PNP.

35. "French Women Fired for Befriending Colored GI's," *BAA*, July 21, 1945, 6.

36. Bland, "Interracial Relationships," 426–430; Huddle, *Roi Ottley's World War II*, 98.

37. TIR, no. 696, July 12, 1945, box 265, entry 189, RG 107; Alfred Duckett, interview by Studs Terkel, in Terkel, *"The Good War,"* 370–371.

38. Robert F. Jefferson, *Fighting for Hope: African American Troops of the 93rd Infantry Division in World War II and Postwar America* (Baltimore: Johns Hopkins University Press, 2008), 199–200; Walter A. Luszki, *A Rape of Justice: MacArthur and the New Guinea Hangings* (Lanham, MD: Madison Books, 1991).

39. Quoted in BPR, May 30, 1945, box 223, entry 188, RG 107; "A Double Standard of Morals," *CD*, Apr. 28, 1945, 12. See also Mary Louise Roberts, *What Soldiers Do: Sex and the American GI in World War II France* (Chicago: University of Chicago Press, 2013), 195–254; Alice Kaplan, *The Interpreter* (Chicago: University of Chicago Press, 2005). It should be noted that rape was a chillingly pervasive fact of World War II, committed by all belligerents in all theaters. The point here is not that black troops were always innocent of these crimes, only that they faced rampant discrimination in the military justice system, especially when the alleged crimes involved sexual matters and white women.

40. Huddle, *Roi Ottley's World War II*, 103.

41. Lester B. Granger, interview by Lawrence D. Reddick, Apr. 4, 1946, box 1, LDR.

42. Quoted in Chris Dixon, *African Americans and the Pacific War, 1941–1945: Race, Nationality, and the Fight for Freedom* (Cambridge: Cambridge University Press, 2018), 107.

43. E. T. Hall Jr., "Race Prejudice and Negro-White Relations in the Army," *AJS* 52 (Mar. 1947): 405; "Negro Troops Can't Dance with Filipinos," *CD*, Mar. 10, 1945, 10.

44. Quoted in Dixon, *African Americans and the Pacific War*, 107.

45. TIR, no. 2558, June 29, 1945, box 265, entry 189, RG 107. On American men fighting for the women in their lives, see Robert B. Westbrook, "'I Want a Girl, Just Like the Girl That Married Harry James': American Women and the Problem of Political Obligation in World War II," *American Quarterly* 42 (Dec. 1990): 587–614.

46. Branch Office of the Judge Advocate General with the United States Forces European Theater, *History Branch Office of the Judge Advocate General with the United States Forces European Theater* (St. Cloud, France, 1945), 1:10, 13, chart 16. On the percentage of black troops overseas, see Strength Accounting & Reporting Office, "Strength of Negro Personnel in the US Army Forces," May 4, 1945, box 15, entry 180, RG 107.

47. L. K. Truscott Jr. to Commanding General, Mediterranean Theater of Operations USA, July 30, 1945, box 34, entry 501, RG 165; Luszki, *Rape of Justice*, 108.

48. Branch Office of the Judge Advocate General with the United States Forces European Theater, *History Branch Office of the Judge Advocate General with the United States Forces European Theater*, 1:9–10, chart 7; Luszki, *Rape of Justice*, 107.

49. On court-martial rules, see *A Manual for Courts-Martial US Army. Revised in the Office of the JAG of the Army and Published by the Direction of the President* (Washington, DC: GPO, 1953), 4, 6. On the problems in the system, see House, *Investigations of the National War Effort: Report of the Committee on Military Affairs*, 79th Cong., 2d sess., 1946.

50. J. Robert Lilly and J. Michael Thompson, "Executing US Soldiers in England, World War II," *British Journal of Criminology* 37 (Spring 1997): 269, 272, 282. On the military music quip, see Kaplan, *Interpreter*, 48.

51. French L. MacLean, *The Fifth Field: The Story of the 96 American Soldiers Sentenced to Death and Executed in Europe and North Africa in World War II* (Atglen, PA: Schiffer, 2013), 264; Kaplan, *Interpreter*, 195n76.

52. Roberts, "Leroy Henry Case," 408.

53. "Negro Officers Assigned to JAG in Paris," *Crisis*, July 1945, 206; Gillem et al., "Policy for the Utilization of Negro Manpower in the Post-War Army," 17.

54. "Who's Criminal, Anyhow?," *BAA*, Aug. 11, 1945, 2.

55. C. W. Ball to Commanding General, Eastern Base Section, memo, May 28, 1943, box 1379, AGH. For background on Ball, see "Corps of Engineers," *Army and Navy Journal* 59 (July 22, 1922): 1155. For a broader sense of anti-black criminalization in the early twentieth century, see Khalil Gibran Muhammad, *The Condemnation of Blackness: Race, Crime, and the Making of Modern America* (Cambridge, MA: Harvard University Press, 2011).

56. Elwood S. McKenney to Officer in Charge, memo, June 21, 1943, box 1379, AGH; Lawrence T. Smith to Commanding General, Eastern Base Section, memo, June 23, 1943, box 1379, AGH.

57. Truman K. Gibson to John J. McCloy, Nov. 24, 1944, box 213, entry 188, RG 107.

58. Quoted in Roberts, *What Soldiers Do*, 208.

59. Alvin (Tommy) Bridges, interview by Studs Terkel, in Terkel, *"The Good War,"* 390. On another example of anti-black racism in court-martial cases abroad, see Dailey, *White Fright*, 128.

60. Roberts, *What Soldiers Do*, 197.

61. Roberts, "Leroy Henry Case," 408.

62. Dixon, *African Americans and the Pacific War*, 120. The charges were so baseless, in fact, that even the US Army officials there contested them.

63. Roberts, *What Soldiers Do*, 197. See also Fabrice Virgili, preface to *Taken by Force: Rape and American GIs in Europe during World War II*, by J. Robert Lilly (New York: Palgrave MacMillan, 2007), xvii.

64. "Who's Criminal, Anyhow?," *BAA*, Aug. 11, 1945, 2.

65. War Department, Advisory Committee on Negro Troop Policies, "Recommendations Extracted from Walter White's Report," Mar. 11, 1944, box 215, entry 188, RG 107. See also "Court-Martial for Rape," *Crisis*, June 1944, 185.

66. TIR, no. 2790, July 16, 1945, box 265, entry 189, RG 107; Francis H. Oxx to Secretary of War, Board Member Report, July 19, 1945, box 34, entry 501, RG 165.

67. Nelson Peery, *Black Fire: The Making of an American Revolutionary* (New York: New Press, 1994), 278–279.

68. Owen L. Crecelius to Commanding General, European Theater of Operations, memo, Sept. 16, 1942, box 32, AGS. For more on this early conflict, see B. O. Davis to Commanding General, European Theater of Operations, memo, Oct. 25, 1942, box 32, AGS; Walter White to Henry L. Stimson, Oct. 2, 1942, box 1073, entry 363, RG 407; Smith, *When Jim Crow Met John Bull*, 139–140.

69. TIR, no. 2479, Apr. 24, 1945, box 265, entry 189, RG 107; Susie J. Thurman to Col. Ganoe, memo, May 2, 1944, box 43, Historical Division, Administrative File, 1942–Jan. 1946, RG 498.

70. Deputy Theater Provost Marshal to Deputy Theater Commander, memo, July 2, 1944, box 204, entry 188, RG 107; Associated Press clipping, n.d., box 27, PNP; Smith, *When Jim Crow Met John Bull*, 145–147; Wynn, "'Race War,'" 333–334.

71. "London Celebration Ends in Rioting," CD, Aug. 25, 1945, 1; BPR, Sept. 9, 1945, box 223, entry 188, RG 107.

72. Kenneth C. Jones to Commanding General, memo, Aug. 9, 1945, box 34, entry 501, RG 165; Max Johnson, "Soldiers Rioting in Europe," NYAN, Aug. 25, 1945, A1. On Germany, see David Brion Davis, "Reflections: Intellectual Trajectories: Why People Study What They Do," *Reviews in American History* 37 (Mar. 2009): 150–151.

73. Walter White, *A Man Called White: The Autobiography of Walter White* (New York: Viking, 1948), 292; W. T. O'Reilly to Adjutant General, memo, Sept. 3, 1945, box 33, entry 501, RG 165. See also Sean Brawley and Chris Dixon, "Jim Crow Downunder? African American Encounters with White Australia, 1942–1945," *Pacific Historical Review* 71 (Nov. 2002): 621; Kay Saunders and Helen Taylor, "The Reception of Black American Servicemen in Australia during World War II: The Resilience of 'White Australia,'" *Journal of Black Studies* 25 (Jan. 1995): 336–340; Dixon, *African Americans and the Pacific War*, 153–157.

74. Bernard C. Nalty, *Strength for the Fight: A History of Black Americans in the Military* (New York: Free Press, 1986), 196. See also White, *Man Called White*, 277–285; "Race Riot on Pacific Isle Laid to Marines," NYT, July 8, 1945, 3; Minutes of Lester B. Granger Press Conference, Nov. 1, 1945, in *Blacks in the Military: Essential Documents*, ed. Bernard C. Nalty and Morris J. MacGregor (Wilmington, DE: Scholarly Resources, 1981), 186; Lester B. Granger, interview by Lawrence D. Reddick, Apr. 4, 1946, box 1, LDR.

75. TIR, no. 247, Apr. 28, 1945, box 265, entry 189, RG 107; Jesus V. Merritt, "1063 Filipino Girls Become Brides of Colored Soldiers," BAA, Feb. 2, 1946, 2; Willie Lawton, interview by Mary Penick Motley, in Motley, *Invisible Soldier*, 101. See also Peery, *Black Fire*, 255–257; Hall Jr., "Race Prejudice and Negro-White Relations," 405–406.

76. Walter White, Memorandum to the President, Feb. 12, 1945, 11, box 27, PNP.

77. "Brother Couch" [William Couch Jr.], interview by Lawrence D. Reddick, Jan. 12, 1946, box 1, LDR; General MacArthur to General Marshall, Mar. 5, 1945, box 15, entry 180, RG 107.

78. Milton Bracker, "Negro Unit Proud of Gains in Italy," NYT, Nov. 1, 1944, 10. See also Thomas North, Memorandum for the Chief of Staff, Apr. 26, 1945, box 28, entry 109, RG 319. On Almond's views in the 1970s, see Dale E. Wilson, "Recipe

for Failure: Major General Edward M. Almond and Preparation of the U.S. 92d Infantry Division for Combat in World War II," *Journal of Military History* 56 (July 1992): 488.

79. Truman K. Gibson Jr. to O. L. Nelson, memo, Mar. 12, 1945, box 15, entry 180, RG 107; E. M. Almond, Approving Action of the Commanding General, 92d Infantry Division of Proceedings of Board of Review, July 2, 1945, box 28, entry 109, RG 319.

80. "First Negro OCS in ETO Turns Out 14 Looeys," *Yank*, July 2, 1943, 5; Minutes of Meeting of Advisory Committee on Negro Troop Policies, Apr. 26, 1944, box 35, entry 88, RG 107.

81. Truman K. Gibson Jr. to General Lee, memo, Mar. 31, 1945, box 32, AGS; Strength Accounting & Reporting Office, "Strength of Negro Personnel in the US Army Forces," May 4, 1945, box 15, entry 180, RG 107.

82. Gillem et al., "Policy for the Utilization of Negro Manpower in the Post-War Army," 17; "Say Army-Released Figures Unfair to Colored Nurses," *BAA*, Dec. 23, 1944, 13.

83. Gillem et al., "Policy for the Utilization of Negro Manpower in the Post-War Army," 18–19; Historical Section, Bureau of Naval Personnel, "The Negro in the Navy," typescript, 1947, NDL; Morris J. MacGregor Jr., *Integration of the Armed Forces, 1940–1965* (Washington, DC: GPO, 1981), 98. On the total number of ma-rine officers, see US Bureau of the Census, *Historical Statistics of the United States, Colonial Times to 1970*, part 2 (Washington, DC: GPO, 1976), 1141.

84. James V. Portly to Leslie M. Perry, n.d., c. Dec. 18, 1944, Box II:B196, NAACPR; Willie Lee Martell to Walter White, Nov. 30, 1944, Box II:B196, NAACPR.

85. Gillem et al., "Policy for the Utilization of Negro Manpower in the Post-War Army," 17.

86. Welton I. Taylor, with Karyn Taylor, *Two Steps from Glory: A World War II Liaison Pilot Confronts Jim Crow and the Enemy in the South Pacific* (Chicago: Winning Strategy Press, 2012), 265.

87. "The 'Work-But-Not-Fight' Policy," *CD*, Feb. 10, 1945, 10; Surveys Division, Bureau of Special Services, Office of War Information, "The Negroes' Role in the War," memorandum no. 59, July 8, 1943, 13, box 1799, entry 164, RG 44. On the wartime idealization of combat GIs, see James T. Sparrow, *Warfare State: World War II Americans and the Age of Big Government* (New York: Oxford University Press, 2011), 12. Allies at times placed black—or nonwhite—troops in the rear; indeed, the French had a name for it—*blanchiment*. See Rick Atkinson, *The Guns at Last Light: The War in Western Europe, 1944–1945* (New York: Picador, 2013), 363.

88. Taylor with Taylor, *Two Steps*, 265; *The World War II Rosters of the Dead (All Services)*, Department of the Army, Microfiche Reference no. 601–607, May 1, 1983, Joint POW/MIA Accounting Command; Congressional Research Service, "American War and Military Operations Casualties: Lists and Statistics," Sept. 24, 2019, https://fas.org/sgp/crs/natsec/RL32492.pdf.

89. Quoted in Jefferson, *Fighting for Hope*, 188. For other blacks making this point, see "The Negroes' Role in the War," 14; Samuel A. Stouffer et al., *The American Soldier: Adjustment during Army Life* (Princeton, NJ: Princeton University Press, 1949), 1:521–535; Christopher Paul Moore, *Fighting for America: Black Soldiers—The Unsung Heroes of World War II* (New York: One World, 2004), 101; Peery, *Black Fire*, 133–134. It should be noted that only a minority of all soldiers were eager for combat assignments. See Stouffer et al., *American Soldier*, 1:337.

90. See, for example, TIR, no. 795, Dec. 1, 1944, box 265, entry 189, RG 107; TIR, no. 2370, Mar. 30, 1945, box 265, entry 189, RG 107; TIR, no. 606, Apr. 10, 1945, box 265, entry 189, RG 107; Charles H. Robinson to Commander Quigley, Mar. 8, 1945, box II:B196, NAACPR; [E. W. Plank], "Leadership of Negro Troops," n.d., but c. July 15, 1943, box 204, entry 188, RG 107.
91. Jacob L. Devers, "Inter-National and Inter-Racial Relations," Oct. 12, 1943, box 53, AGS.
92. *The Fiftieth Seabees*, n.d., but c. July 1, 1945, 28, https://www.history.navy.mil/content/dam/museums/Seabee/Cruisebooks/wwiicruisebooks/ncb-cruisebooks/50th%20NCB.pdf; Walter White to War Department, memo, Apr. 22, 1944, box 58, PNP; TIR, no. 879, July 30, 1945, box 265, entry 189, RG 107; "Negroes at Manila: Navy Version," *CD*, Jan. 27, 1945, 10.
93. Walter White to Henry L. Stimson, May 13, 1942, box 1077, entry 363, RG 407; material attached to Truman K. Gibson Jr. to Assistant Secretary of War, Dec. 17, 1943, box 204, entry 188, RG 107; "Negro's War Record Gives Lie to Those Who Said He Didn't," newspaper clipping, n.d., scrapbook no. 77, AGC.
94. For "animal angle," see Huddle, *Roi Ottley's World War II*, 102. On World War I, see Chad L. Williams, *Torchbearers of Democracy: African American Soldiers in the World War I Era* (Chapel Hill: University of North Carolina Press, 2010), 162.
95. Material attached to Truman K. Gibson Jr. to Assistant Secretary of War, Dec. 17, 1943, box 204, entry 188, RG 107; Huddle, *Roi Ottley's World War II*, 52; Jonathan Welch to Howard Murphy, Dec. 10, 1943, in *Taps for a Jim Crow Army: Letters from Black Soldiers in World War II*, ed. Phillip McGuire (Lexington: University Press of Kentucky, 1983), 119; Huddle, *Roi Ottley's World War II*, 101; Reginald T. Brewster, interview by Lawrence D. Reddick, Dec. 27, 1945, box 1, LDR; Neil R. McMillen, "Fighting for What We Didn't Have: How Mississippi's Black Veterans Remember World War II," in *Remaking Dixie: The Impact of World War II on the American South*, ed. Neil R. McMillen (Jackson: University Press of Mississippi, 1997), 97. See also "Crackers Tell English Tan Yanks Have Tails," *BAA*, Apr. 8, 1944, 2; White, *Rising Wind*, 138–139; Charles A. Gates, interview by Studs Terkel, in Terkel, *"The Good War,"* 268; Timuel Black, interview by Studs Terkel, in Terkel, *"The Good War,"* 279; George W. Goodman, "The Englishman Meets the Negro," *Common Ground* 5 (Autumn 1944): 5–6; Linda Hervieux, *Forgotten: The Untold Story of D-Day's Black Heroes, At Home and at War* (New York: Harper, 2015), 171; Roberts, *What Soldiers Do*, 201.
96. Draft table of contents for Lawrence Reddick manuscript, "Brotherhood under Fire: The Negro and American Democracy in World War II," n.d., box 5, LDR; "French Women Fired for Befriending Colored GI's," *BAA*, July 21, 1945, 6; Alfred Duckett, Interview by Studs Terkel, in Terkel, *"The Good War,"* 371.
97. Stouffer et al., *The American Soldier*, 1:548; "Negro's War Record Gives Lie to Those Who Said He Didn't," newspaper clipping, n.d., scrapbook no. 77, AGC; Jefferson, *Fighting for Hope*, 215; Melton A. McLaurin, *The Marines of Montford Point: America's First Black Marines* (Chapel Hill: University of North Carolina Press, 2007), 103; Brawley and Dixon, "Jim Crow Downunder?," 608. See also William E. Artis, interview by Lawrence D. Reddick, Dec. 12, 1945, box 1, LDR; Leonard Stevens, interview by Lawrence D. Reddick, Dec. 27, 1945, box 1, LDR; "Tales of Tails," *CCP*, Sept. 15, 1945, 3; Gail William O'Brien, *The Color of the Law: Race, Violence, and Justice in the Post–World War II South* (Chapel Hill: University of North Carolina Press, 1999), 105; White, *A Man Called White*, 293; Dixon, *African Americans and the Pacific War*, 79.

98. J. S. Leonard, "Digest of War Department Policy Pertaining to Negro Military Personnel," Jan. 1, 1944, box 15, entry 88, RG 107.
99. Hall, "Race Prejudice and Negro-White Relations," 404. The quotation refers to the European theater but on the following page Hall says the same about the Pacific.
100. Huddle, *Roi Ottley's World War II*, 104; "Seaman Returns from England with Stories of Race Hatred," *People's Voice*, Sept. 26, 1942, 3; Raymond L. Johnson to Robert L. Williams, Dec. 10, 1944, LDR.
101. Christopher Thorne, "Britain and the Black G.I.s: Racial Issues and Anglo-American Relations in 1942," in *Race and US Foreign Policy from 1900 to World War II*, ed. Michael L. Krenn (New York: Garland, 1998), 342; Roberts, *What Soldiers Do*, 240.
102. Huddle, *Roi Ottley's World War II*, 44; Rose, *Which People's War?*, 251–263, esp. 259. See also Bland, "Interracial Relationships," 426–429; "United States Negro Troops in the United States," private and confidential memo, attached to F. A. Newsam to Undersecretary of State, Home Office, Oct. 30, 1942, box 32, no entry, RG 498; Smith, *When Jim Crow Met John Bull*, 39–95; Hachey, "Jim Crow with a British Accent"; Wynn, "'Race War.'"
103. Saunders and Taylor, "The Reception of Black American Servicemen in Australia"; Dixon, *African Americans and the Pacific War*, 150–151.
104. See, for example, Dwight D. Eisenhower to Chief of Staff, memo, Mar. 25, 1942, box 472, entry 418, RG 165; Arthur B. Welsh, "Memorandum for the Record," Feb. 12, 1943, box 200, entry 31 (ZI), RG 112; Thos. T. Handy to Chief of Staff, memo, Oct. 11, 1942, box 148, entry 360A, RG 407; George C. Marshall to John Dill, memo, Sept. 7, 1943, box 1510, entry 360A, RG 407; Ulysses Lee, *The Employment of Negro Troops* (Washington, DC: GPO, 1963), 428–441.
105. Francis N. Salvini to Commanding Officer, 472nd Quartermaster Group, Nov. 28, 1944, box 57, Adjutant General, General Correspondence, RG 493; Aaron S. Sadove to Commanding General, Services of Supply, USAF in Indian-Burma Theater, Nov. 30, 1944, box 57, Adjutant General, General Correspondence, RG 493. On the possibility of black GI–Indian wartime alliances, see Nico Slate, *Colored Cosmopolitanism: The Shared Struggle for Freedom in the United States and India* (Cambridge, MA: Harvard University Press, 2012), 151–160.
106. Report from Commanding General, U.S. Forces, India-Burma Theater, n.d., box 33, entry 501, RG 165. See also W. T. O'Reilly to Adjutant General, Sept. 3, 1945, box 33, entry 501, RG 165; A. C. Kincaid to Commanding General, U.S. Forces European Theater, n.d., box 34, entry 501, RG 165.
107. "Black and White," *Time*, Oct. 19, 1942, 32–33.
108. Huddle, *Roi Ottley's World War II*, 53.
109. TIR, no. 696, July 12, 1945, box 265, entry 189, RG 107. Different sources offer different estimates of the total number of "brown babies." See Paul R. Hawley, "Report on the Incidence of Negro Infants," Nov. 1, 1943, box 119, entry 31 (ZI), RG 112; Roi Ottley, interview by Lawrence D. Reddick, n.d., box 1, LDR; Wynn, "'Race War,'" 338; Smith, *When Jim Crow Met John Bull*, 208; Bland, "Interracial Relationships," 434.
110. Owen L. Crecelius to Commanding General, European Theater of Operations, memo, Sept. 16, 1942, box 32, AGS; Roi Ottley, "Report from England," in *Primer for White Folks*, ed. Bucklin Moon (Garden City, NY: Doubleday, 1946), 396; Edw. N. Wilson to Henry L. Stimson, July 7, 1944, box 1065, entry 363, RG 407.

111. Stouffer et al., *American Soldier*, 1:544. On some black people's desire to stay in Britain, see Joseph Julian, "Jim Crow Goes Abroad," *Nation*, Dec. 5, 1942, 612; Military Attache Report, no. 579, Aug. 17, 1944, box 30, PNP; Wilbur Young, interview by Lawrence D. Reddick, Aug. 9, 1946, box 1, LDR.

112. TIR, no. 1462, Jan. 10, 1945, box 265, entry 189, RG 107. On the signs, see Ottley, "Report from England," 399; White, *Rising Wind*, 12; Smith, *When Jim Crow Met John Bull*, 118; Wynn, " 'Race War,' " 333.

113. "Black and White," *Time*, Oct. 19, 1942, 32; *PC*, Sept. 19, 1942, transcribed in report attached to Lawrence M. C. Smith to Addison Walker, Sept. 28, 1942, box 1, entry 131-O, RG 80; "Speak Out, Mr. Roosevelt," *BAA*, Oct. 10, 1942, 4.

114. Huddle, *Roi Ottley's World War II*, 107; Hervieux, *Forgotten*, 189; Roberts, "Leroy Henry Case," 402, 412.

115. Smith, *When Jim Crow Met John Bull*, 118. See also M. B. Tower to American Ambassador Winant, Sept. 2, 1943, box 32, AGS; "The Trial of a Negro," *Tribune*, June 9, 1944, clipping, box 1065, entry 363, RG 407; "Can't Enter Certain Bars or Dance Halls," Sept. 26, 1942, clipping, box 1073, entry 363, RG 407; Ottley, "Report from England," 400–401.

116. "Negroes Find the British Draw Line Too, but Subtly," *Newsweek*, Nov. 5, 1945, 58–59; Smith, *When Jim Crow Met John Bull*, 95, 119, 128; S. L. Solon, "Because Their Skins [*sic*] Brown . . . ," *News Chronicle* (London), May 8, 1944, clipping, box 4945, file 811.4016, central decimal file 1940–1944, RG 59; "Cruz and Robinson," interview by Lawrence D. Reddick, Jan. 12, 1946, box 1, LDR.

117. John E. Pederson to Commanding General, U.S. Forces, European Theater, Aug. 7, 1945, box 34, entry 501, RG 165; Claude W. White to Commanding General, U.S. Forces, European Theater, Aug. 22, 1945, box 34, entry 501, RG 165; Reverend L. J. Kerr, interview by Lawrence D. Reddick, Mar. 29, 1946, box 1, LDR; Leonard Taylor, interview by Lawrence D. Reddick, Jan. 22, 1946, box 1, LDR; Frances Flats, interview by Lawrence D. Reddick, Mar. 25, 1946, box 1, LDR; George Orwell, "London Letter," *Partisan Review* 11 (Summer 1944): 282.

118. George Padmore, "Bristol Girls Riot as Tan Yanks Leave," *PC*, Sept. 1, 1945, 3. See also Reverend L. J. Kerr, interview by Lawrence D. Reddick, Mar. 29, 1946, box 1, LDR.

119. Fanrose Chargo to Fredi Washington, Jan. 20, 1945, box 3, LDR; Hal Foust, "Negro Soldiers in France Find No Race Barrier," *CT*, July 30, 1945, 5. On the rural northwest of France, see Roberts, *What Soldiers Do*, 244–247.

120. Foust, "Negro Soldiers in France"; John E. Pederson to Commanding General, U.S. Forces, European Theater, Aug. 7, 1945, box 34, entry 501, RG 165; Kenneth C. Jones to Commanding General, U.S. Forces, European Theater, Aug. 9, 1945, box 34, entry 501, RG 165.

121. John Scotzin, Hampton Roads Port of Embarkation, Report no. 771, Dec. 5, 1944, box 262, entry 189, RG 107; David Cason Jr., interview by Mary Penick Motley, in Motley, *The Invisible Soldier*, 271; E. J. Wells, interview by Mary Penick Motley, in Motley, *The Invisible Soldier*, 310. See also L. K. Truscott Jr. to Commanding General, Mediterranean Theater of Operations USA, July 30, 1945, box 34, entry 501, RG 165; Francis H. Oxx to Secretary of War, July 19, 1945, box 34, entry 501, RG 165; William E. Artis, interview by Lawrence D. Reddick, Dec. 12, 1945, box 1, LDR; Leonard Stevens, interview by Lawrence D. Reddick, Dec. 27, 1945, box 1, LDR.

122. Allan Morrison, "The Negro GI in Germany," *Stars and Stripes*, quoted in BPR, Sept. 19, 1945, box 223, entry 188, RG 107; Horace Evans, interview by Lawrence

D. Reddick, n.d., box 1, LDR; *Ebony* quoted in Maria Höhn, *GIs and Fräuleins: The German-American Encounter in 1950s West Germany* (Chapel Hill: University of North Carolina Press, 2002), 91.

123. John E. Pederson to Commanding General, U.S. Forces, European Theater, Aug. 7, 1945, box 34, entry 501, RG 165; Taylor, with Taylor, *Two Steps from Glory*, 224, 296.

124. J. M. Roamer, Notes on interview with Lt. Col. George H. Barrows, Aug. 26, 1944, box 9, Official File 4245g, FDRP. On Australia's settler colonialism, see Patrick Wolfe, *Traces of History: Elementary Structures of Race* (London: Verso, 2016), 31–60.

125. Brawley and Dixon, "Jim Crow Downunder?," 615, 616; Moore, *Fighting for America*, 64. See also Dixon, *African Americans and the Pacific War*, 157–161.

126. Goodman, "The Englishman Meets the Negro," 10; Michael Vinson Williams, *Medgar Evers: Mississippi Martyr* (Little Rock: University of Arkansas Press, 2011), 29.

127. Ollie Stewart, "Races Share Same Bottle," *BAA*, Aug. 7, 1943, 1.

128. "Army Mixed in Tough Spots," *BAA*, Oct. 2, 1943, 1; Unnamed article, dated Mar. 27, 1944, attached to Walter White to War Department, memo, Apr. 22, 1944, box 58, PNP; Roi Ottley, "There's No Race Problem in the Foxholes," *PM*, Jan. 1, 1945, 3–4; August Loeb, "In Italy," *Yank*, Feb. 23, 1945, 7. See also Robert Ferrell, interview by Lawrence D. Reddick, n.d., box 1, LDR. For "large slow target," see Rick Atkinson, *The Day of Battle: The War in Sicily and Italy, 1943–1944* (New York: Picador, 2007), 33.

129. Ottley, "There's No Race Problem in the Foxholes," 4; Woodson quoted in Hervieux, *Forgotten*, 213; Commanding General, Army Forces, European Theater of Operations to War Department, classified message, Aug. 9, 1944, box 15, entry 180, RG 107; Charles A. Gates, interview by Studs Terkel, in Terkel, *"The Good War,"* 268; Kinloch quoted in BPR, Dec. 18, 1944, box 223, entry 188, RG 107. On Kinloch, see Kevin Allen Leonard, *The Battle for Los Angeles: Racial Ideology and World War II* (Albuquerque: University of New Mexico Press, 2006), 320n62.

130. Sources disagree on the total number of black platoons: Gillem et al., "Policy for the Utilization of Negro Manpower in the Post-War Army," 11; Lee, *The Employment of Negro Troops*, 695; MacGregor Jr., *Integration of the Armed Forces*, 52.

131. Dwight D. Eisenhower to Bruce C. Clarke, May 29, 1967, in *Black Soldiers in World War II*, vol. 5 of *Blacks in the United States Armed Forces: Basic Documents*, ed. Morris J. MacGregor and Bernard C. Nalty (Wilmington, DE: Scholarly Resources, 1977), 512; Ralph Martin, "Negroes in Combat," *Yank*, Feb. 23, 1945, 6–7; Wilbur Young, interview by Lawrence D. Reddick, Aug. 9, 1946, box 1, LDR.

132. Research Branch, [Army] Information and Education Division, Headquarters, European Theater of Operations, "The Utilization of Negro Infantry Platoons in White Companies," Report no. E-118, June 1945, 10, box 57, Adjutant General, General Correspondence, RG 493. See also [Army] Information and Education Division, "Opinions about Negro Infantry Platoons in White Companies of 7 Divisions," Report no. B-157, July 3, 1945, box 212, entry 188, RG 107. For more on this experiment, see Gillem et al., "Policy for the Utilization of Negro Manpower in the Post-War Army," 10–13; Lee, *The Employment of Negro Troops*, 688–705; and David P. Colley, *Blood for Dignity: The Story of the First Integrated Combat Unit in the U.S. Army* (New York: St. Martin's Press, 2003).

133. Charles Dollard, interview by Lawrence D. Reddick, June 27, 1946, box 1, LDR.

134. Lee, *The Employment of Negro Troops*, 702.

135. Quoted in John P. Lewis, "Army Jim Crow," *PM*, July 1, 1943, 17; "Force Hears War Correspondent," *Wichita (KS) Negro Star*, Mar. 16, 1945, 1; Fletcher Martin, "Truck Driver Turns Gunner," *BAA*, Nov. 18, 1944, 1.

136. Quoted in BPR, Dec. 4, 1944, 5, box 223, entry 188, RG 107; Ollie Stewart, "Stewart in France," *BAA*, July 15, 1944, 1.

137. Samuel Fuller, interview by Mary Penick Motley, in Motley, *Invisible Soldier*, 215; Private Joseph Poscucci et al., letter to editor, *Yank*, July 28, 1944, 14; "Jim Crow Died . . . in a Mess Hall," *PC*, April 22, 1944, 7.

138. Quoted in BPR, weeks of May 5–May 19, 1945, box 223, entry 188, RG 107; Ripley and Wolf, "Mental Illness among Negro Troops Overseas," 510. White enlisted men expressed similar frustrations with their white officers. See Gerald F. Linderman, *The World within War: America's Combat Experience in World War II* (New York: Free Press, 1997), 209.

139. "Writing the Future in Foxholes," *CD*, Feb. 24, 1945, 10.

140. For the "changing same" concept, see LeRoi Jones (Amiri Baraka), *Black Music* (1968; New York: Akashic Books, 2010), 175–205; and Paul Gilroy, *The Black Atlantic: Modernity and Double Consciousness* (Cambridge, MA: Harvard University Press, 1993), xi, 106, 122.

141. TIR, no. 616, June 18, 1945, box 265, entry 189, RG 107; TIR, no. 828, June 26, 1945, box 265, entry 189, RG 107; quoted in BPR, July 3, 1945, box 223, entry 188, RG 107. For more on black soldiers' low morale, see Stouffer et al., *The American Soldier*, 1:507–550.

142. TIR, no. T/PFI-2440, July 5, 1945, box 265, entry 189, RG 107; TIR, no. 2051, Apr. 9, 1945, box 265, entry 189, RG 107.

143. On the problems with these studies, see Ellen Dwyer, "Psychiatry and Race during World War II," *Journal of the History of Medicine and Allied Sciences* 61 (Apr. 2006): 117–143; and two anonymous brothers, interview by Lawrence D. Reddick, n.d., box 1, LDR.

144. Ripley and Wolf, "Mental Illness among Negro Troops Overseas," 505–506; Eli Ginzberg et al., *Breakdown and Recovery*, vol. 2 of *The Ineffective Soldier: Lessons for Management and the Nation* (New York: Columbia University Press, 1959), 105–108.

145. Isaac McNatt, "I Was a Seabee," *Politics*, June 1944, 139–140. See also Isaac G. McNatt, Affidavit, Nov. 10, 1944, box II:B196, NAACPR; "Statement from 9 Seabees at NAACP Office on Oct. 25, 1943," Oct. 27, 1943, box II:B196, NAACPR; Affidavit from Paul Belcher and Wilson Belcher, Cuyahoga County, OH, Oct. 28, 1943, box II:B196, NAACPR.

146. See Walter White, Address to Wartime Conference, July 16, 1944, 17, box II:A28, NAACPR; Walter White, Memorandum to the President, Feb. 12, 1945, 10, box 27, PNP; "Brother Couch" [William Couch Jr.], interview by Lawrence D. Reddick, Feb. 20, 1946, box 1, LDR; TIR, no. 883, July 30, 1945, box 265, entry 189, RG 107; W. A. Mason Jr. to Sir, n.d., but c. Dec. 4, 1944, box II:B196, NAACPR; Taylor, with Taylor, *Two Steps from Glory*, 232; Dixon, *African Americans and the Pacific War*, 74–75.

147. On an increased sense of unity among black troops, see Winfred Lynn to Nancy Macdonald, June 20, 1944, box 30, series 1, DMP. On masculinity, see McMillen, "Fighting for What We Didn't Have," 100; BPR, June 11, 1945, box

223, entry 188, RG 107; Steve Estes, *I Am a Man! Race, Manhood, and the Civil Rights Movement* (Chapel Hill: University of North Carolina Press, 2005), 11; Peery, *Black Fire*, 271. That many black troops faced constant racist indignities and humiliations—as well as an overrepresentation in rear echelon positions—could also challenge their masculinity. See, for example, Ray Carter, interview by Mary Penick Motley in Motley, *The Invisible Soldier*, 110; Stouffer et al., *The American Soldier*, 2:131–135, 308–309.

148. Marjorie McKenzie, "Pursuit of Democracy," *PC*, Feb. 10, 1945, 7; McMillen, "Fighting for What We Didn't Have," 103. See also Frank James, *Capers of a Medic* (Bloomington, IN: AuthorHouse, 2007), 80.

149. Ollie Stewart, "Races Share Same Bottle," *BAA*, Aug. 7, 1943, 1; Peery, *Black Fire*, 247; TIR, no. 2051, Apr. 9, 1945, box 265, entry 189, RG 107. Servicemen of all backgrounds shared this growing sense of entitlement. See James Lee, "Sure, Mom, Your Soldier's Tough—But He's Alright," *WP*, June 3, 1945, B1–2.

150. "Statement from 9 Seabees at NAACP Office on Oct. 25, 1943," Oct. 27, 1943, box II:B195, NAACPR; Historical Section, Bureau of Naval Personnel, "Negro in the Navy," 78.

151. Lynn Committee to Abolish Segregation in the Armed Forces, Press Release, n.d., but c. Apr. 3, 1945, box 30, series 1, DMP. See also "NAACP, Vets Demand Probe," *BAA*, Mar. 10, 1945, 19; Isaac McNatt, "I Was a Seabee: Hate Practices in Navy Related by Seabee Discharged as 'Unfit' for Service," *BAA*, June 24, 1944, 5; McNatt, "I Was a Seabee"; and materials in folder 4, box II:B196, NAACPR. On McNatt's election to the Teaneck city council, see "McNatt Sets Precedent in Election to N.J. City Council," *BAA*, Dec. 17, 1966, 12.

152. "Forty-Three Soldiers AWOL," *BAA*, Aug. 23, 1941, 4; Military Attache Report, no. 579, Aug. 17, 1944, box 30, PNP; TIR, no. 2479, April 24, 1945, box 265, entry 189, RG 107; TIR, no. T/PFI-1974, May 24, 1945, box 265, entry 189, RG 107; TIR, no. 2558, June 29, 1945, box 265, entry 189, RG 107; TIR, no. 247, April 28, 1945, box 265, entry 189, RG 107; W. T. O'Reilly to Adjutant General, memo, Sept. 3, 1945, box 33, entry 501, RG 165.

153. On Oran, see Allan R. Anderson, interview by Lawrence D. Reddick, May 10, 1946, box 1, LDR. On Cherbourg, see Huddle, *Roi Ottley's War*, 130. On Manila, Duckett, interview by Studs Terkel, in Terkel, *"The Good War,"* 372.

154. See L. K. Truscott Jr. to Commanding General, Mediterranean Theater of Operations USA, July 30, 1945, box 34, entry 501, RG 165; A. C. Kincaid to Commanding General, memo, n.d., box 34, entry 501, RG 165.

155. Deputy Theater Provost Marshal to Deputy Theater Commander, Carrier Sheet to H.Q. ETOUSA, Sept. 20, 1944, box 204, entry 188, RG 107.

156. Transcript of Lynn Committee and Schomburg Collection Meeting on "Military Jimcrowism," Oct. 25, 1945, box 5, LDR.

157. Observations of Negro Personnel by Lt. Commander D. O. Van Ness, Nov. 28, 1944, box 381A, entry 47, RG 319.

158. L. K. Truscott Jr. to Commanding General, Mediterranean Theater of Operations USA, July 30, 1945, box 34, entry 501, RG 165.

159. J. S. Leonard, "Minutes of the Meeting of Advisory Committee on Negro Troop Policies," Apr. 26, 1944, box 35, entry 88, RG 107; Thomas North to Chief of Staff, memo, Apr. 26, 1945, box 28, entry 109, RG 319.

160. Roberts, "Leroy Henry Case."

161. "Jim Crow Died . . . in a Mess Hall," *PC*, Apr. 22, 1944, 7.

162. Franklin D. Roosevelt to Walter White, Mar. 19, 1945, box 173, President's Secretary's Files, FDRP. See also Jonathan Daniels, *White House Witness: 1942–1945* (Garden City, NY: Doubleday, 1975), 214–215.

163. "No Jim Crow on Homeward Voyage," *CD*, Aug. 18, 1945, 3. See also Warren J. Brunson to L. D. Reddick, July 6, 1946, box 1, LDR; Lawrence E. Davies, "Pacific States: New Concern Shown over Racial Issue on the Coast," *NYT*, Mar. 11, 1945, E6.

164. "White Face Passport to Come Home," *CD*, Dec. 15, 1945, 1; "Forrestal Order Rebukes Flattop Chief," *CD*, Dec. 22, 1945, 1.

165. Ottley, "There's No Race Problem in the Foxholes"; Winfred Lynn to Nancy Macdonald, May 11, 1944, box 30, series 1, DMP.

166. August Loeb, "In Italy," *Yank*, Feb. 23, 1945, 7; John H. Sherman, "Our Negro Soldiers," *New Republic*, Nov. 19, 1945, 678; "Writing the Future in Foxholes," *CD*, Feb. 24, 1945, 10.

167. TIR, report no. 360, Mar. 28, 1945, box 265, entry 189, RG 107.

168. Sidney R. Williams to Robert E. Bondy, July 27, 1944, box 1, Central File, 1935–1946, RG 200.

CHAPTER 9

1. For "glowing comradeship," see Grace E. Willis, "Soldier, Shake," *Asia and the Americas*, April 1945, 211.

2. Betty Burleigh Scudder, "The Slant of the Heart," *World Outlook*, April 1945, 137; Gene Casey, "G.I. Japyank," *Colliers*, Aug. 5, 1944, 41–43; Marjorie Avery, "All Hawaiians Jap-Yank Unit Wins GI Praise," *Detroit Free Press*, Mar. 14, 1945, 13; Sidney Carroll, "Purple Heart Battalion," *Coronet* 18 (May 1945): 6; "Japyank Doughboys Shellack Nazis in Italy," *New York Daily News*, April 9, 1945, C12; "'Vinegar Joe' Defends Jap American Servicemen," *Knoxville Journal*, Oct. 11, 1945, 16; "They're GI Pals—Two Nisei and Iowan," *Des Moines Tribune*, Nov. 9, 1944, 11.

3. Donald Culross Peattie, "Lo Takes the Warpath," *American Legion*, July 1943, 9, 30; Burnet Hershey, "Indians on the Warpath Again," *American Mercury*, Oct. 1944, 478. See also Ella Chouteau, "Red Men in Khaki," *Young People's Weekly*, Jan. 19, 1944, 5–6; Ella Chouteau, "Indian's Fame," *Young People's Weekly*, Mar. 18, 1945, 8–9.

4. Harry Franqui-Rivera, *Soldiers of the Nation: Military Service and Modern Puerto Rico, 1868–1952* (Lincoln: University of Nebraska Press, 2018), 148, 146; R.G. Tugwell to Abe Fortas, Oct. 13, 1944, box 35, entry 183, RG 107.

5. John Lardner, "A Reporter at Large: Those of the First Generation," *New Yorker*, Mar. 31, 1945, 55; Office of Censorship, District Postal Censor, Honolulu, T.H., General Information Summary, Dec. 15, 1944–Dec. 31, 1944, box 12, ROC.

6. Masayo Umezawa Duus, *Unlikely Liberators: The Men of the 100th and 442th* (Honolulu: University of Hawaii Press, 1987), 216, 219. For the casualty figures for the lost battalion rescue, see *Personal Justice Denied: Report of the Commission on Wartime Relocation and Internment of Civilians* (Washington, DC: GPO, 1982), 258; US House Committee of the Judiciary, *Providing for Equality under Naturalization and Immigration Laws: Hearings on H.R. 5004*, 80th Cong., 2d sess., 1948, 117; Takashi Fujitani, *Race for Empire: Koreans as Japanese and Japanese as Americans during World War II* (Berkeley: University of California Press, 2011), 208.

7. "Major Fukuda Given Command of the 100th Infantry Battalion," *PCIT*, Oct. 11, 1945, 2. See also Richard Borreca, "Sakae Takahashi, War Hero, Dies," *Honolulu Star-Bulletin*, April 18, 2001, A3.

8. Franklin Odo, *No Sword to Bury: Japanese Americans in Hawaii during World War II* (Philadelphia: Temple University Press, 2004), 237. See also James C. McNaughton, *Nisei Linguists: Japanese Americans in the Military Intelligence Service during World War II* (Washington, DC: GPO, 2006), 168, 294.

9. Clayton Bissell to Commanding General, Thirteenth Air Force, memo, Nov. 23, 1943, box 103, entry 294, RG 18. For the percentages of officers among Japanese American and white military personnel, see "Army Personnel of Japanese Ancestry by Month of Enlistment or Induction," summary, XTM-23, n.d., box 2166, entry 389, RG 407; and Samuel A. Stouffer et al., *The American Soldier: Adjustment during Army Life* (Princeton, NJ: Princeton University Press, 1949), 1:501.

10. Keith Little, interview by Ann Ramsey, July 19, 2004, VHP, transcript, https://memory.loc.gov/diglib/vhp-stories/loc.natlib.afc2001001.28922/transcript?ID=mv0001; Steven Rosales, "Soldados Razos: Chicano Politics, Identity, and Masculinity in the U.S. Military, 1940–1975" (PhD diss., University of California, Irvine, 2007), 65; Christopher Capozzola, *Bound by War: How the United States and the Philippines Built America's First Pacific Century* (New York: Basic Books, 2020), 179. As an exception to this point, Major General Clarence Tinker had Osage ancestry. See "General Tinker Went the Way He Wanted to Go, Friends Say," *Daily Oklahoman*, June 13, 1942, 5; Kenneth William Townsend, *World War II and the American Indian* (Albuquerque: University of New Mexico Press, 2000), 128.

11. Jere Bishop Franco, *Crossing the Pond: The Native American Effort in World War II* (Denton: University of North Texas Press, 1999), 164–165; William C. Meadows, *The Comanche Code Talkers of World War II* (Austin: University of Texas Press, 2003), 208.

12. "Notes on Puerto Ricans and Puerto Rican Troops," n.d., but c. Oct. 1943, box 93, entry 26a, RG 159.

13. Fred Kitada, interview by Darrel Kunitomi, HOHA, June 26, 2004, video, tape 2, 20:31, http://www.goforbroke.org/learn/archives/oral_histories_videos.php?clip=46103. Some Japanese Americans married Europeans. See Thomas D. Murphy, *Ambassadors in Arms: The Story of Hawaii's 100th Battalion* (Honolulu: University of Hawaii Press, 1954), 218.

14. For the quotation about segregation in Genoa, see BPR, weeks of May 5, 1945–May 19, 1945, 6, box 223, entry 188, RG 107. On the Livorno brothel, see Chester Tanaka, *Go for Broke: A Pictorial History of the Japanese American 100th Infantry Battalion and the 442d Regimental Combat Team* (Novato, CA: Presidio Press, 1982), 61.

15. Branch Office of the Judge Advocate General with the United States Forces European Theater, *History Branch Office of the Judge Advocate General with the United States Forces European Theater* (St. Cloud, France, 1945), 1:10, 559, 574, 581; Colonel French L. MacLean, *The Fifth Field: The Story of the 96 American Soldiers Sentenced to Death and Executed in Europe and North Africa in World War II* (Atglen, PA: Schiffer, 2013), 59–61, 111–113, 203–207, 228–229, 233–235. On the Pacific, see Walter A. Luszki, *A Rape of Justice: MacArthur and the New Guinea Hangings* (Lanham, MD: Madison Books, 1991), 173–175; "How He Made His Last Descent," *Smith's Weekly*, Oct. 12, 1945, 15.

16. Branch Office of the Judge Advocate General with the United States Forces European Theater, *History Branch Office of the Judge Advocate General*, 1:386–390.

17. Mary Louise Roberts, *What Soldiers Do: Sex and the American GI in World War II France* (Chicago: University of Chicago Press, 2013), 213. On the Inspector General's report, see MacLean, *Fifth Field*, 121.

18. Edward J. Escobar, *Race, Police, and the Making of a Political Identity: Mexican Americans and the Los Angeles Police Department, 1900–1945* (Berkeley: University of California Press, 1999), 10.

19. For "subhuman . . ." quotation, see John W. Dower, *War without Mercy: Race and Power in the Pacific War* (New York: Pantheon, 1986), 9. For the other characterizations, see E. J. Kahn, "It's a Small World, Isn't It? This Time Much Too Small for the Japs," *Yank*, Oct. 7, 1942, 9; "The General Asks a Pleasant Favor—'Kill Me a Jap—Each of You,'" *Yank*, Sept. 9, 1942, 8; "Mimicking Monkeys," *Yank*, Sept. 9, 1942, 18; David Richardson, "Jap Prisoners at Sanananda Think MacArthur Dead," *Yank*, Feb. 3, 1943, 7; Matthew Hughes, "War without Mercy? American Armed Forces and the Deaths of Civilians during the Battle of Saipan, 1944," *Journal of Military History* 75 (Jan. 2011): 96–100; Gene Larocque, interview by Studs Terkel, in *"The Good War": An Oral History of World War II*, ed. Studs Terkel (New York: New Press, 1984), 190; Craig M. Cameron, *American Samurai: Myth, Imagination, and the Conduct of Battle in the First Marine Division, 1941–1951* (Cambridge: Cambridge University Press, 1994), 89–129; Christopher Thorne, "Racial Aspects of the Far Eastern War of 1941–1945," *Proceedings of the British Academy* 66 (1982): 329–377; Peter Schrijvers, *The GI War against Japan: American Soldiers in Asia and the Pacific during World War II* (New York: New York University Press, 2002), 207–225; Gerald F. Linderman, *The World within War: America's Combat Experience in World War II* (New York: Free Press, 1997), 143–184.

20. Hughes, "War without Mercy?," 98; Dower, *War without Mercy*, 3. Some of these horrific practices also took place in North Africa and Europe against Germans and Italians. See, for example, Rick Atkinson, *An Army at Dawn: The War in North Africa, 1942–1943* (New York: Picador, 2002), 259; Rick Atkinson, *The Day of Battle: The War in Sicily and Italy, 1943–1944* (New York: Picador, 2007), 474; Rick Atkinson, *The Guns at Last Light: The War in Western Europe, 1944–1945* (New York: Picador, 2013), 325, 526–527.

21. Allison Varzally, *Making a Non-White America: Californians Coloring outside Ethnic Lines, 1925–1955* (Berkeley: University of California Press, 2008), 178.

22. For "good Jap" quotation, see McNaughton, *Nisei Linguists*, 71; and Dower, *War without Mercy*, 79. For "good Indian" quotation, see Cameron, *American Samurai*, 118n87. Americans employed this phrase against their European enemies on occasion, too. See Atkinson, *The Guns at Last Light*, 526.

23. John Hersey, *Into the Valley: Marines at Guadalcanal* (1943; Lincoln: University of Nebraska Press, 2002), 6, 31; Dower, *War without Mercy*, 112.

24. Robert G. Ryan, "Bushmasters Master Everything from Jiu-Jitsu to Camouflage," *Yank*, Sept. 30, 1942, 8; Lou Stoumen, "The Puerto Rican Soldier," *Yank*, Mar. 31, 1944, 7.

25. McNaughton, *Nisei Linguists*, 75; Audie Murphy, *To Hell and Back* (1949; New York: Henry Holt, 2002), 79; Ralph G. Martin, "Nisei Combat Team Bared as 'Lost Battalion' Rescuer," *Stars and Stripes* (European Theater of Operations edition), Nov. 8, 1944, 1; "Here's One Jap in New Guinea Who Happens to Be a Nice Guy," *Yank*, Dec. 2, 1942, 10.

26. Ralph G. Martin, *Boy from Nebraska: The Story of Ben Kuroki* (New York: Harper, 1946), 177, 178, 190.

27. McNaughton, *Nisei Linguist*, 271–272, 166 (emphasis in original).

28. WRAWPR, no. 65, Apr. 26, 1944, 14, box 3, entry 5, RG 210. On friendly fire and bodyguards, see McNaughton, *Nisei Linguists*, 147, 174, 176, 361; Moore, *Serving Our Country: Japanese American Women in the Military during World War II* (New Brunswick, NJ: Rutgers University Press, 2003), 116; Tom Ige, *Boy from Kahaluu: An Autobiography* (Honolulu: Kin Cho Jin Kai, 1989), 88; Lyn Crost, *Honor by Fire: Japanese Americans at War in Europe and the Pacific* (Novato, CA: Presidio Press, 1994), 204–205.

29. K. Scott Wong, *Americans First: Chinese Americans and the Second World War* (Cambridge, MA: Harvard University Press, 2002), 189; Donald S. Lopez, *Into the Teeth of the Tiger* (Washington, DC: Smithsonian Books, 1997), 202.

30. Hugh J. Deeney to Commanding Generals, memo, Nov. 17, 1943, box 93, entry 26e, RG 159; "Notes on Puerto Rico and Puerto Rican Troops," n.d., box 93, entry 26e, RG 159.

31. Louis Büttner to Colonel David B. Falk, memo, Feb. 16, 1944, box 93, entry 26e, RG 159; Capozzola, *Bound by War*, 159; Wong, *Americans First*, 152.

32. McNaughton, *Nisei Linguist*, 75.

33. Dower, *War without Mercy*, 147–180.

34. Peggy Pascoe, *What Comes Naturally: Miscegenation Law and the Making of Race in America* (New York: Oxford University Press, 2009), 92.

35. See, for a small sample, Beth Lew-Williams, *The Chinese Must Go: Violence, Exclusion, and the Making of the Alien in America* (Cambridge, MA: Harvard University Press, 2018); Erika Lee, *At America's Gates: Chinese Immigration during the Exclusion Era, 1882–1943* (Chapel Hill: University of North Carolina Press, 2003); Charles J. McClain, *In Search of Equality: The Chinese Struggle against Discrimination in Nineteenth-Century America* (Berkeley: University of California Press, 1994); Kornel Chang, *Pacific Connections: The Making of the U.S.-Canadian Borderlands* (Berkeley: University of California Press, 2012); Lucy E. Salyer, *Laws as Harsh as Tigers: Chinese Immigrants and the Shaping of the Modern Immigration Law* (Chapel Hill: University of North Carolina Press, 1995); Erika Lee, *The Making of Asian America: A History* (New York: Simon & Schuster, 2015), 59–190.

36. See, for example, Rick Baldoz, *The Third Asiatic Invasion: Empire and Migration in Filipino America* (New York: New York University Press, 2012); Roxanne Dunbar-Ortiz, *An Indigenous Peoples' History of the United States* (Boston: Beacon Press, 2014); Kelly Lyttle Hernández, *City of Inmates: Conquest, Rebellion, and the Rise of Human Caging in Los Angeles, 1771–1965* (Berkeley: University of California Press, 2017); Paul A. Kramer, *The Blood of Government: Race, Empire, the United States, and the Philippines* (Chapel Hill: University of North Carolina Press, 2006); David Montejano, *Anglos and Mexicans in the Making of Texas, 1836–1983* (Austin: University of Texas Press, 1987); Patrick Wolfe, *Traces of History: Elementary Structures of Race* (London: Verso, 2016); Katrina Quisumbing King, "Recentering U.S. Empire: A Structural Perspective on the Color Line," *SRE* 5 (Jan. 2019): 11–25.

37. Martin, *Boy from Nebraska*, 190–191.

38. Linderman, *The World within War*, 263.

39. Ollie Stewart, "Races Share Same Bottle," *BAA*, Aug. 7, 1943, 1.

40. [George C.] Marshall to [Jacob L.] Devers, classified memo, July 6, 1944, box 22, entry 180, RG 107; Harrison A. Gerhardt to Abe Fortas, July 11, 1944, box

22, entry 180, RG 107; Commanding General, Allied Armies in Italy to War Department, July 10, 1944, box 22, entry 180, RG 107; Marshall to Devers, top secret message, July 20, 1944, GCMP, 532, https://www.marshallfoundation.org/ library/digital-archive/to-lieutenant-general-jacob-l-devers-15/ (accessed Nov. 11, 2019).

41. Marshall to Devers, top secret message, July 20, 1944, GCMP, 532, https://www. marshallfoundation.org/library/digital-archive/to-lieutenant-general-jacob-l-devers-15/ (accessed Nov. 11, 2019).

42. W. E. Crist to General Strong, memo, Jan. 4, 1943, box 1717, entry 480, RG 389; "Part of the National Policy," *Honolulu Star-Bulletin*, Oct. 19, 1943, 6. On this point, see also Fujitani, *Race for Empire*, 12–16, 83–108, passim and previous chapters of the present volume.

43. Minoru Masuda, *Letters from the 442nd: The World War II Correspondence of a Japanese American Medic*, ed. Hana Masuda and Dianne Bridgman (Seattle: University of Washington Press, 2008), 242. For an example of a press release, see War Department, Bureau of Public Relations, Press Branch, "American Doughboys of Japanese Descent in Vanguard of 5th Army's Advance," press release, May 2, 1945, box 1717, entry 480, RG 389.

44. For *Yank* articles, see James P. O'Neill, "The Nisei Problem," *Yank*, c. July 1945, clipping, box 2, PCC; James P. O'Neill, "The Battle of Belvedere," *Yank*, Aug. 25, 1944, 2–4. For *Stars and Stripes*, see Martin, "Nisei Combat Team Bared as 'Lost Battalion' Rescuer," 1; "Rebuke from the Front," *WP*, June 24, 1945, B4. For *CBI Roundup*, see McNaughton, *Nisei Linguists*, 369.

45. On awards and medals, see "Most Decorated Unit in Military History," *PCIT*, Oct. 6, 1945, 1. That some honors came in part as a consequence of pressure from army and War Department leaders, see George C. Marshall, interview by Sidney T. Matthews et al., July 25, 1949, part II, microfilm reel 32, GCMRL, https:// www.marshallfoundation.org/library/wp-content/uploads/sites/16/2014/05/ Pentagon_Part_2.pdf (accessed Nov. 15, 2019).

46. Meyer Berger, "U.S. Nisei Troops Honored in Italy," *NYT*, Aug. 19, 1945, 11.

47. O'Neill, "The Battle of Belvedere," 2.

48. Headquarters, 92d Infantry Division to Organization Commanders, April 4, 1945, box 1731, entry 427, RG 407. See also Murphy, *Ambassadors in Arms*, 120, 122.

49. "U.S. Japanese Tells How Unit Fought in Italy," *NYHT*, May 23, 1944, 2; Willis, "Soldier, Shake," 212; Murphy, *Ambassadors in Arms*, 121.

50. "They're GI Pals—Two Nisei and Iowan," *Des Moines Tribune*, Nov. 9, 1944, 11.

51. "Ancestry Forgotten by Brothers-in-Arms," *Pittsburgh Post-Gazette*, Dec. 26, 1944, 2.

52. "Crippled in War, Two Enjoy 'Luxuries' on Visit at Home," *Milwaukee Journal*, transcription, WRADND, Feb. 21, 1945, box 3, entry 5, RG 210.

53. "Square Deal for the Nisei," *Newsweek*, transcription, WRADND, Aug. 17, 1945, box 3, entry 5, RG 210.

54. "GI's Fresh from Battle Do the Town Arm-in-Arm," *San Francisco Chronicle*, transcription, WRADND, Sept. 14, 1944, box 3, entry 5, RG 210.

55. Major Ralph R. Hotchkiss, "This Is Our Road Home," *Saturday Evening Review*, transcription, WRADND, June 2, 1945, box 3, entry 5, RG 210.

56. James Lee, "Sure, Mom, Your Soldier's Tough—But He's All Right," *WP*, June 3, 1945, 2B; "War Reporter Sent to Cover Home Front," *LAT*, transcription, WRADND, Feb. 6, 1945, box 3, entry 5, RG 210.

57. *Time*, Feb. 14, 1944, transcription, WRAWPR, Feb. 16, 1944, box 2, entry 5, RG 210; "Germans Feel Deserted," *NYHT*, Feb. 17, 1944, 7; "Loyal Japanese," *Jersey Journal*, transcription, WRADND, Nov. 17, 1944, box 3, entry 5, RG 210; "Japanese-American GI's Entertain at Halloran," *PM*, transcription, WRADND, Sept. 12, 1944, box 3, entry 5, RG 210.

58. "U.S. Nisei Troops Honored in Italy," *NYT*, Aug. 19, 1945, 11.

59. Committee on American Principles and Fair Play, *American Fighting Men Speak Out*, pamphlet, n.d., 2, box 1, entry 8, RG 210; Martin, *Boy from Nebraska*, 160.

60. Martin, *Boy from Nebraska*, 190–191; Richard Goldstein, "Ben Kuroki, 98; Fought Bias to Fight for U.S.," *NYT*, Sept. 7, 2015, B6.

61. Howard Furumoto, interview by Craig Hitada, HOHA, July 6, 1998, tape 6, video, 24:40, http://www.goforbroke.org/ohmsviewer/viewer. php?cachefile=1998OH0002_06_Furumoto.xml.

62. McNaughton, *Nisei Linguists*, 285.

63. Letter to Editor, *PM*, transcription, WRAWPR, May 10, 1944, box 2, entry 5, RG 210.

64. Alison R. Bernstein, *American Indians and World War II: Toward a New Era in Indian Affairs* (Norman: University of Oklahoma Press, 1991), 58; Franco, *Crossing the Pond*, 168–169.

65. Charles Rodriguez, interview by Charlene Riggins, VHP, March 16, 2002, transcript, https://memory.loc.gov/diglib/vhp-stories/story/loc.natlib.afc2001001.43754/ transcript?ID=sr0001; Charlene Riggins and Miguel A. Garcia, eds., *Forgotten Patriots: Voices of World War II Mexican American Veterans of Southern California* (Fullerton, CA: Center for Oral and Public History, 2007), 155; Lopez, *Into the Teeth of the Tiger*, 50.

66. Pauline Kibbe, *Latin Americans in Texas* (Albuquerque: University of New Mexico Press, 1946), 226–227; Staci Schutz, "Guadalupe G. Ramirez," n.d., VOHP, https:// voces.lib.utexas.edu/collections/stories/guadalupe-g-ramirez; Jennifer Yee, "Enrique Rodriguez Falcon," n.d., VOHP, https://voces.lib.utexas.edu/collections/ stories/enrique-rodriguez-falcon; Wong, *Americans First*, 70; Raul Morin, *Among the Valiant: Mexican-Americans in WWII and Korea* (Los Angeles: Borden, 1963), 150.

67. Bill Mauldin, *Up Front* (1945; New York: Norton, 2000), 135; E. J. Kahn Jr., "Open Letter to a Papuan Carrier from Grateful Yanks in New Guinea," *Yank*, Jan. 6, 1943, 7; "Cultured New Guinea Natives Take G.I. City Slickers for a Ride," *Yank*, Nov. 25, 1942, 9; Letter to editor from Frank Genovese, *Yank*, Aug. 25, 1944, 14; Andrew Friedman, "US Empire, World War 2 and the Racializing of Labour," *Race & Class* 58 (2017): 23, 26. See also Thomas Bruscino, *A Nation Forged in War: How World War II Taught Americans to Get Along* (Knoxville: University of Tennessee Press, 2010), 115–125; Linderman, *The World within War*, 222–223; Gary Gerstle, *American Crucible: Race and Nation in the Twentieth Century* (Princeton, NJ: Princeton University Press, 2001), 225; Alex Kershaw, *The Liberator: One World War II Soldier's 500-Day Odyssey from the Beaches of Sicily to the Gates of Dachau* (New York: Broadway Books, 2012), 301; Private Attilio L. Gizzarelli, "Filipinos as Seen by Silver Lake Boy," *La Campana di Silver Lake*, Nov. 4, 1945, 3, St. Bartholomew's Church Records, CMS. On the wartime and postwar expansion of US empire, see Daniel Immerwahr, *How to Hide an Empire: A History of the Greater United States* (New York: Picador, 2019), 171–226.

68. Gerstle, *American Crucible*, 204. The "on the backs of blacks" phrase comes from Toni Morrison, "On the Backs of Blacks," *Time*, Dec. 2, 1993, 57.

69. "Statement from 9 Seabees at NAACP Office on Oct. 25, 1943," Oct. 27, 1943, box II:B196, NAACPR; John V. Alvarado, interview by Abbas Kathiria, VHP, April 26, 2009, audio, 15:04, http://memory.loc.gov/diglib/vhp/bib/loc.natlib. afc2001001.67973 (emphasis mine). From the context of Alvarado's broader point, it appears he meant that black troops were not *treated* equally in comparison with others.

70. George C. Marshall, Interview by Sidney T. Matthews et al., July 25, 1949, part II, microfilm reel 32, GCMRL, https://www.marshallfoundation.org/library/wp-content/uploads/sites/16/2014/05/Pentagon_Part_2.pdf (accessed Nov. 15, 2019).

71. "War Reporter Sent to Cover Home Front," *LAT*, transcription, WRADND, Feb. 6, 1945, box 3, entry 5, RG 210; Milton Bracker, "Negroes' Courage Upheld in Inquiry," *NYT*, March 15, 1945, 12; "Somebody's Gotta Go!" *CD*, March 24, 1945, 12; Proceedings of a Board of Review Appointed by Commanding General, 92d Infantry Division on the Subject Combat Effectiveness of Negro Officers and Enlisted Men," June 24–25, 1945, top secret, box 28, entry 109, RG 319.

72. Chester G. Starr, ed., *From Salerno to the Alps: A History of the Fifth Army, 1943–1945* (Washington, DC: Infantry Journal Press, 1948), 442; Mark W. Clark, *Calculated Risk* (1950; New York: Enigma Books, 2007), 180, 325.

73. Bracker, "Negroes' Courage Upheld"; "Action in Italy," *NYT*, April 11, 1945, 22; "Men from Europe Praise Nisei Unit," *NYT*, June 8, 1945, 5. Occasionally, reporters and others praised different US troops, including both Japanese Americans and African Americans: "Of Valor," *Charlotte News*, Sept 11, 1944, transcription, WRADND, Sept. 18, 1944, box 3, entry 5, RG 210; "Commons Cheers News from Italy," *NYT*, May 3, 1945, 3.

74. *Congressional Record*, 79th Cong., 1st sess., 1945, 91, pt. 5: 6995; *Congressional Record*, 80th Cong., 2d sess., 1948, 91, pt. 6: 7360; Ellen D. Wu, *The Color of Success: Asian Americans and the Origins of the Model Minority* (Princeton, NJ: Princeton University Press, 2014), 4. See also Fujitani, *Race for Empire*, 211–223, 384; Madeline Y. Hsu, *The Good Immigrants: How the Yellow Peril Became the Model Minority* (Princeton, NJ: Princeton University Press, 2015); and Ellen D. Wu, "GI Joe Nisei: The Invention of World War II's Iconic Japanese American Soldier," in *How Race and Gender Shaped American Military Heroism in the Twentieth and Twenty-First Centuries*, ed. Simon Wendt (New Brunswick, NJ: Rutgers University Press, 2018), 33–55.

75. On how the "model minority" idea simultaneously valorizes and ostracizes Asian Americans, see, for example, Claire Jean Kim, "The Racial Triangulation of Asian Americans," *Politics & Society* 27 (Mar. 1999): 105–138. On the concept of leveraging, see Erik Bleich and Kimberly J. Morgan, "Leveraging Identities: The Strategic Manipulation of Social Hierarchies for Political Gain," *Theory and Society* 48 (2019): 511–534.

76. Ulysses Lee, *The Employment of Negro Troops* (Washington, DC: GPO, 1963), 536–589; Daniel K. Gibran, *The 92nd Infantry Division and the Italian Campaign in World War II* (Jefferson, NC: McFarland, 2001).

77. Charles Dollard, interview by Lawrence D. Reddick, box 1, LDR; Walter White to Robert P. Patterson, Oct. 20, 1945, box II:A651, NAACPR; "White Officers Praise Negroes' Fighting Ability," *NYHT*, Oct. 19, 1945, 5.

78. Mike Masaoka with Bill Hosokawa, *They Call Me Moses Masaoka: An American Saga* (New York: William Morrow, 1987), 174–175.

79. It began to appear slightly more frequently after the war. See, for example, E. W. Kenworthy, "The Case against Army Segregation," *Annals of the American Academy of Political and Social Science* 275 (May 1951): 30; Warman Welliver, "Report on the Negro Soldier," *Harper's*, Apr. 1946, 338; David G. Mandelbaum, *Soldier Groups and Negro Soldiers* (Berkeley: University of California Press, 1952), 101; Clark, *Calculated Risk*, 326. Even today some scholars offer decontextualized, and therefore misleading, contrasts between Japanese Americans' and African Americans' fighting records in Italy. See, for example, James M. McCaffrey, *Going for Broke: Japanese American Soldiers in the War against Nazi Germany* (Norman: University of Oklahoma Press, 2013), 291–292.

80. Duus, *Unlikely Liberators*, 227–228.

81. Isamu Inouye, interview by Ian Kawata, HOHA, Nov. 29, 1998, video, tape 7, 11:12, http://www.goforbroke.org/learn/archives/oral_histories_videos.php?clip=02607.

82. Senate Subcommittee of the Committee on Labor and Public Welfare, *Antidiscrimination in Employment: Hearings on S. 984*, 80th Cong., 1st sess., 1947, 211; Mike Masaoka to John J. McCloy, July 10, 1944, box 49, entry 183, RG 107.

83. "No Prejudice on the Frontline but Nisei Veteran Finds Plenty Here," *PC*, July 14, 1945, 14.

84. "No Prejudice on the Frontline but Nisei Veteran Finds Plenty Here," *PC*, July 14, 1945, 14. On the sometimes-pinched parameters of comradeship, see Linderman, *The World within War*, 283–290.

85. Allen H. Okamoto, interview by Jaclyn Hilf, VHP, Jan. 15, 2005, audio, 36:29, http://memory.loc.gov/diglib/vhp/story/loc.natlib.afc2001001.56291/; Avery, "All Hawaiians Jap-Yank Unit Wins GI Praise," 13.

86. Martin, *Boy from Nebraska*, xi. On this point, see also Moon-Kie Jung, *Reworking Race: The Making of Hawaii's Interracial Labor Movement* (New York: Columbia University Press, 2006), 159.

87. Quoted in Chris Dixon, *African Americans and the Pacific War, 1941–1945: Race, Nationality, and the Fight for Freedom* (Cambridge: Cambridge University Press, 2018), 204.

88. See Warren Bryant, interview by Mary Penick Motley, in *The Invisible Soldier: The Experience of the Black Soldier, World War II*, ed. Mary Penick Motley (Detroit: Wayne State University Press, 1975), 257.

CONCLUSION

1. *The Invisible Soldiers: Unheard Voices*, DVD video, 56 mins., WHS media, Sudbury, MA, 2004; Welton I. Taylor with Karyn Taylor, *Two Steps from Glory: A World War II Liaison Pilot Confronts Jim Crow and the Enemy in the South Pacific* (Chicago: Winning Strategy Press, 2012), 362; Warren J. Brunson to L. D. Reddick, July 6, 1946, box 1, LDR.

2. "Men from Unit Praise Nisei Unit," *NYT*, June 8, 1945, 5. The *Times*'s description of "American troops" cheering Tokunaga brings to mind two more recent news headlines involving American figure skater Michelle Kwan: "American Beats Kwan" (1998) and "American Outshines Kwan" (2002). See "Times Won't Forget Readers' Reminder on Kwan Headline," *Seattle Times*, Mar. 3, 2002, https://archive.seattletimes.com/archive/?date=20020303&slug=fancher03.

3. Brehon Somervell, "Negro Policy for Redistribution Stations," memo, July 21, 1944, box 9, Official File 4245g, FDRP; Henry L. Stimson to President Roosevelt, memo, Sept. 20, 1944, box 9, Official File 4245g, FDRP. For "mucky slums," see

Richard Wright, introduction to *Black Metropolis: A Study of Negro Life in a Northern City*, rev. ed., by St. Clair Drake and Horace R. Cayton (1945; Chicago: University of Chicago Press, 1993), xx.

4. A. A. Austin et al. to Franklin D. Roosevelt, Sept. 18, 1944, box 9, Official File 4245g, FDRP; Jonathan Daniels to President Roosevelt, memo, Sept. 21, 1944, box 7, Official File 93b, FDRP. On Roosevelt's meeting with black leaders and his pressure on the War Department, see Walter White to President Roosevelt, Oct. 3, 1944, box 7, Official File 93b, FDRP; Roosevelt to Mr. Secretary [Stimson], draft letter, n.d., box 9, Official File 4245g, FDRP.

5. War Department, Bureau of Public Relations, "Army Will Utilize Existing Camps at Redistribution Centers," press release, Oct. 8, 1944, box 9, Official File 4245g, FDRP; "Foxhole Dreams Come True for GI's at Hotel Dennis," *BAA*, May 26, 1945, 1, 15. On the War Department's unwillingness to admit that its new redistribution policies would be on an "integrated basis," see Diary of John J. McCloy, Oct. 7, 1944, box DY1, JJMP.

6. "Fort Dix Center Turns GI into Civilian in 48 Hours," *BAA*, June 2, 1945, 24; Richard Dier, "Lynn Reveals Army Not Bad," *BAA*, Nov. 24, 1945, 1. For complaints about Dix, see two anonymous brothers, interview by Lawrence D. Reddick, n.d., box 1, LDR; Robert C. Gibson, interview by Lawrence D. Reddick, Jan. 12, 1946, box 1, LDR; Wilbur Young, interview by Lawrence D. Reddick, Aug. 9, 1946, box 1, LDR; Conrad Lynn, *There Is a Fountain: The Autobiography of Conrad Lynn*, foreword by William M. Kunstler (Brooklyn, NY: Lawrence Hill Books, 1979), 106.

7. Peyton Gray, "85-Point Men, 40-Year-Olds of 92nd Arrive at Hampton Roads for Discharge," *BAA*, Aug. 25, 1945, 11; "Investigation Reveals No Wholesale Bias at Ft. Dix," *BAA*, Dec. 15, 1945, 15. On the Great Lakes Separation Center, see "The Story of the Return of a Veteran," *NJG*, Apr. 13, 1946, 20. On soldiers' activism against mess hall segregation at Fort Dix, see Wilbur Young, interview by Lawrence D. Reddick, Aug. 9, 1946, box 1, LDR.

8. Laura McEnaney, *Postwar: Waging Peace in Chicago* (Philadelphia: University of Pennsylvania Press, 2018), 104–105. On protests against discharge delays, see Susan L. Carruthers, *The Good Occupation: American Soldiers and the Hazards of Peace* (Cambridge, MA: Harvard University Press, 2016), 191–200; James T. Sparrow, *Warfare State: World War II Americans and the Age of Big Government* (New York: Oxford University Press, 2011), 237–238; R. Alton Lee, "The Army 'Mutiny' of 1946," *JAH* 53 (Dec. 1966): 555–571.

9. Robert F. Jefferson, *Fighting for Hope: African American Troops of the 93rd Infantry Division in World War II and Postwar America* (Baltimore: Johns Hopkins University Press, 2008), 213; BPR, June 19, 1945, box 223, entry 188, RG 107. Blacks' delayed discharges also delayed their employment searches at home, which compounded their disadvantages in the postwar job market.

10. On the blue discharge figures, see Edward Witsell to Jesse O. Dedmon Jr., Dec. 3, 1945, box 183, entry 188, RG 107. On the military's various kinds of discharges, see Charles Hurd, "Veterans Intelligence," *NYT*, Nov. 12, 1944, 19. Gay soldiers also received a disproportionate share of blue discharges. See Allan Bérubé, *Coming Out under Fire: The History of Gay Men and Women in World War II* (New York: Free Press, 1990), 228–235; Margot Canaday, *The Straight State: Sexuality and Citizenship in Twentieth-Century America* (Princeton, NJ: Princeton University Press, 2009), chap. 4.

11. "Not One Out of a Million," *Crisis*, Dec. 1945, 345. For the statistics on African Americans and army World War II decorations, see Elliott V. Converse et al.,

The Exclusion of Black Soldiers from the Medal of Honor in World War II (Jefferson, NC: McFarland, 1997), esp. 70, 94, 139, 168. For the total number of Medals of Honor awarded across the military during World War II, see James C. McNaughton, Kristen E. Edwards, and Jay M. Price, " 'Incontestable Proof Will Be Exacted': Historians, Asian Americans, and the Medal of Honor," *Public Historian* 24 (Fall 2002): 14.

12. Converse et al., *The Exclusion of Black Soldiers*, 11; James Bennett, "Medals of Honor Awarded at Last to Black World War II Soldiers," *NYT*, Jan. 14, 1997, A1.

13. For the government report, see Francis J. Haas et al., "Report of the Subcommittee Number Two to the Committee as a Whole," n.d., n.p., box 22, PCCR. For all other quotations in this paragraph, see Charles Dollard and Donald Young, "In the Armed Forces," *Survey Graphic*, Jan. 1947, 117.

14. Henry L. Stimson to President Roosevelt, memo, Sept. 20, 1944, box 9, Official File 4245g, FDRP; Margarita Aragon, " 'A General Separation of Colored and White': The WWII Riots, Military Segregation, and Racism(s) beyond the White/ Nonwhite Binary," *SRE* 1 (Oct. 2015): 8.

15. Maggie Rivas-Rodriguez and B. V. Olguín, eds., *Latina/os and World War II: Mobility, Agency, and Ideology* (Austin: University of Texas Press, 2014), ix.

16. For delayed transports, see W. S. Paul, "Nisei Situation on the West Coast," memo, Nov. 15, 1945, box 35, entry 183, RG 107. For quotation about medical care, leave, and garbage detail, see "JACL Protests 'Mistreatment' of Nisei Combat Veterans at Southern California Army Camp," *PCIT*, Jan. 5, 1946, 1. For "un-American attitudes," see Earl M. Finch to Colonel Gerhardt, Oct. 22, 1945, box 48, entry 183, RG 107. For the War Department's direction, see W. S. Paul, "Nisei Situation on the West Coast," memo, Nov. 15, 1945, box 35, entry 183, RG 107. For JACL report, see "JACL Protests 'Mistreatment' of Nisei Combat Veterans at Southern California Army Camp," *PCIT*, Jan. 5, 1946, 1.

17. Shirley Castelnuovo, *Soldiers of Conscience: Japanese American Military Resisters in World War II* (Lincoln: University of Nebraska Press, 2010), 31, 75, 92–96. Not technically related to discharge but a racist line that also restricted postwar access to veterans' benefits was the First Supplemental Surplus Appropriation Rescission Act. Signed by President Truman in February 1946, the act robbed nearly 200,000 Filipino soldiers, who had served as formal members of the US Armed Forces of the Far East during the war, of their rightful GI Bill benefits. See Christopher Capozzola, *Bound by War: How the United States and the Philippines Built America's First Pacific Century* (New York: Basic Books, 2020), 209–210; Katrina Quisumbing King, "The Political Uses of Ambiguity: Statecraft and US Empire in the Philippines, 1898–1946" (PhD diss., University of Wisconsin, Madison, 2018).

18. Blake Clark and Oland D. Russell, "Japanese-American Soldiers Make Good," *American Mercury*, June 1945, 698. For Japanese Americans' Distinguished Service Cross tally, see McNaughton, Edwards, and Price, " 'Incontestable Proof Will Be Exacted,' " 21. Roughly one-quarter of 1 percent of the army, Japanese Americans won a full 1 percent of its Distinguished Service Crosses. On Native Americans and Mexican Americans, see Elizabeth M. Collins, "Hispanic-American Medal of Honor Recipients," U.S. Army, https://www.army.mil/article/176781/ hispanic_american_medal_of_honor_recipients (last modified Oct. 14, 2016); "Native American Medal of Honor Winners," Center of Military History, U.S. Army, https://history.army.mil/html/topics/natam/natam-moh.html (last modified Dec. 12, 2019).

19. McNaughton, Edwards, and Price, "'Incontestable Proof Will Be Exacted,'" 33, 1. On Munemori, see "Nation's Highest Honor Given Japanese American Who Gave His Life to Save Comrades in Italy," *PCIT*, Mar. 16, 1946, 1.

20. L. D. Reddick, letter to the editor, *AJS* 53 (July 1947): 41.

21. Winfred Lynn to Nancy Macdonald, May 11, 1944, box 30, series 1, DMP; TIR, no. 708, July 14, 1945, box 265, entry 189, RG 107; Timothy B. Tyson, *Radio Free Dixie: Robert F. Williams and the Roots of Black Power* (Chapel Hill: University of North Carolina Press, 1999), 48; Edwin M. Embree, "Balance Sheet in Race Relations," *Atlantic Monthly*, May 1945, 91; TIR, no. 323, Dec. 21, 1944, box 265, entry 189, RG 107; Roy Wilkins, "The Negro Wants Full Equality," in *What the Negro Wants*, ed. Rayford W. Logan (1944; Notre Dame, IN: University of Notre Dame Press, 2001), 132; Marjorie McKenzie, "Pursuit of Democracy: Significance of Many Letters from Soldiers Analyzed by Writer," *PC*, Feb. 10, 1945, 7; Neil R. McMillen, "Fighting for What We Didn't Have: How Mississippi's Black Veterans Remember World War II," in *Remaking Dixie: The Impact of World War II on the American South*, ed. Neil R. McMillen (Jackson: University Press of Mississippi, 1997), 103.

22. Nelson Peery, *Black Fire: The Making of an American Revolutionary* (New York: New Press, 1994), 332.

23. Many works cite the importance of black veterans to postwar black politics. For a small sample, see Jefferson, *Fighting for Hope*; Christopher S. Parker, *Fighting for Democracy: Black Veterans and the Struggle against White Supremacy in the Postwar South* (Princeton, NJ: Princeton University Press, 2009); Gail Williams O'Brien, *The Color of the Law: Race, Violence, and Justice in the Post–World War II South* (Chapel Hill: University of North Carolina Press, 1999); Charles Payne, *I've Got the Light of Freedom: The Organizing Tradition and the Black Freedom Struggle* (Berkeley: University of California Press, 1995); John Dittmer, *Local People: The Struggle for Civil Rights in Mississippi* (Urbana: University of Illinois Press, 1994); Taylor, with Taylor, *Two Steps from Glory*; Emilye Crosby, *A Little Taste of Freedom: The Black Freedom Struggle in Claiborne County, Mississippi* (Chapel Hill: University of North Carolina Press, 2005); Jennifer E. Brooks, *Defining the Peace: World War II Veterans, Race, and the Remaking of the Southern Political Tradition* (Chapel Hill: University of North Carolina Press, 2004).

24. Franklin Odo, *No Sword to Bury: Japanese Americans in Hawaii during World War II* (Philadelphia: Temple University Press, 2004), 243; Kenneth William Townsend, *World War II and the American Indian* (Albuquerque: University of New Mexico Press, 2000), 215; Pauline R. Kibbe, *Latin Americans in Texas* (Albuquerque: University of New Mexico Press, 1946), 226–227. For additional work on Native American veterans, see Jere Bishop Franco, *Crossing the Pond: The Native American Effort in World War II* (Denton: University of North Texas Press, 1999), 194–199; John Adair, "The Navajo and Pueblo Veteran," *American Indian* 4 (1947): 5–11.

25. See, for example, Alison R. Bernstein, *American Indians and World War II: Toward a New Era in Indian Affairs* (Norman: University of Oklahoma Press, 1991), 133–139; Henry Christman, "Southwestern Indians Win the Vote," *American Indian* 4 (1948): 6–10; Scott Kurashige, *The Shifting Grounds of Race: Black and Japanese Americans in the Making of Multiethnic Los Angeles* (Princeton, NJ: Princeton University Press, 2008), 190–195; Carey McWilliams, *North from Mexico: The Spanish-Speaking People of the United States*, new ed. (1948; New York: Greenwood Press, 1990), 233; Albert M. Camarillo, "Research Note on Chicano Community Leaders: The G. I. Generation," *Aztlan* 2 (Fall 1971): 145–150; Raul Morin, *Among*

the Valiant: Mexican-Americans in World War II and Korea (Los Angeles: Borden, 1963), 277–280; Steven Rosales, *Soldados Razos at War: Chicano Politics, Identity, and Masculinity in the U.S. Military from World War II to Vietnam* (Tucson: University of Arizona Press, 2017), 7, 178–189; Henry A. J. Ramos, *The American GI Forum: In Pursuit of the Dream, 1948–1983* (Houston: Arte Público Press, 1998).

26. Wilkins, "The Negro Wants Full Equality," 132; Samuel A. Stouffer et al., *The American Soldier: Adjustment during Army Life* (Princeton, NJ: Princeton University Press, 1949), 1:379; Joe McCarthy, "GI Vision of a Better America," *NYTM*, Aug. 5, 1945, 19; Thomas Bruscino, *A Nation Forged in War: How World War II Taught Americans to Get Along* (Knoxville: University of Tennessee Press, 2010), 171, 173–174.

27. Chris Dixon, *African Americans and the Pacific War, 1941–1945: Race, Nationality, and the Fight for Freedom* (Cambridge: Cambridge University Press, 2018), 175; Mary Louise Roberts, "The Leroy Henry Case: Sexual Violence and Allied Relations in Great Britain, 1944," *Journal of the History of Sexuality* 26 (Sept. 2017): 423.

28. John Hope Franklin, "Their War and Mine," *JAH* 77 (Sept. 1990): 578; James Baldwin, *The Fire Next Time* (1963; New York: Vintage, 1993), 20; David Cason Jr., interview by Mary Penick Motley, in *The Invisible Soldier: The Experience of the Black Soldier, World War II*, ed. Mary Penick Motley (Detroit: Wayne State University Press, 1975), 269–270.

29. Castelnuovo, *Soldiers of Conscience*, 64. For biographical information on Kadomiya, see Ron Kadomiya, email message to author, Mar. 26, 2020 (in author's possession); and Yasugo Kadomiya, draft registration card, Oct. 16, 1940, Ancestry, https://www.ancestry.com/interactive/2238/44045_05_00018-00526?pid=36943039&backurl=https://search.ancestry.com/cgi-bin/sse.dll?i ndiv%3D1%26dbid%3D2238%26h%3D36943039%26tid%3D%26pid%3D%2 6usePUB%3Dtrue&treeid=&personid=&hintid=&usePUB=true&usePUBJs=t rue&_ga=2.222305171.965652310.1585791569-629620654.1585229251&_ gac=1.82923236.1585791569.CjwKCAjw95D0BRBFEiwAcO1KDLhyHSEX-WndqSgGjn0i5B6LXFmY3MdPftcZpkLGlqw2pyod9uSWbxoC4PQQAvD_BwE (accessed Mar. 31, 2020).

30. For an opposing argument, that victory, tragically, required an accommodation with anti-black racism, see Daniel Kryder, *Divided Arsenal: Race and the American State during World War II* (Cambridge: Cambridge University Press, 2000), 22; Ira Katznelson, *Fear Itself: The New Deal and the Origins of Our Time* (New York: Liveright, 2013), 8, 10, 24. In calculating costs and benefits, it should also be kept in mind how remarkably conflict- and cost-free the eventual desegregation of the military turned out to be. On this point, see Charles C. Moskos Jr., "Racial Integration in the Armed Forces," *AJS* 72 (Sept. 1966): 132.

31. On the inefficiencies of black-white military segregation, see Charles Dollard and Donald Young, "In the Armed Forces," *Survey Graphic*, Jan. 1947, 68, 111; E. W. Kenworthy, "The Case against Army Segregation," *Annals of the Academy of Political and Social Science* 275 (May 1951): 27–33; *Freedom to Serve: Equality of Treatment and Opportunity in the Armed Services* (Washington, DC: GPO, 1950), 49–50; Sherie Mershon and Steven L. Schlossman, *Foxholes and Color Lines: Desegregating the U.S. Armed Forces* (Baltimore: Johns Hopkins University Press, 1998), 73–92.

32. Karen E. Fields and Barbara J. Fields, *Racecraft: The Soul of Inequality in American Life* (London: Verso, 2012); Mark R. Wilson, *Destructive Creation: American Business and the Winning of World War II* (Philadelphia: University of Pennsylvania Press, 2016); Address by Walter White, Wartime NAACP Conference, July 16,

1944, box II:A28, NAACPR. On the deceptive fragility of racial regimes, see Cedric J. Robinson, *Forgeries of Memory and Meaning: Blacks and the Regimes of Race in American Theater and Film before World War II* (Chapel Hill: University of North Carolina Press, 2007), xii–xvi; and Robin D. G. Kelley, "Beyond Black Lives Matter," *Kalfou* 2 (Fall 2015): 334.

33. Mary Louise Roberts, *What Soldiers Do: Sex and the American GI in World War II France* (Chicago: University of Chicago Press, 2013), 260; Neil A. Wynn, "'Race War': Black American GIs and West Indians in Britain during the Second World War," *Immigrants & Minorities* 24 (Nov. 2006): 339; Samuel A. Stouffer, *The American Soldier* (Princeton, NJ: Princeton University Press, 1949), 2:637–638; Steven White, *World War II and American Racial Politics: Public Opinion, the Presidency, and Civil Rights Advocacy* (Cambridge: Cambridge University Press, 2019), 87; Bruno Bettelheim and Morris Janowitz, *Social Change and Prejudice Including Dynamics of Prejudice* (London: Free Press, 1964), 125, 256–257 (emphasis in original). For later wars' influences on some white veterans' racism, see Kathleen Belew, *Bring the War Home: The White Power Movement and Paramilitary America* (Cambridge, MA: Harvard University Press, 2018).

34. War Department, Military Intelligence Division, Confidential Report, Oct. 7, 1942, box 381, entry 47, RG 319. For a similar observation about Brazil, see Patrick Wolfe, *Traces of History: Elementary Structures of Race* (London: Verso, 2016), 134–139.

35. Mark Brilliant, *The Color of America Has Changed: How Racial Diversity Shaped Civil Rights Reform in California, 1941–1978* (New York: Oxford University Press, 2010), 6.

36. For promising interwar and wartime solidarities, see Luis Alvarez, *The Power of the Zoot: Youth Culture and Resistance during World War II* (Berkeley: University of California Press, 2009); Shana Bernstein, *Bridges of Reform: Interracial Civil Rights Activism in Twentieth-Century Los Angeles* (New York: Oxford University Press, 2011); Matthew M. Briones, *Jim and Jap Crow: A Cultural History of 1940s Interracial America* (Princeton, NJ: Princeton University Press, 2012); Lizabeth Cohen, *Making a New Deal: Industrial Workers in Chicago, 1919–1939* (Cambridge: Cambridge University Press, 1990); Michael Denning, *The Cultural Front* (New York: Verso, 1998); Michael K. Honey, *Southern Labor and Black Civil Rights: Organizing Memphis Workers* (Urbana: University of Illinois Press, 1993); Gaye Theresa Johnson, *Spaces of Conflict, Sounds of Solidarity: Music, Race, and Spatial Entitlement* (Berkeley: University of California Press, 2013); Moon-Kie Jung, *Reworking Race: The Making of Hawaii's Interracial Labor Movement* (New York: Columbia University Press, 2006); Robert Rodgers Korstad, *Civil Rights Unionism: Tobacco Workers and the Struggle for Democracy in the Mid-Twentieth-Century South* (Chapel Hill: University of North Carolina Press, 2003); Kurashige, *The Shifting Grounds of Race*; George Lipsitz, *The Possessive Investment in Whiteness: How White People Profit from Identity Politics* (Philadelphia: Temple University Press, 1998), chap. 9; Nico Slate, *Colored Cosmopolitanism: The Shared Struggle for Freedom in the United States and India* (Cambridge, MA: Harvard University Press, 2012); Ronald Takaki, *Double Victory: A Multicultural History of America in World War II* (Boston: Back Bay Books, 2000); Zaragosa Vargas, *Labor Rights Are Civil Rights: Mexican American Workers in Twentieth-Century America* (Princeton, NJ: Princeton University Press, 2005); Allison Varzally, *Making a Non-White America: Californians Coloring outside Ethnic Lines, 1925–1955* (Berkeley: University of California Press, 2008); Renqiu Yu, *To Save China, To Save*

Ourselves: The Chinese Hand Laundry Alliance of New York (Philadelphia: Temple University Press, 1992).

37. On the Left's and interracialism's struggles in the postwar years, see, for example, Steve Fraser and Gary Gerstle, eds., *The Rise and Fall of the New Deal Order, 1930–1980* (Princeton, NJ: Princeton University Press, 1989); Denning, *The Cultural Front*; Landon R. Y. Storrs, *The Second Red Scare and the Unmaking of the New Deal Left* (Princeton, NJ: Princeton University Press, 2012); Brilliant, *The Color of America Has Changed*. For an excellent analysis of how this sort of "degrading political parcelization" can undermine the growth of mass movements today, see Asad Haider, *Mistaken Identity: Race and Class in the Age of Trump* (New York: Verso, 2018), esp. 40.

38. W. E. B. Du Bois, "Social Planning for the Negro, Past and Present," *JNE* 5 (Jan. 1936): 120. For fatality numbers, see *The World War II Rosters of the Dead (All Services)*, Department of the Army, Microfiche Reference no. 601–07, May 1, 1983, Joint POW/MIA Accounting Command. In these rosters, "white" is distinguished from "Negro," "Chinese," "Japanese," "Hawaiian," "American Indian," "Filipino," "Portorican," and "Other." For whites' proportion of the population, see US Department of Commerce, *Historical Statistics of the United States: Colonial Times to 1970* (Washington, DC: GPO, 1975), part 1, 9.

INDEX

For the benefit of digital users, indexed terms that span two pages (e.g., 52–53) may, on occasion, appear on only one of those pages.